Engraving by William Blake

THE DIVINE COMEDY OF DANTE ALIGHIERI

INFERNO: CANTO III

The Inscription over Hell-Gate

THE DIVINE COMEDY

of Dante Alighieri

TRANSLATED INTO ENGLISH VERSE BY MELVILLE

BEST ANDERSON; WITH NOTES AND

ELUCIDATIONS BY THE TRANSLATOR,

AN INTRODUCTION BY ARTHUR LIVINGSTON,

AND THIRTY-TWO DRAWINGS BY

William Blake

NOW PRINTED FOR THE FIRST TIME

The Heritage Press
NEW YORK

A NOTE ON THIS EDITION

THE translation used in this edition was issued in its first form by Melville Best Anderson in 1921, and was copyright by The World Book Company. Dr. Anderson then made an extensive revision of the text and the notes in 1932 for The Limited Editions Club, and a handsome edition was printed for the members of that Club by the Officina Bodoni in Italy. Dr. Anderson's version is a line-for-line translation which retains the original rhyme form, *terza rima,* or triple rhyme. It is this revised version which is used, by permission, in this edition.

The celebrated drawings by William Blake have never before been printed as illustrations to the text. They were commissioned in 1824 by John Linnell, and remained in the possession of the Linnell family until they were sold at auction in London in 1918, and thus dispersed. They represent Blake's last work: they were still unfinished, when he died in 1827.

For Blake began one hundred and two compositions to illustrate *The Divine Comedy.* Few of them were completely finished, and only seven of them were engraved. The publisher of this edition has selected thirty-two drawings which were finished or nearly finished—and the compositions of which avoid the grisly surrealistic suggestiveness which came into many of the drawings. These are reproduced by the photogravure process, and in reduction; since the originals were 20¾ by 14½ inches in size, impossibly large for a book intended to be held in the hands and read for pleasure.

Before the drawings were dispersed, Sir Emery Walker reproduced them in full size for the National Art-Collections Fund in England. These reproductions are made from those full-size prints. In addition, one of the seven engraved plates is reproduced upon the end papers of this edition.

INTRODUCTION

I. THE VOGUE OF *LA DIVINA COMMEDIA*

We call it the "Divine Comedy". Dante called it simply the "Comedy", because, as he says in one of his letters (if it be his), it proceeds from Hell toward Heaven, from the worse toward the better—a very medieval conception of comedy. The epithet "divine" was added at a later date. Boccaccio began by calling Dante a divine poet. Others burned incense to him as the author of divine works. Finally, in the year 1555, the Tolomei edition was entitled, flatly: *La divina Commedia*. Most fortunate of publishers' blurbs!

Six hundred years—twenty generations of men—have gone by since Dante wrote his "Comedy". Every generation, in the Christian West, has read and evaluated the poem.

For the plain man it has been, as it still is, the story of a traveller returned from the other world, especially from Hell; and the plain man has read it, if possible in illustrated editions, to see what Hell is like.

For the pious soul, of whatever sect or belief, the "Comedy" has been a half-sacred book, probably inspired by God, a book, at any rate, composed by a devout intelligence, and to be read in an earnest devotional spirit quite apart from aesthetic considerations. This has been especially the case in the Latin world, where, in the crises of life, cultivated people inclined to devoutness often turn to the "Comedy" as to a sort of Bible for the educated man. For a complex of historical reasons, the Scriptures themselves have had no great hold on popular affections in Latin countries.

And then comes the man of letters, the critic. In every country of the Christian West to have read Dante has, from the day the work was known, been one of the obligations and one of the insignia of cultivation. The human mind is a capricious thing. The evaluations the literary man has made of the "Comedy" have been endlessly various, according to times and circumstances.

Critics began working at the poem before Dante died, and a first interpretation of it was made three years after his death (Bambagioli's Commentary, 1324). Boccaccio, who was born when Dante was forty-three years old, delivered official public lectures on the "Comedy" in Florence. People of that day, and the generations next following (115 commentaries in all before 1500), approached the "Comedy" from Dante's own point of view. For them it was an "allegorical vision" of traditional form though of surpassing excellence and profoundness. The important thing in their eyes was the doctrine that "lay hidden under the veiling of the verses dark" (*Inf.*, IX. 63). What we moderns call the art was merely sugar for the theological, mystical, or moral pill.

It is now overtrite to think of Dante as the culmination of the Middle Ages; and of Petrarch (who died in 1374), as the initiator of a so-called modern era. The dictum is misleading if by "modern" we mean ourselves: Petrarch was much closer in spirit to Dante than he is to us. It is helpful if by "modern" we mean the generations of men who lived in the fifteenth and sixteenth centuries. Petrarch, an urbane courtier, belonged by virtue of his urbanity to that age of courtiers; while Dante with his long-faced Christianity, and his rugged citizen's virtues, did not.

The revival of classical learning, along with changed social conditions as compared with Dante's times (the rise of court life), gave a new direction to intellectual interests in Europe. Lay culture began to declare, and, as time went on, succeeded in asserting, its independence of Christian culture. Piety and other-worldliness gave ground before the neo-Paganism of the Humanists. Urbanity took precedence over religious earnestness. The cult of fame and power replaced the search for moral perfection and mystic oneness with God. Proud of a sophistication newly acquired, people were learning enough of history to contrast the civilization of their own day with a preceding era of "Gothic" barbarism. Dante was left, for reasons apparent enough, on the "Gothic" side of the dividing line.

In his own country, the development of secular literature in opposition, first to Christian, and then to Humanistic, literature, might, one could suppose, have redeemed him as the creator of the greatest work at the time extant in a modern language; and that eminence was never indeed overlooked. But the scholars and literary men of the Italian Renaissance, thinking especially of rhetoric, diction and good manners, found Dante inferior to Petrarch and Boccaccio, and the same view was passed on to France and England. As time went on, and the younger generations turned, with an enthusiasm today hardly comprehensible, to equipping their languages with rivals to the ancient classics, the Gothic "monstrousness" of the "Comedy" became more and more evident; and as the new literature expanded in bulk and acquired its own glories, Dante continued to be sensed as a great genius, but was regarded as an untrustworthy literary model, as compared with a Sannazaro, an Ariosto, a Politian, or any master, indeed, of the great age. Reformation and Counter-Reform might, again, it would seem, have shifted the balance in Dante's favor: Protestants have ever sensed a kindred spirit in him, by virtue of his pious earnestness; and Catholics have had no fault to find with his orthodoxy. But, really, history does not go backward. The classical revival still intervened between the Europe of Luther and Loyola and the Gothic age. Catholic Europe was to find its distinctive poetry in the "Jerusalem" of Tasso, just as Protestantism was to find its poet in Milton.

With the literary men of the Enlightenment, the regretful reserve of the Renaissance toward Dante turns to vocal animosity. The Renaissance had

VI

disliked Dante's art; but it had respected his doctrine. The Eighteenth century despised both the art and the doctrine. Voltaire found Dante "stupidly extravagant and barbarous"—and, in fact, what "rational" man could linger on the wild imaginings of the *Inferno;* and who but a boor could harp on such things as repentance and death in the presence of a *grande dame* given to fainting spells? Oliver Goldsmith disparaged Dante's immortality on the ground that "in an age of barbarism a small degree of eminence secures success". Goethe, who was joining Milton and Tasso to make up a trinity of modern challenge to Dante, judged the *Inferno* "altogether horrible", the *Purgatorio* as "neither one thing nor another", and the *Paradiso* "intolerably slow". Horace Walpole was more vigorous still: Dante was "extravagant, absurd, disgusting, in short a Methodist parson in Bedlam". And this remark, as a more recent flayer of Dante, Mr. Albert Mordell, suggests, is well to be classed with the damnation of Nietzsche, who, on different sentimental grounds and almost in our own time, was to denounce Dante as a "hyena poetizing in the tombs" (A. Mordell, *Dante and the Waning Classics*, Philadelphia 1916).

But on the Enlightenment follow Revolution and Romanticism. The Nineteenth century at last bridges the gap between the Gothic and the modern spirit. With the collapse of the old feudal aristocracy a new kind of people, the so-called bourgeoisie, comes to constitute the vanguard of culture. The severe urbane ideals of the old gentility give ground before a rich and uncloyed sentimentalism rising from the soil of Europe. Romanticism re-exalted those values of imagination and sentiment which the classic ideal of the Renaissance and the courtly age had rejected as unworthy of thinking people. The Romantics were the first to appreciate at their true value the picturesque, the tragic, and the grandiose elements in Dante; indeed, the surpassing richness of his individuality. But that was not all. With the growth of the modern nation, people come to look differently upon the Middle Ages. That era of "Gothic barbarism" which had seemed to intervene as an intruder between feudal Europe and Imperial Rome now becomes the legendary heroic age which cradled the modern peoples. The "Comedy" of Dante participates in the same revival of Medievalism which glorifies the Gothic cathedrals. While in England, for instance, the Pre-Raphaelites were exalting Giotto over Tintoretto, and Beatrice over Laura, in Italy Dante was attaining apotheosis on the wings of a virulent Italian nationalism, and his poem was becoming what it is today, the holy book of the Italian patriot. And so in other countries of the West, the Christian Middle Ages win recognition as an essential link in the common patrimony of Western culture, and the "Comedy" is regarded as a property of all nations.

The past hundred years have witnessed a vast florescence of so-called historical scholarship in literary criticism, and "Dante literature"—critical and historical literature dealing with Dante—has transcended all conceivable limits of bulk. The avowed pretence of our scholars has been to illumine art with science and to bring the facts of literature under some general law. But one has only to look back upon such literature from the vantage ground of our present day, which it is still our privilege to call superior, to see that science has really had little to do with it. Historical literary criticism has all along been a maidservant to national sentiments, designed to demonstrate the existence of national literary traditions and to validate and assert national sentimental values. It is the "scientific" scholars of Italian Positivism who are responsible for the Dante worship that is prevalent today in Italy. In other Latin countries his fame is being exploited and promoted in the interests of a Catholic element in national sentiment; just as, in our own country, a wide-spread Dante cult connects the "Comedy" with our national tradition by virtue of the "Christian morality" common both to Dante and to Protestants.

II. DANTE ALIGHIERI

No relic of Dante—no manuscript, no signature, no likeness—has survived to our time (letters in his hand were still extant in the fifteenth century). Nevertheless, his external personality has never been vague enough to tempt anyone to attribute the "Comedy" to Roger Bacon.

He was born in Florence during the month of May, 1265. He died in Ravenna, where he was living as guest of a nephew of Francesca da Rimini, on September 13-14, 1321—at the age, therefore, of fifty-six. He came of genteel stock, though his family was not wealthy nor specially prominent. As a gentleman he became a soldier in the Army of the Republic, and saw action somewhere or other in the year 1269. In the year 1297 he married a girl named Gemma Donati. She bore him four children.

Between 1295 and 1301 Dante was "in politics". Florence was a "Guelph" city: that is to say, in the long struggle between Papacy and Empire Florence habitually sided with the Pope. The Republic, at that particular time, had a "popular" coloring: the trades unions, as far back as 1283, had succeeded in excluding non-members of guilds from public office. Dante, accordingly, though a gentleman, enrolled in the Guild of Druggists and Physicians. Local politics were managed by two "machines", the one, of the "White" Guelphs, so-called, run by a Cerchi family, the other, of the "Black" Guelphs, run by a "boss" whose name is known: Corso Donati. The two factions treated each other roughly, as factions in a prosperous well-regulated city will. There were assassinations back and forth. A victory for either faction meant prosecution, and either imprisonment or flight, for the other faction. The situation probably sounds worse on paper than it was in reality. Dante belonged to the "Whites". His best friend, Guido

Cavalcanti, belonged to the "Blacks". His wife was a cousin of the opposing "boss"; the boon companion of his youth was a brother of the same "boss". When they were in power, the "Whites" used Dante as agent ("ambassador") to other republics, and on one occasion, to the Pope. In 1300 he was one of the six "Priors" (almost "select-men") of Florence. At that time he won a contract for widening a street (which sounds Tammany enough). However, the "Whites" were in power only six years. In 1301, supported by an efficiency-morality wave in town opinion, Donati's "gang" threw them bodily out of office, and Dante, with many others, including Petrarch's father, fled for his life.

His party never came back. Scattered about in nearby cities the exiles intrigued now here now there, and, in 1310, turned Ghibelline (Imperial) in hopes of being reinstated in Florence by the army of Emperor Henry VII. To avoid misunderstanding as to his position on the Guelph-Ghibelline issue, Dante wrote at this time his famous political pamphlet called *De Monarchia*. The sudden death of the Emperor in 1313 spoiled the plot. Dante grew discouraged, and thereafter held aloof from other political intrigues. By 1315 his conduct had been so satisfactory that the "Blacks" intimated that for one of the usual considerations the sentence of death which had been passed against him in contumacy would be annulled. Dante refused— the consideration may have been too high—and never changed his mind. His wife, who belonged by birth to a "Black" family, had not been disturbed. She did not follow Dante abroad. Three of his children were with him at Ravenna, when he died. Dante's movements as an exile are vaguely known. Proofs have been unearthed of his presence at one time or another in many towns of Northern Italy. Boccaccio, alone, takes him as far afield as Paris. He lived for long periods with the Scala family at Verona. His last years were spent with the Polentas, lords of Ravenna.

III. THE "SWEET NEW STYLE"

Brilliantly clear, instead, is Dante Alighieri's intellectual or spiritual history —the story of his inner life. Dante's Florence was a booming, active, intelligent city, thrilling with new ideas and ideals. It was a town of business men, who manufactured silks, woolens, jewelry, and sold them in all the markets of Europe; of bankers who were dealing, even in England, with the newly sensed mysteries of credit; and of rich land-owners, who first had been driven by force from their stone houses on the hills and had then taken up a life, after all gayer and more congenial, in the city itself. Placed midway along the traffic lines of Italy, at a time when Italy lay midway along the traffic lines of the world, Florence was a town open to all currents of culture that were anywhere stirring: and the Florentines of that day, knowing the world, had also an inspiring sense of their own superiorities over the peoples in other towns and countries. The men of those generations left their mark upon the town in those square, sharp-cornered towers that still seem somehow to incarnate before our modern eyes the fierce self-confidence of the old Commune—among other buildings, the *Palazzo Vecchio* itself; and they adorned their homes with an art which was also proud of its newness, homes which survive to our day and which we can only call "palaces". The town was, however, a medieval town—shut in behind thick walls. Beyond the walls lay barbarism—the open country that was prey to the strong-armed gangs of the feudal baron, to the freebooter, to anarchy.

Dante's boyhood poems introduce us to the youthful "society" that lived in his rich and busy town. The culture of the old folks, when they are cultured, is in Latin: theology is the principal science; as for letters, there are a few Roman writers (and no Greeks); then the encyclopedia, the "book of knowledge": geography, cosmography, astrology; then lives of the Saints, pious legends. The young people, children of merchants with money to spend, look up respectfully—but they are not convinced. For one thing, it is not altogether easy to know Latin. But, more than that, the breath of a new fashion, a new gentility, is in the air. It is *bon ton* to know French, or rather, the two Frenches, the French of the South, Provençal, in which one can turn such a pretty compliment to a lady, and sing it to the music of a viola, withal; and the French of the North, with its tales of chivalry, its narratives of mirth, its poems of arms and adventure. But not only the French: there are Italians who have learned the art of making verses in the natural language—Guinicelli, at Bologna, was poet and scholar too. And in the good old days, was not Italian the genteel language of Frederick's court in Sicily?

It must have been in some such mood that Dante and his friends first began writing their sonnets and *canzoni* to their sweethearts and to each other, taking their cues from the examples of Guinicelli, the early Sicilians, and the troubadours; and soon they had hit on a new "trick", a new theme, or device of their own—the notion of the "lady angelified", which gave them, even in their own eyes, a certain originality and opened to them depths in the amorous emotions of adolescence which had never before been explored by men. The girl whom Dante made an angel, and who stirred his soul with such rare and mysterious sentiments, he called "Beatrice". Guido, Lapo Gianni, Cina, and the others had similar names for their sweethearts. Who was "Beatrice"? We may be sure that every eligible girl in that society must have asked that question of herself and of Dante; and we may also be sure that in after-church flirtations of those watchful days Dante told every girl whom he knew in his circles in Florence that she was Beatrice. And the historical truth probably is—since boys are boys

—that at one time or another Beatrice was every girl in Florence, every pretty girl, that is; and we have Dante's word for it, that at one time he was writing to two girls at once—not an unique experience, either. Beatrice Everybody-Nobody was to play an important part in Dante's spiritual evolution. At a later day, when he had become famous, people asked in all seriousness, "Who was Beatrice?" And since the question had to be asked, it had to be answered: a Beatrice had to be found. Someone told Boccaccio, in his day, that she was one Beatrice Portinari, a lady who fitted the bill on the score of age. History can go no farther; and those historians who would speculate farther can only be reminded that in history there are many, many things that we shall never know. *Ignorabimus.*

And at this point, instead of proceeding farther here, the reader should turn backwards in the book of his memory to that part before which little is to be read; and if he find there a caption, "Here the New Life Begins", and a recollection of the first revelation of feminine beauty to his spirit; if he has known a love envisaged as mystery and freed of selfish desire, a love which he was fain to associate with the nobler aspirations of his best self; a love which seemed to grow purer and greater in renunciation; a love, finally, hallowed by death and carrying within itself an inner persuasion of immortality—he should then turn to the *Vita nuova* of Dante Alighieri, in the translation of Rossetti, or in the translation of Norton; in order to find there an unforgettably beautiful expression of those adolescent experiences in verse and in prose. The *Vita nuova* was not read, and was hardly known, during the great centuries of Classicism. Europe owes its revival to the Romantics, and Anglo-Saxons, in particular, to the Pre-Raphaelites. For many of us it is the only Dante that is really loved, however much we may admire the "Comedy".

IV. THE THOMIST REVELATION

But this vision of a new gentility in earnest vein, which found expression in the youthful poets of the "sweet new style", was not the only spiritual novelty working in the atmosphere of Dante's Florence. Upon that generation of men fell a new truth, a new intellectual dispensation, which moved all minds deeply, and in the mind of Dante Alighieri in particular wrought a great and proficuous revolution.

The thought of Saint Thomas Aquinas still endures in our day. For some people it is a beacon light marking the safe haven from which modern thought embarked on a hazardous voyage and to which it must someday return. For most of us it is a sand-bar now safely passed by an advancing human spirit. In Dante's day, the *Summa* was still new. It had appeared when Dante was nine years old.

To feel a little as Dante felt when he came upon the *Summa* in those last ten years of the Thirteenth century, we must think of similar experiences of our own times, of books that seem, now to one, now to another of us, to turn the world inside out and lay it bare before our eyes—books such as the "Social Contract" of Rousseau was to the Eighteenth century; the "Critique of Pure Reason" to our great-grandfathers; the "Origin of Species" to our grandfathers. It might be more exact to say that the *Summa* was to Dante's day what the "Capital" of Karl Marx has been to the Socialists and is now to Russia: a book more generally admired than read or understood, and more powerful in its radiations than in its direct influence. The *Summa* is, in fact, the masterpiece of medieval thinking, and one of the great achievements of the human mind at large—something kindred in the sphere of thought to the Ptolemaic system in the sphere of astronomy, a system which, starting from data in large part fanciful, nevertheless reduces the cosmos to something which, on the premises given, is a coherent whole.

For Dante's contemporaries it was a rationalization of the universe. It seemed to remove all contradictions between faith and thought, to harmonize the practical with the ideal, to fit every aspect of human life in this world and the next into its proper place, to solve even the problems of predestination and free will, of good and of evil. Considered as an influence, it had spread abroad the conviction that the universe was a rational manageable quantity—that reality could be grasped by thought.

This inspiration fell upon Dante when he was, let us say at a venture, about twenty-eight (in 1293), when he was just entering upon his manhood's career. He hints at the vision—it came as a veritable illumination—at the end of the *Vita nuova*; for it seems probable that his resolve "to say of Beatrice what had not been said of any woman" relates rather to the philosophical and pseudo-scientific effort left unrealized in "The Banquet" (*Il convito*) than to the much later vision perfected in the "Comedy". Let us keep Dante always in mind as the man he must have been in that active and enthusiastic Florentine society, a popular individual, admired for his originality of mind, praised for the triumphs he had won already in verse and in thought, sure of himself, aggressive. The poetry of the "sweet new style" is a novelty—it has said and felt things that no human being has said or felt before. Dante clings to that novelty. Love is the great and beautiful thing in life—the love of woman. Love of woman is the counter-part, the *verso*, as it were, of the love of which Christianity speaks, the love in which and of which God made the world. "The Banquet" is an abortive work, left, in fact, unfinished. It shows a powerful mind floundering about amid the rubbish which the methods of thinking traditional in Dante's day threw in his path, a mind struggling to cut deep into reality with such tools as pure logic, allegory, erudition, a metaphysic proceeding from words to things rather than a science developing from things to concepts. One senses in the vague biographical background some grumblings from the older generation loyal to orthodox approaches, through the Latin school, to thought; and a spirited defence from the secular bourgeois Florentine of his essentially vernacular culture. Dante defends himself for "thinking in Italian" in the *Convito*. He returns to the same theme in a special treatise, *De vulgari eloquentia*, a general meditation on the whole problem of the vernacular (it was to be discovered, and revived with great effect and enthusiasm, in the Renaissance by Gian Giorgio Trissino, 1521). But, meantime, the general drive of Dante's thought is clear: it is an effort to organize the universe around the concept of love—a sort of Christian Platonism.

Now between the "Banquet" and the "Comedy" there opens in all respects a gulf, which biography ought to fill for us but cannot. Why does the scientific, philosophical research yield to the poetic vision? How does the poet in Dante succeed in asserting himself at the expense of the producer of treatises who was soon to do the *De Monarchia* (1310?), also, and in the end the fatuous *Quaestio de aqua et terra* (1320?)? We must seek the answer, if at all, in Dante's essentially secular background as a man of the world and not of the cloister. Thought, after all, is with him the avocation—that partly explains the immense pride he takes in it. He is not, at bottom, either saint, or professor, or priest: he is the gentleman, a man with a sense of humor, be it not forgotten; and a man who hates and scorns by instinct, and who prays by tradition. And then again he has lived, with his peculiar vividness of observation, and he has read and listened with his unique powers of imagination. It is the panorama of life, present and past, that sets itself over against the edifice of thought he is erecting in his mind, and it, too, clamors within him for expression. His fundamental meditation shortly transcends the scope of the "Banquet" and cries for its own form, such a form as only the poet can give, and which the poet instinctively seeks, again among the literary models available at his time: visions, allegories, didactic journeys.

When Dante began to write the "Comedy" is not known. The *Paradiso* seems to have been written between 1313 and 1321, and somewhat later than the *Inferno* and the *Purgatorio*. The beginning of the *Inferno* may go back as far as 1300. But the character of the "Comedy" is clear: it will be the poem of triumphant knowledge describing a world in which everything is known and exulting in the discovery. Saint Thomas had said it: a part of the truth is knowable through sense and thought. What is not knowable through sense and thought is known through revelation. Surveying the mysteries of life and death, looking through and beyond the turmoils of human passion, Dante is a man who has attained certainty. The world is orderly. The world is rational. Beyond the limits of the world lies the other world. The other world too is orderly. The other world too is rational. There is no element of the unknown in human destiny. Let us take humanity in the concrete—let us take history. The life, the incident, the episode, show a murky blur of passions born of this frail carnality that is so dear to us. Look at them closely, they yield to thought: they find their proper and logical places in the logical scheme of God's universe. Let us describe that universe according to its true scheme. Let us depict it as it is actually experienced by men moved by all their varied passions and possessed of all their varied capacities of intelligence, feeling, action. That will be the "Comedy", the poem of human destiny, the poem of salvation.

V. POET VERSUS THINKER

And, lo, from our modern standpoint, the paradoxes of genius! The "Comedy" is throughout dead! And the "Comedy" is throughout alive!

The "Comedy" is dead, as Dante conceived the "Comedy". As the book of thought and learning and doctrine, which he took, and meant, it to be, it has been entirely overpassed by history. His geography was ruined by Henry the Navigator and by Columbus, and his cosmogony by Copernicus. That philosophy which he thought was explaining everything was found inadequate within a few generations; and within our last three hundred years, if it has been cultivated at all, it has been so apart from the main currents of thought. His theology is dead. The assertion may be disputed— but we are concerned with the question only in its literary bearings: the theology is dead among many people with whom the "Comedy" is alive. The morality of Dante is dead. To be sure, it is still the stronghold of the philistine insensitive by nature to the conscious appreciation of art; and there is no dearth of Dante critics who, as a short cut to a theory of greatness, are willing enough to reduce genius to the commonplace and unveil the secret of a talent like Dante's by seeing in him the exaltation of moral platitudes. But one has only to ask oneself: who believes today in that mechanical, legalistic, altogether extrinsic classification of sins and virtues which form the scheme of the *Inferno*, the *Purgatorio* and the *Paradiso*, even if that scheme be amended by those modifications in feudal law and feudal ethics which modern feeling—the humanitarian spirit in particular—has generally effected? Who, if not since the days of Luther, at least since the day of Kant, any longer believes that morality is even possible on the basis of obedience to injunctions deriving from an external, transcendental authority? Who believes any longer in that delicate balancing of sins and punishments, of virtues and rewards, upon which Dante spent such laborious and painstaking thought?

The "art" of the "Comedy" is dead—the art, in Dante's terms, that is: it was dead, in fact, within a century and a half of Dante's death. Dante conceived the "Comedy" as an allegorical poem. To a certain amount of allegory one must pay attention if one would grasp the logical sequence of the story; but as for the allegory as a whole, no one knows exactly what it is; and even if we take the dilemma by the horns and say "This is the allegory!", the latter results in a complicated theological narrative vague in its terms and dubious in its import, a mechanistic contraption that seems altogether fatuous and ridiculous when we are asked to heed it as we sit spellbound before the majestic song that Dante had to sing. And if this be the case with the allegory, what shall we say of the "anagogy", or divine symbolism, of which Dante was perhaps deservedly proud, since no one has ever been able to say anything intelligent or intelligible about it? And all this we are saying not in reproof of Dante—he was describing life in the terms of the best knowledge of his time, and what more can anyone do?—but in order to fix the limits of an aesthetic problem: to avoid, if we can, the pitfalls into which the Renaissance fell, in disparaging the sentiment and the imagination in Dante; and the error into which the Enlightenment fell, in condemning the art in the light of the doctrine; and into which modern scourgers of the statue of Apollo, such as Mr. Mordell, fall, in holding that because a work of the past has been left behind in the march of progress in some respects, we are wrong in not abandoning it in all respects. All of Mr. Mordell's waning classics are alive, for the simple reason that they are alive—the "Comedy" among them.

Turn to the Francesca episode, for a moment (*Inf.* v), and consider on the one hand Dante's thought, and on the other hand Dante's sentiment: both are clear enough. The thought is, that adulterers who die in their sin are in Hell, a certain distance down, a certain distance up: adultery is worse than ignorance of God, but less sinful than, for instance, gluttony. Not all moderns would agree with this thinking; any more than they would agree, farther along, that suicide with attenuating provocations is more sinful than multiple murder involving killing for the sake of killing. And now the sentiment: two people who loved each other and are united in death, whose love, indeed, is triumphant over death; the tragedy of a defeated love; homesickness for a happiness that is gone beyond recall; wistful recollection of scenes far away; pity for this poor humanity of ours—romanticism asserting itself in the face of, and at the expense of, Thomism.

Or turn to the Ulysses episode (*Inf.* xxvi), where Dante shows, schematically, that evil counsellors are less sinful than traitors but more sinful than, for instance, swindlers; and shows, implicitly, that self-assertion in the face of God-made mystery is fatal to man. But who ever remembers just where, or just why, Ulysses is in Hell? What one remembers is the exciting dash out upon the great ocean; the encircling horizons; star-light over the deep; the trail of the Moon on the waters; the exultant cry of "Land!"; the fascinating horror of a vessel foundering in a gale.

And who could tell, offhand, just where, up along the slopes of Purgatory, Dante encounters Pia dei Tolomei, and who knows, or cares, why she is just there, and not one peg farther up, or another farther down? Yet who can forget, once he has heard it, that sudden lament issuing, deferential, modest, restrained, from the throng of spirits— a lament for a bruised love, an unrancorous protest against a treachery undeserved, the pathos of a bride's blasted hope, the lightning-like sketch of a tragedy in a lonely medieval castle and on a wild landscape of marshland.

Or—to choose one final example from among a thousand—there is that passage in *Purgatorio*, III. 22-45, where Dante propounds the pseudo-scientific query as to why the souls of the dead, which cast no shadow, are nevertheless able to experience the sensations of living bodies; and answers that, after all, one cannot know; whereupon Virgil breaks into a singularly intense lament at the impotence of human intelligence. And here speaks the medieval erudite who wrote the *Quaestio*: but here also speaks the immortal poet, who in a flash of rhetorical divination colors that lament of Virgil with the glows of a Neapolitan sunset and makes the ancient seer look back in a perspective of eternity upon the tomb that holds his mortal dust.

There is, in short, in the "Comedy" a content that is medieval; but then, beyond and apart from the medieval content, there is a content that is of all times and all men. But, having distinguished those elements for purpose of definition, let us not now fall into the error of the Romantics of setting up, beside the "Comedy" that is dead, a "Comedy" of detached romantic episodes that, for historical reasons of our own, we still chance to find sentimentally alive—such a process reduces the poem to too low a plane, cheapens it in fact. For the "Comedy", as for any work of the past, we have to perform an historical reconstruction within ourselves; and just as in re-reading the Dido episode in the *Aeneid* of Virgil, we have to purge ourselves of our Romantic inheritance, and force ourselves to feel in Roman terms that Aeneas was truly great, and not just a cad, in deserting that lady— sense in other words the grandeur of the Roman subjection of the individual to national destiny; so we have to return to that moment in Dante's biography when he caught a comprehensive vision of his universe, saw human existence as certainty with every detail in its logical place, and set out to sing the pilgrimage of man from the dark wood of human error to the light of God's presence. Then only can we really follow Dante in the unrolling of the stupendous panorama which he sees, and grasp each of the three canticles and the majestic structure of the poem as a whole in their historical verity. We have to learn to feel in the *Inferno* a certain mood of desperate finality that emanates from human passions unenlightened by Christian love. We have to learn to feel the peculiar flavor of the melancholy of the *Purgatorio*, where the spirits have a wistful remembrance of Earth and a joyous hope of redemption. We have, finally, to make a great effort, read significance into the theology of the Paradise, accustom our eyes to the blaze of light (which Mr. Mordell finds so offensive), and re-experience with Dante, if not the ecstasy of the divine vision (which, after all, is by definition beyond attainment by the human imagination), at least his faith in the reality of divinity, and his joy and contentment at finding himself in a world made and ruled by a God.

It is then that the "Comedy" comes to true life within us as the music that it really is, a majestic symphony enriched with numberless motifs, which beset the memory, which we finally memorize, and which recur to our minds in now this and now that situation in life, illumining it now with wisdom, now with sentiment, now with humor. Thousands of people, as six centuries have passed by, have read and relived, are reading and reliving, the "Comedy" in just this way. That is why, over the course of its six centuries of age, it continues to endure.

VI. TERZA RIMA

The interlocking rhymed terzet which Dante used in the "Comedy", and which Dr. Anderson has faithfully preserved in this translation, was Dante's own invention. Both Petrarch and Boccaccio were soon to imitate it; and in the course of centuries Italians were to apply it to all sorts of themes. Its use may have given Dante a symbolic thrill as an anagogy of the Trinity. He was addicted to number symbolism. The "Comedy" moreover has three canticles of thirty-three cantos each (if we allow that the first canto of the *Inferno* is prologue). If now the reader will leap aboard a railroad train and journey to the Fiske Dante Collection at Ithaca, New York— the noblest tribute that America has so far paid to Dante— he will find a whole shelf devoted to number symbolism in Dante's works; and if he reads all those many articles which the scholars have written on the subject, with quotations from the Assyrians, the Egyptians, the Greeks and the Latins, and so on down to the Arabs, he will learn: 1, that one plus one plus one makes three; 2, that three times three makes nine (Beatrice's number); 3, that two threes set side by side spell thirty-three. Fortified with that much science he will then be in a position to solve the enigma of the DXV (five hundred ten and five) in *Purgatorio* XXXIII. 43,—which would be so easy, and so fully prophetic, if only it were five hundred five and ten: DVX. And let him not feel too modest to make a try: for his answer, whatever it may be, will be as good as the answers of the most expert Dantologists.

Having now won his spurs as a member of the Dante fraternity, the reader might next turn to the problem in *Inferno* I. 30, where Dante says that he was proceeding in such a manner "that the firm foot was ever the lower". If the reader will try that out, for example on the roof of his bungalow, he will see that such a feat is impossible, if one be walking uphill. Dante, therefore, could not have been walking uphill. It must be, as Lorenzo da Ponte contended, in the first Dante lectures ever delivered in America, that Dante was walking on a level.

And now for that minimum of allegory which is essential to following the story of the "Comedy". The Dante who experiences the vision seems to represent mankind, the human soul. Virgil, his guide through Hell and Purgatory, is Reason. However, in *Inf.* IV. 131, Aristotle is called "master of those who know". Virgil, therefore, would be, not just the rational faculty, but human intelligence as guided and instructed by Roman civilization with its learning, its law, its secular institutions—the Empire, in a word. Cato, who admits the travellers to Purgatory, symbolizes free will. To expound the finer mysteries of upper Purgatory Virgil is assisted by the poet Statius (*Purg.* XXII. ff.), who would seem to represent human (Virgil's) wisdom enlightened by Christianity. The Leah and Rachel who come on the scene in the Earthly Paradise (*Purg.* XXVII) seem to symbolize respectively the Active and the Contemplative Life. The beautiful Matilda might be the Divine Grace that leads to Beatrice, or Revelation.

The Beatrice of the "Comedy" is a very aethereal creature. I will confess, nevertheless, that I am always repeating to myself, understanding not a whit as to what "harmony" can possibly mean, just for the music—the verses in *Purgatorio* XXXI. 139-145: O *isplendor*... etc.—they deal with Dante's reunion with Beatrice; and it seems to me that Dr. Anderson has performed a miracle in rendering them so beautifully.

For me, as for many others, the woman of the "Comedy" is not Beatrice, but Francesca. Or Pia.

ARTHUR LIVINGSTON

TABLE OF CONTENTS

PURGATORIO

PARADISO

NOTES AND ELUCIDATIONS

LIST OF THE PLATES

INFERNO

...molte volte al fatto il dir vien meno.
INFERNO IV. 147

CANTO I

Midway the path of life that men pursue
   I found me in a darkling wood astray,
   For the direct way had been lost to view.
Ah me, how hard a thing it is to say
   What was this thorny wildwood intricate
   Whose memory renews the first dismay!
Scarcely in death is bitterness more great:
   But as concerns the good discovered there
   The other things I saw will I relate.
How there I entered I am unaware,
   So was I at that moment full of sleep
   When I abandoned the true thoroughfare.
But when I reached the bottom of a steep
   Ending the valley which had overcome
   My courage, piercing me with fear so deep,
Lifting mine eyes up, I beheld its dome
   Already covered with that planet's light
   Which along all our pathways leads us home.
Then was a little quieted the fright
   That had been lurking in the heart of me
   Throughout the passage of the piteous night.
And like to one who, panting wearily
   Forth from the deep, at last his safety seeing,
   Turns to the perilous water musingly,
So did my mind, which even yet was fleeing,
   Turn back to view the pass that nevermore
   Has left alive a single human being.
Having a little eased my body sore,
   Along the solitary slope I plied
   So that the firm foot ever was the lower.
And lo! where but begins the mountainside,
   A leopard light and very swift of pace
   And covered with a gaily spotted hide.

Proem: Rescue
of Dante by
Virgil

3

Never withdrew she from before my face;
  Nay, rather blocked she so my going on
  That oft I turned my footing to retrace.
It was about the moment of the dawn;
  Uprose the sun and paled the light benign
  Of those fair stars which were beside him yon
When took they motion first from Love Divine:
  So the sweet season and the time of day
  Caused me to augur as a hopeful sign
That animal with skin bedappled gay:
  Yet not so much but that I felt dismayed
  To see a lion intercept my way.
It seemed to me that he toward me made
  With head erected and with hunger raving,
  So that the very air appeared afraid:
And a she-wolf, made gaunt by every craving
  Wherewith methought she heavy-laden went,
  And much folk hitherto of joy bereaving;
She brought on me so much discouragement
  By terror of her aspect that perforce
  I forfeited all hope of the ascent.
And as one, interrupted in his course
  Of winning, when his fortune is undone
  Is full of perturbation and remorse,
That truceless beast made me such malison,
  And coming on against me pace by pace
  Baffled me back where silent is the sun.
While I was falling back to that low place,
  A being was made present to my ken
  Who through long silence seemed in feeble case.
Seeing that figure in the desert glen,
  'Have pity upon me!' I imploring cried,
  'Whether thou be of shades or real men.'
'Not man,—a man once was I,' he replied,
  'My parents both were born at Mantua,
  And were of Lombard blood on either side.

Sub Julio was I born, though late the day,
    And under good Augustus lived at Rome
    When false and lying deities bore sway.
I was a poet: that just hero whom
    Anchises sired, I sang, who came from Troy
    After the burning of proud Ilium.
But why dost thou return to such annoy,
    Wherefore ascend not the delightful Mount,
    Beginning and occasion of all joy?'
'Art thou indeed that Virgil, and that fount
    Whence pours of eloquence so broad a stream?'
    I made reply to him with bashful front.
'O of the other poets light supreme,
    May the long study now my warrant be,
    And the great love that made thy book my theme.
Thou art my Master and my Authority,
    And thou alone art he from whom I've taken
    The goodly style that has done grace to me.
Behold the beast for whom I have forsaken
    The forward course: assist me, famous sage,
    For look! my veins and pulses all are shaken.'
'Another journey must thy steps engage,'
    When he beheld me weeping, did he say,
    'Wouldst from this savage place make pilgrimage;
Because this beast whereat thou criest, gives way
    Never to any comer, but doth sore
    Impede and harass him until she slay.
Malignant is she so that nevermore
    The craving of her appetite is fed,
    And after food is hungrier than before.
Many are the animals that with her wed,
    And there shall yet be more, until the Hound
    Shall come and in her misery strike her dead.
His food shall not be either pelf or ground
    But what is loving, wise, and valorous:
    Feltro and Feltro shall his nation bound.

5

That humble Italy preserves he thus
   For which the maid Camilla bit the dust,
   Turnus and Nisus and Euryalus:
And out of every city shall he thrust
   That beast, until he drive her back to Hell
   Whence she was first let loose by envious lust.
Wherefore for thee I think and judge it well
   Thou follow me, and I will bring about
   Thy passage thither where the eternal dwell.
There shalt thou hearken the despairing shout,
   Shalt see the souls of yore, each woeful guest
   Who craving for the second death cry out.
Shalt see thereafter those who are at rest
   Amid the flame, because their wishes bend
   To make them, whensoever, of the blest.
If then to these thou wishest to ascend,
   For this a worthier soul than I shall wait,
   And with her will I leave thee at the end:
Because that Emperor who there holds state,
   Seeing I was a rebel to His law,
   Wills that through me none pass His city-gate.
There rules His love, as everywhere His awe;
   There in His capital He sits on high:
   Happy His chosen who may nigh Him draw!'
'O Poet, I entreat of thee,' said I,
   'By that Divinity thou didst not know,
   So this and greater evil I may fly,
That where thou saidst I may a pilgrim go,
   And led by thee Saint Peter's portal find,
   And those thou makest out afflicted so.'
Then moved he on, I following behind.

CANTO II

Day was departing and the dusky air
 Loosing the living things on earth that dwell
 From their fatigues; and I alone was there
Preparing to sustain the war, as well
 Of the long way as also of the pain,
 Which now unerring memory will tell.
O Muses! O high Genius, now sustain!
 O Memory who wrote down what I did see,
 Here thy nobility will be made plain.
Now I began: 'Poet who guidest me,
 Look to my worth if it be plenteous,
 Ere to the hard pass thou confidest me.
Thou tellest that the Sire of Silvius
 Went to the everlasting world, while still
 Corruptible, and in the body thus.
But that the Adversary of every ill
 Should grace him so, viewing the issue high
 And who he was and what he should fulfil,
Seems not unfit to the understanding eye:
 For he was father of imperial Rome
 Elected in the empyrean sky,
Founding that city and her masterdom
 In sooth, for see and sanctuary blest
 Of those who after greatest Peter come.
And by that going, which thou honourest,
 He heard of things whereon were consequent
 His victory and then the Papal Vest.
There afterward the Chosen Vessel went
 Thence bringing comfort to that Faith supreme
 Which of salvation is the rudiment.
But wherefore I? Who grants me such a dream?
 Æneas am I not, nor am I Paul,
 Nor to myself or others worthy seem.

*Virgil describes
the Appeal of
Beatrice*

Whence, if I dare to yield me to thy call,
  I tremble lest the going prove insane:
  My words are to the wise,—thou knowest all.'
And like to those who chop and change again
  On second thoughts, unwilling former will,
  And make their fair beginning wholly vain,
Such became I on that benighted hill:
  Since, taking thought, I cancelled the emprise
  I was before so eager to fulfil.
'If I have comprehended thy replies,'
  Returned that shadow of the lofty mind,
  'Thy soul in caitiff apprehension lies,
Which oftentimes so baffles humankind,
  They turn like animal false sight perceiving,
  Leaving emprise of honour all behind.
To free thee from this timid misconceiving,
  Let me now tell thee what my coming meant,
  And what I heard of thee that set me grieving.
I was with those who are in Limbo pent,
  When a fair Lady from the blest abode
  Called me, and her command was my consent.
More brilliant than the star her glances glowed;
  And gently and serenely she began
  With voice angelic, in her own sweet mode:
"O courteous shade, soul of the Mantuan
  Whose fame endures to-day in human ear,
  And will endure as long as motion can,
One dear to me and not to fortune dear
  Is on the desert hillside in his way
  So hindered that he has turned back for fear,
And may, alas! be now so far astray
  That I am risen for his relief too late,
  From what I've heard the Heavenly voices say.
Now go, and with thine eloquence ornate,
  And what may serve for his escape from woe,
  Aid him, lest I should be disconsolate.

Myself am Beatrice who bid thee go;
   Thence come I whither to return I sigh;
   Love prompted me and makes me urge thee so.
When I shall be before my Lord on high
   I will speak often to Him in thy praise."
   Thereat she paused, and I began reply:
"O Lady by virtue of whom the human race
   Doth in nobility all things excel
   Within the Heaven that rounds the smallest space,
To do thy bidding pleases me so well
   The deed were laggard if already done:
   There is no further need thy wish to tell.
But tell me rather why thou dost not shun
   Descending to this centre from the sphere
   So wide, whereto thou burnest to be gone."
"Seeing it is thy will so far to peer,
   I will proceed to tell thee," she replied,
   "Why I am not afraid to enter here.
Of those things only fear is justified
   Wherein is power of harming less or much:
   At nothing else need one be terrified.
By Grace Divine have I been fashioned such
   That pangs me not the misery of you,
   Nor can the flame of all this burning touch.
In Heaven there is a gentle Lady who
   Berues this barrier whence I bid thee fare,
   So that she bursts on high stern judgement through.
She summoned Lucy to her in her prayer
   And said: 'Thy faithful one now needs thee so
   That I commend him to thy tender care.'
Lucy, of every cruelty the foe,
   Arose and came where I had not been long
   With Rachel, who was set there long ago.
'Beatrice,' she said, 'God's very choral song,
   Why help not him who had such love for thee
   That he forsook for thee the vulgar throng?

9

Dost thou not hear him weep in misery?
　　Dost thou not see how he is combated
　　By Death upon a flood wild as the sea?'
None ever in the world so swiftly sped
　　Avoiding hurt or questing benefit,
　　As came I, after suchlike words were said,
Speeding me down from where the blessed sit,
　　Trusting thy noble speech whose modest lore
　　Honours thyself, and others hearing it."
After she this had spoken, she forbore,
　　And, weeping, turned her shining eyes away,
　　Wherefore to come she made me hasten more;
And, coming to thee even as she did pray,
　　I drew thee from that beast which up the fair
　　Mountain, bereft thee of the briefer way.
What ails thee then? ah, why, why tarry there?
　　Why harbour in thy heart such cowardice?
　　Why not take liberty to do and dare,
When cherish for thee so much care as this
　　In Court of Heaven three Ladies benedight,
　　And mine own speaking pledges thee such bliss?'
Even as the flowerets by the chill of night
　　Bended and closed, when brightens them the sun
　　Uplift both stem and petal to the light,
So with my drooping courage I had done
　　Already, and began like one set free,
　　So much good daring to my heart had run:
'O deep compassion of her who succoured me!
　　And courteous thou, promptly obedient
　　To the true words that she addressed to thee!
Thy words have with such ardent longing bent
　　My heart to the adventure that, in troth,
　　I have returned now to my first intent.
Now go, for one will animates us both:
　　Thou leader and thou lord and master mild!'
　　So said I; and he moving, nothing loath
I entered on the pathway deep and wild.

CANTO III

'Through me the way is to the city of woe;
   Through me the way unto eternal pain;
   Through me the way among the lost below.
Justice commoved my high Creator, when
   Made me Divine Omnipotence, combined
   With Primal Love and Wisdom Sovereign.
Before me nothing was of any kind
   Except eterne, and I eterne abide:
   Leave, ye that enter in, all hope behind!'
On high above a gateway I descried,
   Written in dusky colour, this device:
   Whence I: 'The sense is dire to me, O Guide!'
Then answered he, as of expert advice:
   'Here must thou every fear perforce neglect,
   Here must perforce be killed all cowardice.
Now come we where I taught thee to expect
   To look upon the woeful populace
   Who have forgone the good of intellect.'
Laying his hand on mine with cheerful face,
   Whence I was comforted, he made me keep
   Right on and inward to the secret place.
Here lamentations, sighs, and wailings deep
   Resounding, so the starless welkin fill
   That, at the first, I could not choose but weep.
Strange languages, discoursings horrible,
   Accents of anger, histories of woes,
   Smiting of hands, with voices hoarse and shrill,
Make a tumultuous roar that swirling goes
   Forever in that air of truceless gloom,
   Like to the sandblast when the whirlwind blows.
And I, who felt my head begirt with doom,
   Said: 'Master, what is this I hear, and what
   People who seem with grief so overcome?'

The Dire Inscription and the Dark River

II

And he replied to me: 'In this dim spot
   The miserable souls of those suspire
   Whom infamy and honour both forgot.
They are commingled with that caitiff quire
   Of angels, who nowise rebellious were,
   Nor true to God, but to their own desire.
The Heavens expelled them, not to be less fair,
   Nor find they harbour in the pit of Hell
   Lest over them the damned might glory there.'
'Master,' said I, 'what grievance is so fell
   To these, that their lament should be so great?'
   He answered: 'I will very briefly tell.
These have no hope of death; and this their state
   Of blind existence is degraded so,
   They are envious of every other fate.
Report of them the world does not allow;
   Mercy and Justice hold them in disdain:
   Let us not speak of them, but look, and go.'
And I beheld, on looking there again,
   A whirling banner running swiftly on,
   As scorning all delay; and such a train
Of people in pursuit of it that run,
   Nothing but seeing could belief persuade
   That ever Death so many had fordone.
And recognizing some, I saw a shade
   In whom detected I that one of these
   Who cravenly the Great Refusal made.
This was the sect of caitiffs, who displease,—
   As now forthwith I understood and knew,—
   Not God alone but all His enemies.
Wretches who never were alive, and who
   Were sorely stung upon their bodies nude
   By hornets and by wasps that thither flew.
These bathed the faces of those shades with blood
   Which, blent with streaming tears, was at their feet
   Gathered up by a loathsome vermin-brood.

INFERNO: CANTO II
The Mission of Virgil

And now my glances, pushing further, meet
  People upon the marge of a great stream;
  Whence I: 'Now tell me, Master, I entreat,
What folk are these, and by what rule they seem
  So eager on the passage to be gone,
  As I distinguish by the feeble gleam.'
And he to me: 'These matters shall be known
  Unto thee, when we stay from our advance
  Upon the woeful marge of Acheron.'
Thereon with downcast eyes and modest glance,
  Fearing my words were irksome to him, I
  Far as the stream refrained from utterance.
And lo! upon a bark approaching nigh,
  One white with ancient tresses, passing old:
  'Woe to you wicked spirits!' was his cry.
'Hope nevermore the Heavens to behold:
  I come to lead you to the other bank,
  Into eternal darkness, heat, and cold.
And thou, O living spirit, from the rank
  Dispart thee, of these others who are dead.'
  And when he saw me not as one who shrank:
'Another way, by other ports,' he said,
  'Not here, shalt come for waftage to the shore:
  Upon a lighter keel must thou be sped.'
'Vex thee not, Charon,' said my Monitor:
  'Thus it is willed where will is one and same
  With potence to fulfil,—and ask no more.'
Then quieted the shaggy cheeks became,
  Of him, the boatman of the turbid mere,
  Who round about his eyes had wheels of flame.
But those souls, who are weary all and bare,
  Change colour and their teeth are chattering,
  Soon as the cruel accents strike the ear.
God they blaspheme and their own sires, and fling
  Curses on race and place and time and law
  Both of their birth and their engendering.

Then, flocking all together, they withdraw,
    Bitterly weeping, to the cursèd shore
    Awaiting each who holds not God in awe.
Charon, the demon, with the eyes that glow'r,
    Beckoning to them, every one receives,
    And smites whoever lingers, with the oar.
As in the autumn season when the leaves,
    First one and then another, lightly fall,
    Till all upon the ground the bough perceives:
Likewise the evil seed of Adam all
    Fling them from off that margin one by one
    At signals, like the bird at his recall.
Thus over the dusk water they are gone,
    And ere they can alight on yonder strand
    Forgathers a fresh throng on this anon.
'Son,' said the courteous Master, 'understand
    That those who perish subject to God's ire
    Are all assembled here from every land,
And ready are to pass the river dire,
    Because Celestial Justice so doth goad
    That very fear converts into desire.
No righteous spirit ever takes this road:
    And hence, though Charon may of thee complain,
    Thou knowest now the meaning of his mode.'
When he had ended, all the dreary plain
    So trembled that, but calling it to mind,
    The terror bathes me now with sweat again.
The land of tears gave forth a blast of wind
    With lightning flashes of vermilion deep,
    Whence consciousness I utterly resigned:
Then sank I like one overcome with sleep.

INFERNO

CANTO IV

A pealing burst of thunder loosed my sense
  From heavy sleep, and caused me to rebound
  Like one who is awaked by violence:
And, risen erect, on every side around
  I moved my rested eye, and fixed my sight
  To recognize the features of that ground.
True is it that I stood upon the height
  Above the valley of the Abyss of Woe,
  Which gathers roar of wailing infinite.
It was so dark, deep, cloudy, that although
  My gaze upon the bottom I confined,
  Not anything discerned I there below.
'Now go we down among the people blind,'
  Began the Poet, pallid as the dead:
  'I will go first, and follow thou behind.'
And I, observant of his pallor, said:
  'How shall I come if thou afraid appear,
  By whom I am wonted to be comforted?'
'The anguish of the people downward here,
  Portrays upon my face,' said he at this,
  'That pity which thou deemest to be fear.
The long way urges: come, be not remiss.'
  Thus he set forth, and made me enter thus
  The foremost circle that begirds the abyss.
Here was no sound perceptible to us
  Of wailing, only sighs and sighs again,
  That made the eternal air all tremulous:
And this arose from woe unpanged with pain,
  Felt by the great and thronging multitude
  Of children and of women and of men.
'Askest thou not,' resumed the Master good,
  'What spirits these may be whom thou perceivest?
  Now these sinned not; yet all their rectitude

First Circle:
Limbo; the
Virtuous Pagans

15

(This would I have thee learn before thou leavest),
    For want of Baptism, fails to satisfy
    The sanctions of the faith that thou believest:
And if they came before Christianity,
    God they adored not as His dues require:
    And among spirits such as these am I.
For such defects, and for no guilt entire,
    We are lost, afflicted only in this sense,
    That without hope we linger in desire.'
Thereat my heart was wrung with grief intense,
    For people of much worth I knew full well
    Abiding in that Limbo in suspense.
'Now tell me, Master mine, Lord, speak and tell,'
    Began I, craving utter certitude
    About the faith that can all error quell,
'Went ever any, through his rectitude
    Or through Another, hence to blessed fate?'
    Then he my covert language understood,
Replying: 'I was recent in this state
    When I beheld One come omnipotent,
    With sign of victory incoronate.
The shade of our first father penitent,
    Abel his son and Noah, hence He drew;
    Moses the lawgiver obedient;
Patriarch Abraham, King David too;
    Israel with his sire, with every son,
    With Rachel for whose sake such pains he knew,
And many more, and gave them benison:
    And thou must know that, earlier than these,
    Never a human soul salvation won.'
Not for his speaking did our going cease,
    But ever through the forest did we fare,—
    The forest, I mean, where spirits were the trees.
We had not travelled far as yet from where
    My slumber broke, when I beheld a blaze
    Which conquered from the dark a hemisphere.

INFERNO: CANTO V
Minos

We still were distant by a little space,
   Yet not so far but I discerned in part
   That honourable people held that place.
'O thou who honourest both science and art,
   Who may these be that so great honour claim
   Thus set from fashion of the rest apart?'
And he to me: 'The honourable fame
   Concerning them that in thy life doth ring,
   Wins grace in Heaven that so advances them.'
Hereon I heard a voice thus heralding:
   'Honour to him of poets loftiest!
   His shade returneth home from wandering.'
After the voice had ceased and was at rest,
   Four mighty shades advancing did I see,
   In whom nor grief nor joy was manifest.
The Master good began to say to me:
   'Mark him with sword in hand, appearing sire
   To the others as he walks before the three:
That is old Homer, sovereign of the lyre,
   Next follows Horace on, satiric wit,
   The third is Ovid, Lucan ends the quire.
Since unto each doth, as to me, befit
   The name the one voice sounded, in such wise
   They do me honour, and do well in it.'
So gathered the fair school before mine eyes
   Of that Lord of the very loftiest song
   Who over all others like an eagle flies.
When they together had conversed, erelong
   With welcoming salute they gathered round me,
   Whence smiled my Master on that genial throng.
And yet with honour higher far they crowned me,
   Adopting me to their own brotherhood,
   Whence sixth among these sons of light I found me.
Toward the light we thus our way pursued,
   Discoursing things whereof fits reticence,
   Even as there to speak of them was good.

17

We gained a castle's grand circumference,
    With seven lofty walls encircled round,
    Bemoated with a brooklet for defence.
This passed we over as upon dry ground:
    Through seven gates I with those sages went;
    A meadow of fresh verdure there we found.
People were there of aspect eminent,
    With eyes that moved majestical and slow:
    Taciturn, but with voices sweetly blent.
A little to one side withdrew we so
    Into an open place, and high and sheen,
    Where one and all we might behold and know.
There opposite, upon the enamelled green,
    Were shown to me the mighty souls, whom I
    Feel inwardly exalted to have seen.
I saw Electra with much people by,
    Hector among them, and Æneas descried,
    And armoured Cæsar with the falcon eye.
Camill', Penthesiléa, I espied;
    Over against them King Latinus and
    Lavinia, his daughter, by his side.
I saw that Brutus who the Tarquin banned;
    Lucrece, Cornelia, Julia, Marcia; then
    Saw Saladin apart and lonely stand.
And when I lifted up my brows again,
    The Master I beheld of those who know,
    Sitting amid the philosophic train.
All look to him, to him all honour show:
    Here saw I Plato, Socrates advance,
    Who nearer him before the others go;
Democritus, who puts the world on chance,
    Anaxagoras and Diogenes I saw;
    Dioscorides, good analyst of plants;
Thales, and Zeno of the Stoic law;
    Orpheus, Heraclitus, Empedocles,
    Tully and Livy, and moral Seneca;

Euclid, geometer; Hippocrates,
  Ptolemy, Avicen, Galen; him who wrought
  The Commentary great, Averroës.
In full concerning all report I not,
  For the long theme impels me forward: thus
  Many a time the word comes short of thought.
The band of six gives place to two of us:
  My sage Guide leads me by another way
  Forth from the still air to the tremulous;
And now I come where shines no light of day.

CANTO V

From the first circle thus I made descent
  Down to the second, whose contracted rim
  Girdles so much more woe it goads lament.
There Minos stands and snarls with clamour grim,
  Examines the transgressions at the gate,
  Judges, and sends as he encircles him.
Yea, when the spirit born to evil fate
  Before him comes confessing all, that fell
  Distinguisher among the reprobate,
Seeing what place belongs to it in Hell,
  Entwines him with his tail such times as show
  How many circles down he bids it dwell.
Always before him many wait; they go
  All turn by turn to sentence for their sin:
  They tell and hear and then are whirled below.
'O thou that comest to the woeful inn!'
  As soon as he beheld me, Minos cried,
  Leaving the act of so great discipline,
'Beware to enter, beware in whom confide,
  Be not deceived by wideness of the door.'
  'Why dost thou also clamour?' said my Guide,

*Second Circle:
Francesca da
Rimini*

19

'Bar not his going, fated from before:
 Thus it is willed up yonder where is might
 To bring the will to pass, and ask no more.
And now the notes of woe begin to smite
 The hollow of mine ear; now am I come
 Where I am pierced by wailings infinite.
I came into a place of all light dumb,
 Which bellows like a sea where thunders roll
 And counter-winds contend for masterdom.
The infernal hurricane beyond control
 Sweeps on and on with ravishment malign
 Whirling and buffeting each hapless soul.
When by the headlong tempest hurled supine,
 Here are the shrieks, the moaning, the laments,
 Here they blaspheme the puissance divine.
I learned that to such sorry recompense
 Are damned the sinners of the carnal sting,
 Who make the reason thrall to appetence.
And as great flocks of starlings on the wing
 In winter time together trooping go,
 So did that blast the wicked spirits fling
Now here, now there, now up, and now below:
 Comfort of hope to them is never known
 Either of rest or even less bitter woe.
And as the pilgrim cranes from zone to zone
 Draw out their aery file and chant the dirge,
 So saw I, and I heard them making moan,
Shadows who on that storm-blast whirl and surge:
 Whence I: 'Who, Master, are those tempest-flung,
 Round whom the black air whistles like a scourge?'
'The first,' said he, 'that multitude among,
 Of whom thou seekest knowledge more precise,
 Was empress over many a tribe and tongue.
Abandoned so was she to wanton vice
 That, her own stigma so to wipe away,
 Lust was made licit by her law's device.

That is Semiramis,—as annals say
  Consort of Ninus and successor too;
  Where governs now the Soldan, she held sway.
The next one, lo! herself for love she slew
  And to Sichæus' urn her faith dismissed;
  Next wanton Cleopatra comes to view;
Now lookest thou on Helen, whose acquist
  Brought evil years; and great Achilles see
  Who found in Love his last antagonist.
Look, Paris, Tristan...,' and he pointed me
  A thousand shades, and named me every name,
  Who in our life gave Love the victory.
When I had heard my Teacher many a dame
  Of eld enumerate, and many a knight,
  Pity assailed me and almost overcame.
'Poet,' began I, 'fain would I invite
  Speech with those twain who go a single way
  And seem upon the wind to be so light.'
And he made answer: 'Thou shalt mark when they
  Draw near to us, and then adjure them by
  The Love that leads them, and they will obey.'
Thereafter when a whirlwind swept them nigh
  I lifted up my voice: 'O souls forspent,
  Come and have speech with us if none deny.'
As doves to the heart's call obedient
  Are borne along to the belovèd nest
  On wide and steady pinions homeward bent,
So these came tow'rd us through the air unblest,
  Veering away from Dido and her line,
  So tender and so strong was my request.
'O living creature gracious and benign
  Who goest through the dusk air visiting
  Us who left earth with blood incarnadine,
If friendly were the Universal King
  We would be praying to Him for thy peace,
  Seeing thou pitiest our suffering.

Whatever ye to speak and hear may please,
    That will we speak and hear you close at hand,
    If yet awhile the wind as now may cease.
The town where I was born sits on the strand
    Beside the water where descends the Po
    In quest of peace, with his companion band.
Love that in gentle heart is soon aglow
    Laid hold on this one for the person fair
    Bereft me, and the mode is still my woe.
Love that doth none beloved from loving spare,
    To do him pleasure made my heart so fain
    That, as thou seest, not yet doth it forbear.
Love led us down to death together: Cain
    Awaits the soul of him who laid us dead.'
    These words from them to us returned again.
Hearing those injured souls, I bowed my head
    And held it for so long dejectedly
    That, 'Whereon thinkest thou?' the Poet said.
When I could answer, I began: 'Ah me,
    How many tender thoughts, what longing drew
    These lovers to the pass of agony!'
Thereafter I turned to them, and spoke anew:
    'Francesca, all thy torments dim mine eyes
    With tears that flow for sympathy and rue.
But tell me, in the time of the sweet sighs
    By what, and how did Love to you disclose
    The vague desires, that ye should realize?'
And she to me: 'It is the woe of woes
    Remembrance of the happy time to keep
    In misery,—and that thy Teacher knows.
But if thy yearning be indeed so deep
    To know the first root of a love so dear,
    I will do even as they who speak and weep.
One day together read we for good cheer
    Of Love, how he laid hold on Launcëlot:
    Alone we were and without any fear.

Many and many a time that reading brought
   Our eyes to meet, and blanched our faces o'er,
   But only one point we resisted not.
When reading of the smile long-waited-for
   Being kissed by such a lover chivalrous,
   He, never now from me divided more,
Kissed me upon the mouth, all tremulous...
   Gallehaut was the book and writer too:
   That day there was no reading more for us.'
And while one soul was saying this, for rue
   So wept the other, that I fainted all
   For pity, even as dying persons do,
And fell, as would a lifeless body fall.

CANTO VI

On coming to my senses, closed at sight
   Deplorable of them, the kindred twain,
   Pity for whom had overwhelmed me quite,
New souls in torment and new modes of pain
   Wherever I am moving I behold,
   Wherever I turn and look about again.
In the Third Circle am I, where the cold
   Eternal cursèd heavy rain doth flow,
   In mode and measure ever as of old.
Thick hail and turbid water-drops and snow
   Down through the darkling air forever fall;
   Foul stench receives them on the ground below.
Cerberus, fierce and monstrous animal,
   With triple gullet barks in currish wise
   Above the people here submerged withal.
Greasy and black his beard, and red his eyes,
   And belly big, and fingers clawed amain:
   Clutching the spirits, he doth rend and slice.

Third Circle:
The Intemperate

Howling like dogs by reason of the rain,
    They shelter one side with the other,—thus
    Turn back and forth the reprobates profane.
The open-mouthed great dragon Cerberus
    Displayed his fangs, what time he us descried:
    No limb had he that was not tremulous.
And, spreading palms and fingers out, my Guide
    Took earth up and, full-fisted, flung it right
    Into those gullets ravenous and wide.
As dog that barks for craving appetite
    Grows quiet setting tooth upon his food,
    For but to gorge it doth he tug and fight,
So quiet grew those faces, filth-imbrued,
    Of Demon Cerberus, who bellows so
    The spirits would be deaf if they but could.
We passed above the shadows whom below
    The heavy rain is beating, treading down
    What seems a body, but is empty show.
They all upon the ground were lying prone,
    Except that sudden sat erect one shade
    As soon as it perceived us passing on.
'O thou who through this Hell art led,' it prayed,
    'Recall me, if thou canst, to memory:
    Or ever I was unmade, wast thou made.'
'Perchance,' said I, 'the anguish thou dost dree,
    Doth from my memory thy form efface
    So that, it seems, I never looked on thee.
But tell me who thou art, that in a place
    So woeful liest, punished in such plight
    That none, though greater, were so much disgrace.'
'Thy city,' he returned, 'distended quite
    With envy till the sack no more can hold,
    Held me as hers, when life to me was bright.
Ciacco, ye citizens called me of old:
    For the pernicious guilt of gluttony
    The rain subdues me, as thou dost behold.

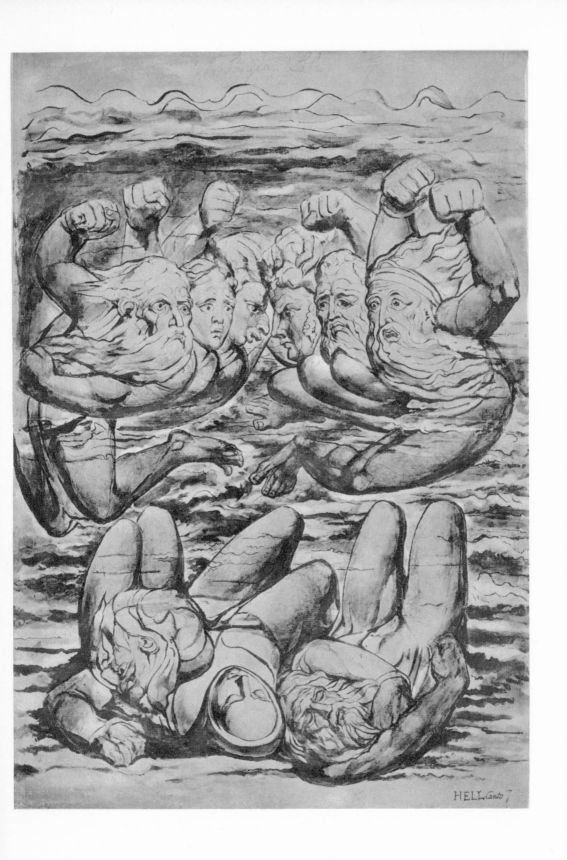

INFERNO: CANTO VII

The Stygian Lake, with the Ireful Sinners fighting

And, wretched spirit, not alone am I,
   Since for like guilt these suffer, all and some,
   Like punishment': no more he made reply.
'Ciacco,' I answered him, 'thy martyrdom
   Doth weigh me down to tears compassionate:
   But tell me, if thou knowest, to what will come
The citizens of the divided state?
   If any one therein be just? and whence
   Such mighty discord makes it desolate?'
And he to me: 'After long turbulence,
   Blood being shed, the rustic faction rising
   Will drive the others forth, with much offence.
Thereafter shall three suns prove term sufficing
   For them to fall and the others rise again
   By force of him who now is temporizing.
Long while shall they a lofty front maintain,
   Keeping the former, spite of tears and shame,
   'Neath heavy fardels bended down amain.
The just are two, but none gives heed to them:
   Envy and avarice and arrogance
   Are triple sparks that set all hearts aflame.'
Here ended he the sad deliverance.
   Whereat I: 'Since I crave instruction yet,
   Pray favour me with further utterance.
Farinata and Tegghiaio, of worth so great,
   James Rusticucci, Arrigo, Mosca, as well
   As others who had hearts on valour set,
Tell where they are,—that I may know them, tell:
   For great desire constrains me now to learn
   Whether Heaven soothe them, or envenom Hell.'
'Among the blackest souls,' he made return,
   'Whom different sins toward the bottom weigh,
   These, goest thou down so far, thou mayst discern.
But when thou art in the sweet world, I pray
   That thou wilt bring me back to human mind:
   No more I answer thee, no more I say.'

His straight eyes thereupon aslant inclined,
   Awhile he scanned me; then did headlong fall
   Down to the level of the other blind.
'No more,' my Leader said, 'he waken shall
   This side of the angelic trumpet sound.
   When shall arrive the judge inimical
Each one shall in his dismal tomb be found,
   His flesh and outward figure reassume,
   And hear what shall eternally resound.'
So fared we onward through that filthy scum
   Of shadows and of sleet, with footing slow,
   Touching a little on the life to come.
Wherefore I questioned: 'Master, will this woe
   After the final Judgement grow amain,
   Or less become, or burning be just so?'
'Turn to thy science,' answered he again,
   'Which holds, the more complete the thing, the
   It feels of pleasure, and the like of pain.   [more
Though these accursèd people nevermore
   Reach true perfection, after that event
   They look to be completer than before.'
A circling course along that road we went,
   Speaking far more than may repeated be;
   Then came we to the point of the descent,
And here found Plutus the arch-enemy.

CANTO VII

'Papé Satan, Papé Satan aleppë!'
   Thus Plutus' clucking voice beginning went;
   And that benignant Sage, experienced
In all things, said for my encouragement:
   'Fear not, for any war that he may wage
   Shall not prohibit thee the rock's descent.'

Then to that bloated visage turned my Sage,
   And said: 'Accursèd wolf, be not so loud!
   And be thou gnawed within by thine own rage.
Not without cause this going is allowed:
   Thus is it willed above where Michaël
   Wrought vengeance for the deed of whoredom
As ocean-faring sails, which the winds swell, [proud.'
   Fall in a tangle if the mainmast crack,
   So to the ground the cruel monster fell.
Descending into the Fourth Gap, we track
   Still farther that declivity of woe
   Which doth our universal guilt ensack.
Justice Divine! can any there below
   Heap up such penalties and travail new?
   And why does guilt of ours consume us so?
As on Charybdis yonder surges do,
   Each against other shattering its crest,
   So here the folk their counter-dance pursue.
Here saw I people more than all the rest
   Who from each quarter, with a howling din,
   Were trundling burdens by main force of breast.
They clash together, and then both begin
   The counter-movement, rolling back again,
   Shouting: 'Why throw away?' and 'Why hold in?'
So on both sides they circled to regain
   The point opposed, along the dismal mew,
   Still shouting their opprobrious refrain:
Then as along his semicircle drew
   Each one to the other joust, he wheeled withal.
   And I, who felt my heart as stricken through,
Said: 'Master mine, now tell me, who may all
   These people be? and on our left-hand side
   These shaven crowns,—were they all clerical?'
'All these were in the first life,' he replied,
   'Of mind so squinting that the middle route
   Of measured spending could not be espied.

With voice exceeding clear they bark this out,
    When to the two points of the circle come,
    Where counter-crime compels them turn about.
These heads bereft of hair were, all and some,
    Priests, popes, and cardinals, whose practices
    Show avarice in sovereign masterdom.'
Then said I: 'Master, among such as these
    There surely must be some I ought to know,
    Who were defiled with these iniquities.'
And he to me: 'Vain thoughts combinest thou:
    The purblind life that made them sordid there
    Bedims them to all recognition now.
To the two buttings will they ever fare;
    Out of the sepulchre will these arise
    Close-fisted, even as those with scissored hair.
Ill-giving and keeping ill have Paradise
    Bereft them, and in such a scuffle joined:
    No beauteous phrase to grace it I devise.
How transient is the farce, here mayst thou find,
    Of goods committed unto Fortune, son,
    Whence buffet one another humankind.
For all the gold the moon looks down upon,
    Or that did ever in the world exist,
    Could of these weary souls give rest to none.'
'Master, now tell me more,' did I insist:
    'This Fortune whereunto thou dost allude,
    What is she, with the world's wealth in her fist?'
And he to me: 'O foolish human brood,
    What ignorance is this wherein ye pine!
    Now let my judgement of her be thy food:
He whose transcendent wisdom is divine,
    Fashioned the skies, and gave them those who
    That every part to every part may shine, [guide
So equally do they the light divide;
    Likewise for earthly grandeur did ordain
    A common regent, who, as times betide,

28

INFERNO: CANTO VIII

Virgil repelling Filippo Argenti from the Boat

Might work vicissitude of treasures vain,
 That they from people and from kindred pass,
 Beyond all human prudence to restrain.
Whence rules one race, another cries "Alas!"
 Obeying her decree, the circumstance
 Whereof is hidden, like the snake in grass.
Your wisdom can no counterstand advance:
 She looks beforehand, judges, and pursues,
 As do the other gods, her governance.
Her permutations have not any truce:
 Necessity makes her precipitate,
 With frequent turns of luck at fast and loose.
Such is that one against whom people prate
 Who rather ought to praise her, doing amiss
 To deal in blame and to vituperate.
But she is blest and takes no heed of this:
 With other primal creatures jocundly
 She rolls her wheel, rejoicing in her bliss.
Now go we down to deeper misery:
 Already sinks each star that made ascent
 When I set forth, —no loitering may be.'
Across the circle to the bound we went,
 Above a bubbling fountain that careered
 Down through a gully where it found a vent.
The water far more dark than perse appeared:
 And as the dusky waves companioned us,
 We entered downward by a pathway weird.
A marish, Styx by name, this dolorous
 Rivulet fosters when its waters flow
 To foot of the gray slope precipitous.
And standing there intently gazing, lo!
 I saw a folk bemired upon that fen,
 All of them naked, and with look of woe.
Each smote his fellow with the hand, and then
 With both the feet and with the chest and head,
 Rending with teeth and rending once again.

CANTO VII
115-130

'Now seest thou, son,' the kindly Master said,
  'The souls of those whom Wrath did overquell:
  And I would also have it credited
That underneath the water people dwell
  Who sigh, and make it bubble at the brim,
  As wheresoe'er it turn, thine eye may tell.
Fixt in the ooze, they murmur forth this hymn:
  "Sweet sun-rejoicing air did we respire
  Sullenly, drowned in sluggish vapours grim:
Now lie we sullen here in the black mire."
  They gurgle in their gullets this refrain,
  Because they cannot speak with words entire.'
Thus, in wide compass round the filthy fen,
  Between the dry bank and the bog we passed,
  Scanning the guzzlers of the puddle: then
We reached the bottom of a tower at last.

CANTO VIII

Fifth Circle:
The Wrathful

Long while before (I say continuing)
  We reached the bottom of that tower so high,
  Our gaze upon its top was lingering
By reason of two lights we could descry;
  And other signal gleamed far opposite,
  So far away it hardly caught the eye.
Turned to that Sea of Wisdom infinite,
  I said: 'What means this? what may answered be
  By yonder beacon? and who kindled it?'
'The thing we await thou mayst already see
  Over the turbid waves,' he answered, 'so
  The marish-vapour hide it not from thee.'
Cord never shot an arrow from the bow
  That ran so swift a course athwart the air,
  As o'er the water at that moment, lo!

I saw a little bark toward us fare,
  Under a single boatman's pilotage,
  Who shouted: 'Now, fell spirit, art thou there?'
'Phlegyas, Phlegyas,' replied to him my Sage,
  'This time thou shoutest vainly: it is meet
  Thou have us but to pass the ferriage.'
As one who listens to some foul deceit
  That has been done him, and resents it sore,
  Such became Phlegyas in his gathered heat.
Embarking thereupon my Monitor
  Caused me to take my station at his side,—
  And only then the boat seemed laden more.
When I was in the wherry with my Guide,
  The ancient prow upon the passage sped,
  More than with others furrowing the tide.
While we were running through the channel dead,
  Arose before me one whom mud did steep:
  'Who art thou, coming ere thy time?' he said
And I: 'Though come, I stay not in the deep:
  But who art thou who art grown filthy so?'
  And he: 'Thou seëst that I am one who weep.'
Then I to him: 'With weeping and with woe
  Accursèd spirit, tarry here for aye:
  For thee, all filthy as thou art, I know.'
Then stretched he forth both hands, the boat to stay:
  But him my wary Master from us pressed,
  Crying: 'Away, with the other dogs, away!'
Then said 'Indignant soul!' as he caressed
  My bosom with embrace, my cheek with kiss,
  'Blessèd be she that bore thee 'neath her breast!
A person arrogant on earth was this,
  No least report of good his memory graces:
  Therefore his shade down here in fury is.
How many now up yon hold kingly places,
  Who are to wallow here in mire like swine,
  Leaving behind them horrible dispraises.'

'Much should I like,' said I, 'O Master mine,
   To see him in this hellbroth dipped and dyed,
   Before we issue from the marsh malign.'
And he to me: 'Thou shalt be satisfied
   Ere comes the shore to view; for it is fit
   That such desire of thine be gratified.'
Short while thereafter I beheld him smit
   By that bespattered folk with stroke so fell
   That still I praise and thank the Lord for it.
'At Philip Argenti! at him!' all did yell:
   That spirit Florentine exasperate
   Turned on his very self with tooth and nail.
We left him there, nor more do I narrate:
   But lamentation smote mine ears upon,
   Whence I look forward with mine eyes dilate.
And the good Master said: 'Now, O my son,
   The city named of Dis is nigh at hand,
   With heavy citizens, great garrison.'
And I: 'Already in the valley stand
   Its mosques, O Master, and to me they show
   Vermilion, as if issuing from the brand.'
And he made answer: 'The eternal glow
   Of inward flame kindles that ruddy glare,
   As thou perceivest in this Hell below.'
Then came we into the deep fosses, where
   They compass round that town disconsolate:
   The walls appeared to me of iron there.
Not without making first a circuit great,
   We came unto a place where loudly cried
   The boatman: 'Get ye out, here is the gate.'
I saw above the portals and beside,
   Thousands rained down from Heaven, who wrath-
   'Who is this man that, never having died, [ful said:
Is going through the kingdom of the dead?'
   And my sage Master signalled he would fain
   Talk with them privately.—Thus they were led

A little to abate their great disdain,
  And cried: 'Come thou alone; let him go back
  Who has made bold to enter this domain.
Alone shall he retrace his reckless track:
  Let him attempt it; for thou here shalt stay
  Who hast revealed to him a land so black.'
Imagine, Reader, what was my dismay
  At hearing that accursèd language: for
  I felt that I could never find the way.
'O my belovèd Leader, thou who more
  Than seven times hast made me safe, and hast
  Rescued from peril deep,' did I implore,
'Do not forsake me thus undone at last;
  And if the going farther be denied,
  Let us retrace our steps together fast.'
And that Lord who had thither been my Guide,
  Answered: 'Fear nothing, for the way we go
  By Such is given, none turneth us aside.
Wait here, and let thy soul, forwearied so,
  Be fed with better hope and comforted:
  I will not leave thee in the world below.'
And thus the gentle Father forth is sped,
  There leaving me who in conjecture dwell;
  For Yes and No contend within my head.
What he proposed to them I could not tell;
  But long he had not tarried with them, when
  Back inwards all went scurrying pell-mell.
The gates they shut, those enemies of men,
  On my Lord's bosom, who, excluded thence,
  With tardy steps returned to me again.
His eyes were on the ground, of confidence
  His forehead shorn, and amid sighs he spake:
  'Who has denied me the grim tenements?'
And then to me: 'What though my wrath awake,
  Be not dismayed, for I shall find the way,
  Whatever obstacle within they make.

This insolence is nothing new, for they
    Displayed it at less hidden gate of yore,
    Which stands unbolted to this very day.
Thou sawest the deadly writ above the door;
    And now descends the steep upon this side,
    Passing without a guide the circles o'er,
One who shall fling the city open wide.'

CANTO IX

Sixth Circle:
The Furies and
the Angel

The cowardice that blanched my outward hue
    Seeing my Guide returning back from thence,
    The sooner checked in him his colour new.
He halted like a listener intense,
    For but a little way the eye could pierce
    So darkling was the air, the murk so dense.
'Yet it behoves us win the fight, though fierce,'
    Began he: 'Nay but… so great help was sent…
    How long it seems here till Some one appears!'
I plainly saw how what at first he meant,
    He sought with after thoughts to cancel through
    In phrases from the former different.
But still his language roused my fear anew,
    For in the broken phrase I traced a scope
    Perchance more harmful than he had in view.
'Into this hollow, down the dismal slope
    Doth ever any come from the first grade
    Whose only punishment is crippled hope?'
So questioned I; and in reply he said:
    'Rarely does any out of our abode
    Perform the journey whereon I am sped.
Once previously, indeed, I took this road
    Conjured by that Erichtho void of grace
    Who erst their bodies to the shades bestowed.

My flesh was bare of me but little space,
 When she compelled me enter yonder mure,
 To draw a spirit forth from Judas' place.
That is the lowest round, and most obscure,
 And farthest from the all-circling Heaven: the path
 I know full well: therefore be thou secure.
This marish, breathing forth the fetid scath,
 Begirds the woeful city of the dead,
 Where now we cannot enter without wrath.'
I bear not now in mind what more he said,
 Because so fast were riveted mine eyes
 To that high tower with summit glowing red,
Where on a sudden up erect arise
 Infernal Furies three of bloody dye,
 Who have the limbs of women and their guise;
Bright green the hydras they are girded by;
 Little horned serpents pleated in a braid
 Like tresses round their cruel temples lie.
And recognizing every cruel maid
 Of her, the Queen of everlasting woe,
 'Behold,' he bade me, 'the Erinyes dread.
This is Megæra on the left, and lo!
 Alecto weeping yonder on the right;
 Tisiphone is between,' he ended so.
Each with her talons rips her breast; they smite
 Upon themselves, with shrieks so loud in tone,
 I clung close to the Poet in affright.
'Medusa come and turn him into stone!'
 All shouted looking downward; 'to our bane
 We made not Theseus his assault atone.'
'Turn round, and let thine eyes close shut remain:
 For should the Gorgon come, and shouldst thou
 There would be no returning up again.' [see,
Thus said the Master; and thereafter he
 Turned me, nor trusted to my hands alone,
 But also with his own blindfolded me.

O ye who hold sane intellect your own,
  Consider heedfully the hidden lore
  Beneath the veil of the strange verses thrown!
And now there came the troubled waters o'er
  A crashing clangour of a fearful kind,
  Whereat were trembling yon and hither shore:
Not otherwise it was than when the wind,
  By dint of adverse heats grown wild and high,
  Tosses the forest boughs, and unconfined
Shatters, and dashes down, and sweeps them by:
  Superbly whirls along in dust and gloom,
  Making the wild beasts and the shepherds fly.
He loosed mine eyes: 'Across that ancient foam
  Be now the nerve of sight directed yond,'
  He bade me, 'where most pungent is the fume.'
As frogs before their serpent-foe abscond,
  All slipping through the water in retreat
  Till squatted on the bottom of the pond,
So saw I thousands of lost spirits fleet
  Before a single Being who did fare
  Over the Stygian ford with unwet feet.
He wafted from his face that fetid air
  Moving the left hand forward ceaselessly,
  And only for that noyance seemed to care.
That he was sent from Heaven I well could see
  And to the Master turned, whose beckoning hand
  Bade me do homage to him tacitly.
Ah, how indignant seemed he! With light wand
  He toucht and opened wide to us the gate,
  Wherein was no resistance to withstand.
'O abject race, from Heaven how alienate!'
  Began he, standing on the horrible sill,
  'How harbour ye this insolence so great?
Wherefore recalcitrate against that Will
  Which from its purpose never can be shut,
  And which has many a time increased your ill?

36

What profits it against the Fates to butt?
   Your Cerberus, as ye are well aware,
   For this still goes with chin and gullet cut.'
Then he turned back by the foul thoroughfare,
   Speaking no word to us, but did advance
   Like one constrained and urged by other care
Than that of any who before him stands.
   Toward the city paced we afterward,
   Enheartened by the holy ordinance.
Therein we entered, finding none to guard:
   And I, because of my desire to know
   The lot of any in such fortress barred,
Being within, cast round mine eye; and lo!
   Before me far and wide spread out a land
   Full of atrocious torment and of woe.
Even as at Arles, where Rhone becomes a pond,
   Even as at Pola near Quarnaro Bay
   Which limits Italy and bathes her strand,
Sepulchres strew the ground in rough array:
   Here upon every hand it was the same,
   Except that here more bitter was the way:
For scattered in among the tombs was flame,
   Whereby such utter heat in them arose
   That never craft can more from iron claim.
Their lids were lifted all, and out of those
   Were issuing such dire lamenting cries,
   As told of wretched ones and full of woes.
'Master,' said I, 'what people on this wise
   Finding within these burial-chests their bed,
   Make themselves audible with woeful sighs?'
'Here the arch-heretics,' to me he said,
   'With followers of every sect are pent:
   More than thou thinkst the tombs are tenanted.
Like unto like are here in burial blent,
   And heated more and less the monuments.'
   Then, when he to the right had turned, we went
Between the tortures and high battlements.

CANTO X

My Master now along a hidden track
    Between the city rampart and the fires,
    Goes forward, and I follow at his back.
'O Virtue high, that through these impious gyres
    Dost wheel me at thy pleasure,' began I,
    'Speak to me, — give content to my desires.
The people in the sepulchres that lie,
    Might they be seen? With lifted covers burn
    They ever, and no one keeps guard thereby.'
'All will be shut within, when they return
    Back from Jehosaphat,' thereat he said,
    'Bringing their bodies from the burial urn.
Herein with Epicurus have their bed
    His followers one and all, who represent
    The spirit with the body to be dead.
But soon shalt thou within here have content
    As to the question which thou hast proposed,
    And to the wish whereof thou'rt reticent.'
And I: 'Good Leader, I do not keep closed
    My heart from thee, except that words be few:
    Nor hast thou me now first thereto disposed.'
'O Tuscan, thou who goest living through
    The city of fire, speaking becomingly,
    May it please thee stay thy steps in this purlieu!
The fashion of thy speech proclaimeth thee
    A native of that land of noble pride
    Which haply suffered too much harm from me.'
Suddenly in such accents some one cried
    From out one of the coffers; startled now,
    I drew a little closer to my Guide.
Whereat he said: 'Turn round; what doest thou?
    Look, Farinata! thou canst see him well
    Towering up full height from belt to brow.'

His face already held me with a spell:
 Erect of breast and forehead there he stands
 As if he entertained great scorn of Hell.
My leader with adroit and daring hands
 Thrust me among the sepulchres to him:
 'Brief be thy words!' that Monitor commands.
When I was standing at his footstone's rim,
 He eyed me a little, and then as in disdain:
 'Who were thy fathers?' came the question grim.
And I, to be compliant wholly fain,
 Hid nothing, but made full acknowledgement;
 Whereat he slightly frowned, and said again:
'Seeing that they were foes maleficent
 To me, my sires, my party, 'twas my will
 Twice to disperse them into banishment.'
'Though driven abroad,' I quick retorted, 'still
 Both times from everywhere returned my kin;
 But yours have never rightly learned that skill.'
Thereat a shade, seen only to the chin,
 Beside the former in the tomb appeared,—
 Arisen, I think, upon its knees therein.
As if by longing urged, it round me peered
 To see if one were with me there behind;
 But after that surmise was wholly cleared,
Weeping it said: 'If through this prison blind
 Thou go by loftiness of genius borne,
 Where is my son, and why not with thee joined?'
'Not of myself tread I this land forlorn;
 Yonder he waits who leads me here,—perchance
 Your Guido held him overmuch in scorn.'
His language and the penal circumstance
 Had told his name already: my reply
 Was for that reason full of relevance.
But he was on his feet now with the cry:
 '*Held* dost thou say? and lives he then no more?
 Strikes the glad light no longer on his eye?'

Become aware of some delay before
    I made reply, he forthwith backward sank
    Into the tomb, and stood forth nevermore.
That other soul magnanimous and frank
    Who caused my stay, stood undisquieted
    And neither moved his neck nor bent his flank.
'And if,'—continuing what before he said, —
    'They've badly learned that skill, — if this be so
    It is more torment to me than this bed.
But not yet fifty times anew shall glow
    The wan face of the Lady reigning here,
    Ere thou the burden of that skill shalt know.
And so the world may sweet to thee appear,
    Say why the statute of that people runs
    So pitiless against my kindred dear?'
'The havoc and the massacre that once
    Stained,' I replied, 'the Arbia-water red,
    Are causing in our fane such orisons.'
And sighing thereupon, he shook his head:
    'Not I alone in that, and in no case
    Should causeless with the rest have moved,' he said:
'But I it was, when in that other place
    To wipe out Florence one and all agreed,
    Alone defended her with open face.'
'Ah! so may ever rest in peace your seed,'
    Entreated I, 'pray loose that knot for me,
    Which doth my judgement at this point impede.
It seems that ye prophetically see
    What time brings with it, if I hear aright,
    And as to present things act differently.'
'We see, like him who has imperfect sight,
    The things,' said he, 'that are remote from view,
    So much still shines for us the Sovran Light:
When they draw nigh, or are, quite cancelled through
    Our vision is; if others bring it not,
    Unto your human state we have no clue.

Whence thou canst comprehend that blotted out
  Will be our knowledge, from that moment when
  The portal of the future shall be shut.'
As conscious of my fault, I said: 'Now, then,
  I wish that you would tell that fallen one
  His son is numbered still with living men.
And if just now I rendered answer none,
  Tell him it was because my thoughts were tied
  Still by that error which you have undone.'
Already was recalling me my Guide:
  Wherefore more hurriedly did I request
  That spirit tell who else therein abide.
'With thousands here,' he said to me, 'I nest:
  The Second Frederick herein is pent,
  And the Cardinal: I speak not of the rest.'
He hid himself; and thereupon I went
  Toward the ancient Poet, pondering
  That word which seemed to me maleficent.
He moved along, and then, thus journeying,
  Inquired of me, 'Why art thou so bestirred?'
  Whereat I satisfied his questioning.
'Let memory preserve what thou hast heard
  Against thyself,' that Sage adjured me so,
  Lifting his finger; — 'and now mark my word!
When thou shalt standing be in the sweet glow
  Of her whose beauteous eye on all is bent,
  From her the journey of thy life shalt know.'
Then turned he leftward: from the wall we went,
  Striking across toward the middle by
  A pathway leading to a pit that sent
Its loathsome stench ascending even so high.

CANTO XI

Upon an eminence with margin steep,
   Formed by rock-masses in a circle rent,
   We came above a still more cruel deep.
And here, by reason of the horrible scent
   That was belched forth from the profound abyss,
   Behind the lid of a great monument
We stood aside, and saw inscribed on this:
   'I hold within Pope Anastasius,
   He whom Photinus led to go amiss.'
'We must delay our going down, that thus
   A little more familiar to the sense,
   The dismal blast no longer trouble us.'
The Master thus; and I: 'Some recompense
   Do thou devise to balance this delay,
   Lest time be lost.'—'My very thought!' he assents.
'My son, within these rocks,' began he say,
   'From grade to grade three lesser circles wind,
   Like those above from which we come away.
All swarm with cursèd souls of humankind:
   But that the sight alone suffice from hence,
   Learn how and wherefore they are thus confined.
Of every malice that gives Heaven offence,
   Injury is the aim; such aim again
   Grieves others or by Fraud or Violence.
But because Fraud is man's peculiar bane,
   God loathes it more; and so the fraudulent
   Are placed beneath, assailed with greater pain.
The whole First Circle is for the violent:
   But since to persons threefold force is done,
   In triple rounds it has apportionment.
To God, to neighbour, and to self, can one
   Do violence: I say, their property
   And them,—as thou shalt hear made clearly known.

By violence, death and grievous wounds may be
  Dealt to one's neighbour; to his goods and rights
  Injury, arson, and rapacity:
Whence homicides and each who wrongly smites,
  Marauders and freebooters, all their train
  The foremost rondure plagues in various plights.
A man may lay a violent hand again
  On self and on his goods: wherefore below
  In the second rondure must repent in vain
Whoso deprives him of our world, whoso
  Gambles and dissipates his affluence,
  And comes to grief where he should jocund go.
The Deity may suffer violence
  With heart's denial and with blasphemies,
  And scorning Nature, and His beneficence:
And hence the smallest rondure signet-wise
  Stamps Sodom and Cahors, and all of those
  Who, speaking from the heart, their God despise.
That Fraud whose gnawing every conscience knows,
  A man may use on others who confide,
  Or on them who no confidence repose.
This latter method seems but to divide
  The link of love that in our nature is:
  Whence in the Second Circle there reside
Wizards, hypocrisy, and flatteries,
  Cheating, and simony, and thievishness,
  Panders, and the like filth, and barratries.
In the other mode there lies forgetfulness
  Of love which nature makes, and furthermore
  Of what begets especial trustfulness:
Whence in the Smallest Circle, at the core
  Of the whole universe, and seat of Dis,
  Whoso betrays is wasted evermore.'
'Master, thy reasoning of the abyss
  Runs clear, 'said I, 'defining what belongs
  To place, and to the folk possessing this.

But tell me: of the fat lagoon the throngs,
   Those the rain beats upon, those tempest-led,
   Those who encounter with such bitter tongues,
Wherefore are they within the City red
   Not punished, if the wrath of God they bide?
   If otherwise, then wherefore so bestead?'
'Why wandereth thine intellect so wide
   Beyond the wonted mark?' he said, 'or what
   Hath thine attention elsewhere occupied?
Hast thou the tenor of those words forgot
   Wherewith thine Ethics thoroughly explain
   The vices three that Heaven endureth not, —
Incontinence, and malice, and insane
   Bestiality? and how incontinence
   Less angers God, and less doth censure gain?
If thou consider well this evidence,
   And what they are recall to memory,
   Who up outside are bearing punishments,
Thou wilt discern why they divided be
   From all these felons, why God's hammers smite
   Upon them somewhat less avengingly.'
'O Sun! thou healer of all troubled sight,
   So gladdens me thy bringing truth to view,
   That doubt no less than knowledge is delight.
Yet turn a little back,' said I, 'pursue
   Thy argument that usury offends
   Divine beneficence, — that knot undo.'
'Philosophy,' said he, 'if one attends,
   Not merely in one passage has defined
   How Nature in her origin descends
From art Divine, and from the Master Mind;
   And if unto thy Physics thou refer,
   After not many pages wilt thou find
That your art, as it can, pursueth her,
   As the disciple doth the master; so
   That your art is God's grandchild, as it were.

INFERNO: CANTO X
Farinata degli Uberti

To these twain, if thy memory backward go
   To Genesis where it begins, perforce
    Must men their life and their advantage owe.
Since usurers adopt another course,
   They Nature and her follower disdain,
    Because they draw their hope from other source.
But follow, for the journey am I fain:
   The Fishes on the horizon writhe by this,
    While wholly over Caurus lies the Wain,
And yonder far descends the precipice.'

CANTO XII

The place we came to that we might descend
   Was alpine, what beside was on that bank
    Was such that it would every eye offend.
Such as that rock-fall which upon the flank
   Struck on the Adigë, this side of Trent,
    Whether by earthquake or support that sank;
For, from the summit whence the ruin went,
   Down to the plain, the cliff has fallen between,
    So from above there might be some descent;
Such was the causeway into that ravine:
   And on the border of the rugged brow
    The infamy of Crete was prostrate seen,
That was conceived in the fictitious cow:
   He bit himself, when eyes on us he laid,
    Subdued within by anger. 'Haply thou,'
My Master sage toward him shouting said,
  'Believest here the Duke of Athens, who
    Up in the world of mortals struck thee dead?
Monster, begone! for guided by no clue
   Given by thy sister, comes this man below,
    But passes by, your punishments to view.'

45

Just as the bull that feels the deadly blow,
    Breaks from his halter, and not very far
    Can move, but merely plunges to and fro:
So doing I beheld the Minotaur.
    'Run!' cried my Master, who the passage showed,
    'While he is raging, hasten down the scar.'
Thus downward we, our way pursuing, trode
    That dump of stones, which often as I went
    Moved underfoot beneath the novel load.
I musing passed. And he: 'Thou art intent
    Perhaps upon this ruin, sentinelled
    By that brute wrath, now rendered impotent.
Now I would have thee know, that when I held
    My first course hither to the deep abyss,
    This mass of rock had not as yet been felled.
But certainly, discern I not amiss,
    A little ere He came who mighty prey
    From the upper circle levied upon Dis,
The deep and loathsome valley every way
    So trembled, that the Universe, I thought,
    Was thrilled with love, whereby there are who say
The world was many a time to chaos brought:
    And in that moment, here and elsewhere, thus
    Upon this ancient crag was ruin wrought.
But fix thine eyes below; for neareth us
    The river of blood, wherein all boiling be
    Who were by force to men injurious.'
O wicked, blind, and mad cupidity,
    That in our brief existence spurs us so,
    And in the eternal steeps so bitterly!
I saw a wide moat curved into a bow
    And such that it doth all the plain embrace,
    According as my Guide had let me know.
Between it and the precipice did race
    Centaurs in file with arrows, as of yore
    It was their wont on earth to follow chase.

Seeing us coming down, they moved no more:
    And three detached themselves from out the row
    With bows and with long arrows, chosen before.
And from afar one shouted: 'To what woe
    Descending thus the precipice come ye?
    Tell it from thence; if not, I draw the bow.'
My Master answered: 'Our reply will be
    To Chiron yonder at close quarters made:
    Thus ever rash thy will, the worse for thee!'
'That one is Nessus,' nudging me he said,
    'Who died because of Dejanira fair,
    And for himself, himself his vengeance paid.
And gazing on his breast between the pair
    Is mighty Chiron who Achilles taught:
    Pholus the wrathful is the other there.
By thousands go they round the fosse about,
    Piercing with darts whatever soul withdraw
    From out the blood, more than its crime allot.'
Nearing those fleet wild animals, we saw
    Chiron take up a shaft and with the notch
    He ruffled back his beard behind his jaw.
When his huge mouth he had uncovered, 'Watch!
    Are ye aware,' thus to his mates he said,
    'That he behind moves whatsoe'er he touch?
Not so are wont the footfalls of the dead.'
    And my good Leader, level with his breast
    Where the two natures are together wed,
Replied: 'Indeed he lives, and by behest
    Alone I show him thus the dark defile:
    Necessity, not choice, impels the quest.
From singing Alleluia paused awhile
    One who commits to me this office new;
    He is no robber, I no spirit vile.
But by that Virtue which gives motion to
    My feet along so wild a thoroughfare,
    Give us for escort any one of you,

That he may show us where to ford, and bear
    This man upon his back across the tide:
    For 'tis no spirit that can walk the air.'
'Turn about, Nessus, so to be their guide,'
    Said Chiron, round upon his right breast bent,
    'If other troop encounter, warn aside.'
Together with the trusty guide we went
    Along the boiling of the crimson flood,
    Wherein the boiled were making loud lament.
I saw who plunged there to the eyebrows stood:
    'Once these,' the Centaur great took up the tale,
    'Were tyrants steeped in pillage and in blood.
The ruthless wrongs they wrought they here bewail,
    Here Alexander, fell Dionysius who
    Made woeful years in Sicily prevail;
And yonder brow with hair so black of hue
    Is Ezzelin; that other, fair of face,
    Obizzo of Este, whom his bastard slew
Up in the world, to truly state the case.'
    Then turned I to the Poet, and he said:
    'Give him the first and me the second place.'
A little farther on the Centaur led
    And paused above a folk whose evil fate
    Plunged them throat-high within that boiling red.
He showed a shade alone and separate,
    Saying: 'That spirit cleft within God's breast
    The heart that still by Thames they venerate.'
Then saw I people who with head and chest
    Wholly uplifted from the river stood;
    And many I recognized among the rest.
Thus evermore grew shallower that blood
    Until it only cooked the feet: and lo!
    Here was our passageway across the flood.
'Just as thou seest the boiling river grow
    Still lower on the farther side, and lower,'
    The Centaur said, 'so I will have thee know

INFERNO: CANTO XII
The Minotaur

That on this other, with a circling shore
   Its bottom sinks, until it makes its way
   Where tyranny must groan for evermore.
Justice divine here goads that Attila
   Who was a scourge upon the earth, and stings
   Pyrrhus and Sextus, and milks forth for aye
From Rinier of Corneto tears, and wrings
   Hot tears from Rinier Pazzo, — Riniers twain
   Who on the highways wrought such plunderings.'
Back then he turned and passed the ford again.

CANTO XIII

Not yet had Nessus gained the farther side,
   When we began to pass a forest through,
   Wherein not any path could be descried.
Not green the foliage, but of dusky hue;
   Not smooth the boughs, but gnarled and intricate;
   No fruits therein, but thorns with poison grew.
Those fierce wild animals that hold in hate
   Tilled lands 'tween Cécina and Corneto, no
   Thickets infest so dense and desolate.
Hither the loathsome Harpies nesting go,
   Who drove the Trojans from the Strophades,
   With direful prophecy of coming woe.
Broad wings, and human face and neck have these,
   And feet with claws, huge belly feathered all;
   They utter rueful cries on the weird trees.
'Ere yet,' the Master good began withal,
   'Thou tread the Second Round, consider well
   That here thou shalt employ the interval
Until thou comest to the sand-waste fell.
   So look aright, and there shall be descried
   Things thou wouldst not believe, if I should tell.'

*Seventh Circle:
Ring 2. The
Suicidal Wood*

49

Thereat I wailings heard, on every side,
    And person who might utter them saw not:
    Whence stood I still, completely mystified.
I think now that he thought perhaps I thought
    That through those trunks so many voices came
    From people who from us concealment sought.
Wherefore thus said the Master: 'If thou maim
    Of any of these plants one little spray,
    The thoughts thou hast will all be rendered lame.'
Lifting my hand a little then, away
    A branchlet from a mighty thorn I tore;
    Then did the trunk of it, lamenting, say:
'Why rendest thou?' Thereafter, dark with gore,
    Began again to cry: 'Why mangle me?
    Hast thou no spirit of pity then? Of yore
Men were we, and each now is turned to tree:
    Well might thy hand have shown itself more kind,
    Though souls of veritable serpents we.'
As out of a green brand, which burns behind,
    And from the other side the drops exude,
    The while it sputters with the escaping wind:
So from that broken sliver words and blood
    Were flowing forth together: whence I let
    The tip fall down, and like one frighted stood.
'O wounded soul!' my Sage replied, 'if yet
    Before he had been able to believe
    What he has only in my numbers met,
Thou wouldst not this offence from him receive;
    The wonder of the thing made me advise
    His doing that whereat myself I grieve.
But tell him who thou wast, so that in guise
    Of some amends, he yet may vindicate
    Thy fame on earth, where he again shall rise.'
The trunk: 'Thy honeyed words hold out such bait,
    I cannot choose but speak; then let it be
    Not burdensome if I expatiate.

I am that one who held the double key
  Of Frederick's heart, and, turning both ways, knew
  To lock and loosen with such suavity,
His confidence from others I withdrew:
  To that high trust fidelity I bore,
  Losing my vigour and repose therethrough.
The harlot who yet never from the door
  Of Cæsar's dwelling turned her wanton eyes,
  The curse and bane of courts for evermore,
Inflamed all minds against me; in such wise
  Inflamed, they made Augustus flame again,
  So that glad honours turned to dismal sighs.
My spirit, through her temper of disdain,
  Believing to escape disdain by dying,
  Made me, though just, to self-injustice fain.
By the strange roots this thorn-tree underlying,
  I swear to you I never forfeited
  Faith to my Lord, his honour magnifying.
If either of you yet the earth shall tread,
  Let him the memory of me restore,
  Still by the stroke of Envy prostrated.'
When he a little to discourse forbore,
  The Poet said: 'Let not the moment go,
  But speak and ask him what thou wouldest more.'
And I to him: 'Do thou entreat him show
  What e'er thou thinkest may content my will,
  For I cannot, for pity of his woe.'
Whence he resumed: 'So may the man fulfil
  What thou hast prayed for, and full willingly,
  Imprisoned spirit, may it please thee still
To tell us in what way the soul may be
  Bound in these knots; and tell, if licit, too,
  If ever any from such limbs breaks free.'
The trunk a mighty suspiration blew,
  Whereon that wind was changed to voice like this:
  'Brief the reply that shall be made to you.

When the fierce spirit separates amiss
From out the body whence itself has torn,
Minos consigns to it the seventh abyss.
It falls into the forest, where no bourn
Is chosen for it, but where chance may throw,
Here it sprouts up, as doth a grain of corn;
Doth to a sapling and a wild tree grow:
The Harpies, browsing then its leafy crest,
Cause woe, and give a window to the woe.
We shall go seek our bodies like the rest,
But with them never to be re-arrayed:
For 'tis not just to have what we divest.
Here shall we drag them, and the forest glade
Shall see our bodies hanging dismally,
Each on the thorn-tree of its injured shade.'
We were attentive still unto the tree,
Thinking that haply it would tell us more,
When a tumult overtook us, so that we
Were like to one aware of hunt and boar
Approaching to the place where he had stood,
Who hears the branches crash the beasts before.
And now behold two spirits scratched and nude
On the left hand, in flight so furious
They broke through every barrier of the wood.
The first: 'Now hurry, hurry, Death to us!'
And the next, who thought himself in speed out-
Was shouting: 'Lano, not alertly thus   [done,
Thy legs did at the jousts of Toppo run.'
And haply for his breath too short he found,
A thicket and himself he grouped as one.
After them, filling all the forests round,
Were running ravening bitches black, and fleet
As, after slipping from the leash, the hound.
In him who cowered down their tushes meet,
All into pieces rending him: again
They bear away those limbs dilacerate.

Taking me by the hand, my Leader then
  Led forward to the bush, with many a sigh
  Lamenting through its bleeding wounds in vain.
'O James of Sant'Andrea,' was its cry,
  'Of making me thy screen what is the good?
  For all thy wicked life what blame have I?'
The Master said when he beside it stood:
  'Who wast thou that, through wounds so numerous,
  Art blowing forth thy woeful words with blood?'
'O souls that hither come,' he said to us,
  'To view the shameful havoc that from me
  Has rended all away my foliage thus,
Gather it up beneath the wretched tree.
  Mine was the town that her first patron for
  The Baptist changed: and for this reason he
Will plague her with his art forevermore.
  And, were it not that still of him remain
  Some features where men cross the Arno o'er,
Those citizens who built the town again
  Upon the ashes left by Attila,
  Would have performed the labour all in vain.
With mine own house I made myself away.'

CANTO XIV

Because for native country reverent,
  Perforce I gathered up the scattered leaves
  And gave them back to him, whose voice was spent.
Thence came we to the boundary which cleaves
  The Second Rondure from the Third, where dread
  Mode of eternal justice one perceives.
To show the new things clearly, be it said
  That we arrived upon a desert plain
  Which banishes all plants from off its bed.

*Seventh Circle:
Ring 3. Defiers
of God*

The woeful wood enwreathes it, as again
  The dismal moat encloses that around:
  Here, hard upon the verge, did we remain.
An arid and dense sand composed the ground,
  Nor was it formed and fashioned otherhow
  Than that of old where Cato footing found.
Vengeance of God! O how much oughtest thou
  By every person to be held in awe
  Who reads that which was manifested now!
Manifold flocks of naked souls I saw
  Who all did woeful lamentations pour,
  And they seemed subject unto diverse law.
Supine were lying some upon the floor,
  And some were sitting all together bent,
  And others went about forevermore.
The more were those who round about there went.
  And fewer those who lay in torment low,
  But had their tongues more loosened to lament.
Above that waste of sand, descending slow,
  Rained everywhere dilated flakes of fire,
  As upon Alps, without a wind, the snow.
As Alexander, where the heat is dire
  In India, upon his host beheld
  Flames fall, as far as to the ground entire;
Whereat he with his legions was compelled
  To trample down the soil, for better so
  The flames, remaining single, could be quelled:
Such was descending the eternal glow;
  Whereby, like tinder under steel, the sands
  Were kindled for redoubling of the woe.
Forever tossing were the wretched hands
  Now hither and now thither without rest,
  Fanning fresh burning off in counter-dance.
'Master,' began I, 'thou who conquerest
  All things except the stubborn demon train
  That from the gate against our entering pressed,

Who is the mighty one that in disdain
   Lies scowling, nor appears the fire to dread,
   So that he seems unripened by the rain?'
And that same one, perceiving what I said
   In question to my Guide of him, did shout:
   'What once I was alive, that am I dead.
Should Jupiter his blacksmith weary out,
   From whom the sharpened thunderbolt he tore
   Wrathful, and me upon my last day smote;
Or weary out the others o'er and o'er
   In Mongibello at the stithy swart,
   Crying, "Help, help, good Vulcan", as of yore
On Phlegra's battlefield; and should he dart
   His bolts at me with vigour multiplied,
   That vengeance never should make glad his heart.'
My Leader then with so much strength replied
   That I had never heard his voice so great:
   'O thou Capaneus, just because thy pride
Remains unquenched, the woefuller thy fate:
   No torment save thy very rage would be
   Unto thy fury pain proportionate!'
Then with a better look he turn'd to me:
   'That one was of the seven monarchs who
   Laid siege to Thebes; he held and seemingly
Holds God in scorn, and gives contempt to view:
   But, as I said to him, his spiteful mood
   Is for his breast adornment very due.
Now follow me, and let thy heed be good
   Not on the burning sand thy feet to set,
   But keep them ever back, close to the wood.'
In silence came we where a rivulet
   Gushes from out the wood: a rill so red
   That thinking of it makes me shudder yet.
As from the Bulicamë there takes head
   A brooklet which the sinful women share,
   So this ran down across the sandy bed.

The bottom and both shelving banksides were
   Hardened to stone, and the margins at the side
   Whence I perceived our passageway was there.
'Among all other things by thee descried
   Through me, since entering within the gate
   Whose threshold unto no one is denied,
Thine eyes not anything yet contemplate
   Noteworthy as the present stream, which quite
   Doth all the flames above it suffocate.'
This language of my Leader did incite
   Petition from me that he let me taste
   The food for which he lent the appetite.
'In the mid-sea there lies a country waste,'
   Thereon he said, 'that bears the name of Crete,
   Under whose king the world of old was chaste.
There is a mountain, Ida, once the seat
   Of laughing waters and of leafy shade;
   To-day it lies deserted and effete.
Once Rhea in this faithful cradle laid
   Her son; and to conceal him should he raise
   His voice to weep, caused clamours to be made.
A tall old man within the mountain stays,
   Who doth his back to Damietta hold,
   And upon Rome, as in a mirror, gaze:
His head is fashioned of the finest gold,
   And of pure silver are the arms and breast,
   Whence to the fork he is of brazen mould;
Thence downward all is iron, of the best,
   Save the right foot of terra cotta, and more
   Doth he on that than on the other rest.
Every part, except the golden ore,
   Is broken by a cleft where tears distil,
   And, gathering, perforate that cavern floor.
They fall cascading to this valley, — fill
   Dark Acheron and Styx and Phlegethon;
   Then flow along this narrow channel, till

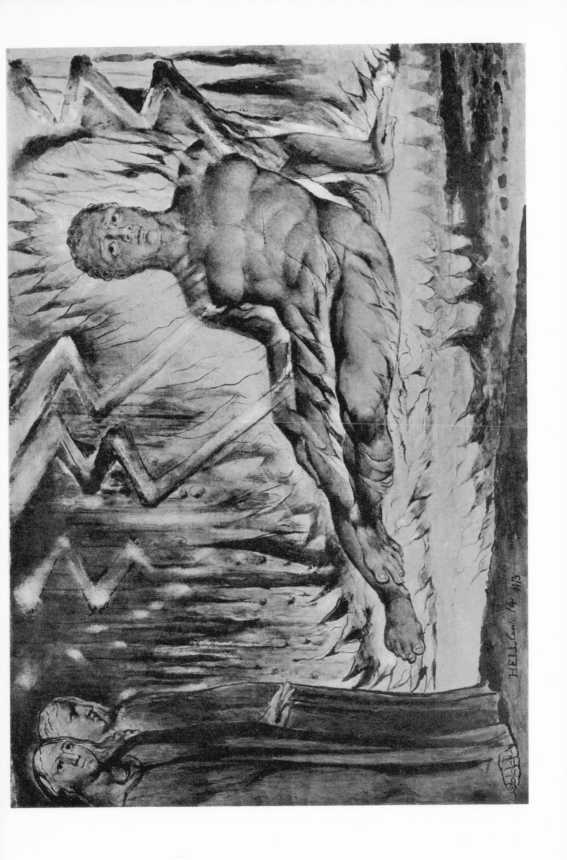

INFERNO: CANTO XIV
Capaneus the Blasphemer

They come where there is no more going down:
   They form Cocytus,—that pool shalt thou know
   By seeing: so be here description none.'
And I: 'If thus the present brooklet flow
   Down from our world wherein its source is found,
   Why does it only on this border show?'
And he to me: 'Thou knowest the place is round
   And though thou comest from a distant place,
   Still to the left toward the bottom bound,
Thou dost not yet the circle fully trace:
   Wherefore if something novel comes to view,
   It ought not to bring wonder to thy face.'
'Where found is Phlegethon,' said I anew,
   'And Lethë? for of one thou'rt silent, Lord,
   And sayest the other to this rain is due.'
'Thy questions please,' he said, 'in every word,
   Although the crimson brook's ebullience
   Might well the answer unto one afford.
Lethë shalt see, but from this fosse far hence,
   There where to lave themselves the souls repair,
   When guilt has been removed by penitence.'
Then added he: 'The time is come to fare
   Out of the wood: take heed thou follow me:
   The banks, not burning, form a thoroughfare,
And all the space above from flame is free.'

CANTO XV

Now bears us over one of the hard banks,
   And fumes above the brooklet, shading well,
   Shelter from fire the water and the flanks.
As Flemings, who 'twixt Bruges and Wissant dwell,
   Fearing the floodtides that upon them run,
   Throw up the dyke the ocean to repel,

*Seventh Circle:
Ring 3. Dante
Meets a Great
Teacher*

And as by Brenta does the Paduan,
   His villas and his villages to spare
   Before Carinthia ever feels the sun:
Of like formation those were fashioned there,
   Though not so high nor of so broad a base
   The Master made them, whosoe'er he were.
We were so distant from the forest chase
   By this, that I could never have descried
   The spot, though backward I had turned my face;
And now we met along the margin side
   A company of spirits coming by,
   Who each peered at us, as at eventide
Beneath new moon, we one another spy;
   And they were puckering their brows at us
   Like an old tailor at the needle's eye.
By such a family inspected thus,
   Well-known I proved to one of them, who caught
   My garment's hem, and cried: 'How marvellous!'
And when he stretched his arm, a glance I brought
   To bear so fixed upon his branded hue,
   That his scorched countenance prevented not
His recognition by my inner view;
   And to his visage bending down my head
   I answered: 'Ser Brunetto, is it You?'
'O son, let it displease thee not,' he said,
   If Brunetto Latino a little way
   Turn back with thee and let the troop be sped.'
'For that,' said I, 'with all my heart I pray;
   And if you bid me sit, it shall be done,
   So he I go with do not say me nay.'
Then he: 'Whoever of this herd, O son,
   But pauses, then a hundred years must lie
   Unfanned, when smites the fiery malison.
Therefore pass on: I at thy skirts will hie,
   And then rejoin my fellows yonder wending
   While weeping their eternal penalty.'

I durst not from the causeway risk descending

   To a level with him, but in reverent mode
   Beside him walked, my forehead humbly bending.
'What fortune,' he began, 'what fatal goad
   Drives thee down here before the hour extreme,
   And who is this who teaches thee the road?'
'Up in the life serene,' I said to him,
   'Ere to the middle term of manhood come,
   I found myself lost in a valley dim.
But yestermorn I turned my face therefrom:
   This one appeared to me returning there,
   And leads me now along this pathway home.'
'If following thy star thou onward bear,
   Thou canst not fail of glorious port,' he said,
   'If well discerned I in the life so fair:
And but that I was far too early dead,
   Beholding Heaven so unto thee benign,
   I would thee in the work have comforted.
But that ungrateful populace malign,
   Who came of yore down from Fiesolë,
   And savour still of mountain and of mine,
For thy good deeds will be thy enemy;
   And rightly: for 'mid crabbèd sorbs confined,
   Befits not the sweet fig to fructify.
Old rumour in the world reports them blind;
   A people envious, arrogant, and hard:
   Take heed thou from their manners be refined.
Fortune reserves thee honour and reward,
   Such that both parties yet will hungry go
   For thee: but far from goat shall be the sward.
Let the Fiesolan beasts their litter strow,
   Rending themselves; nor let them touch the blade,
   If ever any on their dunghill grow,
Wherein may yet revive the holy seed
   Of Romans, — those therein still resident
   When it became such nest of evil deed.'

'If all my prayer had found accomplishment,'
   Replied I to him, 'not yet would you be
   From human nature placed in banishment:
For I have held in loving memory
   Your kind paternal image, and now yearn
   For you, who in the world instructed me
From hour to hour how man becomes eterne:
   And while I am alive, it is but right
   Men in my words my gratitude discern.
What you relate about my course, I write,
   And keep—with other text—for a Lady, who,
   If I attain her, can the gloss indite.
Thus much would I have manifest to you,
   That if so be my conscience do not frown,
   I am ready, whatsoever Fortune do.
Not newly is such hansel paid me down:
   Therefore let twirling Fortune ply her wheel
   At pleasure, and his mattock ply the clown.'
Thereat my Master, back upon his heel
   Turning toward the right, upon me bent
   His eyes; then said: 'Who notes it, listens well!'
Nor speaking less on that account, I went
   With Ser Brunetto on, and question made
   Of his companions known and eminent.
'To know of some of them is well,' he said,
   'Of others best be silent, for the time
   With so much speaking were too quickly sped.
Know then, in brief, that all were clerks, sublime
   In their renown, and men of letters great,
   On earth polluted with the one same crime.
Priscian goes with yon troop disconsolate,
   And Francis of Accorso; who observes
   Such vermin, might have seen that reprobate
Who, by the Servant of each one who serves,
   Was banned from Arno to the Bacchiglion',
   Where he laid by his ill-excited nerves.

INFERNO: CANTO XVIII
The Flatterers

Of more would I relate, but going on
   And speech can be no longer, for I see
   New smoke from the great sand uprising yon.
A people comes with whom I may not be;
   Now to thy care my "Treasure" be commended,
   Where still I live, and crave not more of thee.'
Then, wheeling, it would seem that he contended
   The field with those who at Verona run
   For the green cloth; and well his pace he mended
More like the winner than the losing one.

CANTO XVI

I was already where we heard a sound
   Such as the bees make in the hive, a hum
   Of water falling into the next round;
Then did three shades together running come,
   Quitting a passing company that went
   Beneath the rain of the sharp martyrdom.
Approaching, in this cry their voices blent:
   'Stop thou, who by thy garb appearst to be
   Some one from out our city pestilent.'
What sores flame-branded on their limbs, ah me!
   Still recent ones and ancient, met my view:
   It grieves me for them yet in memory.
Their cries attention from my Teacher drew,
   Who turned his face to me and said: 'Now stay:
   To such as these all courtesy is due;
And if it were not for the fiery spray
   The nature of the place darts, I should feel
   That thou wert better hurry, and not they.'
They re-began to dance the ancient reel
   Soon as we paused, and, drawing near us so,
   All three resolved themselves into a wheel.

*Seventh Circle:
Ring 3. Three
Great Citizens
of Florence*

As champions stripped and oiled are wont to do,
  Who for their grip and for their vantage look,
  Before they ever bandy thrust and blow:
Thus, wheeling round, not one of them forsook
  The sight of me, so that in counterchase
  The neck and feet continual journey took.
'Ah! if the misery of this shifting place
  Make us and our desires contemptible,'
  Began one, 'and our black and blistered face,
Let our renown incline thy mind to tell
  Who art thou that, with such security,
  Trailest along thy living feet through Hell?
He treading in whose track thou seëst me,
  Excoriated though he be, and nude,
  Was higher than thou thinkest in degree.
The grandson was he of Gualdrada good;
  His name was Guido Guerra: much he planned
  Astutely, and his sword was likewise shrewd.
The other who behind me treads the sand,
  Tegghiaio Aldobrandi is, whose fame
  Ought to be grateful in the upper land.
And I, thus put upon the cross wtih them,
  Was called James Rusticucci: that I grieve,
  Truly my savage wife is most to blame.'
If from the fire I could have had reprieve,
  I should have flung me down to them below,
  And think my Teacher would have given me leave.
But since I should have parcht and burnt me so,
  Terror availed to check the kindly thought
  Which prompted me to their embrace to go.
'Contempt,' began I, 'it indeed was not,
  That your condition thrilled me with, but rue
  So deep that it will not be soon forgot,
When this my Lord spake words to me, where-
  The expectation was within me stirred [through
  That people might be coming such as you.

I am your fellow-townsman; every word
   That told your honoured names and actions all,
   With love I ever have rehearsed and heard.
I go for the sweet fruit, leaving the gall,—
   Fruit by the truthful Leader promised me:
   But to the Centre first I needs must fall.'
'So may thy limbs long while directed be
   By living soul,' that one thereon replied,
   'And so may thy renown shine after thee,
Tell whether courtesy and valour abide
   Within our city as of wont, or thence
   Banished and altogether thrust aside?
For William Borsierë, who laments
   Of late with us, and goes with yonder train,
   Speaks that which much our misery augments.'
'The upstart people and the sudden gain
   Excess in thee and arrogance have bred,
   O Florence, as thou findest to thy bane!'
Thus cried I out aloud with lifted head:
   And holding this for my reply, the three
   Looked at each other, as when truth is said.
'If otherwhile so little costs it thee
   Others to satisfy,' all answered then,
   'Happy thou, speaking with impunity.
Whence if, escaped this place of gloom, again
   Returned to see the starry heavens fair,
   Thou shalt rejoice to utter, "I have been,"
Pray speak of us unto the people there.'   [broken,
   Then they took flight and, when the wheel was
   Their nimble legs appeared to wing the air.
No glib 'Amen' could ever have been spoken
   So quickly as their vanishing occurred,
   Which for departing gave my Master token.
I followed, and but little way we stirred,
   Before so near us was the water's sound
   That, speaking, we could hardly have been heard.

Even as that stream which holds its proper ground
    The first, from Monte Viso to the sea
    Eastward, upon the Apennines' left bound, —
Stillwater called above, before it be
    Precipitated to its lower bed,
    But of that name is vacant at Forlì, —
Above Saint Benedict from the mountain head
    Goes bellowing down a single waterfall
    Where for a thousand should be room instead:
Thus, leaping downward from a scarpèd wall,
    We heard that tinted water make such din,
    That it would soon have stunned the ear withal
I had a cord that girt my garment in,
    For with it I had once thought requisite
    To take the leopard of the painted skin.
As soon as I had loosed it from me quite,
    To the commandment of my Guide submiss,
    I reached it to him, coiled and wound up tight.
Whereon he turned toward the right, and this,
    A little out beyond the verge, did fling
    Down into that precipitous abyss.
'Now surely it must be that some new thing,'
    I said within, 'answer the signal new
    Which thus the Master's eye is following.'
Ah me! how cautious should men be and do
    Near those who witness not alone the deeds,
    But with their wisdom to the thoughts look
He said to me: 'What I expect must needs [through!
    Come upward soon, and what thy dreams now ask
    Must soon be such that very eyesight heeds.'
Aye to that truth concealed beneath false mask,
    A man should close his lips, if in him lies,
    Lest he, though blameless, should be brought to
But here I cannot: by the harmonies   [task;
    Of this my Comedy, Reader, I swear,
    So may their grace be lasting, that mine eyes

Saw through the gross and gloomy atmosphere
   A shape come swimming up, of such as be
   To every steadfast heart a thing of fear:
As he returns who sometimes dives, to free
   The anchor-fluke, lest vessel come to harm
   On reef, or aught else hidden in the sea,
Who draws his foot in, and flings up his arm.

CANTO XVII

'Behold the beast with pointed tail, whose guile
   Doth mountains cleave & valls & weapons rend;
   Behold him who doth all the world defile.'
So spoke to me my Leader and my friend;
   And that it come in shoreward beckoned it,
   Near where the trodden marbles make an end.
Then forward came that filthy counterfeit
   Image of Fraud to land its head and bust,
   But drew not up its tail from out the pit.
Its face was like the face of person just,
   So outwardly benignant was its hue,
   But like a serpent all the rest outthrust.
Paws shaggy to the armpits it had two;
   And many a painted nooselet, many a quirk
   The back, the breast, and both the flanks bestrew.
Never was cloth by Tartar woven or Turk,
   More variously coloured, warp and woof,
   Nor yet such tissue did Arachne work.
As along shore the wherries lie aloof
   At times, in water part and part on land;
   And as the beaver in his hunt's behoof
Doth yonder 'mid the guzzling Germans stand:
   So lay that worst of beasts along the stone
   That forms the margin fencing in the sand.

All quivering in the void the tail was thrown,
   Twisting aloft the point of it, that bare
   A venomed fork as in the scorpion.
'Now,' said my Leader, 'it behoves us fare
   Somewhat aside, far as that maledight
   Wild beast which couches on the border there.'
So therefore we, descending on the right,
   Ten steps along the outer border pace,
   The sand and flakes of fire avoiding quite,
As soon as ever we have reached the place,
   A little farther on the sand I see
   A people sitting near the empty space.
'Of this third round,' the Master said to me,
   'That thou mayst carry full experience,
   Go now, consider what their manners be.
Out there concise must be thy conference:
   I will persuade this brute his shoulders strong
   To lend us, against thy returning thence.'
Thus farther yet, the utmost verge along
   Of that same Seventh Circle, did I go,
   And all alone, where sat the sorry throng.
Out of their eyes is bursting forth their woe:
   Now here, now there, with hands they agonize
   Against the flames, against the soil aglow.
Dogs in the summer do not otherwise,
   Now with the paw and presently with snout,
   At bite of fleas, of gadflies, or of flies.
When I had singled certain faces out
   Of these on whom the woeful fire is shed,
   Not one of them I knew; but slung about
Each neck perceived a pouch, emblazonèd
   With certain hue and certain cognizance,
   And therewithal, it seems, their eye is fed.
And as, among them looking, I advance,
   Beheld I *Azure* on a wallet *Or*,
   Bearing a lion's mien and countenance.

And as the sweep of vision onward bore,
   Another bag, blood-red, beheld I now.
   Display a goose, as butter white, and more.
Then one upon whose wallet white a sow,
   In brood and azure, was in blazon set,
   Exclaimed: 'Here in this ditch what doest thou?
Now get thee gone: and since thou'rt living yet,
   Know that my neighbour Vitaliano, here
   Upon my left-hand side a seat shall get.
A Paduan with these Florentines, mine ear
   Ofttimes they deafen, crying in each close,—
   "Let him come down, the sovran cavalier
Who with the triple-beakèd budget goes!" '
   Here pursing up his mouth, he made display
   Of tongue, like cattle when they lick the nose.
And apprehensive lest my longer stay
   Displease him who had bid me little bide,
   I turned me from those weary souls away.
On back of that fell beast I found my Guide
   Already mounted: 'Take good heed,' said he,
   'That thou be steady and unterrified.
Now by such flight of stairs descent must be:
   Mount thou in front, for I between will sit,
   So that the tail may do no harm to thee.'
Like one about to have the ague fit
   Of quartan, blue of nail, all shuddering
   At shadow, catching but the sight of it,—
Such I became, on hearing such a thing;
   But his monitions wrought in me that shame
   Which makes brave servant before noble king.
I set myself upon that monstrous frame:
   'Clasp me!' I tried to say, but utterance
   Refused to come, though I believed it came.
But he who otherwhile in other chance
   Assisted, with his arms encircled me
   As soon as I had mounted. 'Now advance,

O Geryon! ample let thy wheelings be,'
   He bade, 'and slow be thy descending here;
   Remember the new load that burdens thee.'
As draws a little vessel from her pier,
   So, backing, backing, thence did Geryon draw;
   And when he felt that he was wholly clear,
Turned tail to where before his breast I saw,
   And tail outstretching, moved it like an eel,
   And gathered in the air with play of paw.
No greater fear, I ween, did any feel,
   When Phaëton, abandoning the rein,
   Branded the sky, as still the nights reveal;
Nor when poor Icarus perceived each pen
   Fall from his flank, the molten wax withal, —
   'Thy way is wild!' his father shouted then, —
Than mine, when I beheld me to be all
   Adrift in air, and saw extinguished so
   Every sight but of the animal.
He swims along, slow undulating, slow,
   Wheels and descends, — this I could but surmise
   By wind upon my face, and from below.
Already on the right I heard arise
   Out of the cataract a frightful roar,
   Whence I outstretched my head with downward
Thereon the precipice dismayed me more,   [eyes.
   For burning did I see and moaning hear,
   Whereat my thighs gripped closer than before.
Now I discerned, what first did not appear,
   The sinking movement and the wheeling, by
   Great woes from every quarter drawing near.
Like falcon, overlong enforced to fly,
   That without spying either bird or bait,
   'Ah me, thou stoopest!' makes the falconer cry,
Descending weary whence it sped elate,
   Alights, full many a circle having rounded,
   Far from its master, aloof, exasperate:

Hard by the cliff upon the bedrock founded,
　　Thus Geryon set me down beside my Lord,
　　And, disencumbered of our persons, bounded
Up and away like arrow from the cord.

CANTO XVIII

There is in Hell a region all of stone,
　　By name Malpouches, of an iron hue
　　Like the precipitous encircling zone.
Right in the middle of the fell purlieu
　　There yawns a Pit, exceeding deep and wide,
　　Whose structure I shall tell in order due.
The belt is therefore circular, outside
　　The Pit to foot of the high rocky steep,
　　And in its bottom valleys ten divide.
Of like configuration is that deep
　　As otherwhere, for safeguard of the wall,
　　Several moats begird a castle-keep:
Such an appearance have these valleys all;
　　And as from thresholds of such fortalice
　　Run to the outer rampart bridges small,
So from the bottom of the precipice
　　Causeys across the banks and fosses run,
　　Converging and cut short at the abyss.
Here, shaken from the back of Geryon,
　　We found ourselves: then took the Poet's feet
　　The leftward turn, and I behind moved on.
On the right hand, new sorrow did I meet,
　　New torments and new wielders of the thong,
　　Wherewith the foremost pocket was replete.
The sinners naked at the bottom throng:
　　This side the middle come they facing me,
　　Swifter, beyond, they stride with me along.

Eighth Circle:
Pouch 1.
Panders and
Seducers.
Pouch 2. Flatterers

The Romans thus, in year of Jubilee,
    To make the people pass the bridge devise,
    By reason of the countless company,
So that on one side all direct their eyes
    Toward the Castle and Saint Peter's fane;
    On the other toward the Hill their passage lies.
Hither and yon along the gloomy lane,
    I saw horned demons with great whips, who dealt
    Behindward on them furious blows amain.
Ah! how these made them after the first pelt
    Lift up their heels! then truly waited none
    Until the second or the third he felt.
While I was going on, mine eyes by one
    Encountered were; and instantly I said:
    'For sight of him I have not hungry gone!'
Wherefore to make him out my feet I stayed;
    And my kind Leader, slackening his pace,
    Consented to some steps I backward made.
And that scourged spirit, lowering his face,
    Bethought to hide, but with small benefit;
    I saying: 'Thou that dost thine eyes abase,
Must, if those features are not counterfeit,
    Venedico Caccianimico be:
    But what brings thee to such a smarting pit?'
'Unwillingly I tell, though forced,' said he,
    'By thy explicit speech which brings the old
    Foregone existence back to memory.
To do the Marquis pleasure, I cajoled
    Fair Ghisola, — in whatsoever way
    The shameful tale be peradventure told.
No lonely Bolognese I weep here: nay,
    For rather do we so this region fill,
    That not so many tongues are taught to say
Sipa 'twixt Savena and Reno; still
    If thou wouldst have me pledge or proof subjoin,
    Recall to mind our avaricious will.'

While he was speaking thus, upon his loin
  A demon laid the lash, and said: 'Begone,
  Pander, there are no women here to coin!'
I came back to mine Escort; and thereon
  Few paces brought us where we could discern
  A craggy causey from the embankment run.
Ascending this full easily, we turn
  Upon its jagged ridgeway to the right,
  Departing from those circling walls eterne.
When came we where a gap beneath the height
  Yawns for the sinners driven by the thong,
  My Leader said: 'Lay hold, until the sight
Strike on thee of another misborn throng,
  Of whom thou hast not yet beheld the face
  Because they still have gone with us along.'
From the old bridge we viewed the file, apace
  Who neared us on the further side below,
  And whom the scourges in like manner chase.
Without my asking, the Good Master so
  Addressed me: 'Yonder mighty one behold,
  Who seems to shed no tear for all his woe:
How kingly is his bearing, as of old!
  'Tis Jason, who by prowess and by guile
  Despoiled the Colchians of the Fleece of Gold.
He skirted once the coast of Lemnos isle,
  After the merciless women unafraid
  Devoted all their males to death erewhile.
There, with love-tokens and fair words, the maid
  Hypsipylë did he betray, that one
  Who first, herself, had all the rest betrayed.
And there he left her, pregnant and alone:
  Such guilt condemns him to such martyrdom,
  And for Medea too is vengeance done.
With him go such deceivers all and some:
  Of the first valley let so much suffice,
  And of those by its vengeance overcome.'

Already had we reached the place where lies
   The narrow path across the second dike,
   Which buttress for another arch supplies.
Thence heard we people whimper plaintive-like
   In the next pocket, and with snorting roar
   Of muzzle, with their palms upon them strike.
The banks were with a mould encrusted o'er
   By vapours from below that on them rest,
   With both the eyes and nostrils waging war.
The bottom is so hollowly depressed
   There is no room to see, except one go
   Up where the arching bridge is loftiest.
Thither we came, whence in the ditch below
   I saw folk weltering in excrement
   That out of human privies seemed to flow.
While I was looking down with eye intent,
   I saw one head so smeared with ordure all,
   If clerk or layman 'twas not evident.
'Wherefore so greedy art thou,' did he bawl,
   'At me more than the filthy rest to stare?'
   'Because,' I answered, 'if I well recall,
I have already seen thee with dry hair;
   Alessio Interminei of Lucca, late
   Wast thou: whence singled out from others there.'
And thereon he, belabouring his pate:
   'To this has plunged me down the sycophance
   Wherewith my tongue was never satiate.'
Hereon my Leader said to me: 'Advance
   Thy face still further forward, till thou bring
   Thine eyesight full upon the countenance
Of that uncleanly and dishevelled thing,
   Who scratches yon with nails smeared filthily,
   And now is standing up, now cowering.
Thus is the harlot Thaïs seen of thee,
   Who answered once her minion when he said:
   "Dost greatly thank me?"—"Nay, stupendously."
And herewith let our sight be surfeited.'

CANTO XIX

O Simon Magus, O disciples vile!
 Ye who the things of God, which ought to be
 The brides of righteousness, lo! ye defile
For silver and for gold rapaciously;
 Now it befits the trumpet sound your doom,
 Because in this third pouch of Hell are ye.
Now had we climbed above the following tomb
 Upon the rocky causey, to that part
 Which doth the middle-moat quite over-loom.
Wisdom Supreme! what evidence of art
 In Heaven, on earth, and in the bad world found!
 And how great justice doth thy power impart!
I saw upon the sides and on the ground,
 With many a hole the dark stone drilled, and all
 Of one dimension, and each one was round.
None ampler seemed to me, nor yet more small,
 Than those that in my beautiful St. John
 Are made to the baptizers for a stall;
And one of these, not many years agone,
 I broke for one who stifling would have died:
 Be this a seal to undeceive each one.
Thrust forth from every opening, I descried
 A sinner's feet, and saw the ankles twain
 Far as the calf: the rest remained inside.
The soles of all were both consumed amain,
 And so with flames the joints were quivering
 No ropes and withies would have stood the strain.
As flame of oily things is wont to cling
 Alone upon the face exterior,
 So here from heel to point 'twas flickering.
'Master,' said I, 'who is that one who more
 Infuriate writhes than his companions there,
 And whom a redder flame is licking o'er?'

Eighth Circle:
Pouch 3.
Simoniacal Popes.

73

And he to me: 'If thou wilt let me bear
  Thee down by yonder bank that lies more low,
  From him of him and of his crimes shalt hear.'
'Thy pleasure, lord, is mine, and thou dost know
  That I depart not from thy will,' I said,
  'And knowest my unspoken thought, I trow.'
Thereon the fourth embankment did we tread,
  Turned, and descended leftward from the bank
  Down to the narrow, perforated bed.
The Master good not yet from off his flank
  Deposed me, till he brought me to the hole
  Of him who so was weeping with his shank.
'Who e'er thou art, thus planted like a pole
  Top downward,' then began I, 'do thou strive
  To speak out, if thou canst, O wretched soul!'
My posture was the friar's, at hand to shrive
  The false assassin, who, when planted, tries
  To call him back, still to remain alive.
'Art thou already standing there?' he cries,
  'Art standing there already, Boniface?
  By several seasons, then, the writing lies.
And art thou glutted with that wealth apace,
  For sake whereof thou didst not fear betray
  The Lady beautiful, and then disgrace?'
Such I became as people brought to stay
  Because an answer from the mark seems wide,
  As if bemocked, not knowing what to say.
'Say to him quickly,' hereon Virgil cried,
  '"I am not he thou thinkst, I am not he!"'
  And as enjoined upon me, I replied.
The spirit writhed his feet exceedingly;
  Then sighing, and with voice disconsolate,
  Said to me: 'What then wantest thou of me?
If thou desire so much to know my state,
  That for this cause thou hast the bank traversed,
  Know, I was vested with the Mantle Great.

INFERNO

True son of the She-bear, I had such thirst
  Insatiate to advance the Cubs, mine own,
  That wealth above, and here myself, I pursed.
Beneath my head the others down are thrown,
  Preceding me in simony, and all
  Flattened along the fissures of the stone.
Down thither shall I likewise drop withal,
  When comes that other whom I thought to meet
  What time I let the sudden question fall.
But longer now do I already heat
  My footpalms, standing here inverted thus,
  Than he shall planted stay with ruddy feet:
For after him a Pastor impious
  Shall come from Westward, fouler in his deed,
  Such as befits to cover both of us.
New Jason will he be, of whom we read
  In Maccabees: and pliant as that lord,
  Will he who governs France give this one heed.'
I know not if foolhardy was my word,
  But I made answer only in this key:
  'I pray thee tell me now how rich a hoard
Saint Peter paid into the treasury,
  Ere gave Our Lord the keys to his control?
  Nothing in truth He asked save "Follow me!"
Nor Peter nor the rest did levy toll
  Of gold or silver, nor Matthias grant,
  For the lost office of the guilty soul.
Then stay, well punished, and be vigilant
  In guardianship of the ill-gotten gold
  That made thee against Charles so arrogant.
And were I not forbid to be so bold,
  Because of reverence for the Keys Sublime
  Which in the happy life thou diddest hold,
Yet harsher language would befit my rime:
  Pastors, your greed afflicts the world; it brings
  Good underfoot, while still exalting crime!

75

Of you the Evangelist had prefigurings,
   When her that sits the waters did he view
   Committing fornication with the kings:
She with the seven heads begotten, who
   From the ten horns her sign and sanction bore
   Long as her spouse delight in virtue knew.
A god of gold and silver ye adore;
   And from the idolaters how differ ye,
   Save where they one, a hundred ye implore?
Ah, Constantine, to what iniquity
   Gave birth — not thy conversion — that domain
   Which the first wealthy Father took from thee!'
And while I sang to him in such a strain,
   Whether that frenzy or that conscience bit,
   With both his footpalms struggled he amain.
I think my Leader well applauded it,
   He listened still with look of such content
   To the clear accents which the truth befit.
Thereon to take me up, both arms he bent,
   And when he had me wholly on his breast,
   Remounted by the way of his descent;
Nor did he tire of holding me thus pressed,
   Till up the summit of the arch he bare,
   Which crosses from the fourth to the fifth crest.
Here he laid down his charge with tender care,
   Tender, for rugged was the crag and steep,
   That goats had found a toilsome passage there:
Thence was disclosed to me another deep.

INFERNO: CANTO **XX**

The Necromancers and Augurs

CANTO XX

New punishment must needs by me be dirged,
   Providing matter for the twentieth strain
   Of the first Song, which tells of the submerged.
I was already placed and wholly fain
   To look down into the disclosed abyss
   Bedewed with tears of anguish and of pain,
And through the circling vale I saw at this
   A silent, weeping folk, who onward pressed
   As pace in this our world the litanies.
As lower down on them my sight did rest,
   Each wondrously distorted seemed between
   The chin and the beginning of the chest:
For every visage had been twisted clean
   Round to the loins, and backward they must go,
   Since looking forward had forbidden been.
Thus utterly distorted by some throe
   Of palsy, some one may have been perchance;
   I never saw, nor think it can be so.
Imagine, Reader, so God's sufferance
   Permit that, reading, thou be edified,
   How I could keep unwet my countenance,
When near at hand our image I descried
   Contorted so, the weeping eyes did wet
   With tears the hinder parts where they divide.
Truly I wept, leaned on the parapet
   Of the hard bridge, so that mine Escort said:
   'Art thou among the other fools even yet?
Here piety lives on in pity dead.
   Who is a greater reprobate than one
   That grieves at doom divine? Lift up thy head,
Lift up thy head, and do thou look upon
   Him earth engulfed before the Theban's sight,
   Whereat all shouted: "Whither dost thou run,

Eighth Circle:
Pouch 4. Diviners
Origin of Mantua

77

Amphiaräus? Why forsake the fight?"
 From plunging downward he was only stayed
 By Minos, who lays hold on every wight.
Mark how his shoulders to a breast are made!
 Because he wished to see too far before,
 Forever backward doth he look and tread.
Tiresias see, who altered semblance wore
 When from a male he was made feminine,
 While all his members transformation bore;
And afterward he had to strike again
 With wand the intertwining serpents two,
 Ere he regained his plumage masculine.
With back to this one's belly is Aruns, who
 In mountain land of Luni (on whose height
 Drudges the Carrarese who dwells below)
Had once a cavern among marbles white
 For his abode, from which he could behold
 Ocean and stars with unobstructed sight.
And she whose locks unfilleted enfold
 Her bosom from thy sight, — the hairy coat
 O'er all her skin on the other side unrolled, —
Was Manto, who through many countries sought,
 And after tarried where I had my birth:
 Whereof to please me take a little note.
After her father had from life gone forth,
 And Bacchus' city came to slavery,
 This woman for a long time roamed the earth.
There lies a lake up in fair Italy,
 At bottom of the Alps that fence Almain,
 Tyrol above, — Benaco names that sea.
I think a thousand founts the Pennine drain
 Of water which within that lake is pent,
 Garda and Val Camonica between.
There is a middle place where he of Trent
 Or Brescia pastor, or the Veronese,
 Might give his blessing, if that way he went.

Peschiera, fair and mighty fortalice,
  Sits where lies lowest the surrounding shore,
  To front the Brescians and the Bergamese.
There whatsoever cannot tarry more
  In bosom of Benaco, down must flow
  And make a river through green meadow floor.
The waters gathering head, as Mincio,
  No longer called Benaco, flow apace
  Far as Governo, falling into Po.
Coursing not far, they find a level place
  Where in a wide lagoon they stagnant spread,
  And where in summer oft is noisomeness.
Passing that way, the Virgin, never wed,
  Perceived a tract of land amid the fen,
  Wholly untilled and uninhabited:
And there, to shun all intercourse with men,
  Stayed with her servants, arts of magic plied,
  Lived, and there left her empty body then.
The people, who were scattered far and wide,
  Thereafter gathered in that place, which lay
  Defended by the marsh on every side.
O'er those dead bones the city builded they,
  And, after her who first had chosen the place,
  Called it, without more omen, Mantua.
Denser therein was once the populace,
  Ere ever Casalodi witlessly
  From Pinamonte suffered such disgrace.
Hence if thou ever hear, I monish thee,
  My city given foundation different,
  Let falsehood not defraud the verity.'
'Master, thy reasons are so evident,
  And so lay hold of my belief,' said I,
  'That others were to me but embers spent.
But tell me, of the people going by,
  None seest thou worthy of note? for to their woe,
  Only to that, returns my inner eye.'

79

Whereon he answered: 'He whose beard doth flow
   Down from his cheeks upon his shoulders dun,
   Was, what time Greece of males was emptied so
That in the cradles tarried almost none,
   An augur, and with Calchas gave the sign
   To cut, in Aulis, the first cable, — one
Eurypylus, — thus in a certain line
   My lofty tragedy records the name:
   Well knowest it thou who knowest each verse of
That other, in the flanks so light of frame, [mine.
   Was Michael Scot, and of a truth he knew
   Of magical deceptions well the game.
Guido Bonatti view; Asdente view,
   Who now would wish his leather and his awl
   Had held him — all too late repents he too.
See wretched hags who let the needle fall,
   The spool and distaff, for divining fain,
   With herb and image working spells withal.
But come, for with his thorns already Cain
   Doth hold of both the hemispheres the bound,
   And yonder under Seville touch the main,
And only yesternight the moon was round:
   Thou shouldst recall, for she did thee no wrong
   One certain time within the wood profound.'
While thus he spake to me, we moved along.

CANTO XXI

Eighth Circle:
Pouch 5. Barrators

Discoursing thus of matters different
   Whereto my Comedy cares not to hark,
   Holding the height, from bridge to bridge we
But halted other vain laments to mark [went,
   In Evil-pouches, other cloven den;
   And there I saw that it was weirdly dark.

As in the Arsenal of Venice, men
  Boil sticky pitch in winter, which they use
  To make their vessels water-tight again
When unseaworthy; some perhaps may choose
  To build anew, — some make it their concern
  To caulk ribs buffeted in many a cruise;
Some hammer at the prow, some at the stern,
  Some fashion oars and others cordage twine,
  And some to mend the jib or mainsail turn:
Thus not by fire, but by an art divine,
  Boiled clammy pitch down there, which every side
  Smeared over the embankments that confine.
I saw it, but naught else therein descried,
  Except the bubbles which the boiling raised,
  As all heave up and then comprest subside.
While thither downward steadfastly I gazed,
  My Leader saying, 'Beware, beware!' did swerve
  Me round to him from where I stood amazed.
Then like one fascinated to observe
  The very thing that one perforce should flee,
  Till sudden terror takes away his nerve
So that he puts not off his flight to see,
  I looked behind and saw a devil swart
  Come running up the causeway after me.
Fierce-visaged was he, and oh! how my heart
  Sank at his action so unpitying, —
  So light of foot with wings spread wide apart!
Astride his shoulder high and tapering
  A sinner sitting on both haunches rode:
  To the ancle-tendon did the demon cling.
'Maltalons,' he cried, as on our bridge he strode,
  'Look ye, one Elder of Saint Zita, — dash
  Him under, while I get another load
From the town I stock with plenty of the trash:
  Barrators all there but Bonturo, — in brief
  There they convert the No to Aye for cash.'

Flinging him down, upon the flinty cliff
    He wheeled, and never gave so hot a chase
    An unleashed mastiff running down a thief.
That sinner plunged, and aired his back apace;
    But demons, lurking there the bridge below,
    Cried: 'No invoking here the Holy Face!
Here swim ye not as in the Serchio:
    Therefore take heed, unless thou mean to try
    Our grapples, not above the pitch to show.'
Then, pricking him with hundred prongs, did cry:
    'Here must thou dance about in covert guise,
    That, if thou can, thou swindle on the sly!'
Cooks make their scullions do not otherwise,
    When with their hooks they plunge the carcass clean
    Down in the caldron, that it may not rise.
Then said the Master good: 'Lest it be seen
    That thou art with me, do thou downward cower
    Behind a block, that thou mayst have some screen;
And what though wrong may seem to overpower
    Be not afraid: to these things am I wont,
    Having been in such wrangle once before.'
Beyond the bridge-head then he faced the brunt,
    And when arrived upon the sixth levee,
    He had full need to show a steadfast front.
With such a tempest and as furiously
    As when dogs rush upon a beggar man,
    Who, where he halts, cuts very short his plea,
From underneath the bridge those demons ran,
    And turned against him every hook and rake;
    But, 'None of you be felons!' he began:
'Ere with your forks ye loose upon me break,
    To listen to me send forth one of you:
    Then as to tearing me your counsel take.'
They shouted all: 'Let Malacoda go!'
    And halted: whereupon one forward goes,
    Murmuring on the way, 'What good will it do?'

'And dost thou, Malacoda, then suppose,
   Thou wouldst have found me,' said that Lord of
   'Safe hitherto, however ye oppose,   [mine,
Without propitious fate and Will Divine?
   Let me pass on, for Heaven has sent behest
   That I show some one else this road malign.'
Thereat so fallen was his haughty crest,
   That, letting fall the grapple at his feet,
   'No striking now!' he shouted to the rest.
'O thou!' exclaimed my Leader, 'from thy seat
   Where crouching on the craggy bridge dost hide,
   Now unto me securely make retreat.'
Wherefore I moved, and promptly sought his side;
   But all the devils sprang toward me so
   I trembled lest the compact were defied.
Even thus I saw the soldiers long ago,
   By compact from Caprona issuing,
   Exhibit fear amid so many a foe.
With all my body I drew up to cling
   Unto my Leader close, nor turned mine eye
   From off their look, which was not promising.
Forks levelled, they kept saying: 'Shall I try
   And touch him up upon the hinder side?'
   'Yes, nick it into him,' was the reply.
But that one who was talking with my Guide,
   Turned about quickly and commanded thus:
   'Bide quiet, Scarmiglionë, quiet bide!'
Then: 'There's no thoroughfare,' he said to us,
   'Across this bridge, because the sixth arch lies
   Now on the bottom, wholly ruinous:
If going forward still to you seem wise,
   Along the present bank ye journey may;
   Hard by there doth another bridgeway rise.
Later by five than this hour yesterday,
   Twelve hundred six and sixty years their line
   Completed since here broken was the way.

Thither I'm sending some of these of mine
    To see who airs him in the pitchy den:
    Go with them, for they will not be malign.
Alichino and Calcabrina, forward then,
    And thou Cagnazzo,' he began to add;
    'And Barbariccia, do thou lead the ten.
Libicocco and Draghignazzo come,' he bade,
    'Tusked Ciriatto and Graffiacanë too,
    And Farfarello and Rubicantë mad.
Explore all round about the boiling glue
    Let these be safe to the next bridging way
    Spanning the dens, a craggy avenue.'
'Alas, my Lord, what see I?'— did I say:
    'Go we alone and without escort now;
    If thou art able, none for me, I pray!
If with thy wonted heed observest thou,
    Dost thou the gnashing of their tusks not hear,
    And see them threaten mischief with their brow?'
And he to me: 'I would not have thee fear;
    Let them gnash with their tushes at their will,
    They do it for the parboiled wretches there.'
Upon the left-hand margin turned they still;
    But each began by thrusting tongue to lump
    The cheek, as signal to their leader ill,
Whereat he made a trumpet of his rump.

CANTO XXII

*Eighth Circle:
Pouch 5.
Comedy of the
Devils*

I have seen horsemen into battle go,
    And when on dress parade, and striking tent,
    And scurrying to anticipate the foe;
And foragers who on you made descent,
    O Aretines, and many a mounted scout,
    Running of tilt and clash of tournament,

With boom of bell and trumpet blaring out,
  With castle beacons and with drums of war,
  And instruments from home and from without:
But never yet to bugle so bizarre
  Did I see horse or foot set forward thus,
  Nor ship by any sign of land or star.
On went we, the ten demons guiding us:
  Ah, the fell company! but in the fane
  With saints, in tavern with the gluttonous.
Intent upon the pitch did I remain,
  To see the whole condition of the moat
  And of the people in their burning pain.
Like dolphins when to sailors they denote,
  With arching body bounding into sight,
  That they look sharp to keep their ship afloat:
So ever and again, for easement slight,
  Some sinner would present his back outside
  And hide it fleeter than a flash of light.
And as at marge of flooded moat abide
  The squatting frogs and only show the snout
  So that their feet and other bulk they hide,
The sinners thus were lying all about;
  But at the approach of Barbariccia
  They dove, and only bubbles showed without.
I saw (whereat I shudder to this day)
  One lingering thus — as when one takes the water
  Another frog will often chance to stay;
And Graffiacanë, watchful counterplotter,
  Hooked him by pitchy tresses and updrew,
  So that he had the semblance of an otter.
(The names of all and sundry of that crew, —
  So had I noted them when they were picked
  And listened when they called, — by this I knew.)
'O Rubicantë, see that thou inflict
  Thy talons on his back and soundly flay!'
  Shouted together all the maledict.

And I: 'Endeavour, Master, if thou may,
  To learn what luckless spirit thus doth lie
  To clutches of his enemies a prey.'
My Leader up beside him drawing nigh,
  Demanded whence he came, and this his word:
  'Born in the Kingdom of Navarre was I.
My mother placed me servant to a lord,
  For she had borne me to a worthless blade,
  Destroyer of himself and of his hoard.
Of good King Tybalt then retainer made,
  In barratry attained I mastership,
  Wherefore down here hot reckoning is paid.'
And Ciriatto, each way from whose lip
  A tusk, as of a boar, protruded long,
  Gave him to feel how one of them could rip.
The mouse was fallen evil cats among,
  But Barbariccia locked him in embrace,
  Saying: 'Stand off from him, while I emprong!'
Then to my Master turning round the face,
  Added: 'Ask on, if thou wouldst have him show
  Yet more, before the other fiends deface.'
'Now of the other sinners, dost thou know,'
  My Leader said, 'any Italian here
  Beneath the pitch?' And he: 'Short while ago
I quitted one who was their neighbour near;
  Would I were still with him in cover laid,
  So neither claw nor grapple should I fear.'
'We bear too much!' then Libicocco said,
  As with the hook he caught his arm amain,
  And, rending, bore away a sinew-shred.
And Draghignazzo for a grip was fain
  Down at the legs; whence their Decurion
  With grim demeanour turned and turned again.
When they were somewhat pacified anon,
  My Guide inquired of him, without delay,
  Who ruefully his wound was gazing on:

86

'Who was that soul from whom, as thou dost say,
   Ill parting madest thou to come abroad?'
''Twas Friar Gomita,' answered he straightway,
'He of Gallura, adept in every fraud,
   Who had in hand his master's every foe,
   And dealt so with them that they all applaud:
Taking the cash, he suavely let them go,
   So says he; by no petty standard clever
   In office jobbery, but hugely so.
Don Michael Zanchë of Logodoro ever
   Keeps him boon company; Sardinia draws
   Them on to wag their tongues that weary never.
But look! I fear that other fiend because
   His teeth are gnashing; I would add a word,
   But for my scurf he seems to whet his claws.'
To Farfarello turning then, who stirred
   His eyes asquint as if for striking home,
   Their master marshal said: 'Off, wicked bird!'
'If ye would see or hearken all and some,'
   The frightened spirit re-began thereon,
   'Tuscans or Lombards, I will make them come.
But the Maltalons must be well withdrawn
   Lest my companions their vendetta fear,
   And I, not stirring from this spot, for one
That I am, will make seven more appear
   By whistling, which, when one of us gets out,
   Is customary signal with us here.'
Cagnazzo at these words perked up his snout,
   Wagging his head, exclaiming: 'Hear the thing
   The knave to fling him down has thought about!'
Whence, fertile in device, he answering
   Said: 'Over-knavish am I, it is true,
   When I procure my friends more suffering.'
Alichino could not hold, but counter to
   The others, said to him: 'If thou depart,
   I shall in no wise galloping pursue,

But shall above the pitch on pinions dart:
    Leave we the ridge, a shelter be the shore,
    And see what match for us alone thou art!'
Reader, new sport is presently in store!
    Bended their eyes the other way all these, —
    He foremost who had been most loath before.
Selected well his time the Navarrese,
    Planted his foot-soles firm, and in a flash
    Leaped, and released him from their purposes.
Whereat they all with self-reproaches gnash,
    He most who made them so discomfited;
    And he leaped forward, yelling: 'Not so rash!'
But little it availed: fear faster fled
    Than wing could follow; down he dove amain,
    And on, with upturned breast, the demon sped.
Not other fashion is the wild duck fain
    To dive down nimbly, when draws nigh the hawk
    Who, vexed and baffled, glides aloft again.
But Calcabrina, furious at the mock,
    Followed behind him flying, in delight
    At this escape, the scuffle not to balk;
And when the barrator had vanished quite,
    His claws upon his fellow turned, — whence yond
    Above the moat they grappled for the fight.
But the other was a sparrow-hawk full fond
    To claw him well, and both together went
    Plump to the middle of the boiling pond.
The heat caused sudden disentanglement;
    But all the same they had no power to soar,
    So wholly did the pitch their wings cement.
Barbariccia, woeful with the rest, made four
    Incontinently on their pinions glide,
    With hooks and all, far as the other shore;
Down to their posts they dart on either side
    And stretch their forks toward the limèd pair
    Who were already cooked within the hide:
And thus we left them in embroilment there.

INFERNO

CANTO XXIII

Silent, alone, and uncompanioned, so
   Went we, the one before and one behind,
   As on their way the Minor Friars go.
Upon the tale of Æsop now my mind
   Was fixed, by reason of the present fray,
   Where of the frog and mouse we fabled find:
For not more similar are Aye and Yea
   Than this to that, if with attention due
   The outset and the end we rightly weigh.
And even as thoughts on other thoughts ensue,
   Now out of that was born another: thus
   My former terror double in me grew.
For I was thinking: 'These because of us
   Are flouted, damaged, and at naught are set,
   So that, methinks, they must be furious.
If rancour should their evil purpose whet,
   They will come after us, more pitiless
   Than dog when snapping up the leveret.'
Already did I feel my every tress
   Stiffen with terror, while I backward peer
   Intently, saying: 'Master mine, unless
Thou quickly hide thyself and me, I fear
   Maltalons, for they hard upon us tread:
   I so imagine them, I feel them near.'
'If I were fashioned out of glass and lead,
   I could not catch thine outward lineament
   More quickly than thine inward now,' he said.
'Even now thy thoughts among my own were blent,
   With similar action and with similar face,
   So that of both I made one sole intent.
If but the dexter bank so slope to base
   That we may down to the next pocket go,
   We shall escape from the imagined chase.'

Eighth Circle:
Pouch 6.
Hypocrites under
Copes of Lead

89

He had not yet made end of saying so,
    When I beheld them come with wings spread wide,
    Not far away, with will to work us woe.
Then caught me up full suddenly my Guide
    (Even as a mother wakened by a shout
    To see the flames enkindled close beside,
Who snatching up her little son runs out,
    And, having less for self than him regard,
    Tarries not even to wrap a smock about),
And from the ridge of the embankment hard
    Glided face upward down the rocky shore
    Which on that side the adjacent valley barred.
So swift through sluice slipped water nevermore
    The wheel of any bankside mill to run,
    Even when nearest to the floats, as bore
My Master me, that border land upon,
    Lying securely clasped upon his breast,
    Not merely as companion but as son.
No sooner had his feet the bottom prest
    Than our pursuers were upon the hill
    Above us; but his fears were now at rest,
Because exalted Providence, whose will
    Put them in the fifth moat to servitude,
    Made leaving it to all impossible.
A painted folk we found here, who pursued
    Their circling round with steps exceeding slow,
    Weeping, and looking weary and subdued.
They had on mantles with the hoods drawn low
    Before their eyes, and fashioned by such law
    That in Cologne monastics wear them so.
Gilded without, they dazzled them who saw;
    But were within of lead, so loaded down
    That those of Frederick were light as straw.
O everlasting mantle, heavy gown!
    We went along in their companionship
    Leftward once more, hearing their dreary moan:

But with the weight forspent, that fellowship
   So slowly came, that overtook we new
   Pilgrims at every movement of the hip.
Wherefore unto my Leader I: 'Now do
   Find some one not unknown by name or deed,
   And thus advancing, let thine eyes rove too.'
And one who gave the Tuscan accent heed,
   Cried to us from behind: 'O ye who race
   Thus through the dusky air, now stay your speed!
Perchance thou'lt get from me the wished-for grace.'
   Whereat my Leader turned and said: 'Now stay,
   And then proceed according to his pace.'
I stopped, and by their look saw two betray
   Great eagerness of spirit to advance;
   But the load hindered, and the crowded way.
Having come up, awhile with eye askance
   They gaze upon me, but their words control;
   Then say between themselves, exchanging glance:
'He seems alive by action of his jole:
   And by what privilege, if they are dead,
   Go they divested of the heavy stole?'
To me then: 'Tuscan, to the college led
   Of the sad hypocrites, do not thou scorn
   To tell us of thy origin,' they said.
And I replied: 'In the great city born,
   Did I by the river of fair Arno grow,
   And have the body I have always worn.
But who are ye from whom distils such woe
   As I see trickling down along the cheek?
   And what the pain that glitters on you so?'
And one replied to me: 'Of lead so thick
   The orange hoods are, that without surcease
   The weights thus cause their balances to creak.
Jovial Friars were we, and Bolognese,
   I Catalan, he Loderingo named,
   And by thy town together for its peace

Taken, where but a single man is claimed
    By custom; and it still may be descried
    Around Gardingo how we should be blamed.'
'O Friars, your iniquities...' I cried,
    But went no further, for there struck my sight
    One on the ground with three stakes crucified.
Beholding me, he writhed with all his might,
    Blowing into his beard with many a sigh:
    But Friar Catalan, who saw his plight,
Said to me: 'That staked felon thou dost eye,
    Counselled the Pharisees that it was meet
    That one man for the populace should die.
He is laid naked and across the street,
    As thou beholdest, and has first to note
    Of all who pass, how heavy weigh their feet.
His father-in-law is staked within this moat,
    And so the others of that Parliament
    Which for the Jews was seed of evil fruit.'
Virgil thereafter I beheld intent
    With wonder on that spirit crucified
    So vilely in eternal banishment.
Then to the Friar: 'Be it not denied,
    So please you, if it be legitimate,
    To tell if lie upon the right-hand side
Some passage, that we may go out that gate
    Without constraining any angel swart
    To come, and from this bottom extricate.'
'Still nearer than thy hope,' said he, 'doth start
    A bridgeway from the belt of the abyss,
    Spanning the cruel valleys overthwart,
All save that, broken, it bespans not this:
    Ye can ascend the ruin from hereunder
    For up it slopes against the precipice.'
My Leader bent his brow awhile to ponder,
    And then said: 'Evilly did he advise
    Who grapples with his hook the sinners yonder.'

INFERNO: CANTO XXIII

Dante and Virgil escaping from the Devils

And the Friar: 'Once I heard them stigmatize
   The Devil at Bologna, and perpended
   That he's a liar and first father of lies.'
Hereon with larger stride my Leader wended,
   Some ire perturbing his expression sweet;
   Whence from those leaden souls my pace I mended,
Following the prints of the beloved feet.

CANTO XXIV

In that young year-time when the sun his hair
   Tempers beneath Aquarius, and when
   The nights already tow'rd the southland fare,—
The hoarfrost on the greensward copies then
   His sister's image white, but by and by
   Abates the dainty temper of his pen,—
The husbandman, who sees starvation nigh,
   Rising and looking out, beholds the plain
   All whitened over, whence he smites his thigh:
Returning in, doth to and fro complain
   Like one who cannot mend his wretched case;
   Then out he comes and picks up hope again,
Beholding how the world has altered face
   In little while, and catching up his crook
   Drives forth his sheep to pasturage apace:
Thus when I saw perturbed my Master's look
   Did I lose heart, and thus the balm applied
   Suddenly from the wound the ailment took.
For when we reached the ruined bridge, my Guide
   Turned round and fixed me with that kindly glance
   Which first I saw beneath the mountain side.
He spread his arms out, and, as laying plans
   Within himself, first viewed the ruined fell,
   Then laid his hold upon me to advance.

Eighth Circle:
Pouch 7.
The Robbers and
the Serpents

Like one who labours and considers well,
  Seeming forever to provide anew,
  My Leader, lifting me toward the swell
Of one crag, had another rock in view,
  Saying: 'Now clamber over that one, but
  Try first if it be firm to grapple to.'
No way was this for one in mantle shut,—
  For scarcely we, he light and I pushed on,
  Were able to ascend from jut to jut.
And were it not that in that quarter, one
  Ascent is shorter than the other, I know
  Nothing of him, but I had been fordone.
But since upon a slant Malpouches go
  All to the entrance of the lowest Pit,
  So must the site of every valley show
One bank upreared above the opposite:
  We clomb, however, the last craggy stair
  At length, which from the ruined cliff is split.
My lungs so utterly were milked of air
  When I was up, no farther could I get;
  Nay, sat me down on first arriving there.
'Thus now behoves that sloth aside be set,'
  The Master said, 'to fame we never come
  Sitting on down nor under coverlet,
Which wanting, whoso goes to his long home
  Leaves of himself on earth as little trace
  As smoke in air or in the water foam.
Up then, thy panting overcome apace,
  With spirit that will every battle dare
  Unless the heavy body deep abase.
Behoves thee yet to climb a longer stair:
  Suffices not that forth from these we went;
  If thou hast understood, now forward fare.'
Then up I rose, and showed my breath less spent
  Than 'twas indeed, and said: 'Go on once more,—
  Look, if I be not strong and confident.'

Upward we took our course, the bridgeway o'er,
  A craggy, difficult, and narrow way,
  And far, far steeper than the one before.
Speaking I went, no faintness to betray,
  When out of the next moat a voice I heard
  Ill suited aught articulate to say.
Of what it said I do not know a word,
  Though now atop the arch that crosses nigh;
  But he who spake appeared to anger stirred.
I had bent downward, but no living eye
  Could through the darkness to the deep attain:
  'Master, contrive to come,' said therefore I,
'To the next dike, the inner wall to gain;
  For even as hence I hear, but cannot heed,
  So peering down I shape out nothing plain.'
To this he said: 'No answer is of need
  Except the doing, for the fit request
  Should tacitly be followed by the deed.'
The bridge we now descended from the crest
  Where with the eighth bank it united stood,
  And then to me the pouch was manifest:
And there I saw so terrible a brood
  Of serpents, of diversity so great,
  That the remembrance still freezes my blood.
Let Libya with her sand no longer prate:
  Though Amphisbœna, Cenchres, Pharëæ,
  Chelydri, Jaculi, she generate,
Never so many plagues and dire showed she,
  Even with all regions of the Ethiope,
  Nor yet with those which border the Red Sea.
Amid these, cruelly that swarm and grope,
  Were running naked and affrighted folk
  Hopeless of hiding-place or heliotrope.
Serpents the hands of these behind them yoke,
  With head and tail transfix them through the loin,
  And into knotted coils before them lock.

And lo! at one who loitered near our coign
    Of vantage, sprang a snake and pierced him through
    Just where the collar and the shoulders join.
Never was I so quickly written, or O,
    As he took fire and burnt, and he was doomed
    All into ashes dropping down to go;
And then the dust, so on the ground consumed,
    Collected of itself together there,
    And instantly that former shape resumed.
So verily the sages great declare
    The Phœnix dies, and then doth life repeat
    On drawing nigh to her five-hundredth year;
Lifelong no grain nor grasses doth she eat,
    But tears of incense and amome alone,
    And nard and myrrh are her last winding-sheet.
As one who falls, he knows not how, and prone
    Upon the ground by force of demon lies,
    Or by some other stoppage binding one,
Who, when he rises, looks around, with eyes
    Wholly bewildered by the mighty throes
    Which he has undergone, and looking sighs:
Such was that sinner after he arose.
    O Power of God, how just art thou to men,
    That showerest for vengeance down such blows!
'Who mayst thou be?' my Leader asked him then;
    Whence he replied: 'I rained from Tuscany
    Short while ago into this cruel glen.
Life of the brute, not man, delighted me,
    Mule Vanni Fucci, bestially propense:
    Pistoia was my den, and fittingly.'
I to my Leader: 'Let him not slip hence,
    And ask what crime here thrust him down so low:
    I knew him man of blood and insolence.'
The sinner feigned not, hearing me speak so,
    But full upon me bent his face and thought,
    And coloured with shame's melancholy glow;

Then said: 'It grieves me more that I am caught
   In misery which I must now display,
   Than when I from the other life was brought.
To thy demand I cannot say thee nay:
   I am put down so deep as this because
   I robbed the Chapel of the Fair Array,—
And falsely to another imputed 'twas.
   But that thy joy in such a sight abate
   If ever thou escape these gloomy jaws,
Open thine ears and listen to thy fate:
   Pistoia shall be thinned of Blacks at first,
   Then Florence men and manners renovate.
Mars out of Magra's vale with thunderburst
   Arises, in black clouds embosomed round,
   And with a storm impetuous and cursed,
A battle shall be fought on Picene ground;
   Whence sudden shall the mist be riven, so
   That every White thereby receives a wound:
And this I have foretold thee to thy woe.'

CANTO XXIV
133-151

CANTO XXV

As soon as those his words concluded were,
   Both figs with lifted fists the robber sends,
   Yelling: 'Have at thee, God; at thee I square!'
From that time forth the serpents were my friends
   For one of them did then his neck entwist,
   As who should say, 'Herewith thy speaking ends!'
Another, coiling, riveted each wrist,
   Clinching in front of him to such degree,
   He could not any longer jerk the fist.
Ah, why, Pistoia, dost thou not decree
   To burn thyself to ashes and so fall,
   Since thy ill deeds outdo thine ancestry?

Eighth Circle:
Pouch 7.
Transformation of
the Five Thieves

Throughout the dark infernal circles all,
 I saw no spirit Godward flaunt such pride,
 Not him who fell at Thebes down from the wall.
He fled away, all further word denied;
 Then saw I come a centaur, full of spleen:
 'Where is, where is the callous wretch?' he cried.
Harbours so many serpents not, I ween,
 Maremma, as he had his back along
 As far as where our lineaments begin.
Behind the nape, upon the shoulder clung
 A dragon with his pinions wide outspread:
 On every one he meets his fire is flung.
'That one is Cacus,' then my Master said,
 'Who in the cavern of Mount Aventine
 Has made full many a time a pool blood-red.
He goes not with his brothers in one line,
 By reason of his wily practice, when
 He stole the neighbouring great herd of kine:
Wherefore his crooked actions ended then
 Beneath the blows of Hercules, who plied
 Perhaps a hundred,—but he felt not ten.'
While he was speaking thus, and past us hied
 The centaur, there below came spirits three
 Whom neither I perceived, nor yet my Guide,
Until they shouted to us: 'Who are ye?'
 Whereby our story to a stand was brought,
 And them alone thereafter heeded we.
And now it happened (for I knew them not),
 As it is wont to happen, that one shade,
 To name another by some chance took thought,
Exclaiming: 'Where can Cianfa still have stayed?'
 Whence I, to make my Guide attentive so,
 Upward from chin to nose my finger laid.
If thou to credit what I say art slow
 Now, Reader, need there be no wonderment,
 For I, who saw, can scarce consent thereto.

The while I raised my brows on them intent,
  There darted a six-footed serpent out
  In front of one, and grappling with him blent.
With middle feet it clasped his paunch about,
  And flung the forward ones his arms around;
  Then gashed both cheeks of him the gaping snout.
With hinder feet outspread the thighs it bound,
  Thrusting its tail between them, and behind
  Upward extending it, the loins enwound.
So never did the barbèd ivy bind
  A tree up, as the reptile hideous
  Upon another's limbs its own entwined;
They clave together,—hot wax cleaveth thus,—
  And interfused their colours in such wise
  That neither now appeared the same to us:
Just as in burning paper doth uprise
  Along before the flame a colour brown
  Which is not black as yet, and the white dies.
The other two each shouted, looking on,
  'O me, Agnello, how thou alterest!
  Lo, thou'rt already neither two nor one!'
Already the two heads had coalesced,
  Whereby two faces seemed to be compelled
  Into one face, wherein were two suppressed.
Now the two arms from strips quadruple swelled;
  The thighs and legs, the chest and belly grew
  To members such as never man beheld.
All former aspect there was cancelled through:
  Two and yet none the shape perverted showed,
  And such with tardy steps away it drew.
As the eye-lizard, under the great goad
  Of dog-day heat, from hedge to hedge again
  Darts like a flash of light across the road:
So, tow'rd the bellies of the other twain
  Darting, a little fiery serpent went,
  Livid and tawny like a pepper-grain.

And in that part whence first our nourishment
   We draw, it one of them transfixed, then down
   In front of him fell back, and lay distent.
The pierced one gazed, but language uttered none:
   Nay, rather yawned and never stirred a limb,
   As if with fever or with sleep fordone.
He eyed the reptile, and the reptile him:
   One from his wound, the other from its snout
   Smoked fiercely, and the smoke commingled dim.
Be still now, Lucan, where thou tellst about
   Wretched Sabellus and Nasidius,
   And wait to hear what now shall be shot out!
Of Arethuse be still, Ovidius!
   If, fabling, he converts her to a fount,
   Cadmus to snake, I am not envious:
Because two natures never front to front
   Has he transmuted, so that both forms grew
   Each o'er the other's substance paramount.
In such wise answered each to each the two,
   That to a fork the serpent cleft his tail,
   And the stricken one his feet together drew.
The legs compacted, and the thighs as well,
   In such a manner that in little space
   The juncture left no mark discernible.
Now in the cloven tail the form we trace
   The other forfeited; the former's skin
   Elastic grew, the other's hard apace.
I saw the arms drawn through the armpits in,
   And the reptile's two short feet becoming long
   By so much as the arms had shortened been.
Thereafter the hind feet together clung
   To form the member that a man conceals,
   And to the wretch from his, two feet were sprung.
Now while the smoke with a new colour veils
   The one and the other, causing hair to spring
   On one, which from the other part it peels,

One rose, and fell the other grovelling,
  Though turning not aside the cruel glare
  Whereunder each his face was altering.
The erect one drew his where the temples were,
  And from stuff overmuch that thither went,
  Ears issued from the cheeks, hitherto bare:
And what, not running back, remained unspent,
  Sufficed to form a nose unto the face
  And give the lips their fit apportionment.
He that lay prone, thrust forward his grimace,
  And then his ears into his head are drawn
  As draws the snail his feelers into place.
Lastly the tongue, which heretofore was one
  And fit for speech, is cleft, and the cloven kind
  In the other closes: and the smoke is gone.
The soul thus with a reptile form combined,
  Exploding hisses fled the valley through,
  And the other, sputtering, remains behind:
Then, turning to the snake his shoulders new,
  Said to the third: 'As I along this way
  Have crawling run, will I have Buoso do.'
The seventh ballast did I thus survey
  Shifting, reshifting: here let novelty
  Excuse me, if my pen go aught astray.
And notwithstanding that mine eyes might be
  Somewhat bewildered, and my mind the same,
  Those could not flee away so covertly
But that I plainly saw Puccio the Lame:
  And of the three companions did he keep
  His form, alone of those at first who came;
The other, O Gaville, thou dost weep!

CANTO XXVI

Rejoice, O Florence, since thou art so great,
  Thy wings are beating land and sea around,
  And even in Hell thy name is celebrate.
Among the robbers five like these I found,
  Thy citizens,—whereat comes shame to me,
  Nor doth great honour upon thee redound.
But if near dawning dream be verity,
  Within short while from now shalt thou perceive
  What Prato, if no other, craves for thee.
If it must be, let come without reprieve;
  Serene the mind when of the worst aware:
  The older I become, the more 'twill grieve.
We parted thence, and up along the stair
  The spur-stones made before for our descent,
  My Guide remounted now, and drew me there.
And as the solitary way we went
  Amid the crags and splinters of the span,
  The foot without the hand had been forspent.
Then sorrowed I, and sorrow now again,
  When I direct my thoughts to what I viewed,
  And curb my genius from the course it ran,
Lest it from Virtue turn to truanthood;
  So that if favouring star or higher grace
  Have given me aught, I forfeit not that good.
During that season when from us his face
  He least conceals whose light the world doth fill,
  What time the fly unto the gnat gives place,
The peasant who is resting on the hill
  Sees many a firefly down along the dale,
  Perhaps where he doth gather grapes and till:
With flames so many the eighth pit of Hell
  Was everywhere agleam, as I beheld
  On coming where I saw the bottom well.

And even as he whom bears avenged of eld
   Looked on Elijah's parting chariot
   When straight the way to Heaven the horses held;
For with the eyesight could he follow not
   So that aught other than the flame was seen
   Flitting aloft, a fading cloudy spot:
Thus moved along the throat of the ravine
   Each flame, for none of them the theft unlock,
   Though every flame a sinner wraps within.
I stood to look upon the bridge of rock,
   Erect, so that, did not a jut prevent,
   To make me fall had been no need of shock.
And when my Leader saw me thus intent,
   He said: 'The spirits in the fires abide,
   Each swathed within the burning element.'
'Through hearing thee, my Master,' I replied,
   'Am I more certain; but what thou dost say
   I had surmised and would have asked, O Guide,
Who is within that flame which comes this way,
   Whose cloven top seems rising from the pyre
   Where once Eteocles with his brother lay?'
'Ulysses pines,' he said, 'within that fire,
   And Diomed; thus neither goes alone
   In punishment, as neither went in ire:
And in their flame together do they groan
   The ambush of the horse, whence was to come
   The noble seed by the old Romans sown;
There weep the guile whereby, though dead and
   Deidamía still Achilles wails;   [dumb,
   And there they pay for the Palladium.'
'If they within those sparks can tell their tales,'
   Said I, 'O Master, much I pray thee, pray
   Until my prayer a thousandfold avails,
That thou wilt not refuse me leave to stay
   Until the hornèd flame comes hither nigh:
   Thou seest with what desire I lean that way.'

'Thy prayer deserves all praise,' he made reply,
  'And therefore I accept it; none the less
  Take heed thou to thy tongue all speech deny:
Leave me to speak, for I already guess
  What thou desirest: seeing that these were Greek,
  Perhaps they might be shy of thine address.'
After the flame with the divided peak
  Had come where time and place to him seemed due,
  I heard my Leader in this manner speak:
'O ye, within one fire remaining two,
  If I deserved of you in life, if I
  Or much or little merited of you
When in the world I wrote the verses high,
  Do not move on, but one of you declare
  Whither, being lost, he went away to die.'
One horn, the mightier of the ancient pair,
  With murmuring began to quiver then,
  Even as a flame made weary by the air.
Waving the summit back and forth again,
  Thereafter, like a speaking tongue, the flame
  Flung forth a voice and spoke as follows: 'When
Of Circe I had taken leave,—the same
  Who held me near Gaeta a year and more,
  Ere yet Æneas gave it such a name,—
Nor tender love of son, nor pity for
  My aged father, nor affection due
  That should have cheered Penelope, o'erbore
The ardour that was in me to pursue
  Experience of the world, that I might be
  In human vices versed and virtue too:
But I put forth on the deep open sea
  With but one vessel, and that little train
  Which hitherto had not deserted me.
Both of the shores I saw as far as Spain,
  Morocco, and Sardinia's isle, and so
  The other islands bathing in that main.

I and my company were old and slow
   When in upon that narrow pass we bore,
   Where Hercules set up his bounds to show
That man beyond might venture nevermore.
   Here left I Seville back upon the right,
   And had left Ceuta on the other shore.
"O Brothers," said I, "Who are come despite
   Ten thousand perils to the West, let none,
   While still our senses hold the vigil slight
Remaining to us ere our course is run,
   Be willing to forgo experience
   Of the unpeopled world beyond the sun.
Regard your origin,—from whom and whence!
   Not to exist like brutes, but made were ye
   To follow virtue and intelligence."
With this brief speech I made my company
   So keen to go, that scarce to be denied
   Would they have been thereafter, even by me.
And having turned the stern to morning-tide,
   For the mad flight we plied the wingèd oar,
   Steadily gaining on the larboard side.
Night saw the constellations more and more
   Of the other pole, and ours at such descent
   That it rose not above the ocean-floor.
Five times rekindled and as many spent
   The light beneath the moon did wane away,
   Since to the passage of the deep we went,
When there appeared to us a mountain, gray
   With distance, and upreared a loftier brow
   Than I had ever seen until that day.
At this rejoiced we, but it turned to woe,
   For out of the new land a whirling blast
   Arose and struck the vessel on the prow:
Thrice with the waters all, it whirled her fast;
   The fourth upheaved the stern and sunk amain
   The prow, as pleased Another, till at last
The ocean had above us closed again.'

CANTO XXVII

The flame became erect and quiet now
　　To speak no more, and now was passing on,
　　Nor did the gentle Poet disallow;
When after it there came another one
　　Which made us eye its summit, whence found
　　A vague and indistinguishable tone.　　[vent
As the Sicilian bull, which with lament
　　Of him was first to bellow ('twas his due!)
　　Who gave it fashion with his instrument,
Bellowed with voice of every victim new,
　　So that, for all it was of brazen plate,
　　Yet it appeared with anguish stricken through:
Thus, having at their source not any gate
　　Nor outlet from the fire, into its mode
　　Of speech were turned the words disconsolate.
But afterward, when they had found a road
　　Up through the point, transmitting it the same
　　Quiver in passing which the tongue bestowed,
We heard it say: 'O thou at whom I aim
　　My voice, who spakst the tongue of Lombardy,
　　Saying,—"Now go, no more I urge, O flame!"
To pause and speak be irksome not to thee,
　　What though I come a little late withal:
　　Thou seest, although I burn, it irks not me.
If from that sweet Italian land thou fall
　　But now into this world of blinded souls,—
　　For thence I came with my transgression all,—
Say, have they peace or war, the Romagnoles?
　　For I was from the mountains there between
　　Urbino and the range whence Tiber rolls.'
Still was I bended down, with eager mien,
　　When now my Leader touched me on the side,
　　Saying: 'Speak thou,—Italian he has been.'

And I, well knowing what should be replied,
  Began discoursing without hesitation:
  'O spirit, thou who dost thereunder hide,
In thy Romagna ever inclination
  For war her tyrants harbour; but no plans
  For open war left I in preparation.
As stood she many a year, Ravenna stands:
  There doth the Eagle of Polenta brood
  So that she covers Cervia with her vans.
The town that gave proof of long fortitude,
  And in a bloody heap the Frenchmen threw,
  Under the Green Paws now is re-subdued.
Verrucchio's ancient Mastiff and the new,
  Who ill disposal of Montagna made,
  Still flesh their fangs where they are wont to do.
Lamone's and Santerno's towns are swayed
  By the young Lion on an argent ground,
  'Twixt summer and winter proved a renegade.
That town whereof the Savio laves the bound,
  As set between the mountain and the plain,
  Is between tyranny and freedom found.
Now who thou art I beg thee tell us twain:
  Show not more hardness than another showed,
  So thy repute may in the world remain.'
After the fire in its peculiar mode
  Had roared awhile, the pointed tip was quaking
  Hither and yon, and then such breath bestowed:
'If I supposed myself as answer making
  To one who ever could return on high
  Into the world, this flame should stand unshaking:
But since none from this yawning cavity
  Ever returned alive, if truth I hear,
  Fearless of infamy, do I reply.
I was a man of arms, then Cordelier,
  Hoping to make amends, begirded so:
  And this my hope was coming true, no fear,

But for the Priest Supreme, betide him woe!
   Who put me back into my sins of old;
   And how and wherefore I would have thee know.
While I was yet a tenant of that mould
   Of bone and pulp my mother gave, my bent
   Was ever of the fox, not lion-bold.
I knew all wiles and ways to circumvent,
   And plied the craft of them with such avail
   That to the ends of earth the rumour went.
When I began to feel the years prevail,
   Arrived that time of life when one had need
   To coil the tackle up and take in sail,
What pleased before, now grieved me: so with heed
   To penance and confession I withdrew;
   Ah, hapless! and it had availed indeed.
The Prince of the new Pharisees, in view
   Of Lateran, having a war in hand,—
   And not with Saracen, and not with Jew,
For all his enemies were Christian, and
   Not one of them at Acre's fall was nigh,
   Nor yet a trader in the Soldan's land,—
Neither his Holy Orders nor his high
   Office regarded, nor that cord of mine
   Which used to make more lean those girt thereby.
But as within Soractë, Constantine
   Besought Sylvester heal his leprosy,
   Likewise, his fevered pride to medicine,
Did this man seek out as physician me:
   Counsel he craved, and I deemed silence just,
   Because his language drunken seemed to be.
At length he said: "Let not thy heart mistrust;
   Henceforward I absolve thee: teach me how
   To level Palestrina with the dust.
I have the power to shut, as knowest thou,
   And open Heaven: whence double are the keys
   Which my foregoer held not dear enow."

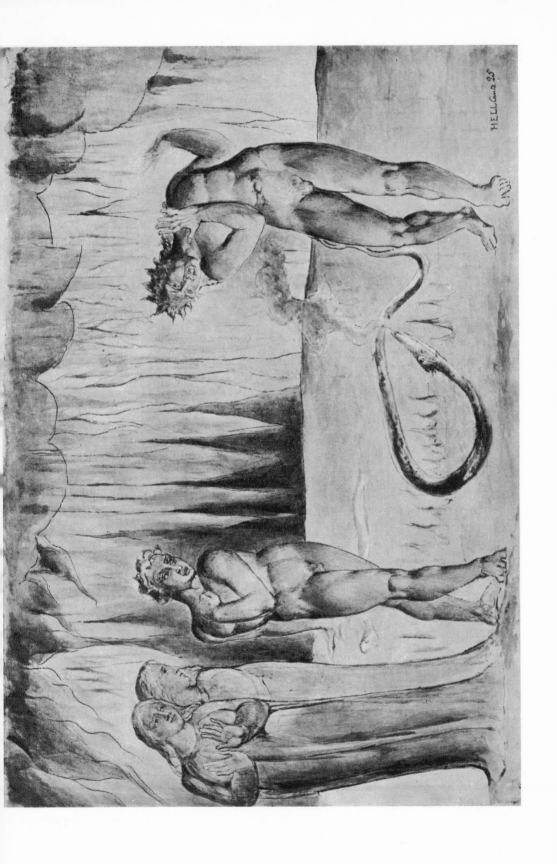

INFERNO: CANTO XXV

The Serpent attacking Buoso Donati

Constrained me weighty arguments like these,
  To such a point that silence seemed unfit:
  "Father, since thou assurest me release
From that transgression which I must commit,
  Long promise with short keeping," so I said,
  "Will make thee triumph in thy lofty Seat."
Saint Francis came for me, when I was dead;
  But shouted one of the black Cherubim:
  "Convey him not, nor wrong me; for instead
He must go down among my minions grim,
  Because he gave the counsel fraudulent,
  From which time forth I have been dogging him.
For none can be absolved but he repent,
  Nor can a man repent and will withal,
  For contradictories do not consent."
Alas for me! O how I trembled all
  What time he took me, saying: "Can it be
  Thou didst not think that I was logical?"
Down unto Minos then he carried me,
  Who twined with eightfold tail his stubborn frame,
  And, after he had gnawed it furiously,
Said: "'Tis a sinner for the thievish flame":
  Whence, where thou seëst me, am I forlorn,
  And, going thus attired, bemoan my shame.'
When he had thus his testimony borne,
  The flame with anguished utterance withdrew,
  Twisting about and tossing the sharp horn.
We passed along, my Guide and I, up to
  The next arch of the viaduct, whence showed
  That moat of Hell wherein is paid their due
To those who, severing, make up their load.

CANTO XXVIII

Who ever in words released from laws of rime
    Could fully of the blood and wounds report
    That now I saw, though telling many a time?
Every tongue would certainly fall short,
    Because the heart and speech of humankind
    Have little compass to contain such hurt.
Could ever all the people be combined
    Who in Apulia wept their blood poured out
    Upon the fateful land time out of mind
By Trojans, and in that long war, the rout
    Which issued in the mighty spoil of rings,
    As Livy writes, whose word we cannot doubt;
With those who bore the brunt of buffetings
    Resisting Robert Guiscard; and that horde
    Whose bones the ploughshare to this day upflings
At Ceperano, where each Apulian lord
    Proved faithless; and at Tagliacozzo's field
    Where aged Erard conquered without sword:
And all their mutilated limbs revealed,
    It would be naught to that dismemberment
    In the ninth pouch obscenely unconcealed.
No cask that middle board or stave forwent
    Was ever cleft so wide as one I saw
    Ripped from the chin clean down to fundament:
Between the legs hung down the viscera;
    The vitals showed and the foul pouch thereunder
    That turns to ordure what goes in the maw.
While I am gazing at him full of wonder
    He eyes me, and both hands in breast he plants,
    Saying: 'Look how I tear myself asunder,
How mangled is Mohammed! In advance
    Of me with weeping goes along Alee,
    Cleft chin to forelock in the countenance.

And all the others whom thou here dost see
  Were sowers of scandal and schismatic feud
  While living, and hence are cleft so cruelly.
A devil is behind us, who with crude
  Cleavage is carving, to the edge of sword
  Putting each member of this multitude,
When we have circled round the path abhorred;
  For lo! the gashes reunited are
  Ere we revisit that infernal lord.
But who art thou who musest on the scar,
  Perchance because reluctant to go hence
  To punishment, self-sentenced at the bar?'
'Death has not reached him yet, nor has offence,'
  My Master answered, 'to this torment led;
  But to procure him full experience,
It is my bounden duty, who am dead,
  To lead him down through Hell from round to
  As I speak with thee, this is truly said.' [round:
More than a hundred, when they heard this sound,
  Stood still within the moat at me to peer,
  Forgetting in their wonder every wound.
'Well then, to Fra Dolcin this message bear,
  Since thou, perchance, wilt shortly see the sun,
  That if he would not quickly join me here,
Let him be armed with food, or be undone
  By the Novarese, because of stress of snow:
  Else were their victory not so lightly won.'
When he had lifted up one foot to go,
  Mohammed spoke to me such words as those,
  Then stretched it to the ground, departing so.
Another, who with slitted gullet goes,
  And who withal has but a single ear,
  And close beneath the eyebrows cleft the nose,
Stopping for wonder with the rest to stare,
  Opened before that mutilated throng
  His gullet, which was crimson everywhere,

And said: 'O thou by pangs of guilt unwrung,
   Whom up in Latin country long ago
   I saw, unless undue resemblance wrong,
Remember Pier da Medicina's woe
   If thou return to see the lovely plain
   That from Vercelli slopes to Marcabò.
And speaking then to Fano's worthiest twain,
   Ser Guido and Ser Angiolello, say
   That, if our foresight here be nothing vain,
With sack and stone shall they be cast away
   Out of their ship, by a fell tyrant's guile,
   And perish hard by La Cattolica.
From Cyprus westward to Majorca's isle,
   Saw never Neptune so great outrage done
   By pirates or Argolic folk erewhile.
That traitor who sees only with the one,
   And lords the city, sight of which one here
   Would be delighted never to have known,
Will summon them in parley to appear;
   Then so will deal that neither vow shall be
   Required against Focara's wind, nor prayer.'
And I to him: 'Show and declare to me,
   If thou wouldst fain that word of thee be brought,
   Him who deplores that sight so bitterly.'
Therewith on a companion's jaw he caught,
   And with rude hand the mouth he open rent,
   Crying: 'This is the wight, and he speaks not;
This, this is he who, being in banishment,
   Quenched doubt in Cæsar, saying: "To men
   Delay was ever found a detriment."'   [prepared
Oh, how disconsolate to me appeared,
   With tongue asunder in his gullet lopt,
   Curio, who in his speech so greatly dared!
And one whose hands from both his wrists were chopt,
   The stumps uplifting so athwart the gloom
   That blood upon the face defiling dropt,

112

INFERNO: CANTO XXIX

The Pit of Disease: The Falsifiers

Cried out: 'To memory let Mosca come,
　　Who said, alas! "A thing once done is sped!"
　　Which was to Tuscan people seed of doom.'
'And death to all thy kin,' I adding said:
　　Whereon he went like person crazed with rue,
　　Heaping up sorrow upon sorrow's head.
But I remained to look upon that crew,
　　And saw a thing I should feel insecure
　　Even to tell without assurance new,
If Conscience did not wholly reassure,
　　That good companion which emboldens man
　　Beneath the conscious helm of feeling pure.
I truly saw, and seem to see again
　　A headless body going by, as passed
　　The others of that melancholy train;
And dangled by the tresses holds he fast
　　The severed head, which like a lantern shows,
　　And groans, 'Woe me!' gazing at us aghast.
Of self he made himself a lamp,—and those
　　Were two in one, and one in two were they;
　　How that can be, Who so ordains, He knows.
Arriving just below the bridging way,
　　The arm with head and all uplifted he,
　　To bring the nearer what he had to say,
Which was: 'Now see the grievous penalty,
　　Thou who to view the dead dost breathing go,
　　If any be as great as this one, see!
And that thou mayst bear tidings of me, know,
　　Bertran de Born am I, who counsel fell
　　Did craftily on the Young King bestow,—
Made son and father each to each rebel:
　　Not upon Absalom and David more
　　With wicked promptings wrought Ahithophel.
Because I parted those so bound of yore,
　　Woe worth the day, I carry now my brain
　　Cleft from its source within my body's core.
Thus retribution doth in me obtain.'

CANTO XXIX

The many people and strange wounds did steep
    Mine eyes with tears, and made them drunken so
    That they were craving, but to stay and weep.
But Virgil asked me: 'Whereon gazest thou?
    What may it be that still thy sight beguiles
    To rest upon sad mangled shades below?
Thou wast not wont to do so otherwhiles:
    Consider, wouldst thou make the count complete,
    The valley circles two and twenty miles,
And now the moon is underneath our feet;
    Brief is the time vouchsafed us for the way,
    And more to see than here thy glances meet.'
'Hadst thou but heeded,' did I answering say,
    'The reason why my gaze was bended there,
    Perchance thou wouldst have granted longer stay.'
Already did my Leader forward fare,
    I following while making my reply,
    Subjoining then thereto: 'Within that lair
Whereon so steadfastly I bent mine eye,
    Methinks a spirit of my blood complains
    About the crime that costs down there so high.'
Then said the Master: 'Baffle not thy brains
    Henceforth with anxious thought concerning this;
    Mind other thing, although he there remains:
For him I saw beneath the pontifice
    Menacing thee with finger vehement,
    Geri del Bello named in the abyss.
But thou wast at that moment all intent
    On him who once held Hautefort — thus the name
    Thou heardst not, nor didst look, until he went.'
'Dear Guide, the violent death that on him came,
    For which,' said I, 'unpaid remains the score,
    By any one a partner in the shame,

Made him indignant; whence he passed before
   Getting speech with me, if I guess aright,
   And so has made me pity him the more.'
Thus we conversed as far as the first height
   Which from the bridge the neighbour valley shows
   Quite to the bottom, were there but more light.
When we were over the last cloister-close
   Of the Malpouches, so that to our view
   All its lay brothers could themselves disclose,
Strange lamentations pierced me through & through,
   Which had their arrows barbed with pity all:
   Whence with my hands I shut mine ears thereto.
If from Chiana's every hospital,
   'Twixt July and September, all the sick,
   Maremma's and Sardinia's withal,
Were in one trench together crowded thick:
   So woeful was it here, and such a scent
   As out of putrid limbs is wont to reek.
Upon the final bank we made descent
   From the long bridge, and still did leftward fare;
   And then my vision, growing keener, went
Down tow'rd the bottom of the pocket, where
   The High Lord's handmaid, Equity condign,
   Punishes falsifiers apportioned there.
It was no greater sorrow, I opine,
   To see Ægina's people all infirm,—
   What time the atmosphere was so malign
That animals, down to the little worm,
   Fell stricken, and the ancient people then,
   As poets for a certainty affirm,
Were from the seed of ants restored again,—
   Than now to see, throughout that dim abode,
   Languish in ghastly stacks the souls of men.
They lie across the paunch, the shoulders load,
   Of one another, and some are creeping round
   Shifting their place along the dismal road.

Step after step we went without a sound,
　　Looking, and listening to the sick ones, who
　　Could not lift up their persons from the ground.
I saw, on one another leaning, two
　　(As pan is propped against a pan to dry)
　　All scab from head to heel: I never knew
A stable-boy so vigorously ply
　　The currycomb because his master watches,
　　Or one who keeps awake unwillingly,
As each of these incontinently scratches
　　Himself with biting nails, for frenzy mad
　　Of itching, which no other succour matches.
So was the tetter which their bodies clad
　　Flayed from them, as from bream knife scrapes
　　Or other fish, if any larger had.　　[the scales,
'O thou whose every finger thee dismails,'
　　So did my Guide to one of them begin,
　　'And sometimes makest pincers of thy nails,
Say if there be among those here within
　　Any Italian, so suffice thee thus
　　Thy nails forevermore upon thy skin.'
'Italians both, whose plight so hideous
　　Thou seëst,' weeping, one replied; 'but tell,
　　Who art thou that dost ask concerning us?'
My Leader answered, 'Down from fell to fell
　　I with this living man am travelling,
　　And I came purposing to show him Hell.'
Thereat the mutual trestle sundering,
　　That couple turned round to me tremblingly,
　　With others who by echo heard the thing.
The gentle Master then drew close to me,
　　Suggesting: 'To thy mind expression give.'
　　And as he willed, began I: 'So may be
Your fame in the first world not fugitive,
　　Fading from human mind without a trace,
　　But may it under many a sun still live,

Declare me who ye are and of what race:
   Do not, I pray, the revelation dread
   Because of the foul punishment's disgrace.'
'I was an Aretine,' one answering said,
   'Siena's Albert cast me in the fire;
   But what I died for nowise hither led.
'Tis true I said, as did the whim inspire,
   That I could wing the air in flight: whereon
   He, who had little wit, but fond desire,
Would fain be taught that cunning, and alone
   For I made him no Dædalus, made me
   Burn at the stake, through one who called him son.
But Minos damned me down for alchemy,
   Which in the world I practised, to the clutch
   Of the tenth pouch and last, nor erreth he.'
Then to the Poet I: 'Was ever such
   A foolish gentry as the Sienese?
   Surely not so the French, by very much!'
The other leper, hearing words like these,
   Spoke up: 'Except me Stricca, resolute
   For temperance in spending, if you please;
And Niccolò, the first to institute
   The costly application of the clove
   Within the garden where such seed takes root;
Except the club where Caccia d'Ascian strove
   To squander his great wood and vinery,
   And Abbagliato his vast wit to prove.
But that thou know who thus doth second thee
   Against the Sienese, now sharpen so
   Thine eye that well my face responds, and see!
I am the shadow of Capocchio
   Who did by alchemy false metals shape;
   And, if I well descry thee, thou shouldst know
The curious skill that made me Nature's ape.'

CANTO XXX

In time when Juno had so angry grown
    For Semelë, against the Theban strain,
    As she had more than once already shown,
Then Athamas was stricken so insane
    That he, his very wife encountering,
    Burdened on either hand with children twain,
Cried out: 'Spread we the nets for capturing
    The lioness and whelps upon this ground';
    Then, stretching forth his claws unpitying,
He took the one Learchus named, and round
    Whirled him, & round, & dashed him on a stone:
    Herself, then, with her other charge, she drowned.
Again, when Fortune had so overthrown
    The arrogance of Trojans all too brave,
    That king and kingdom were alike undone,
Poor Hecuba, a wretched captive slave,
    When she had looked on dead Polyxena,
    And afterward, beside the ocean wave,
The body of her Polydorus saw,
    Barked like a dog, out of her senses then;
    So grief had wrung the soul of Hecuba.
But never furies came to Theban ken,
    Or Trojan, of so much ferocity
    In goading brutes, much less the limbs of men,
As in two pallid, naked shades saw I,
    Running along and biting in such kind
    As does the boar when loosened from the sty.
One seized upon Capocchio, and behind
    His neck-joint fixed a fang so murderous
    It made the solid rock his belly grind.
Said the Aretine, who stood there tremulous:
    'That goblin's Gianni Schicchi, and insane
    He goes about to mangle others thus.'

'Oh!' said I, 'so the other may refrain
   From planting fangs in thee, let me persuade
   Thee tell who 'tis ere it dart hence again.'
And he to me: 'That is the ancient shade
   Of Myrrha, who in her abandoned mood
   Illicit love unto her father made.
Coming to sin with him, she understood
   To take an alien form; as who withdrew
   Yonder, to win the queen mare of the stud,
Made bold Buoso Donati's form to indue
   In counterfeit presentment, making will
   And testament in legal order true.'
And when the rabid pair had passed, who still
   Had riveted my gaze, I turning eyed
   The other malefactors starred so ill.
One fashioned like a lute I then espied,
   If only at the groin were amputate
   The thighs, just at the point where they divide.
The heavy dropsy which doth so mismate
   The limbs with ill-concocted humour thin
   That face and loin are disproportionate,
Compelled him so to hold his lips atwin
   As hectics do, for out of thirst he bent
   Upward the one, the other tow'rd his chin.
'O ye exempted from all punishment
   In this grim world and why I do not know,'—
   So he began,—'ah! look and be intent
Upon the mode of Master Adam's woe:
   Living, I had enough of what man wills,
   Now crave one drop of water here below.
The rivulets to Arno from the hills
   Descending through the Casentino green,
   Cooling and freshening their little rills,
Ever and not in vain, by me are seen,
   Because their image is more withering
   Than the disease that makes my visage lean.

Rigorous Justice with its goading sting,
    Takes vantage of the very region where
    I sinned, to give my sighs a nimbler wing.
There is Romena, where the coin that bare
    The Baptist's image did I counterfeit:
    For which I left my body burnt up there.
But could I Alexander's wretched sprite,
    Or Guido's, or their brothers', down here see,
    For Fontëbranda I would not give the sight.
One is already in, if truthful be
    What the mad shades that circle round me say,
    But since my limbs are tied, what steads it me?
If yet enough of nimbleness had they
    To carry me an inch a hundred year,
    Already had I started on the way
To seek him 'mid this squalid rabble here,
    Although eleven miles the round deploy,
    Nor less than half a mile across appear.
Through them in such a family am I:
    'Twas they who instigated me to stamp
    The florins with three carats of alloy.'
'What wretched two,' said I, 'lie, scamp by scamp
    Together, hard upon thy right confine,
    Reeking, like to wet hand in winter's damp?'
And he replied: 'I found them here supine,
    When to this trough I rained; they've moved no
    Since then, nor ever will they, I opine.   [more
She, who false witness against Joseph bore,
    He, Sinon the false Greek from Troy: intense
    The fever is that makes them reek so sore.'
And one of them, who seemed to take offence
    At being mentioned in a mode so mean,
    Fisted forthwith his hidebound corpulence,
Which rumbled, as it were a tambourine;
    But Master Adam planted in his face
    An elbow no less vigorous, I ween,

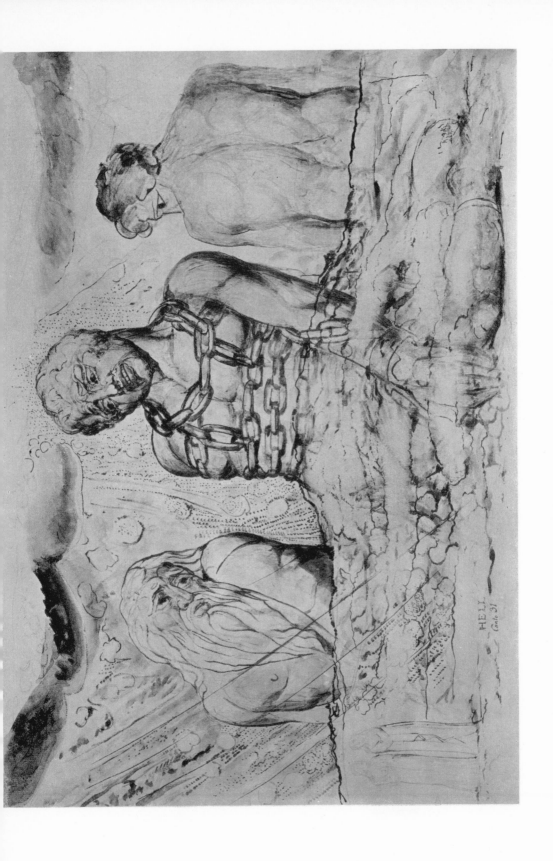

INFERNO: CANTO XXXI
Ephialtes and two other Titans

Saying to him: 'Though I be held in place
  Because of my obesity of loin,
  I have a limber arm for such a case.'
'When going to the stake,' did he rejoin,
  'Thou didst not have an elbow half so free;
  But so, and more, when thou wast making coin.'
'That,' quoth the dropsied one, 'is verity;
  Thou didst not witness to the truth so well
  When of the truth at Troy they questioned thee.'
'Told I false tale, false coinage didst thou tell,'
  Said Sinon, 'for one fault am I undone,
  But thou for more than other fiend of Hell.'
'Bethink thee of the horse, thou perjured one,'
  The sinner of inflated belly cries,
  'That the world knows it, be thy malison.'
'Thy malison the thirst that cracks and dries
  Thy tongue,' the Greek said, 'and the filthy swill
  Which makes that paunch a barrier to thine eyes.'
'Thy mouth is gaping open to thine ill
  As usual,' thereon the coiner said,
  'For if I thirst and flux my belly fill,
Thou hast the fever and the aching head;
  To lap the mirror of Narcissus, few
  The words of invitation thou wouldst need.'
While I was listening absorbed,—'Now do
  Go staring on!' the Master said to me,
  'A little more and we shall quarrel too.'
Now when I heard him speak thus angrily,
  I turned me round toward him with such shame
  That still it circles through my memory.
And even as he who of his harm doth dream,
  And, dreaming, doth to be a dreamer sigh,
  Craving what is, as if it did but seem,
Such, without power of utterance, grew I:
  Longing to bring, I brought excuses in,
  Yet did not think myself excused thereby.

'Less shame would purge away a greater sin
    Than thine has been,' at this the Master cried,
    'Therefore disburden thee of all chagrin;
And count that I am ever at thy side,
    If it fall out again that Fortune place
    Thee where in such a brabble people bide:
Because desire to hear the like is base.'

CANTO XXXI

One selfsame tongue first bit these cheeks of mine
    Suffusing both of them with bashful blood,
    And then held forth to me the medicine.
Even so the lance (as I have understood)
    Of Achilles and his father, was the source
    At first of evil guerdon and then good.
With backs to that sad vale, we took our course
    Up by the bank engirding it around,
    Traversing this with truce to all discourse.
Here less than night and less than day we found,
    Whence little way before my sight could fare;
    But now I heard a bugle so resound
That thunder would be feeble to its blare:
    Whereat mine eyes were counter to it cast
    Upon one spot, and wholly centred there.
After the woeful battle, when at last
    Was lost to Charlemagne the holy array,
    Roland blew not so terrible a blast.
Not long I held my head bended that way
    When many a lofty tower appeared to rise;
    Whence I: 'What is this city, Master, say?'
And he replied to me: 'Because thine eyes
    Traverse the darkness through too wide a space,
    Befalls that fancy wanders in such wise.

Well shalt thou see, arriving at that place,
How from afar the sense deceived may be:
Whence somewhat forward spur thyself apace.'
Taking me by the hand then tenderly,
'Ere yet,' continued he, 'we farther go,
So that the truth appear less strange to thee,
Not towers are these, but giants, must thou know,
And in the Pit about the bank are they,
From the navel downward, one and all below.'
As when the mist is vanishing away,
Little by little through the blotted air
The gaze shapes out whatever hidden lay:
So, through the dense and darksome atmosphere
Piercing, while ever nearer to the bound,
Forsook I error to encounter fear.
For, as with circling mural turrets crowned
Montereggionë stands, from the opening
Emerged half figures, turreting around
The margin that doth all the Pit enring,
Of horrible giants whom Jove from the sky
Still with his thunderbolt is threatening.
I could the face of one by now descry,
Breast, shoulders, and of belly portion great,
And either arm depending by the thigh.
Certainly Nature, ceasing to create
Such living beings, showed exceeding sense
These ministers of Mars to abrogate:
And if of elephant and whale repents
She nowise, he who subtly looks will find
Of justice and discretion evidence;
Because where the equipment of the mind
Combines with force and malice criminal,
No bulwark can be made by humankind.
His face appeared to me as huge and tall
As is Saint Peter's Pine-cone there at Rome,
With the other bones in due proportion all:

So that the bank, which was an apron from
 His middle down, showed upward of his size
 So much that, boasting to his hair to come,
Three Frisians would have made it good nowise:
 For I beheld of him thirty full palms
 Down from the place where man the mantle ties.
'Rafel mai amech zabi almi,'
 The mouth ferocious began bellowing,
 To which are not befitting sweeter psalms.
To him called out my Leader: 'Stupid thing!
 Stick to thy horn; contrive to make it serve
 Thine anger, or whatever passion sting.
Search at thy neck and there wilt thou observe
 The cord that makes it fast, O soul confused!
 And see the horn thy mighty breast becurve.'
And then to me: 'He hath himself accused;
 This one is Nimrod, through whose evil mood
 One language in the world is not still used.
Leave him, for empty speaking were not good:
 Since every language is to him the same
 As his to others, of none understood.'
We therefore journeyed on, with constant aim
 Toward the left, and at a crossbow shot
 We found one far more fierce and huge of frame.
The master smith to bind him know I not,
 But he was holding out his left hand bound
 In front of him, the right behind drawn taut
By a cable chain, which held him so enwound
 From the neck down, that on the part displayed
 As many as five coils begirt him round.
'This arrogant soul was bent,' my Leader said,
 'To try conclusions with almighty Jove,
 Whence in such fashion is his meed repaid.
His name is Ephialtes; he did prove,
 When giants frighted gods, his force immense:
 The arms he brandished never will he move.'

INFERNO: CANTO XXXI

Antaeus setting down Dante and Virgil

And I to him: 'I would, if naught prevents,
   That of the measureless Briäreus
   These eyes of mine might have experience.'
'Antæus shalt thou see,' he answered thus,
   'Hard by, articulate, unfettered,—he
   To bottom of all bad shall carry us.
'Tis a far cry to him thou wouldest see;
   Made fast is he, and fashioned like this one,
   Save that his features more ferocious be.'
Earthquake aforetime there was surely none
   Of force to rock a turret as when grim
   Ephialtes sudden shook himself thereon.
I feared death never as I did from him,
   Nor need had been of more beyond the dread,
   Had I not seen his gyves on every limb.
Farther along we then our footsteps sped,
   And reached Antæus standing forth ells five
   Above the rocky verge, without the head.
'O thou who sawest the fateful valley give
   Glory to Scipio, made heir of fame
   When Hannibal and his host turned fugitive,
And broughtest a thousand lions there as game,
   And through whom, hadst thou helped thy brothers
   In the high warfare, some appear to deem   [once
That victory had gone to the earthborn sons:
   Do not disdain now down to carry us
   Where frost Cocytus locks. Such orisons
Are not for Typhon nor for Tityus;
   This man can give what here ye are craving for:
   Wherefore stoop down, nor curl thy muzzle thus.
He in the world can yet thy fame restore:
   For still he lives and waits long life, unless
   Grace call him to herself his time before.'
The Master thus; and he in eagerness
   Took up my Leader in those hands outspread
   Whence Hercules once felt the mighty stress.

And when he felt their pressure, Virgil said:
'Come hither, that I may enclasp thee quite';
Then of himself and me one fardel made.
Such as the Carisenda seems to sight
Of one beneath its leaning, when a cloud
Goes over, and the tower hangs opposite:
Just so Antæus seemed to me who stood
Watching to see him lean; and it was then
I could have wished to go by other road.
But lightly down he laid us in the fen
That Lucifer with Judas prisons fast:
Nor lingered there thus leaning, but again
Rose up and up, as in a ship the mast.

CANTO XXXII

*Ninth Circle:
Caïna; Antenora*

Had I such harsh and grating rimes as must
Be most in keeping with the dismal Pit
Where all the other crags converging thrust,
I would press out the juice of my conceit
More perfectly: but since 'tis otherwise
Not without fear I come to speak of it:
Because it is no frolic enterprise
To plot the ground of all the universe.
Nor for a tongue that *Mama* and *Papa* cries.
But be those Ladies helpers in my verse,
Who helped Amphion Thebes to close and keep,
That from the fact the word be not diverse.
O dwellers in the unrecorded deep,
Rabble beyond all others born amiss,
Better had ye on earth been goats or sheep!
When we were down within the dark abyss
Beneath the giant's feet, but far below,
And yet I gazed at the high precipice,

I heard it said to me: 'Look how thou go:
   Let not thy feet betrample by mistake
   The heads of brothers weary and in woe.'
Whereat I turned, and saw a sheeted lake
   Before and underfoot, whereon the ice
   Did sheen of glass and not of water make.
At wintertide in Austria never lies
   On current of the Danube veil so thick,
   Nor upon Don far under freezing skies,
As here there was: so that if Tambernic
   Or Pietrapana had tumbled in that glade,
   Not even the border would have given a creak.
And as the frogs to croak are often laid
   With muzzle out of water, when alone
   Of frequent gleaning dreams the peasant-maid:
Livid to where the blush of shame is shown,
   Here shades in ice betrayed their sufferance
   Setting their teeth to the stork's monotone.
Every one was casting down his glance:
   The cold is proved by chattering of the jaw,
   And the heart's agony by the eye askance.
When I had looked around awhile, I saw
   Down at my feet two shades so close-embraced
   Their fell of hair was mingled. 'By what law,'
Said I, 'have ye the breasts so interlaced;
   Who are ye, tell?' Back then their necks they bent,
   And when their faces up to me were raised,
Their eyes, whose moisture yet within was pent,
   Brimmed over at the lids, whereon the cold
   Congealed the tears between and locked the vent.
Never did clamp two strips of scantling hold
   So stiffly; whence like he-goats rancorous
   Butted the two, in anger uncontrolled.
And one, bereft both ears by frost, spoke thus,
   Still holding down the face lest I discern:
   'Why make a looking-glass so long of us?

Dost thou for knowledge of this couple yearn,
  The valley whence descends Bisenzio
  Their father Albert held, and they in turn.
They issued from one body: thou mayst go
  Questing Caïna through, and find no shade
  Deserving more in gelatine to show:
Not him the hand of Arthur open laid,
  At one blow piercing breast and shadow, nor
  Focaccia even, not him who with his head
So hinders me that I cannot see before:
  One Sassol Mascheroni,—estimating
  That thou art Tuscan, I need say no more.
And that I be not put to further prating,
  Know me for Camicion de' Pazzi, still
  Exoneration from Carlino waiting.'
Then saw I myriad faces for the chill
  Grinning like dogs: whence shudders manifold
  Seize me at frozen pools, and ever will.
While way toward the Centre did we hold
  Whereto all weights converge in unison,
  And I was trembling in the eternal cold,
Whether by will, or fate, or fortune done,
  I know not; but among the heads somehow
  I struck my foot full in the face of one.
Wailing he yelled at me: 'Why tramplest thou?
  Unless to double vengeance for the day
  Of Montaperti, why molest me now?'
And I: 'Now, Master, make a little stay,
  That I through him may rid me of a doubt:
  Then shalt thou haste me as thou wilt away.'
My Leader stopped; and I, now turned about
  To him, still bitterly blaspheming there,
  Said: 'Who art thou on others crying out?'
'Nay, who art thou?' he answered, 'that dost fare
  Through Antenora, trampling jowl and crown,
  So that, wert thou alive, 'twere ill to bear!'

'Alive I am, and cravest thou renown,'
  I answered, 'dear to thee may be the boon
  If with my other notes I put thee down.'
'The contrary I crave,' quoth that poltroon,
  'Take thyself off the nuisance to abate,
  For thou cajolest ill on this lagoon.'
Then by the scalp I seized upon him straight
  Exclaiming: 'Thou must tell what thou art called
  Or little hair be left upon thy pate!'
But he retorted: 'Thou canst strip me bald,
  Yet shall not what I am be shown or said
  What though a thousand times my head be mauled.'
My hand, now coiled with tresses of his head,
  By many a tuft was leaving it dishevelled,
  He howling, with eyes downward riveted,
When some one this loud taunt against him levelled:
  'What ails thee? not content with clattering jowl,
  Bocca, needs must thou bark? art thou bedevilled?'
'Thy tongue', I cried, 'no more would I control,
  Malignant traitor, and for shame to thee
  Shall I bear back true tidings of thy soul.'
'Begone, and babble what thou wilt,' said he,
  'But, going hence, fail not discourse to hold
  Of him who had the tongue just now so free.
He is lamenting here the Frenchman's gold:
  "I saw him of Duera," canst thou note,
  "There where the sinners lie out in the cold."
And should they ask thee other anecdote,
  Him at thy side there name in thy reports,
  The Becchería,—for Florence cut his throat.
Gianni de' Soldanier, I think, consorts
  With Ganelon, and Tribaldello yon
  Who while men slept unbarred Faenza's ports.'
Already we away from him were gone
  When, frozen in one hole, beheld I two
  So that one head was hood to the other one:

And even as people bread for hunger chew,
The uppermost upon the one below
Set teeth where brain and neck together grew.
Not otherwise once Tydeus gnawed the brow
Of Menalippus, in his rage malign,
Than skull and other parts gnawed this one now.
'O thou who showest by so bestial sign
Hatred to him whom thou devourst,' said I,
'Tell me the cause, upon this pledge of mine,
If thou complainest with good reason why,
That I, with both acquainted, and his guile,
May yet requite thee in the world on high,
If this my tongue be not dried up erewhile.'

CANTO XXXIII

*Antenora.
Ugolino and his
Children
in the Tower*

That sinner lifted from the foul repast
His mouth up, wiping it upon the hair
Behind the head whereon I looked aghast;
Then he began: 'Thou wilt that I declare
Desperate grief that wrings the heart of me,
Even in the thought, before I lay it bare.
But if my words a seed of infamy
May sow unto the traitor whom I gnaw,
Speaking and tears together shalt thou see.
I know not who thou art, nor by what law
Thou comest down here; but a Florentine,
On hearing thee, it seemed to me I saw.
Thou hast to know I was Count Ugolin,
And this Archbishop Roger: why so fell
A neighbour am I, let me tell his sin.
That I, in his good faith confiding well,
By his devices was in prison flung
And done to death, there is no need to tell.

But what thou hast not heard from any tongue,
   That is, the cruel death he put me to,
   Shalt hear, and learn if he have done me wrong.
A narrow aperture within the mew
   Which holds the name of Hunger because of this
   Offence,—and others must be shut there too,—
Had shown me already through its orifice
   Many a moon, when came the ill dream to me
   That rent the veil of future destinies.
This man seemed master of the hounds to be,
   Chasing the wolf and wolflings to the mount
   Wherethrough the Pisan cannot Lucca see.
With eager sleuthhounds gaunt and trained to hunt,
   Had he Gualandi on before him sent,
   Sismondi with Lanfranchi, to the front.
After brief coursing, sire and sons forspent
   Appeared to me, and all the while they fled
   I saw their flanks with whetted tushes rent.
When I awoke before the dawn was red,
   I heard my children moaning in their sleep,
   For they were with me, and imploring bread.
Right cruel must thou be if thou canst keep
   The tears back, thinking what my bodings were,
   And if thou weep not now, when wouldst thou weep?
The wonted hour to bring our food drew near,
   And all by this were from their slumber stirred,
   And each one from his dream was full of fear:
When, sounding through the horrible tower, I heard
   One nailing up the doorway of the mew:
   So gazed I at my sons without a word.
I wept not, so of stone within I grew:
   They wept; and Anselm, darling little one,
   Said: "How now, father, art thou ailing too?"
Nor yet for this I wept, made answer none
   Throughout that day and all the following night,
   Till dawned upon the world another sun.

Soon as a slender ray of feeble light
    Entered the dreary prison, to disclose
    My looks reflected in four faces white,
I bit both hands for anguish. Thereat those,
    Supposing that I did it for desire
    Of breaking fast, with one accord uprose
And said: "Father, our pain were far less dire
    If thou wouldst eat of us: from thee we got
    These wretched bodies,—take them from us, sire."
I calmed me then, lest they be more distraught:
    Through that day and the next all mute were we:
    Ah, cruel earth, why didst thou open not?
On the fourth day, when dawn broke dismally,
    Fell Gaddo at my feet, and I must brook
    Hearing: "O father, hast no help for me?"
There died he; and as thou on me dost look,
    I lookt and saw them falling, falling through
    The fifth day and the sixth: whence I betook
Myself, now blind, to groping, and for two
    Whole days called to them, after they were gone:
    Then hunger did what sorrow could not do.'
Having said this, with eyes askance drawn down,
    That miserable skull he grappled dumb,
    With teeth strong as a dog's upon the bone.
Ah, Pisa! of the folk opprobrium
    In the fair country where the *si* doth sound,
    Since neighbours lag in punishment, let come
Caprara and Gorgona, shifting ground,
    And choke up Arno's channel, quite across,
    That every living soul in thee be drowned.
For if folk tax Count Ugolin with loss,
    By treachery to thee, of places strong,
    Shouldst not have put his sons on such a cross.
Thou modern Thebes! their youth made free from
    Uguccion and Brigata, and withal   [wrong
    The two already mentioned in my song.

Yet onward went we, where the icy pall,
  Rough swathing, doth another people keep,
  Not downward bended, but reverted all.
The very weeping there forbids them weep,
  And finding on the eyes a barrier, woe
  Turns inward to make agony more deep:
Because the first tears to a cluster grow,
  And, like a visor crystalline, upfill
  The whole concavity beneath the brow.
And though, as in a callus, through the chill
  Prevailing there, all sensibility
  Had ceased its function in my visage, still
I felt some wind, so now it seemed to me:
  'Master, who moveth this?' I therefore said,
  'Is not all vapour quenched down here?' Whence he:
'Speedily art thou thither to be led
  Where shall thine eye to this an answer find,
  Seeing the cause wherefrom the blast is shed.'
And of the wretches of the frozen rind
  One shouted to us: 'O ye souls so fell
  That the last station is to you assigned,
Lift from my visage up each rigid veil,
  That I may vent the sorrow in a trice,
  Which swells my bosom, ere the tears congeal.'
'Tell who thou art,' I said, 'I ask this price:
  If thee therefore I do not extricate,
  May I go to the bottom of the ice.'
And he: 'Fra Alberigo I of late,
  He of the fruit of the ill garden: so
  I here am getting for my fig a date.'
'Already,' said I, 'art thou here below?'
  And he made answer: 'How my flesh may thrive
  There in the upper world, I do not know.
This Ptolomea hath such prerogative
  That oftentimes the soul falls to this place
  Ere ever Atropos the signal give.

And that more willingly from off my face
   Thou now remove away the glazen tears,
   Know that as soon as any soul betrays,
As I betrayed, forthwith a fiend appears
   And takes her body, therein governing
   Throughout the revolution of her years.
Headlong to such a cistern doth she fling;
   And haply still above the trunk is shown
   Of yonder shade behind me wintering.
To thee, if just come down, he should be known:
   Ser Branca d'Oria: and many a year
   Since he was thus locked up, is come and gone.'
'I think,' said I, 'that thou deceivst me here:
   For Branca d'Oria not yet is dead,
   But eats and drinks and sleeps and dons his gear.'
'Into the moat of Maltalons,' he said,
   'Up there where boils the sticky pitch away,
   Had Michael Zanchë's spirit not yet sped,
When this one left a devil in full sway
   In his own body, and one next of blood
   Who served him as accomplice to betray.
But now reach here thy hand, as understood,
   Open mine eyes': my hand I reached not forth
   And courtesy it was to be thus rude.
Ah, men of Genoa, strangers to all worth
   And full of all depravity accurst,
   Why have ye not been scattered from the earth?
For, with that spirit of Romagna worst,
   One such of you I for his dealing found,
   Whose soul is in Cocytus now immersed,
Yet seems he alive in body above ground.

INFERNO

CANTO XXXIV

'Tow'rd us the banner of the King of Hell
  Advances; therefore forward bend thine eyes,'
  My Master said, 'if thou discernest well.'
As, when thick fog upon the landscape lies,
  Or when the night darkens our hemisphere,
  A turning windmill seems afar to rise,
Such edifice, methought, did now appear:
  Whereat, by reason of the wind, I cling
  Behind my Guide,—no other shelter near.
Already (and it is with fear I sing)
  I found me where the shades all covered show
  Like straws through crystal faintly glimmering.
Some stand erect, others are prone below;
  One here head up, soles uppermost one there;
  Another face to foot bent, like a bow.
When we had made our way along to where
  I was to see, as pleased my Master good,
  The Being that once bore the semblance fair,
He halted me, and from before me stood,
  Saying: 'Lo! Dis, and lo! the place of blame
  Where thou must weapon thee with fortitude.'
How frozen and how faint I now became,
  Ask me not, Reader, for it balks my pen,
  All language would fall short of such an aim.
I did not die, nor living was I then:
  Think now, if thou hast any wit therefor,
  What thing, bereft of both, did I remain.
He, of the woeful realm the Emperor,
  Emerged midbreast above the ice-field yon,
  And liker to a giant I, than bore
The giants with his arms comparison:
  Consider, with respect to such a limb,
  How huge that whole which it depends upon.

*Ninth Circle:
Judecca. Passage
from Lucifer to
the Light*

If he were fair once, as he now is grim,
      And raised his brow against That One who made,
      Well may all woe have fountainhead in him.
O what a wonder, when upon his head
      Three faces to my sight were manifest!
      The one in front, and it was fiery red;
The other two with this one coalesced
      Just o'er the middle of each shoulder, while
      They all conjoined together at the crest:
The right-hand face appeared to reconcile
      With yellow, white; the left was such of hue
      As folk who come whence floweth down the Nile.
Vast wings came forth, beneath each visage two,
      Such as were fitting to a bird like that:
      Sails of the sea so broad I never knew.
They bore no feathers, but as of a bat
      Their fashion was; and flapping them he stood
      So that three winds proceeded forth thereat,
Whence frozen over was Cocytus flood.
      The cadent tears were trickling from six eyes
      Over three chins, to mix with drooling blood.
At every mouth his tushes heckle-wise
      Upon a malefactor champ and tear,
      So that he thus makes three to agonize.
To him in front the bite could not compare
      Unto the clawing, for at times the hide
      Dilacerated, left the shoulders bare.
'That soul up yon, most sorely crucified,
      Is Judas the Iscariot,' said my Lord,
      'His head within, he plies his legs outside.
Of the other two, whose heads are netherward,
      Brutus it is who hangs from the black jowl:
      Look how he writhes and utters not a word!
The other Cassius, stalwart-seeming soul,
      But now another night is darkening;
      We must depart: for we have seen the whole.'

About his neck I, at his bidding, cling:
 And he of time and place advantage takes:
 And soon as wing is wide apart from wing,
Lays hold upon the shaggy flanks, and makes
 His way from shag to shag, descending by
 The matted hair among the frozen cakes.
When we were come to that point where the thigh
 Revolves, exactly where the haunches swell,
 My guide, with effort and distressful sigh,
Turned round his head to where his footing fell,
 And like one mounting, grappled to the hair,
 So that, methought, we back returned to Hell.
'Keep fast thy hold, because by such a stair,'
 The Master said, panting like one forspent,
 'Forsaking so great evil, must we fare '
Out through the crevice of a rock he went,
 And set me on its brink; then warily
 Planting his feet, his steps toward me bent.
I lifted up mine eyes, thinking to see
 Lucifer, just as I had seen him last,
 And saw him with his legs upturned to me.
And what perplexity now held me fast,
 Let dullards fancy who have notion none
 What point it was I had already passed.
'Rise up,' the Master said, 'thy feet upon:
 The way is long, and difficult the road,
 And now to middle tierce returns the sun.'
It was no palace chamber where we stood,
 Rather a natural dungeon vault was this,
 Wanting in light and without footing good.
'Before I pluck myself from the Abyss,
 Master,' when risen to my feet I said,
 'Talk with me somewhat, lest I judge amiss.
Where is the ice? and how is This One stayed
 Thus upside down and how, in moments few,
 The sun from even to morning transit made?'

'Thou still believest thee,' he said thereto,
   'Yon-side the Centre, where I gripped the hair
   Of the fell Worm that pierces the world through.
So long as I descended wast thou there:
   Soon as I turned, the point we overran
   Whereto all weights from all directions bear:
Thou'rt come beneath the hemisphere whose span
   Is counterposed to that which doth embrace
   The great dry land, beneath whose cope the Man
Was slain, pure born and without need of grace:
   Thy feet upon a little disk abide
   That for Judecca forms the counter face.
Here it is morn when yonder eventide:
   And still doth This One stand as fixedly
   As ere he made a ladder with his hide.
Down out of Heaven upon this side dropped he,
   And all the land that here of yore arose
   Was veiled, through terror of him, with the sea
And joined our hemisphere; and some suppose
   Perhaps that land to-day on this side found
   Fled up from him, and left this empty close.'
There is a place below, whose further bound
   From Beelzebub far as his tomb extends,
   By sight unnoted, but betrayed by sound
Made by a rivulet that here descends
   A crannied rock, which it has gnawed away
   With gently sloping current, as it wends.
My Guide and I upon that hidden way
   Entered, returning to the world of light:
   And without caring for repose to stay,
He first, and I behind him, scaled the height,
   Till a round opening revealed afar
   The beauteous things wherewith the heavens are
                                [bright:
Thence came we forth to re-behold each star.

PURGATORIO

E quant'uom più va su, e men fa male.

PURGATORIO IV. 90

P-g. Canto I

PURGATORIO: CANTO I
Dante and Virgil again beholding the Sun as they issue from Hell

CANTO I

Sets sail the little vessel of my mind
    And henceforth better waters furrowing
    Leaves such a cruel ocean far behind.
And of that Second Kingdom will I sing
    Wherein the human spirit, purged of stain,
    Grows worthy to ascend on heavenward wing.
Here let dead poesy arise again,
    O holy Muses, since I am your own,
    And here Calliope uplift her strain,
Companioning my singing with that tone
    Whence the poor Magpies felt so stricken through
    That they were desperate of pardon grown.
The tender oriental sapphire hue
    Suffusing the calm heaven from midmost height
    To the first circle down, so pure and blue,
Cheered up mine eyes with long-unfelt delight
    Soon as I issued forth from the dead blur
    That had afflicted both my heart and sight.
The planet fair that is Love's comforter
    Lit with her smiling all the eastern skies,
    Veiling the Fishes then escorting her.
Turning toward the right, I fixed mine eyes
    On the other pole, thereby four stars discerning
    Ne'er seen by man save first in Paradise.
The heaven appeared enraptured with their burning:
    Clime of the northland, O how widowed thou,
    Since these have been withholden from thy yearning?
When from their view I could avert my brow,
    Glancing a little toward the north, that shone
    Where the bright Wain had sunk from sight ere now,
Near me appeared an elder all alone,
    Worthy of so great reverence by his mien
    That more to father owes not any son.

The Dawn of Easter

141

Long was his beard, with grizzled streaks between,
   And like thereto the crown of hair he wore
   Fell to his breast in double tresses sheen.
Beams of the holy luminaries four
   Adorned his face and so great lustre shed,
   I saw him as though the sun had been before.
'Who are ye, against the darkling river fled
   From out the eternal prison void of day?'
   Moving those venerable plumes, he said.
'Who was your lantern or who led the way
   Issuing forth from the abysmal gloom
   That makes the infernal valley black for aye?
Are broken thus below the laws of doom?
   Or has in Heaven gone forth some new decree
   That ye, being damned, to my rock-caverns come?'
Straightway my Leader laid his hold on me,
   And with word, hand, and signal, to position
   Of reverence compelled my brow and knee;
Then answered: 'I came not of my own volition:
   A Lady made descent from the Divine,
   And I assist this man at her petition.
But since it is thy will that I assign
   More reason for our veritable plight,
   My will cannot be at variance with thine.
This man has never seen his final night,
   But by his folly had come near it, so
   That little time was left to turn aright.
I was sent to him, as I let thee know,
   For his redemption, and there was no road
   Save this whereon I set myself to go.
I have shown him all the bad and their abode;
   And now intend to show him the array
   Of spirits who are purged beneath thy code.
How I have brought him would be long to say:
   From up aloft comes virtue adjuvant,
   To give him sight and speech of thee to-day.

Please to his coming now thy favour grant:
  He goes in quest of Freedom, boon how dear
  Knows that man who for her his life doth scant.
Thou knowest it, for death did not appear
  Bitter to thee in Utica, vacating
  The vesture that great day to be so clear.
No eternal edicts are we violating:
  For this man lives, and Minos binds me not,
  But I am of the circle where are waiting
Marcia's pure eyes, which still with prayer seem fraught
  That thou wouldst hold her thine, O holy breast!
  Then grace us, if her love be unforgot.
Let us throughout thy seven kingdoms quest:
  Thee by report to her will I requite,
  If word of thee below thou sanctionest.'
'Marcia was aye so winsome in my sight
  Long as I tarried yonder,' he replied,
  'That doing all her will was my delight.
Now can she, from beyond the baleful tide,
  Move me no more, by law which took effect
  When I passed over from the further side.
But if a Lady of Heaven prompt and direct,
  As thou hast said, thy bland persuasion hush:
  Sufficient answer for her sake expect.
Go then and see that with a simple rush
  Thou gird this mortal, washing in such wise
  His face that for no soilure it may blush:
For it were unbecoming that with eyes
  Beclouded, he appear before the Prime
  Angel who is of those of Paradise.
This islet, ere the slope begins to climb,
  About the margin where the billow heaves,
  Is fringed with rushes in the oozy slime.
No other plant, of such as put forth leaves
  Or harden, could survive there, since not bent
  To every buffet that the stalk receives.

Put all returning here from your intent;
   The sun, now rising, will instruct you how
   To take the Mount by easier gradient.'
So vanished he; and I, uprising now
   Without a word, and firmly taking stand
   Close to my Leader, bent on him my brow.
'Follow my footsteps, son,' was his command,
   'Let us turn backward, for from here this lea
   Slopes to the lower limit of the land.'
Now did the shadowy hour of morning flee
   Before the dawn, so that from far away
   I caught the gusty ripple of the sea.
We walked the lonely plain as wander they
   Who turn back to the pathway lost, and who
   Until they find it seem to go astray.
When we had reached that region low where dew
   Contends with sun, nor in the chilly air
   Disperses while the beams are faint and few,
Softly upon the tender herbage there
   Both of his outspread palms my Master placed;
   Whence I, who of his purpose was aware,
Lifted my grimy cheeks, with tear-stains laced;
   There to my features he restored that hue
   Which by the spume of Hell had been effaced.
Then to the lonely seashore came we two,
   Which never yet upon its waters found
   One mariner who afterward withdrew.
Here as that other bade, he girt me round:
   O miracle! that such as from the earth
   He culled the humble plant, quick from the ground
Whence it was plucked, it came again to birth.

PURGATORIO: CANTO IV

Dante and Virgil ascending the Mountain of Purgatory

PURGATORIO

CANTO II

The sun by now to that horizon came   *The Angel Pilot*
   The arc of whose meridian is at height
   Just at the point above Jerusalem:
And, circling opposite to him, the Night
   Was issuing forth from Ganges with the Scales
   Which fail her hand when she exceeds in might;
So, where I was, the cheek that glows and pales
   Of fair Aurora, sallowed with the ray
   Of orange, because age on her prevails.
Beside the sea we pondered on the way
   Like folk who, lingering still along the shore,
   Hasten in heart and in the body stay;
And as, a little while the dawn before,
   Mars through dense vapour glows with ruddy
   Low in the west above the ocean-floor,   [light
I saw,—O may it bless again my sight!
   A lustre coming on across the main
   With speed unparalleled by any flight.
And when I let mine eye awhile remain
   Detached from it, to question of my Guide,
   Larger and brighter now it showed again.
Then there emerged to view on either side
   A whiteness indistinct, and down below
   Little by little another I descried.
My Master uttered not a word, till lo!
   The first white spots appeared as wings to shine,
   Then, when he surely did the Pilot know,
He cried: 'Make haste, make haste, the knee incline,
   Fold hands,—it is God's Angel! thou shalt use
   Henceforth to see such ministers divine.
Look, how doth he all human means refuse,
   Scorning device of sail or oar, nor drew
   Aught but his wings upon so far a cruise;

Look, look how heavenward he holds them true,
  Fanning the welkin with those plumes eterne
  Which do not moult as mortal feathers do!'
Then, near and nearer come, might I discern
  The Bird of God more dazzling than before,
  Until mine eyes that with the blaze now burn
Fall down undone. But he drew near the shore
  On pinnace light and rapid,—such an one
  The water swallowed nothing of the prore.
Astern the Pilot stood, with benison
  Of Heaven inscribed upon his face devout:
  A hundred and more spirits sat thereon.
'When Israël from Egypt issued out,'
  They chanted as with single voice the lay,
  With what there afterward the Psalmist wrote.
When sign of holy cross he made them, they
  Flung themselves one and all upon the strand,
  And swiftly as he came he swept away.
There huddled they together close at hand
  Gazing about, like strangers to the place
  Endeavouring new things to understand.
The sun was shooting everywhere his rays,
  And with the arrows of his radiance now
  Did Capricorn from middle-heaven chase,
When the new people lifted up their brow
  Toward us, saying:'If expert ye be
  In faring up the Mountain, show us how.'
And Virgil said:'Ye deem perchance that we
  Have knowledge of the place where now we stray,
  But we are also pilgrims as are ye.
We came short while before you, by a way
  So rough and difficult that the ascent
  Henceforward will appear to us but play.'
The souls, to whom it became evident,
  Seeing me breathe, that still alive was I,
  Turned deadly pale for sheer astonishment.

146

And as, to hear good tidings, people hie
   To reach the olive-bearing messenger,
   And not a man of jostling appears shy,
So one and all the happy spirits there
   Fastened upon me hungrily their view,
   As if forgot the quest to make them fair.
And I saw one of them who forward drew
   To my embrace with love so manifest
   That I was influenced the like to do.
O insubstantial souls in shadowy vest!
   Thrice did I clasp my hands behind that shade
   And drew them back as often to my breast.
Wonder, I think, was on my face portrayed;
   Whereat it only smiled and drew away
   While I pursued in hopes it would have stayed.
In mellow tones he gently said me nay,
   And knowing him thereby, did I implore
   That he for speech a little while would stay.
'As loved I in the mortal flesh of yore,
   So loosed I love thee still,' he answered clear,
   'I stay then; but why pacest thou the shore?'
'To this place where we are, Casella dear,
   To come once more I make this pilgrimage;
   But why is so much time bereft thee here?'
And he: 'No injury can I allege,
   If he who takes up when and whom he please
   Somewhile denied to me the ferriage,
For of right will his own is made. Yet these
   Three happy months accepts he verily
   Whoever longs to enter, with all peace;
Whence I, who had just now betaken me
   Where Tiber water savours of the brine,
   Have been received by him benignantly.
That is the goal where now his wings incline;
   For at that outlet ever gathers what
   Falls not perdue to punishment condign.'

And I: 'If novel law abolish not
    Practice or memory of the song of love
    That used to solace all my yearning thought,
I pray thee grace me with the comfort of
    Thy song, for in the body travelling
    So far, my heart is weary here above.'
'Love, deep within the spirit reasoning,'
    So sweetly he began to sing it thus
    That still the dulcet tones within me ring.
My Master and I and that unanimous
    Company with him drew such rapture thence
    As if no other care encumbered us.
Still hung we on that music in suspense,
    When lo! that stately Elder: 'Laggard crew
    Of spirits, what portends this negligence?
Think what, delaying, ye neglect to do!
    Speed to the Mount to slough the film,' he cried,
    'That lets not God be manifest to you.'
As pigeons that are feeding side by side
    And pecking at the darnel or the ear,
    Quiet and strutting not with wonted pride,
If aught whereof they are afraid appear
    All of a sudden let alone their food
    Because of being assailed by greater care,
So saw I that newly-landed multitude
    Forsake the song and scurry tow'rd the height
    Like them who go but wot not where they would:
Nor any less precipitate our flight.

CANTO III

While sudden flight was all dispersing thus
　That flock of spirits through the countryside
　Toward the Mount where reason searches us,
I drew up close to my Companion tried;
　And how without him had I kept the course?
　Who up the mountain would have been my guide?
He seemed to me disturbed with self-remorse:
　O soul of honour, tender conscience good,
　How little fault to have such bitter force!
After his feet the hurry had subdued,
　That of all action mars the dignity,
　My mind, which hitherto in durance stood,
Eagerly rendered its attention free;
　Then turned my sight toward the Hill, supreme
　Of peaks emerging skyward from the sea.
Behind us flamed the sun, whose ruddy gleam
　Before me broke in the configurement
　Formed of me by the stoppage of its beam.
I turned, in terror of abandonment
　Sidewise and half around, become aware
　The ground was shadowed only where I went.
Then turning round to me, my Comforter
　Began: 'Why givest thou suspicion room?
　Dost thou not think I, guiding, with thee fare?
Already it is evening at the tomb
　Where lies the body of me that cast a shade:
　Naples received it from Brundusium.
Now if no shadow is before me made,
　Like wonder in the heavens dost thou behold,
　Whose rays are not by one another stayed.
The Power who will his workings not unfold
　Makes bodies apt to suffer, as we do,
　Torments arising both from heat and cold.

149

One Substance, in Three Persons, travels through
    Illimitable ways, where it were wild
    To deem that human reason might pursue.
Be to the fact, O mortals, reconciled,
    For, had ye power to see all things and learn,
    No need had been for Mary to bear child.
And ye have seen without fulfilment yearn
    Those whose desire would have been satisfied,
    Which now is given to them for grief eterne.
Of Aristotle and Plato I speak,—beside
    Many another.' Here his brow he bent,
    Deeply perturbed, and further speech denied.
Meanwhile toward the mountain-foot we went:
    A cliff so steep that nimble legs would be
    Of small avail attempting such ascent.
The way between Turbía and Lerici
    Most lonely and deserted were a stair,
    Compared with that, accessible and free.
'Where slopes the mountain, who can tell me where,'
    The Master murmured, staying his advance,
    'So that the wingless foot may clamber there?'
And while he, casting down his countenance,
    Was questioning his mind about the road,
    And up along the rock I ran my glance,
Off to the left a flock of spirits showed
    Moving their feet our way, though otherwise
    Appearing, so deliberate their mode.
'Look, Master,' I exclaimed, 'lift up thine eyes:
    Some who will put us right are coming yon,
    If thou canst find within thee no device.'
He looked, and said, with confidence re-won:
    'Go we to meet them, for their steps are slow,
    And do thou keep good hope, beloved son.'
We moved along a thousand steps or so,
    Finding that company as far by this
    As a good thrower with his hand could throw,

When at the foot of the high precipice
   Gathered they all, compact and circumspect,
   Gazing like men who fear to go amiss.
'O ye who ended well, O souls elect!'
   Virgil began, 'in name of that sublime
   Peace which, I think, ye one and all expect,
Tell us if it be possible to climb
   The Mountain somewhere by a slope less bold:
   For irksome to the wise is loss of time.'
As sheep are wont to issue from the fold
   By one and two and three, the rest pursue
   Meekly, and eye and muzzle downward hold,
And what the first one does the others do,
   And if she stop all huddle at her side,
   Nor question why, the quiet silly crew:
So moving now toward us I descried
   The column-leaders of that happy flock,
   Modest in face, in action dignified.
When those in front beheld my body block
   The light upon my dexter hand, whereby
   The shadow stretched from me toward the rock,
They halted and withdrew somewhat more nigh
   Those following behind, and all the rest
   Did in like manner, without knowing why.
'I frankly tell you, without your request,
   This is a human body that ye see,
   As by the broken light is manifest.
Then do not wonder, but persuaded be
   That not by heavenly Power unwarranted
   To mount this barrier endeavours he.'
The Master thus; and that good people said:
   'Then turn about and enter in before,'
   And with the backs of hands the signal made.
'Whoever thou mayst be,' did one implore,
   'While pressing forward, hither turn anew:
   Consider if thou sawst me there of yore.'

I turned to scan him, and there met my view
    Fair features and of gentle mien and blond,
    Although one eyebrow had been cloven through.
And when I ventured humbly to respond
    With a denial, 'Look!'—and he laid bare
    Above his breast a sanguinary wound.
'Manfred am I,' said he with smiling air,
    'Grandson of Empress Constance: whence I pray
    Thee go, returning, to my daughter fair,
Mother of both the monarchs who bear sway,
    One in Sicilia, one in Aragon,
    And tell her truth, whatever else they say.
When these two mortal stabs had quite undone
    My body, yielded I with tears contrite
    To Him who willingly gives benison.
Horrible were my sins, but Infinite
    Bounty has arms of an embrace so broad
    That it accepts whoever turn to it.
And if Cosenza's Pastor, who at nod
    Of Clement went to hunt me down, had known
    How to peruse aright this page in God,
Even now were of my body every bone
    At the bridgehead near Benevento trenched,
    Beneath the safeguard of the heavy stone.
Now scattered by the wind, by the rain drenched,
    Beyond the kingdom hard by Verde's flow,
    Whither he carried them with tapers quenched.
By curse of theirs no soul can perish so
    But that Eternal Love for them may bloom
    While hope one particle of green can show.
True is that such as died beneath the doom
    Of Holy Church, though they at last repent,
    Must here outside the precipice find room,
Full thirtyfold the time that they have spent
    In their presumption, if to briefer span
    Good prayers do not reduce such banishment.

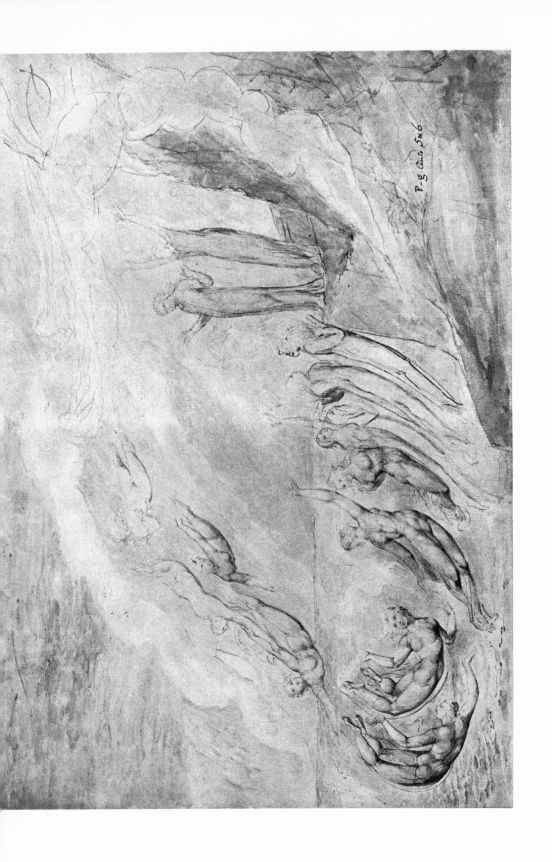

PURGATORIO: CANTOS V & VI

The Souls of those who only repented at the Point of Death

Hereafter pray rejoice me, if thou can,
   Revealing to my gracious Constance dear
   How thou hast seen me and alas! this ban:
For much those yonder may advance us here.'

CANTO IV

When an impression of delight or dole
   Works on some faculty of ours, and thus
   Wholly that faculty absorbs the soul,
It seems of other force oblivious;
   And this is counter to that erring thought
   Which would enkindle soul on soul in us.
Therefore, when hearing or when seeing aught
   That draws the soul's attention potently,
   Time passes by, and one perceives it not;
For that which notes it is one faculty,
   Another that which holds the souls intent:
   This is preoccupied, and that is free.
Hereof I made a true experiment
   Listening in wonder to that spirit fair;
   For now the sun had fully made ascent
Fifty degrees, and I was not aware,
   When came we where cried out those spirits true
   With one accord: 'Look, your desire is there!'
The hedger oft a wider passage through
   With a single forkful of his thorns can block
   What time the clustered grape is turning blue,
Than was the passage where up through the rock
   My Guide alone ascended, and then I,
   Turning away from that departing flock.
You drop to Noli, mount San Leo high,
   And on Bismantova may scale the height
   On feet alone, but here a man must fly:

*The Ascent of the
Mountain begun*

153

I mean on nimble pinions fledged for flight
  By great desire, and following that Guide
  Who held out hope to me and gave me light.
Through the cleft rock we climbed; on either side
  Hemmed us the lofty wall; and here the ground
  Demanded that both foot and hand be plied.
Emerging on the upper rim, we found
  The slope expanding freely to the sky:
  'Master,' I queried, 'whither are we bound?'
'Not a step downward!' was his quick reply:
  'Upward behind me be the mountain won
  Until some trusty escort we descry.'
So high the peak that vision was outrun,
  And steeper far the slope than line away
  From centre to the middle quadrant drawn.
Weary was I when I began to pray:
  'Dear Father, O turn hitherward and see
  How I am left alone unless thou stay!'
'My son, draw up as far as here,' said he,
  Pointing me to a ledge just overhead
  Circling on that side all the acclivity.
So sharply spurred me on the words he said,
  That I crept after him with might and main
  Until the terrace was beneath my tread.
There to sit down awhile we both were fain,
  Facing the East whence we had made ascent;
  For, looking back, a man takes heart again.
Mine eyes at first to the low shores were bent,
  Thereafter lifted to the sun, whose glow
  Struck us from leftward, to my wonderment.
The Poet well perceived me gazing so
  Upon the car of light with wonder, where
  It entered between us and Aquilo.
Whence he: 'If Castor and if Pollux were
  Companions with that mirror which sheds back
  The light divine to either hemisphere,

Thou wouldst behold him blaze in Zodiac,
  Unto the Bears revolving still more nigh,
  Unless the sun should quit his ancient track.
If thou wouldst understand the reason why,
  With centred thought imagine Zion-hill
  On earth set over against this mountain high,
So that they both have one horizon still
  And hemispheres diverse; then wilt thou see,
  If to take heed thine intellect have skill,
How the highway that Phaëton, ah me!
  Knew not to course, must pass upon that side
  This mountain, and this side of Zion be.'
'Truly, my Master, never yet,' I cried,
  'Saw I so clearly as I now discern,
  Since of the mark my wit seemed ever wide,
That the mid-circle of the heaven supern,
  Equator in a certain science known,
  And which doth still 'twixt sun and winter turn,
Is distant, for the reason thou hast shown,
  Northward from here as far as once the Jews
  Beheld it looking tow'rd the torrid zone.
But if it please thee well, I fain would choose
  To know how far we clamber; for so high
  Rises the Hill, that sight in vain pursues.'
'This mountain slope is such,' he made reply,
  'That low beginnings ever painful seem;
  The toil decreases climbing tow'rd the sky.
But when it comes about that thou shalt deem
  Climbing as easy as to ship and crew
  Seems gliding with the curent down the stream,
There is the end of this hard avenue,
  There may thy weary limbs expect repose:
  More I reply not, knowing this for true.'
No sooner had he said such words as those,
  Than sounded out a voice near by: 'Perchance
  He'll have to sit before so far he goes!'

Both of us, turning at this utterance,
    Saw at the left a stone of massive size
    Which neither had perceived at the first glance.
Thither we drew apace, till met our eyes
    Persons behind a rock, with shadow blent,
    Lying along as one in idlesse lies.
And one of them, who seemed to me forspent,
    Was sitting, and was clasping both his knees,
    Holding his face deep down between them bent.
'Look, Master mine,' said I, 'if one of these
    Seems not more overcome with lassitude
    Than if his sister had been slothful Ease.'
At this he bent to us, and understood,
    Moving his visage up along his thigh,
    And said: 'Now up, for thou hast hardihood!'
Then showed he features that I knew him by,
    And my still panting breath impeded not
    My going to him; and as soon as I
Had reached him, he uplifted but a jot
    His brow, and murmured: 'Seest thou how the Sun
    O'er thy left shoulder drives his chariot?'
His lazy mien and phrase compactly spun
    Relaxed my lips to show a little glee;
    'Belacqua,' I began, 'from this time on
I grieve no more for thee; but answer me,
    Why sitst thou here? awaitest thou a Guide?
    Or has thy wonted mood recaptured thee?'
'Brother, what use in climbing?' he replied,
    'The Bird of God, at threshold of the gate,
    Would not admit me to be purified.
First Heaven must needs as often circulate
    Round me outside, as it in life had done,
    Since I put off repentance till too late;
If earlier aid me not some orison
    Breathed forth from soul with living grace at core;
    What boot is other prayer, unheard up yon?'

PURGATORIO: CANTOS VII & VIII

The Lawn with the Kings and Angels

Already went the Poet up before,
    Saying: 'Come on now: look, the Sun is bright
    On the meridian, and at the shore
Morocco lies beneath the foot of Night.'

CANTO V

Now from those shades departing, I betook
    Myself my Leader's footmarks to pursue,
    When one behind me, pointing, shouted: 'Look,
The sunbeam seems not to be shining through
    Leftward from him below; and more by token
    He seems to bear him as the living do!'
I turned about to look when this was spoken,
    And saw them gaze at me for marvel—yea
    At me, and at the sunbeam that was broken.
'Why is thy mind diverted from the way
    To make thee loiter?' said my Master kind;
    'What carest thou up here how whisper they?
Come after me and let them speak their mind;
    Stand like a tower unwavering and stout
    Against whatever buffets of the wind.
For he who thinks about it and about
    Falls short, forever thwarted of his aim,
    Since one thought by the next is cancelled out.'
I said, 'I come!'—how answer else for shame?
    And said it with that flush which may restore us
    To pardon, if we worthily lay claim.
Behold now people who, short way before us
    Across the Mountain passing, as they go
    Sing *Miserere* verse about in chorus.
Seeing my body interrupt the flow
    Of sunlight, and enshadowing the plain,
    They changed the singing to a long hoarse *Oh!*

*Tragic Deaths of
Three Noble
Souls*

157

And in the form of messengers came twain
   Running toward us from that multitude,
   Desiring knowledge of our state to gain.
'Ye can go back,' replied my Master good,
   'To those who sent you forth, and certify
   That this man's body is true flesh and blood.
And if to see his shadow made them shy
   As I suppose, enough: let them endeavour
   To do him honour, profiting thereby.'
So swiftly enkindled vapours saw I never
   At early evening cleave the sky serene,
   Nor yet the sunset clouds of August sever,
As these returning up again were seen;
   Then wheeled to usward with the rest along,
   Like troops that gallop without drawing rein.
'These crowd upon us in a mighty throng,'
   The Poet said, 'to make thee one request;
   Yet go, and going, listen to their wrong.'
'O pilgrim soul who goest to be blest
   With those limbs fashioned in thy mother's mould,
   Stay but a moment!'—cried they as they pressed.
'Look if thou sawest one of us of old,
   That thou to earth mayst tidings of him bear:
   Pray why dost thou go on? pray why not hold?
We all were slain by violence whilere,
   And sinners till the final hour of grace;
   Then light from Heaven made us so well aware
That, penitent and pardoning, apace
   We quitted life at peace with the Most High,
   Who heartens us with yearning for his face.'
'Although I scan your lineaments,' said I,
   'Not one do I recall; but pray ye speak,
   If aught to please you in my power there lie,
And I will do it, happy spirits meek,
   By hope of peace which, following up the Hill
   Behind such Guide, from world to world I seek.'

And one began: 'We all are trusting still
  In thy good offices, no need to swear,
  Provided weakness do not cancel will:
Whence I alone before the rest make prayer
  That, if thou see the countryside one day,
  Lying 'twixt Charles's and Romagna fair,
Thou of thy courtesy for me wilt pray
  In Fano, so that there be orisons
  To help me purge my heavy sins away.
Thence came I; but the gashes wherethrough once
  Issued the blood wherein I had my seat,
  Were dealt to me among Antenor's sons,
There where I fancied safest my retreat:
  The Este had it done, who held me then
  In anger more by far than justly meet.
But had I fled toward La Mira, when
  At Oriaco by pursuers found,
  Still were I yonder among breathing men.
I ran to the marsh; the mud and reeds around
  So hampered me I fell, and there saw I
  My blood become a pool upon the ground.'
'Ah, by that yearning,' did another sigh,
  'Whereby to the High Mountain drawest thou,
  Do thou aid mine with pious sympathy.
I was of Montefeltro, merely now
  Buonconte; heeds me none, not even Joan,
  Whence among these I go with downcast brow.'
And I: 'From Campaldino lost alone
  By chance wast thou, or violence malign,
  So that thy burial place was never known?'
'Oh,' said he, 'runs athwart the Casentine
  A stream called Archiano, rising o'er
  The Hermitage aloft in Apennine.
There where it answers to that name no more
  Came I with throat empiercèd, as I fled
  On foot along the plain, marked with my gore.

There eyesight failed me, and the prayer I said
  Paused on the name of Mary; there I fell,
  And there my flesh remained untenanted.
The truth I speak among the living tell:
  God's Angel took me: "Why wilt thou be stealing
  Mine own, thou son of Heaven?" cried he of Hell;
"With his immortal art thou skyward wheeling;
  That part I forfeit for one little tear;
  But with the other use I other dealing."
Thou knowest how gathers in the atmosphere
  That vaporous moisture, soon to water turning
  By the chill pressure of the upper sphere.
That Evil Will, for evil only yearning,
  Endowed with native power intelligent,
  Joined and moved cloud and wind with fell discern-
So he, thereafter, day being fully spent,   [ing.
  From Pratomagno to the Great Yoke fills
  With fog the valley and veils the firmament
And into water the teeming air distils;
  Down through the gullies comes the fallen rain
  All thirsty earth could drink not,—and the rill
Into great torrents gathering amain,
  Headlong toward the royal river bore
  With such a rush that weir and dike were vain.
Wild Archiano found my body frore
  Hard by his outlet, sweeping it inert
  Into the Arno, and from my bosom tore
The cross I made me, conquered by the hurt;
  Whelmed me along by many a bank and shoal,
  Then with his shingle covered me and girt.'
'Ah, when thou turnest to an earthly goal,
  And shalt have rested from the weary way,'—
  The second ceasing, followed a third soul,—
'Remember me, who am Pia, when thou pray;
  Siena made me, by Maremma undone:
  He knows who ringed me, ringless till that day,
Espousing me with gem and benison.'

CANTO VI

When breaks the game of hazard, he who lost
   Remains behind in sorrow, and essays
   The throws again, thus learning to his cost;
With the winner all the others go their ways:
   One in advance, one plucks him from the rear,
   And for reminder one beside him stays.
He hastens,—all soliciting his ear,—
   His hand goes out to some, who leave him free,—
   And so from pressure of the crowd gets clear.
So I, amid that thronging company,
   Was turning to them here and there my face,
   And making promise, extricated me.
The Aretine who in the grim embrace
   Of Ghin di Tacco perished, with them stood,
   And the other who was drowned while giving chase.
There prayed, with hands in suppliant attitude,
   Frederick Novello, and that Pisan son
   Who proved the good Marzucco's fortitude.
I saw Count Orso, and the soul of one
   Bereft of life by spite, as he averred,
   And envy, not for any trespass done,—
Pier de la Brosse, I mean: and may this word
   Prompt the Lady of Brabant to heedfulness
   Lest she for this consort with baser herd.
As soon as I was free from all the stress
   Of shades, who prayed that other prayer benign
   Might speed them on the way to holiness,
Thus I began: 'It seems, O light of mine,
   In one text thou expressly questionest
   That orison may bend decree divine;
And yet these people only this request:
   Can it be possible their hope is vain?
   Or is to me thy word not manifest?'

Dante
the «Stormy Voice»
of Italy

And he responded: 'What I wrote is plain,
    And not fallacious is the hope of these
    If one consider it with reason sane,
For Top of Judgement stoops not when the pleas
    Of burning love do in a moment what
    These do who here await the slow decrees.
And in the instance where I tied that knot,
    Prayer did not counterbalance the defect,
    Since, from God disunited, prayer was not.
Howbeit, waive decision in respect
    To doubt so deep, till she interpret this,
    Who shall be light 'twixt truth and intellect.
Be assured that here I speak of Beatrice:
    Her shalt thou see above, upon the crown
    Of this same Mountain, smiling and in bliss.'
And I: 'Lord, let us hasten to be gone,
    For I am not as hitherto forspent,
    And look, the hill now casts a shadow down.'
'As much as possible of the ascent,
    Will we perform to-day,' responded he,
    'But other than thou thinkest is the event.
Ere thou canst climb up yonder, thou wilt see
    Return that light so hidden that its ray
    Is interrupted now no more by thee.
But see! there is a spirit making stay
    All, all alone, and looking tow'rd this side;
    It will point out to us the speediest way.'
We thither came: O Lombard soul, what pride
    And lofty scorn thine attitude expressed,
    And thy slow-moving eyes how dignified!
As we came on he proffered no request,
    But let us go our way, calmly surveying
    In manner of a lion when at rest.
Steadily drew up Virgil tow'rd him, praying
    Direction where ascent might best be made;
    But he, no word by way of answer saying,

News of our life and of our country prayed.
   And when thereto the gentle Guide began,—
   'Mantua—' upleaped that all-secluded shade
From where before he stood: 'O Mantuan,
   I am Sordello of thy city!'—said he,
   And to embrace of each the other ran.
Hostel of woe, ah, servile Italy,
   Vessel unpiloted in a great storm,
   No Lady of provinces, but harlotry!
Eager that noble spirit was and warm
   To welcome there his own compatriot,
   So did the sweet name of his city charm!
While now in civil tumult are distraught
   Thy living citizens,—at daggers drawn
   Those whom one wall incloses, and one moat.
Make search around thy seaboard, wretched one,
   And after in thy bosom look again,
   If anywhere within be unison!
What boots Justinian adjust the rein
   If ever empty be the saddle? Without
   Such bridle not so black would be the stain.
Ah, gentry, ye that ought to be devout
   And let but Cæsar in his saddle sit,
   Nor leave unheeded what God pointed out,
Look well to this wild beast, consider it,
   Ungoaded by the spur how fell it grows
   Since ye laid hand upon the bridle-bit!
O German Albert, who to such as those
   Yieldest this wild unruly animal,
   And oughtest to bestride her saddlebows,
May from the stars upon thy issue fall
   Just judgement, and be it strange and manifest
   Such that it may thy follower appal!
Thy father suffered, and thou sufferest,
   Held back up yonder by the greed of you,
   The garden of the Empire go to waste.

Come look at Capulet and Montague,
    Monaldi and Filippeschi, man remiss
    These dreading that which those already rue.
Come, cruel prince, see the iniquities
    Thy nobles suffer, cure their hurts,—nay, come
    See Santafiora how secure it is!
Come hear the outcries of thy weeping Rome
    By day and night, a widow and alone:
    'My Cæsar, why forsakest thou thy home?'
Come, see how much the folk to love are prone,
    And if for us no pity in thee lie
    Come and take shame to thee for thy renown.
And if it be allowed me, Jove most High,
    Thou who for us on earth wast crucified,
    Is otherwhere averted thy just eye?
Or is it discipline thou dost provide
    In thy deep counsel, for some useful plan
    To our perception utterly denied?
Swarm in Italian towns the tyrant clan,
    And a Marcellus comes incipient
    In every churl who plays the partisan.
My Florence, thou indeed mayst be content
    With this aside,—thy withers are unwrung,
    Thanks to thy people all so provident.
The bow of justice is but slowly strung
    By many, who let no random arrow fly:
    Thy people have justice pat upon the tongue.
Many would put the public burden by,
    But answers eagerly thy populace
    Unbidden: 'Shoulder to the wheel!' they cry.
Good reason hast thou to take heart of grace:
    If sooth I say the facts do not conceal,
    Thou wealthy and thou wise and thou at peace!
The Athenian and the Spartan commonweal,
    Long famed for art and law, gave feeble proof
    Of civil life to what thy deeds reveal,

Who with such foresight weave in that behoof,
   That reach not to the middle of November
   The filmy threadlets of October's woof.
How often hast thou changed (canst thou remember?)
   Law, coinage, offices, time out of mind,
   And usage, renovating every member.
And were thy memory not so short or blind,
   Thou wouldst see thyself in that sick woman, fain
   A little rest upon her couch to find,
Who would by tossing ward away her pain.

CANTO VII

After the courtly and glad greetings now
   Again a third time and a fourth began,
   Sordello drew back saying: 'Who art thou?'
'Ere to this Mount turned any soul of man
   Worthy to rise with God to be enskied,
   My bones were buried by Octavian.
For want of faith and for no fault beside,
   Did I, who am Virgil, forfeit Paradise.'
   So forthwith made reply to him my Guide.
Like one confronting with bewildered eyes
   Some sudden wonder unbeheld before,
   Who murmurs,' 'Tis, 'tis not!' believes, denies,
Sordello stood; then bowed his forehead lower,
   Turning to greet my Leader with embrace
   More humble, where lays hold the inferior.
'O glory,' exclaimed he, 'of the Latin race,
   Through whom our language showed its worth
   O praise eternal of my native place,   [so well,
What merit shows thee or what miracle?
   If I be worthy held thy news to know,
   Say from what cloister comst thou, if from Hell?'

*The Negligent
Princes*

165

'Through all the circles of the world of woe
    Am I come hither,' so he made reply,
    'Moved by a power of Heaven whereby I go.
Omitting, not committing, forfeit I
    Sight of the Dayspring where thy longings rise,
    And which was known by me too tardily.
There is a place below not otherwise
    Tormented save with gloom, where the laments
    Are uttered not in wailing but in sighs;
There I abide with little innocents
    Bitten by fangs of Death and all undone
    Ere yet exempt from man's maleficence;
There I abide with those who put on none
    Of the three holy virtues, yet who knew
    The others, following guiltless every one.
But if thou know and can, afford some clue
    To us, whereby we may arrive apace
    Where Purgatory has beginning true.'
He answered: 'We are bound to no fixed place;
    I lawfully may wander up and round,
    And join you as guide for my allotted space.
But look! the day declining to the bound,
    And we are powerless to ascend by night;
    Then let us think of pleasant resting-ground.
Souls dwell secluded yonder to the right:
    Unto them will I lead if thou consent,
    Nor will acquaintance be without delight.'
'How so?' was asked, 'if any made ascent
    By night, would he be then inhibited
    By another, or would want of power prevent?'
'Look!' and the good Sordello's finger sped
    Along the ground, 'the sun being parted hence
    Thou couldst not even cross this line,' he said;
'Not that there else would be impediments
    To going up save shades nocturnal,—they
    Would trammel up the will with impotence.

166

One might indeed in darkness downward stray,
  And make the tour of the whole mountain-ring,
  While the horizon prisons up the day.'
Then said my Master, as if wondering:
  'Now lead us on whither, by thy report,
  We may have some delight while tarrying.'
Thence on the Mountain was the distance short
  When of a hollow I became aware,—
  Valleys down here are hollowed in such sort.
'Yonder,' proposed that shade, 'let us repair
  Where inward-curving slopes a dell surround,
  And dawning of new day await we there.'
Now level and now steep, a pathway wound
  That led us to a margin where the height
  Half falls away before that hollow ground.
Gold, silver fine, scarlet and pearly white,
  Clear Indian wood of azure loveliness,
  Or fresh-flaked emerald would be less bright
Than were the grass and flowers in that recess:
  In colour each of these would be outdone
  As by the greater is outdone the less.
Nor yet was Nature a mere painter yon,
  But did from thousand odours sweet distil
  A subtly blended fragrance known to none.
Salve Regina, with such chanting thrill
  The souls on bloom and greensward there at rest,
  Concealed before by hollow of the hill.
'Before the faint sun settle to his nest,'
  The Mantuan said who made us thither swerve,
  'Do not my guidance among these request.
From vantage of this bank ye will observe
  The features and the acts of all and some,
  Better than down among them in the curve.
He highest placed, to whom seems burdensome
  That he neglected what he ought, for song
  Upon the lips of others finds him dumb,

167

Was Rudolph, Emperor, who feels the prong
  In unhealed wounds, fatal to Italy,
  While healing through another tarries long.
The next, who seems his comforter to be,
  Governed the country whence the waters spring
  Moldau bears Elbe, Elbe to the sea,—
His name was Ottocar, far better king
  As babe, than bearded Wenceslaus, his child,
  In luxury and idlesse battening.
That small-nosed one, with him of aspect mild
  So close in counsel, as seems manifest,
  Died fleeing and left the fleur-de-lis defiled:
Look there, how he is beating at his breast!
  And yonder at his sighing partner glance
  Who on his palm has laid his cheek at rest.
Father and father-in-law of the plague of France
  Are these,—they know his vicious life and lewd,
  And hence the grief that pierces like a lance.
He who so stalwart seems, whose song in mood
  Accords with that of him of virile nose,
  Wore girt the cord of every manly good;
And if the youth who yonder doth repose
  Behind him had long governed in his stead,
  Worth would have passed from vase to vase in
This of the other heirs cannot be said: [those;
  While James and Frederick the kingdoms sway,
  None has the better share inherited.
Not often rises up through branch and spray
  Prowess of man: such is the Will Divine
  In order that from Him the gift we pray.
My words apply as well to the aquiline
  As to his fellow-singer, Peter: yet
  Apulia and Provence thereat repine.
Less is the plant than seed that did beget
  By how much Constance still her spouse may praise
  More than can Beatrice and Margaret.

Look at the monarch of the simple ways,
 Harry of England, sitting there alone:
 Better the issue that his branches raise.
That one of them whose eyes are upward thrown
 Is Marquis William, humblest among these,
 For whom Alessandria and her war make moan
Both Monferrato and the Canavese.'

CANTO VIII

*Happy Interview
with Departed
Shades*

Now was the hour that melts the heart anew
 In voyagers with yearning for the shore
 The day belovèd friends have said adieu,
And the new pilgrim feels the pang once more
 Of love, on hearing from the far-off land
 Bells that belike the parting day deplore,
When I began no more to understand
 His words, on seeing a soul among them there
 Uprisen, who craved a hearing with its hand.
It joined both palms and lifted them in air,
 Fixing its eyes toward the orient,
 As saying to God, 'I have no other care!'
Te lucis ante in notes so sweetly blent
 Came from those lips devout, all my concern
 Lapsed and was lost in rapturous content.
As led that soul, the others in their turn
 With sweet devotion did the hymn pursue,
 Holding their eyes upon the wheels supern.
Sharpen thine eyes here, Reader, to the true,
 For now so thin the veil that penetration
 Is surely easy to the inward view.
I saw that gentle host with adoration
 Silent while upward did their look ascend,
 Pallid and meek, as if in expectation:

169

And saw emerge and from aloft descend
   Two angels, with two swords of flame unfailing
   But broken off and blunted at the end.
Green as new leafbud only now unveiling,
   Their raiment, fanned by throbbing pinions green,
   In airy wafture was behind them trailing.
Above us one took post with guardian mien,
   The other on the margin opposite,
   So that the people were contained between.
Well I perceived their tresses blond, but sight
   Could only be confounded by the face,
   Like faculty blind with excess of light.
'From their embosoming in Mary's grace,'
   Sordello said, 'to guard the vale these two
   Come, for the Serpent will arrive apace.'
Whence I, because nowise their way I knew,
   Strove by the trusty shoulders to remain
   Close sheltered, for I felt me frozen through.
'Now go we down,' Sordello said again,
   'And with the mighty shades exchange replies:
   To bid you welcome will they all be fain.'
Three paces peradventure might suffice
   For my descent; and one did gazing pore
   Upon me, as in hope to recognize.
Already was the air endarkened more,
   But not so that between his eye and mine
   It failed to show what it had locked before.
Tow'rd me he comes and I to him incline:
   Noble Judge Nino, happy was my case
   When I beheld thee not of the malign!
Silent between us was no word of grace;
   Whereon he asked: 'How long since camest thou
   Through the far waters to the Mountain's base?'
'Oh!' said I, 'out of dismal caves below
   This morning come, in the first life am I,
   But hope to gain the other, going so.'

As soon as ever heard they my reply,
　　Sordello and that spirit backward drew
　　Like startled folk whose impulse is to fly.
One turned to Virgil, and the other to
　　A soul there seated: 'Conrad, look, the Lord
　　Has willed through Grace a wondrous thing to do!'
Then turned to me: 'By thanks thou must accord
　　To Him for special grace, who doth so hide
　　His own first wherefore that it has no ford,
When thou shalt be beyond the billows wide,
　　Say to my Joan that she for me implore
　　Where answer to the pure is not denied.
I think her mother cares for me no more,
　　Since she has laid aside her wimples white
　　Which she, poor thing, shall yet be craving for.
By her example may be seen aright
　　How brief the fire of love in woman's breast
　　Unless rekindled oft by touch or sight.
Less fair an emblem for her burial chest
　　The Viper leading Milan to the field,
　　Than would have been the Cock, Gallura's crest!'
While he was speaking thus, his face revealed
　　That upright zeal wherewith the heart may be
　　Aflame, and in due measure stamped and sealed.
Ranging the heavens my eager eyes could see
　　Only the place where most the stars are slow,
　　As in a wheel nearest the axletree.
'Son,' said my Guide, 'at what art gazing so?'
　　'At those three starry torches,' I replied,
　　'Wherewith the hither Pole is all aglow.'
'Low are the splendid stars on yonder side,
　　Those four thou sawst at early dawn to-day,
　　And in their places these are now enskied.'
Sordello seized him as he thus did say,
　　Exclaiming, 'See our enemy advance!'
　　With finger guiding him to look that way.

171

At that part where the little valley slants
    Devoid of barrier, crept a Snake along,—
    Such offered Eve the bitter food perchance.
The evil streak the grass and flowers among,
    With head reversed like beast that licks its fell,
    Came undulating on with dartling tongue.
I did not see and cannot therefore tell
    How the celestial hawks their stations left,
    But saw the motion of each sentinel.
Feeling the air by their green pinions cleft,
    The Serpent fled; both wheeling up as one
    The angels lighted, having barred the theft.
The shade, that close beside the Judge had drawn
    When he exclaimed, had not removed its eyes
    Cleaving to me till that assault was done.
'So in the taper lighting to the skies
    The wax of thy free will may not abate
    Until thou reach the flowery Paradise,'
Began he, 'canst thou tidings true relate
    Of Valdimagra, or of region nigh,
    Tell it to me, for there I once was great.
Conrad the Malaspina called was I;
    The elder not, although from him descended;
    My love of kindred here I purify.'
'Oh,' cried I, 'through your land I never wended,
    But where in Europe dwells one so forlorn
    As never to have heard their fame commended?
Renown and honour that your house adorn
    Proclaim the land, proclaim her every lord,
    So that he knows who never reached that bourn.
And by my pilgrim hope I give my word
    Your honoured kindred do not strip away
    The virtue of the purse and of the sword.
Chartered by custom and by nature, they,
    Though the bad leader warp the world aside,
    Alone go straight, and scorn the evil way.'

PURGATORIO: CANTO IX

Lucia carrying Dante in his Sleep

And he: 'Now look,—seven times shall not abide
   The sun, returning back within the bed
   The Ram's four feet now cover and bestride,
Ere this opinion, courteously said,
   With better nails than hearsay hammered home,
   Shall pierce the very middle of thy head,
Unless arrested be the course of doom.'

CANTO IX

Now did the mistress of Tithonus hoar
   Show at the eastern window, clad in white,
   Forth from the arms of her dear paramour;
Her brow was glittering with jewels bright
   Set in the figure of that monster cold
   Which strikes at people with his tail; and Night
Had two already of the paces told
   Wherewith she rises where our steps were stayed,
   And the third hour began her wings to fold,
When I, on whom something of Adam weighed,
   Conquered by slumber, sank upon the lawn
   Where all we five the nightly vigil made.
Upon the hour when, very near to dawn,
   Begins the twittering swallow to repine,
   Perchance in memory of her woes foregone,
When anxious thoughts less narrowly confine,
   And when the pilgrim soul, from flesh more free,
   Is in her visions very near divine,
Then poised aloft did I appear to see
   An eagle, with gold plumage, in my dream,
   With open wings, intent to swoop at me;
And I was in that place, or so did seem,
   Where Ganymede was torn from friends away,
   Up to the synod of the gods supreme.

The Symbolic Gate

'Perchance this bird strikes here,' I seemed to say,
  'Only by habit, and from otherwhere
  Scorns with his claws to carry up the prey.'
Methought then, having wheeled a little there,
  He, terrible as thunderbolt, descended
  And snatched me upward to the fiery sphere.
There he and I seemed with the burning blended,
  And so the imagined fire seemed scorching me
  That of necessity my sleep was ended.
Even as Achilles shuddered once, when he
  Found himself gazing round with wakened eye
  Not knowing in what quarter he might be,
What time his mother him, her sleeping prize,
  From Chiron in her arms to Scyros bore,
  Whence later the Greeks took him,—in such wise
I shuddered when fled sleep away before
  The face of me; and pallid did I stand,
  Even as a man with terror stricken frore.
My Comforter alone was near at hand;
  The sun above two hours had made ascent,
  And I was facing now toward the strand.
'Fear nothing,' was my Lord's admonishment,
  'Be reassured, for we are in good state;
  Relax not, but be every sinew bent.
Now art thou come to Purgatory-gate:
  Lo, yonder the enclosing cliff, and lo
  The entrance where it seems to separate!
At dawn of day a little while ago,
  As slept thy soul within thee on the bed
  Of flowers that deck the meadow down below,
A Lady came, and "I am Lucy" said;
  "Let me take up this sleeper; it is meet
  That so he be upon his journey sped."
With the other noble forms in that retreat
  Sordello stayed; she took thee, and with day
  Came upward, and I came where fell her feet.

She laid thee here; that open entrance-way
　　With her fair eyes first having pointed out,
　　Together then with sleep she went away.'
Like one who wins assurance after doubt,
　　And into confidence converts his fear
　　When truth is known, so did I change about;
And when my Leader saw me free from care,
　　He started up along the cliff again
　　Toward the height, and I pursued him there.
Reader, thou seest how I exalt my strain,
　　And therefore do not hold it strange if by
　　More cunning art I now the theme sustain.
We reached a point, as we were drawing nigh,
　　Whence what first seemed a wall that had incurred
　　A fissure, now threw open to the eye
A door, and steps beneath, first, second, third,
　　For access to it, all diverse of hue,
　　And a Gatekeeper who yet spoke no word.
And as I opened more mine eye thereto,
　　I saw him sitting on the upper stair,
　　Such in the face I could not bear the view.
He held a sword whereof the blade was bare,
　　Which shed a sheen so dazzling to our viewing
　　That oft in vain I raised my glances there.
'Stand there and tell what aim ye are pursuing;
　　Where is the escort?'—he began to say,
　　'Beware lest coming up be your undoing!'
My Master answered him: 'This very day
　　A Lady of Heaven, aware how to proceed,
　　Bade, "Thither go, there is the entrance-way!"'
'And may she all your steps with blessing speed,'
　　Rejoined the Gatekeeper in courteous tone,
　　'Come to our stair then, as it is decreed.'
Thither we came: a great white marble stone
　　Was the first stair, so polished and so terse
　　That in it was my very image shown.

The second, tinct of deeper hue than perse,
    Was rugged rock, scorched with corrosive stain,
    And cloven through both lengthwise and traverse.
The third, which from above thrusts down amain,
    Seemed to me porphyry, as luminant
    As red blood spirting from a master-vein.
Upon this last one both his feet did plant
    Th' Angel of God, who sat the threshold warding,
    Which seemed to me of stone of adamant.
Up the three steps, mine own good will according,
    Drew me my Guide, and said: 'Humbly request
    That he unlock, admittance thus affording.'
Devoutly fell I at the footpalms blest;
    For mercy craved the opening to me;
    But first I smote me thrice upon the breast.
With sword-point he inscribed the letter P
    Sevenfold upon my forehead: 'Once inside,
    Take heed to wash away these wounds', — said he.
Ashes, or earth which has been digged and dried,
    Would match the hue of his habiliment,
    And, drawn from underneath it, I descried
Two keys, one gold, one silver instrument:
    Now with the white, then with the yellow too,
    He plied the gate until I was content.
'Should either key the fastening not undo,
    Within the wards inadequately plying,'
    Said he to us, 'blocked is the passage through.
More dear is one, the other one relying,
    Ere it unlock, on passing craft and wit,
    For this one brings the knot to its untying.
Peter, who gave them, said 'twere better fit,
    When people at my feet were prostrate lain,
    To err by opening than shutting it.'
He pushed the portal of the holy fane:
    'Enter,' said he, 'this knowledge with you bringing, —
    Whoso looks backward goes outside again.'

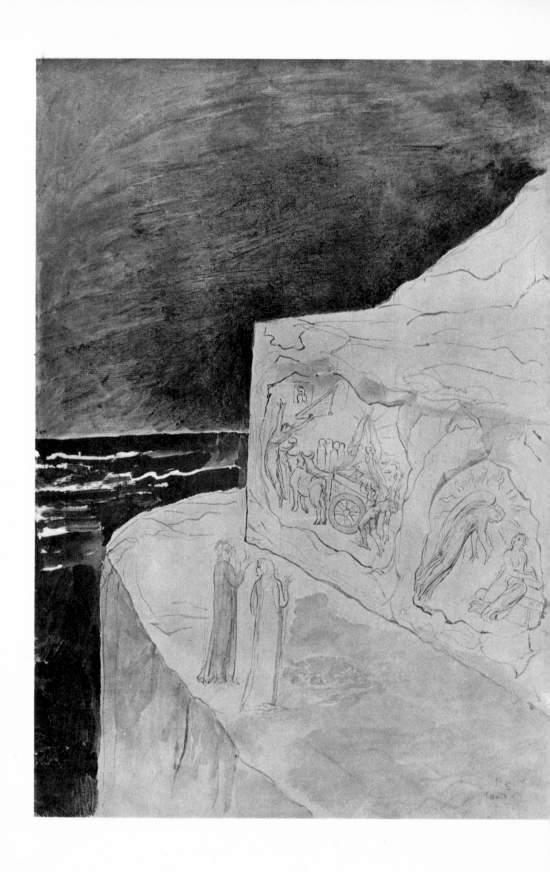

PURGATORIO: CANTO X

The Rock sculptured with the Recovery of the Ark and the Annunciation

And when upon their sockets were set swinging
The pivots of that consecrated door,
Hinges of metal stout, sonorous ringing,
Not so discordant seemed, nor did so roar
Tarpeia, when away from her was rended
The good Metellus, whence grew lean her store.
I turned away, and the first note attended:
Te Deum laudamus on mine ear was stealing
In voices with sweet music interblended.
Then listened I with such a raptured feeling
As often overcomes the souls down here,
When sing the people to the organ pealing,
And now the words are muffled, now ring clear.

CANTO X

When once within the threshold of the gate,
The Marvellous
Carved Walls
Which souls disuse through evil inclination
To make the crooked pathway appear straight,
I felt it closed by its reverberation:
And if I had turned back mine eyes thereto,
What for the fault were fitting exculpation?
A fissured rock were we ascending through,
Which did to this side and the other sway
As waves advancing and receding do.
'Now must a little skill come into play,
In keeping close, now here,' my Leader said,
'Now yonder, to the side that curves away.'
So scantily our steps were making head
That the moon's waning disk had time thereby
To settle down to rest within her bed,
Before we issued from that needle's eye.
But when we reached a free and open land
Above, where gathers back the mountain, I

Being weary, both uncertain on which hand
   The way led, stopped we, not to go amiss
   By roads more lonely than through desert sand.
From where the void borders the precipice
   To base of the high cliff ascending sheer,
   The human form thrice told would measure this;
And, as I winged my glances far and near,
   Now to the leftward, now toward the right,
   Still did this cornice such to me appear.
Our feet had not yet moved upon the height,
   When that sheer cliff around us, there become
   Too steep for climbing, proved of marble white
And decked with carvings past the masterdom
   Not only of cunning Polycletus,—nay,
   Nature herself had there been overcome.
The Angel who proclaimed on earth the sway
   Of peace long ages sighed to constitute,
   Which swept the ancient ban of Heaven away,
Before us stood with truth so absolute
   Carved in the acting of the gracious theme,
   That it appeared to be no image mute.
You'd swear that he cried 'Hail!' for how misdeem
   When there was imaged forth that Lady dear
   Who turned the key to open Love supreme?
'Behold the handmaid of the Lord is here!'
   Such was the language by her mien attested,
   Clearly as figure stamped in wax is clear.
'Attend not to one part alone,' requested
   The kindly Master who was holding me
   On that side where the human heart is nested;
Whereat, my glance removing, did I see
   Next beyond Mary, and toward the Guide
   Who urged me on, another history
Set in the rock; whence, turning to that side,
   I passed by Virgil and drew nigh alone,
   So that it might the better be descried.

There in the living marble carved, were shown
   The cart and kine the holy ark that drew,
   Whereby we fear an office not our own.
People were grouped about the foreground, who,
   In seven choirs, made my two senses say,
   One, 'They sing not,' the other, 'Yes, they do.'
And likewise, where the marble did portray
   The smoke of incense, eyes and nostrils bore
   Discordant witness both of yea and nay.
The lowly Psalmist, high-girt, on before
   The sacred vessel, bounded in the dance,
   And, doing so, was less than king and more.
Michal was figured, looking on askance
   From window of great palace opposite,
   Perturbed and scornful in her countenance.
From there the movement of my feet was slight
   Till I could scan another tale anigh,
   Which, beyond Michal, gleamed upon me white.
Herein was historied the glory high
   Of the princely Roman who, beneficent,
   Moved Gregory to his great victory:
Trajan, the emperor, hereby is meant:
   And a poor widow to his bridle clung
   In attitude of grief and of lament.
He seemed to ride with many a knight, among
   A trampling throng; eagles of golden hue
   Above him streaming to the wind seemed flung.
'Avenge me, Sire!'—amid that retinue
   Appeared that wretched mother to implore,
   'For my slain son my heart is stricken through.'
'Be patient,' answered her the Emperor,
   'Till my return.' And she, with urgent moan
   Replied: 'How, Sire, if thou return no more?'
Then he: 'Whoso shall sit upon my throne
   Will do it.' And she: 'What boot shall be to thee
   Another's bounty, if thou stint thine own?'

'Now be thou comforted,' consented he,
   'For ere I go my duty must I do,
   So Justice wills, pity restraining me.'
That Being who can look on nothing new
   Produced that visible speech engraven yon,
   Unknown here, therefore novel to our view.
While I delighted me to look upon
   These portraits of humility so fair
   And dear, considering Who this had done,
'Lo, many people, but with footsteps rare,'
   Murmured the Poet, 'on this side of us;
   These will direct us to the lofty stair.'
Mine eyes, that were intent on gazing thus,
   Turned round toward him, loath to be delayed
   To see new objects still solicitous.
I would not have thee, Reader, shrink dismayed
   From thy good purpose, though thou come to
   How God ordains it that the debt be paid.   [know
Take heed not to the fashion of the woe;
   Think on what follows; at the worst take thought
   Beyond the Judgement Day it cannot go.
'Master,' began I, 'what I see seems not
   Persons approaching us with motions slight,
   But sight is so at fault, I know not what.'
And he replied to me: 'So dire a plight
   Doubles them down with punishment condign,
   That I could not at first believe my sight.
But closely look till vision disentwine
   What yonder comes beneath those boulders bent:
   Already canst thou see how all repine.'
O ye proud Christians, wretched and forspent,
   Infirm in vision of your inward eyes,
   Who in backsliding steps are confident,
Perceive ye not how we from worms arise
   To form the fair angelic butterfly
   Which unto judgement undefended flies?

Why is the spirit in you puffed on high,
   Since ye are ungrown insects at your best,
   Defective grubs that undeveloped die!
As ceiling or roof timbers often rest
   On corbels, carved to indicate the strain
   In figure quaint, contorting knee to breast,—
Whence out of the unreal, real pain
   Is bred in him who looks,—beneath such stress
   Did I see these, on giving heed again.
True is it, they were bowed down more and less
   As more or less upon their backs they bore,
   And he whose look seemed most to acquiesce,
Weeping, appeared to say: 'I can no more!'

CANTO X
127-139

CANTO XI

'Our Father, Thou who dwellest high in Heaven,
   Not circumscribed, save by the Love immense
   That to Thy first creation Thou hast given,
Praised be Thy name and Thy omnipotence
   By all created beings, emulous
   To render thanks to Thy sweet effluence.
Let peace from Thine own kingdom come to us,
   For with all reach of soul that in us lies
   We cannot win it, if it come not thus.
As Thine own holy angels sacrifice
   Their will to Thee, while they *Hosanna* sing,
   So let men do with penitential sighs.
This day to us our daily manna bring,
   For in this desert rough, in utter dearth,
   We backward go when most endeavouring.
As we forgive to every one on earth
   The wrongs we bore, so graciously do Thou
   Forgive us, and look not upon our worth.

The Proud made
Humble

Put not to proof before our ancient foe
 Our power of will, so easily undone,
 But liberate from him who spurs it so.
We make, dear Lord, this final orison
 Not for ourselves, because there is no need,
 But all for dear ones left behind us yon.'
Beseeching for themselves and us good speed,
 Those heavy-laden shades went their slow way
 Under such loads as oft from dreams proceed,
And with unequal anguish circled they
 Wearily that first cornice of the Hill,
 Purging the soilure of the world away.
If good for us be spoken yonder still,
 What may be done and said for them down here
 By those who have a good root to their will?
Surely we ought to give them aid to clear
 The stains they carried hence, that light and chaste
 They issue forth upon the starry sphere.
'Ah, so may justice and may pity haste
 To disemburden you and speed your wing
 Whither your heart's desire is wholly graced,
Tell us which passage to the stair may bring
 Us soonest; and if more than one there be,
 Show that where least is need of clambering:
For in the flesh of Adam comes with me
 This person, by the burden so oppressed
 That, although willing, he mounts charily.'
The answer to these words, wherewith addressed
 Those weary souls my Leader and my Friend,
 Came back, from whom was yet not manifest;
But it was said: 'If to the right ye wend
 With us along the cliff, ye shall be shown
 A passage where the living could ascend.
And if I were not hampered by the stone
 Taming my neck, erewhile imperious,
 So that perforce I hold my visage down,

Then would I scan that one, not named to us
   But still alive, to see if him I knew,
   And make him of this burden piteous.
To a great Tuscan Sire my birth is due,
   William Aldobrandesco: I know not
   Whether his name was ever known to you.
My ancient blood, and prowesses that wrought
   My forebears, swelled my arrogancy so
   That, of our common mother losing thought,
I felt disdain for every man below,
   And died of it, as know the Sienese
   And every child in Campagnatico.
Humbert am I; nor harmed my haughtiness
   Me only, but all those my kinsmen bred
   Are dragged in consequence to deep distress.
And here I cannot choose but bow my head
   Beneath this load till satisfied be Grace,—
   Since not alive I did it, with the dead.'
Listening to him, I bended down my face;
   And one of them beneath the weight they brook
   (Not he who spoke) twisted himself apace
And saw me and recognized and called, his look,
   Albeit with effort, at my figure aimed
   Which going withal their crouching posture took.
'Art thou not Oderisi,'—I exclaimed,
   'Glory of Gubbio for that art of thine
   In Paris now "illuminating" named?'
'Brother,' said he, 'the leaves more smiling shine
   By Franco of Bologna's brush made fair:
   His now is all the boast, eclipsing mine.
I had not been so courteous over there
   While living, for the yearning strong in me
   For excellence, which was my utmost care.
Here of such pride is paid the penalty;
   And had I not, while free to sin, been fain
   To turn to God, even here I should not be.

O glory of the human powers, how vain,
    How little green may at the top endure,
    Unless rude after-ages supervene!
In painting Cimabuë held secure
    The field, and now is Giotto in request,
    So that the other's fame is grown obscure.
So did one Guido from the other wrest
    The palm in language; there may be, who knows?
    One born to drive both eagles from the nest.
Worldly renown is windy breath that goes
    Now hither and now yon, and changes name
    According to the quarter whence it blows.
If old thou strip thy flesh, shall then thy fame
    Be much more glorious than hadst thou died
    While pap and prattle still thy lips became,
A thousand years to come? a briefer tide
    To all eternity, than wink of eye
    To circle round the Heaven most slowly plied.
With him who little road doth occupy
    Before me, rang all Tuscany of yore,
    Though few for him now in Siena sigh
Where he was master once, and overbore
    The rabidness of Florence, prostitute
    At present, even as she was proud before.
As colour of the grass is your repute
    Which comes and goes; He makes it yellow and sere
    Who summons from the earth the greening fruit.'
And I: 'Thy truthful words make lowlier
    My spirit, and abate my swelling pride:
    But who is he of whom thou spokest here?'
'That? Provenzan Salvani,' he replied,
    'Put here because presumptuous to hold
    All Siena underfoot. So since he died
Has he been going, and ever as of old
    Unresting goes; with such coin he atones
    Who in the other life has been too bold.'

PURGATORIO: CANTO X

The Proud under their enormous Loads

And I: 'If every spirit who postpones
   Repentance till he reach life's utmost rim
   Cannot, unaided by good orisons,
Ascend the Mount, but must an interim
   Equal to all his life remain below,—
   How has the coming been vouchsafed to him?'
And he: 'When living in the greatest show,
   Upon the Campo of Siena fain
   Was he to stand and all respect forgo:
For, wishing to deliver from the pain
   Of Charles's prison house, a friend, he there
   Compelled himself to quake in every vein.
I say no more, of darkling words aware;
   But shortly will thy neighbours bring about
   That thou the pregnant comment canst prepare!
This action from those limits let him out.'

CANTO XII

Abreast, like oxen going in a yoke,   *The Pictured Floor*
   I with that heavy-laden soul went on,
   By the kind Teacher's leave. But when he spoke:
'Now it behoves us leave him and be gone;
   To ply the bark with sail and oar is best
   Here, far as possible, for every one,'
Upright, prepared for walking, I redressed
   My body, howsoever inwardly
   My thoughts remained both lowly and depressed.
I had moved on, and followed willingly
   The footsteps of my Master, and so fleet
   We went as showed us light of foot to be,
When said he: 'Cast thine eyes down; it is meet,
   In order well the pathway to beguile,
   To look upon the bed beneath thy feet.'

As, that their memory remain awhile,
   Earth-level tombs above the buried show
   The carven traces of their former style,
Whence tears for them here often freshly flow
   Through pricking of remembrances, that stir
   Only the tender-hearted: even so
Beheld I, but of semblance goodlier
   There, in accordance with the Workman's worth,
   Figured the way along that mountain-spur.
I saw on one side him of nobler birth
   Than any other creature, swift as light
   Fall like a thunderbolt from Heaven to Earth.
I saw Briareus, smitten by the bright
   Celestial dart, with chill of death subdued,
   Heavy upon the ground there opposite.
I saw Thymbræus, Pallas, Mars, who stood
   In armour round their Father, and they were
   Gazing at members of the Giants strewed.
I saw, at foot of his great labour, stare
   Bewildered Nimrod, where on Shinar plain
   Lay those who with him had been haughty there.
O Niobe, with eyes how full of pain,
   Portrayed upon the path I saw thee too,
   Between thy seven and seven children slain!
O Saul, how on your proper sword did you
   There lifeless upon Mount Gilboa show,
   That felt thereafter neither rain nor dew!
O mad Arachne, I beheld thee so,
   Half spider, wretched on the ruin wrought
   Upon the web thou wovest to thy woe!
O Rehoboam, here thy form does not
   Appear to threaten, but fulfilled with fear,
   Snatched from pursuers by a chariot!
Showed the hard pavement, too, what guerdon dear
   Alcmæon made unto his mother once
   The ill-predestined ornament appear;

Showed how upon Sennacherib the sons
  Fell in the temple, where, when he was slain,
  They left him without any orisons;
Showed how great ruin and what cruel pain
  Wrought Tomyris, when she to Cyrus said:
  'Thy thirst for blood with blood I slake again';
Showed how in panic the Assyrians fled
  As soon as Holofernes was undone,
  And showed the remnants of that victim dead.
I saw in caves and ashes Ilion:
  O Troy, thy state how low and pitiful
  Showed in the sculptured imagery yon!
What Master could with brush or graving-tool
  Those lines and shades so deftly have bestowed,
  To make the cleverest wit cry 'Wonderful'?
The dead seemed dead, alive the living showed:
  Better than I, saw not who saw the true,
  All that I trod while bent above my road.
Now lift your haughty looks, insolent crew
  Of sons of Eve, nor glance ye at the ground
  To see the wicked way that ye pursue!
More of the mount by us was circled round,
  And the sun's course now far more nearly spent,
  Than deemed my spirit, which was not unbound,
When he who ever vigilantly went
  Before me, 'Lift thy head,' began to say,
  'The time is past for going thus intent.
Lo! yonder is an Angel in array
  To come toward us: lo! returning seen
  The sixth handmaid from service of the day.
Adorn with reverence thine act and mien,
  That he may gladly speed our way on high:
  Think that this day will never dawn again.'
Well wonted to his monishing was I,
  On no account to squander time; and thus
  He could not on that theme speak covertly.

Toward us came the being beauteous,
　　Vested in raiment white, and in his face
　　Such as appears the dawn-star tremulous.
His wings he opened, opened his embrace,
　　Bidding: 'Approach, for hard by is the stair,
　　And from henceforward ye ascend apace.
To these glad tidings the response is rare:
　　Born to soar up, why are ye overthrown,
　　O human race, at every puff of air?'
He led us to where cloven was the stone;
　　Here with his wings did on my forehead smite,
　　Then promised me secure the going on.
As beyond Rubacontë, to the right,
　　Where sits the temple built to overlook
　　The well-directed city, the sharp flight
Of that ascent less pantingly we brook
　　By means of stairways fashioned in the days
　　Safe for the bushel and the audit-book;
So here the mountainside a little stays
　　Its dizzy drop from the succeeding round,
　　But high rocks either side the pathway graze.
As we are turning thither, voices sound,
　　'*Blessed the poor in spirit!*'—sweet concent
　　Such that to tell it words could not be found.
Ah me, these entrances how different
　　From that Infernal! for with anthems here
　　One enters,—there below with wild lament.
We were ascending now the holy stair,
　　And now I seemed to walk with lighter spring
　　Than even on the level plain whilere:
Wherefore I questioned him: 'What heavy thing
　　Has been uplifted from me, Master, say,
　　That now I go almost unwearying?'
He answered: 'When the other P's that stay,
　　Though indistinctly, on thy forehead still,
　　Shall, like the one, be cancelled quite away,

Thy feet will be so subject to good will,
  Not only will they not be wearied out,
  But feel delight to be urged up the hill.'
Then did I as do those who go about
  Hooded they know not how, till by and by
  The beckonings of others make them doubt;
Wherefore the hand is raised to verify,
  And finds the thing it seeks, thus lending aid
  To supplement the office of the eye;
So found the fingers of my right outspread,
  Six only of the letters that erewhile
  He of the Keys had graven on my head:
And this my gesture made the Leader smile.

CANTO XIII

We now were at the summit of the stair,
  There where the mount that heals as one ascends
  Is cut away the second time. And there
A terrace round about the hillside trends
  In the same manner as the former one,
  Save that more suddenly its contour bends.
Shaded or graven form appeared there none:
  So bare the bank, and so the pathway showed
  With but the livid colour of the stone.
'If to inquire of people we abode
  Still here,' the Poet said, 'I fear perchance
  It would too much delay our choice of road.'
Then fixing on the sun a steady glance,
  And centering his movement on the right,
  He caused his left side round it to advance.
'O Thou, confiding in whose kindly light
  I enter the new pathway, lead,' he said,
  'For leading here within is requisite.

Sapìa of Siena

The world thou warmest, lamping overhead;
   If other reason urge not, by thy smile
   We ought forever to be onward led.'
As far as here we reckon for a mile
   So far there did we on our journey move
   By dint of ready will, in little while;
And tow'rd us were heard flying thereabove
   Spirits invisible, with courteous
   Persuasion, bidding to the board of Love.
The first voice that went flying onward thus,
   With loud proclaim cried out: '*No wine have they,*'
   Repeating it long after passing us.
And ere, far off, it wholly died away,
   I heard another that was flying by,
   'I am Orestes,'—nor did this one stay.
'O Father mine, what voices these?' said I;
   And while I questioned, did a third one urge,
   'Love him that uses you despitefully.'
And he: 'This round doth castigating purge
   The sin of Envy, and from Love sublime
   Are therefore drawn the lashes of the scourge.
The curb must need be of a counter-chime,
   And thou wilt hear it, if I well surmise,
   Or ever thou the Pass of Pardon climb.
But through the air intently fix thine eyes,
   And thou shalt see along this avenue
   People, all sitting where the rocks arise.'
Then opened wider than before my view,
   Taking in shades in front, with mantles on
   That did not differ from the stone in hue.
And when we had a little farther gone,
   I heard a moaning: 'Mary, for us pray!'
   To Michael and Peter and all the saints a moan.
I cannot think there walks the earth to-day
   A man so hard as not to have been stung
   With pity at what I saw beside the way:

For when I drew so nearly them among
   That all their actions became manifest,
   Out through mine eyes full bitter tears were wrung.
In haircloth mean I seemed to see them dressed;
   Each lent his shoulder unto him behind,
   And all supported by the cliff did rest.
Thus at indulgences the poor and blind
   To crave their needment by the portal wait,
   Each with his head upon the next reclined,
That others may be made compassionate
   Not by the sound of words alone so soon
   As by their looks that no less supplicate.
As profits not the blind the sun at noon,
   So to the shades who sat where I have said,
   The light of Heaven will not confer its boon;
For pierces all their lids an iron thread,
   And sews them up, as to a savage hawk
   Is done, since it will not be quieted.
Methought it unbecoming so to walk
   Beholding others while concealed from view;
   Whence turned I, with my counsel sage to talk.
What the mute wished to utter, well he knew,
   Whence did he not my questioning abide,
   But said: 'Speak to the point; let words be few.'
Virgil was walking with me on that side
   Whence one may fall, because a parapet
   To girdle round the terrace is denied.
Upon the other side of me were set
   The pious shades, who through the suture dread
   Strained forth the tears until their cheeks were wet.
To them I turned me, and, beginning, said:
   'O people sure to see the lofty Glow
   Whereto your longing thoughts are wholly led,
May Grace soon loosen all the soilure so
   From off your conscience, that descending clear
   Through it the stream of memory may flow,

Tell me for welcome will it be and dear,
  If soul Italian here among you be;
  It might be well for him that I should hear.'
'Citizens all, O brother mine, are we
  Of one true city; but be this thy word,—
  One who a pilgrim dwelt in Italy.'
By way of answer this, methought, I heard
  A little farther on than where I stood;
  Whence I directed me yet thitherward.
Among the others there, one shadow showed
  A waiting look; should any ask 'How so?'
  It lifted up its chin in blind man's mode.
'O soul, subdued that thou mayst upward go,'
  Said I, 'if thou it be that answerest,
  Vouchsafe that I thy name or country know.'
'I was a Sienese, and with the rest,'
  She answered, 'here I cleanse my life unfit,
  Weeping to Him to come and make us blest.
Sapient was I not, though named of it
  Sapìa; greeting with far greater glee
  Another's bane than mine own benefit.
And that thou think me not deceiving thee,
  Hear whether I was foolish as I tell
  What time the years were sloping down with me.
One day the men who in my country dwell
  Joined battle near to Collë with their foes,
  While I was praying God for what befell.
Routed were they, and felt the bitter woes
  Of fugitives; beyond comparison
  My joy, on witnessing the chase, arose:
So that I lifted my bold face thereon,
  Crying to God, "I fear Thee not from hence!"
  As doth the blackbird for a little sun.
At utmost verge of my expiring sense
  I yearned for peace with God nor would I be
  Even yet discharged of debt by penitence,

Had it not been that, out of charity
   Grieving, with supplications holiest,
   Pier Pettinagno still remembered me.
But who art thou that comest making quest
   About our state, with unimpeded eye
   As I believe, and breathing reasonest?'
'Mine eyes will be withheld,' I made reply,
   'But briefly here, for small offence done when
   With Envy they were yonder turned awry.
My spirit, too expectant of the pain
   They suffer underneath, is terrified;
   That load already weighs on me amain.'
And she to me: 'Who then hath been thy guide
   Up here among us, if return is meet?'
   'He with me who is silent,' I replied;
'And living am I; whence do thou entreat
   Of me, O chosen soul, wouldst have me yon
   Yet move in thy behalf my mortal feet.'
'O strange is this to hear!'—she said thereon,
   'And of God's love to thee a happy sign
   Whence aid me sometime with thine orison.
And I implore by most desire of thine,
   If thou shalt tread the Tuscan earth anew,
   That thou make good my fame with kindred mine.
Seek them among that futile people, who
   Place hope in Talamonë, forfeiting
   More hope than when the Dian they pursue:
But the admirals will lose a greater thing.'

CANTO XIV

'Who is this that, ere Death have given him wing,
 Doth circling round about our Mountain go,
 Shutting his eyes at will, and opening?'
'I know not who he is, but he, I know,
 Is not alone: ask thou, who art more nigh,
 And greet him gently, that he answer so.'
Thus, leaning each to each, held colloquy
 Two spirits, sitting on the right hand there;
 Then, to address me, with the face on high,
One said: 'O soul, that dost already fare
 Heavenward, nor dost the body yet resign,
 For charity console us, and declare
Who art thou and whence come; for so divine
 A miracle as never known before,
 Must needs appear to us this grace of thine.'
And I: 'Through Tuscan mid-interior
 A river, born in Falterona-ground,
 Wanders in course of hundred miles and more.
This body bring I from that river-bound:
 To tell you who I am were speech in vain,
 Because my name does not yet far resound.'
Then he who first had spoken said again:
 'Thou speakst of Arno, if I picture well
 The colour of thy sense within my brain.'
Whereto the other: 'Why did he not tell
 The very word we know that river by,
 But keep it back as something horrible?'
And the shadow that was questioned made reply:
 'I know not, but indeed 'tis fitting for
 The very name of such a vale to die.
For from its fountain,—where the waters pour
 So amply from that rugged mountain chain
 Torn from Pelorus, seldom teeming more,

194

As far as where it renders up again
   That which the heaven absorbs from out the flood,
   Wherefrom the rivers have their flowing train,
Virtue is driven like a serpent brood,
   The enemy of all, or through mischance
   Of place, or scourge of evil habitude.
Whence so disnatured are the habitants
   Of that unhappy vale, it would appear
   That Circe had them in her maintenance.
Among foul hogs, of acorns worthier
   Than other viands made for use of men,
   It first directs its puny thoroughfare;
Curs it encounters, coming downward then,
   More snarling than their power gives warranty,
   And turns from them its muzzle in disdain;
The more it flows on downward swellingly,
   The more the dogs grown wolves are found by this
   Accursèd ditch of evil destiny,
Which then, descending many a deep abyss,
   Finds fraudful foxes such as do not fear
   To be entrapped by any artifice.
Nor do I curb my tongue lest others hear:
   And good for this man to remember well
   The things true prophecy is making clear.
I see thy grandson, who becomes a fell
   Hunter of those wolf-creatures, terror giving
   To all who by the cruel river dwell.
He traffics in their flesh while it is living,
   Then slaughters them as would a wild-beast hoar;
   Many of life, himself of praise bereaving.
From the grim wood he issues red with gore,
   Leaving it such not thousand years will show
   That river-bank rewooded as before.'
As at announcement of impending woe,
   The hearer's face betrays his troubled mood,
   From wheresoever peril threaten; so

I saw in the other soul, in attitude
   To listen, signs of grief and perturbation
   When that prophetic word he understood.
The words of the one, the other's agitation
   Made me desire to know the names they bore
   Whereof I made request, with supplication.
Thereat the spirit that spoke to me before,
   Began again: 'Thou wilt not do the same
   Favour to me that thou art craving for;
But if God will that forth in thee should flame
   Such grace, I will not as a niggard do:
   Know then, Guido del Duca is my name.
So Envy did the blood of me imbue,
   That, had I seen a man grow joyful there,
   Thou wouldst have seen me tinged with livid hue.
From my own sowing reap I such a tare:
   Why set your hearts, O human progeny,
   On what ye are permitted not to share?
This is Rinier, of the house of Calboli
   The glory and the honour; from their blood
   Has sprung no heir of his nobility.
'Twixt Po and mountain, Reno and the flood,
   His family is not the only race
   Stripped of integrity and gentlehood;
For in these bounds replete is every place
   With poisonous scions, so that late and slow
   Could ever tilth eradicate their trace.
Henry Mainardi and good Lizio,
   Pier Traversar', Guy di Carpigna, where
   Be they, O Romagnoles, who bastard grow?
When will Bologna now a Fabbro bear?
   Faenza a Bernardin di Fosco when?
   Of humble family the noble heir.
Tuscan, let not my tears amaze thee then,
   When Guy da Prata I recall to mind,
   With Hugh of Azzo as he lived with men,

And Frederick Tignoso and his kind,
   The Traversara, the Anastagi (those
   Two houses in their lineage declined!),
The knights and ladies, labour and repose,
   That kindled in us love and courtesy,
   Where every human heart so wicked grows.
O Brettinoro, why dost thou not flee,
   Seeing that, not to be corrupted, go
   Many to exile with thy family?
Well does Bagnacaval being barren so,
   But Castrocaro ill, and bent to spawn
   Such breed of counts, still worse does Conio.
Will do well the Pagani, when is gone
   Their Demon from them; but not so that pure
   Can ever the report of them live on.
O Hugh of Fantolini, now secure
   Thy name is, which no fear may entertain
   Of sons degenerating to obscure!
Now, Tuscan, go thy way, for I am fain
   Rather to weep than our discourse pursue,
   So has it left my spirit wrung with pain.'
That those dear souls could hear when we withdrew,
   We were aware; and therefore confident
   Their silence made us of the avenue.
When we became alone, as on we went,
   A voice came counter to us that did say,
   Even as when lightning cleaves the firmament:
'Every one that findeth me, shall slay';
   All of a sudden thereupon it passed,
   As thunder with the storm-rack rolls away.
Soon as our ears had truce from such a blast,
   Behold another of so loud a tone,
   It seemed the thunderclap that follows fast:
'I am Aglauros, who became a stone!'
   Backward instead of forward, at that sound
   I stepped, and pressed the Poet hard upon.

Now was the air grown quiet all around;
    And he to me: 'That was the galling bit
    Which ought to keep a man within his bound.
But ye accept the baited hook, and it
    Draws you toward the Adversary old,
    Whence curb or call doth little benefit.
The Heavens are calling to you, and unfold
    Their never-fading beauties to your view
    Which ever fixed upon the earth ye hold;
Whence the All-seeing One is scourging you.'

CANTO XV

*Treasure in
Heaven: Visions
of Forbearance*

As much as shows, between the dawn of day
    And when the third hour closes, of the sphere
    That like a child is evermore at play,
So much seemed left the sun of his career
    Toward the night, remaining to be run:
    There it was vespers, and 'twas midnight here.
The rays were striking full our face upon,
    For so we circling round the mountain went
    That we were going toward the setting sun;
When yet far more I felt my forehead bent
    Beneath the splendour that did on it smite,
    And the strange matters were my wonderment:
Wherefore I made a visor to my sight,
    Lifting my hands above these brows of mine
    So as to temper the excess of light.
As when on glass or water sunbeams shine,
    Then in the opposite direction dart,
    Ascending in a corresponding line
To that of their descent, and so depart
    Equally from the falling of the stone,
    As demonstrate experiment and art;

So I felt struck by light reflected, thrown [gleaming
   From straight before, whence from the vivid
   Quick fled my sight. 'What is that, O mine own
Father,' said I, 'intolerably beaming
   So that I find no shelter for mine eyes?
   And coming on to usward, or so seeming.'
'If dazzle thee the household of the skies
   As yet, be it no wonder,' came reply;
   'That is a Messenger to bid man rise.
Soon will it not be grievous to thine eyes
   To look on these things, but complete delight
   Up to the top of thy capacity.'
When we had reached the Angel benedight,
   His glad voice said: 'From here thou enterest
   A stair than others far less steep of flight.'
Departing thence, we mounted now, and *Blest
   Are the compassionate*, did it intone
   Behind us, and *Rejoice, thou conquerest!*
My Master and myself, we two alone,
   Were going up, and going, I took thought
   How from his words to gain some benison;
And turned me to him, thus inquiring: 'What
   Could he have meant, the spirit Romagnole,
   Speaking of sharing as permitted not?'
Then he: 'Of his own greatest sin, that soul
   Conceives the harm; whence let it not surprise
   If he rebuke it, that there be less dole.
For inasmuch as your heart's treasure lies
   Where through companionship ye lose a share,
   Doth Envy work the bellows for your sighs.
But if love for the most exalted sphere
   Should make your aspiration upward turn,
   Ye would not harbour in your breast that fear;
Because the more there yonder be who yearn
   To murmur "Ours", the more has each, and more
   Of charity doth in that cloister burn.'

'I am further from contentment than before
　　I ceased from being silent,' then I said,
　　'And more of doubt within my mind I store.
How can a single boon, distributed,
　　Give many holders wealth more unconfined,
　　Than if it be by few inherited?'
And he: 'Because thou centerest thy mind
　　Only on earthly things, thy inward sight
　　Is, in the plenitude of brightness, blind.
That inexpressible and infinite
　　Boon up above there, so to love outflows,
　　As to a lucid body runs the light.
Much as it finds of ardour, it bestows:
　　So that, however wide spreads charity,
　　Above it the Eternal Bounty grows.
And the more people set their hearts on high,
　　The more love purely, and their loves augment
　　As rays reflected from a mirror fly.
Now if appease thee not my argument
　　Shalt look to Beatrice, and dissipated
　　Be this and every other discontent.
Two of thy wounds are now obliterated:
　　But strive that speedily, the same as these,
　　The five may close, by sorrow expiated.'
As I was fain to say, 'Thou dost appease,'
　　Behold! another Circle did I gain,
　　And eager eyes compelled me hold my peace.
There suddenly I felt me overta'en
　　By an ecstatic vision, whence beguiled,
　　I saw a crowd of people in a fane;
And at the door a Lady, with the mild
　　Mien of a mother, seemed to say this thing:
　　'Ah, why hast thou so dealt with us, my child?
Thy father and myself, lo! sorrowing
　　Were seeking thee.' As here she ceased to speak,
　　That which had first appeared was vanishing.

Another then appeared, adown whose cheek
   Those waters coursed that grief distils, when great
   Resentment upon others it would wreak:
'If Master of the town that such debate
   Caused to the gods about its name,' said she,
   'And whence doth every science scintillate,
Upon that bold embrace avenge thou thee,
   That clasped our daughter, O Pisistratus!'
   Her lord benign and gentle seemed to me
To answer her with temperate manner thus:
   'What shall we do to them who wish us ill,
   If they who love us are condemned by us?'
Then I saw angry folk aflame with will
   To slay a youth by stoning, raising cries
   Hoarsely to one another: 'Kill him, kill!'
And saw him bowed to earth, and now he lies
   Under the weight of Death, yet, thus undone,
   Still making gates to Heaven with his eyes;
Lifting to the High Lord his orison,
   With look such as unlocks our sympathy,
   For pardon to his slayers every one.
Soon as returned my spirit outwardly
   To things external to it, which are true,
   Did I my not erroneous errors see.
Thereon my Leader, who could see me do
   Like one disputing slumber's masterdom,
   Exclaimed: 'What ails thee? canst not stand? go to!
For half a league and farther art thou come
   With eyes veiled over, and with legs that sway,
   Like one with wine or slumber overcome.'
Then said I: 'O my gentle Father, pray
   Listen to me, and I will tell thee what
   I saw, when thus my legs were ta'en away!'
'A hundred masks upon thy face would not
   Avail to shut thy mind from me,' he said,
   'However trivial might be thy thought.

What thou hast seen was that thou mayst be led
  To ope thy heart to waters of repose
  That pour from the eternal fountainhead.
I did not ask "What ails thee?" as do those
  Who only look with inattentive glance
  When reft of consciousness the body shows,
But asked that vigorous thy foot advance:
  Thus it behoves to spur the laggard, slow
  To put to proof returning vigilance.'
Still forward through the vesper did we go,
  Straining as far as possible the eye
  Against the late and shining rays; and lo!
By slow degrees toward us coming nigh
  A cloud of smoke, as gloomy as the night,
  Nor was there any place of shelter by:
This of pure air bereft us and of sight.

CANTO XVI

*Lawlessness of the
Temporal Power
of the Clergy*

The gloom of Hades and of shades that shroud
  Every star beneath a barren sky,
  Darkened as much as possible with cloud,
Made never veil so thick unto mine eye
  Nor of so rough a tissue to the feeling,
  As did that smoke we there were covered by,
From the closed eyes all vision quite concealing;
  Whereat mine Escort sapient and tried
  Offered me help, his shoulder tow'rd me wheeling.
Even as a blind man goes behind his guide,
  And lest he haply stumble against aught
  Might hurt or kill him, does not go aside,
So faring through that bitter fume, I caught
  The accents of my Guide, who did but say:
  'Take care that we be separated not!'

Voices I heard, and each appeared to pray
   That might in peace and in compassion come
   The Lamb of God who takes our sins away.
Just *Agnus Dei* was their exordium,
   One measure was for all, and one desire,
   So that in harmony seemed all and some.
'Master, can what I hear,' did I inquire,
   'Be spirits?' 'Thou hast said it,' he replied,
   'And they go loosening the knot of ire.'
'Now who art thou cleaving our smoke aside,
   Who art discoursing of us even as though
   Thou didst by calends still the time divide?'
Speech by a single voice was uttered so:
   Whereat the Master said: 'Thy answer be
   To ask if here the pathway upward go.'
And I: 'O creature that art cleansing thee,
   To return beautiful to Him who made,
   Shalt hear a wonder if thou follow me.'
'I'll follow thee far as I may,' it said,
   'And if the smoke make still our seeing vain,
   To keep us joined shall hearing serve instead.'
'Swathed in the bands that Death unbinds again,'
   Began I, 'do I go the upward road,
   And hither came I through the eternal pain;
And since enfolds me so the grace of God,
   Showing His will that I behold His court
   By way quite other than our modern mode,
What man thou wast ere death do thou report,
   Concealing naught, and tell me if I go
   Right for the pass; and let thy words escort.'
'Lombard was I, called Marco; and did know
   The world's concerning, and that virtue love
   Whereat each one has now unbent the bow:
For mounting up do thou straight forward move.'
   Thus answering, 'I pray thee,' added he,
   'To pray for me when thou shalt be above.'

And I to him: 'I pledge my faith to thee
To do that which thou cravest; but I burst
With inward doubt till from it I am free.
Elsewhere suggested, it was simple first,
But now confirmed by words which thou hast said,
Redoubled, and to know the cause I thirst.
The world in very deed is forfeited
To vice by virtue all, as thou dost say,
And is with evil big and overspread:
But put thy finger on the cause, I pray,
That I, discerning it, let others know
Whether the blame to heaven or earth to lay.'
Voicing his deep sighs in a cry by woe
Wrung from him, he began: 'The world is blind,
Brother, and sooth thou comst from there below.
All causes are by you who live assigned
To heavens above, as if their motion still
Did of necessity all natures bind.
If this were true, your freedom of the will
Would be destroyed, and it would not be right
To have or joy for good, or grief for ill.
The heavens do your first impulses excite,—
I say not all; but grant that this I said,
For good or evil there is given you light
And free volition; which to battle led
Against the stars, though weary it commence,
Finally conquers all, if rightly fed.
Though free, ye are subject to omnipotence
And better nature, which doth in you mould
The mind, exempt from starry influence.
Hence if the present world go uncontrolled,
In you the cause, let it be sought in you:
And true intelligence I now unfold.
Forth from the hand of her Creator, who
Loves her before she be, in maiden guise,
With gleeful laughter and with tears of rue,

Issues the innocent soul, in nothing wise
  Save that, from blithesome Maker, turns she fain
  To things wherein some specious pleasure lies.
Cheated at first, she tastes the savour vain
  Of trivial good, and runs to that desire,
  With appetite unswayed by guide or rein.
Hence law by way of bridle we require;
  Require a king discerning from aloof
  Of the true City of God at least the spire.
Laws are,—but who to put them to the proof?
  None: since the shepherd, he who goes before,
  Can chew the cud but cleaveth not the hoof.
Whence folk who see their leader striking for
  That having which they greedily pursue,
  Being fed with that, hunger for nothing more.
Well canst thou see that governance untrue
  The cause is that hath made the world malign,
  And not that nature is corrupt in you.
Rome, that redeemed the world, once gave to shine
  Two suns, which both the one and the other course
  Made manifest,—the worldly, the divine.
The one hath quenched the other; and perforce,
  The sword together with the crozier wed,
  Ill can but come of it till they divorce,
Since, joined, the one doth not the other dread.
  Consider well, if thou believe not so,
  The fruit, for every plant is known by seed.
In the land laved by Adigë and Po,
  Valour was once in vogue, and courtesy,
  Ere Frederick had quarrelled with his foe;
Now can fare through it with security
  Any whom sense of shame may set at strife
  From speaking with the good or drawing nigh.
Survive still, to rebuke the manners rife,
  Three veterans, and long appears the road
  To them, till God conduct to better life:

Conrad, named of Palazzo, Gerard good,
    And Guido of Castello,—better say
    The loyal Lombard, after the French mode.
The Church of Rome, declare thou from this day
    That would in double government engage,
    Falls with its burden in the miry way.'
'O Marco mine,' said I, 'thy words are sage;
    And now I see why Levi's children should
    Have been excluded from the heritage.
But who is Gerard, that example good,
    Thou sayest, of a generation spent,
    Who lives to upbraid our barbarous period?'
'Cheat me thy words, or make experiment,
    In that thou, speaking Tuscan,' he replied,
    'Of the good Gerard seemest ignorant.
I know him not by any name beside,
    Unless 'twere from his daughter Gaia drawn.
    I come no farther; so be God your guide.
Already through the smoke the splendour yon
    Is whitening,—the Angel is there,—before
    He has perceived me, I must needs be gone.'
So he turned back, and would not hear me more.

CANTO XVII

Profitable Discourse
during the Second
Night

Recall to mind if ever shut thee in,
    Reader, a cloud upon the Apennine,   [skin;
    Wherethrough thou sawest but as mole through
How, when the dank, dense vapours discombine,
    And slowly fall away, the solar sphere
    Comes struggling in again with feeble shine;
And to thy fantasy it will be clear
    Immediately, how I saw once more
    The sun, that was already setting here.

To the sure footsteps of my Counsellor
  Matching my own, from such a cloud I thus
  Emerged to rays now dead on the low shore.
O power of fancy, oft withdrawing us
  So from without, we show indifference
  Though a thousand trumpets round are clamorous,
Who moves thee if impel thee not the sense?
  Moves thee a heaven-informed illumining,
  Led down by will or starry influence.
Appeared the trace in my imagining
  Of her, the pitiless, who changed, some say,
  Into the bird that most delights to sing;
And here my intellect in such a way
  Was locked within, that nothing was descried
  Of any object that outside it lay.
In my raised fantasy, one crucified
  Rained down thereafterward, of scornful mood
  And rancorous in mien, and so he died.
Around him great Ahasuerus stood,
  Esther his wife, just Mordecai, he who
  In word and deed was of such rectitude.
And as this image of itself withdrew,
  Collapsing like a bubble when it wants
  The film of water it was fashioned through,
Uprose a youthful maiden in my trance,
  Bitterly weeping, and she cried: 'O Queen,
  Why wouldest thou be naught in petulance?
To lose Lavinia not, thyself hast slain:
  Now thou hast lost me; she who mourns am I,
  Mother, for thee, ere for another's teen.'
And even as slumber breaks, when suddenly
  Upon closed eyelids strikes the morning light,
  And, broken, wavers ere it wholly die,
So fell away from me this fancied sight,
  Soon as there struck upon my face a glare
  That, matched with what we know, seemed infinite.

When I had turned to see the way to fare,
   I heard: 'Here go ye up!' in accents blest
   Withdrawing me from every other care,
Making my will so eager in request
   To know the speaker, and to look and see,
   That, until face to face, it cannot rest.
But as before the sun, excessively
   Resplendent, veiling so its form from sight,
   Thus was the power deficient here in me.
'This is a spirit divine, who tow'rd the height,
   Without our prayer, points where we should be hieing,
   And wraps himself about with his own light.
He deals with us as self to self replying;
   For who waits prayer, while to the need alive,
   Malignly leans already to denying.
To such inviting let the foot now strive:
   Upward endeavour we ere day be dim,
   Else could we not until new day arrive.'
So having said, my Guide, and I with him,
   Together tow'rd a stairway turned our feet;
   And soon as I set foot on the first rim,
I felt a fanning on my face like beat
   Of wings, and heard: 'Blest the Peacemakers are,
   For wrath unrighteous hath in them no seat!'
Now were uplifted over us so far
   The parting beams whereon the night pursues,
   That upon every side shone forth a star.
'Alas, why are my sinews grown so loose?'
   Within me I began to murmur, for
   I felt my power of limb was put in truce.
Come were we where ascended now no more
   The stairway up, and there we fast were stayed,
   Even as a vessel moored upon the shore;
And for a little while I gave full heed
   If aught were heard within the circle new;
   Then to my Master turned about, and said:

'Inform me here, belovèd Father true,
    What fault is in this circle purified?
    Though pause the feet, let not thy word so do.'
And he to me: 'The love of good, denied
    Its due activity, is here restored;
    Here the ill-slackened oar again is plied.
Wouldst thou more clearly comprehend my word,
    Be but attentive and, although we wait,
    Thou shalt derive some profit and reward.
Neither Creator, no, nor thing create,
    Son,' he began, 'was ever void of love,—
    Thou knowest it,—or of spirit, or innate.
Innative love doth ever faultless prove;
    But the other, by ill aim, or little might,
    Or by excessive might, is prone to rove.
While tends to primal goods the appetite,
    In secondary things self-moderator,
    It cannot be the cause of ill delight;
But when it turns to evil or, with greater
    Or less than proper zeal, on good is bent,
    The creature works against its own Creator.
As seed in you of all that's excellent,
    Thou mayest infer that Love must needs have served,
    And of each act that merits punishment.
Since never can the eye of love have swerved
    From its own person, it must be concluded
    That from self-hatred all things are preserved;
And since no being can be thought secluded,
    Standing alone, cut from First Cause away,
    From hate of Him is every heart precluded.
Hence if, distinguishing, I rightly say
    It is your neighbour's harm you love, takes root
    This love in triple fashion in your clay.
There are who, seeing their neighbour underfoot,
    Hope to excel, and for this reason, down
    From his high pinnacle would have him put.

There are who power, grace, honour, or renown
    Fearing to forfeit, if another rise,
    Crave the reverse, and on his fortune frown;
Then those who seem to chafe at injuries,
    Greedy for vengeance, so that it behoves
    Them evil to another to devise.
Yonder below are wept these threefold loves:
    Now of the other do I thee to wit,
    That to the good in faulty measure moves.
Vaguely each one conceives a benefit
    Wherein the mind may rest, and yearns thereto
    Whence each endeavours to attain to it.
If languid be the love inciting you
    To look upon it, or to make pursuit,
    This Cornice pains you on repentance due.
There's other good wherein there is no boot:
    It is not happiness, is not the good
    Essence, of every good the fruit and root.
The love that yields unduly to such mood
    Is up above bewept in circles three;
    But how it were tripartite understood,
I leave unspoken, to be sought by thee.'

CANTO XVIII

The lofty Teacher, ending argument,
    Gave me a searching look, as for inferring
    From play of feature if I seemed content.
And I, whom new thirst was already spurring,
    Was mute without, but said within: 'Perchance
    I burden him, too many a question stirring.'
But that true Father, who took cognizance
    Of the shy wish that was concealed from view,
    Speaking, put heart in me for utterance.

'Master,' said I, 'my sight so lives anew
    Within thy light that I discern by it
    All that thy words enunciate as true.
Define, however, if that prayer be fit,
    The love whereto thou tracest, Father kind,
    Every good action and its opposite.'
'Direct to me the keen eyes of the mind,'
    Said he, 'and see the error demonstrated
    Of those who would be leaders, being blind.
The soul, susceptible to love created,
    Responds to all things pleasing in its view,
    When once to act by pleasure stimulated.
Now your perception doth from something true
    Derive an image and within you unfold
    So as to cause the soul to turn thereto;
And if, when turned, she sends there uncontrolled,
    That tendency is love, 'tis Nature's bent
    Through pleasure getting in you a fresh hold.
Then, even as fire has motion of ascent,
    By virtue of its form which makes it wing
    To where it dwells more in its element:
So the rapt soul doth into longing spring,
    A spiritual motion, never still
    Till she rejoice in the belovèd thing.
Now may be evident how very ill
    They view the truth, who would aver to thee
    That all love in itself is laudable,
Because its matter may ideally
    Appear good always: but not every seal
    Is good, however good the wax may be.'
'Thy words, and my wit following, reveal
    Love and its nature to me,' answered I,
    'But therefore all the greater doubt I feel;
For if Love offer from without, and by
    Another foot the spirit travel not,
    She has no merit, go she straight or wry.'

And he to me: 'As far as pierces thought,
    Myself can tell: beyond that fix thy mind
    On Beatrice, that faith in thee be wrought.
Every substantial form that is conjoined
    With matter, and yet from it cut away,
    Holds inward virtue of specific kind,
Which, save in act, is not brought into play,
    By its effect alone in evidence,
    Like life in plant evinced by the green spray.
Thus, whence originates intelligence
    Of first ideas, is unknown to thee,
    And bent of the primordial appetence,
Which are in you as study in the bee
    To make its honey; and such primal bent
    Of neither praise nor blame receives the fee.
Now, that with this may all desires consent,
    The power that counsels is innate in you,
    And ought to hold the threshold of assent.
This is the principle wherefrom accrue
    The grounds of your desert, as gathering
    And winnowing the false loves from the true.
Who to the bottom went in reasoning,
    Took notice of this inborn liberty,
    Thus morals to the world delivering.
Assuming, then, that from necessity
    All love is kindled rightly or amiss,
    To hinder it ye have ability.
This noble virtue is called by Beatrice
    The Freedom of the Will; take heed aright
    If she begin to speak to thee of this.'
The slow moon tow'rd the middle of the night,
    Shaped like a bucket all ablaze, more wan
    Now made the constellations to our sight,
And counter to the heavens that pathway ran
    Fired by the setting sun, which he of Rome
    Sees 'twixt Sardinian and Corsican;

When he, that noble shade by fame of whom
  Pietola every Mantuan town outwent,
  Had put aside my fardel burdensome:
So that I, who explicit argument
  And lucid to my questioning had found,
  Remained like one who rambles somnolent.
But from this somnolence I was unbound
  All of a sudden by a multitude
  Toward us from behind now coming round.
Of old Ismenus and Asopus viewed
  Such hurrying throng at night their banks beside,
  If Thebans but in need of Bacchus stood,
As these who round that Cornice curve their stride,
  From what I saw of those approaching me,
  On whom goodwill and right affection ride.
They were soon upon us, for that great company
  Was coming at a run; and with lament
  Two in advance cried out alternately:
'Mary in haste to the hill country went,'
  And, 'Cæsar, to conquer Lerida, in haste
  Struck at Marseilles, and then swept Spainward
'Quick, quickly, lest the moment go to waste [bent.'
  Through little love!' did the others then intone,
  'That zeal for doing good be freshly graced.'
'O people, in whom keen fervour doth atone
  Perchance, delay and negligence which you
  By lukewarmness in doing good have shown,
This man who lives (I surely tell you true!)
  Would fain go up, if shine again the sun;
  So tell us where is nearest passage through.'
These words were spoken by my Guide; and one
  Among those spirits answered: 'Follow us,
  And thou shalt find the opening anon.
We are so full of zeal for running thus
  We cannot stay; pardon, we therefore cry,
  If this our duty seems discourteous.

San Zeno's abbot at Verona I,
    Beneath good Barbarossa's empire, whom
    Yet Milan cannot name without a sigh.
And one has foot already in the tomb
    Who shall erelong that monastery rue,
    And rue the having had there masterdom,
Because his son, in body lame, thereto
    Mind lamer still, and who was born amiss,
    He put in office of its pastor true.'
I know not whether yet he held his peace,
    So far beyond us he was hurrying,
    But gladly I remember hearing this.
And he who was my help in everything
    Now said: 'Turn hitherward and look,—two more
    Are coming onward, giving sloth a sting.'
'Dead were the folk whom ocean opened for,'
    They, bringing up the rear, were crying thus,
    'Ere Jordan looked on its inheritor,'—
And,—'Those who found it too laborious
    To bide the issue with Anchises' son,
    Gave themselves up to life inglorious.'
Then, when so distant were those shades that none
    Could more be seen of all that multitude,
    My mind began upon new thoughts to run,
Whence many more were born, a motley brood;
    And so did one upon another teem,
    I lapsed with closed eyes into drowsihood,
Transmuting meditation into dream.

CANTO XIX

It was the hour wherein the heat of noon,
  By Saturn haply, or by earth undone,
  Can warm no more the coldness of the moon;
When geomancers see before the dawn
  Their Greater Fortune rising eastward through
  A course she will not long go darkling on;
I saw in dream a stammering woman, who
  Was squint of eye, and of distorted feet,
  Bereft of hands, and sallow in her hue.
I gazed at her: as from the sun streams heat
  Into the limbs made chilly by the night,
  Even so my gazing served to liberate
Her tongue, and erelong wholly set her right,
  And with the pallor of her features blent
  The flushes that to love are requisite.
Thereon her speech became so eloquent,
  And so her song began to charm mine ear,
  That scarce could I away from her have bent:
'Sweet Siren I, who witch the mariner
  Amid the billows,' she began to sing,
  'So full of pleasantness am I to hear;
I turned Ulysses from his wandering
  By power of song: who listen to my strain
  Seldom depart from me, all-solacing.'
Her parted lips had not yet closed again,
  Ere for her quick confusion, at my side,
  A Lady holy and alert was seen.
'O Virgil, Virgil, who is this?'—she cried
  Indignantly; and he was drawing near
  With looks but to that modest Virtue tied.
He seized the other one and laid her bare,
  Rending her garb, the belly to display;
  This waked me with the stench arising there.

A Repentant Pope
(Adrian V)

Eyeing the Master good, I heard him say:
'Thrice have I called thee; rise and come, to find
The opening where goes thy passageway.'
I rise: lo! round the sacred Mountain wind
The Cornices in open day; and now
We go our way with the new sun behind.
Following after him, I bore my brow
Like one who makes himself, o'erborne with
Into the half-arch of a bridge to bow; [thought,
When 'Come, here is the passage!'—this I caught
In accents mild, of such benignity
As in this mortal region hear we not.
With swan-like pinions widely open, he
Upward directed us, so having said,
Between two walls of solid masonry.
With moving wings, he wafture on us shed,
Affirming that *the mourners shall be blest*,
For they shall have their spirits comforted.
'What ails thee that thou earthward rivetest
Thy glance?'—began to say to me my Guide,
When somewhat past the Angel we had pressed.
And I: 'With such misgiving am I plied
By novel vision of compulsive stress,
So that my thoughts as by a spell are tied.'
'Hast seen,' said he, 'that ancient sorceress?
She who alone is now bewept up yond,
And seen how man is loosed from her duress?
Be it enough,—beat heels upon the ground,—
Lift eyes toward the lure up, that with vast
Circles, the Eternal King is whirling round.'
Like hawk that, eyeing first her feet, at last
Turns to the call and spreads her pinions out,
By longing yonder drawn to break her fast;
Such I, and such, far as affords a route
The cloven rock to them who upward go,
I went where starts the circling round about.

When opened to me the Fifth Cornice, lo!
 People who wept upon it there, nor stirred
 From lying prone, with faces turned below.
'*My soul hath to the pavement cleaved!*' I heard
 Their voices uttering with such deep sighs,
 That one could hardly understand the word.
'O ye elect of God, whose agonies
 Are made by justice and by hope less grim,
 Direct us where the lofty stairs uprise.'
'Come ye exempt from lying prone of limb,
 And wish to find the road with little stay,
 Let your right hand be ever tow'rd the rim.'
So prayed the Poet, and from little way
 Before so came reply; whence I detected
 That hidden thing the speaker failed to say,
And then mine eyes unto my Lord directed:
 Whereat with cheerful sign he gave consent
 To what the look of my desire expected.
When I could act according to my bent,
 I said, and stood above that being there,
 Whose words already rendered me intent:
'Spirit, whose weeping ripens thee to bear
 Fruit without which to God is no returning,
 Suspend awhile for me thy greater care.
Who wast thou? why your backs thus upward turning?
 When I go yon whence moved my living feet,
 Can I do aught to satisfy thy yearning?'
'Shalt learn,' said he, 'why Heaven esteems it meet
 We turn our backs to it; but meanwhile know
 I was successor to Saint Peter's seat.
'Twixt Sestri and Chiàvari doth flow
 A river fair, whose title of renown
 Springs from my race. A month sufficed to show
How heavy the Great Mantle weighs on one
 Who seeks to guard it from the miry street,
 So that all other burdens seem but down.

My own conversion came, ah me! full late;
But, having been created Pastor at Rome,
I grew aware that life is mere deceit.
There for the longing heart I found no home,
Nor in that life a loftier ascent;
So love of this sprang up in me therefrom.
Till then I was a spirit malcontent,
Alien from God, devoted all to gain,
Whence thou beholdest here my punishment.
The effect of avarice is here made plain
In purging of converted souls: upon
The Mountain nowhere is more bitter pain.
Even as our eye was not uplifted yon
To Heaven, but fixed upon the things of earth,
So Justice here has sunk it earthward down.
As avarice quenched our love to all of worth
So that our power of doing good was spent,
So Justice binds us here in utter dearth
Of freedom on this ledge, thus impotent:
So long as please our Father just and good,
So long we stay immobile and distent.'
I had knelt down, and would have fain pursued
The conversation, but he seemed to know
By hearing, of my reverent attitude:
'What cause,' said he, 'has bowed thee downward so?'
And I: 'By reason of your Dignity
My upright conscience urged the posture low.'
'Make straight thy legs; rise, brother!' answered he,
'Err not; because I fellow-service hold
Under one Power with others and with thee.
If thou that holy Gospel word of old
Which saith, "*They neither marry,*" ever weighed,
Why thus I speak thou mayst full well behold.
Now go: I would not have thee longer stayed,
For while thou tarriest my tears I stay,
Whereby I ripen that which thou hast said.

I have a niece there named Alagia,
    Good in herself, if but our family
    By ill example lead her not astray:
And she alone is left to pray for me.'

CANTO XX

Counter to better will strives will in vain:
    Whence I, for his content, with discontent
    Dry from the water drew the sponge again.
I moved, and with my Leader onward went
    Along the cliff through gaps none occupy,
    As by a wall hugging the battlement;
Because that folk distilling through the eye
    The ill wherewith the world is all possessed,
    On the other side too near the margin lie.
Thou old She-Wolf, may curses on thee rest,
    That more than all the other beasts hast prey,
    Because thy hungry maw gapes hollowest!
O Heaven, in whose revolving, people say,
    Conditions are transmuted here below,
    When comes he who shall drive this wolf away?
We went along with paces few and slow,
    And I attentive to the utterance
    Of shadows weeping and lamenting so;
When on in front of us I heard, by chance,
    'O blessed Mary!'—even as makes her moan
    A childing woman; and in continuance,
'What poverty was thine may well be known
    By thy poor entertainment at the inn
    Where thou didst lay thy holy burden down.'
Then: 'Good Fabricius, who wouldest win
    The meed of virtue linked with poor estate,
    Far rather than great opulence with sin!'

*The Founder of a
Great Royal House*

219

These words were of delight to me so great,
    That I pushed on, more knowledge to possess
    Of that soul whence they seemed to emanate.
It went on speaking of the largesses
    Of Nicholas to the girls, their maidenhood
    Thus leading in the path of righteousness.
'O soul abounding in report so good,
    Tell who thou wast, and why alone,' I said,
    'By thee these worthy praises are renewed?
Thy words shall have a meed well merited,
    If I return to finish the brief race
    Of mortal life that tow'rd the end is sped.'
'I'll tell thee, not that I from yonder place
    May hope relief,' he said, 'but since there shoot
    Forth from thee ere thy death such gleams of grace.
I was of that malignant plant the root,
    Shadowing so all Christian lands that they
    Yield niggard harvesting of wholesome fruit.
But ah! if Bruges and Ghent and Lille and Douay
    Were potent, there would light on it swift doom;
    And this of Him who judges all I pray.
I was called there Hugh Capet: from me come
    The Louises and Philips every one
    Who recently in France hold masterdom.
A mere Parisian butcher called me son.
    When ceased the ancient monarchs to exist,
    Save one, betaken unto orders dun,
Then found I tightly clenched within my fist
    The bridle of the realm, with power that goes
    With multitude of friends, and new acquist;
So to the widowed diadem arose
    The head of mine own son; from whom took birth
    The consecrated bones of all of those.
Till the Great Dowry of Provence caused dearth
    Of shame among the kith and kin of me,
    They did no harm, although of little worth.

Began by fraud and by rapacity
   Their rapine then; and after, for amends,
   Took Ponthieu, Normandy, and Gascony.
Charles came to Italy, and, for amends,
   Made Conradin a victim; then a prey
   Of Thomas, thrust to Heaven, for amends.
I see a time, not distant from this day,
   That shall lead forth another Charles from France,
   Both him and his the better to betray.
Unarmed he goes alone, but with the lance
   Wherewith Iscariot jousted, and that same
   Within the bursting paunch of Florence plants.
He thence not any land, but sin and shame
   Shall win, so much the heavier therethrough
   That he the lighter reckons all such blame.
The other, plucked once from his ship, I view
   Vending his daughter in the market place,
   As corsairs with the other bondmaids do.
O Avarice, since thou hast brought my race
   To hold its issue at so cheap a rate,
   What further canst thou do for our disgrace?
That past and future ill appear less great,
   I see the Fleur-de-Lis Alagna gain,
   And in His Vicar Christ incarcerate.
I see how there they mock Him yet again,
   I see the vinegar and gall renew,
   And between living thieves I see Him slain.
I see so pitiless the Pilate new
   That, yet unsated, he without decree
   Into the Temple steers his greedy crew.
When, O my Lord, shall I rejoice to see
   The vengeance that doth in thy counsels hide,
   Calming thine anger in thy secrecy?
What I was saying of that only bride
   Of the Holy Spirit, prompting thee to pray
   Some comment of me, that is still replied

To all our orisons while lasts the day;
    But in the place thereof, when night comes on
    We ring the changes on a counter lay:
We tell the tale then of Pygmalion
    Who traitor, thief, and parricide was made
    By gluttony for gold; and harp upon
Poor Midas, how he covetously prayed,
    And what fulfilment followed to his bane,
    Wherefore men laugh for ever at his greed.
We all record then Achan the insane,
    Who seems, because he took the accursed thing,
    Wrung by the wrath of Joshua again;
Sapphira with her spouse to judgement bring;
    Then praise the hoof-beats Heliodorus bore;
    And Polymnestor's shame doth all enring
The Mountain, for the murdered Polydore;
    Lastly we cry: "Tell us, for thou must know,
    Crassus, the savour of the golden ore!"
Sometimes we speak, one loud, another low,
    According as affection may be spurred
    To make the pace of speaking fast or slow;
Wherefore, if I alone erewhile was heard
    Citing the good whereof we tell by day,
    None else at hand was lifting up the word.'
Departed from him, we had gone our way,
    And on the thoroughfare I spent my breath
    To overcome it far as in me lay,
When now behold! the Mountain shuddereth
    As to its fall; whence over me is driven
    A chill, as over him who goes to death.
Such shock was surely not to Delos given
    Before Latona couched therein, to be
    Delivered there of the twin eyes of Heaven.
Uprose a pæan simultaneously
    Such that toward me drew the Master good,
    Saying: 'Fear not while I am guiding thee.'

'*Glory in the highest to God!*' that multitude
   Chanted, as I from neighbours comprehended,
   Of whom the pæan might be understood.
We listened motionless, with breath suspended,
   Like the poor shepherds first that song perceiving,
   Till ceased the quaking, and the singing ended.
Thereon the holy thoroughfare retrieving,
   We eyed the shades recumbent in that spot
   Who had returned now to their wonted grieving.
Never did ignorance yet feud so hot
   Wage with my passionate desire to know,
   If here my memory be deluded not,
As now in thought seemed battling to and fro:
   Nor yet for hurry any question daring,
   Nor of myself discerning aught there, so
Timid and pensive went I onward faring.

CANTO XXI

The natural thirst unsatisfied for aye
   Save with that water for whose boon was fain
   The lowly woman of Samaria,
Tormented me, and by the encumbered lane,
   Haste goaded me behind my Leader on,
   And I was grieving for that righteous pain;
When lo! in manner even as Luke sets down
   That in the way to twain did Christ appear,
   From the tomb's mouth of late arisen and gone,
A shade appeared and came behind us where
   We were intent the prostrate crowd to view,
   And spoke to us before we were aware,
Saying: 'My brothers, peace be unto you.'
   And Virgil, turning with me suddenly,
   Gave back the word of greeting that is due.

The Poet Statius

'May the true court in peace establish thee
  In council of the blest,' then Virgil said,
  'Though to eternal exile dooming me.'
'How!' said that spirit, while we onward sped,
  'If ye are shades God will on high not deign,
  Who has so far up by His stairway led?'
'But note the marks,' my Teacher said again,
  'Which this man bears as doth the Angel write,
  Well shalt thou see he with the good must reign.
But because she who spins both day and night,
  Drew off not yet his distaff-full of twine
  Which Clotho winds compact for every wight,
The soul of him, thy sister-soul and mine,
  In coming upward, could not come alone,
  Not seeing in the fashion of our eyne.
I, therefore, from wide-throated Hell was drawn
  To show him the way onward, and shall show
  As far as by my school it can be done.
But tell us why the Mountain, if thou know,
  So quaked erewhile, and all appeared to cry
  With one voice, to its wave-washed foot below?'
So questioning, he hit the needle's eye
  Of my desire, and by the hope withal
  My thirst was made less hard to satisfy.
The spirit began: 'There is nothing here at all
  Not subject to the holy ordination
  Of the Mountain, or that is exceptional.
This place is free from every permutation;
  In what from Heaven back to itself doth flow,
  And in naught else, there may be found causation:
For falls not any rain or hail or snow,
  Nor can the dew nor yet can hoarfrost lie
  Above the little triple stairway; no
Clouds ever thicken here nor rarefy,
  Lightning is not, nor Thaumas' daughter fleet
  Who changes region oft in yonder sky;

224

Parched vapour does not overtop the seat
 Of the three steps I touched upon just now,
 Whereon the Vicar of Peter sets his feet.
It trembles more or less, one may allow,
 Beneath; but up here never trembled through
 Wind prisoned in the ground, I know not how.
It trembles when some soul feels pure and true
 For setting forward, freely up aloof
 Ascending, whereupon such shouts pursue.
Of purity the will alone gives proof:
 Quite free for change of cloister, this intent
 Takes by surprise the soul to her behoof.
She first wills well, but divine government
 Sets will against desire, which, as before
 It craved for sinning, craves for punishment.
And I, who have five hundred years and more
 Beneath this torment lain, but now could trace
 Free will for threshold of a better door.
Hence didst thou feel the quake, and spirits of grace
 Didst hear along the Mountain celebrate
 The Lord,—ah! may He send them up apace,'
He said; and since joy is proportionate
 In drinking, with the thirst to be allayed,
 My gain by him I could not say how great.
'I see the net now,' my wise Leader said,
 'That snares you here, and how ye are set free,
 Wherefore it quakes, and whereat glad ye are made.
Now tell me who thou wast, I beg of thee,
 And in thy words I pray thee be it told
 Why thou layest here so many a century.'
'When the good Titus in the time of old,
 Helped by the King Supreme, avenged each wound
 Whence issued forth the blood by Judas sold,
With name most durable and most renowned
 I yonder lived,' that spirit answering said,
 'And passing fame, but not yet faith had found.

So sweet a music from my soul was shed
 That from Toulouse Rome beckoned me away,
 Where I deserved brows myrtle-garlanded.
There people call me Statius to this day:
 Of Thebes I sang, and great Achilles' might,
 But with my second load fell by the way.
The seeds that raised my genius to its height
 Were sparks from that celestial flame shot forth,
 Whence more than a thousand have been set alight:
The *Æneid*, I mean, that mothered me from birth,
 The nurse that suckled me in poesy;
 Without it were I not a drachma worth.
To have lived when Virgil lived, would I agree
 To penance of one sun more than I owe,
 Ere from my place of banishment set free.'
Turned Virgil to me, he discoursing so,
 With 'Be thou silent,' in his tacit glance;
 But there are limits to what will can do:
For tears and laughter are such pursuivants
 Upon the passions out of which they rise,
 That truest will has weakest vigilance.
I could but smile, with meaning in mine eyes;
 Whereat the shadow paused, and looked me straight
 Into the eye, where most expression lies.
'So mayst thou well such labour consummate,'
 He said, 'tell wherefore I but now descried
 A laughter-flash thy face irradiate?'
Now am I caught on this and the other side:
 One bids 'Be still,' and the other 'Speak to me!'
 Whence I was comprehended when I sighed.
'Thou needst,' my Master said, 'not fearful be
 To speak, but tell, and let thy words attest
 What he besought with such anxiety.'
'O ancient soul,' said I, 'thou marvellest
 Perchance, because my smile thou sawest shine;
 But I will move more wonder in thy breast!

This one who guides on high these eyes of mine,
   Is that Virgilius who made thee fit
   To sing concerning men and gods divine.
If else thou deemedst of my smiling, quit
   The untrue suspicion: deem what thou hast said
   To be the veritable cause of it.'
To kiss my Teacher's feet he bent his head;
   'Brother,' the Master urged with tenderness,
   'Do not; thou seest me like thyself a shade.'
Then Statius rising said: 'Now canst thou guess
   The love that warms me to thee, how intense,
   When I can so forget our emptiness,
Treating a shadow as a thing of sense.'

CANTO XXII

Behind us had we left the Angel now   *The Three Poets*
   Who up to the sixth round had turned our quest,   *converse as they*
   Having erased a stigma from my brow;   *walk*
And had announced to us that they are Blest
   Who long for justice in whate'er they do,—
   But saying it with 'thirst' without the rest.
And, lighter than at other passes through,
   Following those swift spirits up above,
   I went without fatigue. Then did renew
Virgil his speaking: 'Worth-enkindled love
   Can kindle in us love reciprocal,
   Its ardour being revealed. In proof whereof,
Among us when descended Juvenal
   Down into the Infernal Limbo, where
   He made thy feeling known to me withal,
Never did man to unseen person bear
   More love than did my heart toward thee bend,
   So that now short to me will seem the stair.

But tell me, and forgive me as a friend
    If I give rein to overconfidence,
    And talk we heart to heart now to the end:
Oh, how could Avarice find residence
    Possibly, in a bosom such as thine,
    Replete with wisdom through thy diligence?'
These words made Statius at first incline
    To smile a little; then replied he thus:
    'Each word of thine to me is Love's dear sign.
Often indeed do things appear to us
    That offer for suspicion grounds deceiving,
    Since their real causes are not obvious.
Thy question proves it to be thy believing
    That Greed in the other life had been my curse
    Perchance because of the round where I was griev-
Know, then, that my offence was the reverse   [ing.
    Of Avarice; my prodigality
    Thousands of courses of the moon amerce.
And if I had not, pondering upon thee,
    Set right my conduct, misdirected first,
    Where thou exclaimst against humanity
Almost in wrath: "To what, unholy thirst
    For gold, dost thou not mortal craving bring?"
    I should be rolling in the tilts accurst.
Then saw I that the hands too wide of wing
    Might be in spending, and repented thence
    Of that and every other evil thing.
Because of ignorance of this offence,
    How many shall arise devoid of hair,
    In life and death bereft of penitence!
And know that sin, in opposition square
    Rebutting other sin, dries up its green
    Together with the opposing trespass there.
Wherefore if I, to purge myself, have been
    With those who weep their Avarice in throngs
    I suffered it for contradictory sin.'

'Now when thou sangest of the cruel wrongs
   Of war that wrought Jocasta's double woe,'
   The Singer said of the Bucolic Songs,
'The chords there touched with Clio do not show
   Thee yet as of that Faith a devotee,
   For want whereof good works are not enow.
What candles or what sun, if so it be,
   So pierced thy darkness that thy sails were spread
   After the Fisher of the eternal sea?'
'Thou first directedst me,' he answering said,
   'Parnassus-ward, to drink upon its height,
   Then on my way to God thy light was shed.
Thou diddest like to him who walks by night,
   Bearing the torch, not for his proper good,
   But to the after-comers giving light,
When saidest thou: "The world is all renewed;
   Justice returns, and man's primeval spring,
   And out of Heaven descends another brood."
Poet was I, then Christian, following
   Thy guidance; but that thou the better view
   My sketch, I set my hand at colouring.
The world by now was teeming with the true
   Religion, by the sowers of the Lord
   Eternal, scattered every country through;
And thy words, touched upon above, concurred
   With the new gospellers in such a wise
   That I became a hearer of the Word.
They came to seem so holy in mine eyes
   Then, when Domitian persecuted sore,
   That tears of mine accompanied their cries;
And while I lingered upon yonder shore
   I succoured them, whose upright manners made
   All other sects seem worthless; and before
I, poetizing, yet the Greeks had led
   Far as the Theban streams, baptized was I;
   But hid my Christian faith, because afraid,

Long while appearing Pagan outwardly;
  And for this lukewarmness I circling went
  The Fourth Round more than the fourth century.
Do therefore thou who madest evident
  That good wherein I find so great reward,
  While we have something left of the ascent,
Tell me where Terence is, our elder bard,
  Cæcilius, Plautus, Varius, if thou know:
  Tell me if these are damned, and in what ward?'
'These, Persius, I, and many another,'—so
  Answered my Guide,— 'are with that Greek con-
  Whom most the Muses suckled long ago,   [fined
In the first girdle of the Prison Blind.
  We often talk about the Mountain where
  Forever haunt the nurses of our kind.
Euripides and Antiphon are there,
  Simonides and Agathon and more
  Grecians who once with laurel decked their hair.
There see we people sung by thee of yore,
  Antigone, Deiphile, Argeia,
  And there Ismene, mournful evermore.
There see we her who pointed out Langeia;
  There is Tiresias' daughter, Thetis there,
  And with her sisters there Deidameia.'
By this time silent both the poets were
  Eager to gaze about them far and wide,
  From the walls liberated, and the stair;
And four of the Day's handmaids now abide
  Behind, the fifth still pointing up the bright
  Horn of the chariot-pole; whereon my Guide:
'Methinks it now behoves us turn the right
  Shoulder toward the outer verge, intent
  To round, as we are wont to do, the height.'
By custom in such manner led, we went
  Our way with the less fear of going wrong,
  Because that noble spirit gave assent.

230

In front they, and alone went I along
    Behind, hearing their words, which gave to me
    Intelligence about the craft of song.
But their kind talk was broken by a tree
    That midway in the road we encountered now,
    With fruitage smelling sweet and gratefully.
As fir-tree tapers upward, bough on bough,
    So this one appeared downward tapering,
    Methinks that none thereon might climbing go.
There where our way was closed, a water spring
    Down from the lofty cliff was falling clear,
    And on the upper foliage scattering.
The poets twain unto the tree drew near,
    Whereon a voice cried out the branches through:
    'Dearth of this viand ye shall have to bear.'
'Mary was more concerned,' it said anew,
    'To grace the wedding feast with plenitude,
    Than for her mouth which now entreats for you.
Of water the old Roman womanhood
    Were satisfied to drink; and Daniel nursed
    Wisdom within him by despising food.
Golden in beauty was the world at first;
    To appetite it made the acorn sweet,
    And every brook like nectar to the thirst.
Honey and locusts were the only meat
    That John the Baptist in the desert knew;
    Whence now he is in glory, and so great
As by the Gospel is revealed to you.'

CANTO XXIII

Because these eyes of mine yet never stirred
   From the green foliage, like such an one
   As wastes his life to hunt the little bird,
My more than Father said to me: 'My son,
   Come on now; for the time assigned had need
   To be allotted for more benison.'
Then turned I face and foot with equal speed
   After those speakers sage, so eloquent
   As made it cost me nothing to proceed.
And hearken! now both singing and lament
   Grown audible: 'Open my lips, O Lord!'
   Such as gave birth to grief and to content.
'O Father dear, what is it I have heard?'
   And he replied: 'Shades going to undo
   The knot, perchance, of debt they have incurred.'
Like pilgrims pensively advancing who,
   When overtaking strangers on the road,
   Will look but will not linger, so here too
Up from behind, devout and silent, strode
   A crowd of souls more swiftly passing on,
   But gazing at us eagerly. They showed
Instead of eyes black caverns; very wan
   Was every visage, and so hunger-pined,
   Over the bone the skin was tightly drawn.
I cannot think that to such utter rind
   Was shrivelled Erysichthon's withered cheek
   By fasting, when it most appalled his mind.
'Behold,' within me did I musing speak,
   'The folk who forfeited Jerusalem,
   When in her child Maria struck her beak.'
Each eyepit seemed a ring without the gem:
   Who OMO reads in face of man, might well
   Here in each countenance make out the M.

Who ever could believe that from the smell
  Of apples or of water there could grow
  Such craving, knowing not how this befell?
I still was wondering what pined them so,
  The cause that rendered them so scurvily
  Withered and meagre being yet to know,
When, look now, from its deep skull cavity
  A spirit made its eye upon me keen,
  Then cried aloud: 'What grace is this to me!'
Never should I have known him by his mien,
  But something lingered in his utterance
  That in his lineament had cancelled been.
This spark enkindled to my inward glance
  Something familiar in his altered look,
  And I recalled Forese's countenance.
'Ah, do not mind,' he prayed, 'the scurf that took
  The fresh complexion of my skin away,
  Nor yet the lack of flesh I have to brook,
But tell me truth of thee, and who are they,
  Yon spirits twain by whom thou'rt hither led?
  Ah, tarry not, speak, speak to me, I pray!'
'Thy face, bewept by me when thou wast dead,
  Gives me for weeping now no lesser rue
  Beholding it disfigured so,' I said.
'By hope of Heaven, then tell what withers you:
  Bid me not speak while marvelling, for ill
  One speaks, by other craving stricken through!'
And he to me: 'By the Eternal Will
  Falls virtue to the water and the plant
  Behind us, that emaciates me still.
All of these people who lamenting chant,
  For being out of measure gluttonous,
  Grow holy here through thirst and hunger gaunt.
Craving for food and drink is stirred in us
  By fragrance from the fruit, and from the spray
  That sprinkles over all the verdure thus.

And not once, as we circle round this way,
 But many times our penance is renewed.
 Penance I say, who solace ought to say:
For to the tree that same solicitude
 Leads us, that led rejoicing Christ to cry
 "Elì", when He redeemed us with His blood.'
'Not yet five years from that day forth,' said I,
 'When for a better world thou tookest flight,
 Forese mine, have until now rolled by.
If sooner ended were in thee the might
 Of sinning, than the hour had supervened
 That weds again to God the heart contrite,
How then art thou arrived up hither, friend?
 I thought to find thee on the slope below,
 Where time doth dissipated time amend.'
'My Nella, with her tears that overflow,
 Hath brought me,' he replied, 'so speedily
 To drink of the sweet wormwood of this woe,
With pious prayers and tears withdrawing me
 Up from the hillside where the people wait,
 And from the other circles setting free.
Dearer to God, and of more estimate,
 My widow whom so well I loved, as there
 She more alone to good is dedicate.
More modest in its dames beyond compare
 Is the Barbagia of Sardinia,
 Than the Barbagia where I left her.
O brother dear, what wilt thou have me say?
 My foresight by a future is possessed,
 When not yet very old shall be this day,
When warning from the pulpit is addressed
 To the unblushing women Florentine,
 Who go about displaying paps and breast.
What Pagan women, aye, or Saracen,
 Have stood in need, to make them covered go,
 Of spiritual or other discipline?

But if these unabashed ones did but know
   What holds in store for them the hastening sky,
   For howling would their jaws be open now;
For if herein my foresight do not lie,
   They will be sad ere yet his cheek have down
   Who now is quieted with lullaby.
Now brother, pray, be more concealment none:
   Look, not I only, but these people all
   Are gazing there where veilest thou the sun.'
Whence I to him: 'If thou to mind recall
   What once to one another were we two,
   The present memory will yet appal.
That one who goes in front of me withdrew
   Me from that life the other day, when round
   The sister of him yonder appeared to you
(I pointed to the sun). Through the profound
   Midnight he led me from the dead apart,
   With this real flesh that after him is bound.
Thence having drawn me, comforts he my heart
   To circle up the Mountain, that again
   Straightens you whom the world had wrenched
He speaks of going with me until when   [athwart.
   I shall be there where will be Beatrice;
   Without him there must I perforce remain.
He Virgil is who sayeth to me this
   (And him I showed); that other shadow, know
   Is he for whom shook every precipice
Recently, when your Kingdom let him go.'

235

CANTO XXIV

Cheerful Abstainers
from Good Cheer

Neither for talking did we lag behind,
    Nor lagged our talk, but stoutly on we went,
    Like vessel urged along by favouring wind.
And shades that seemed by double death forspent,
    Beholding me alive, were all betraying
    Deep in their eyepits their astonishment.
I, going on with what I had been saying,
    Said: 'Peradventure he doth upward go,
    For sake of some one else, with more delaying.
But tell, where is Piccarda, if thou know;
    And mention any in this multitude
    Of note, among those gazing at me so.'
'My sister,—if most beautiful or good
    I know not,—in her crown is triumphing
    On high Olympus in beatitude.'
So said he first, then: 'No forbidden thing
    Is giving names here, so obliterate
    Is our resemblance by the dieting.
This,' pointed he, 'is Bonagiunta, late
    Bonagiunta of Lucca; and further thence,
    That face more than the rest emaciate,
Once used his arms the Holy Church to fence;
    He was from Tours, and atones the Vernage wine,
    And Lake Bolsena's eels, by abstinence.'
And many another name did he assign;
    And all seemed pleased, for not one sombre look,
    Despite the naming, saw these eyes of mine.
There saw I bite the void and hunger brook
    Ubaldin of La Pila, and Boniface
    Who shepherded much people with his crook.
I saw Lord Marquess who of old had space
    For drinking with less dryness at Forlì,
    With craving still unsated ne'ertheless.

PURGATORIO: CANTO XXVII

The Angel inviting Dante to enter the Fire of the Proud

But as he does who scans selectingly,
   So did my choice on him of Lucca fall,
   Who seemed most eager to have speech with me.
I heard him murmur, what I know not all,
   About Gentucca, where he most was wrung
   By Justice that so withers them withal.
'O soul,' said I, 'that seemest so to long
   To speak with me, give pleasure to my ears
   And to thy heart by loosening thy tongue.'
'A maid is born, nor yet the wimple wears,
   Who shall make pleasant to thee,' did he say,
   'My city, whatsoever blame it bears.
With this my presage shalt thou go thy way;
   And did my murmur error in thee move,
   Facts will explain it at some future day.
But tell me, do I speak with him who wove
   The rhymes in the new manner, that begin,
   Ladies who have intelligence of love?'
'I am of those who, when Love breathes within,
   Take note,' I answered, 'and shape heedfully
   My cadences to those he dictates in.'
'O brother mine,' exclaimed he, 'now I see
   What bar held back from the sweet manner new
   Guittone, and the Notary, and me.
I see distinctly how your pens pursue
   The one who dictates, following his bent;
   The which was certainly of ours untrue.
And who most looks to find them different,
   Finds else no choice of one and the other style';
   And holding here his peace, he seemed content.
Even as the birds that winter by the Nile
   Go flocking through the welkin now, then fly
   With quicker wing that they may go in file,
Thus all that multitude of people I
   Saw turn their faces, while their steps they pressed,
   And, light by will and leanness, hastened by.

237

And, as a weary runner lets the rest
   Of his companions go, that he may walk
   Until abate the panting of his chest,
So did Forese let the holy flock
   Pass by, and pausing with me, said: 'When more
   May we thus face to face together talk?'
'I know, not,' said I, 'when my life is o'er,
   Though not so speedily can I arrive
   But that my heart is sooner on the shore;
Because the place where I was made alive,
   From day to day more stripped of goodness is,
   And seems to dismal ruin doomed to drive.'
'Take heart; I see him most to blame for this
   Dragged at a horse's tail along,' said he,
   'Toward the never pardoning abyss.
At each bound goes the beast more rapidly,
   Ever increasing, till it strikes amain
   The body, and leaves it mangled hideously.
Not often shall those wheels revolve again,'
   He raised his eyes to heaven, 'ere is made clear
   To thee, that which my words cannot explain.
Now stay behind, because the time so dear
   Is in this kingdom, that too much I lose
   Going at even pace thus with thee here.'
As sometimes cavalier at gallop goes
   Forth from a troop of horse, to make his worth
   Renowned by first encounter with the foes,
So he with longer strides departed forth;
   And I remained there with those two behind,
   Who were such mighty marshals here on earth.
And when he had passed on so far that blind
   To follow him mine eyes grew, as, I trow,
   To follow on his words had been my mind,
Appeared, with many a laden and living bough,
   Another apple tree, not far away,
   Because my road curved round on it but now.

Beneath were folk with lifted hands, and they
  Cried out toward the leaves, I know not what,
  Like fond and eager little ones who pray,
And that one whom they pray to answers not,
  But holds aloft and does not hide their boon,
  That it may be more longingly besought.
Then, as if disappointed, they were gone:
  So reached we the great tree that doth deny
  So many a tear and many an orison.
'Go your way onward without drawing nigh;
  The tree is higher up whence Eve devoured
  The fruit, and whence this plant was reared on high.'
Thus spoke some one amid the fronds embowered;
  Whence Virgil, Statius, and I, close pressed
  Together, moved along the cliff that towered.
'Recall those cloud-begotten ones unblest,
  Who being drunken,' so it re-began,
  'Strove against Theseus with their double breast;
Those Jews who, drinking, showed some want of man,
  Whence Gideon their company was spurning
  When he went down the hills 'gainst Midian.'
So, close by one of the two margins turning,
  We passed, hearing of sins of gluttony,
  Followed of old by miserable earning.
At large then on the lonely road, we three
  Moved further on a thousand steps or so
  Without a word, all walking pensively.
'Ye three alone, why do ye pensive go?'
  I started when a sudden voice thus said,
  As, startled from repose, shy creatures do.
To see who this might be, I raised my head;
  And never yet in furnace was the hue
  Of glass or metal such a glowing red,
As one I saw who spoke: 'So please it you
  To mount aloft, here must ye turn aside:
  This way goes he who would his peace pursue.'

239

To look on him was sight to me denied:
    Whence turned I in my Teacher's steps to fare,
    Like one who goes with hearing for his guide.
And as, from herbs and flowers, the harbinger
    Of early dawn, the zephyr of the May
    Steals odours that make balmy all the air,
Even such a breeze I felt directly play
    Upon my brow, and felt myself caressed
    By plumage breathing of ambrosia.
And heard proclaimed thereafter: 'They are blest
    Whom Grace so much illumes, that appetite
    Kindles not overmuch within their breast,
Hungering ever in accord with right.'

CANTO XXV

*The Mental
Physiology of the
Shades*

Now since the Sun had left the circle of noon
    To Taurus, and the Night to Scorpio,
    Henceforward the ascent brooked hindrance none.
Wherefore, as people on their journey go
    And tarry not, whate'er beholding, while
    The spur of need is urgent on them; so
Now one by one we entered the defile,
    Taking the stairway where the narrow lane
    Compels the climbers to go single file.
And, like the little stork, for flying fain,
    Lifting its wing, and, daring not to fly
    From off the nest, letting it droop again;
Such, with desire kindled and quenched, was I,
    And nothing further than the movement made
    That will to speak is indicated by.
'Do thou discharge,'—my gentle Father said,
    Forbearing not, although we swiftly went,
    'The bow of speech bent to the arrowhead.'

Then opened I my mouth, made confident,
   Beginning: 'How can there be withering,
   Of bodies with no need of nourishment?'
'Wouldst Meleager's plight to memory bring,
   How by a wasting brand he wasted was,
   This would not seem,' said he, 'so hard a thing;
And wouldst thou call to mind how in the glass
   Tremble your forms whenever tremble ye,
   What seems hard would seem lightly brought
But that thy will be satisfied in thee,   [to pass;
   Lo! here is Statius, whom I call and pray
   That of thy wounds he now the healer be.'
'If here where thou art present I display
   The eternal view,' responded Statius,
   'Be my excuse I cannot say thee nay.
Son, if thou well receive,'—began he thus,
   'And if thy mind consider this my word,
   'Twill make the "How" thou askest, luminous.
Ne'er drunk up by the thirsty veins, but stored
   The purest essence of the blood remains,
   Like viands that thou takest from the board;
And power informing in the heart obtains
   To shape all human organs, being that flood
   Which, to become them, courses through the
Digested still, descends where it is good   [veins;
   To leave unsaid; thereafter trickles thence
   In natural vessel on another's blood,
Where both together have their confluence.
   Passive is one,—but the other active, through
   The perfect place whence pours its influence,
Begins to operate when joined thereto,
   Coagulating, quickening the whole
   That it for shaping to consistence drew.
This active principle, become a soul
   As of a plant (but so far different
   That it half-way and that is at the goal),

Begins to move and to be sentient
  Like the sea fungus, then to organize
  The powers whereof it is the rudiment,
Dilates, my son, and spreads the force that lies
  Within the heart of the begetter now,
  Where Nature would the organs all devise.
But how grow child from animal?—That "How"
  Seest thou not yet; that is the problem great
  Which once misled a wiser man than thou,
Who by his teaching thought to separate
  Soul from potential intellect, for no
  Organ he saw thereto appropriate.
Open thy breast to coming truth, and know
  That when the organizing of the brain
  Has been completed in the embryo,
Toward it turns the Primal Motor then,
  By Nature's so great art made debonair,
  Breathing new spirit full of power to drain
Whatever virtue it finds active there
  Into its substance, and one soul there grows,
  Living, and feeling, and of itself aware.
To make less marvellous what I disclose,
  Consider how the sun's heat becomes wine,
  Joined to the juice that from the vine outflows.
This soul from out the flesh doth disentwine
  Whenever Lachesis hath thread no more
  And latent bears the human and divine:
So voiceless each and every other power;
  But will and memory and intelligence
  Far keener in their working than before.
Incontinent the spirit falls propense
  To one or the other shore in wondrous wise,
  And first takes knowledge of its pathway thence.
Soon as the region round about it lies,
  Virtue informative beams round it there,
  As in the living limbs in shape and size.

And as, when saturate with rain, the air
  By the refraction of the solar rays
  Is decked with variegated colours fair,
Even so upon the circumjacent haze
  A wraithlike form is printed by control
  Of shaping soul that in the region stays;
And as the flamelet's little aureole
  Follows the fire upon its shifting flight,
  So its new form accompanies the soul.
Because thus rendered visible, the sprite
  Is called a shade; and organs of each sense
  Fashions thereafter, even to that of sight.
So thence proceed our words, our laughter thence,
  Thence do we fashion forth the tears and sighs
  Whereof the Mount may give thee evidence.
According as desires within us rise
  Or feeling, takes the shade configurement:
  And this is what occasions thy surprise.'
Now were we come to the last punishment,
  And now toward the right-hand were we starting,
  And were upon another care intent.
There from the cliffside arrowy flames are darting,
  And from the shelf breathes up a blast thereon,
  Hurling them back, a pathway thus disparting;
Whence it was needful to go one by one
  On the open side, so that I felt dismay
  Of burning there, and here of falling down.
'To hold tight rein on the eyes along this way,'
  My Leader said, 'must now be our concern,
  Because for little one might go astray.'
Then from among those flames that hotly burn,
  Came singing: '*God of clemency supreme!*'
  Which filled me with no less desire to turn;
Then saw I spirits walking through the flame:
  Wherefore apportioning my sight I go,
  Now looking to my steps, and now at them.

They cried aloud: '*A man I do not know!*'
    As soon as they had to the end pursued
    That hymn; then recommenced, with voices low.
This done, anew they shouted: 'In the wood
    Diana stayed and banished Helicë,
    For Venus had deflowered her maidenhood.'
Then recommenced the song; then would it be
    The praise of wives and husbands who were pure,
    As virtue bids, and married chastity.
And in like mode, methinks, they must endure
    The while they burn within the fiery blast:
    With diet such as this, with such a cure,
The wound of sin must be healed up at last.

CANTO XXVI

While thus along the border we proceeded
    In single file, my Master kept repeating:
    'Take care, take care! the warning here is needed.'
The sun was now on my right shoulder beating,
    And over all the west a splendour shed
    That blanched the blue; whereon my shadow
The pallid flame made it appear more red; [meeting
    Then saw I many shades such indication
    Take notice of, as through the fire they sped.
This was the cause that gave initiation
    To speech of me; and they began to say:
    'His body does not seem an adumbration!'
Then certain of them, far as in them lay,
    Came nearer me, always with vigilance
    Never to issue from the fiery way.
'O laggard not, but reverent perchance,
    Who followest the others round this slope,
    Answer my burning, thirsting suppliance!

Nor wilt thou anwer only to my hope;
    Since greater thirst for it endure these all
    Than for cool drink Hindoo or Ethiope.
Tell us, how dost thou make thyself a wall
    Against the sun, as wert thou still without
    That passage where the snares of Death befall?'
So hailed me one of them; and I, no doubt,
    Had made me known, but that I was intent
    Upon a novel thing that came about:
For, midway through the burning element,
    Facing this company, a people hied
    Who made me stop to gaze for wonderment.
I saw there hasten up from either side
    Each shade to kiss a shade, for dalliance
    Unresting, with brief greeting satisfied.
So pausing, as their dusky troops advance,
    Emmet encounters emmet, nose to nose,
    Their road and fortune to espy, perchance.
No sooner does the friendly greeting close,
    Or ever the first footstep passes by,
    Strive these to lift up louder cries than those:
'Sodom and Gomorrah!' the newcomers cry;
    The rest: 'Pasiphaë enters the cow,
    So that the bullock to her lust may hie.'
As cranes to the Riphæan mountain brow,
    Might fly in part, part to the sandy plain,
    These shunning frost and those the sun, so now
One people goes and one comes on amain,
    And weeping they return to their first chants
    And to their more appropriate refrain;
And close about me as before advance
    The very same who had entreated me,
    With will to listen in their countenance.
I, who now twice had seen their urgency,
    Began to speak: 'O spirit brotherhood
    Secure of peace, whenever it may be,

These limbs of mine, neither mature nor crude,
  Left I down yonder on the earth behind,
  But bring them here with all their joints and
I go hence up to be no longer blind: [blood.
  A Lady is on high who wins us grace
  Whence through your world I bring my mortal
But so may be your fond desire apace   [rind.
  Fulfilled, so harbour you the heavenly height
  Most ample, which is Love's full dwelling place,
Tell me, that yet on paper I may write,
  Who may ye be and what that multitude
  Behind your backs, and going opposite?'
As stands agaze the mountaineer in mood
  Bewildered, stricken silent and dismayed,
  When come to town in rustic garb and rude,
So did now in its semblance every shade;
  But when they had their wonder well in hand,
  Which soon in lofty hearts is quieted,
Resumed that one who made the first demand:
  'Blessed art thou who, for life's better ending,
  Layest up experience of our border-land!
The folk who come not with us were offending
  In that for which once Cæsar suffered blame,
  Hearing "Regina" with his triumph blending.
Whence in their parting from us, they exclaim
  "Sodom!" as thou hast heard, in self-despite,
  And make the burning hotter with their shame.
Our own transgression was hermaphrodite;
  But since we heeded not the human code,
  Following like the brutes our appetite,
Departing, we, in self-reproachful mode,
  Ourselves pronounce the name of her who so
  Did bestialize herself in beastlike wood.
Our deeds now, how far guilty, knowest thou:
  Wouldst thou, perchance, by name know who we
  There is no time to tell, nor should I know.   [be,

246

I grant, indeed, thy wish concerning me:
　　I'm Guido Guinizelli, purged by fire
　　Through penitence before th' extremity.'
Such as, amid Lycurgus' frenzied ire,
　　Two sons became their mother to regreet,
　　Such became I, but do not so aspire,
When I heard name himself that father, meet
　　For me and other men my betters, who
　　Ever used gracious rhymes of love and sweet;
And, hearing not, did I my way pursue
　　Long while with pensive gaze and nothing said,
　　But for the fire no nearer there I drew.
Thereafter, when of gazing fully fed,
　　I offered myself all to do him grace
　　With such an oath as makes one credited.
And he to me: 'Thy words have left a trace
　　Upon my spirit charactered so clear
　　That Lethë cannot dim it nor efface.
But if it be a true avouch I hear,
　　What is the cause of thy avowal, pray,
　　By word and look that thou dost hold me dear?'
And I to him: 'Your every dulcet lay,
　　Which, if our modern use endure so long,
　　Will render dear their very ink for aye.'
'He yonder, brother,' back to me he flung
　　With finger pointing to a spirit before,
　　'Was a better shaper of his mother tongue.
In love-rhymes and romantic tales of yore
　　Surpassed he all, and let fools prate who view
　　Him of Limoges as the superior.
They hold by rumour more than by the true,
　　And in that way their fixed opinion mould,
　　Ere art or reason have been listened to.
Thus with Guittone many did of old,
　　Basing his praise upon *they say, they say*,
　　Until at length with most the truth controlled.

247

Now if thou have such charter that the way
   Into that cloister is vouchsafed to thee
   Where Christ is abbot of the college, pray
A Paternoster unto him for me,
   As far as profits here the orison
   Where power to sin no more for us may be.'
Then peradventure to give place to one
   Who followed close, he vanished in the burning
   As fish through water to the bottom run.
I went a little on, to that one turning
   Who had been shown me, saying, if I knew
   His name it would be solace to my yearning.
And he of free accord replied thereto:
   'Your courteous request delights me so
   I can not, will not hide away from you.
I am Arnaut who weep and singing go;
   Contritely I see past folly, and I see
   Rejoicingly the hoped-for morning glow.
I pray you now by that Divinity
   Who guides you to the summit of the stair,
   Keep at due time my pain in memory.'
Then hid he in the fire that makes them fair.

CANTO XXVII

---

*The Will of the
Pilgrim of Eternity
is Purified*

As when the earliest rays of dawning quiver
   Where shed His blood the Maker of the light,
   High Libra lamping over Ebro-river,
And Ganges-wave at noontide burning bright,
   So hung the sun; and day being nearly o'er,
   Appeared to us God's Angel benedight.
Standing without the flame upon the shore,
   He sang: *'Blest they who pure in heart abide!'*
   In voice melodious, than ours far more.

Then: 'No one farther goes, souls sanctified,
  Unbitten by the fire; be thither sped,
  Not deaf to chanting from the farther side.'
As we drew nearer to him, this he said:
  Whence I became, to hear a thing so dire,
  Like one within the fosse deposited.
Clasping my hands and gazing at the fire
  I forward bent, recalling vividly
  Bodies of men once seen upon the pyre.
My kindly Leaders now turned round to me,
  And Virgil spoke as follows: 'Son of mine,
  Here may be torment, not mortality.
Recall, recall! when layest thou supine
  On Geryon's shoulders, still I safely led;
  And how then now, more near to the Divine?
What though a thousand years within the bed
  Of this same fire thou didst abide, believe
  It could not hurt a hair upon thy head.
And if perchance thou deem that I deceive,
  Draw nigh it, and with proper hands assay
  Upon the border of thy garments. Give
Fear to the wind,—put every doubt away;
  Turn hither and come forward, safe withal.'
  Yet against conscience did I rooted stay.
Seeing me rooted, stubborn to his call,
  He said, perturbed a little: 'Look now, son,
  'Twixt Beatrice and thee remains this wall.'
As the eyes of Pyramus, when death drew on,
  Opened at Thisbe's name, upon her dwelling
  While the mulberry became vermilion,
So did I turn, my stubborn fear dispelling,
  To my wise Leader, by the name beguiled
  That in my memory is ever welling.
Whereon he shook his head at me, and smiled:
  'What, would we tarry here?'—as when we win
  With proffered apple an unwilling child.

Then in advance of me he entered in
   The fire, entreating Statius to come last,
   Who for a long way back had been between.
When I was in, I would have gladly cast
   Myself in molten glass for solacement,
   So beyond measure was the burning blast.
To comfort me, my kindly Father went
   Ever discoursing but of Beatrice,
   Saying: 'Her eyes seem now upon us bent.'
Beyond, a voice was singing, and by this
   Conducted, and to this attentive quite,
   We issued forth where mounts the precipice.
'Come, all ye of my Father benedight!'
   Rang out within a light there manifest
   So that I could not look, it was so bright.
'Night comes,' it added, 'and goes the sun to rest;
   Then quicken up your pace and do not stay,
   While yet not wholly darkened is the west.'
Straight upward through the rock mounted the way,
   Directed so that I, before me there,
   Cut off the sinking sun's last level ray.
And both I and my Sages grew aware
   Of sunset, by my shadow vanished thence,
   When we had made brief trial of the stair.
And ere within one dim circumference
   The wide horizon mingled sea and shore,
   And Night held sway with all her influence,
Each of us on a stair was bedded; for
   The mountain-law deprived us of the will
   And of the power of there ascending more.
Just as, while ruminating, goats grow still,
   However bold and nimble they had run
   Over the heights before they browsed their fill,
Hushed in the shade while blazes hot the sun,
   Watched by the herdsman leaning on his rod,
   Who, leaning thus, attends them every one;

And as the shepherd, stretched upon the sod,
 Watches by night his quiet flock beside,
 That no wild beast may scatter it abroad:
Even so did we at such an hour abide,
 I like the goat, they shepherdlike, all three
 Hemmed in by lofty rock on either side.
Little without could there be seen by me;
 But in that little saw I more intense
 The stars, and larger than their wont to be.
So musing and so gazing, somnolence
 Fell on me, such as oftentimes before
 They come about, gives tidings of events.
That hour, I think, when through the eastern door
 First on the mountain Cytherea beams,
 Who fired with love seems burning evermore,
A Lady young and fair I saw, in dreams,
 Who through a meadow land appeared to go
 Gathering flowers, and singing said, meseems:
'If any ask my name, then let him know
 That I am Leah, and I move alway
 Fair hands to wreathe myself a garland so.
Here at my glass I joy in my array;
 But never does my sister Rachel rise
 Up from her mirror where she sits all day.
She yearns to look in her own lovely eyes,
 As I to deck me with my hands am yearning:
 Her, seeing, and me, doing satisfies.'
Through splendours of the dawn already burning
 (That rise to pilgrim hearts so much more sweet
 As less remote their hostel, home returning),
The shades of night were now departing fleet;
 And slumber having with them fled away,
 I rose, seeing my great Masters on their feet.
'That sweet fruit which, through many a branching
 Ye mortals go seeking with little ease, [spray,
 Shall set at peace thy hungerings to-day.'

Virgil began to me in words like these,
    And never were there guerdons that could cope
    With suchlike rapture-giving largesses.
Such longing upon longing for the slope
    Came over me, at every step I could
    Perceive my wings becoming fledged with hope.
When all the stairs were traversed, and we stood
    Upon the uppermost, did Virgil turn
    His eyes on me with wistful fatherhood;
'Son, thou hast looked upon the fire eterne
    And temporal, and comest to a place
    Where, of myself, no further I discern.
I brought thee here by intellect and grace;
    Henceforth let thy good pleasure guide thy going:
    Thou art beyond the steep, the narrow ways.
Look how the sun is on thy forehead glowing,
    Look at the grass, the tender shrubs, the bloom
    That here the soil is willingly bestowing.
Until the lovely eyes rejoicing come,
    Which weeping made me come to lead thee thence,
    Here canst thou sit and canst among them roam.
Await no more my word or influence:
    Upright is now thy will, and sound, and free,
    And wrong to disobey its bidding: whence
Lord of Thyself I crown and mitre thee!'

CANTO XXVIII

Now eager for exploring the divine
    Evergreen forest dense, that screened the day,
    So newly-risen, for these eyes of mine,
I leave the Mountain-brow without more stay,
    And slowly, slowly through the plain advance,
    That everywhere breathes fragrance of the May.

PURGATORIO: CANTO XXVII

Dante at the moment of entering the Fire

A soft air, subject to no variance,
   Continually stroked me on the brow
   As lightly as when gentle zephyr fans;
And tremblingly responsive, every bough
   Was bending all its foliage what way
   The Holy Mount cast the first shadow now;
Yet did they not so violently sway
   That any little bird on topmost limb
   Was fain forsake the practice of his lay,
But might, while chanting the full joy in him,
   Welcome the breath of morn the leaves among,
   That ever bore a burden to his hymn:
From bough to bough goes gathering such song
   Through the pine forest on Chiassi's shore,
   When forth by Æolus Scirocco is flung.
So far already through the woodland hoar
   My lingering feet had borne me, that I knew
   Where I had entered into it, no more;
When lo! a brooklet cut my pathway through,
   Rippling along toward my left, and bending
   The grasses that along the margin grew.
All waters here in purity transcending,
   Would seem commingled in comparison
   With that, whose limpid wave conceals no blending,
Although it darkly, very darkly run
   Beneath perpetual shade, unpenetrated
   Ever by radiance of moon or sun.
My footsteps tarried, but mine eyes elated
   Passed to alight beyond the rivulet
   On the fresh May profusely variegated;
And there appeared (as when a thing is met
   All of a sudden, leading thought to stray
   For the great wonder, and all else forget)
A Lady, who went her solitary way
   Singing and culling flower from flower, whereof
   The colouring made all her pathway gay.

I said: 'Pray, Lady fair, in rays of love
   Basking, if I may credit looks that still
   Are wont the pledges of the heart to prove,
Draw forward hither, if it be thy will,
   Toward the margin of this brooklet borne,
   That I may understand thy canticle.
Thou bringest back Proserpina, the morn,
   The dewy meadow where she forfeited
   The spring, and left her mother all forlorn.'
As turns upon the floor with even tread
   A lady in the dance who hardly sets
   Foot before foot, even so above the bed
Of scarlet and of yellow flowerets,
   She turned to me with maidlike innocence
   And drooping eyes, and to the rivulet's
Border approaching, did so recompense
   My praying, that the dulcet melody
   Was borne to me, together with the sense.
When she was where the grass begins to be
   Bathed by the ripples of the beauteous river,
   She raised the guerdon of her eyes on me.
I think there glowed so bright a lustre never
   Beneath the lids of Venus, by her son
   Empierced with dart from his unwilling quiver.
She smiled, erect upon the margin yon,
   With fair hands trailing many a colour pied
   Of flowers upon that highland never sown.
We were parted by a stream three paces wide;
   But Hellespont where Xerxes passed,—a spot
   To this day curbing every human pride,—
Never more hatred in Leander wrought,
   Because 'twixt Sestos and Abydos swelling,
   Than this in me since then it opened not.
'Ye are newcomers,' she began her telling,
   'And so my smiling in this place elect
   For human nature as a native dwelling,

Perchance awakens in you some suspect;
   But the Psalm *Delectasti* sheds a ray
   Of light that may discloud your intellect.
And thou in front, who didst entreat me, say,
   Wouldst thou hear more?—By thy solicitude
   Prompted, I came to do it quite away.'
'The water,' said I, 'and the murmuring wood
   Impugn within me new belief, thereto
   In contradiction, as I understood.'
Whence she: 'How from their proper cause ensue
   The things occasioning thy wonderment,
   Will I declare and purge thy inward view.
The Good Supreme, sole in itself content,
   Created man for good, and peace eterne
   Pledged him by giving him this tenement.
Here, by his fault, short while did he sojourn;
   By his own fault, to travail and to woe
   Did innocent joy and pleasant pastime turn.
That the disturbances produced below
   By exhalations of the land and sea
   (That after heat, as far as may be, go)
Might wage no war upon humanity,
   Rose heavenward up so high this Mountain here,
   And is above the guarded gateway free.
Now since, in circuit with the primal sphere,
   The universal air is rolling round,
   While it remains unbroken anywhere,
This motion strikes the summit, disembound
   In living ether all, and makes the dense
   Forest, being a thicket, to resound.
Within the smitten plant has residence
   Power to impregn the breeze, and this henceforth,
   In whirling, sheds abroad that influence.
Conceived and childed so on yonder earth
   Are various trees of virtue various,
   According as its clime and soil have worth.

Rightly considering the matter thus,
That without visible seed some plants take root
In yonder earth, should not seem marvellous.
And thou must know that where thou setst thy foot
The holy upland every seed contains,
And never yonder can ye pluck such fruit.
The water that thou seest wells not from veins
Which vapours, by the cold condensed, restore,
Like river that now loses breath, now gains,
But from a fountain constant evermore;
And Will Divine replenishes that source
By all that forth its double rivers pour.
On this side, it flows downward with the force
That takes man's memory of sin away:
The other, that of all good done, restores.
It is called Lethë here, as Eunoë
On the other side, nor doth the working speed
Till of the taste of both ye make assay:
This every other savour doth exceed.
Now, though thy thirst may be so satisfied
That of more telling there be little need,
A corollary will I grant beside,
Nor deem I the less dear to thee my granting,
If it beyond the pact be amplified.
Who anciently the golden age were chanting,
And its felicity, about this place
Dreamed peradventure, while Parnassus haunting.
Here without guile took root the human race;
Here is all fruitage, here the prime unbroken;
This is the nectar they unite to praise.'
Then looking to my Poets for a token,
I noted how with smiling mien they brooked
The parable that lastly had been spoken;
Then to the Lady fair again I looked.

PURGATORIO: CANTO XXVII
Dante and Statius sleeping, Virgil watching

CANTO XXIX

The Lady, in the manner of a lover,
    Resumed her singing, when her words were done:
    'Blessed are they whose sins are covered over.'
And as the nymphs were wont to go alone
    Among the woodland shadows, with endeavour
    Some to behold, some to avoid the sun,
She moved then up along the little river,
    Following the bank, and I with her abreast,
    Brief paces with brief paces matching ever.
Between us not a hundred steps were paced,
    When both alike the margins made a bend,
    So that toward the east again I faced.
Nor yet, so going, had we far to wend
    Before the Lady fully turned about
    Toward me, saying: 'Look, brother, and attend.'
And lo! a sudden lustre ran throughout
    Every quarter of the forest vast,
    So that of lightning I was put in doubt.
But since the lightning, as it comes, is past,
    And this still brightened more and more the wood,
    I said within me: 'What may this forecast?'
Then did a melody delightful flood
    The illumined air, whence holy ardour made
    Me fain to reprobate Eve's hardihood;
For there, where both the Earth and Heaven obeyed,
    The woman only, and but just created,
    Would underneath not any veil be stayed;
Whereunder, had she but devoutly waited,
    So should I that ineffable content
    Have sooner had, and had it unabated.
While I amid so many first-fruits went,
    Of the eternal joy, and all upstrung,
    And evermore on greater joyance bent,

In front of us, the verdant boughs among,
　　The air as if by fire enkindled grew,
　　And the sweet sound was now perceived as song.
O holy Virgins! now did I for you
　　Hunger or cold or vigils never shun,
　　Need goads me to implore the guerdon due.
Pour forth for me thy waters, Helicon,
　　Urania sustain me with thy chorus,
　　To put in rhyme things hard to think upon!
The wide tract of the middle distance bore us
　　The show of seven trees of gold, not far
　　Beyond, in false presentment there before us;
But when so near approached to them we are,
　　That common traits which lead the senses wrong
　　Forfeit by distance no particular,
The force that makes discourse of reason strong
　　Perceived at length that candlesticks were they,
　　And heard 'Hosanna' in voices of the song.
Aloft was flaming now the fair array,
　　Far brighter than the Moon who lamps the skies
　　At midnight in her monthly course midway.
Thereon I turned about with wild surmise
　　To the good Virgil, who thereto replied
　　With like amazement in his startled eyes.
Thence turning back my vision, I descried
　　Those high things moving on to us so slow
　　They would have been outstripped by the new
The Lady chided me: 'Why yearning so　　[bride.
　　Only to gaze upon each living light,
　　That what comes after them thou dost forgo?'
Then, as behind their leaders, came to sight
　　A people in white raiment,—never seen
　　Was here upon the earth so pure a white.
The water on my left was full of sheen,
　　Reflecting back the left-hand side of me
　　As in a mirror, when I looked therein.

When I had gained such place upon the lea
  That separated me the brook alone,
  I stayed my steps, the better thus to see,
And saw the flamelets forward move, a zone
  Of coloured air behind them leaving, so
  That they appeared by brush of painter drawn;
And thus the air above remained aglow
  With seven stripes, containing every hue
  Of Delia's girdle and Apollo's bow.
These pennons farther than my range of view
  Were streaming rearward; by my estimate
  Ten steps asunder were the outer two.
Under so fair a sky as I relate,
  By two and two came Elders twenty-four,
  Their brows with flower-de-luce incoronate.
They all were singing: 'Blessed thou before
  The daughters all of Adam; blessed be
  Thy loveliness for ever and evermore.'
Now when no more the chosen company
  Footed the flowers and tender herbage seen
  Upon the margin opposite to me,
As follows light on light in the serene
  Heaven, came after them four living things,
  Each one incoronate with frondage green.
Every one was feathered with six wings
  Studded with eyes; the eyes of Argus thus,
  If living, might be full of visionings.
I lavish no more verses to discuss
  Their form, O Reader! other charges bind
  So, that perforce I am penurious.
But read Ezekiel, and call to mind
  How he beheld them from the quarter cold
  With cloud approaching, and with fire and wind;
As thou shalt find it in his pages told,
  Such were they,—save as to their pinions, John
  Varies from him, and with the saint I hold.

Within the space among those four came on,
　　Triumphal, rolling on two wheels, a Wain
　　That forward by a Gryphon's neck was drawn.
Up he extended both his wings between
　　The middle striping and the three and three,
　　That none took hurt from being cleft amain.
How high they rose no human eye could see;
　　Where he is bird his limbs of gold are wrought,
　　The others white, but mingled ruddily.
With car so beautiful Rome honoured not
　　Or Scipio or even Augustus,—nay,
　　Poor were the Sun's to such a chariot,
The chariot of the Sun which, driven astray,
　　Was burnt at Earth's devoted orison,
　　When Jove was just in his mysterious way.
At the right wheel, in dance came whirling on
　　Three ladies: one of such a ruddy glow
　　As haply in the fire were seen of none;
Such flesh and frame the second one did show
　　As out of emerald she had been made;
　　The third appeared like freshly fallen snow.
Now by the white appeared they to be led,
　　Now by the ruddy lady, by whose lay
　　The others timed their swift or tardy tread.
Beside the left wheel four made holiday
　　In purple raiment, following as guide
　　One in whose head three eyes looked every way.
Behind all those described thus, I descried
　　Two aged men clad with a difference,
　　But like in bearing grave and dignified.
One seemed adept in the experiments
　　Of high Hippocrates, whom Nature made
　　For th' animals she holds in preference;
The other, who was carrying a blade
　　Gleaming and sharp, showed care so opposite
　　That, though this side the stream, I was afraid.

Thereafter saw I four of humble plight;
  And behind all an aged man alone
  Walking in trance, but yet acute of sight.
These seven, like the company first shown,
  Were habited in white; yet not like those
  Around the forehead wore a lily crown,
But rather flowers of crimson, and the rose:
  Onlooker would have sworn, if near them not,
  That they were all aflame above their brows.
When over against me was the Chariot,
  Thunder was heard; whereby that worthy band
  Was interdicted further march, methought,
There with the vanward ensigns brought to stand.

CANTO XXX

When the Septentrion of highest Heaven
  That set or rising never knew, nor pall
  Of any cloud save that of sin, had given
To every creature there processional
  Such due direction as is ever sought
  From that below by homing pilots all,—
When that stood still, the people true of thought
  First come 'twixt Gryphon and Septentrion,
  As to their peace turned to the Chariot.
'Come with me, with me, Bride, from Lebanon,'
  Did one, like messenger from Heaven, cry thrice
  Singing, and so the others every one.
As shall the blest at the last trumpet rise,
  Every one lightly from his hallow urn
  With *Hallelujah* on revestured voice,
So on the Car Divine did I discern
  A hundred at such Elder's call upstand,
  Angels and ministers of life eterne.

*The Reproaches
of Beatrice*

261

'*Blessed be thou that comest!*' cried that band,
  Filling the air with flowers along the way,
'*O give ye lilies all with liberal hand!*'
As I have often seen at break of day
  The eastern region of the sky all rose,
  With the other heaven in limpid fair array,
And the new sun, shadowed with mist, disclose
  A face so temperate these eyes of ours
  Could long endure the radiance it throws;
So in the bosom of a cloud of flowers
  Flung in the air and drifting to the ground
  From the angelic hands in blossom showers,
In veil of white, with olive fillet crowned,
  Appeared to me a Lady in mantle green,
  With colour of living flame invested round.
And to my spirit that so long had been
  Out of her presence, which did ever move
  Me to stand trembling and abashed of mien,
Virtue descending through her from above
  Attested, without witness of the eye,
  The great tenacity of early love.
No sooner smote my sight the virtue high
  Which had already pierced me through the breast
  Before my early boyhood had gone by,
Than to the left as trustfully I pressed
  As to the mother does the child, distraught
  By terror or by grief, to manifest
To Virgil: 'In my pulses beats no jot
  Of blood that does not quiver; I perceive
  The early flame beneath the ashes hot.'
But gone was Virgil, leaving me to grieve,
  Virgil, to me a father passing dear,
  Virgil from whom salvation I retrieve,
Nor all that lost our ancient mother here
  Availed to keep my cheeks, though cleansed with
  From being stained again with many a tear. [dew,

262

'Dante, because Virgilius withdrew,
  Do not weep yet, not yet a-weeping fall:
  Another sword has yet to pierce thee through.'
As stands at stern or prow an admiral
  To inspect the service, and to cheer the men
  Upon the other ships to prowess all,
At the left margin of the chariot,—when
  I turned about on hearing mine own name
  Which here indeed I cannot choose but pen,—
I saw the Lady, she before who came
  Veiled underneath the angelic festival,
  Direct her eyes to me across the stream.
Though, circled with Minerva's coronal,
  The ample veil descending from her head
  Gave forth but faint glimpse of her form, withal
Austerely, and with queenly bearing dread
  Continued she, as who in saying this
  Still left the hottest utterance unsaid:
'Look at us well, we are, we are Beatrice;
  How didst thou deign to come unto the Mount?
  Knewest thou not that man is here in bliss?'
Mine eyes fell down into the limpid fount,
  But seeing myself reflected, did I turn
  Back to the lawn again with bashful front.
As to the child appears the mother stern,
  So she appeared to me; for bitter food
  Is pity, and tart in flavour, though it yearn.
She held her peace, and the angel multitude
  Chanted: '*In Thee, Lord, do I put my trust,*'
  But beyond '*set my feet*' did not conclude.
As, on the back of Italy, the gust
  Slavonic doth the living rafters sheathe
  With drifted snow soon frozen to a crust,
Which melts and trickles down if only breathe
  The land where shrink the shadows, and appears
  Like wax that liquefies the flame beneath,—

So I remained with neither sighs nor tears
  Before the song of them who chanting go
  After the notes of the eternal spheres.
But when I heard their tuneful pity flow
  More sweetly than as if it were expressed:
  'Lady, why dost thou break his spirit so?'
The ice that was about my heart compressed,
  To breath and water changing, gushed forth hot
  Through lips and eyes with anguish from my breast.
Still from the same side of the Chariot,
  Turned she to that compassionate array
  Her words, her attitude yet moving not:
'Ye keep your watch through the eternal day
  So that nor night nor slumber robs from you
  One step the world may walk along its way;
Thus to my answer greater heed is due
  That yonder weeper understand me, whence
  Of equal measure may be guilt and rue.
By work not only of the wheels immense
  Guiding all seeds toward their destined places
  According as the stars reign influence,
But by the guerdon of celestial graces,
  Which have so lofty vapours for their showers
  That nevermore our sight their fountain traces,
Such, virtually, was this friend of ours
  In his new life, that issue marvellous
  Was to be looked for from his native powers.
But all the wilder and more mischievous
  Is an unweeded garden grown to seed,
  The more the soil is rank and vigorous.
Whiles I sustained him with my face indeed,
  The light of my young eyes upon him turning;
  And tow'rd right issues followed he my lead.
When I had crossed my second threshold, spurning
  That earthly life, the heavenly to inherit,
  Then he forsook me for another yearning.

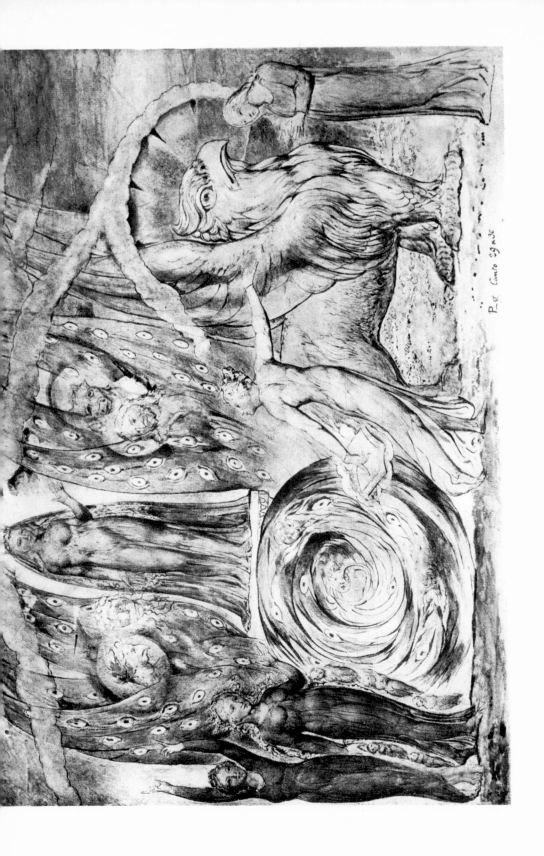

P.o Canto 29.30

PURGATORIO: CANTOS XXIX & XXX

Beatrice addressing Dante from the Car

So, when arisen out of flesh to spirit,
    Waxing in beauty and in worth, I grew
    Less precious to his mind, and of less merit;
And his feet wandered by a way not true
    After false images of good, pursuing
    Promises unredeemed with payment due.
To summon him away from his undoing,
    The invocation of no dream or vision
    Availed to me,—so little was he ruing.
He fell so low, no means for the remission
    Of sin in him yet in my power was lying,
    Save showing him the people of perdition.
For this I gained the portal of the dying,
    And to that one who led him here were spoken
    My supplications mingled with my sighing.
High fiat of the Almighty would be broken
    Were he to traverse Lethë without scoring
    Due payment of such viand, certain token
Of deep repentance with hot tears outpouring.'

CANTO XXXI

'O thou who art yon side the sacred river,'   *Dante's Bitter*
    Aiming her speech at me by thrust, that through   *Confession*
    The cutting edge alone had made me quiver,
Pursuing without truce began she anew,—
    'To such a heavy charge is requisite
    Thine own confession: speak, speak, is it true?'
So great the perturbation of my wit,
    Though my tongue moved, it was with such delay
    That first my voice had died away on it.
Granting short shrift, she urged: 'What dost thou say?
    Answer me, for the memories that gnaw
    Are not yet by the water purged away.'

Together intermingled shame and awe
    Constrained my lips to shape forth such a 'Yes'
    As could be heard only by her who saw.
As crossbow, tightened up with too great stress,
    Is shattered when the arrow forth is flung,
    Which strengthless from the target falls, no less
Was I beneath this heavy charge unstrung,
    Pouring forth tears and sighs, and so undone
    The faltering voice was slow upon my tongue.
'In thy desires of me that led thee on
    To love the Good Supreme,' then did she say,
    'Beyond which aspiration there is none,
What thwarting trenches or what cables lay
    Across the avenue of thy advance,
    That thou hadst need to strip thy hope away?
And what allurements in the countenance
    Of others, or what advantage didst thou spy
    That thou shouldst linger for their dalliance?'
After the heaving of a bitter sigh
    My lips for utterance were almost sealed
    And with great effort shaped out a reply.
Weeping I murmured: 'Present things that yield
    Fallacious joy, allured my steps aside
    Soon as your countenance became concealed.'
And she: 'Hadst thou been silent, or denied
    What is confessed, the record would allege
    Thy guilt no less, by such a Judge descried.
But when the sinner's scarlet cheeks are pledge
    Of self-accusal, in our Court and Fane
    The grindstone is whirled back to blunt the edge.
Howbeit, in order that thou now sustain
    Shame for thy fault, and be of stouter soul
    When thou shalt hear the Sirens sing again,
Awhile the sowing of thy tears control,
    And hearken how my flesh when laid away
    Ought to have led thee to the counter-goal.

Never did Nature, never Art convey
  Such rapture to thee as those features fair
  That held me, and are scattered in decay,
And if my dying left thy soul so bare
  Of joy supreme, what mortal hankerings
  Ought ever have allured to baser care?
At the first shaft of perishable things
  Thou oughtest truly to have soared aloof
  With me from such concern; nor should thy wings
Have been weighed downward to abide the proof
  Of further strokes, whether of dainty maid
  Or other vanity of brief behoof.
For two or three the fledgeling may be stayed,
  But in the sight of the full-plumaged bird
  Vainly the bolt is sped or net is laid.'
As children stand abashed without a word,
  But listening with eyes upon the ground,
  Conscious and sorry for the fault incurred,
So stood I; and she said: 'Since thou hast found
  Pain in the hearing, lift thy beard,—thou must
  Receive, by looking, yet more grievous wound.'
With less reluctance is an oak robust
  Wrenched up by gale that scours across the sprays
  From Libia, or stricken by our Alpine gust,
Than did I at her word my chin upraise;
  And when by 'beard' invited to the viewing,
  Full well I felt the venom of the phrase.
And my uplifted eyes, their gaze renewing,
  Plainly distinguished those primordial creatures
  How they were pausing from their blossom-strewing;
And these mine eyes, as yet uncertain teachers,
  Showed Beatrice turned to the Animal
  That is one single Person in two natures.
Beneath her veil, beyond the stream withal,
  She seemed beyond her ancient self to go
  More than outwent she here the others all.

CANTO XXXI
49-84

The nettle of remorse there pricked me so
    That what once most with love seductive drew
    Now most of all things seemed to be my foe.
Such self-conviction gnawed my conscience through,
    I fell undone; what then upon me passed,
    That knows she best who gave me cause thereto.
When heart revived my outward sense at last,
    Appeared the Lady whom I had found alone,
    Above, me saying: 'Hold fast to me, hold fast!'
Me throat-high in the river had she drawn,
    And, haling me behind her, was she light
    As any shuttle o'er the water gone.
When I drew nigh the margin benedight,
    'Purge me', so sweetly did I hear the sound,
    Remember it I cannot, much less write.
The Lady fair then put her arms around
    My head, and plunged me under, so embraced,
    Till fain to drink the water; then she crowned
The whole by leading me, thus rendered chaste,
    Into the dance of the four Ladies fair
    Who each with guardian arm my shoulder graced.
'Here we are nymphs, and stars in Heaven: or ere
    Beatrice had descended to the earth,
    We were ordained as handmaidens to her.
We lead thee to her eyes; but by the worth
    Of yonder three who gaze with deeper quest,
    Thine will be sharpened for their lustrous mirth.'
So first they sang; then to the Gryphon's breast
    Led me along with them; and at that spot
    Toward us turned, was Beatrice at rest.
'Be vigilant to spare thy gazing not:
    We have stationed thee before the emeralds, whence
    Love formerly his arrows at thee shot.'
Thronging desires, beyond all flame intense,
    Fixed mine upon those shining eyes, whose gaze
    Was fastened on the Gryphon's lineaments.

PURGATORIO: CANTO XXXII

The Harlot and the Giant

As back from mirror flash the solar rays,
    The twofold Animal therein was glowing
    Now in the one, now in the other phase.
Think, Reader, of the wonder on me growing,
    The thing, itself so tranquil to my sight,
    Mutation in its image undergoing!
While full of awe, amazement, and delight,
    My soul was breaking fast upon the food
    That both contents and quickens appetite,
The other Three came forth, their attitude
    In dancing their angelic roundelay
    Approving them to be of nobler brood.
'Turn, Beatrice, O turn,' so ran their lay,
    'Thy holy eyes upon thy servant leal
    Who moved his steps to thee from far away.
Of thy grace to us, graciously reveal
    Thy smile to him, so that he may discern
    The second beauty which thou dost conceal.'
O splendour of the living light eterne,
    What dreaming poet ever has so paled
    In shadow of Parnassus, or at its urn
So drunken, that his heart would not have failed
    Endeavouring to render thee, how fair,
    Beneath the harmony of heaven unveiled
When opening thy beauty to the air?

CANTO XXXII

So steadfast and attentive was my eye
    To satisfy my thirst decennial,
    All other sense did in abeyance lie;
And so her holy smiling made me fall
    In the old toils, that my indifference
    Inclosed me on every side as with a wall;

*Allegory of the
Evil Days of the
Church*

When force perforce my sight was shifted thence
   Tow'rd my left hand by those Divinities,
   Because I heard from them a 'Too intense!'
And that condition of the sight, which is
   In eyes but lately smitten by the sun,
   Cancelled awhile my vision after this.
But when my sight was for the less rewon
   (The less compared with that superior
   Splendour from which perforce I had withdrawn),
Turned on the right flank face about, once more
   The glorious army stood to me revealed
   With sun and with the seven flames before.
As changes front, 'neath cover of the shield,
   A squadron with the standard, while yet not
   The body of the army can have wheeled,
The knighthood of the heavenly realm that brought
   The van up, all had wheeled and passed us by
   Ere the front beam had turned the Chariot.
Back to the wheels did then the damsels hie,
   Whereat the Gryphon moved his blessèd charge
   So that no feather of him shook thereby.
The Lady fair who drew me to the marge,
   And Statius and I were following all
   Behind the wheel that curved with arc less large;
And thus, while passing through the forest tall,
   Void by her fault who pledged the Snake amiss,
   Our feet to angel music timed their fall.
Three flights might carry along as far as this
   An arrow, haply, loosened from the string:
   At such remove alighted Beatrice.
I heard them one and all there murmuring
   'Adam!'—then circled they about a tree
   Bare on each bough of bloom and burgeoning.
Its foliage, which spreads accordingly
   As it is towering upward, would for height
   To Indians in their woods a marvel be.

'Blest art thou Gryphon, that thou dost not smite
  With beak this tree that to the taste is sweet,
  For anguish follows on such appetite.'
So round the sturdy tree the rest repeat;
  Whereat the Animal of natures two:
  'Thus to fulfil all justice it is meet.'
And, turning to the wagon-pole, he drew
  It up beneath the widowed trunk,—whereon
  That which came from it left he bound thereto.
Even as, when falls the great light of the sun
  Downward, commingled with that radiance far
  Which beams behind the heavenly Carp, anon
Burgeon our trees, and each its singular
  Colour renews, before the sun has set
  Yoke on his coursers under other star:
So did the tree, of fronds so naked yet,
  Revive and open out into a hue
  Less than of rose and more than violet.
What hymn that throng then sang, I never knew,—
  A matter not intoned in human chants,—
  Nor could I bear the melody all through.
O could I picture sinking into trance
  Those cruel eyes, of Syrinx hearing tell,
  Those eyes that paid so dear long vigilance,
Into what drowsihood hereon I fell,
  Like painter from the life would I portray:
  Who would, must know to image slumber well.
Whence pass I to my waking, and I say
  A dazzling splendour rent the veil from me
  Of slumber, and a calling: 'Rise, why stay?'
As, to see blossoms of the apple tree
  That makes the angels eager to be fed,
  And marriage feasts in Heaven eternally,
Peter and James and John were upward led,
  And, overcome, recovered at the word
  Of Him who broke the slumbers of the dead,

And saw their band to what it was restored
   By loss of Moses and Elias too,
   And changed again the raiment of the Lord:
So I recovered, and so did I view
   Above me standing that compassionate Guide,
   Who my first steps along the river drew.
'And where is Beatrice?'—perplexed I cried;
   'Sitting beneath the foliage freshly sprung,
   Upon its root behold her,' she replied.
'Behold around her the companion throng;
   The others with the Gryphon upward speeding,
   Singing a sweeter and a deeper song.'
And if she spoke more words than the preceding
   I know not, so mine eyes were fixed upon
   Her who had shut me off from other heeding.
Alone upon the bare earth sat she down,
   Left there as warder of the Chariot
   I saw made fast by Creature two-in-one.
The seven nymphs a ring around her wrought,
   And in their hands the seven lampads lay
   That Aquilo and Auster extinguish not.
'Here art thou forester but a brief day,
   And of that Rome where Christ is Roman, then
   Shalt thou a burgess with me be for aye:
Whence, for the benefit of erring men,
   Observe the Car, and what thou canst descry,
   Having returned to earth, take heed to pen.'
So Beatrice commanded, and so I,
   To very foot of her commands devote,
   Whither she willed gave all my mind and eye.
Never with fall so swift the lightning smote
   Out of a heavy cloud-bank, when it showers
   Down from that bourn which stretches most remote,
As now beheld I through the leafy bowers
   Swoop down the bird of Jupiter amain,
   Rending the bark and the fresh leaves and flowers,

Thereon with all his might smiting the Wain;
   Whereat it reeled, like ship storm-buffeted,
   Wave-tossed to starboard and to port again.
I saw a vixen glide with stealthy tread
   Quite into the triumphal Car thereon,
   And she appeared with wholesome food unfed.
But for so foul a fault, with malison,
   My Lady put her to such flight as bore
   The fleshless framework of her skeleton.
Then, by the course that he had come before,
   I saw the eagle swoop into the ark
   Of the Chariot, and leave it feathered o'er.
And out of Heaven a voice of sighing, hark!
   Such sighs as from a grieving bosom steal:
   'How badly art thou fraught, my little bark!'
Thereon the earth seemed cleft 'twixt wheel and wheel,
   And thence I saw a dragon issuing,
   That upward through the Chariot thrust his tail;
And like the wasp withdrawing forth the sting,
   He with malignant tail drew forth amain
   Part of the floor, and went off wandering.
As fertile soil takes grass, the rest again
   Took on the plumage, given to satisfy
   Intent perchance benevolent and sane,
And both the wheels were overrun thereby
   So quickly, and the chariot pole o'errun,
   The lips are longer parted with a sigh.
The holy structure, thus transformed, anon
   Heads over all its different portions bore,
   Three on the pole, at every corner one.
The three were horned like bullocks, but the four
   With single horn had each the forehead crowned:
   Monster like this was never seen before.
Secure as citadel on lofty mound,
   Sitting upon the Car appeared to me
   A wanton whore, darting her oglings round.

And, as her warder, lest she taken be,
    Was standing at her side a giant brute,
    And now and then their kissing did I see.
But since her roving eye and dissolute
    Was turned on me, that savage paramour
    Did scourge her from her head unto her foot.
Then jealously and fierce with anger, tore
    The Monster loose, and dragged so far withal
    That with the forest shielded he the whore
From me, and shielded the strange Animal.

CANTO XXXIII

*The Poet made
pure for the Ascent
to the Stars*

'O God, the heathen are come,' alternately
    The ladies, now the three and now the four,
    Weeping, began the dulcet psalmody;
And Beatrice, all compassionate, forbore
    Nowise to sigh, and heard them with such look
    That Mary at the Cross changed little more.
But when the other virgins song forsook
    To let her speak, now upright on her feet,
    With face the colour of fire, thus she spoke:
'A little while and me ye shall not meet;
    And yet a little while,' again she said,
    'And ye shall look upon me, sisters sweet.'
Then sent she all the seven on, and made
    To follow after, merely by a sign,
    Me and the Lady and the Sage who stayed.
So went she, and had taken, I opine,
    Scarcely ten paces, through the woodland faring,
    When with her piercing eyes she smote on mine:
'Approach,' commanded she, sedate of bearing,
    'In order that, if I discourse with thee,
    Thou mayst remain within an easy hearing.'

274

When I was with her, as I ought to be,
  'Brother,' said she, 'why art thou diffident
  To question, seeing that thou walkst with me?'
As befalls people over-reverent
  In speaking in the presence of the great,
  When, ere it reach the lip, the voice is spent,
So I, inapt for sound articulate,
  Began: 'You know, my Lady, what beseems
  To me, because you know my poor estate.'
'I would not have thee henceforth by extremes
  Of fear and shame,' she answered, 'made to quail,
  Nor would I have thee speak like one in dreams.
Know that the vessel rent by dragon-tail,
  Was and is not: but be the guilty aware
  That Divine Vengeance fears no coat of mail.
Not always shall remain without an heir
  The Eagle that emplumed the Chariot, whence
  It grew a monster and then a prey: I bear
Sure witness, and foretell an influence
  Of stars already close at hand to give
  An era free from all impediments,
Wherein One, a Five-hundred Ten and Five,
  God-sent, shall with the harlot do to death
  That giant who doth now with her connive.
Perchance in cloudy talk I waste my breath,
  Like Sphinx and Themis, unpersuasive thus,
  Since in their mode the mind it darkeneth;
But fact erelong will be the Œdipus
  Of this enigma, the hard knot untying,
  Nor be to fold or field injurious.
Mark thou: and even as I am prophesying,
  So do thou teach to those who run the race
  Of life, which is a hastening to dying;
And bear in mind, when thou the writing trace,
  Not to conceal how thou hast seen undone
  The Plant, that twice was pillaged in this place.

Whoever robs or rends it, malison
  Of very deed upon High God is casting,
  Who hallowed it to purpose of His own.
For tasting it, in pain and longing wasting
  Five thousand years and more, the first soul sighed
  For Him who punished on Himself that tasting.
Thy wit must slumber, having not descried
  How for a special reason passing high
  Rises the Tree, and has the top so wide.
And did thy vain conceits not petrify
  Like Elsa water round thy mind, were not
  Their joy a Pyramus to the mulberry,
So many circumstances would have taught
  The justice of the interdict Divine
  Upon the Tree, symbolically wrought.
But though I see that intellect of thine
  Grown stony, and so windowless and blind
  To radiance wherewith my teachings shine,
Yet, if unwritten, painted on the mind,
  Pray bear them, by what token palmers do
  Their staves with frondage of the palm entwined.'
And I: 'As to the seal the wax is true,
  Holding the form and pressure evermore,
  So is my memory now stamped by you.
But why do your desirèd words outsoar
  The utmost pinion of my sight, that so
  I fail of them, the more I strive therefor?'
'It is,' she said, 'to enable thee to know
  The school that thou hast followed,—to display
  How lamely it can follow where I go;
And that thou mayst perceive your human way
  As far from the Divine, as is remote
  From Earth the Heaven that highest speeds away.'
Whereat I answered her: 'I have forgot
  That ever I estranged myself from you;
  And qualms of conscience for it have I not.'

'And if it has been blotted from thy view,
   Now recollect,' her smiling answer went,
   'How thou hast drunk of Lethë but anew;
So that, if smoke of fire is argument,
   Thus to forget affords clear evidence
   Of guilt in thy desire elsewhere intent.
Be that as may, my oracles from hence
   Shall be unveiled, far as to show their faces
   May be appropriate to thy rude sense.'
More brilliant now and with more lingering paces
   The sun along the noonday circle drew,
   That shifts as viewed from this or other places,
When halted (even as halts a person who
   As guide to travellers goes on before,
   Finding new thing or trace of something new)
The seven ladies by a shadowy shore:
   Green foliage and glooming branches throw
   Such shadow over mountain torrents frore.
In front, methought I saw Euphrates flow
   And Tigris, from a single starting-place,
   And separate, like friends at parting slow.
'O light, O glory of the human race!
   What flood is this that gushes here away
   Out of one fount, and separates apace?'
To such a prayer reply was made me: 'Pray
   Matilda that she tell.' As one who scatters
   Suspicion of some fault imputed: 'Nay,'
Said the fair Lady,—'this and other matters
   Were told him by myself, and sure am I
   They were not hid from him by Lethë waters.'
And Beatrice: 'Perchance some care more high,
   Which often renders inward vision dim,
   May have bereft him of his memory.
But lo! where Eunoë doth overbrim;
   Lead him to it, and in thy wonted fashion
   Cause fainting virtue to revive in him.'

CANTO XXXIII
130/145

Like gentle soul who does not make evasion
   But lets another's will her will subdue
   Obedient to outward indication,
So, taking me, the lovely Lady drew
   Nearer the water, and with womanly grace
   Invited Statius: 'Come with him, too.'
If, Reader, I had only ampler space
   For writing I would sing, at least in part,
   The sweet draught never cloying: in this case
Since full are all the pages set apart
   For the Second Cantica, my further going
   Is here arrested by the curb of art.
From the most holy flood for ever flowing
   Did I return renewed, as new plants are
   When foliage is new and blossoms blowing,
Pure and prepared to mount from star to star.

PARADISO

E 'n la sua volontate è nostra pace.

PARADISO III. 85

CANTO I

The glory of Him who moves the universe
  Doth penetrate the whole, and shine intense
  In different regions in degrees diverse.
That Heaven partaking most His effluence
  I entered into, things therein discerning
  None knows, nor can report, descending thence;
Because in drawing near to its own yearning
  The intellect is gulfed in such a sea
  That for the memory is no returning.
Yet whatsoever in my memory
  I could entreasure of the Kingdom blest
  Henceforth the matter of my song shall be.
O good Apollo, for the final quest
  Make me such vessel of thy worth as thou
  For the loved laurel-gift requirest!
One summit of Parnassus until now
  Sufficed me, but henceforth the twain beneath
  Into the last arena must I go.
Into my bosom enter thou, and breathe
  As when thou didst pluck Marsyas amain
  And from the scabbard of his limbs unsheathe!
Virtue Divine! if thou wilt lend me a strain
  To manifest the blessèd realm above,
  Whose shadowy signature is in my brain,
Shalt see me pluck the laurel of thy love
  And crown me with those leaves, which this my
  Matter and thou shalt make me worthy of. [higher
So seldom do we gather of them, Sire,
  For Poet's triumph or for Emperor
  (The fault and shame that spring from man's desire),
That the Peneian frond should breed the more
  Joy in the joyous Delphic deity
  When it makes any one athirst therefor.

From tiny spark flame follows hot and high:
    After me better voices shall perchance
    Lift up such prayer that Cyrrha may reply.
Through different entrances to mortal glance
    The world's lamp rises, but from out that station
    Where join three crosses with four circling bands
With a better course, with a better constellation
    It comes conjoined, sealing with stamp more clear
    And tempering mundane wax more to its fashion.
This gate had almost made it evening here
    And morning yonder; all was there aglow
    While darkness overcast our hemisphere,
When, turned about toward the left hand, lo!
    Beatrice who was gazing on the sun:
    Never did eagle fasten on it so.
And just as ever from the former one
    Issues a second ray and upward flies,
    Like pilgrim turning homeward, journey done,
So did her act, informing through the eyes
    Mine own imagination, give me grace
    To eye the sun beyond our wonted wise.
Much is permitted yonder, in this place
    Prohibited our powers, thanks to the spot
    Fashioned expressly for the human race.
Not long did I endure this, and yet not
    So little but I saw it sparkling nigh,
    As iron from the fire pours boiling hot;
And of a sudden day to day thereby
    Seemed to be added, as if He who can
    Had with another sun adorned the sky.
Fixed where the everlasting circles ran
    Were the rapt eyes of Beatrice, and mine
    Withdrawn from heaven were turned her own
Gazing at her I grew within divine   [to scan.
    As Glaucus did, tasting the herb, and thence
    Peer of the other gods beneath the brine.

No word 'transhumanizing' represents:
   The example then to him sufficient be
   Whom Grace reserves for like experience.
If I was merely what most recently
   Thou madest, Love, who governest the skies,
   Thou knowest, who with Thy light upliftedst me.
Now when the Wheel Thou dost eternalize
   By being desired, made me on it intent
   By music Thou dost tune and harmonize,
So kindled seemed to me the firmament
   By the sun's rays, that never rain nor stream
   Flowed over into a lake of such extent.
The newness of the sound and the great gleam
   Kindled my wish their causes to assign
   To poignant longing never so extreme.
Whence she who could my question well divine,
   The perturbation of my mind to lull,
   Parted her lips and took the word from mine,
Beginning thus: 'How dost thou make thee dull
   With false imagination, not perceiving
   What thou wouldst see wert thou less fanciful.
Thou art not on the earth, though so believing;
   But lightning from its proper home ne'er flew
   Such flight as thou, thy proper home retrieving.'
If disentangled from my first doubt through
   Such little words as these, more smiled than phrased,
   The more was I enmeshed within a new;
'Already I had ceased to be amazed,'
   Said I, 'but am again with wonder filled
   How through these lightsome bodies I am raised.'
Whence Beatrice, with a sigh of pity mild,
   Bending her eyes upon me with such glance
   As a mother casts on her delirious child,
Began: 'All things soever have ordinance
   Among themselves; here is the form displayed
   Which makes the world like God's own countenance.

Herein the exalted creatures see the tread
    Of the Eternal Worth, which is the goal
    Whereto the aforesaid rule is fashionèd.
The ordinance I speak of doth control
    All natures, which through fates of different sorts
    Neighbour, both near and far, their Primal Soul;
Wherefore they shape their course to different ports
    Of the vast sea of being, each with boon
    Of instinct that informs it and supports.
This bears aloft the fire toward the moon,
    This power doth mortal hearts forever move,
    This bind the earth together and attune.
Not merely things created empty of
    Intelligence, this mighty crossbow hurls,
    But those endowed with intellect and love.
The Providence that shapes all ends, enfurls
    That heaven in dateless quiet with its light,
    Within which what has greatest hurry, whirls;
And thither now, as to appointed site,
    Bears us along the vigour of that cord
    Which aims at happy mark its arrow-flight.
True is it that, as form does not accord
    At all times with the artisan's intent,
    The stuff being deaf to the creative word,
Even so the creature from the way it went,
    Though thus impelled, possesses power of turning
    Away sometimes, to follow other bent
(Just as one may behold the lightning burning
    Down from the cloud), if the prime thrust be quite
    Earthward diverted by deceptive yearning.
Thou shouldst not wonder more, deem I aright,
    At thy ascent, than if a brooklet be
    Plunged to the bottom from a mountain-height.
As great a marvel it would be in thee,
    Unhindered, to be seated on the plain,
    As in live fire on earth tranquillity.'
Thereon she turned her face to heaven again.

PARADISO: CANTO XIV
Dante adoring Christ

CANTO II

O ye who in your little bark till now,
   Eager for listening, have made your way
   Behind my vessel with the singing prow,
Turn to your native shore while yet ye may:
   Do not put out to sea, lest haply there
   By losing me, ye should remain astray.
None ever coursed the water where I fare:
   Minerva breathes, Apollo pilots me,
   And all nine Muses point me to the Bear.
Ye other few, with neck stretched yearningly
   For bread of angels whereon ye are fain
   To live while here, nor ever sated be,
Your ship may well put out upon the main,
   Following close upon my wake before
   The salt-sea water returns smooth again.
Those glorious ones at Colchis who of yore
   Saw Jason made a ploughman, no such burning
   Amazement felt, that ye shall not feel more.
The concreate and everlasting yearning
   For the Realm Deiform bore us well-nigh
   As swiftly as moves heaven to your discerning.
I gazed on Beatrice, and she on high:
   And in such time perchance as crossbow shot
   Alights and is unloosened and let fly,
I found myself arrived where sight was caught
   Compulsively by something marvellous:
   Whence, since my doing could be hidden not
From her, she faced me, blithe as beauteous:
   'Lift up thy grateful mind to God!' she said,
   'Who with the prime star has united us.'
Around us there appeared to me to spread
   A cloud smooth, dense, consolidate, and bright
   Like diamond whereon the sun is shed.

*Heaven of the
Moon*

285

Into the pearl of everlasting white
   We glided, even as water though unstirred
   Is penetrated by a ray of light.
If I was body (on earth it seems absurd
   That one bulk brook another, as must be
   If body into body glide!) more spurred
Should be the longing of our hearts to see
   That Essence where we shall behold the plan
   Of our own nature blent with Deity.
There shall be seen what now by faith we scan,
   Not proved, but primal truth self-evident
   And by direct cognition held by man.
I answered: 'Lady, with devout intent
   I render thanks to Him who did ordain
   That from the mortal world I should be sent.
But tell me, what those dusky marks which stain
   This body, whereby on earth below the while
   People are prone to fable about Cain?'
'And if,' she answered with a little smile,
   'Where key of sense effects no opening
   Mortal opinion may so far beguile,
Surely the shafts of wonder should not sting
   Thee longer, since even following the sense
   Thou seest that reason has too short a wing.
But tell me, what is thine own inference?'
   And I: 'Methinks what here seems different
   Is brought about by bodies rare and dense.'
'Well shalt thou see what credence thou hast lent
   To error,' she answered, 'giving heed unto
   What I adduce in counter-argument.
The Eighth sphere shows forth many a light to you
   Which in their quantity and in their kind
   May be observed from different points of view.
If only rare and dense herein combined,
   One single virtue in all were absolute,
   Now more, now less, now equally assigned.

But Virtue different must needs be fruit
  Of fundamental forms, and these, save one,
  Thy reasoning would pluck up by the root.
Besides, if rarity produced that dun
  Thou mootest, would this planet through and
  Be perforated, leaving matter none,   [through
Or otherwise, as fleshly bodies do
  The fat and lean apportion, so would this
  Alternate leaves within its book renew.
Supposing true the first hypothesis,
  The sunlight in eclipse would be descried
  Right through, as through whatever orifice.
This false, consider we the other side,
  And if I chance to find an error there
  Then thy opinion will be falsified.
Now if this rareness find no thoroughfare,
  There needs must be some limit hindering
  The counter-penetration of the rare;
Thence will the ray of other body spring
  Reverberated backward, in such kind
  As back from leaded glass comes colouring.
But thou wilt say that here appears more blind
  The radiance than in regions othersome,
  From being reflected further from behind.
Such an objection may be overcome
  Experimentally, if thou wouldst try
  That fountain of all human masterdom.
Take mirrors three, and two of them set by
  At equal distance, and between the twain
  The other further off, before thine eye.
Turning toward them, let a light remain
  Behind thy back, kindling the mirrors three
  And smitten by them all to thee again.
Whereas the further light will seem to thee
  Less ample as to size, yet will it show
  An equal lustre, of necessity.

Now, even as the ground beneath the snow
    Is stripped of previous colour and of cold
    Beneath the beating of the warm rays, so
Thy mind, being stripped of error fold on fold,
    Will I inform with light so crystalline
    That it shall quiver now thou canst behold.
Within the Heaven that harbours Peace Divine
    Circles a body in whose virtue lies
    The being of whatever it enshrine.
The following heaven, which has so many eyes,
    Imparts that form through various types, and these
    Distinct from it, which yet it doth comprise.
The other spheres in different degrees
    Dispose of their distinctive elements
    According to their seeds and purposes.
Thou seest these universal instruments
    Thus drawing from above, while raining down
    From grade to lower grade their influence.
Look at me finding passage for thine own
    Arrival at the truth thou art fain to scan,
    And know henceforth to keep the ford alone!
The breath of blessèd Movers needs must fan
    Motion and influence of holy sphere,
    As craft of hammer moves by artisan.
And that same Heaven the many lights make fair,
    From the Deep Mind that gives it whirl and thrust
    So takes the image and so seals it there.
And as the soul within your human dust
    Makes different members work in unison,
    Distributed through each in measure just,
So doth the Mind deploy its benison
    Multiplied through the starry firmament,
    But turns upon Itself, remaining One.
Each different power makes mixture different
    With precious body rendered quick thereby,
    Wherewith, like life within you, it is blent.

By glad endowment of the Nature High,
   This mingled virtue through the body glows,
   As gladness lights the pupil of the eye.
From this proceeds whatever difference shows
   'Twixt light & light, & not from rare & dense:
   This is the intrinsic principle whence flows
The dark and bright, as by its excellence.'

CANTO III

The sun that erst with love had warmed my breast
   Had now the fair sweet face of truth, by proof
   And refutation, rendered manifest;
And to confess, so far as was behoof,
   Myself corrected thus and confident,
   My head for speech was lifted more aloof.
But something gleamed on me, whence so intent
   To gaze thereon my baffled vision grew,
   That my confession out of memory went.
As through transparent polished glass, or through
   Still and pellucid waters, of too mean
   A depth to have the bottom lost to view,
Come back the contours of our faces, seen
   So pallidly that pearl on forehead white
   Is caught as quickly if the eye is keen,—
Such faces, fain for speaking, came to sight;
   Whence I in counter-error fell thereby
   To what befell the fount-enamoured wight.
The instant that aware of them was I,—
   Reflected images by my surmise,—
   To see of whom they were, I turned mine eye;
But, seeing nothing, went with my surprise
   Straight to the light of her, my Leader sweet,
   Whence smiling kindled in her holy eyes.

Spirits of Women
in the Lunar
Heaven

She said: 'No wonder if with smiles I meet
 This exhibition of thy childish mind
 Unwilling yet to truth to trust its feet,
But turns thee back in vain, after its kind.
 True substances are what thou dost perceive,
 Here for some forfeiture of vows assigned.
Whence talk with them, and listen, and believe;
 For that which gives them peace, the one true Fire,
 Suffers their feet its purlieu not to leave.'
And to that shade who seemed most to require
 Question with me, began I, tow'rd it bended
 Like one bewildered by too great desire:
'O spirit born to bliss, with radiance blended
 Of life eterne in sweet felicity
 That, tasted not, is never comprehended,
Thou wilt be gracious to content in me
 The craving for thy name, and for your lot.'
 Whereon with smiling eyes and promptly, she:
'To just desire our charity doth not
 Deny the door, more than His love doth so
 Who wills His Court all in His image wrought.
I was a virgin sister there below;
 And if thou recollect, it will appear
 That greater beauty doth not hide me: know
I am Piccarda, relegated here
 Together with these others who are blest,
 And myself blessèd in the slowest sphere.
All our affections, kindled as may best
 Conform to pleasure of the Holy Spirit,
 Rejoice being fashioned after His behest.
And this low-seeming lot that we inherit
 Is given to us because we did our vow
 Make in some manner void, or did defer it.'
'Your wondrous faces shine, I know not how,'
 Was my reply, 'with some diviner grace,
 Transmuting them from what we knew ere now;

Whence was my memory of laggard pace;
    But what thou tellest helps me to make clear
    Thy features which now better I retrace.
Tell me: ye whose felicity is here,
    Do ye desire a dwelling-place above
    To grow in vision or to God more dear?'
Her flitting smile lit up the faces of
    Those others; then she spoke so blithesomely
    She seemed to kindle with first fire of love:
'Brother, the influence of charity
    Contents our will, alone solicitous
    For what we have,—no craving else have we.
Did we desire a place more glorious,
    Then our desires would be at variance
    With will of Him who here assigneth us;
These circles have no room for dissonance,
    As thou shalt see, for herein love is fate,
    If thou behold its nature not askance.
Nay, 'tis the essence of this blessèd state
    To dwell within the Will Divine alone,
    Whereby our wills with His participate.
So that throughout this realm, from zone to zone,
    We pleasure the whole realm without surcease,
    And please the King who inwills us with His Own;
And in His Will is our eternal peace;
    And everything is moving to that sea,—
    All it creates as nature gives increase.'
Then only was the truth made clear to me
    That everywhere in Heaven is Paradise
    Where Grace Supreme rains not in one degree.
But, as will happen, should one food entice,
    Other than that wherewith we have been fed,
    Grateful for that, we crave for this: precise
The parallel to what I did and said,
    Seeking to learn what web it was whereof
    She had not drawn the shuttle to the head.

'Life perfect and high worth enheaven above,'
  She said thereto, 'a Lady among the blest,
  Under whose rule in your world women love
To robe and veil, till death to watch and rest
  Beside that Spouse, accepter and rewarder
  Of vows which love conforms to His request.
To follow her, of maiden weeds discarder,
  Fleeing the world and in her habit dressing,
  I pledged me to the pathway of her Order.
Thereafter men more used to ban than blessing
  Ravished me from the cloister sweet: God knoweth
  What my life then, without mine own confessing.
This other splendour on my right who showeth
  Her beauty to thee, luminously burning
  With all the light that in our circle gloweth,
Takes to herself these words myself concerning:
  A sister she, and so from her was riven
  The veil by hands its holy shadow spurning.
But when she back into the world was driven
  Despite her wish and wont legitimate,
  She never from her heart the veil had given.
This is the radiance of Constance great,
  Who to the Second Blast of Swabia
  Bore the Third Puissance, and ultimate.'
So spake she, and in chant began to say
  Ave Maria, and chanting from me stole
  As through deep water sinks a weight away.
My vision, straining to pursue that soul
  To the utmost, when she vanished into bliss,
  Turned to the mark of a more longed-for goal,
Reverting wholly round to Beatrice;
  But such a lightning flashed she on my look
  That first my sight endured it not; and this
So gave me pause that question I forsook.

CANTO IV

Between two foods alike to appetite
  And like in distance, a free man, I suppose,
  Would starve before of either he would bite;
So would a lamb, between the hungry throes
  Of two fierce wolves, feel equipoise of dread,
  So hesitate a hound between two does.
Whence by my doubts alike solicited
  Inevitably, censure can be none
  Nor commendation, if I nothing said.
And I said nothing; but desire upon
  My face was pictured, questioning as well,
  Set forth more fervently than words had done.
Like Daniel when he did the miracle,—
  Nebuchadnezzar from the anger turning
  That first had rendered him unjustly fell,—
So Beatrice did, and said: 'I see one yearning
  And the other draw thee so, that eagerness
  Ties up thy tongue to breathe no dear concerning.
Thou urgest: "By what justice can duress
  Imposed by others, if persist good will,
  Render the measure of my merit less?"
Perplexes thee another question still:
  "Do souls rejoin the stars, as it would seem,
  And the idea of Plato thus fulfil?"
These questions balance equally the beam
  Of thy desire; and therefore I incline
  To treat that first whose venom is extreme.
Not he of Seraphim the most Divine,
  Not Moses, Samuel, and either John
  Thou mayest choose to take, not Mary in fine,
Do hold their seats in any other zone
  Of Heaven than those thou didst but now discern,
  Nor more nor fewer years of being own.

All make the Primal Circle fair, and earn
   Life of sweet bliss in different measure here,
   Through feeling more or less the breath eterne.
Not as allotted here did they appear
   Within this heaven, but as a sign intending
   The least exalted though celestial sphere.
My words perforce unto your wit are bending,
   Which grasps but by perception of the sense
   What then it worthy makes for comprehending.
The Holy Scriptures, condescending hence
   To your conceit, with foot and hand endue
   The Deity, with mystic difference;
And Holy Church so represents to you
   Michael and Gabriel with human traits,
   And the other who gave Tobit health anew.
That which Timæus of the soul debates
   Is different from that seen here by far,
   For seemingly he thinks it as he states.
He says the soul returns to its own star,
   Whence nature actuated its descent,
   Giving it in the flesh an avatar.
And in his doctrine haply more is meant
   Than meets the ear, and may have sense whereto
   Befits it not to be irreverent.
If, for the influence they rain on you,
   He means these wheels may blamed or honoured
   Perchance his arrow hits a target true.   [be,
This principle, perverted, formerly
   Led almost the entire world astray
   In naming Jove and Mars and Mercury.
The other dubitance that gives thee stay
   Empoisons less, for its malicious thrust
   Could never put thee from myself away.
That our high justice should appear unjust
   In eyes of mortals, is an argument
   Of faith, not of heretical distrust.

But since ye, humanly intelligent,
   Can pierce into this truth, as thou dost choose
   I undertake to render thee content.
If violence be when he who bears abuse
   Has nothing to the wrong contributed,
   These souls could claim on that score no excuse:
For will, unwilling, never can be dead,
   But doth as nature doeth in the fire,
   Which by a thousand gusts is buffeted.
For, little or much as it may yield, desire
   Abets the violence: and these did thus,
   Free to their sanctuary to retire.
Had but their will been whole and vigorous,
   Like that which fastened Lawrence to his grill
   And ruthless to his hand made Mucius,
Then up the road whence they were dragged, their will
   Would have impelled them, soon as they were free;
   But all too rare is will so inflexible.
And by these words, if thou hast duteously
   Gathered them up, is quashed the argument
   That would yet many a time have troubled thee.
But now another cross-entanglement
   Puzzles thine eyes, wherethrough thou couldst not
   An issue by thyself, until forspent.   [find
I have for certain put into thy mind
   That never could speak false a soul in bliss,
   Since to the source of truth forever joined;
Then mayst have understood Piccarda amiss
   That Constance to the veil was ever true:
   So that she seems to contradict me in this.
Many a time, my brother, urged thereto
   By hope of scaping peril, under stress,
   Men have done what they ought not, would not do;
Even as Alcmæon,—who by prayer express
   Of his own sire, his mother life refused,—
   Not to lose piety, grew pitiless.

Think, pray, when come to this, that force is fused
   With will together, and so the two are blent
   That the offences cannot be excused.
Will absolute doth not to ill consent:
   Consenting just so far as it may rue,
   If it resist, some greater detriment.
Therefore Piccarda, saying what is true,
   Means absolute volition; I, however,
   The other,—whence in truth agree we two.'
Such was the rippling of the holy river
   Out of the fountain whence all truth flows over,
   Setting at rest both my desires forever.
'Divine one, O belov'd of the First Lover,'
   I straightway said, 'whose words are in me burning
   And flooding till I life on life recover,
Not deep enough the channel of my yearning
   For thanks of mine coequal with your favour:
   May He requite who can and is discerning!
I see our mind unsated still with savour
   Of any truth, till of that truth aware
   Beyond which is no light that doth not waver.
Therein it rests, like animal in lair
   When it attaineth; and it can attain,
   Else frustrate every craving for it were.
Whence like a shoot doubt ever springs again
   At foot of truth; and so from height to height
   Doth nature urge us summitward amain.
This doth assurance give me, this invite
   To ask with reverence of another theme,
   O Lady, wherein truth is dark to sight.
Fain would I know if man may ever dream
   With good to so amend vows forfeited,
   They shall not in your balance kick the beam.'
Beatrice gazed at me with eyes that sped
   Flashes of love, divine of radiance,
   So that my vanquished force of vision fled,
And all but lost was I, with bended glance.

CANTO V

'If in the warmth of love on thee I beam
   So beyond earthly mode as must defeat
   The valour of thine eyes, be this no theme
For wonder, since it issues from complete
   Vision divine, which in the Good whereof
   It has attained perception, moves its feet.
I see how shines already from above
   Into thine intellect the Eternal Light
   That needs but to be seen to kindle love;
And if some other thing your love delight,
   Naught is it but some vestige of that same
   Effulgence, comprehended not aright.
Thou askest whether men for vows they maim
   May pay such other service as to gain
   Exemption of the soul from any claim?'
So Beatrice began this further strain;
   And even as one discoursing, who would not
   Break off, took up the holy theme again:
'The gift most precious to Creative Thought,
   Most signal of God's bounties, and the one
   After the pattern of his goodness wrought,
Was Freedom of the Will,—a benison
   Wherewith all creatures of intelligence
   Both were and are endowed, and they alone.
Now will appear to thee by inference
   The high worth of the vow so framed, supposing
   That with thine own consenting, God consents;
For, between God and man the bargain closing,
   Of what I call this treasure an oblation
   Is made in sooth, made by its own proposing.
What may be offered then in compensation?
   Weening to use well what thou offeredest,
   Thou seekest for thy plunder consecration.

Vows and Free Will; Ascent to the Heaven of Mercury

Now art thou assured concerning the main quest:
    But since herein doth Holy Church acquit,
    Which seems against the truth I manifest,
Thou canst not choose but still at table sit
    Awhile, for the tough viand thou hast chewed
    Wants further aid for thy digesting it.
Take what I tell thee in receptive mood
    And hold it fast; it is the very vice
    Of wit to lose what has been understood.
Pertain to essence of this sacrifice
    Two elements: one what it treats about,
    The other from the covenant takes rise.
The latter never can be cancelled out
    Save by fulfilment; and already so
    I spoke about it as to banish doubt;
Hence had the Hebrews still to offer, though
    Something whereof the sacrifice was made
    Might be commuted, as thou shouldest know.
The former, which as matter I portrayed,
    May well be such that no offence is done
    If with some other matter counterweighed.
But wilfully let on his shoulder none
    Shift burden, without sanction of the Power
    That turns the white key and the yellow one.
And folly all commuting deem, before
    The thing remitted in the thing ye essay
    Shall be contained, as in the six the four.
Therefore whatever by its worth may weigh
    So much as can make every balance swing,
    Can never be redeemed with other pay.
Let men deem not the vow a trifling thing:
    Be loyal, and in being so not blind
    As Jephthah was in his first offering,
Who did worse honouring the vow unkind,
    But should have said: "I sinned"; like foolish plight
    The mighty leader of the Greeks entwined,

Whence rued Iphigenia her beauty bright,
    And made for her both wise and simple rue,
    So many as hear report of such a rite!
Christians, be graver in your moving; do
    Not featherlike to every wind consent,
    And ween not every water washes you.
Ye have the Old and the New Testament,
    The Shepherd of the Church to shape your aim
    Therewith for your salvation be content.
If sorry greed aught else to you proclaim,
    Be men, and be not silly sheep, that so
    The Jew among you laugh you not to shame.
Behave not like the lamb who doth forgo
    The mother's milk, and wantonly delight
    In making of himself a mimic foe.'
Thus Beatrice to me, just as I write;
    Then all in longing up to that expanse
    Where most the world is quickened, turned her
Her silence and transfigured countenance   [sight.
    Imposed like silence on my eager wit,
    Though ready with new questions to advance.
And as the mark is by the arrow smit
    Before the cord forgets to quiver, thus
    Into the Second Kingdom did we flit.
I saw my Lady there so rapturous
    As to the lustre of that heaven she drew
    That even the planet grew more luminous.
And if the laughing star was altered too,
    What then became I, by my native mood
    Ever susceptible to something new!
As in clear pool where the still fishes brood,
    Aught dropping in impels the finny drove
    To dart toward it, deeming it their food,
So saw I there a thousand splendours move
    To meet our coming, and every one was hymning:
    'Behold one who will multiply our love.'

And every shade of them, now nearer swimming
    Appeared as with effulgent glory fraught
    Streaming out of its rapture overbrimming.
If what is here begun proceeded not,
    Think, Reader, what an agonizing dearth
    Of knowing more would be within thee wrought;
And from thyself infer how these gave birth
    To yearning in me to hear each circumstance
    Concerning them, when they revealed their worth.
'O happy-born, whom sovereign Grace thus grants
    To see the thrones triumphant and eterne
    Ere thou abandonest thy militance,
By light that ranges through all heaven we burn
    Enkindled so; and therefore, if thou please,
    Content thy heart with light from out our urn.'
One of the souls devout spoke words like these
    To me; and Beatrice: 'Speak, speak out free
    And trust to them as to divinities.'
'Well I perceive how thou art nesting thee
    In thine own light, and drawing it again
    Through eyes that coruscate so laughingly.
But who thou art, blest soul, I cannot ken,
    Nor wherefore thou art graded in the sphere
    That is in alien radiance veiled to men.'
Thus spoke I straight toward the lustre fair
    That first addressed me; whereupon it grew
    By far more radiant than it was whilere.
Then like the sun concealing himself through
    Excess of light, when heat has gnawed away
    The tempering shade to heavy vapours due,
Concealed himself from me in his own ray
    The holy shape for very jubilance;
    And, thus fast folded, did in answer say
In fashion as the following canto chants.

CANTO VI

'When Constantine had wheeled the Eagle away
   Against Heaven's course, where it was following
   That ancient who espoused Lavinia,
Two centuries and more saw hovering
   The Bird of God at Europe's border line,
   Near to the mountains whence it first took wing;
And, overshadowing with wings divine,
   Governed from hand to hand the world of man,
   And in due turn alighted upon mine.
Cæsar was I, and am Justinian,
   Who, to the primal Love obedient,
   Winnowed the laws, and bolted to the bran.
And ere yet wholly on that labour bent
   Did I a single nature in Christ misdeem,
   Not more, and with such faith remained content;
But blessèd Agapetus, the supreme
   Shepherd of souls, directed me and drew
   To the pure faith, discoursing of the theme.
Him I believed, and what by faith he knew
   Now clearly see, as seest thou every pair
   Of contradictories both false and true.
When with the Church my footsteps moving were,
   I gave me single-minded to the laws,
   Inspired by Grace Divine to that high care;
Committing weapons in the imperial cause
   To Belisarius mine, so comforted
   By Heaven's right hand that I had leave to pause.
Here then to thy first question comes to head
   My answer; but its terms make apposite
   That something as a sequel should be said,
That thou mayest see with what amount of right
   Against the hallowed ensign move both they
   Who make it theirs and who against it fight.

The Function of
Rome in Human
Redemption

Think what large reverence we ought to pay
   Its prowess, starting from the moment when
   Died Pallas to secure it sovereign sway.
In Alba 'twas, thou knowest, a denizen
   Three hundred years and more, until the close
   When fought the three to three for it again.
From Sabine rape down to Lucretia's woes
   Thou knowest how with seven kings it went
   Subduing round about the neighbour foes.
Thou knowest how, borne by Romans eminent,
   'Gainst Brennus, against Pyrrhus it o'ercame,
   And against others, prince or government;
Torquatus, and that Quintius who took name
   From hair unkempt, Decii and Fabii so
   Wrought deeds that gladly I embalm their fame.
It laid the pride of the Arabians low,
   Who passed in train of Hannibal among
   The rocky Alpine peaks whence pours the Po.
It led to triumph while they yet were young
   Pompey and Scipio, and bitterly
   Wrought to that hill beneath which thou art sprung.
Then near the time when heavenly harmony
   Would tune the world to concord with its own,
   Cæsar laid hold of it at Rome's decree;
And what it wrought from Var to Rhine is known
   To Isère, to the Saône, and to the Seine,
   And every valley brimming up the Rhone.
Its prowess, issuing from Ravenna, when
   It leapt the Rubicon, so swiftly flew
   That follow it could neither tongue nor pen.
It wheeled the legions back to Spain; then threw
   Them on Durazzo; and smote Pharsalia
   So that to torrid Nile was felt the rue.
Antandros and the Simois it saw,
   Its starting point, where Hector sleeps so fast;
   Then, woe to Ptolemy, roused beak and claw;

Thence fell, like thunderbolt on Juba cast;
   Then wheeling back into your West it came
   On hearing the Pompeian trumpet-blast.
What the next bearer with it did, proclaim
   Brutus and Cassius in the hellish deep,
   And Modena and Perugia wail the same.
Ever doth wretched Cleopatra weep
   Because of it—she, fleeing on before,
   Took from the adder suddenly black sleep.
With him it coursed far as the Red-sea shore;
   With him composed the world in peace so great
   That barred on Janus was his temple door.
But what the standard that I celebrate
   Had done before and was about to do
   For mortal man in every subject state,
Dwindles away, beclouded to the view,
   If one in hand of the third Cæsar seek
   With vision clear and with affection true;
For Living Justice, moving me to speak,
   Gave it, in person of that emperor,
   The glory vengeance for just wrath to wreak.
Now marvel here at what I tell thee more:
   Later it flew with Titus, doing again
   Vengeance on vengeance for the sin of yore.
And after, when the Lombard fang would fain
   Bite Holy Church, to rescue her from foes
   Beneath those wings came conquering Charle-
Now then thou mayest judge of such as those [magne.
   Whom I before accused, and of their faults
   Which are the origin of all your woes.
Against the public ensign one exalts
   The yellow lilies; another this assigns
   To party,—hard to say who most is false.
Under another ensign Ghibellines
   May ply and ply devices,—for amiss
   He follows it who from justice discombines.

And let that younger Charles not trample this,
  He and his Guelfs, but fear the claws that wield
  Force to flay tougher lion-fell than his.
Children have oft bewailed by flood and field
  The father's fault, nor let him ever ween
  His lilies to be quartered in God's shield.
This little planet is made passing sheen
  With the good spirits who have striven that fame
  And honour follow them; whenever lean
The truant wishes toward such an aim,
  Then true affection needs must radiate
  Upward to Heaven less vividly aflame.
But that our guerdon is commensurate
  With worth, is part of our beatitude,
  Seeing it nor too little nor too great.
Whence Living Justice sweetens so the mood
  Of love in us that no perversity
  Can tangle it in any turpitude.
Voices diverse below make melody;
  So in this life of ours each various grade
  Renders among these wheels sweet harmony.
And from within the present pearl is rayed
  The light of Romeo, whose labours great
  And generous were shabbily repaid.
But those of Provence cannot gratulate
  Who wrought against that noble minister:
  Evil to them who other's good abate!
Four daughters, Queens, had Raymond Berenger
  And he who crowned them was no citizen
  But Romeo, a lowly pilgrimer.
By crooked counsel moved, the Master then
  Calls to account the servant just, who clears
  His credit,—seven and five for every ten.
Then he departed poor and stricken in years;
  But if the world could know the heart he bore
  Begging his bread and eating it with tears,
Much as it praises, it would praise him more.'

CANTO VII

Hosanna, holy God of Hosts, Thou who
    Dost all the blessèd fires that are burning
    Within the Kingdom with Thy light outdo!
Even so, in time to its own music turning,
    That being on whom two splendours form a crest
    Chanted, as well I saw, the while discerning
How he began to dance with all the rest,
    And like swift sparklets with velocity
    And sudden distance veiled them from my quest.
In doubt I was repeating inwardly:
    'Tell it, tell it, tell to my Lady, whose
    Distilments are so sweetly slaking me;'
But reverence, whereby I cannot choose
    But mastered be at sound of 'Be' or 'Iss',
    Bowed me like one who falls into a doze.
But little while so left me Beatrice
    Till, with a radiant smile of such a kind
    As would have put a burning man in bliss,
She said: 'By my unfailing sight I find
    The question how a vengeance that was just
    Could justly be avenged, perturbs thy mind;
But if I speed to thy release, so must
    Thou listen well, because these words of mine
    Will guerdon thee with reasoning august.
By not submitting to a curb benign
    Upon his power of will, that man ne'er born
    Damning himself, condemned thus all his line,
Whereby the human race below forlorn
    Lay many a century in error great,
    Until the Word Almighty did not scorn
Going down to join in Person increate,
    By the sole act of His eternal love,
    That nature from its Maker alienate.

*Mystery of the
Redemption*

305

Now turn thy look to what I reason of:
    This nature, which its Maker made His own,
    Did, as created, pure and sinless prove;
But it was exiled by its fault alone
    From Paradise, for that it, wandering
    From way of truth and life, astray had gone.
Thus, by the adopted nature measuring,
    The penalty upon the cross exacted
    Did never any yet so justly sting;
And likewise never was such wrong enacted,
    Considering Who suffered, and the worth
    Of Him to whom this nature was contracted.
Thus from one act diverse effects took birth;
    The same death pleased the Hebrews and the Lord:
    Heaven opened at the sight, and quaked the earth.
No longer deem then difficult the word
    When it asseverates that vengeance just
    Was afterward avenged by a just sword.
But now I see how thought on thought is thrust
    Upon thy mind, entangled in a skein
    Whence it awaits release with eager trust.
Thou sayest within: "Yea, what I hear is plain,
    But it is Hidden from me why God chose
    This only way our ransom to attain."
My brother, this decree from eyes of those
    Lies buried deep, whose wit is not mature
    Within the flame of love that ripening glows.
Nevertheless as at this cynosure
    Mortals long gaze, though little they discern,
    Will I declare why this way was the truer.
Bounty Divine, that doth all envy spurn
    Away from Him, sends burning sparks therefrom,
    So lighting up the loveliness eterne.
That which distils without a medium
    From Him, has then no end, for permanence
    Gives form and pressure where His seal has come.

That which rains down without a medium thence
   Is wholly free, since not beneath the bar
   Of changing secondary influence.
Things please Him most that in His likeness are,
   For the all-irradiant sacred glow must be
   Most living in the things most similar.
These coigns of vantage all humanity
   Inherits, and, if one of these it wants,
   Falls force perforce from its nobility.
Sin only is man's disinheritance,
   Rendering him unlike the Highest Good
   And less blanched therefore by its radiance,
And never he gains his former altitude
   Except he fill the guilty void again,
   Just penalty for pleasure ill-pursued.
Your nature, sinning in your Sire amain,
   From such advantages as these was barred
   Even as from Paradise; and such the stain
That in no manner could they be restored,
   If thou with subtle wit the matter heed,
   Except by passing one or the other ford:
Either that God's sole clemency concede
   Redemption, or that human foolishness
   Should expiated be by human deed.
Now let thine eye pierce into the abyss
   Of the eternal counsel, close intent
   As possible to my discourse of this.
Man could, within his finite limits pent,
   Never atone, his pinions downward weighing
   With meekness and thereafter obedient,
Far as he planned to soar by disobeying;
   And this is why, though man himself would pay
   His own atonement, he was barred from paying.
Whence Deity must needs in His own way
   Bring man in perfect life again to birth,—
   In one way, or indeed in both, I say.

But since the doer's deed is graced with worth
    The more in measure as it more infers
    The heart of bounty whence it issued forth,
Bounty Divine that stamps the universe,
    Was fain to put in force His every mode
    To liberate you from the primal curse;
Nor was nor shall be, since the first day glowed
    Till the last night, so high and glorious
    A progress on the one or the other road:
For, giving Self, was God more bounteous,
    So making man sufficient up to rise,
    Than if He simply had forgiven us;
Nor any other method might suffice
    For justice, had the Son of the Most High
    Not humbled Him, assuming mortal guise.
And now, with all thy yearning to comply,
    Let me turn back to make one matter clear,
    That we may see it together, eye to eye.
Thou sayest: "I see the water, I see the air,
    The fire, the earth and all their mixtures stay
    But little while, then to corruption fare,
Yet nothing but created things were they;"
    Wherefore, if what I have averred is sure,
    They ought to be secure against decay.
The angels, brother, and the country pure
    Wherein thou art, may be called generated
    In all their being, as they are, mature;
But the elements whose names thou hast related,
    And all the things that from their minglings flow,
    Informed with power that was itself created.
Created was the matter in them so,
    Created the informing influence
    Within these stars that sweeping round them go.
Plucked out from their potential elements
    By light and motion of the holy fires
    Are souls of every brute and of the plants.

But the Supreme Benignity inspires
   Your soul directly, and enamours her
   With Him, whom she forever then desires.
And furthermore thou mayest hence infer
   Your resurrection, if thou think once more
   How human frames divinely fashioned were
When our first parents both were framed of yore.'

CANTO VIII

The world was in its peril wont to hold
   That the fair Cyprian was raying out
   Wild love, in her third epicyle rolled;
Wherefore the ancient people went about
   In antique error, not alone to pay
   To her the sacrifice and votive shout,
But Cupid and Dionë honoured they,
   This as her mother, that one as her son,
   Telling how he in Dido's bosom lay;
And named from her with whom I have begun
   That planetary star which, now at brow
   And now behind the shoulder, woos the Sun.
I had no sense of rising there till now,
   But of our being there my Lady's favour
   Gave proof, because I saw her fairer grow.
And as in flame we see the sparkles waver,
   Or as within a voice a voice discern
   One holding note, one shaking out a quaver,
So in that radiance other torches burn
   In circle speeding variably fast,
   Methinks in measure of their sight eterne.
Never from icy cloud so swift a blast
   Swept, seen or unseen, that the interim
   Would not have seemed long-drawn before it passed,

*The Heaven of
Venus*

To one who should have seen approaching him
    Those lights divine as they forsook the gyre
    Begun among the lofty Seraphim.
And from among the foremost of that quire
    Rang forth *Hosanna,* so harmonious
    That ever to rehear it I desire.
Then one of them drew near alone, and thus
    Began: 'We all with eagerness are burning
    To do thy will that thou have joy in us.
Of one orb, of one circling, of one yearning
    With the celestial Princes are we rolling
    To whom once thou, from worldly matters turning:
"Ye the third Heaven by intellect controlling";
    And to delight thee shall a quiet space
    Be no less sweet, our love is so ensouling.'
After mine eyes had sought my Lady's face
    With reverence, and she of her assent
    Had satisfied them, and assured her grace,
Then to the light which did such hope present.
    I turned about, and,—'Tell me, who are you?'
    Inquired in tone of tender sentiment.
Ah, when I so had spoken, how it grew
    Transfigured to my vision, and enhanced
    In size and brilliance, joy and joy thereto!
'The World,' he answered, thus enradianced,
    'Held me short while, and had it longer been
    Much harm that will befall had never chanced.
I am concealed from thee behind a screen
    Of gladness that irradiates me round,
    As swathes a creature its own silken sheen.
Much didst thou love me, with good reason fond,
    For had I stayed below I would have shown
    More of my love to thee than in the frond.
That left bank which is watered by the Rhone
    When it has drunk the Sorgue up, would have held
    Me in good time the master of its own;

And that horn of Ausonia, citadelled
  By Bari, Gaeta, and Catona, and where
  Tronto and Verdë in the sea are quelled.
Already gleamed the crown above my hair
  Of that dominion which the Danube purges
  Abandoning its German banks; and fair
Trinacria, which on occasion merges
  Pachynus and Pelorus in one gloom
  Over the gulf that Eurus chiefly scourges
(Not by Typhoeus, but by sulphur fume),
  Would for her sovereigns be looking still,
  Through me from Charles and Rudolph yet to
Had not the subject folk, by lordship ill   [come,
  Exasperated, been provoked to cry
  Insurgent in Palermo: "Kill them, kill!"
And had my brother been forewarned thereby,
  He now were fleeing, lest it work him woe,
  The greedy Catalonian poverty.
For he or his must make provision so,
  Forsooth, his overladen bark aboard,
  That none shall further lading seek to stow.
His nature, niggard from a generous lord,
  Should be supported by such counsellors
  As would give little heed to till or hoard.'
'The lofty rapture that thy telling pours
  Into me, is no clearer, master mine,
  To my own vision than it is to yours,
Since thou beholdest it in the Divine;
  Grateful am I,—more grateful still that thou
  Seest it where good has end and origin.
Thou hast made me glad, and in like manner now
  Clear up the doubt awakened in my mind,
  How from sweet seed can bitter fruitage grow?'
So I; and he to me: 'If I can find
  An answer setting truth in evidence,
  Thou'lt have before thee what is now behind.

The Good that turns the whole and that contents
    The Realm thou mountest, in these bodies vast
    Makes active virtue of its Providence;
And Mind in Itself perfect has forecast
    The natures not alone, but has in charge
    Along with them their welfare first and last.
Whence whatsoever thing this bow discharge
    Alights to predetermined end, like dart
    Unerringly directed to the targe.
If, not, the Heaven where thou a pilgrim art
    Would so in its effects come short of goal
    That they would not be beautiful, but thwart,
Which could not be unless the minds that roll
    These stars were in default, defaulting too
    For leaving them at fault, the Primal Soul.
Dost thou require more proof that this is true?'
    'Not so; it is impossible, I see,
    That Nature weary in aught of need to do.'
'Now say, were't worse for man,' continued he,
    'Were he on earth unsocial?'—'It were so,'
    I answered; 'that is obvious to me.'
'And can he be so if he live below
    Without diversity of offices?
    If well your master write about it,—no!'
So he by inference drew up to this:
    'Therefore perforce the roots of what is done
    Among you are diverse; whence not amiss
Is one born Solon, Xerxes one, and one
    Melchizedek, another who would fly
    Fanning the welkin, losing thus his son.
Revolving Nature well her craft doth ply
    Stamping her seal on wax of mortal clay,
    Nor takes account of hostel, low or high.
Whence it occurs that Esau falls away
    At birth from Jacob, and Quirinus rose
    From Sire so mean that sired him Mars, they say.

Careers of children would conform to those
  Of their begetters, like to like in kind,
  But that Divine prevision overthrows.
Now frontest thou the truth that was behind;
  But that thou know my joy in thy behoof,
  With corollary will I cloak thy mind.
If she find Fortune from herself aloof,
  Ever will Nature, like another seed
  Out of its region, come to evil proof.
And if the world down yonder would take heed
  To what the rudiments of nature teach,
  Following these, well would her people speed.
But ye pervert him to a priest, whose reach
  Of nature warrants him the sword to wield,
  And make a king of him who fain would preach:
Therefore your footsteps go so far afield.'

CANTO IX

After thy Charles had thus, O Clemence fair,
  Enlightened me, he told the frauds, he said
  That his posterity would have to bear;
Adding: 'Be silent till the years are sped';
  So that I naught can say, save that of right
  Tears for these wrongs of yours shall yet be shed.
And now the spirit of that holy light
  Had turned toward the Sun, that plenteous
  Fountain of good to all things requisite.
Ah, souls deluded, creatures impious,
  To wrench your hearts from such a blessèd state,
  Your brows tow'rd vanity directing thus!
And lo! another of those splendours great
  Drew nearer, while its will for my content
  Seemed from its features forth to radiate.

*A Great Lady
and a Poet
prophesy*

313

The eyes of Beatrice were on me bent
 As heretofore, and to the thing I sought
 Gave me assurance of her sweet assent.
'Soon be thy longing to fulfilment brought,
 Blest spirit,' said I, 'and give me certitude
 That in thyself I can reflect my thought.'
Whence the new light, from deep beatitude
 Wherein it had before been singing, said
 In manner of one delighting to do good:
'In that depraved Italian region spread
 Between Rialto and the highlands whence
 The streams of Brenta and Piava head,
Rises a hill of no great prominence,
 Wherefrom a firebrand came down formerly,
 Doing that district injury immense.
From one same root arose both I and he:
 Cunizza was my name, here overbowed
 With splendour, since this star prevailed on me.
But gladly have I to myself allowed
 The cause of this my lot, without dismay,
 Though hard the saying, haply, to your crowd.
This precious jewel of pellucid ray
 Our heaven adorning and to me most near,
 Left great renown, and ere it fade away
Shall be quintupled this centennial year.
 Ah, let man look to make him excellent
 That the first life bequeath a second there!
So reason not the present rabblement
 Whom Tagliamento and Adigë contain,
 Nor yet for being scourged are penitent.
But soon shall Padua at the pool distain
 The water that should wash Vicenza sweet,
 Since mutinous to duty are the men.
And there where Silë and Cagnano meet
 One plays the lord and walks with insolence,
 Although the snare is set to trap his feet.

Moreover Feltro shall bewail the offence
   Of her unconsecrated pastor,—none
   So foul has entered Malta's prison-pens.
Too large would be the measure of the tun
   That of the Ferrarese should hold the gore
   (To weigh it ounce by ounce would weary one!)
Which this obliging priest will have to pour
   To prove him partisan; such gifts are due
   To match the life that land is noted for!
Above are mirrors—thrones as called by you—
   Whence God in judgement doth upon us shine
   So that seem good to us these sayings true.'
Herewith she held her peace, and gave me sign
   Of being turned to other heed, whirled on
   As heretofore along the dance divine.
The other joy, already known as one,
   Swam into vision as a thing illumed,
   Like a choice ruby smitten by the sun.
Brightness up there by rapture is assumed
   Like laughter here on earth; but they who live
   Below are shadowed as the soul is gloomed.
'All-seeing God,' said I, 'to thee doth give
   Vision so inwardly with Him imbued,
   Can no desire from thee be fugitive.
Therefore thy voice that gives beatitude
   To Heaven, in concert with those fires divine
   Who with their six wings make themselves a hood,
Why does it leave me in desire to pine?
   Not now would I be waiting thy demand
   Did I indwell thy soul, as thou dost mine.'
'The greatest valley into which expand
   The waters,' his reply to me began,
   'Forth from that sea engarlanding the land,
Extends 'twixt alien shores so long a span
   Against the sun, that what was just before
   Horizon, soon appears meridian.

315

I was a dweller midway on that shore
   'Twixt Ebro and Magra, which with passage short
   Bars to the Genoese the Tuscan door.
For rise and set of sun of one report
   Would be Buggeä and my native town,
   Whose blood once warmed the waters of the port.
Folco they called me where my name's renown
   Was noted, and this heaven is stamped by me
   As on me once its influence rained down.
More burned not Belus's daughter, balefully
   Both to Sichæus and Creüsa too,
   Than I while it became my locks; nor she,
The Rhodopeian maid who had to rue
   Demophoön's deceit; Alcides not
   When Iolë into his heart he drew.
Yet nowise grieve, but smile we in this spot,
   Not at the fault which ne'er returns to mind,
   But at the Worth that ordered and forethought.
Here we behold the skill which has assigned
   Itself so fair result,—discern the Good
   Which with the world above atones mankind.
But that thou bear away in plenitude
   Fulfilled those wishes native to this sphere,
   With something further I perforce conclude.
Thou wouldest know who in this radiance here
   Beside me scintillates, as in pure stream
   A sunbeam tremulous in water clear.
Now learn that rests at peace within that beam
   Rahab, and that our order, made her own,
   Bears signet of her in degree supreme.
Into this heaven, where ends the shadowy cone
   Cast by your earth, all other souls before,
   She, in Christ's triumph, was received alone.
Meet was it in some heaven forevermore
   Leave her as palm of the victorious hope
   Achieved with one palm and the other; for

She lent her aid to the first glorious scope
  Of Joshua upon the Holy Land,
  That little stirs the memory of the Pope.
Thy City, the plantation of his hand
  Who turned his back on his Creator first,
  And from whose envy spring your woes, doth
And scatter far and wide that flower accursed [brand
  Whereby the shepherd into wolf is turned,
  So that the sheep and lambs are all dispersed.
The Gospel and the doctors great are spurned,
  And only the Decretals studied well
  For this,—as by their margin is discerned.
Thereon the Pope and cardinals do dwell:
  Never on Nazareth is fixed their scan,
  Where opened once his pinions Gabriel.
But holy parts of Rome, both Vatican
  And other, chosen as the burial spot
  Of the army whereof Peter led the van,
Soon shall be purged of the adulterous blot.'

CANTO X

The primal and unutterable Worth
  Gazing upon His Son's benignant face
  With Love which both eternally breathe forth,
Made all things that revolve through mind or space
  With so much order that whoso looks aright
  Can never want some image of His Grace.
Then, Reader, lift straight up with me thy sight
  To the high wheels, where the two motions come
  To that point where they each on other smite,
And there begin to enjoy His masterdom
  Who loves His work within Him with such love
  As never to withdraw His eye therefrom.

Heaven of the Sun:
Starry Garland
of Sages

Look, how that circle oblique, the bearer of
   The planets, is at present branching thence
   To appease the world that calls them from above;
And were their road not bent, much influence
   In Heaven would be unfruitful, and down here
   Almost all virtue drained to impotence;
Did it at less or greater angle veer
   From the right line, deficiency were dire
   Both up and down, in either hemisphere.
Now on this foretaste of the heart's desire,
   Remain, O Reader, on thy seat to brood,
   For it will charm thee long before thou tire;
I set it forth; do thou partake the food;
   For I have made me scribe of such a theme
   As claims the whole of my solicitude.
The Minister of Nature all supreme,
   Who with the worth of Heaven the world is sealing
   And measuring our time out with his beam,
Joined with that region named above, was wheeling
   Along the spirals of that thoroughfare
   Where daily earlier is his revealing;
And I along with him, but unaware
   Of the ascending, more than one perceives
   Thought in the mind before its advent there.
'Tis Beatrice herself who leading gives
   From good to better, so immediately
   Her act no vestige of duration leaves.
Within the sun where I had entered, see
   How brighten spirits into recognition,
   By light, not colour, manifest to me!
What though I summon genius, art, tradition,
   That splendour could be imaged nevermore,
   But faith may see,—ah, let us crave the vision!
No wonder our low fancy cannot soar
   To such an altitude, for never yet
   Was eye that did not quail the sun before.

So bright was the fourth family, here set
  By the High Sire, imbuing them with bliss,
  Showing how He doth breathe, and how beget.
'Give thanks to Him,' began now Beatrice,
  'Thank Him who of the angels is the Sun,
  Who by His Grace has lifted thee to this!'
So ardently subdued to orison
  Devoted, heart of mortal yet was not,
  So eager for divine surrender none,
As at these words my own desire was hot;
  And so my love to Him was wholly plighted
  That Beatrice was in eclipse forgot.
Nor this displeased her; but her eyes so lighted
  With laughter, that the splendour of her mien
  Drew off to other things my mind united.
For other living lustres, passing keen,
  Centred upon us like a chaplet round,
  Still sweeter in their voice than bright in sheen.
The daughter of Latona thus enwound
  Is seen at moments when so teems the air
  It holds the thread wherewith her zone is bound.
Manifold are the jewels dear and fair
  In Court of Heaven, whence I returning come,
  And none to carry them away could dare;
Of these the carols of those light were some:
  Who takes not wing up thitherward to fly
  May better ask for tidings of the dumb!
When, chanting so, those blazing suns on high
  Had wheeled about us thrice, in radiance
  Like stars the steadfast pole for ever nigh,
Ladies they seemed, who break not from the dance,
  But stop in silence listening for the chord
  Whereto their tripping steps again advance.
And from within one light came forth this word:
  'Since radiance of Grace, enkindling so
  True love to be the multiplied reward

Of loving, doth in thee so brightly glow,
    Leading thee up that stairway where none save
    To reascend can ever go below, —
Whoever should deny thee if thou crave
    Wine from his flagon, would be free no more
    Than water seeking not the level wave.
Thou wouldest know what blossoms now enflower
    This garland, circling with blithe roundelay
    The Lady beautiful, thy heavenly dower.
Lamb of the holy flock was I, whose way
    Is shepherded by Dominic, and here
    Fair is the fattening, if they do not stray.
The brother to my dexter hand most near
    Was Albert of Cologne, my master best,
    And I was Thomas of Aquino there.
And if to name and number all the rest
    Thou cravest of me, let thy look awhile
    Circle up here along the garland blest.
That other splendour issues from the smile
    Of Gratian,—one and the other court he lent
    Such aid as Heaven with rapture to beguile.
And of our chorus the next ornament
    Was Peter, who gave Holy Church his mite
    Like the poor woman of the Testament.
The fifth and loveliest of our circle bright
    Breathes from such love that all the world below
    Looks eagerly for tidings of its plight:
Within it is the lofty spirit, so
    Imbued with wisdom that, if truth be true,
    No second rose so much to see and know.
Next it the radiance of that taper view
    Which, still in mortal flesh, did best divine
    The angelic nature, and its service due.
Next in that little light see, smiling, shine
    That advocate of Christian ages whose
    Fair Latin edified Saint Augustine.

Now, if in sequence as my praise pursues
   From light to light, thy mental eye is veering,
   Thou cravest for the eighth, and canst not choose,
Therein the sight of Good Supreme is cheering
   The holy soul who renders evident
   The world's deceit to whoso well give hearing.
The body whence on earth it hunted went
   Lies in Cieldauro, and from torture came
   Into this peace and out of banishment.
And yonder see the fervent spirits flame
   Of Isidore, of Bede, of Richard who
   In contemplation more than man became.
This one, wherefrom to me returns thy view,
   Shines from a soul to thought so dedicate
   That death, he thought, too slowly on him drew:
This is the light of Siger, beyond date,
   Who in the Street of Straw once lecturing,
   Had enviable truths to demonstrate.'
Then as a chiming horologe doth ring
   To rouse the Bride of God to matin-song
   Unto the Spouse, His love soliciting,
Where one part draws another and thrusts along
   With tintinnating note harmonious
   Whence love in well-tuned spirit waxes strong, —
The glorious wheel I saw revolving thus
   And render voice to voice, in concord blending
   With sweetness never to be known of us,
Save in that place where joy is never-ending.

CANTO XI

St. Thomas
Aquinas in praise
of St. Francis

Insane solicitude for mortal things,
  Alas, how all the reasonings are vain
  That make thee heavily beat down thy wings!
One followed priesthood and one followed gain,
  One aphorisms of Hippocrates,
  One strove by violence or craft to reign,
One throve by theft, one by juristic pleas,
  One in the pleasures of the flesh enwound
  Was wearing out, and one gave up to ease,
While I, set free from all that dreary round,
  Aloft in Heaven, with Beatrice at hand,
  So passing glorious a welcome found.
When every member of that circling band
  Had gained the point where he had been before,
  He stayed, as stays the taper in the stand.
And now I heard the former voice once more
  Within that lustre, while yet more intense
  Became the brilliance of the smile it wore:
'As I am kindled in His effluence,
  So, gazing into the Eternal Light,
  I trace thy thoughts back to their rudiments.
Thou doubtest, and wouldst have me sift aright
  My utterance, and in plain language bring
  The matter to the level of thy sight
Where lately I said,—"Where is good fattening",
  And where again I said, "No second rose";
  And here is need of clear distinguishing.
That Providence which rules the world with those
  Mysterious laws that baffle mortal eye
  Before it ever to the bottom goes
(So that to wed with Him who espoused her by
  The blessèd blood with loud proclaim, the Bride
  Might go with greater nuptial loyalty,

And with more self-security beside),
   Ordained two princes who should both attend
   One upon either hand to be her guide.   [her,
All fire seraphical was one defender;
   The other one with wisdom all aflame,
   Light to the world cherubic in its splendour.
Of one I mean to speak, for both may claim
   Our praises, whichsoever one intending,
   Because their labours had a single aim.
Between Topino and the stream descending
   The hill that blessèd Ubald erewhile chose,
   A fertile slope is from the mountain bending,
Whence hot and cold upon Perugia blows
   Through Porta Solë, while behind it groan
   Gualdo and Nocera their heavy woes.
Where drops the highland less abruptly prone,
   A sun upon the world began ascent,
   As somewhiles out of Ganges dawns our own.
Wherefore let any, when this place is meant,
   Say not "Ascesi", which were short to say,
   But, fitlier to speak, say "Orient"!
He, from his rising not yet far away,
   Began to give the world some handsel of
   The comfort-giving virtue of his ray;
And, still a boy against his father strove
   For such a Lady, men unbar the door
   As willingly to death as to her love;
And in the spiritual court, before
   His father's face, united with her stood,
   Whereon from day to day he loved her more.
Reft of first husband she in widowhood
   Till after the eleven hundredth year,
   Contemned, obscure, awaited him unwooed;
Nor aught availed that men of her should hear
   As with Amyclas found unterrified
   By voice of him who struck the world with fear;

Nor aught availed her faith and courage tried,
    So that, let Mary at the foot remain,
    She mounted up where Christ was crucified.
But lest too enigmatic be my strain,
    From my long parable shalt thou infer
    That Poverty and Francis are these twain.
So blithe and so harmonious they were,
    Their love, their wonder, their communion sweet
    In all around set holy thoughts astir;
Whence venerable Bernard first thought meet
    To go unshod, and after so great peace
    He ran, and running blamed his lagging feet.
O wealth untold, good fruitful of increase!
    Giles bares his feet, Sylvester his, behind
    The Bridegroom, such the Bride's peculiar grace.
Then with his Lady and with the house assigned,
    All with the humble cord begirded now,
    Went forth that Father and that Master kind;
Nor did he cravenly abase his brow
    As son of Peter Bernardone, or feel
    Cast down by strange contempt. But his stern vow
With regal dignity did he reveal
    To Innocent the Pope, by whom was granted
    For his religious order the first seal.
As multiplied the poor folk who had panted
    To follow him whose life-work marvellous
    Were better in the glory of Heaven chanted,
This Master-shepherd's holy zeal for us
    Was sealed with crown of the Eternal Spirit
    A second time through Pope Honorius.
Then preached he to the Soldan proud (to merit
    The palm of martyrdom he would have borne)
    Christ and his followers; but since to hear it
He found unripe that folk, who put to scorn
    Salvation, and lest vain should be the quest,
    Returned to harvest of the Italian corn;

'Twixt Tiber and Arno on the rocky crest
  From Christ's own hand the final seal he won,
  Borne for two years upon his limbs impressed.
When God, allotting him such benison,
  Vouchsafed to draw him to the meed above
  That he had gained by being a lowly one,
Unto his brethren, as right heirs thereof,
  Bequeathed he all his wealth, his Lady dear,
  Bidding them hold fidelity in love;
And from her breast the lofty spirit clear
  Desired to pass to its own realm divine,
  And for its body willed no other bier.
Judge now the worth of one who could combine
  With him to pilot over the high seas
  The Bark of Peter by the starry sign!
Such was our Patriarch; and they who please
  To follow him, obeying his command,
  Take on such freight of good commodities.
But now so greedy is become his band
  For novel fodder, nothing can withhold
  The sheep from roaming through wild pastureland;
And these, the more by distant lure cajoled,
  And truant more from him in field and wood,
  Emptier of milk return they to the fold.
Some truly, boding evil likelihood,
  Cleave closely to the Shepherd, but so few
  That scanty cloth would furnish every hood.
Now if my words not feeble are, if due
  Hearing thou gavest them with mind entire,
  And if the memory call them up anew,
In part contented shall be thy desire,
  Seeing the plant with scions torn away,
  And seeing what signifies the qualifier:
"Fair is the fattening, *if they do not stray.*"'

CANTO XII

Before the final cadence ceased to sound
    Forth from the blessèd spirits radiant,
    Began the holy millstone to whirl round,
But of full circling something yet did want,
    When now another ring around it fuses
    And matches dance with dancing, chant with chant,
Chant that as passing far excels our muses,
    Our sirens, in those mellow flutings blew,
    As the first sunbeam by reflection loses.
As curve two bows the filmy cloud-rack through,
    Both parallel in line and colour, done
    As Juno bids her maid the picture do,
The outer taking birth from the inner one
    In hues reëchoed like that wandering voice
    Consumed by love, as vapour by the sun,
Giving mankind a signal to rejoice
    That what God promised Noah shall abide,
    Whence deluge nevermore the world destroys:
So the two garlands bright about us plied
    Of roses an eternal coronal,
    And the outer to the inner so replied.
Then, when the dance and lofty festival
    Both of the flaming lights and of the quires
    Light beside light jocund and blithesome, all
Of one accord grew quiet, song and fires
    (Even as the eyelids cannot choose but shut
    Or lift themselves again as will requires),
From one of the new lights a voice came out,
    Which made me, needle to that pole, incline
    My body round toward its whereabout;
And it began: 'The Love that makes me shine
    Prompts me to laud the other Leader great,
    For whose sake here is spoken fair of mine.

Each with the other should be celebrate
   That, as united they were militant,
   Their glory may together radiate.
The army of Christ, at cost exorbitant
   Equipped anew, was moving slow of pace
   Mistrustful, and too few the flag to plant,
When He who kings it over time and space
   Provided for His knighthood jeopardied,
   Not for their worth, but only of His Grace,
Coming, as said, to succour of His Bride
   With champions twain, whose prowess and behest
   Rallied the stragglers who had turned aside.
Where first the winds breathe gently from the west
   To open the fresh foliage of spring,
   Whence smiles Europa being newly dressed,
Not far from where the waves are thundering
   Wherein the sun, because his course is great,
   Somewhile from man concealed is slumbering,
There Calahorra sits, the fortunate,
   Protected by the great escutcheon where
   The lion doth succumb and subjugate.
Therein was brought to birth the lover dear
   Of Christian Faith, athlete in holiness,
   Kind to his own, to enemies severe.
Such life-power in his mother did possess
   The infant spirit at its first creation
   As to transform her to a prophetess.
Fulfilled at holy font the declaration
   Between him and the Faith, of sacrament
   Wherein each pledged the other with salvation,
The woman who for him had given assent
   Beheld the admirable fruit, in dream,
   Of him and of his heirs; and with intent
That what he was he might in grammar seem,
   A spirit went bearing the possessive word
   Of his Possessor hence to christen him,

And called him Dominic: for I record
   The story of the husbandman whom Christ
   Chose for his aid in vineyard of the Lord.
True messenger he seemed and friend of Christ,
   For the first love obtaining masterdom
   In him, was the first counsel given by Christ.
His nurse discovered him, awake and dumb,
   Many a time recumbent on the ground,
   As who should say, "To this end am I come!"
O thou, his father, Felix truly found!
   And thou, his mother, verily art Joan,
   If that interpretation be the sound.
Not as men now are spent for worldly boon
   Following Thaddeus and the Ostian,
   But, loving the true manna, very soon
He grew a mighty teacher, and began
   About the vineyard to be vigilant,
   Where bleach the vines if bad the husbandman;
And of the Seat that once to righteous want
   Benigner was (not by her own offence
   But that of her degenerate occupant!),
He begged,—not two or three for six dispense,
   Not income of first vacant benefice,
   Not tithes, of God's own poor the competence,—
But leave against the world, that goes amiss,
   To battle for the Faith, from seed whereof
   Sprang twice twelve plants that garland thee with bliss
Then, both with learning and with zealous love,
   By apostolical authority,
   Like torrent urged by fountain up above,
Dashed in among the shoots of heresy,
   Smiting with greater vehemence, the more
   Resistance proved to be refractory.
From him thenceforward various runnels pour
   To irrigate the Catholic garden spot,
   Making its bushes greener than before.

PARADISO

If such was one wheel of the Chariot
  Wherein rode Holy Church for her defence
  Over the field where civil strife was hot,
Clearly shouldst thou perceive the excellence
  Of the other wheel, which Thomas had discussed
  Before I came, with courteous eloquence.
But, where the outmost rim its pressure thrust,
  The track is now deserted by the wheel,
  So that there is the mould where was the crust.
His household, who set forth with footing leal
  Upon his footprints, now are turned again
  So that they cast the toe upon the heel.
And soon the crop will prove, when gathered in,
  How bad the tillage when the tares will weep
  Because they are excluded from the bin.
Yet any eyes that through our volume sweep
  Leaf after leaf, will on some page have caught
  The legend still: "Unto my vow I keep."
But from Casale or Acquasparta not,
  Whence come such as the writing so apply
  That one evades, the other draws it taut.
The effluence of Bonaventura am I,
  From Bagnorea, who did evermore
  Put last the left-hand care in office high.
Here, of the earliest of the barefoot poor,
  Illuminato and Augustin, made dear
  To God while circled with the cord of yore.
Hugh of Saint Victor is among them here,
  And Peter Mangiadore, and Peter of Spain
  Who in twelve books down there is shining clear;
The Prophet Nathan, Metropolitan
  Chrysostom, Anselm, that Donatus who
  Stooped to the first art, a grammarian;
Here is Rabanus, here beside me too
  Shines the Calabrian abbot Joachim,
  Gifted with spirit of prophetic view.

In rivalry such paladin to hymn,
    Moved me with courtesy-enkindled mood
    Friar Thomas, by the fair discourse of him,
And with me prompted all this brotherhood.'

CANTO XIII

*Discourse of the
Angelic Doctor set
to Celestial Music*

Let him imagine, who would fain be shown
    What now I saw (and hold the image fast
    While I am speaking, carven as in stone!),
Fifteen stars that in various regions vast
    Do make the heavens alive with lustre, serving
    To pierce the air, however overcast;
Imagine the great Wain whereto the curving
    Vault of our heaven is so ample, night and morn
    That from the veering tongue 'tis never swerving;
Imagine too the broad bell of that Horn
    Beginning at the axle-hub, whereby
    The first revolving sphere is round us borne:
These to have made two clusters in the sky,
    Like that which the daughter of Minos fashionèd
    When, chilled, she felt herself about to die,—
One cluster with the other garlanded
    And in such fashion whirling both the two
    That one was leader and the other led:
Then will he have some shadow of the true
    Star clusters, as in counter-dance they gleam,
    Circling the point that I was rooted to,
Since these outstrip the things we see or dream,
    As does that Heaven which is the swiftest o'er us
    The moving of Chiana's oozy stream.
Not Bacchus, not Apollo was their chorus,
    But Persons three in being all divine,
    In one, divine and human, to restore us.

The song and circle measured, turned in fine
  To us those holy lustres, more by token
  Passing from heed to heed with joy benign.
'Mid those concordant powers was silence broken
  Then by that light whence the achievements of
  The marvellous mendicant of God were spoken:
'One sheaf being thrashed,' the words fell from above
  'And that its grain is to the garner gone,
  To beat the other beckons me dear love.
Thou thinkest of the bosom whence was drawn
  The rib wherewith to fashion the fair face
  Whose palate cost the world so dear a pawn,
And of that lance-pierced bosom, by whose grace
  Sin past and future was so compensated
  That the atonement in the scale outweighs,
Thou thinkest man may be illuminated
  By no more light than was infused in those
  By that same Power who both of them created:
And hence thy wonder when my story goes
  That the Fifth Light with vision so profound
  Was gifted, that *"No second ever rose"*.
Open thine eyes now and behold how bound
  Is thy belief with what I shall reply,
  Both in the truth like centre in the round.
That which can die, and that which cannot die,
  Are nothing save the splendour of that Word
  In love begotten by our Father High;
Because that Living Light which is transferred
  So from its Source, it may not be undone
  From it or from that Love which is their third,
Its mirrored rays by its own benison
  In nine subsistencies together brings,
  Itself eternally abiding One;
Thence passes through successive lowerings
  To the ultimate potential elements,
  Producing naught but brief contingent things;

331

And these contingent things I take in sense
   Of generated things, in seedlessness
   Or seed produced, through heavenly influence.
The wax of these things with the plastic stress
   Stands not at one,—its trace may be defined
   Beneath the ideal pattern, more and less.
Whence comes about that, after its own kind,
   The selfsame tree bears worse and better fruit,
   And ye are born endowed with various mind.
Now were the wax exactly worked to suit,
   Did stars supreme their influence assemble,
   The lustre of the seal were absolute;
But Nature mars,—wherein she doth resemble
   The craftsman who about his labour goes
   And keeps the knack, although his fingers tremble.
Yet if the fervent Love seal and dispose
   Clear insight of the Primal Power, achieved
   Perfection on that substance fully shows.
Dust of the ground, made worthy thus, received
   Full animal perfection once therethrough;
   Thus wrought upon, the Virgin once conceived.
So that I give my sanction to thy view
   That human nature never yet has been,
   Nor can be, such as in those persons two.
Now if no farther forward should I win,
   "How then consider him without a peer?"
   Upon this question would thy words begin.
But to see clearly what is not yet clear,
   Think who he was and why petitioning
   When he was bidden ask the guerdon dear.
Thus have I spoken but exhibiting
   That he was king, and asked for plenitude
   Of wisdom to become a worthy king,—
Not for the number of the multitude
   Moving these spheres, nor if *necesse* chained
   With a contingent ever could conclude,

Nor if prime motion is to be maintained,
   Nor if in semicircle could be drawn
   Triangle, save right angle be retained.
Whence, taking this with my discourse foregone,
   A kingly prudence is that peerless prize
   The shaft of my intention hits upon.
And if on *"rose"* thou turnst discerning eyes,
   Thou wilt perceive that it is spoken of
   Kings,—who are many, and but few the wise.
Thus qualified, in what I said above
   Agreement with thy view is found complete
   As to our primal Sire and Him we love.
Let this be ever lead upon thy feet
   To make thee like a weary man move slow
   When *Yes* and *No* the inner vision cheat;
For he among the fools is very low
   Who affirms or who denies in either kind
   Without distinction of the *Yes* and *No*,
Since often to false bias are inclined
   Opinions men too hastily attain,
   And mere conceit then trammels up the mind.
His putting forth from shore is worse than vain
   Who wanting skill goes fishing for the true,
   Since as he went returns he not again;
Melissus gives the proof of this to view,
   And Bryson and Parmenides, who recked
   Not of their goal, however fast they flew.
So with Sabellius, Arius, and each sect
   Of fools who were as swords to Scripture pure,
   Distorting features otherwise correct.
Let folk in judgement never be too sure,
   As when into the field the peasant goes
   To reckon up the ears not yet mature;
For I have seen beneath the winter snows
   The wild brier rugged seem, and troublesome,
   And then upon its summit bear the rose;

CANTO XIII
136-142

And once I saw a gallant vessel come
　　Straight over-seas, completing her emprise,
　　To perish entering the port at home.
Seeing one thieve, another sacrifice,
　　Let not Dame Joan and Gaffer John presume
　　To penetrate them with divining eyes,
For one may rise, the other fall to doom.'

CANTO XIV

The Spiritual Body. Galaxy of the Cross in Mars

From centre unto rim, or back about,
　　Vibrates the water in a rounded vase,
　　As smitten from within or from without.
Into my mind came suddenly the case
　　That here I moot, soon as the effluence
　　Of glorious Saint Thomas held his peace,
Because of likeness in the incidence
　　Of his discourse and that of Beatrice,
　　Whom it pleased after him thus to commence:
'This man has need (yet does not tell you this
　　Either by voice or thinking) to pursue
　　Another truth to where it rooted is.
Inform him if the light which doth endue
　　Your substance with its blossom, will remain
　　As now it is for evermore with you;
And if it shall remain with you, explain
　　How ye can bear it and conserve your sight
　　When ye shall be made visible again.'
Just as, impelled by urgence of delight,
　　They who are wheeling in the dance as one,
　　Lift up the voice and make the movement light,
So at the prompt devoted orison
　　The holy rings gave proof of rapture new,
　　Turning in wondrous choral unison.

Whoso laments our death down here, therethrough
　　To win new life above, did never see
　　Refreshment there of the eternal dew.
That ever-living One and Two and Three
　　Reigning in Three Two One beyond all date,
　　Unbounded and all-bounding Trinity,
Did each among those spirits celebrate
　　Three times, with such melodious utterance
　　As were fit meed for merit passing great.
And where divinest was the radiance
　　Of the inner ring, a quiet voice replies
　　(To Mary such the Angel's voice perchance!):
'Long as the festival of Paradise
　　Shall have continuance, so long our love
　　Engarments us with such a radiant guise.
Its brightness will keep pace with movement of
　　Our zeal, and zeal with vision, which is full
　　As it has grace its proper worth above.
When with the glorious holy flesh the soul
　　Shall be reclothed, our personality
　　Will dearer grow, since wholly beautiful.
Thereby will wax the light, that largess free
　　Vouchsafed us by Supremest Excellence,
　　Light which enables us His Face to see;
Wherefore the vision needs must wax intense,
　　The fervour wax that from the vision came,
　　And wax the radiance proceeding thence.
But even as a firebrand, darting flame,
　　Is by its living glow victorious
　　So that its visible form remains the same,
So will this lustre now enswathing us
　　Be vanquished by the flesh, that now from sight
　　This many a day by earth is covered thus.
Nor can we weary of so great a light;
　　Strong shall the bodily organs be concerning
　　All that may minister to our delight.'

So ready and with such an eager burning
   To cry 'Amen' appeared to me both quires,
   As for the mortal body showed their yearning,
Not for themselves alone, but for their sires
   And mothers and perchance for others dear
   Ere they became imperishable fires.
And lo! a lustre all around, of sheer
   Surpassing splendour dawned upon the view,
   Like an horizon that is growing clear.
And even as at early nightfall, new
   Gleamings begin to spot the sky again,
   While true appears the vision, yet not true,
Methought up there, beginning to grow plain,
   Novel existences, a circling host
   Outside of those circumferences twain.
O very sparkling of the Holy Ghost,
   Smiting mine eyes with such an instant flare
   They might not brook it, in the lustre lost!
But Beatrice showed so smiling and so fair,
   It must be left with visions that elude
   The memory, which cannot follow there.
Therefrom mine eyes, resuming aptitude
   To lift their lids, showed me with her alone
   Lifted to loftier beatitude.
That I was lifted to a higher zone
   Was told me by that star's enkindled smile
   Which ruddily beyond the common shone.
In that deep language of the heart whose style
   Is one in all, to God I here addressed
   Oblation for the gift bestowed the while;
Nor yet was consummated in my breast
   The sacrifice, before I knew the prayer
   To be propitious and with favour blest,
For with a rubeate glory past compare
   Showed splendours forth, within two rays of light,
   Such that I cried: 'O Sun that makes them fair!'

As, 'twixt the two poles of the world, gleams white
   The Galaxy with less and greater stars,
   Putting in doubt the very erudite,
Thus, constellated in the depth of Mars,
   Fashioned those rays the venerated sign
   Formed in a round by crossing quadrant bars.
Here memory overcomes all wit of mine:
   Because that Cross was lamping so with Christ
   I cannot find similitude condign;
But whoso takes his cross and follows Christ
   Shall yet forgive me what I leave unsaid,
   Seeing that dawnlight flashing with the Christ.
From arm to arm, and between base and head,
   Lights were in motion, brightly scintillant,
   Passing and counterchanging as they sped.
So swift and slow and level and aslant
   Are seen here, ever altering their mien,
   The atomies of bodies long or scant
Adance upon the ray that cleaves the screen
   Of shadow often, which for their defending
   Men cause by handicraft to intervene.
And, as the harp or violin, with blending
   Of many chords, sweet tinkling makes to him
   Who hears the music without comprehending,
So from the lights there shining bright or dim
   Gathered along the Cross a melody
   That raptured me, oblivious of the hymn.
High laud it was,—so much was clear to me,
   Because 'Arise and conquer' was the strain
   Which still I heard uncomprehendingly.
So charmed was I therewith that until then
   Naught had there ever been that could impose
   On me the fetters of so sweet a chain.
Perchance too bold appear such words as those,
   Disparaging the charm of those fair eyes
   Gazing wherein my longing has repose.

CANTO XIV
133-139

But whoso comprehends how as they rise
　　Those living seals of every beauty augment,
　　Nor had I turned to where their lustre lies,
May excuse me from the indictment I present
　　For my excuse, and find my truth the surer:
　　The holy bliss has here no banishment
Because, ascending, it becomes the purer.

CANTO XV

*Cacciaguida recalls
the Heroic Age of
Florence*

Benignant will, distilling into blest
　　Love-breathing charities that never cease,
　　As greed in wicked will is manifest,
Silence imposed on that sweet lyre, and peace
　　Upon those holy chords, which one by one
　　The hand of Heaven doth tighten and release.
How can be deaf to righteous orison
　　Those Beings who, to hearten me the more
　　For supplication, paused in unison?
Right is it that he endlessly deplore,
　　Who, out of love for what does not abide,
　　Forfeits that other love for evermore.
As through the pure and tranquil eventide
　　A flash is seen from time to time to race,
　　Setting the calmest eyelids staring wide,
Appearing like a star that changes place,
　　Save that, where first enkindled is its light
　　Nothing is missed, and it goes out apace,—
So shot from the arm extending to the right
　　To bottom of the cross, a star of them
　　That make the constellation there so bright;
Downward it ran along the radiant stem
　　Like fire in alabaster shining through,
　　Nor from the fillet once broke forth the gem.

338

Such love the shade of old Anchises drew,
  If credit we our poet passing great,
  When in Elysium his son he knew.
'O kinsman mine! Grace incommensurate
  Upon thee shed! to whom, as unto thee,
  Was ever opened twice the Heavenly gate?'
So spake that light; whence thereto eagerly
  I turned,—then to my Lady,—in such wise
  That from both quarters awe came over me;
For such a smile was glowing in her eyes
  That, with mine own, methought I touched the [bound
  Both of my grace and of my Paradise.
Thereafter, blithe of look and blithe of sound,
  That soul to salutation added speech
  Past my conception, it was so profound;
Of choice concealed he not what he would teach,
  But force perforce, because the lofty sense
  So overshot the mark of mortal reach.
But when the bow of burning love less tense
  Became, and his discourse came down and stood
  Upon the plane of our intelligence,
The first expression that I understood
  Was: 'Benediction on Thee, Trine and One,
  For guerdoning my kinsman with such good!'
'A grateful and long fast,' he followed on,
  'From reading the Great Book where black on
  Is set down ineffaceably, my son,   [white
Hast thou now satisfied within this light
  I hail thee from, thanks to her favour who
  Clad thee with plumage for the lofty flight.
Thou deemest that thy thought to me flows through
  From the First Cause, even as from unity,
  If that be known, the five and six to you,
Not asking who I am, nor why in me
  Appears a gratulation more elate
  Than elsewhere in this jocund company.

Thou deemest true: in this life small and great
 Are gazing in that Mirror whence, before
 Thou thinkest, thy reflections emanate.
But that the Holy Love mine eyes adore
 In vigil never broken, hunger-spent
 With sweet desire, may be fulfilled the more,
O let thy voice, secure, glad, confident,
 For will and yearning find the fitting word
 Whereto is predetermined my consent.'
Thereon I turned to Beatrice, who heard
 Before I spake and gave assent, whereby
 The growing wings of my desire were stirred.
'When dawned on you the Prime Equality,
 Love and intelligence for each of you
 Became of equal poise,'—so answered I;
'Because the Sun that lit and warmed you through
 Holds in its heat and light such balance fit
 That all comparison falls short of true.
But mortal wing of will and wing of wit,
 For reason well apparent to your sight,
 Fail of the balanced pinions requisite.
Whence I, who with the heart alone requite
 Thy dear paternal welcome, feel my lame
 Mortal disparity of will and might.
I do entreat thee, living topaz-flame,
 Set as a gem upon this jewel choice,
 To satisfy my craving with thy name.'
'O leaf of mine, who made me even rejoice
 Expecting thee, thy root behold in me!'
 Beginning thus, replied to me the voice;
Then said: 'That soul who gave thy family
 The surname, and has round the Mountain gone
 On the first terrace, a long century,
Was thy great-grandfather, and was my son:
 Befits that respite thou for him bespeak
 From his long travail, with thy orison.

Florence, encircled by her wall antique,
    Whence tierce and nones are tolling evermore,
    Lived peaceable and temperate and meek.
Her arm no clasp, no crown her forehead bore,
    No silken petticoat, with girdle gay
    More tempting to the eye than she who wore.
Not yet did little daughter's birth dismay
    The father; not too early did they mate,
    Nor yet was dowry ruinous to pay.
No house was then of children desolate;
    Not yet Sardanapalus came to show
    What in a chamber he can perpetrate.
Not yet outflown was Monte Mario
    By your Uccellatoio,—which as outflown
    In soaring up, shall be in falling low.
I saw in belt of skin and clasp of bone
    Bellincion Berti, and his lady quit
    The mirror with complexion still her own;
I saw the Nerli and the Vecchio fit
    The leathern jerkin with good countenance,
    With spindle and with flax their ladies sit.
O happy women! each yet in advance
    Sure of her burial, and none beguiled
    Of comfort in her bed because of France.
One, keeping watch above her cradled child,
    Would soothe it with the babbling idiom
    Whereto the fathers and the mothers smiled;
And one, the thread from distaff drawing home,
    Gathered her brood and prattled fables how
    Came Trojans to Fiesolë and Rome.
A marvel then Cianghella's brazen brow,
    Or Lapo Salterello, as complete
    As Cincinnatus and Cornelia now.
To life of citizen in house and street
    So fair and quiet, to so great a fame
    For neighbour loyalty, to home so sweet,

341

My mother gave me, calling Mary's name;
    And so, within your ancient Baptistry,
    Christian and Cacciaguida I became.
Moronto and Eliseo brothered me;
    My Lady came from Valley of the Po,
    Whence was thy surname handed down to thee.
I followed Kaiser Conrad then, with so
    Good service that he belted me a knight,
    So much my prowess made his favour grow.
Beneath his banner followed I to fight
    That ill-famed law whose folk usurp control,
    To pastors' shame, of what is yours by right.
There disentangled by those caitiffs foul
    Was I from the delusive world, whose quest
    Infatuate debases many a soul,
And came from martyrdom unto this rest.'

CANTO XVI

O petty our nobility of blood!
    If thou prompt men to make their boast of thee
    Down here, where faints our yearning for the good,
Never shall this seem wonderful to me,
    For where desire is not perverted, yea
    In Heaven itself, I felt such vanity.
In truth, thy cloak so quickly shrinks away,
    That, add we not a frequent piece thereto,
    Time with the shears goes round it day by day.
With *You*, which Rome at first permitted, *You*,
    Wherein her children now least persevere,
    Proudly began I my discourse anew.
Whence Beatrice, a little distant here,
    By smiling called to mind that dame who coughed
    At first recorded fault of Guenevere.

'You are my Father,' so began I soft,
　'You fill me for discourse with courage high,
　You lift me far above myself aloft.
So many rivulets are pouring joy
　Into my heart that happy is my tongue
　Seeing I can bear and not be rent thereby.
Tell then, belovèd root whence I am sprung,
　Who were your forebears, what the years foregone
　That signalized themselves when you were young.
Tell me about the sheepfold of Saint John,
　What were the numbers and who were the folk
　Within it who the highest places won?'
As is by breathing of the wind awoke
　Flame in a coal, so did I see that blaze
　Kindle at the caressing words I spoke,
And growing ever fairer to my gaze,
　With sweeter accent gentlier it said,
　But in no dialect of nowadays:
'From the first *Ave* to that childing-bed
　Whereon my mother, now ensainted, through
　Delivering of me was comforted,
Five hundred times and fifty and thirty drew
　This circling fire to its own Lion apace,
　Beneath his paw to kindle up anew.
My sires and I were native to that place
　Where the last ward first intersects the course
　Of the hot runner in your annual race.
Enough about my elders this perforce
　For as to whence they came and who they were,
　Silence is more becoming than discourse.
All those at that time competent to bear
　Weapons, the Baptistry and Mars between,
　Numbered a fifth of them now living there.
But the community, where intervene
　Campi, Certaldo, and Figlinë now,
　Pure to the humblest artisan was seen.

343

O how much better let such neighbours plough
    Around Galluzzo, and let your border lie
    At Trespiano, rather than allow
Their entrance, so to be offended by
    The stench of Aguglion, and Signa's clown,
    Who has for jobbery so sharp an eye.
Were folk who most on earth have fallen down
    Not stepmother to Cæsar, but instead
    Benignant, like true mother to her son,
One, made a Florentine by truck and trade,
    Would have turned back to Semifontë again,
    Where went about his grandsire begging bread.
Still would the Counts on Montemurlo reign,
    The Cerchi be in Aconë's parish still,
    Perchance the Buondelmonte on Greve's plain.
When mingled populations overfill
    The city, evermore begins its woe,
    As added victual makes the body ill.
And the blind bullock falls more headlong low
    Than the blind lamb, and more one sword will
    And often deeper than the five will go.   [cleave,
If Luni and Urbisaglia thou perceive,
    How they have gone, and likewise pass away
    Chiusi and Senigallia, to believe
That in like fashion families decay
    Will seem opinion neither strange nor new,
    Seeing that even cities have their day.
All your affairs are mortal even as you,
    The very brevity of life concealing
    In some the creeping steps of death from view;
And as the lunar heaven, for ever wheeling,
    Covers and bares incessantly the shore,
    So fickle Fortune is with Florence dealing.
Hence what I tell should seem no fable-lore
    Concerning the renownèd Florentines   [more.
    Whose fame through lapse of time is known no

I saw the Hugos, saw the Catellines,
    Filippi, Greci, Ormanni, Alberichi there,
    Illustrious citizens in their declines,
And saw, as mighty as they ancient were,
    With one of La Sannella, of Arca one,
    Ardinghi and Bostichi and Soldanier.
Above the gateway newly weighed upon
    By felony so heavy in its shame
    That from the bark shall soon be jettison,
Dwelt then the Ravignani, from whom came
    Count Guido down, and whoso to this hour
    Has taken lofty Bellincionë's name.
He of La Pressa wisely wielded power
    Already, and the Galigaio claimed
    Sword-hilt and pummel gilt in hall and bower.
Greatly the pale of Minever was famed,
    Sacchetti, Giuochi, Fifanti, and Barucci,
    And Galli,—and others by the bushel shamed.
The parent stock whence budded the Calfucci
    Was great already, and to curule chair
    Already drawn Sizii and Arrigucci.
Ah, mighty did I see them who despair
    Because of their own pride! and the Balls of Gold
    In all her prowess made our Florence fair.
So likewise did the ancestors of old
    Of those who, when your see is vacant, find
    Fat profit by abiding in the fold.
That haughty breed, so dragon-fierce behind
    The fugitive, but let your teeth be seen
    Or purse belike, seem lambs, they grow so kind,
Was on the rise, although from people mean,
    Whence Ubertin Donato felt disgrace
    When his wife's father made them kith and kin.
Down from Fiesolë to market-place
    Had gone now Caponsacco,—Judah there
    And Infangato, burghers in good grace.

Incredible, yet true, what I declare:
   The little circuit had an entrance way
   Called after them whose emblem is the Pear.
All wearers of the fair insignia
   Of the great Peer, whose name and valour grim
   The feast of Thomas calls to mind to-day,
Knighthood received and privilege from him;
   Though with the populace to-day unite
   That man who guards the scutcheon with a rim.
Gualterotti and Importuni were at height;
   And had they for new neighbours suffered dearth
   More tranquil would the Borgo be to-night.
The house from which your tears have had their birth,
   Because its just resentment killed your joyance
   And with the blood of many stained the earth,
Was honoured in itself and its alliance:
   O Buondelmontë, by what evil daring
   Didst flee at others' prompting its affiance!
Glad would be many who are now despairing,
   If God had to the Ema relegated
   Thyself, when first toward the city faring.
But meet it was that Florence consecrated
   A victim, while her last peace was prevailing,
   To that bridge-warding marble mutilated.
With folk like these, nor yet were others failing,
   Did I see Florence in such deep repose
   That she had no occasion yet for wailing;
I saw her people glorious with those,
   And just, so that the Lily never stood
   Reversed upon the lances of her foes,
Nor dyed vermilion yet by party feud.'

PARADISO

CANTO XVII

As who makes fathers chary of undue   *Dante's Exile and*
  Promise to children, questioned Clymenë   *Justification*
  If what he heard against himself was true,
Even such was I, and such perceived to be
  By Beatrice and by the Holy Lamp
  Who previously had changed his place for me.
Then said my Lady to me: 'Do not damp
  The flame of thy desire, but let it soar
  Well making manifest the inward stamp;
Not that thy words may make our knowledge more,
  But that thou mayst acquire the habitude
  To tell thy thirst that we for thee may pour.'
'Dear parent stock, raised to such altitude
  That, as to earthly minds is evident
  No triangle may two obtuse include,
Thus do contingent things before the event
  Exist for thee, still gazing where take head
  All times together with the present blent;
While in the company of Virgil led
  Up and along the spirit-healing slope
  And down throughout the region of the dead,
I heard discourses grievous in their scope
  Touching the remnant of my life, although
  Well squared against the blows of chance by hope:
Wherefore my will were well content to know
  What fortune is approaching to molest:
  For bolt foreshadowed strikes a lighter blow.'
So to that selfsame light that had addressed
  Beforehand me, I said as willed to say
  By Beatrice, and mine own will confessed.
Not with blind riddles which in former day
  Ensnared the credulous, ere yet was slain
  The Lamb of God who takes our sins away,

347

But with clear utterance and language plain
  That fatherly affection made reply,
  In his own smile withdrawn and shown again:
'Contingency, which is embounded by
  The volume of your matter, is beheld
  All pictured forth before the Eternal Eye,
Yet not thence of necessity compelled,
  More than the vessel down the current steering
  Is by the mirror in the eye propelled.
Therefrom comes, even as comes upon the hearing
  Sweet organ music, to my sight the course
  Of time already now for thee preparing.
As through stepmother proof to all remorse
  Hippolytus from Athens fled of old,
  So out of Florence shalt thou go perforce.
Already this is willed and sought,—nay hold
  It good as done by him who schemes the plot
  Where every day the Christ is bought and sold.
The wonted cry of blame will follow hot
  The party wronged; but vengeance yet will bring
  Witness to Truth that shall the wage allot.
Thou shalt leave far behind thee everything
  Most dearly loved: the sharpest barb is there
  That first the bow of banishment lets fling.
Thereby shalt thou make proof what bitter fare
  Is bread of others, and how hard a road
  The going up and down another's stair.
Yet for thy shoulders the most crushing load
  Will be companions witless and malign
  With whom thou hast to fall to such abode,
Who, graceless and ungrateful, will combine
  All furious against thee; but their own
  Foreheads will soon be red for it, not thine.
Of their stupidity will proof be shown
  In what they do, till thou shalt find it best
  To have made a party by thyself alone.

Thy first asylum and first house of rest
   Shall be the mighty Lombard's courtesy
   Who on the Ladder bears the Eagle blest,
Who will have so benignant heed for thee
   That of the doing and asking 'twixt you two
   First will be what is wonted last to be.
Beside him shalt thou see that hero who
   From this strong star received at birth such seal
   That his emprise will be renowned therethrough.
His tender age does not as yet reveal
   Him to the people: only while are told
   Nine childish years, these circles round him wheel;
But ere the Gascon pontiff have cajoled
   The lofty Henry, sparks of worth shall shoot,
   Showing him careless both of toil and gold.
Fame of his glorious deeds so absolute
   Shall grow, that foes shall not prove dominant
   Enough to keep the tongues of people mute.
On him and on his favours do thou plant
   Thy trust; through him shall many change degree,
   Altering state, both rich and mendicant.
And bear thou written in thy memory
   Of him, but tell it not,'—and he revealed
   Things past believing, even of those who see.
Then added: 'Son, these glosses may be sealed
   To what was told thee; snares are waiting thus
   Behind few circles of the spheres concealed.
Yet be not of thy neighbours envious,
   Seeing thy future life will long outlast
   The forfeit of their deeds perfidious.'
Soon as that holy soul to silence passed,
   Showing the pattern it had woven above
   The web whereof myself the warp had cast,
Did I begin like one misdoubting of
   His course, who craves advice from one of those
   That, seeing, do correctly will, and love:

'Well see I, Father, how my time of woes
    To deal me such a buffet spurs along
    As is the heavier when one heedless goes;
Whence it is good with foresight to be strong,
    That, though the dearest place bereft me be,
    I forfeit not the others by my song.
Down through the world embittered endlessly,
    And up the Mountain from whose lovely height
    My Lady with her eyes uplifted me,
And then throughout these heavens from light to light,
    Have I learnt what, retold by me, would reek
    With savour rank to many an appetite;
And if to Truth I prove a friend too meek,
    I fear the forfeiture of life with those
    Who after us shall call this time antique.'
That light, which by its smiling did disclose
    My treasure-trove, then flashed out, coruscating
    As in the sun a golden mirror glows.
'A conscience clouded, whether contemplating
    Its own shame or another's,' he replied,
    'Will feel thy language veritably grating.
But none the less, put every lie aside,
    And make thy vision clearly manifested,
    Letting them scratch who have an itching hide;
For, though thy word be grievous, barely tasted,
    It will leave vital nourishment behind
    When it shall thoroughly have been digested.
This cry of thine will do as doth a wind
    Which buffets most the peaks of loftiest crown,
    Wherein no little honour shalt thou find.
Whence in these wheeling Circles have been shown,
    As well as in the Mount and Valley of Ill,
    Only those spirits who by fame are known:
Because the hearer's mind is volatile
    So that it will not yield to argument
    From case unrecognized and hidden, nor will
Pin faith to proof that is not evident.'

CANTO XVIII

Now in his inward thought with joy replete
    Was that blest Mirror, and I savoured mine
    By seasoning the bitter with the sweet;
And the Lady leading me to the Divine
    Said: 'Shift thy thought to see my link unbroken
    With him who lightens every load malign.'
Thereat I turned to look at the fond token
    Of my Consoler, and what love I viewed
    In the holy eyes is here perforce unspoken,
Partly that words would be misunderstood,
    Partly that memory is unreturning
    If others guide not to such altitude.
This only can I tell that point concerning,
    That, rebeholding her, my own affection
    Grew fetterless and free from other yearning.
While the Eternal Joy, without deflection
    Rayed upon Beatrice, and mirror-wise
    From her fair look appeased me by reflection,
Subduing me with light of smiling eyes,
    'Turn round and hearken,' thus to me she said,
    'Not in mine eyes alone is Paradise!'
As sometimes in the visage here is read
    The inclination, if of so much force
    That the whole soul thereby is riveted,
So turning to my great progenitor's
    Sanctified radiance, the wish I found
    Yet somewhat further with me to discourse.
Then he began to speak: 'In this fifth round
    Branching the Tree that draws life from the crest
    And fruits for aye, and never sheds a frond,
Are souls who, ere they came among the blest,
    Were in the world below of so great fame
    Could noble Muse no richer theme request.

The Mystic Symbol
of Justice in the
Temperate Star
of Jove

351

Observe the arms o' the Cross, and those I name
    Will at the signal in such mode proceed
    As in the cloud its fulminating flame.'
I saw along the Cross a lustre speed
    At name of Joshua: to ear and eye
    The word did not anticipate the deed.
And at the name of Maccabæus high
    Another spiral whirling flashed amain,
    And that which whipped the top was holy joy.
Likewise for Roland and for Charlemagne
    Did my enraptured gaze two lights pursue,
    As eye doth after flying falcon strain.
Afterward William drew, and Renouard drew,
    And great Duke Godfrey drew mine eye by fire
    Along that Cross, and Robert Guiscard too.
Then mingling with the other lights, the Sire
    Whose spirit had discoursed with me made known
    His artistry among the heavenly quire.
To my right hand I turned me at that tone,
    My duty to behold in Beatrice
    Either by language or by gesture shown,
And all her past and recent wont by this
    Her present look was vanquished, such a ray
    Flashed from her eyes lit with exceeding bliss.
And as by greater comfort in essay
    Of righteous doing, man becomes aware
    Of virtue waxing in him day by day,
So, wheeling in a wider circle there,
    A heaven of more extended scope I knew,
    Seeing that miracle become more fair.
For now a shift of colour met my view,
    As when a woman's countenance, oppressed
    With blushful shame, resumes its pallid hue,
Such, when I turned about was manifest
    Dawning in the white star of temperance,
    The sixth that had received me to its breast.

I saw within that Jovial radiance
   The flying sparks of love that there abound
   Shaping our language out before my glance.
As birds, rejoicing in their pasture ground,
   Start up together from a river dell
   And gather in a flock, now long, now round,
So holy creatures in the lights that dwell,
   Were flitting and were chanting, fashioning
   Their flock to figures,—D and I and L.
First sang they, to their own notes fluttering,
   Then, having fashioned one or the other sign.
   Would hold their peace awhile and stay their wing.
O Pegaseä, glorifier divine
   Of human wits, their life to render long,
   As towns and kingdoms they, by aid of thine,
Brighten me with thyself to tell in song
   Their shapes as I deciphered them in Heaven,
   In these brief verses let thy breath be strong!
These then displayed themselves in five times seven
   Vowels and consonants: I noted down
   The members as they seemed by utterance given.
DILIGITE JUSTITIAM, first noun
   And verb of all the figure were enscrolled,
   QUI JUDICATIS TERRAM, followed on.
These in the M of the fifth word did hold
   Such settled order there, that Jupiter
   Seemed to be silver patterned out with gold.
And other lights I saw descending where
   The apex of the M appeared their goal,
   Chanting, I think, the Good that draws them there.
Then, as by stirring of a burning coal
   Innumerable sparks are upward sped,
   Prophetic omens to the simple soul,
So thence thousands of lights seemed spirited
   To mount aloft, some lower and some higher,
   By their enkindling Sun distributed;

And lo! when settled into place each flyer,
   I saw an Eagle as to head and breast
   Delineated by that patterned fire.
He there who paints has none to guide, but best
   Guideth Himself, and from Him we divine
   The secret of the moulding of the nest.
The other blessèd flock, content to twine
   A lily flower at first upon the M,
   With a slight flutter filled out the design.
Sweet star, what jewels, and how many of them,
   Informed me that our Justice is the birth
   Of that sixth heaven whereof thou art the gem!
Wherefore I pray the Mind wherein thy worth
   And motion start, that He take note whence come
   The fumes that dim thy radiance on earth;
That he once more be wroth with all and some
   Who buy and sell within the Temple-door
   Built round with miracles and martyrdom.
O heavenly host on whom I gaze, implore
   For them who still are here on earth, each one
   Misled by ill example! War of yore
Was waged by dint of sword, but now 'tis done
   By keeping back from one and the other guest
   The bread the pitying Father locks to none.
But thou who writest and then cancellest
   Take heed that Peter and Paul are living yet,
   Who died for the vineyard thou art laying waste.
Well mayst thou urge: 'I have my heart so set
   On that ascetic who in royal hall
   Was danced into the martyr's coronet,
That I know not the Fisherman nor Paul.'

CANTO XIX

The image fashioned by the engarlanding
  Souls who in sweet fruition took delight,
  Stood fair before me, spreading either wing.
Each seemed a little ruby where a bright
  Sunbeam appeared so burningly to sink
  As to flame back again upon my sight.
And what I now am bound to tell, by ink
  Was never traced, by ear was never heard,
  Nor entered into heart of man to think:
For lo! I heard and saw that beakèd Bird
  Give voice to I and MY, though understood
  Were WE and OUR as men conceive the word.
So it began: 'Through being just and good
  Raised am I to that glory far transcending
  All mortal yearning for beatitude,
And left remembrance of my great intending
  Upon the earth, but wicked people there
  Follow the story not, although commending.'
As many an ember makes us feel the glare
  Of one sole heat, so rang one melody
  From many loves out of that image fair:
Whereon I prayed: 'O flowers perpetually
  Blooming from joy eternal, breathing forth
  Your odours that one fragrance seem to me,
So breathing, banish from me the great dearth
  Which makes me for so long in hunger pine,
  Finding not any food for it on earth.
Well know I that, though Justice the divine
  Be in another Heavenly kingdom glassed,
  No veil for you endarkens the design.
Ye know how eagerly do I forecast
  The hearing, and ye know what is that doubt
  Which is within me such a long-drawn fast.'

The Symbolic
Eagle discourses
of Divine Justice

355

CANTO XIX
34'69

As from the hood the falcon issuing out
  Conceals not her desire, but makes her fair,
  Lifting her head and fluttering about,
So in my sight became that emblem, where
  Praises of Grace Divine were interwound
  With songs familiar to the happy there.
Then it began: 'Who turned the compass round
  The world, and Who in its circumference
  Set much both clear to sight and too profound,
Could not in all the Universe condense
  His Worth so far but that His Infinite
  Wisdom remained in overplus immense.
In proof whereof, behold that first proud Wight
  Among all creatures supereminent,
  Falling unripe, through not awaiting light:
Therefore too scanty a recipient
  Appears each lesser nature for that Good
  Which has no bound but by self-measurement.
From this it follows that our sight, which should
  Out of that Mind supernal radiate
  Wherewith all things whatever are imbued,
Can by its nature have no power so great
  But that its origin sees far afield
  Beyond the scope of all we contemplate.
Therefore no vision to your world revealed
  Can plumb eternal Justice to the ground,
  Just as the ocean to your eye is sealed;
Awhile from shore ye may the bottom sound,
  And out of soundings in the unplumbed sea
  We know it still is there, though never found.
Save from the never-clouded Source, may be
  No light, but rather everywhere is shade,
  Venom and shadow of carnality.
Now amply is the covert open laid
  That kept the living Justice from thy sight,
  Whereof thou hast so frequent question made.

"For," saidest thou, "on Indus-bank a wight
   Is brought to birth, where none is to direct
   To Christ, nor who may read of Him, nor write,
And all his acts and wishes are correct
   As far as human reason may perceive,
   Whether in word or life without defect;
Faithless he dies, nor baptism can receive:
   What is this justice which condemns the man?
   What is his fault if he do not believe?"
Now who art thou to mount the bench and scan
   A thousand miles from what thou wouldst discuss,
   With thy short vision reaching but a span?
Surely for him who cavils with me thus,
   Were not the Scripture over you, the food
   For subtle questioning were marvellous.
O earthly animals! O spirits rude!
   Never the Primal Will was self-betraying,
   Nor altered from Itself the Supreme Good.
Weighed is your human justice with Its weighing,
   By no created goodness is It led,
   Rather from It created good is raying.'
As wheels the mother-stork just overhead
   When she has given her nestlings all their fill,
   And they look up toward her comforted,
So thither was my brow uplifted still,
   And circling so the blessèd image flew
   On wings propelled by force of many a will.
Wheeling it chanted, adding thereunto:
   'My notes thou hearest heeding not their sense,
   So mortals by Eternal Justice do.'
When quiet was that glowing effluence
   Of Holy Ghost, still in the heraldry
   That gained the Romans world-wide reverence,
'Up to this Kingdom,' it resumed to me,
   'Rose never one who had not faith in Christ
   Before or since they nailed Him to the tree.

357

But many, mark, who cry aloud Christ! Christ!
  Shall be less near Him at the Great Assize,
  By very far, than some who know not Christ.
The Ethiop shall such Christians stigmatize
  When the two colleges apart are led,
  One poor, the other with the eternal prize.
To Christian monarchs what will not be said
  By Persians, when the Book is open placed
  Upon whose page their evil deeds are spread?
There 'mid the deeds of Albert shall be traced
  That which will start the moving pen once more,
  To show the realm of Prague become a waste;
There seen how men along the Seine deplore
  The doing of that counterfeiter accurst
  Foredoomed to die by bristle of the boar;
There seen the arrogance that quickens thirst,
  Driving both Scot and Englishman insane,
  Whence both anon across the border burst;
There the soft life and lust of him of Spain
  And the Bohemian,—never known to them
  Was prowess, or held ever in disdain.
There to the Cripple of Jerusalem
  Shall with an I the good be credited,
  While the reverse is rated at an M.
There shall the greed and cowardice be read
  Of him who wards the fiery Island,—tomb
  Where the long journey of Anchises led;
And to denote him paltry, let the doom
  In curt abbreviations be set down,
  Infinite matter in a little room.
And foul to all be noted the renown
  Of uncle and of brother, who deflower
  Illustrious lineage, and each a crown.
And he who holds in Portugal the power,
  And Norway shall be shown; and Rascia there
  Who saw Venetian coin in evil hour.

O blest were Hungary, if she would bear
   No buffets longer; and Navarre in bliss
   If her own mountain but a rampart were!
And let each one recall, in proof of this,
   How Nicosìa and Famagusta groan
   Already for their beast, and take it amiss
That he beside the others hold his own.'

CANTO XX

When he who sheds through all the world his ray
   Is from our hemisphere descending so
   That everywhere the daylight fades away,
The sky, ablaze with him short while ago,
   Is suddenly rekindled to our ken
   By many lights that answer to one glow:
And I recalled this heavenly action when
   The ensign of the world and of its head
   Grew silent in the blessèd beak again;
For all those living luminaries, made
   Brighter than ever, were beginning chants
   Out of my memory to lapse and fade.
O sweet Love, veiled in smiling radiance,
   How ardent didst thou seem in those canorous
   Flutes that breathed only holy meditance!
After the bright and precious brilliants o'er us,
   Wherewith I saw the sixth heaven glittering,
   Had made an end of their angelic chorus,
It seemed to me I heard a murmuring
   Stream that runs limpid down from stone to stone
   Showing the plenty of its mountain spring.
And as upon the cittern's neck the tone
   Assumes its form, and in reed instrument
   The vent-holes mould the breathing through it blown,

*The Eagle continues
to discourse*

Thus, brooking no delay, incontinent
   Did that soft murmur of the Eagle float
   Up through the neck, as if it were a vent;
There became voice, and issued from the throat
   Out through the beak, with words in unison
   With longing of the heart whereon I wrote.
'That part in me which sees, and braves the sun
   In mortal eagles,' it prelusive said,
   'Should now attentively be gazed upon;
For of the fires whereof my form is made,
   Those are in all their grades of most renown
   Wherewith the eye is sparkling in my head.
Who midmost as the pupil glitters down,
   He was the Holy Spirit's laureate
   Who bore about the Ark from town to town;
Now knows he his song's merit adequate,
   So far as subject to his will's control,
   By the reward which is proportionate.
Of five who curve along my brow, that soul
   Neighbouring nearest to the beak of me
   Did the poor widow for her son console;
Now knows he dear the ransom is if we
   Follow not Christ, by the experience
   Of this sweet life, and of the contrary.
Who next, along on the circumference
   In question, follows on the upward way
   Delayed his death by very penitence;
Now knows he that Eternal Judgement may
   Be altered never, though a worthy prayer
   On earth below to-morrows the to-day.
The next, to set the Pastor in the chair,
   Ill fruitage gathering from good intents,
   Made Greek himself, the laws, and me down there;
Now knows he that the evil consequence
   Of his good deed gives him no cause to grieve,
   Although the world go all to ruin thence.

Next in the downward curve dost thou perceive
  Him who was William, whom those lands regret
  Which weep that Charles and Frederick still live;
Now knows he how the love of Heaven is set
  On a just king, and the effulgency
  Of his appearance makes it patent yet.
Down in the erring world who would agree
  That Trojan Rhipeus in this round were fit
  The fifth among the holy lights to be?
Now knows he much whereof our human wit
  In Grace Divine can catch not any gleam,
  Although his vision cannot fathom it.'
Like to the lark that in the morning beam
  Upsoars, first singing and thereafter still,
  Rapt with the sweetness of her song supreme,
Such seemed the imaged Emblem of the Will
  Eternal, in accordance with whose bent
  Created things their final ends fulfil.
And notwithstanding that my wonderment
  Showed through me like the colour through the
  Yet could it not abide the time content,   [glaze,
But forced by virtue of its weight the phrase
  Forth from my lips,—'What wonders these!' Oh
  I saw great revelry of flashing rays!   [thence
Thereon with kindling eye still more intense,
  To me the Blessèd Emblem made reply,
  To hold me not in wondering suspense:
'I see that thou believ'st these things, since I
  Report them to thee, but dar'st not avow,
  For, though believed, they are hidden from the eye.
Thou doest like that one who may well allow
  A thing in name, but who cannot define
  Its essence if another show not how.
The Kingdom of Heaven suffers force benign
  From living hope and loving fervency,
  Able to overcome the Will Divine;

Not as man over man wins victory,
  That which is craving to be quelled they quell,
  Which, conquered, conquers through benignity.
The brow's first living soul and fifth may well
  Astonish thee, because thou seest with those
  Adorned the region where the angels dwell.
These left their bodies not, as men suppose,
  Gentile, but Christian, each in firm faith cleaving
  To crucifixion's past or future throes.
For one from Hell, whence none returns retrieving
  Good will again, did yet his bones resume,
  And living hope this guerdon was receiving,
The living hope whence vital power should bloom
  Through prayer to God for his upraising made,
  So that his will could move to change his doom.
The glorious spirit whereof this is said,
  Short while abiding in the flesh on earth,
  Put faith in Him who had the power to aid,
And so belief enkindled on his hearth
  True love, that when returned he to the grave
  He was found fit to come unto this mirth.
So deep a fountain yielded grace to save
  The other soul, no eye, however bright,
  Of any creature pierced its primal wave;
And so in righteousness was his delight
  That our redemption in the future, more
  And more by Grace was opened to his sight:
Wherefore he put his trust therein, nor bore
  Thenceforth the stench from heathendom arising,
  Reproving the perverted folk therefor.
To him, a thousand years ere solemnizing
  Of baptism, those three maids thou sawst, who wheeled
  Beside the dexter wheel, stood for baptizing.
Predestination! Ah, how far afield
  Thy root from vision of their intellect
  To whom the First Cause is not all revealed!

And be ye, mortals, closely circumspect
In judging, forasmuch as we, who see
The very God, know not yet all the elect;
And in such lack is our felicity,
For in this good our own good we refine
So that with Will Divine our wills agree.'
Thus by that emblematic form divine,
To make me feel the limits of my vision,
Was dealt to me delightful medicine.
As on the chorded lute the good musician
Pinching the strings supports the singer good,
Thus making more delightful the rendition,
So I remember, while he thus pursued,
Beholding those two blessèd lustres dance
Accordant, as the eyes in winking would,
Moving their flamelets with that utterance.

CANTO XXI

Already on my Lady's countenance
Mine eyes were bended, and my mind withdrew
With them from every other circumstance;
Nor was she smiling, but began thereto:
'Were I to smile thou wouldst become like fair
Semelë, when she dust and ashes grew;
Because my beauty on the Palace stair
Eternal, shining in more bright relief
As thou hast seen, with our ascending there,
If not attempered, would be past belief
Effulgent, so that thy poor mortal sense
Would be but as the thunder-blasted leaf.
Raised are we to the Seventh Splendour, whence,
Now warmed beneath the Lion's burning breast,
Rains down its mitigated influence.

Heaven of Saturn

Let thy mind follow where thine eyes request,
  And let them mirrors be for that reflection
  Which in this mirror shall be manifest.'
Whoso could know how great was the refection
  Mine eyes found in her features sanctified,
  When drawn away perforce in new direction,
Might comprehend, by weighing the one side
  With the other, how delighted I became
  To do the bidding of my heavenly Guide.
Within the crystal that doth bear the name
  The world around of its bright Leader, who
  So ruled that perished every deed of blame,
I saw a Ladder all of golden hue
  Burnished with light, and lifted up so high
  Mine eyes were unavailing to pursue;
Then saw so many splendours downward fly
  Along its rungs, all light the stars distil
  Had, it appeared to me, been shed thereby.
And as, at bidding of their nature's will,
  Jackdaws together flock at break of day,
  Bestirring them to warm their plumage chill;
Thereafter there are some who fly away
  Without returning, others fly off where
  They started from, and others, wheeling, stay:
In such a fashion came together there,
  Methought, that scintillating company,
  Soon as it lighted on a certain stair;
And one, which nearest us appeared to be,
  Became so bright, I murmured in my thought:
  'Well I perceive thy love that signals me.'
But she, by whom the How and Where is taught
  Of speech and silence, pauses, whence aright
  I do, against desire, inquiring not.
Whence she who saw my silence in the sight
  Of That One to whose seeing all is shown,
  Bade me,—'Appease thy yearning appetite!'

PARADISO: CANTO XIX
The Recording Angel

And I began: 'No merit of mine own.
  Renders me worthy that thou make reply,
  But for her sake who bids me ask, make known
To me, O soul in bliss, enshrouded by
  The joyfulness within thyself abounding,
  What cause has put thee near me thus? and why
Keeps utter silence, where this sphere is rounding,
  The dulcet symphony of Paradise
  Down through the others so devoutly sounding?'
'Thy mortal eye and ear are both amiss,'
  He answered, 'here aloft no songs are sung
  For the same cause that smiles not Beatrice.
Down on the sacred ladder rung by rung
  So far descended I to make thee graced
  With words, and with the radiance round me flung;
Nor was it greater love that made me haste,
  For equal love, or more, burns up above,
  As makes the flaming clearly manifest;
But we, as prompted by Exalted Love,
  To serve the purpose of the world so burn:
  'Tis love allots,—thou seest the mode thereof.'
'Full well, O holy lamp, do I discern
  How love, left free, may in this Court suffice
  For following the Providence eterne;
But ever this is baffling to mine eyes:
  Wherefore among thy consorts thou alone
  Hast been predestinate to this emprise?'
Before I uttered forth the final tone,
  The light an axis of its middle made,
  Rapidly whirling as in mill the stone.
Thereon the loving spirit in it said:
  'Focused on me is radiance divine
  Piercing the mesh of that around me shed,
Whereof the virtue and my sight combine
  To lift me so above myself, I see
  The Fount Supreme whence doth this lustre shine.

Thence comes the rapture all aflame in me,
    For to my vision as it grows more bright
    I match a flame of equal clarity.
But soul in Heaven with most access of light,
    Seraph whose eye is most on God intent,
    Could to thy question not reply aright,
For it is gulfed in the arbitrament
    Unfathomed, of eternal law's control,
    Where all created sight is vainly bent.
Carry this back to every mortal soul
    On thy return, that men no more presume
    To lift their feet toward so high a goal.
The mind that here is flame, on earth is fume;
    Consider then if it down there can see
    That which it cannot, although Heaven assume.'
His words imposed such limit upon me,
    I put the question by, and did no more
    Than humbly ask of his identity.
'Crags rise in Italy 'twixt shore and shore,
    And from thy fatherland not far away,
    So high, the thunderstorms below them roar,
Swelling aloft to a height called Catria,
    Whereunder is a sacred hermitage
    Once destined only as a place to pray.'
So for the third time spoke to me that sage;
    Continuing: 'There, on God's service bent,
    So used was I my hunger to assuage
On bread with olive juice for condiment,
    That here I passed the seasons hot and cold
    Lightly, in thoughts contemplative content.
That cloister once bore fruitage manifold
    Unto these heavens, but now it yields no more,
    As must perforce hereafter soon unfold.
There Peter Damian was the name I bore;
    Peter the Sinner was I in the fane
    Of Our own Lady on the Adrian shore.

To me did little mortal life remain,
  When called to take, against my own accord,
  That hat which shifts from bad to worse again.
Came Cephas, the great Vessel of the Lord
  Came lean and barefoot, taking bit and sup
  From whatsoever hospitable board.
Now serving-men are needed to hold up
  Fat modern pastors, one on either side
  And one before and one behind to prop.
Their furs o'erflow the palfreys which they ride
  (How much, O Patience, hast thou yet to bear!)
  So that two beasts go underneath one hide.'
Flames saw I at such cry from stair to stair
  Descending and whirling round in multitude,
  At every whirl becoming still more fair.
Around this soul they flocking came, and stood,
  And lifted up such high resounding shout
  That here there could be no similitude,
Nor, thunderstricken, could I make it out.

CANTO XXII

Plunged in bewilderment I turned me thence
  Round to my Guide, even as a little child
  Runs ever where he feels most confidence;
And promptly as a mother's cadence mild
  Is wonted to give courage to her son
  Pallid and gasping,—so her words beguiled
My fear: 'Enfolds thee not the benison
  Of Heaven where all is holy? and canst thou doubt
  That zeal for good prompts what in Heaven is done?
What perturbation had been brought about
  Both by the singing and my smiling eye,
  When thou hast been so startled by the shout?

CANTO XXI
124-142

St. Benedict;
Dante's Natal
Constellation

Wherein, if thou hadst understood their cry
    Which is a prayer, already would be clear
    The vengeance thou shalt see before thou die.
Smites never down in haste the sword from here,
    Nor tardily, excepting in his view
    Who waits for it in longing or in fear.
But look about thee now to something new;
    Thou shalt see spirits most illustrious,
    Turning thy face round as I bid thee do.'
Compliant to her will, I turned me thus,
    And saw a hundred little globes of fire
    By interchange of light more beauteous.
Like one who blunts the edge of his desire
    Within himself, became I, diffident
    Of question, lest I overmuch aspire.
And the most lustrous and preëminent
    Among those pearly lights began to advance,
    To make my wish concerning it content.
Within it then I heard: 'Could but thy glance
    Like mine perceive our interflaming Love,
    Thy tacit thought would have found utterance;
But lest thou linger from the goal above
    I will make answer even to the scope
    Of the request thou art so chary of.
Where lies Cassino on the mountain slope,
    Up to the very summit dwelt of yore
    The folk perverse who in delusion grope;
And I am he who first up thither bore
    The name of Him who brought the human race
    The Truth enabling us so high to soar:
Then shone upon me so abounding Grace
    That from the impious worship which misled
    The world, I drew each neighbour dwelling-place.
These other fires were men whose spirits fed
    On Contemplation, kindled by that heat
    Whence holy flowers and holy fruits are bred.

Here Romuald and here Macarius meet
  All my good brethren of the cloister who
  Kept steadfast heart and stayed their truant feet.'
And now I spoke: 'The love thou givest to view
  Talking with me, and the benevolence
  Which I perceive aglow in all of you,
Dilate as genially my confidence
  As the sun doth the rose, till she uncase
  Her petals and exhale her perfume thence.
Therefore I pray,—and tell me if such grace,
  O Father, may perchance upon me shine,—
  That I may see thee with uncovered face.'
'Brother, up in the final sphere divine,'
  Said he, 'shall thy exalted wish be granted,
  Where all the others are fulfilled, and mine.
There is mature and perfect and unscanted
  Every desire; and in that realm of day
  Alone all parts eternally are planted;
For it is not in space, nor doth it sway
  On poles; and thither doth our ladder go,
  Whence it is fading from thy sight away.
The Patriarch Jacob saw it long ago
  Extend its upper reaches heavenward yon,
  When angels up and down seemed thronging so.
But now to clamber thither raises none
  His feet from earth, and, though my Rule remain,
  Waste is the paper it is written on.
The abbey walls, that used to be a fane,
  Are become robber dens, and every cowl
  A sack that doth corrupted meal contain.
But heavy usance levies smaller toll
  Counter to Will Divine, than fruits that curse
  With such insanity the monkish soul.
What Holy Church may have to disemburse
  Belongs to them who in God's name invoke;
  Not to one's kindred, nor to others worse.

The flesh of mortals is so frail that folk
　　Make good beginnings there, which do not hold
　　Till acorns ripen on the sapling oak.
Peter made his beginning without gold
　　Or silver, I with fast and orison,
　　And Francis humbly set about his fold.
And scanning the beginning of each one,
　　And then where it has wandered, thou wilt see
　　How white has been converted into dun.
But Jordan backward turned, in verity,
　　And ocean at God's will in flight perdue,
　　More wondous were than rescue here would be.'
He spoke, and turned to his companions, who
　　Surrounding him, together closed their throng,
　　Then upward like a whirlwind all withdrew.
My gentle Lady urged me then along
　　With a mere wafture up that mystic stair,
　　So was her power upon my nature strong;
Nor in our rising and descending here
　　By natural law, has ever been a flight
　　So swift as with my pinion to compare.
Reader, as I to that devout delight
　　Hope to return, for whose sake I deplore
　　Oft-times my sins, and on my bosom smite,
Thou wouldst have plucked thy finger nevermore
　　Out of the fire, ere I beheld the Sign
　　After the Bull, and was within its core!
O glorious stars, whose influences shine
　　Pregnant with power, to whom is honour due
　　For whatsoever genius may be mine,
With you was dawning, darkening with you
　　He who is Sire of all mortality,
　　When my first breath of Tuscan air I drew;
And then, when gift of Grace had made me free
　　Of the high wheeling sphere wherein ye roll,
　　Your very region was assigned to me.

To you devoutly now suspires my soul,
   Virtue soliciting and consecration
   For the hard passage to the final goal.
'Thou art so near the Ultimate Salvation,'
   So Beatrice began, 'that it is meet
   To have eyes keen and purified from passion.
Hence, before deeplier immersed in it,
   Look down below and see what world expanse
   I have already put beneath thy feet;
So that thy heart with utmost jubilance
   Confront the Triumph of the multitude
   Who through this ether-sphere blithely advance.'
Then one and all the Seven Spheres I viewed
   With backward gaze, and saw this globe of dust
   Such that I smiled at its poor likelihood;
And to his counsel I most largely trust
   Who holds it cheapest; and who turns him thence
   To other thoughts may well be reckoned just.
Latona's daughter kindled on my sense
   Without that shadow making her appear
   Such that I held her once both rare and dense.
Hyperion, I could endure up here
   The radiance of thy son, and marked how move
   Maia and Dionë round about him near.
Thence I perceived the tempering of Jove
   Father and son between, and thence the mode
   Of all their variations as they rove.
Thence to me all the seven planets showed
   How vast they are, how swift they are, and how
   Far, far apart they are in their abode.
With the Eternal Twins revolving now,
   I saw our madding little threshing floor
   Spread out from river mouth to mountain brow:
Then turned I to the beauteous eyes once more.

CANTO XXIII

Even as a bird the well-loved leaves among,
  Having reposed with her sweet nestling brood
  While night has over all her mantle flung,
Who, that she may adventure for their food,
  Delighting in hard toil, and that she may
  See the loved pledges of her motherhood,
Anticipates the hour on open spray,
  And fired with eagerness awaits the light,
  Vigilant ever until break of day:
So was my Lady standing at full height
  Alert and watchful, lifting up her face
  Thither where most the sun retards his flight;
Whence I, observant of her eagerness,
  Became like one who wistfully doth pant
  For his desire, and so takes heart of grace.
But now the interval of time was scant,
  I mean of my suspense until aware
  That more and more the heaven grew radiant.
And Beatrice said: 'Behold the army fair
  Of Christ Triumphant,—all the harvest raised
  By whirling influence of every sphere.'
It seemed to me that all her features blazed
  And such a flood of rapture filled her eye
  That I must pass it by perforce unphrased.
As at still midnight when the moon is high
  Trivia smiles among the nymphs eterne
  Who brighten every quarter of the sky,
Above a thousand lustres saw I burn
  One Sun, enkindling round it all and some,
  As does our sun the other lights supern.
And that illuminating Masterdom
  Shot down a living splendour so intense
  Into mine eyes that they were overcome.

Oh, Beatrice, dear guiding influence!
   'That which subdues thee here,' she said to me,
   'Is virtue against which is no defence.
Here is the Wisdom and Supremacy
   That opened between Heaven and Earth the road
   Whereto men yearned of old so urgently.'
As fire expands till it unlocks the cloud
   That cannot longer hold it, and doth fall
   Earthward against its nature, in such mode
My spirit found amid that festival
   Enlargement, and the bound of self forsook,
   Nor what it then became can now recall.
'Open thine eyes,' resumed she then, 'and look
   Upon my very nature; thou hast seen
   Things that enable thee my smile to brook.'
I was like one who feels the spell again
   Of a forgotten vision, and doth try
   To bring it back to memory, in vain,
When I received this proffer, worth so high
   Tribute of thanks as could not be effaced
   Out of the chronicle of time gone by.
Not all the tongues by Polyhymnia graced,
   That both from her and from her sisters drew
   Their lyric milk most honied to the taste,
Could tell a thousandth part of what is true,
   Hymning the holy smile of Beatrice
   And on her holy face what light it threw.
Whence, in depicting Paradise, at this
   The sacred Poem leaps perforce the theme,
   Like one whose way is cut by an abyss.
But whoso notes its weight will never deem
   Me blameable if mortal shoulder bear
   But tremblingly a burden so supreme.
For little bark can be no passage where
   The wave is cleft by my adventurous prow,
   Nor yet for pilot who would labour spare.

'Why so enamoured of my face art thou,
 And turnest not to the fair garden-close
 Blooming beneath the rays of Christus now?
The Word Divine became in yonder Rose
 Incarnate; yonder are the lilies white
 Whose fragrance did the way of life disclose.'
So Beatrice: and I, submitting quite
 To what she urged, again free scope allowed
 To the contention of my feeble sight.
Just as mine eyes, themselves beneath a shroud
 Of shadow, have beheld a flowery lea
 Laughing in light that streamed through rifted
So many a splendid throng now seemed to be [cloud,
 Lit from above by burning radiance, though
 No fountain of those flashings could I see.
O Power benignant who dost mark them so,
 Thou hadst withdawn thee upward to give way
 Before mine eyesight baffled by the glow!
The mention of the Rose whereto I pray
 Morning and evening, utterly subdued
 My soul to contemplate her greater ray.
When with her quality and magnitude
 As she transcended here up there transcending,
 That living star had both mine eyes imbued,
Behold athwart the heaven a torch descending,
 Formed like a coronet, wherewith it crowned her,
 About her in a fiery circle bending.
Whatever melody is sweet hereunder
 Most wooingly to wake the heart's desire,
 Would seem a cloud-bank rended by the thunder
Compared to the resounding of that lyre
 Engarlanding the Sapphire beauteous
 Whose holy azure tints the Heaven of Fire.
'I am the Love angelic circling thus
 The lofty rapture of the womb, that blest
 Hostel of Him who was desired of us;

374

And I shall circle until thou followest
    Thy son, O Lady of Heaven, diviner making
    The Sphere supreme because thou enterest.'
So now the circling melody was taking
    The seal, and all the other lights in fine
    With name of Mary into song were breaking.
That regal mantle which doth all entwine
    The rolling worlds, and hath its appetite
    Most quickened in the breath and deeds divine,
Held far remote from us and at such height
    Above my standing place its inner shore,
    That vision of it dawned not on my sight.
Therefore mine eyes did not have power to soar
    After the flame incoronate, who rose
    Up to her Son where He had risen before.
As little child toward the mother throws
    Its arms up, soon as it with milk is fed,
    And grateful love in such a transport shows,
When each and all of those fair splendours shed
    Their light upstretching, so an infinite
    Love toward Mary in the act I read.
Before me still remained those splendours white,
    And 'Queen of Heaven' they all so sweetly chanted
    That present with me yet is the delight.
Oh, how great plenty is laid up unscanted
    In those abounding coffers that of old
    Were husbandmen upon the ground they planted!
There live they, glad in treasure manifold
    Which in captivity at Babylon
    They gathered up with tears, forsaking gold.
There triumphs, under the exalted Son
    Of God and Mary, now victorious
    And with the council old and new, that one
Who holds the keys of gate so glorious.

CANTO XXIV

'O chosen fellowship of the Lamb Blest
  At the great supper where He feeds you so
  That your desire is ever set at rest,
Since Grace Divine doth on this man bestow
  Foretaste of viand from your feast above,
  Or ever death cut short his time below,
Give heed to his immeasurable love,
  Bedew him somewhat: ye are quaffing bowls
  Brimmed from the fount that he is dreaming of.'
So Beatrice besought; and those blithe souls
  Flashed out like comets streaming in the sky,
  Whirling in circles round determined poles.
And even as wheels in clock escapement ply
  In such a fashion geared that motionless
  Appears the first one, and the last to fly,
Likewise those wheeling carols let me guess,
  By variable measure of the dance
  Or swift or slow, their wealth of blessedness.
The carol that seemed fairest to my glance
  Was flaming forth such plenitude of bliss
  That none was left of greater radiance,
And swept three times encircling Beatrice
  Accompanied with singing so divine
  That fantasy in me falls short of this:
I write it not, my pen must skip the line,
  For hues of fancy would too coarsely glare,
  Let alone words, on drapery so fine.
'O holy sister, thy compelling prayer
  Devout, and with so fervent feeling made,
  Detaches me from yonder circle fair.'
After the blessèd fire its motion stayed,
  Did it directly to my Lady turn
  Breathing forth what I have already said.

And she replied to it: 'O light eterne
  Of the great peer to whom our Master gave
  Keys he brought down of this delight supern,
Invite this man, on questions light or grave
  As pleases thee, about the Faith to tell
  Wherethrough thou once didst walk upon the
If loves he, hopes he, and believes he well,   [wave.
  Is hidden not from thee who hast thine eye
  Where all things seen as in a picture dwell.
But it becomes him thus to testify
  For the true Faith, that it be glorified,
  Seeing this Realm is citizened thereby.'
As arms the bachelor, whose tongue is tied
  Until the master doth the question stir,
  To sanction it with proof, not to decide,
Even so did I, hearing these words from her,
  Equip me all with answer in advance
  In such a shrift to such examiner.
'Speak up, good Christian, give it utterance,
  What thing is Faith?' Whereat I raised my brow
  Whither was breathing forth that radiance,
And then turned round to Beatrice, who now
  Wafted prompt signals to me that I lift
  The inward sluice gate and my creed avow.
'May Grace, which is vouchsafing to me shrift
  In presence of the chief Centurion,'
  Began I, 'mould the expression of my drift.
Father, as wrote the truthful pen thereon
  Of thy dear brother who set the feet of Rome
  In the right path with thee, Faith's benison
Is substance of the things we hope will come,
  And of invisible things the evidence:
  Its essence such appears to me in sum.'
Then heard I: 'Rightly dost thou catch the sense,
  If comprehending why he classed it now
  With substances and now with arguments.'

And I thereon: 'The deep things which allow
   That glimpses of themselves should here be shown
   Are so concealed from mortal eye below
As to exist there in belief alone,
   Whereon our hope sits, founded high aloof,
   Whence Faith is by the name of substance known;
From which belief is laid on us behoof
   To argue without seeing more than it,
   Wherefore it takes the notion on of proof.'
Then heard I: 'If whatever men admit
   For doctrine were so understood on earth,
   No room would there remain for sophist wit.'
This was from that enkindled Love breathed forth,
   Subjoining then: 'Right well dost thou rehearse
   The carats of this coinage and the worth:
But tell me if thou hast it in thy purse?'
   And I: 'That have I, both so bright and round
   That of its stamp to me no doubt occurs.'
Thereafter issued from the light profound
   Glowing above, this utterance thereto:
   'This precious gem, wherein all worth we found,
Came to thee whence?' And I: 'The ample dew
   Of the Celestial Spirit, which is shed
   Over the Ancient Parchments and the New,
Is argument that hath within me bred
   Belief so strong that, set against its force,
   All demonstration seems to me but dead.'
I heard thereon: 'The old and the new course
   Of argument with such conclusion fraught,
   Why dost thou hold it for divine discourse?'
And I: 'The very proof is to be sought
   In th' after-works, whereto might never be
   Hot iron yet on Nature's anvil wrought.'
'Who vouches, pray,' it was replied to me,
   'That these works were performed? Thou dost attest
   The very text affirming it to thee.'

'Though without miracles the world confessed
  Christianity, this were a hundredfold
  More wonderful,' I answered, 'than the rest;
For poor and hungry once into the wold
  Didst thou go forth to sow there the good plant,
  A bramble now, which was a vine of old.'
The high and holy Court, then celebrant,
  Made a 'Praise God' throughout those circles ring
  In such a melody as there they chant.
And that great Lord who, thus examining,
  Had so far drawn me now from spray to spray
  That near the topmost frondage poised our wing,
Resumed: 'The Grace whose dalliance doth so play
  Upon thy soul, thus far to conference
  Hath opened thy lips duly; and I pay
My commendation to what issued thence;
  But now to tell thine own belief is meet,
  And why it captured thine intelligence.'
'O holy Father, soul with so complete
  Discernment of thy faith, thou didst outfare,
  Anigh the Sepulchre, more youthful feet,'
Began I, 'thou wouldst have me here declare
  The very essence of my prompt believing,
  And also have the grounds of it laid bare.
And I reply: by faith am I receiving
  One God, sole and eterne, the Heavens all
  Who moves (Himself unmoved) by love and
And for such faith have I proofs physical   [craving.
  And metaphysical, nor am denied
  The verity that showers from here withal
Through Moses, Psalms, and prophecies, beside
  The Evangel, and what you Apostles writ
  When by the fiery Spirit sanctified.
In three Eternal Persons, and to wit
  One Essence I believe, so One and Trine
  That *are* and *is* the syntax must admit.

This, the mysterious state of the Divine,
    Doth many a time the Gospel teaching leaven,
    Which stamps upon my mind its seal and sign.
This is the focus whence the spark is driven
    Which then doth into living flame dilate
    And shine within me like a star in Heaven.'
Even as a lord who hears good tidings, straight
    The story ended, presses to his breast
    The servant whom he would congratulate,
So, by his singing rendering me blest,
    Three times encircled me, when ceased my voice,
    That apostolic Light at whose behest
I spoke: so did he in my words rejoice.

CANTO XXV

—————

St. James examines
him concerning
Hope

If ever it happen that the Sacred Song
    Which Heaven and Earth have set their hand to so
    That it has made me lean for seasons long,
Vanquish the cruelty that bars me now
    From the fair sheepfold where, a lamb, I lay
    Enemy to the wolves that work it woe,
With other voice, with other fleece, that day
    Returning poet, will I from my font
    Baptismal take the coronal of bay;
For there the Faith I entered, that is wont
    To make souls known of God, and through that
    Did Peter then encircle thus my front.   [rite
Then from that spheral garland moved a light
    Tow'rd us, from whence had issued the first Head
    Whom Christ left of His vicars. At such sight
My Lady full of rapture to me said:
    'Look, look, behold the Baron for whose grace
    Galicia below is visited.'

380

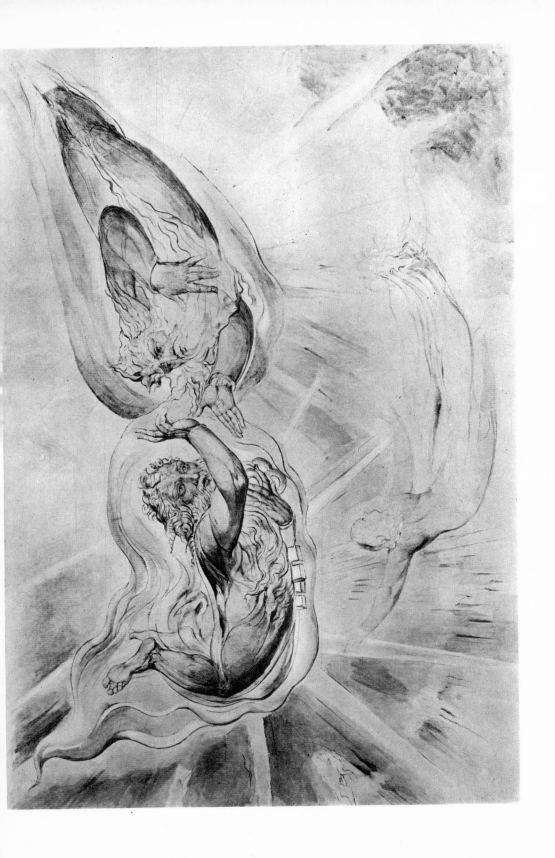

PARADISO: CANTO XXV
St. Peter, Beatrice and Dante with St. James also

As, circling nearer to the nesting place
   And cooing to his mate, alights the dove,
   And both pour forth affection, in like case
I saw one great and glorious Prince with love
   And welcome by that other grandeur greeted,
   Praising the food which feeds them thereabove.
But when the gratulation was completed,
   Silent in front of me they both stopped short,
   Enkindled so, mine eyes fell down defeated.
Then Beatrice smiled forth what I report:
   'Illustrious Life, who didst in bounty write
   The perfect gifts of our Imperial Court,
Do thou make Hope resound upon this height,
   For thou dost hope as often typify
   As Jesus granted to the three most light.'
'Be of good cheer and lift thy head on high,
   For all ascending here from mortal stress
   Must in our mellowing rays to ripen lie.'
The Second Fire did with this comfort bless;
   Whence to the hills I raised mine eyes, before
   Bowed heavily by radiant excess.
'Since of his grace desires our Emperor
   That thou meet face to face before thy death
   His baronage within the secret door,
That, seeing this Court truly, thou draw breath
   Till in thyself and others thou relume
   The Hope which well below enamoureth,—
Tell what hope is, and how therewith abloom
   Thy spirit, and tell whence it came to thee':
   So speaking, did the Second Light resume.
And she who with compassionate sympathy
   To so high flight my fledgy wings beguiled,
   With answer thus anticipated me:
'Church militant has not a single child
   Richer in hope, as read we in the fire
   Of that Sun which throughout our host has smiled;

And hence it was vouchsafed to his desire
   To come from Egypt to Jerusalem
   To see, before the limit of his hire.
The other two points,—since thou askest them
   Not for thy knowing, but that he report
   To men this virtue as thy dearest gem,—
To him I leave; he will not find them thwart
   Nor matter of boast; let him reply thereto,
   Nor may the grace of God in him come short.'
I answered even as willing pupils do
   The master, who are glad, when competent,
   That their proficiency be brought to view:
'Hope is the expectation confident
   Of future glory, fountain that doth stream
   From Grace Divine and merit that forewent.
Stars many Cause this light on me to beam,
   But who first made it through my bosom shine
   Was supreme singer of the Guide Supreme.
So speaks he in his Psalmody divine: [and who
   "Hope they in Thee who know Thy name,"—
   Can know it not, having like faith with mine?
Thou then didst so bedew me with his dew
   In thine Epistle that I am full, and pour
   On others rain that showers from both of you.'
While thus I spoke, within that living core
   Of fire there quivered forth a flash of light
   Quick as chain lightning. Whereupon once more
It breathed: 'The love wherewith I flame so bright
   For that same Virtue still my comforter
   Unto the palm and issue of the fight,
Again on thee whose joy abides in her
   Moves me to breathe; and I would fain be told
   What is it Hope gives promise to confer?'
And I: 'The Scriptures, new as well as old,
   Set forth the emblem whence I understand
   The bliss of souls, God's friends, the double-stoled:

Isaiah promises that all shall stand
  In their own land with double raiment on,—
  And this sweet life is their own fatherland;
Far more distinctly does thy brother John,
  Where he is treating of the robes of white,
  Make manifest to us this benison.'
Now first, my words being ended, from the height
  'Hope they in Thee' a voice was heard to say,
  The carols all responding; then a light
Among them shot forth so intense a ray
  That, if the Crab held one such diamond,
  Winter would have a month of one sole day.
As winsome maiden rises with a bound
  To go and join the dancing, honour due
  Giving the bride, and from no motive fond,
So saw I drawing near the other two
  The brightened splendour, where they wheeled
  As it became their burning love to do.   [along
It mingled with their measure and their song;
  And gazing on them did my Lady rest
  Even as a bride unmoved and still of tongue.
'This, this is he who lay upon the breast
  Of our own Pelican; to him the award
  Of the great trust was from the cross addressed.'
My Lady thus; not more was her regard
  Moved to withdraw itself from its delight
  Before these words of hers, or afterward.
Like one endeavouring to view aright
  The eclipsing of the sun a little space,
  Who through long gazing grows bereft of sight,
Such, by that latest fire, became my case,
  While it was said: 'Why dost thou dazzle thee
  To see a thing that here can have no place?
My body is on earth, and there will be
  With all the rest, until our number grow
  Such as to tally with the eterne decree.

383

With the two robes in blessèd cloister glow
  Only those two great Splendours who ascended:
  Bear this report back to your world below.'
And at this voice the flaming whirl was ended,
  And therewithal was brought to quiet close
  The trinal breath harmoniously blended,
As when, avoiding risk, or for repose,
  The oars, that smote till now upon the wave,
  All pause together when a whistle blows.
Alas! how much the mind in me misgave
  When I turned round to look on Beatrice,
  At having no power to see her, although I clave
Close to her side, and in the world of bliss.

CANTO XXVI

While I was trembling for my sight, forspent
  By the effulgent flame, there issued thence
  A breathing voice that made my heed intent,
Saying: 'While thou recoverest the sense
  Of vision which thou hast burnt out on me,
  Let conversation serve for recompense.
Begin then, and declare where centred be
  Thy heart's desires; and let assurance stand
  That dazzled and not dead is sight in thee,
Because the eyes of the Lady, through this land
  Divine conducting thee, irradiate
  The power that was in Ananias' hand.'
'Unto these eyes of mine, which were the gate
  When she brought in the fire that burns undying,
  Come healing at her pleasure, soon or late.
The Good, to this high court all satisfying,
  Is Alpha and Omega of the scroll
  Love reads me loudly or softly,' I said replying.

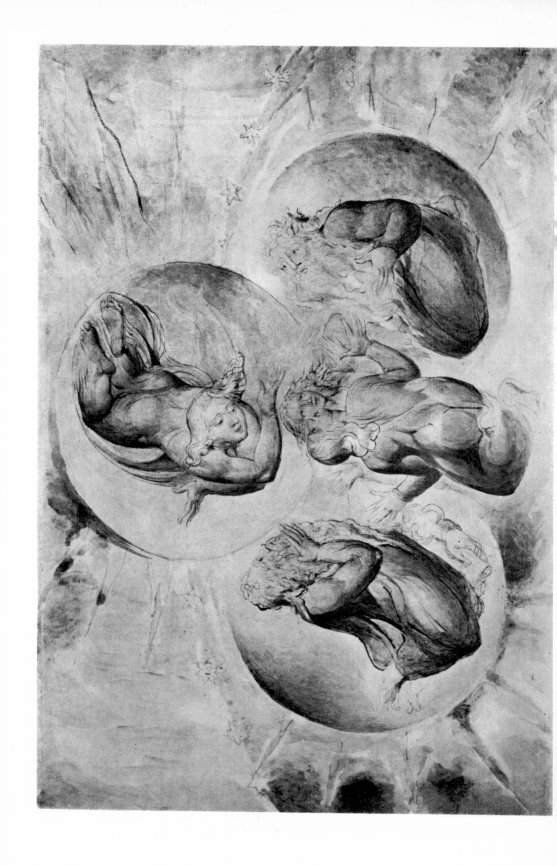

PARADISO: CANTO XXVI

St. Peter, St. James, Dante, Beatrice with St. John the Evangelist also

The selfsame voice, first lifted to control
  My fear when dazzled suddenly, to large
  Discourse of reason called again my soul:
'Nay, but thy sieve more finely must discharge,'
  So it resumed, 'and needs must thou reply,
  Who aimed thy arrows at so high a targe?'
'By teachings of Philosophy,' said I,
  'And by authority descending hence
  I bear perforce the print of love so high,
For Good, as such, when brought in evidence,
  Makes love flow forth to it in fuller stream
  As it embraces more of excellence.
Hence to the Essence which is so supreme
  That every good outside it to be traced
  Is but an emanation from its beam,
More than to any other needs must haste
  In love the soul of every one not blind
  To truth whereon this argument is based.
This truth has been unfolded to my mind
  By him who demonstrates to me what drew
  The primal love of all the eternal kind.
It is unfolded by the Author true
  To Moses, speaking of His proper worth:
  "All goodness will I set before thy view."
Thou too unfoldest it at setting forth
  To cry Heaven's secret in that herald word,
  The loftiest of all heralding to earth.'
'By human understanding,' then I heard,
  'In concord with authoritative writing,
  Thy sovran love is looking heavenward.
But further, if thou feelest other plighting
  That draws thee Godward, by thy words attest
  With just how many teeth this love is biting.'
Not hidden from me was the purpose blest
  Of the Eagle of Christ; nay, whither he would
  My declaration became manifest.   [guide

'All of those bitings,' therefore I replied,
  'Of force to turn the heart to God alone,
  Combine to make such love in me abide:
Because the world's existence and mine own,
  His death that I might live for evermore,
  And what I hope with every faithful one,
As well as the aforesaid living lore,
  Drew me from love perverse wherein I drowned,
  And of right love have set me on the shore.
My love for blooms embowering the ground
  Of the eternal Gardener, is strong
  In measure as His gifts in them abound.'
Soon as I paused, a strain of sweetest song
  Rang through the Heaven, and my Lady said,
  'O Holy, Holy, Holy!' with the throng.
As slumber breaks when vivid light is shed,
  So runs the spirit of sight to meet the burning
  Splendour, through tunic after tunic sped
Until the waker flinch,—for undiscerning
  Is consciousness before the sudden day
  Till judgement to his succour is returning,—
Thus from mine eyes drove Beatrice away
  All motes with lustre of her own so bright
  That myriads of miles was shed the ray;
Whence better than beforehand was my sight:
  And I made question like one in a maze,
  Perceiving there before us a Fourth Light.
My Lady answered: 'Shrouded in those rays
  The first soul that was made by Virtue Prime
  On his Creator doth in rapture gaze.'
Even as the tree-top bows from time to time
  Beneath the passing breeze, then rises slow
  To place again through native power to climb,
While she was speaking did I waver so,
  And then grew confident, though struck with
  Such will to question set me all aglow.   [awe,

386

And I began: 'O fruit that ripe, not raw,
  Alone hast been produced, O Father of yore
  To whom each bride is daughter and daughter-
Devoutly as I may do I implore   [in-law,
  Thy speech with me; thou seest that I have stayed
  Mine utterance to speed thy speaking more.'
Sometimes a covered animal is swayed
  So that its feeling necessarily
  Is by its undulating wrap betrayed;
And so the primal soul gave me to see,
  Transpiring through his screen of radiance,
  How blithesome he became to pleasure me.
Then he breathed forth: 'Without thine utterance
  Can I more readily detect thy yearning,
  Than canst thou any surest circumstance,
Because in the True Mirror this discerning,
  Which forms of all things images sublime,
  And naught such mirror unto Him is turning.
Thou wouldest know what ages since the time
  God placed me in the lofty Paradise,
  Where taught thy Lady so long stair to climb,
And how long it was pleasant to mine eyes,
  And the true reason of the scorn divine,
  And the idiom I used and did devise.
Now, not the tasted tree, O son of mine,
  Was solely cause of so great banishment,
  But only overstepping of the line.
Down there, whence by thy Lady Virgil went,
  Four thousand and three hundred circles and two
  Of sun, I yearned for this high Parliament;
And on the solar pathway to my view
  Nine hundred times the lights all reawoke,
  And thirty, and still breath on earth I drew.
Long silent were the accents that I spoke
  Before the work not to be consummated
  Was undertaken first by Nimrod's folk;

For never aught by reason fabricated
 Endured, because of human choice renewing
 As heavenly influences operated.
The use of speech by man is nature's doing;
 But Nature lets you shape it thus or so
 As suits the fashion you may be pursuing.
Before I sank down to the Eternal Woe,
 Men gave the name of "Jah" to the Chief Good
 Whence comes the rapture round me all aglow;
Then called Him "El" as fitted to their mood;
 For mortal fashions are like leaves that cling
 To branch, and fall in swift vicissitude.
The Mount above the wave most towering
 Held me, with life first pure, and then undone,
 From the first hour to that next following
The sixth, at altered quadrant of the sun.'

CANTO XXVII

*Ascent to the
Crystalline Heaven*

'To Father, Son, and to the Holy Ghost
 Glory,' began, with sweetness exquisite
 Intoxicating me, the Heavenly Host.
Seemed what I witnessed with so deep delight
 A laughter of the Universe; for this
 Elation entered through both ear and sight.
O joy supreme! O inexpressive bliss!
 O life of love and peace in ample store!
 O wealth secure exempt from avarice!
Above my enraptured eyes the torches four
 Stood kindled, and the one that first had come
 Began to grow more vivid than before,
And to take on such look as might assume
 Bright Jupiter were he and ruddy Mars
 Transformed to birds, with interchange of plume.

The Providence allotting to the stars
   Of heaven their function and their office due,
   Had stilled all voices of the blessèd choirs,
When I heard say: 'If I transform my hue,
   Marvel not, for behold incarnadine
   While yet I speak will grow the others too!
He who on earth usurps that place of mine,
   That place of mine, that place of mine, just now
   Vacant in presence of the Son Divine,
Has turned my burial ground into a slough
   Of blood and filth, whence the Perverted One
   Who fell from here takes comfort there below,
With such a crimson as the adverse sun
   Paints on the cloud at morn or eventide,
   Did I behold all Heaven suffused thereon.
And as a modest lady doth abide
   Sure of herself, but through another's shame
   At the mere hearing becomes mortified,
So Beatrice changed semblance; and I deem
   That such eclipse took place in Heaven perchance
   When suffered the Omnipotence Supreme.
Thereon proceeded forth his utterance
   With voice so greatly altered that behold!
   Was not more changed his very countenance:
'The Bride of Christ was nurtured not of old
   On blood of mine and that of Linus good
   And Cletus, to be used for acquist of gold;
But for acquist of this beatitude
   Did Sixtus, Pius, and Calixtus weep,
   And Urban, and thereafter shed their blood.
Nor purposed we the Christian folk to keep
   To right and left of our successors,—these
   Stigmatized goats, the others favoured sheep;
Nor were confided to my hand the Keys
   To be an emblem on a banneret
   For war on the baptized; nor do I please

To figure as a signet that is set
   On privileges venal and untrue,
   Whereat my frequent blush is burning yet.
From here aloft in all the folds a crew
   Of ravening wolves in shepherd garb is seen:
   Vengeance of God, why dost thou lie perdue?
To drink our blood Gascon and Cahorsine
   Are making ready. Alas, must needs the end
   Of fair beginning be indeed so mean?
But lofty Providence that once did fend
   Rome's empire of the world with Scipio,
   Will quickly here, I deem, some succour lend.
And thou who must return once more below
   Through mortal load, open thy mouth, my son,
   Fail not to say what I fail not to show.'
As when our atmosphere is snowing down
   In flakes the frozen vapours, when the horn
   Of Heaven's goat is gilded by the sun,
Such swarming flakes in triumph upward borne
   Seemed those who with us there had sojourn made,
   And now awhile the ethereal sky adorn.
My sight was following what their wraiths displayed,
   And followed till the vastness manifold
   All power of penetrating farther stayed.
Whereon my Lady, seeing me withhold
   From gazing up, commanded me: 'Now cast
   Thine eye down at the distance thou hast rolled.'
I saw that, so revolving, I had passed
   From the first hour I looked, the whole arc through
   Which the first climate makes from midst to last,
Hence could the wild course of Ulysses view
   Past Cadiz, and well-nigh the hither shore
   Whereon Europa so dear burden grew.
And further surface of this threshing-floor
   Had been uncovered, but the sun sped, turning
   Beneath my feet, removed a Sign and more.

Now my enamoured spirit always yearning
   After my Lady, to bring back and sate
   Mine eyes on her, was more than ever burning.
What nature made, or art, to captivate
   The eye and give a banquet to the mind
   In human flesh real or delineate,
All would appear as nothing, though combined,
   To the divine enjoyment glowing through me
   On turning round her smiling face to find.
The power wherewith I felt that look endue me
   From the fair nest of Leda tore me away
   And to the fleetest heaven of all updrew me.
So uniform its parts I cannot say
   Which one had Beatrice chosen for my place,—
   Full of exceeding life and lofty they.
Then she, who saw my longing, of her grace
   Began with smile of so blithe innocence
   That God appeared rejoicing in her face:
'The nature of the world which holds suspense
   The centre and makes all else around it fare,
   Doth here as from its starting-point commence.
And in this heaven there is no other Where
   Than in the Mind Divine, wherein both move
   The Love that turns and Power that sheds the
Engird it with one cincture light and love,   [sphere.
   As it engirds the others; He alone
   Who girdles it is governor thereof.
No other measures motion all its own,
   But by this mete are measured all the rest,
   As ten by its half and by its fifth is shown.
And how in such a vessel Time can nest
   Its roots, its foliage in the others grow,
   Henceforward may to thee be manifest.
O Greed, who overwhelmest mortals so
   Beneath thyself that none has masterdom
   To lift his eyes again from out thy flow!

Will does indeed in men to blossom come;
  However long-continued rain and reek
  Convert to blighted fruit the perfect plum.
Only in little children are to seek
  True faith and innocence; then both too soon
  Vanish before the down is on the cheek.
Many keep fast while yet they babble and croon,
  Who swallow, when the tongue is free to play,
  Whatever food under whatever moon;
And many babblers cherish and obey
  Their mother, who, when they can speak aright,
  Long for the dawning of her burial day.
Even so the skin grows swarthy, which was white
  At the first aspect, of the daughter fair
  Of him who ushers morning and leaves night.
But lest thou shouldst as at a marvel stare,
  Consider none on earth is governor,
  Whence human household strays from thorough-
But before January be no more   [fare.
  In winter, by the hundredth part neglected
  Down there, so shall these upper circles roar
That Fortune, who has been so long expected,
  Shall whirl the stern about where lies the boom
  So that the fleet will run the course directed;
And perfect fruit will follow on the bloom.'

CANTO XXVIII

When she who doth imparadise my mind
  Had ended the veracious charge she brought
  Against the life of wretched humankind,—
As one whose eye has in a mirror caught
  The image of a torch behind him, long
  Before he has it or in sight or thought,

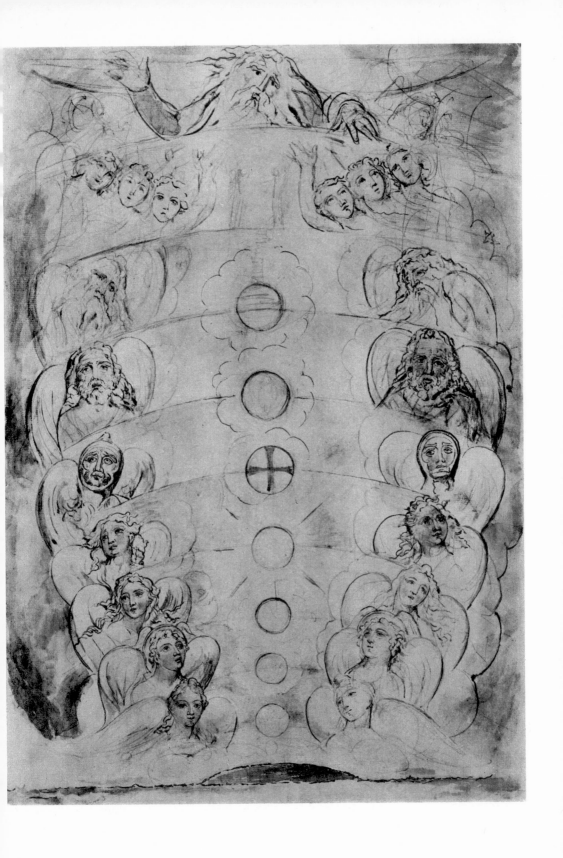

PARADISO: CANTO XXVIII

The Deity, from whom proceed the Nine Spheres

And turns to verify if right or wrong
  The mirror speak, and finds it to agree
  With truth, as chimes the metre with the song,—
So did I, as I call to memory,
  On looking in those eyes with beauty burning
  Wherewith Love made the noose for snaring me.
And, as I shifted round my look, discerning
  The contents of that volume, read aright
  With eye that is intent upon its turning,
I saw a Point which radiated light
  So piercing that the vision, fired thereby,
  Is closed perforce by vividness so bright.
That star appearing smallest to our eye
  Would seem a moon beside its light intense,
  As star is matched with star along our sky.
Perchance in distance equal to that whence
  Halo engirds the light that has impearled
  Its colour when the vapour is most dense,
So distant round the Point a circle whirled
  Of fire so swift its motion had outpaced
  That which goes quickliest around the world;
Round this another circle swept in haste,
  Round that a third, a fourth the third enwound,
  The fourth a fifth, and that a sixth embraced;
The seventh came afterward so wide of bound
  That Juno's herald, though complete, would run
  Too narrow to engirdle it around;
Likewise the eighth and ninth; and slowlier on
  Did each one move according as accrued
  Its number farther from the point of One;
And shone that flame with clearest plenitude
  From the Pure Spark at shortest interval,
  I think because more with its truth imbued.
Perceiving me become the anxious thrall
  Of dubitance, my Lady spoke this word:
  'From that one Point hang Heaven and nature all.

Look at that circle which doth next engird
　　The Point, and know it has such eager haste
　　For the enkindled love whereby 'tis spurred.'
But I made question: 'If the world were based
　　Upon the order yonder wheels disclose,
　　Enough were what has been before me placed;
But in the world of sense one sees and knows
　　The orbits to be ever more divine
　　The more their distance from the centre grows.
Whence wouldst thou still the longing that is mine,
　　Within the wonderful angelic fane
　　Which light and love and these alone confine,
I need to hear thee furthermore explain
　　Why copy is not here with pattern vying,
　　Since I unaided gaze thereon in vain.'
'Suffice not thy own fingers for untying
　　Such knot, there is no wonder, seeing it
　　So tangled has become for want of trying.'
My Lady thus; and then: 'Take what seems fit
　　For me to tell, wouldst thou be satisfied,
　　And going round it sharpen thou thy wit.
The spheres corporeal are strait or wide
　　According to the virtue less or more
　　Which throughout all their regions is supplied.
Superior good wills weal superior,
　　And if like perfect organs it dispose,
　　Holds larger body weal in larger store.
Therefore this sphere which carries as it goes
　　All the universe beside, must correspond
　　To that small circle which most loves and knows.
Hence if thou seek to measure with thy wand,
　　Not the appearance, but the excellence
　　Of substances which to thine eye seem round,
Of more with greater, wondrous congruence,
　　As of the less with lesser, wilt thou seek
　　In every heaven, with its Intelligence.'

Then as remains serene and cleared of reek
  The hemisphere of air, soon as the blast
  Is puffed by Boreas from the gentler cheek,
Whereby the cloudy rack that overcast
  The welkin is dissolving, and the blue
  Of heaven in all its beauty smiles at last,
So cleared was I of all confusion through
  The lucid answer that my Lady made,
  And like a star in heaven appeared the true.
Thereon, when her discourse to me was stayed,
  As iron rays forth sparklings under stress
  Of fire, such sparklings now the circles rayed.
Each spark did with their blazing coalesce,
  And running into millions manifold
  More than the duplication of the chess.
From quire to quire I heard *Hosanna* rolled
  To the fixed Point which holds them to the *Where*
  From evermore, and will forever hold.
And she, of my perplexity aware,
  Said: 'The first gyres enlighten thee concerning
  The Seraphim and Cherubim, who fare
After their bonds so swiftly, because yearning
  To grow as like the Point as most they may,—
  And so they may, exalting their discerning.
Those other loves that whirling round them play
  Are Thrones, wherein God's grace is manifest,
  For that the primal triad ended they.
And thou must know that one and all are blest
  According as they penetrate the true,
  Wherein all understanding is at rest.
Herein perceive we how the act of view
  Is source wherefrom beatitude draws being,
  Not act of love thereafter to ensue;
And merit is the measure of this seeing,—
  Merit begot by Grace and right endeavour:
  Such are the steps progressively agreeing.

The second triad, burgeoning for ever
  To flower in this sempiternal spring
  Which the nocturnal Ram doth ravage never,
Is here perpetually carolling
  Hosanna, sounded with three melodies
  Whence orders three with trinal rapture ring.
This priesthood musters three divinities:
  The Dominations first, the Virtues then,
  And third the order of the Potencies.
Next, all but ultimate, in dances twain,
  Are Princedoms and Archangels wheeling on;
  Rejoicing Angels last in sportive train.
Upward are gazing all these orders yon,
  And down prevail so that to the divine
  They all are drawing as they all are drawn.
Such zeal to contemplate these orders nine
  Showed Dionysius, that coincided
  His definitions and his names with mine.
Thereafter Gregory from him divided;
  Wherefore that saint, first opening his eye
  Within this Heaven, himself with smiles derided.
And that on earth a mortal might descry
  Such inward truth, need not astonish you
  Since learned from him who saw it here on high,
With much more of these circles that is true.'

CANTO XXIX

------

*Creation and
Nature of Heavenly
Intelligence*

When, by the Ram and by the scales o'erbrooded
  The twin-born children of Latona fair
  In one horizon girdle are included,
Long as the zenith balances them there
  Until both swerve from that circumference
  Unbalancing and shifting hemisphere,

396

So long, with smiles lighting her countenance,
  Paused Beatrice, concentering her ken
  Upon the Point that had subdued my glance.
'I tell and do not ask,' began she then,
  'What thou wouldst hear; by vision I assist
  Where centres every *where* and every *when*.
Not to possess Himself of good acquist,
  Which cannot be, but in the splendour of
  His glorious declaration, "I exist",
Beyond all limits, and all time above,
  As pleased Him, in His own eternity,
  Unfolded in new loves the Eternal Love.
Nor yet before as if inert lay He,
  Since nor before nor after moved the flow
  Of spirit divine to brood upon that sea.
Matter and form, combined and simple, so
  Came into being flawless and unblighted,
  Like arrows three from triple-corded bow;
And as glass, amber, crystal may be lighted
  So that between the earliest radiation
  And full effulgence all remains united,
Even so the Father's threefold operation
  All at a flash its being consummated
  Without an interval in the creation.
Order was constituted and created
  In substances; the universe was crowned
  With these, wherein pure act was generated.
Pure potentiality held lowest ground;
  Midway did act and potence interweave
  Such withies as can never be unbound.
Jerome wrote to you that we must believe
  The angels to have been created ages
  Before the other world; thou mayst perceive,
However, if thou but peruse the sages
  Through whom the Spirit spoke in Holy Writ,
  The very truth displayed on many pages;

And also reason gets a glimpse of it,
Which that Prime Movers for so long could be
Without their perfect work, could not admit.
Now where these loves were formed is known to thee,
And when and how; and in thy longing hence
Already are extinguished ardours three.
Ere they reach twenty who to count commence,
So quickly of the angel host a part
Disturbed the lowest of your elements.
The rest, who stayed, began to ply this art
Which thou beholdest,—so beatified
That never from their circling they depart.
The Fall originated in the pride
Accursèd of that One whom thou hast seen
Crushed by the weights of all the world beside.
Those thou beholdest here have humble been
To acknowledge them as from that Goodness kind
Which made them apt for knowledge so serene;
Wherefore illuminative Grace combined
With their own merit to exalt their view
So that they have a full and steadfast mind.
I would not have thee doubt, but hold it true
That grace accepted thus is merited
By laying open the longing heart thereto.
Henceforth, if thou my words hast harvested,
Canst round this Sacred College take thy fill
Of contemplation without further aid.
But since on earth your schools attribute still
To the angelic nature, memory
Together with intelligence and will,
I will speak further to make clear to thee
The truth, confused by men below who indite
Prelections fraught with ambiguity.
These substances, since first they drew delight
From God's own face, wherefrom is hidden naught,
Have never turned away from it their sight;

Whence they have vision intercepted not
  By concept new, and need not undertake
  To call back memory through divided thought.
So men down there are dreaming, wide awake,
  Weening, or weening not, truth to declare;
  But in the one more guilt and shame partake.
Below ye travel not one thoroughfare
  Philosophizing; so far does the love
  Of show delude you, and its specious air.
Yet even enduring this, the Heavens above
  Are less indignant, than when set aside
  Is Holy Writ or idly prated of.
What blood was spent to sow it far and wide
  Is given no heed, nor how their prayer is heard
  Who in humility by it abide.
Each is agog to shine, and ply absurd
  Inventions, and these form the staple theme
  Of preachers,—of the Gospel not a word!
During Christ's passion, some would have us deem
  The moon turned back again and cancelled through
  The intercepted sunlight; and some dream
That of its own accord the light withdrew,
  And hence would this eclipse alike appear
  To Spaniard and to Indian, as to Jew.
So many a Lapo and Bindo every year
  Breeds Florence not, as fables of this kind
  Are bawled out from the pulpit, far and near;
So that from pasture, flatulent with wind,
  The silly sheep flock, witless of salvation;
  Yet is it no excuse that they are blind.
Christ did not say to his first congregation:
  "Preach to the world with idle utterance,"
  But laid for their behoof the true foundation;
And that had from their lips such resonance,
  That, to enkindle faith, their battle-quest,
  The Gospel formed their buckler and their lance.

Now preachers sally forth to break a jest,
    Buffoons who, so they may provoke a grin,
    Puff out their cowls and reck not of the rest;
But could the people see what bird of sin
    Is nestling in the hood-tail, they would guess
    What kind of pardon they are trusting in;
Whence in the world so waxeth foolishness
    That, seeking not approof of any sign,
    Men jump at promise of indulgences.
Hereby St. Anthony makes fat his swine,
    And others also, far more swine than they,
    Paying their scot with counterfeited coin.
But since we have gone very far astray,
    Let us look back to the straight thoroughfare,
    So with the time to shorten up the way.
The angelic nature runs up such a stair
    Of number, scaling so remote a height,
    Never could tongue or thought pursue it there.
And Daniel's revelation, read aright,
    Shows, in the thousands he enumerates,
    That definite number is withheld from sight.
The Primal Light, which all irradiates,
    By modes as many is received in these
    As are the splendours whereunto it mates.
And since love follows on the act that sees,
    Therefore the sweetness of their love is spoken,
    More and less warm in diverse degrees.
Let this the height, henceforth, and breadth betoken
    Of Worth Eternal, fashioning great store
    Of mirrors whereupon its light is broken,
One in Itself remaining as before.'

CANTO XXX

When, eastward ho! six thousand miles perchance   *The Celestial Rose*
   Noon blazes, and toward the level bed
   The shadow of this world already slants,
The deep of central heaven above our head
   Grows so suffused that here a star and yon
   Begins to pale the radiance it shed,
And, as the brightest handmaid of the sun
   Advances, so are quenched the heavenly graces
   Star after star, even to the fairest one.
Not else the Triumph that for ever races
   Around the Point which overcame me quite,
   Seeming embraced by that which it embraces,
Was imperceptibly immerged in light;
   Whereat to turn mine eyes on Beatrice,
   Love laid constraint on me, and lack of sight.
Could what is said of her as far as this
   All in one single act of praise conclude,
   It would but serve the present turn amiss.
The beauty that I saw doth so elude
   Our measure, that its Maker, I surely deem,
   Alone can taste its full beatitude.
I yield me vanquished at this pass supreme;
   Comic or tragic poet overborne
   Was never thus by crisis of his theme.
For, as to dazzled sight the sun of morn,
   So doth her sweet remembered smile erase
   My memory, of its very self forlorn.
From the first day when I beheld her face
   In this life, even until the present viewing,
   My song yet never faltered on her trace;
But now I must give over from pursuing
   Her beauty in these cadences of mine,
   Like every artist tasked beyond his doing.

Such as I leave her to a more divine
   Renown than any that my trumpet grants,—
   Which now concludes its arduous design,—
She said, with leader's voice and vigilance:
   'Quitting the body most immense and fleet,
   We reach the heaven that is pure radiance:
Radiance of intellect with love replete,
   Love of true good replete with ecstasy,
   Ecstasy far exceeding every sweet.
Here both the one and the other soldiery
   Of Paradise, and one host of the two
   Robed as at Final Judgement, shalt thou see.'
As when a sudden lightning routs the crew
   Of visual spirits, putting them to flight
   So that the clearest things are cancelled through,
So beamed there all about me living light,
   Leaving so thick a veil around me closing,
   That I saw nothing for that glory bright.
'The Love wherein this heaven is aye reposing
   Is wonted so to welcome those who come,
   Duly the taper for its flame disposing.'
No sooner had this brief exordium
   Within me penetrated, than I knew
   Myself upraised beyond my masterdom;
And I rekindled with new power of view
   Such that no light could be so unalloyed
   But that mine eyes were tempered thereunto.
And I saw light in river-form with tide
   Of fulgent fire between two margins streaming
   Which wondrously with flowers of spring were dyed
Out of that current living sparks were teeming
   And flashing from the flowers with hues intense
   Like very rubies from gold patines gleaming.
Thereon, appearing drunken with the scents,
   They plunged again into the wondrous eddy,
   And as one sank another issued thence.

'The lofty wish aflame in thee already
  For knowledge of this vision, in like wise
  Extends my joy as its increase is steady;
But thou must of this water of Paradise
  Drink deep, to slake a thirst that so consumes.'
  Thus spoke to me the sunshine of mine eyes,
Adding: 'The river and the smiling blooms,
  The plunging and emerging jewels bright,
  Are types of truth that in their shadow looms;
Not that these things are hard to see aright,
  But on thy part there is inaptitude
  Since not yet so exalted is thy sight.'
There is no child far later than it should
  Awakening, with face toward the breast,
  That plunges with more hunger-stricken mood,
Than did I, that mine eyes might mirror best
  That vision, bending me my fill to take
  Out of that flood which pours to make us blest.
No sooner had I felt its ripple slake
  Mine eyelids, than both margins seemed to yield
  From long to large and rounded to a lake.
Then, even as masqueraders are revealed
  Quite other than beforehand, letting fall
  The alien guise wherein they were concealed,
So changed for me to ampler festival
  The flowerets and the flashes, till I saw
  Clearly the two Courts of the heavenly Hall.
O splendour of very God, whereby I saw
  The Kingdom true in triumph high, increase
  In me the power to tell it as I saw!
A light up yonder shows without surcease
  The Maker to that creature, who alone
  In seeing Him inherits its own peace;
And this light broadens in a circling zone
  So far and wide that its circumference
  Would be too large a girdle for the sun.

Its semblance, all of radiant effluence,
    Doth to the top of Primal Motion pass,
    Which takes vitality and vigour thence.
And as a hillside makes a looking-glass
    Of water at its foot, as if discerning
    How fair and rich it is in flowers and grass,
So mirrored, round and round above the burning
    On myriads of thrones, beheld I those
    Of us who there above have won returning.
And if the lowermost degrees inclose
    Lustre so large, what amplitude of light
    Spread in the outer petals of the Rose!
My vision in the vastness and the height
    Strayed not, at home and fully conversant
    With essence and with scope of that delight.
There near and far do neither add nor scant,
    For where God is directly governing
    The law of nature is not relevant.
Into the yellow Rose unwithering,
    Whose petals are unfurled with fragrance cast
    Of praise unto the Sun of dateless spring,
Like one long silent, moved to speak at last,
    Did Beatrice conduct me, saying: 'View
    The Congregation of white robes, how vast!
Look the wide circuit of our city through!
    Look at our benches which are so replete
    That here henceforward are expected few!
There where thine eyes are drawn to that great Seat
    By the already overhanging crown,
    Ere thou shalt at this wedding supper eat,
The soul of noble Henry shall sit down,
    Who comes, august, to render straight the way
    For Italy, ere she be ready grown.
Blind Greed, who doth her spell upon you lay,
    Has made you like the child who, though he pine
    With hunger, pushes yet the nurse away.

Then shall be Pontiff in the Court Divine
    One such that open word and covert deed
    Walk not on equal feet to one design.
But little while will God permit him speed
    In Holy Office, for he shall be thrust
    With Simon Magus, and make, by way of meed,
Him of Alagna bite the baser dust.'

CANTO XXXI

In fashion therefore of a pure white Rose
    Unfolded to my view the sacred throng
    Whom Christ in His own blood espoused. But
Who witness as they fly, and tell in song   [those
    The glory of Him who makes them love, and sing
    His excellence who made them fair and strong,—
Even as a busy swarm of bees a-wing
    That merge in flowers awhile, then speed away
    To where their labour sweet is savouring,—
Plunged into the Great Flower, with fair array
    Of Petals, and were reascending thence
    Where sojourns their own Love for ever and aye.
Their features were alive with flame intense,
    Golden their wings, the rest so white that banks
    Of drifted snow have not their innocence.
Alighting on the Flower, to ranks on ranks
    They proffered of the ardour and repose
    Which they had won by winnowing their flanks.
Nor did the coming in, between the Rose
    And That which dwelt above, of flight so great
    Obstruct the vision; still the splendour glows,
For through the universe doth penetrate
    In measure of its worth the Light Divine
    So that no bar can ever separate.

Beatrice sends
St. Bernard to
Dante

405

This safe and happy Kingdom, where combine
    Both ancient folk and modern thronging thus,
    Had look and love all turned unto one sign.
O Trinal Light, in one Star luminous,
    Soothing their vision with such benison,
    Look down upon the storm that buffets us!
If the barbarians from out that zone
    Where spreads for ever Helicë her span
    Revolving with her well-belovèd son,—
If, entering Rome, her mighty works to scan,
    These stared in wonder, in that era when
    Transcended mortal things the Lateran,—
I, who to the divine had come from men,
    From time unto eternity had come,
    From Florence to a people just and sane,
With what amazement was I overcome!
    Truly the wonder and the joy between,
    'Twas rapture to hear nothing and stand dumb.
And as the wayworn pilgrim grows serene
    Gazing around the temple of his vow,
    And muses how he shall describe the scene,
I, bending on the living light my brow,
    Followed along the lines, and sought to trace,
    Now up, now down, and round the circle now.
I looked on many a love-persuading face
    Decked with Another's light, and their own eyes
    Smiling, and action of all noble grace.
The universal form of Paradise
    My glance had gathered as a whole immense,
    But did no single part yet signalize;
And round I turned with will rekindled thence
    To ask my Lady what these matters be
    Concerning which my mind was in suspense.
One thing I meant, another fronted me:
    Weening to look again on Beatrice,
    A glory-vested Elder did I see.

His lineaments were overspread with bliss
    Benignant, kindly was his mien and eye,
    Betokening a father's love in this.
'And she,—where is she?' was my sudden cry;
    Whereat he answered: 'To fulfil thy yearning
    Beatrice urged me from my place on high:
Third from supreme the circle, which discerning,
    Thou shalt again behold her countenance
    Shine down from where her worth a throne is
Without reply I lifted up my glance   [earning.'
    And saw her, where a coronal she wore
    Woven from out the eternal radiance.
From welkin whence the highest thunders roar
    Has never mortal eye so distant been,
    Though sunken deep beneath the ocean-floor,
As mine from Beatrice; but 'twas so keen
    No distance mattered, since her features beaming
    Shone down on me without a blur between.
'O Lady in whom my living hope is teeming,
    And who didst once endure to leave the trace
    Of thy dear feet in Hell for my redeeming,
In all the worth and beauty finding place
    In things thou hast enabled me to see,
    I recognize thy virtue and thy grace.
Thou leddest me along from slave to free
    By all those ways, by all expedients
    Whereby the power to do so lay in thee.
Preserve in me thine own magnificence,
    So that my spirit, through thy healing, may
    Content thee as it slips the coil of sense.'
Far as she seemed, on hearing me so pray,
    She smiled and looked: then to the Fountain-head
    Eternal turned her shining eyes away.
'In order,' now the holy Elder said,
    'That thou complete thy course,—whence holy love
    Dispatched me and true orisons have sped,—

Let thy fleet glances through this garden rove,
    For better will such sight thy vision steel
    Upon the ray divine to mount above.
And she, the Queen of Heaven, for whom I feel
    Love's utter flame, will grant us furtherance,
    For reason that I am her Bernard leal.'
Like him who from Croatia, perchance,
    Comes to see our Veronica, well known
    Through old report, and cannot sate his glance,
But thinks within, so long as it be shown,
    'My Lord and very God, Christ Jesus mine,
    And were these features once Thy very own?'
Such was I, gazing at that living shrine
    Of charity, who in the world below
    By contemplation tasted peace divine.
'This blithesome being wilt thou never know,
    O son of grace,' such was his further note,
    'With eyes but fixed here at the bottom so;
But mark the circles to the most remote
    Until thou shalt the enthronèd Queen descry,
    To whom this realm is subject and devote.'
I raised mine eyes; and as the morning sky
    Displays a point of the horizon bright
    Beyond that of the westering sun, so I,
As going with my glance from vale to height,
    Beheld a region at the verge extreme
    Surpassing all the other front in light.
And as, where we expect the chariot-beam
    That Phaëton guided ill, the glows increase,
    Fading away on either hand, the gleam
Illumined so that Oriflamme of peace
    In the live centre, while on either side
    In equal measure did the splendour cease.
And at that centre I saw, on wing flung wide,
    A thousand jocund angels sweep along,
    In glow and ministry diversified.

There, smiling on their games and at their song,
   I saw a Beauty that was bliss indwell
   The eyes of all the other holy throng.
Yet were my wealth of diction parallel
   With wealth of fancy, rash were the emprise
   The least of her delights to strive to tell.
Then holy Bernard, when he saw mine eyes
   Fastened upon the object of his yearning,
   His own in her did so imparadise
As to make my desire to look more burning.

CANTO XXXII

———

That contemplator took the office free
   Of teacher, while intent upon his bliss,
   Beginning with these holy words to me:
'The wound by Mary balmed and covered, this
   That woman fair reposing at her feet
   Inflicted, opening the cicatrice.
Beneath her third in order has her seat
   Rachel, and thou beholdest at her side
   Beatrice. Below these in order meet
Sara, Rebecca, Judith, and that bride,
   Great-grandame of the singer who for grief
   Of his own guilt the *Miserere* cried:
From rank to rank descending, these in chief
   Mayst thou behold, as, naming each one, I
   Go downward through the Rose from leaf to leaf.
And from the seventh degree, as from on high
   To it, are Hebrew women cutting through
   All petals of the Flower successively;
For these, according to the point of view   [blended
   Whence looked their faith to Christ, compose a
   Wall that divides the sacred stair in two.

*Order of Places
in the Mystic
Amphitheatre*

Upon this side where every petal splendid
    Is full in bloom, are seated in their places
    All who believed in Christ not yet descended;
And those half-circling ranks, with vacant spaces
    On the other side, with happy intuition
    To Christ already risen turned their faces.
And just as here the glorious position
    Of Heaven's Lady, and the others one by one
    Below it, constitute so great division,
So counterposed is that of mighty John,
    Who bore the desert, martyrdom in fine,
    And, holy still, two years in Hell thereon;
And Francis, Benedict, and Augustine,
    With others hitherward from row to row
    Continue downward the dividing line.
Now see high Providence Divine, and know
    That one and the other phase of our believing
    Shall to this garden equally bestow.
And know that down from yonder circle, cleaving
    Across, midway on the partitions two,
    Sit they, no meed of merit so retrieving,
But meed of others, by conditions due;
    For these are souls who did the flesh divest
    Before they could make any choices true.
This by their countenances may be guessed
    And by the tune their childish voices hum,
    If thou but lookest well and listenest.
Now doubtest thou, and doubting makes thee dumb;
    But I will shatter for thee the strong chain
    Of subtle thought which is so cumbersome.
The boundless amplitudes of this domain
    No particle of accident admit,
    More than of hunger, thirst, or any pain,
For Law Eternal has established it
    In what thou seest, that with exactitude
    Duly the ring doth to the finger fit.

Wherefore this swiftly hasting multitude,
   Seeking true life, are not without causation
   Placed at a higher or lower altitude.
The King through whom reposing is this nation
   In so great love and in such Paradise
   That none aspires to loftier consummation,
All minds creating in His own glad eyes,
   At His good pleasure doth with grace endue
   Diversely; and here let the fact suffice.
And this expressly is made clear to you
   In Scripture, by that twin-embrothered pair
   Who even in their mother angry grew.
Whence fittingly the light supremely fair
   May crown us with a chaplet of that grace
   According to the colour of the hair.
They stand then, not by merit of their ways,
   At different stages, only differing
   Themselves in primal keenness of their gaze.
So, when the centuries were at the spring,
   Sufficient was the parents' faith, along
   With native innocence, for rescuing;
And when the centuries were no longer young,
   'Twas needful that the males by circumcision
   Should have their innocent pinions rendered
But since the era of free grace has risen, [strong;
   If lacking perfect baptism into Christ,
   Such innocence has been kept down in prison.
Look now upon the face most like to Christ
   In its fair lineaments, whose radiance bright
   Alone can make thee fit to look on Christ.'
I saw rain down upon her such delight
   Carried by those intelligences good
   Created all for soaring through that height,
That whatsoever I before had viewed
   Did never so suspend my soul in wonder
   Nor show me of God so great similitude.

And that Love who had flown before thereunder
Singing: '*Hail Mary, full of grace benign!*'
Now spread in front of her his wings asunder.
Responses to the minstrelsy divine
Rang through the blessèd Court from all and some,
Making all features more serenely shine.
'O holy Father, who endurest to come
For me down here, quitting the blissful quire
Where by divine allotment is thy home,
Who is that Angel who with glad desire
Looks in the eyes of our own Empress yon,
Enamoured so, he seems a flame of fire?'
So turned I to the teaching of that one
Who gathered beauty out of Mary's face
As does the star of morning from the sun.
And he to me: 'All confidence and grace
Are in him, much as ever was conferred on
Angel or soul, and willing is our praise.
For this is he who brought the palm as guerdon
To Mary down, when took without distrust
The very Son of God our fleshly burden.
But follow with thine eyes now, for I must
Pursue the theme, and mark the throng of those
Great peers of this most holy realm and just.
The twain who most enraptured there repose,
Through being next neighbours to Augusta fair,
Are as the double roots of this our Rose.
He who upon the left is next her there
Is that First Sire by whose audacious taste
Mankind is savouring such bitter fare.
That ancient Father of Holy Church, once graced
By Christ with keys of this fair realm, beside
Our Lady, and upon her right, is placed.
And that one who beheld before he died
All grievous days of her purchased for us
At cost of lance and nails, Christ's own fair Bride,

412

Sits next that Father; and over against him thus
   That Leader under whom were fed with manna
   The folk ungrateful, headstrong, mutinous.
Opposite Peter seest thou seated Anna,
   So happy in her daughter that no whit
   She moves her eyes away to sing *Hosanna.*
Our greatest of housefathers opposite
   Sits Lucy, who impelled thy Lady down
   When thou wast heading straight toward the Pit.
But since Time speeds along thy trance to drown,
   Here let us pause, like prudent tailor who
   Patterns according to the cloth the gown;
And to the Primal Love turn we our view,
   So that, on visionary wing upspeeding,
   Thou pierce as in thee lies his radiance through.
Yet lest thou, peradventure, while receding,
   Flutter thy wings, advancing but in thought,
   Let grace be our petition, grace exceeding
Through her with power to help thee must be sought;
   And do thou follow me with adoration
   That from my word thy heart be severed not.'
Here he began this holy supplication.

CANTO XXXIII

'Daughter of thine own Son, thou Virgin Mother,   *The Ultimate*
   Of the eternal counsel issue fated,   *Vision*
   Lowlier and loftier than any other,
To such nobility hast thou translated
   Man's nature that its Maker did not spurn
   To make Himself the thing that He created.
Beneath thy heart was made again to burn
   The Love by virtue of whose warmth withal
   This Flower has blossomed in the peace eterne.

413

A living torch here art thou to us all
 To kindle love, and down where mortals sigh
 Thou art a fount of hope perennial.
Thou art so prevailing, Lady, and so high
 That who wants grace and will to thee not run
 Would have his longing without pinions fly.
Thy loving-kindness fails to succour none
 Imploring it, but often is so free
 As to anticipate the orison.
In thee is mercy, pity is in thee,
 In thee munificence, in thee a host
 Of human virtues are in unity.
This man, who hither from the nethermost
 Pool of the world comes making observation
 Of spiritual natures, ghost on ghost,
Now doth to thee of grace make supplication
 That he by vision may uplift his being
 Still higher toward the Ultimate Salvation.
And I, who never burned for mine own seeing
 More than I do for his, imploring pray
 With all my soul, and pray for thine agreeing,
That thou drive every mortal cloud away
 Which darkens round him, with thine interceding,—
 Be the Chief Joy unveiled to him to-day.
Hear, all-prevailing Queen, my further pleading,
 Keep his affections through thy vigilance
 Sound for him, after vision so exceeding.
Quell by thy watchcare baser human wants:
 Lo, yonder, Beatrice with all the blest
 Clasping their hands to thee are suppliants.'
The venerated eyes, belovèd best
 Of God, attent on him who made the prayer,
 Showed us her pleasure in devout request;
Then plunged into the Light Eternal, where
 We may not think of any creature turning
 An eye that penetrates so clearly there.

And I who to the goal of every yearning
  Was drawing near, slaked, as was meet for me,
  And satisfied the thirst within me burning.
Then Bernard beckoned to me smilingly
  To look aloft; but I already grew
  Of my own accord as he would have me be;
Because, becoming purified, my view
  Now more and more was entering the ray
  Of the deep Light that in itself is true.   [say,
Thenceforth my seeing was more than tongue can
  Yields our discourse before the Light Supreme,
  And violated memory falls away.
Like him who sees while dreaming, and the dream
  Remains thereafter traced upon his feeling,
  While memory holds thereof no other gleam,
Even such am I; for though the great revealing
  Fades almost all away from me, yet flow
  Its drop of sweetness in my heart distilling.
Thus in the sun evanishes the snow;
  Upon the light leaves by the zephyr drifted
  The wisdom of the Sibyl perished so.
O Light Supreme, who art so high uplifted
  From mortal thought, still let my mind with some
  Of what thou didst appear to me, be gifted,
And dower my tongue with so great masterdom
  That one sole sparkle of thy glory be
  Thereby transmitted to the folk to come;
For by some glimpses caught by memory,
  And by some echo in these rimes, perchance
  Better shall be conceived thy victory.
Pierced by the vivid living radiance
  Methinks I had been lost, if by the sight
  Bewildered, I had turned aside my glance;
And I remember, till I could unite
  My gaze therewith, my hardihood to dare
  The vision of the Goodness Infinite.

O plenteous grace, whence I presumed to bear
    The stress of the Eternal Light, till thirst
    Was consummated in the seeing there!
I saw in its abysmal deep immersed,
    Together in one volume bound with love,
    What is throughout the universe dispersed:
Substance and accidents all thereabove
    So interfused in property and mood,
    That what I say gives but scant glimpse thereof.
Of this same fusion do I think I viewed
    The universal form, for uttering
    This word, I feel ampler beatitude.
To me more Lethë doth one moment bring
    Than five and twenty centuries for the emprise
    Whence Argo's shade set Neptune wondering.
So was my spirit gazing, all surmise,
    Steadfast, intent, in absolute repose,
    And evermore enkindled through the eyes.
In presence of that radiance one grows
    So rapt, it is impossible the soul
    Could yield to turn aside to other shows;
Because the Good, which is volition's goal,
    All gathers there, and the deficient rest
    Outside it, there becomes a perfect whole.
Now will my words fall even shorter, in quest
    Of my remembrance, than the infant lore
    Of him whose tongue is moistened at the breast.
Not that the Living Light I saw gave more
    Than one sole semblance to my contemplation,
    For it is always what it was before;
But by my gathered strength of observation,
    One sole appearance, unto me thus seeing,
    Was ever changing with my transformation.
To me within the luminous deep being
    Of Lofty Light appeared three circles, showing
    Three colours, and in magnitude agreeing;

And from the First appeared the Second flowing
   Like Iris out of Iris, and the Third
   Seemed fire that equally from both is glowing.
O but how scant, how feeble any word
   To my conceit! and this to what I viewed
   Is such, to call it little were absurd.
O Light Eterne, who dost thyself include,
   Who lovest, smiling at thine own intents,
   Self-understanding and self-understood!
That circling which in Thee seemed effluence
   Of light reverberated, by my view
   Surveyed awhile in its circumference,
Within itself of its own proper hue
   Seemed painted with the effigy of man,
   Whereat my sight was wholly set thereto.
As the geometer, intent to scan
   The measure of the circle, fails to trace,
   Think as he may, some feature of the plan,
Such I at the strange vision of the Face:
   How the image fits the circle, fain aright
   Would I perceive, and how it there finds place;
But my own wings were not for such a flight—
   Except that, smiting through the mind of me,
   There came fulfilment in a flash of light.
Here vigour failed the lofty fantasy;
   But my volition now, and my desires.
   Were moved like wheel revolving evenly
By Love that moves the sun and starry fires.

NOTES AND ELUCIDATIONS

INFERNO

CANTO I

TIME: *Morning of Good Friday of the Jubilee year, 1300, Dante being midway to three-score and ten.*
PLACE: *The 'wandering wood of this life', where Dante comes to himself from that sleep which is spiritual death. To understand the Poet one must 'go into the poet's country',—a country where all material things and transitory wants are looked at* sub specie eternitatis. *Dante himself is at once an individual and a type of humanity erring, repenting, winning salvation. Virgil is at once the poet whom Dante most admired and the type of human wisdom* (philosophy). *Beatrice is at once the woman whom Dante loved and the mouthpiece of Divine wisdom* (theology). *Earth is still the centre of the universe; the sun is a larger planet; astronomy is hardly distinguished from astrology.*

1-3] The proper comment would be chapters 23 and 24 of the Fourth Book of the Convivio, where human life is likened to an arch rising to its apex in the thirty-fifth year and thence descending to the period fixed by the Psalmist. As Dante, the protagonist of his own Poem, was born in 1265, he is now thirty-five, the year that is the key-stone of the arch.
The first word of the third line would be 'where' (in which) if the Oxford text were here followed.

3] Oxford text reads *che.*

20] The rime-scheme here compels the translator to omit the striking image, 'the lake of the heart'.

30] But that this line has been discussed so much, it would seem superfluous to remark that this is the Poet's way of saying that he is gradually ascending. In going up hill the bodily weight rests upon whichever foot is standing still below the one which is being thrust forward.

31-58] Just what sins the three beasts typify is disputed. Elsewhere in the Poem the wolf is the type of avarice, by which Dante means all forms of selfish advantage at the expense of others. It is the sin which he most frequently stigmatizes; obviously, therefore, the allegory here cannot be merely personal. If the leopard symbolizes lust, the lion pride, the wolf avarice, the correspondence is sufficiently plain with the grand division of sins in Canto xi into sins of Incontinence, of Violence, and of Fraud.

38-40] The sun was placed in the sign of the Ram (Aries) at the Creation, and rises now accompanied by the same stars. At Eastertide all nature rises with the risen God; the vernal equinox is the true beginning, not only of the year, but of all things. Our Chaucer afterwards chose the same date for his pilgrimage to Canterbury, when 'the yongë Sonne Hath in the Ram his halfë cors yronnë'.

48] Cf. Shakespeare's *Henry the Fifth*, Chorus I, lines 12-14; and Tennyson's *Godiva.*

79] Dante's choice of Virgil as his guide is a noble instance of that humanity which is above all creeds. The Roman poet is made the type of human reason and he therefore retires, in the Earthly Paradise, in favour of Beatrice who typifies 'the good of intellect', i.e., the knowledge of God.

101-11] The Hound is to be a great national deliverer, such as Dante at one time hoped Henry of Luxemburg would be. Here he seems to have in mind Can Grande della Scala, but the reference is purposely vague. There is a town Feltre on the Piave and the famous castle of Montefeltro was in the mountains of the Romagna. Torraca does not capitalize the initial letters of these words (*feltro e feltro*).
Taking 'nazion' in the primary sense of nativity, the meaning would be, 'his birth shall be between felt and felt'. It is explained that felt was used for fine cushions and rugs, so that the Poet is prophesying a deliverer 'born in the purple'. Casella, whose critical text is made accessible to English readers in the edition of the Nonesuch Press, follows this reading, as does Passerini in the monumental edition printed at Florence in 1911 (Olschki).

117] Probably annihilation is meant. But see Book of Revelation xx. 6 and 14, and xxi. 8.

CANTO II

TIME: *Evening of Good Friday, 1300.*

13] The allusions in Dante's address to Virgil are to the sixth book of the *Aeneid* and to the twelfth chapter of Second Corinthians.

22] That the Roman Empire is a fundamental part of the Divine plan for human redemption is a principle in Dante's philosophy of history, as will be fully developed in Cantos vi and xviii of *Paradiso.*

37-42] For another notable passage on this theme see *Purgatorio* v. 16-18.

58] All the words of Beatrice breathe womanly sweetness and have that 'divine liquidity' which, since Chaucer, is so rare in our literature. Translation inevitably falls far short of the music and simplicity of the original.

67] Not mere fine phrasing; no one could despise it more than Dante did. Poetry to him is the perfect utterance of the truth: hence the choice of a poet as the organ of human reason.

94] The blessed Virgin Mary whose name, like

that of Christ, recurs so often in other parts of the Poem, may not be directly mentioned in Hell. Likewise God is referred to commonly as 'Another'. Santa Lucia, who reappears, notably in *Purg.* ix, is a saint to whom Dante was especially devoted.

134] This is Dante's third use of the word 'cortese' in the present canto. Surely the salutation given Virgil by the blessed spirit,

'O anima cortese mantovana' (l. 58)

must suggest to the thoughtful mind that the word has an almost religious connotation. Courtesy is even attributed to the Divinity in line 17, in *Par.* vii. 91 and in *Par.* xv. 48. The influence of this gracious virtue in softening the hard hearts of that time must have been notable. It is hardly possible to fathom its significance in the poetry of those centuries without being immersed in the soul of the Middle Ages. Much that now passes for religion might be none the worse for some infusion of a virtue once so celebrated and now perhaps somewhat antique.

CANTO III

Before reaching Limbo proper, we pass through what is neither Hell nor not-Hell, where those who were too cowardly to take sides or to have pronounced opinions, run to escape wasps and other petty plagues.

60] The Great Refusal was made in 1294 by Pope Celestine V, whose abdication was probably managed by his immediate successor, Boniface VIII, a chief object throughout the Poem of scorn and denunciation.

64-9] The repulsive imagery symbolizes the vain remorse of those who in life were 'lukewarm and neither hot nor cold'.

70-81] On approaching the dark river separating us from the First Circle, dialogue is, with definite artistic intention, cut short.

82-129] Charon is the first of the demons enumerated in the note to Canto v. 4. The contrast between Charon and the guardian of Antepurgatory, Cato of Utica, is noteworthy. There is a long series of contrasts in detail between the persons and things of Hell and those of Purgatory and Paradise. Few of these contrasts can be referred to in these notes.

93] The 'lighter keel' is that of the angel-pilot of *Purgatorio* ii.

112-17] The poetic charm of the Inferno is due, in no small degree, to the art with which the Poet flashes at intervals the light of beauty upon the gloomy scenery of the mind. Cheering relief is given to the dark sublimity of this canto by the images of the leaves in autumn and of the bird obedient to the signal of the falconer.

136] The Poet leaves the reader to imagine how he was carried across. Being asleep, he did not himself know. Description is wisely reserved for another ferriage (Canto viii). He begins Canto iv with his awakening on the other side. There has been much throwing about of brains concerning this passage on the part of anxious commentators.

CANTO IV

Unbaptized innocents and virtuous pagans, in a quiet and not unpleasant retreat (Limbo), where they suffer nothing but want of hope.

34-45] No wonder great woe laid hold of our gentle Poet to find devoid of hope in that other world so many heroes and sages whom he held in honour. How the word 'honour' goes ringing through this sad bede-roll! See lines 70-93.

53] Referring of course to the descent of Christ, who must not be named in Hell.

86-96] The selection here made of members of the fair school of Homer is, of course, marked by medieval limitations. To Dante, Greek literature was either unknown, or known through references or fragments in the Latin writers, or from Arabian sources. Of the Greek tragic and comic poets he appears to have known nothing. Among the Latins, Lucretius seems to have been unknown to him. It is pathetic to see him looking up to writers like Lucan and Statius and Ovid, and Livy 'the unerring' (*Inf.* xxviii. 12). But if his literary horizon was contracted, he cultivated it to the utmost verge.

106-11] The gates of the Castle, conceived as a magnificent University, typify the seven liberal arts of the Trivium (grammar, logic, rhetoric) and the Quadrivium (arithmetic, geometry, astronomy, music). These formed the regular curriculum of the schools, as being the avenues to all human knowledge.

121-44] This resounding enumeration of famous worthies of the ancient and non-Christian world is interesting as being distinctive of the period, especially by reason of the names conspicuous for their absence. It is noteworthy that the only moderns are three illustrious Saracens: Saladin, Avicenna, Averroës. Dante and the 'learnèd clerks' of his century were greatly indebted to Arabian culture for what they knew of 'the master of those who know' (Aristotle). As to the famous Avicenna, his *canon* continued to be a text-book of medicine for a century after Rabelais studied it at Montpellier.

141] Oxford text reads *Lino*.

CANTO V

Victims of sensuality, continually buffeted about by fierce gales.

4] Upon entering each of the five circles outside the City of Dis the Poet is confronted and challenged by a mythological guardian : (1) Charon, (2) Minos, (3) Cerberus, (4) Plutus, (5) Phlegyas. Each of these is in turn rebuked and humbled by Virgil. Within Dis the (7) Minotaur is similarly encountered and defeated, but a far more powerful hand had been needed to open the gate of that city against the (6) Furies (Erinyes). (8) Geryon, at entrance to Malpouches (Malebolge) is tamed to service; as finally is (9) Antaeus at entrance to the Pit. In shining contrast with these are the noble custodians of the terraces of Purgatory.

28-51] With this passage compare that in which Shakespeare rises, as only he could do, to an equal height upon such a theme (*Measure for Measure*, III. i. 118-32). Here, as everywhere, Dante, with a justice that, if not Divine, is certainly poetic, makes the punishment fit, or typify the crime. With l. 28 compare Canto i. 60.

65-6] Dante did not have access to the poems of Homer. He follows the tradition then current that Achilles met death at the hands of Paris, who decoyed the Grecian hero into a temple for a meeting with the Trojan princess Polyxena, of whom he was enamoured.

97] Ravenna, where Dante spent his latter years in the service or under the protection of its lord, Guido Novello da Polenta, a nephew of Francesca. The mode of her death is so grievous to her because it deprived her of a chance to repent.

139-42] Although Francesca speaks for both the lovers, her words are marked by a womanly reticence that approves her to be, like Pia in *Purg.* v, a true sister to Desdemona and hapless Ophelia. To enlarge here upon the delicate dramatic truth of this poignant recital would be impertinent. But it may be remarked that the Poet's swooning has a far deeper root than mere pity or even sympathy. He may well mean to suggest that he felt himself already wounded by the sword with which Beatrice is soon to pierce him. Cf. *Purg.* xxx-xxxi; especially the reference to the 'pargoletta' (dainty maid), xxxi. 59.

CANTO VI

The Gluttons are lying on the ground whipped by filthy rain, pelted with hail and snow, and persecuted by Cerberus, cruel of claw and deafening in his clamour.

34] The *spirits, souls, shades*, as they are variously called, although but shadows of what they were in life, seem subject to being physically maltreated, as by Cerberus, or, as here, trodden upon. We are in a region where other laws obtain than those we know, or suppose ourselves to know. Cf. Virgil's pathetic remarks on the subject near the beginning of *Purg.* iii. It must never be forgotten that all the physical imagery of Hell is the Poet's only means of vividly figuring the tortures of self-condemnation. Until psychology is able to adjust its boundary dispute with physiology we are hardly justified in carping at Dante for leaving the frontier undetermined.

52] Ciacco is a familiar form of Giacomo (cf. Jack). Such names are of course not necessarily nicknames. It also means *hog*, possibly by onomatopoeia. This person seems to have been well known but his identity is uncertain.

64-75] This prophecy refers to incidents in the bitter, fluctuating, dramatic struggle for mastery in Florence between the aristocratic Black Guelfs, captained by Corso Donati, and the Whites, led by the Cerchi—whose rustic origin is so often referred to as to convince us that they retained some of the faults of breeding that stamp in all ages the newly rich.—The trimmer, 'he who now is temporizing' (l. 69), is Pope Boniface. Who the two just men are is matter of conjecture.

79-87] If we go down far enough, we shall meet all of these worthies except Arrigo, of whom nothing is recorded.

106-11] *Thy science*, as later in Canto xi, *thy physics, thy ethics*, is always with reference to Aristotle, 'master of those who know'.—The doctrine is that the soul understands best which inhabits the most perfect body, and thus if the body lacks an organ, understanding is impaired. The damned cannot attain perfection in their damnation until soul shall be reunited with body.

CANTO VII

1] These words of Plutus and those of the giant Nimrod (xxxi. 67) are doubtless intended as senseless gibberish, as becomes the nature of these creatures. What in the light of Eternity (*sub specie eternitatis*) could be more foolish than the love of money? See note to Canto v. 4.

22-35] The Avaricious from one side, the Prodigal from the other, are rolling great weights until their lines clash together like the counter-currents of the Strait of Messina, between Scylla and Charybdis (greatly feared by the ancients).

39] Cropped hair is a symbol of lavishness. 'He has spent his whole substance, even to the hair of his head' (Italian saying).

49-54] So the ignoble usurers of noble family are known only by their heraldry. Canto xvii. 52 ff.

68-96] Fortune, regarded as an angelic intelligence whose function it is to bring down the
mighty and exalt those of low estate.

115-26] The Wrathful and the Sullen are immersed in the muddy Styx. The Sullen appear to
be entirely submerged. *Accidia,* which I translate
as *sullenness,* is deliberate, repressed, rankling
wrath or rancour.

CANTO VIII

*The Wrathful, plunged in the muddy Stygian lagoon
and continually fighting among themselves, only unit-
ing to persecute some particularly odious neighbour.*

4-6] The other beacon is from the high tower in
the City of Dis: Canto ix. 36. Compare ll. 70-5
of the present Canto. Such signals were the tele-
gaphy of that age.

19] Phlegyas is utilized, as later Geryon and
Antaeus. See note to Canto v. 4.

32-63] Filippo Argenti, of the great house of the
Adimari, a swaggering, insolent noble who shod
his horse with silver. Boccaccio describes him as
a tall, swart, sinewy fellow of enormous strength,
prone to anger on the slightest occasion. Boccaccio tells an illustrative anecdote of him (*Decameron* ix. 8). Franco Sacchetti (*Novelle,* 114) tells a
quaint story of the ironical plea of Dante for a
young man of the Adimari family, who was either
identical with, or of nature akin to, this personage.—We may have before us the only instance,
in which Dante can fairly be suspected of personal
animosity against one of the 'submerged'. The
case of Bocca degli Abati (Canto xxxii), whom
Dante never saw, is not in point. Dante's usual
attitude towards the shades of sinners is sympathetic. For a terrible characterization of the Adimari, see *Par.* xvi. 115-20.

71] The reference to the mosques in the Capital
of the Infernal Empire is in harmony with the
elaborate poetical parallelism between Heaven
and Hell, the things of God and those of Lucifer,
which is one of the features of Dante's art. To the
mind of the medieval Christian the mosque is the
temple of a wicked heresy. Thus Hell has 'clois-
ters'; the members of the 'college' of the hypocrites wear 'cowls'; Dante goes so far as to parody
one of the Latin hymns of the Church to emphasize the contrast between Christ and Satan (beginning of Canto xxxiv).

115] Virgil's repulse here seems to shadow forth
a spiritual crisis so terrible that the noblest human
reason is unavailing. There are dreadful gates
where the wisest can only cast his eyes to the
ground. In the middle of the next Canto the
Poet emphasizes the importance of the allegory
in this crucial passage.

124] The fallen angels, become demons, had
likewise made bold to oppose the descent of
Christ into Hell.

CANTO IX

7-18] The anacoluthon, to denote dismay and
confusion of mind, reminds one of the famous
beginning of the first speech of Satan in *Paradise
Lost.* Dante's question (ll. 16-18) implies some
doubt as to Virgil's competence as guide.

22-7] That the Thessalian witch Erichtho may
thus have used the soul of Virgil for her purposes was suggested to Dante by a passage in
Lucan (*Pharsalia* vi).

52-63] It seems to be agreed that the Furies represent pangs of conscience. But what is the Gorgon? Some say doubt, which turns the heart to
stone; others make it an emblem of the harden-
ing effect of despair. Almost every commentator
has a special interpretation of the 'strange verses'.
Compare the note to Canto viii. 115.

80] This Divine messenger is without doubt one
of the Angels. The need must have been indeed
urgent that prompted this singular instance of
Divine interposition. We shall arrive at the shore
of the island of Purgatory before meeting another
such sublime minister of grace (*Purg.* ii).

89] The touch of the wand is effectively contrasted with the crash of the then familiar bat-
tering-ram. The same disdain of human instruments is expressed in *Purg.* ii. 31.

98-9] Cerberus had met more than his match
when he attacked Hercules, who amused himself
by chaining the monster and dragging him over a
very rough road and releasing him far from home.

112-15] At Arles the Rhone no longer 'ponds',
although its tendency to do so is manifest in La
Camargue, a little below. A few relics of the
ancient cemetery are still to be seen there. In the
Great War Italy finally regained its boundary on
the Gulf of Quarnaro, beyond Pola. Benvenuto
states that some seven hundred tombs existed
there. Impressive still are the Roman remains,
especially the well-preserved amphitheatre.

127-31] Just why heretics receive this form of
punishment may be left to the imagination of the
student of religious history. Heresy does not fit
into the classification of sins in Canto xi. Dante
gives it a place between sins of passion and sins
of malice, and obviously avoids dwelling upon
its nature. In Canto x the reader's interest is
shifted from the heretics to Florentine history and
to the fate of the Poet himself. Those interested in
Dante's treatment of the heretics are referred to the
chapter on this Circle in Reade's *Moral System
of Dante's Inferno.*

INFERNO

CANTO X

The heretics lie in open tombs filled with fire. Dante exhibits the great heretics, as he does the virtuous pagans, with frank admiration. The lofty figure of Farinata is portrayed with the same sympathy, not to say partiality, with which Milton draws his imposing Satan. The Poet's attitude is much the same towards Ulysses (Canto xxvi).

13] Epicurus, not being a Christian, was no more a heretic than were the other great pagans. The statement must be attributed to Virgil with deliberate purpose. That Dante's philosophic guide should be baffled in the Circle of Heresy is of deep significance.

36] How an ideal, a purpose, a great hope, or even a poignant remembrance, can make a man superior to fate!

52-72] The personage by the side of Farinata is the father of Guido Cavalcanti. Guido, who was Dante's intimate friend, seems to have belonged to that Florentine type of the lofty-minded, cultivated, able, somewhat sceptical patrician, of which Lorenzo il Magnifico is the most conspicuous example. The broken spirit of the elder Cavalcanti here sets the superb figure of Farinata in relief. It is significant also that the families were related by the marriage of Guido very early in life to the daughter of Farinata. As Messer Cavalcante de' Cavalcanti was a Guelf patrician, it was vainly hoped by such a politic marriage to bring about peace if not union between the factions.

79-81] 'The Lady reigning here' is Proserpina, queen of Erebus—night's Plutonian shore—here identified with the moon. Before fifty moons shall have waxed and waned Dante will have had painful experience of the difficult art of returning from exile. In answer to Dante's question concerning this and other dark prophecies about his life, his great kinsman Cacciaguida in the Heaven of Mars discourses of the Poet's exile (*Paradiso* xvii).

85-7] The bloody battle of Montaperti, near Siena, in 1260, where the Florentine Guelfs were utterly put to rout by the Sienese and the Florentine Ghibellines under the leadership of Farinata.

91-3] But for the opposition of Farinata, Florence would have been destroyed after Montaperti. The Florentine Guelfs rewarded their saviour with the blackest ingratitude, treating the whole Uberti clan with rigour unexampled even in those cruel times.

94-108] They can prophesy, but are unaware of present conditions on earth. Canto xix. 52-7.

110] Dante addresses both Farinata and the father of Guido Cavalcanti with the respectful 'you', 'your'. For the great significance of this, see the first dozen lines of *Paradiso* xvi.

119] The Emperor, of whom Dante often speaks and whom he admired greatly; and the Cardinal Ottaviano of the Ubaldini, who said, when about to die: 'If there be a soul, I have lost mine a thousand times for the Ghibellines.' He had looked at the Gorgon! The terse reference to him implies the fact that he was the outstanding prelate of his age, although never attaining the papal dignity. The Ubaldini were, perhaps, after the Aldobrandeschi, the most powerful Ghibelline clan in Tuscany.

CANTO XI

3] This is the Seventh Circle (of the Violent), which we enter in Canto xii.

8] An echo of the disputes about the nature of Christ which rent the ancient church and which still persists. The story is that Pope Anastasius II was too friendly to the person and too tolerant of the doctrine of the monophysite prelate Photinus. There is another echo of this baneful controversy in *Paradiso* vi (13 ff.). To question the orthodox view that there are two natures, divine and human, united in Christ, was anathema.

17] Lesser circles, because Hell narrows funnelwise, but still vast spaces. We have seen, outside the City of Dis, the punishments of the Incontinent; we are next to traverse the three rounds or rings of the Violent (Cantos xii to xvii), composing the First Circle (seventh of the whole). At the end of Canto xvii we descend by a living airship to Evil-pouches, ten in number, where as many varieties of Fraud are punished (Cantos xviii to xxx). These all belong to the Eighth Circle from the beginning. The final Cantos (xxxii to xxxiv) deal with Treacherous Fraud punished in the Ninth Circle of the whole, called Cocytus.—The classification of the Heretics (Canto x) is left undetermined.

39] Foremost Rondure, i.e., first Round or Ring of the great plain of the First Circle of the Violent (seventh of the whole).

42] Second Rondure, encircled by the first.

49] Smallest Rondure, because surrounded by the second.

50] Cahors, in South Central France, was a noted seat of usury. The attitude of Dante towards usury is the result of a prejudice which is traceable back to Aristotle and which propagated itself until the middle of the eighteenth century, when Turgot gave it the *coup de grâce*. Dante, indeed, failed to read correctly some of the economic signs of his own time.

57] Second Circle (or eighth of all Hell) is Malebolge (Malpouches). Eight of the classes punished in these ditches are enumerated here, the others being evil counsellors and sowers of discord.

64] Smallest Circle—ninth of Hell—the ultimate Pit at bottom of which Dis (Satan) stands at the centre of the earth, like a monstrous worm at the core of the whole Creation.

80] Thine Ethics—the Ethics of thy master Aristotle. This is an elaborate, scholastic way of pointing out that sins of impulse, due to want of self-control, are less heinous than those of malignant intention.

82] The classification of sins is clear. The significance of the quite different classification in Purgatorio will be pointed out in a note to Purg. xvii.

97] The argument about usury, and the classification of this with sodomy, so strange and repellent to us, is a notable example of that scholastic reasoning imposed upon Dante by the leaders of thought in his time, to whom the authority of 'the master of those who know' was little less sacred than that of Holy Writ.

113] This is an elaborate way of saying that it is an hour or two before sunrise. The Fishes are on the morning horizon, the Ram (with the sun) just below it, the Wain (Septentrion, 'Dipper') is with the northwest wind (Caurus).

115] This and Canto vi are the shortest in the Poem. The average length is a little over 142 lines. On the other hand, the penultimate Canto (xxxiii) is the longest of the Inferno, as the penultimate of Purgatorio (xxxii) is longest of the whole Poem (160 lines).

The correspondence everywhere traceable between sins and penalties can only be meant to suggest that the awful imagery is but a shadow of spiritual experience. The hint is put, for example, into the mouth of poor Francesca. It is no physical agony that extorts the moan, 'Nessun maggior dolore' (v. 121). That the tortures of Hell are mental is told, as only poetry can tell it, by the attitudes as well as the words of Farinata and Cavalcante and a hundred others whom the reader is to meet. Dante had no need to cry with Marlowe: 'Why this is Hell, nor am I out of it!'; nor with Milton, 'Myself am Hell'; nor with Swinburne,

> 'The heart is the prey of the gods
> Who crucify hearts, not hands.'

CANTO XII

1-3] Plunged more or less deeply in Phlegethon, river of boiling blood.

4] This interesting rock-fall, called Slavini di Marco, is in the defile through which the Adige passes near Rovereto. The brief geological explanation (l. 6) is due to Albertus Magnus, the Universal Doctor, who died when Dante was a youth and is one of the great circle of lights of Par. x.

12 ff.] The Minotaur, symbol of violence, the more bestial for being half human. The symbolic union of Pasiphaë and the bull is twice referred to in Purg. xxvi. The Minotaur is the fit guardian of the entrance to this region of Hell, where sins of violence and bestiality are punished. Theseus is called Duke of Athens also by Shakespeare.

20] Ariadne.

22] Probably referring to a sacrifice.

30] The movement of the stones beneath the physical weight of the living body does not escape notice as we shall see. This is one of a hundred observations that show our Poet to be familiar with mountain-climbing.

34] As explained near the beginning of Canto ix.

37] Cf. Canto iv. 52 ff.

42] He who said so was Empedocles. Possibly Dante means to hint that love in Hell would be, locally at least, a disorganizing force.

52] Now we are looking down upon the edge of the great plain skirted by the boiling river of blood, beyond which the wood of the suicides lies around the great sand-waste, as explained at the beginning of Canto xiv.

55-87] The centaurs, like the Minotaur, half beast and half human, are equally appropriate watchmen here. The Poet evidently feels the essentially noble poetic nature of the centaur. Dante does not allow condemnation to eternal punishment to prejudice him illiberally against the inmates of Hell, whether centaur or human.

88-9] Beatrice.

103-20] Of the violent here the two most interesting to us are Ezzelino da Romano, called a 'firebrand' by his sister, the blessed Cunizza, whom we shall meet in the Heaven of Venus; and Guy de Montfort, who slew in church at Viterbo the young English prince, Henry of Cornwall, innocent victim of vendetta. To mention Alexander and the tyrant of Syracuse alongside of modern tyrants is an example of the Poet's outlook sub specie eternitatis. Orosius, whom we shall meet among the sapient souls in the Heaven of the Sun, who was regarded as a great historical authority, enlarging upon the cruelty of Alexander, had given justification to Dante for placing the conqueror here. Elsewhere Dante praises Alexander for liberality. Cf. the case of the emperor, Frederick II (Canto x. 119).

118-20] Guy (Guido) de Montfort, mentioned in the preceding note, is son of that Simon de Montfort who played so important a rôle in the time of Henry III of England. Simon, 'protector gentis angliae', had been slain at the Battle of Evesham, where Prince Edward (later Edward I) led the opposing royalist forces. Since Guy cannot get at Edward, he takes the life of Henry, who was cousin to both of them. Villani reports that the heart of the victim was set in a golden cup on a column at the head of London Bridge. Crimes combining violence with sacrilege were regarded with especial horror; hence this miscreant is set apart from the others.

126] (and compare ll. 67 and 97, together with the context of each.) Dejanira, wife of Hercules, was riding the Centaur, Nessus, across a river, when he was overpowered by that passion for her which ended so disastrously for all concerned. Ovid's remark that Nessus was *scitus vadorum* (acquainted with fords) made the choice of him for such an office the more suitable. The thought of riding the same great horse that had once carried a lady so long celebrated must have been rather fascinating to the Poet (Ovid, *Metam.* ix).

135-8] Sextus Pompeius and Pyrrhus, alias Neoptolemus, son of Achilles and Deidamia. His violence and cruelty are brought out by Virgil in the account of the sack of Troy (*Aeneid*, Book II, from l. 469). The two Rinieri were egregious robber chieftains of noble family, who patrolled the two roads from Tuscany to Rome. Rinier Pazzo is said to have been in the service of Frederick II in war against the Pope, and was perhaps not much worse than many other Ghibelline nobles whose castles commanded the routes of traffic.

CANTO XIII

The violent against themselves (suicides) and against their goods (spendthrifts).

8] The Maremma, a district wild, marshy, malarial, along the Tuscan seaboard between the river Cécina and the town Corneto, its northern and southern landmarks. It is referred to repeatedly in the Poem, the enjoyment of which is greatly enhanced by familiarity with the map of Italy.

28-45] Dante adapts to his purpose the strange tale of Polydore (*Aeneid*, Bk. III, from l. 22). Polydore had been murdered by Polynestor (*Purg.* xx. 115) for the treasure with which the young prince had been sent from Troy just before its fall. Cast upon the seashore, the body was covered with sand, and the javelins which had been left in the wounds sprouted up as myrtle and cornel shoots. When Aeneas begins to pluck these shafts, preparatory to a sacrificial rite, first blood issues and then the voice of the murdered prince.—Our

Poet is therefore here an imitator—at least his inventive power is less independent than usual.

48] In the *Aeneid*, Book III.

58] The shade of Pier della Vigna, chancellor and confidant of the great Emperor Frederick, and an able and eloquent man whose letters may still be read. Perhaps it is out of homage to him as a stylist that Dante makes him tell his story in so ornate a manner. Homage is done to the illustrious man by allowing him to speak at length—forty-five lines, much for Dante. The other chief speakers in Hell, aside from Virgil and Dante himself, are Francesca, Farinata, Ser Brunetto, Ulysses, Guido of Montefeltro, Master Adam, Ugolino. Of these, all save Farinata, speak at greater length than Francesca, whose immortal lines number less than forty.

Inasmuch as Dante deemed the *apologia* of Pier (Peter) della Vigna worthy of a space relatively so large, possibly some readers may be willing to hear a very little more about this great figure. As Logothete (i.e. Chancellor) of Sicily, then the most civilized kingdom in Europe, and as Protonotary of the Empire, Peter was easily the most important administrative officer of the Western World. In other ways also he acted as confidential agent and adviser to Frederick of Hohenstaufen. He seems to have been the driving force in the compilation of the *Liber Augustalis*—the first medieval codification of the Roman Law—a code which the magnanimous Frederick liberalized in important directions. Peter went to England to negotiate the marriage of the Emperor with Isabella, sister of Henry III. His final fall was as sudden and fatal as that of Wolsey, three centuries later. In the heart of Frederick there were chambers of which the keys were entrusted to none.

64] The harlot (*meretrix*, from *mereri*, to earn) is of course Calumny—to men of old much more than a mere abstraction. Cf. the vivid allegorical picture by Botticelli—one of the chief treasures of the Uffizi.

120-42] This Lano is said to have been a member of the Spending Club (Brigata Spendereccia) of Siena, described in Canto xxix. Having spent his wealth speedily, he flung himself upon certain death when ambushed in the engagement at the ford of Toppo over the river Chiana. The other spirit who provokes the remonstrance of the bush, James of Sant'Andrea, was a Paduan spendthrift of extraordinary ingenuity in shortening his *peau de chagrin*. The speaker in the bush was a judge of Florence, one Lotto of the Agli family, whose stately tower still stands in a suburb of Florence.

143] It was a characteristic popular superstition

at Florence that the continual strife that raged there was due to the jealousy of the ancient patron god, Mars. The present Baptistry, the old Cathedral, was pretty certainly built on the foundation of an ancient temple of Mars. Compare the significant reference to the maleficence of the mutilated statue of the god on the Ponte Vecchio (*Par.* xvi, near end of Canto).

CANTO XIV

The dreadful waste of sand (orribil sabbione) *pelted by the Sodomitic rain of fire.*

8] Here at length, leaving the Suicidal Wood infested by filthy harpies and fierce black dogs, we emerge upon the sand-waste, to the dwellers in which the next four Cantos are devoted.

15] Cato of Utica, who led the retreat of Pompey's army across the desert (Lucan, *Pharsalia*, Bk. x). We shall meet him on the shore of the Purgatorial island.

22-5] The violent against God are flat on their backs; the violent against art (usurers) are sitting crouched over their money-bags; the violent against nature (guilty of unnatural sexual indulgence) are incessantly roving.—There is, unfortunately, too much testimony, and by no means only in Dante, that the violent practices against nature, known as the 'sin of Sodom', were exceedingly common in the middle ages, especially among the clergy and the literary class.

31-6] Legends of Alexander and buildings attributed to him are still extant in the Punjab. Dante was probably influenced by his historical authority, Orosius, to omit Alexander from his enumeration of illustrious Pagans (Canto iv), although in the *Convivio* (iv, 11) Alexander is praised for liberality, along with Saladin, whom we saw in Canto iv, and Bertran de Born whom we shall meet in Canto xxviii.

56] Mongibello is another name for Etna, where the Cyclopes had their forge. The word Gibello, itself meaning mountain, is a memorial of the Saracen occupation of Sicily (Arabic *Jebel*).

58] Phlegra, scene of the attempt of the giants to scale Olympus.

70] Capaneus defied Jove—whom Dante here apparently identifies with God, as he does again in Canto xxv, and in *Purg.* vi. It is true these other instances are more purely poetical; here an interesting theological question might be raised.

79] Bulicamë: name of a hot mineral spring at Viterbo, from which water seems to have been conducted to the houses of unfortunate women.

103] The tall old man in the cavern of the Cretan Mount Ida seems to symbolize historically the human race facing westward, its tears supplying the rivers of Hell. The cleft is the result of the Fall of Man; hence these tears. The golden age is of course before the Fall. The image is copied from that in Nebuchadnezzar's dream in the Book of Daniel. The reader may amuse himself by tracing the interesting symbolism in detail. Crete, by its central geographical position as well as by its place in the history of culture, is a well-selected site for such an emblem.

126] Lefthand turns are the rule in Hell; the reverse is the rule in Purgatory.

130-5] Our Poet, like Shakespeare, turns every scrap of knowledge to account. Being unacquainted with Greek, he probably owes to Virgil his knowledge of the meaning of the word Phlegethon. Cf. *Aeneid*, Book vi, l. 551. There is an ancient gloss to l. 265 of the same book: 'Phlegetonta vocat ignem.' The present passage is an acknowledgement of indebtedness for this bit of linguistic lore. Virgil's reply is a courteous way of hinting to Dante that, aware of the meaning, he might have spared the question. In l. 132 the rain referred to is that of the tears of mankind collected in the Colossus of Crete. The hasty reader should not confuse this with the 'rain of fire' described early in this Canto.

136] We shall encounter and pass Lethë after the great central passage of the Poem (*Purg.* xxxi).

CANTO XV

Traversing the horrible sand waste upon a dyke of Phlegethon.

1] Upon the dyke along the red rivulet of Phlegethon the Poets can pass safely, sheltered by certain fumes rising from the stream, as pointed out by Virgil in the preceding Canto, l. 90.

4] Wissant, anciently a haven of importance near Cape Grisnez, west of the later town of Calais, marks the western border of the great countship of Flanders. Bruges, near the eastern end of the long Flemish dyke, was perhaps the most prosperous city of the North, and was sometimes known as the Venice of the North. It was the seat of one of the principal Florentine factories. Both ports were used by the Florentines in their extensive commerce with England.

9] That is before the snow melts upon the mountains in which it heads. The medieval Duchy of Carinthia extended westward to the headwaters of the Brenta, the river which passes near Padua and flows into the Venetian lagoon.

30-6] Brunetto Latino (or Latini) was a distinguished citizen and man of letters who had powerfully influenced Dante in the latter's earlier years. Brunetto's principal work was written in

INFERNO

French—*Le Livre dou Tresor*—a compilation of encyclopaedic character held at that time in high esteem. Dante addresses him with the *Voi* (you), in token of profound respect, as he has so far addressed only the two Florentine worthies in Canto x (cf. note to x. 110).

62] Fiesolë is a very ancient city, with massive Etruscan remains and a Roman theatre, built on the lofty hill above Florence. In the commune of Fiesolë are the immense quarries which furnished the material for the building of Etruscan and Roman Fiesolë, as well as of Florence, to which the stone is still daily transported by cartloads. Ser Brunetto makes a sharp distinction between the descendants of the Roman colonists of Florence and the Fiesolans, rough and hard as their mountain and their rock.

72] Both parties at Florence will have to go hungry for Dante, who will be safe at Ravenna under the powerful Guido Novello, 'the eagle of Polenta' (xxvii. 41).

79] This tribute to Ser Brunetto exemplifies the detachment with which Dante distinguishes between his personal gratitude to a great intellectual guide and his reprobation of the sin which involves such punishment. As in the cases of Francesca, Farinata, and several others, our Poet exhibits pity, sympathy, veneration, even affection for the condemned.

89] For Beatrice. The other text is the prophecy of Ciacco (Canto vi) and that of Farinata (Canto x). Some of the interpretation or gloss which Dante hopes for is supplied in *Par.* xvii by his great ancestor.

106] In the middle ages most men of letters belonged to the clergy which, by reason of enforced celibacy, was peculiarly vulnerable to carnal temptation.

109] Priscian is the famous grammarian of the sixth century. Francesco d'Accorso (or Accursi) was a legal adviser to the greatest of English kings, Edward I (d. 1307).

111] The word here translated 'vermin' (tigna, pustule or scab of itch) seems more applicable to the thoroughly contemptible bishop who, by the *servus servorum* Boniface VIII, was deposed at Florence and sent to Vicenza, where he soon died. Benvenuto speaks of him as bestial in stupidity as well as in morals. But he belonged to the powerful Mozzi family, his brother being an eminent jurist.

123] The green cloth was the prize of a foot-race. Palio (pallium, cloth or cloak) is the name of the famous horse-races run to this day in the Campo of Siena.

More of the violent against Nature dancing under the pelting fire in the dreadful arena.

1] Byron in his noblest lyric recalls voices that 'sound like a distant torrent's fall'. Dante here tells what *that* sound is like.

8] The garb in question is doubtless the distinctive and beautiful habit of the Florentine gentleman, as we see it in Giotto's portrait of young Dante in the Chapel of the Bargello.

9] These patriots, like Dante himself, supremely love the city which they denounce. Torraca cites a still unpublished sermon, delivered in front of the church of Santa Maria Maggiore in 1305, stigmatizing Florence as almost another Sodom. —In that church, the thoughtful pilgrim to Florence may like to know, still stands the contemporary cruciform monument of Dante's *maestro*, Brunetto Latino.

19-27] It seems that these spirits cannot remit, as Ser Brunetto had done, the swift action of their limbs; and since all are equally eager to gaze at the apparition of a living man their movement is converted into the wheeling dance so vividly pictured. The nude and anointed champions are perhaps such as Virgil had described in the account of the games (*Aeneid*, Book III, ll. 281-2).

28-45] These three worthies were distinguished citizens, of Florence to whom Dante had looked up in his youth. Gualdrada was daughter of the ancient Bellincione Berti, described in *Par.* xv and xvi, and was ancestress of the Conti Guidi, a famous lineage. Her beauty and virtue are Florentine traditions. Aldobrandi counselled against the fatal expedition to Siena in 1260, resulting in the terrible defeat at Montaperti—a reason why Florence should honour him. In the excuse he makes for Rusticucci the Poet does not appear to be quite 'on the side of the angels'. No cloister in Hell seems set apart for shrews! For interesting tradition and gossip about these personages cf. Toynbee's *Dante Dictionary*.

70] To him Boccaccio devotes one of the tales of the *Decameron* (I. 8), where he is described as a worthy well-bred witty gentleman.

94-105] Monte Viso (Chaucer's 'Vesulus the colde') is at the head of the Po. The river here referred to, the Montone, was the first river north of the Apennines which had an independent course to the sea. Dante makes his geographical references an element of poetry, as after him did Milton. As to the waterfall of San Benedetto, it is now, owing to the deforesting of the Apennines, no longer very impressive. We know from familiar examples how erosion changes in the course of centuries the form and aspect of a waterfall. Of the various interpretations of l. 102, the simplest is that this is a heightened way of saying that the mass of water, forced through the narrow gorge, would have been sufficient to cover a much wider channel. The word 'thousand' is frequently used in the Poem for an indefinitely large number.

106] The cord is supposed to be the girdle of St. Francis, who intended it as an emblem of the binding of the wild beast of the body. The old commentator, Buti, states that Dante was once a member of that order of Franciscans called, from the cord, Cordeliers. So the celebrated Guido da Montefeltro, who tells his dramatic story in Canto xxvii.

127-9] The superficial comment is that the poet takes oath to a fiction by a fiction. But there is a world of difference between fiction and falsehood. He swears to what he wishes us to accept as an emblem of a truth by what is to him dear and sacred: the Poem upon which he bases his hope of fame. Were it not for the spur which Milton calls 'that last infirmity of noble mind', how poor would be our culture and how unprofitable our annals!

CANTO XVII

The money-sharks of great family crouching over their emblazoned wallets.

21-2] According to medieval bestiaries the beaver was in the habit of using its tail to strike and stun its prey.

The word *lurchi,* here translated 'guzzling', doubtless connotes both eating and drinking. Portia's unflattering description of 'the young German, the Duke of Saxony's nephew', would have delighted Dante. (*Merchant of Venice,* I. ii). The sober Tuscan was as much offended by intemperance in drink as Portia or Hamlet could have been.

52-7] See Canto vii. 49-54, note.

58-73] These are the cognizances, respectively, of the Florentine families Gianfigliazzi and Ubriachi, and of the Paduan family, Scrovigni, all degraded by the inordinate practice of usury. The shield of the Scrovigni is an example of canting heraldry, like the wild boar on the escutcheon of the Bacon family. Of Vitaliano nothing is surely known; apparently he was still alive. The 'sovran cavalier', supreme usurer, Giovanni Buiamonte of Florence, is also condemned while living.— These wretches are not Jewish Shylocks, but members of proud families of the nobility!

74-5] The base and cruel practices incident to extortionate money-lending and collecting have blotted out, with the personal features, the sense of shame in this member of a proud family. Lost to personal dignity or decency, these money-grubbers are even more degraded than the traitors far below in the ice of Cocytus.

85-93] Dante is none the less brave for being thoroughly scared. The intrepidity of the unimaginative rash is but a low form of courage.

115-26] The Poet anticipates and faithfully describes the actual impressions of the modern aviator.

136] Geryon is in every way the most dantesque of the symbolic creatures enumerated in the note, Canto v. 4. The docility of the monster, quelled by the cord of St. Francis, is of course allegorically significant. The cord seems to be a magic sign such as the cross traditionally is.

CANTO XVIII

Sloping series of ten concentric ditches or pouches which 'ensack' various classes of the fraudulent.

1-18] The Malebolge (Malpouches) are ten great concentric gulches or canyons, each in succession a little lower, and of course smaller in circumference, than the one surrounding it. From the foot of the cliff where Geryon leaves us, we cross these successive bolge upon rough stone bridges, ascending and descending in each case the high-flung curve of the arch. The ancient Ponte della Maddalena (alias Ponte del Diavolo) over the Serchio a few miles above Lucca is an interesting example of such a bridge. Finally, after crossing the tenth and innermost bolgia, we reach the brink of the deep Pit of lowest Hell (Canto xxxi).

28-33] The fact that, owing to the enormous crowds of pilgrims in the Jubilee year (which is the identical year of this mystic journey), the elementary precaution was taken to make the people file across the Ponte Sant'Angelo in an orderly way seems very remarkable to the Florentine mind. To this day there is no agreement among pedestrians as to right and left. To attempt to pass systematically on either hand at Florence one must be very determined and a little rude. The hill (l. 33) on the left bank of the Tiber was doubtless higher then than now. Or possibly the distant Capitoline Hill is meant.

51] The word *salse,* here translated *pit,* is a local reference to a golgotha at Bologna where the bodies of criminals were thrown. Bologna, where Dante was a student, is often referred to with intimate satire.

55] Ghisola (or Ghislabella) was his sister, whom he persuaded to become the mistress of the Este, the powerful lord of Ferrara.

61] *Sipa* was the Bolognese form of the present

subjunctive of the verb meaning 'to be'. The modern form is said to be *sepa*. Bologna lies between the two rivers Rèno and Savena.

62-6] The wide significance to the medieval mind of the wolfish lust of Avarice (*Avaritia*) should not be lost sight of. It is a primary root of almost all evil. As to Bologna, the intelligent fourteenth-century commentator, Benvenuto da Imola, himself a professor there, asserts that in pursuit of their personal pleasures the Bolognese are in the habit of selling their daughters, sisters, and wives.

72] 'Circling walls': the lofty surrounding cliff that shuts in this vast cavernous funnel.

83-96] Hypsipylë had betrayed her female fellow-conspirators against superfluous males by saving her father the king. Of another vicissitude of her remarkable career we shall hear in *Purgatorio* xxvi. Jason, in his more heroic capacity, is mentioned in the noble invocation at the beginning of *Paradiso* ii, and his ship Argo thrillingly reappears in the last glorious Canto of the Poem.

113] It is hardly necessary to remind the sympathetic reader that no poet could well be more delicate and pure-minded than Dante. But it is impossible to pass through Hell without encountering filth and obscenity, as here and at the close of Canto xxi.

122] A nobleman of the great Interminelli (Antelminelli) family of Lucca, who, according to Benvenuto, was an unctuous flatterer even of menials. Of this family came the great Ghibelline leader, Castruccio Castracane, whose gallant exploits were just a few years too late to be recorded, as they deserved, by the Poet.

135] This anecdote is from Cicero, *De Amicitia*, xxvi, evidently referring to a comedy by Terence with whose plays Dante shows no familiarity. In the comedy not Thaïs but the go-between makes the flattering reply. Dante seems to mistake Thaïs for a real person. The reply, which seemed to Cicero and to our Poet so extravagant, seems commonplace now. In fact the words of the text, 'anzi meravigliose', are nothing more than our everyday 'thanks awfully!'

CANTO XIX

Pope Nicholas III (of the Orsini) thrust head first into a hole in the rock, kicking out his blazing feet, waiting to be plugged in by Boniface VIII.

1] For Simon Magus see Acts viii. From his name is derived the word *simony*, the perversion of the gift of God into an object of merchandise. The topsy-turvy position of the sinners is a symbol of this perversion.

17] The Baptistry of Florence where until recent times all Florentine children were christened. The marble holes or 'stalls' are no longer there, but similar holes may still be seen in the beautiful Baptistry of Pisa. Of Dante's bold enterprise in breaking one of them we know nothing beyond the record here, which apparently put an end to malicious rumours. At all events the answer lives, the rumours are dead.

49-51] One of the legal punishments of that implacable period was the 'planting' thus of the perfidious murderer. Dante's similitudes imply, of course, familiarity on the part of the reader of his time with the scene referred to. The customs, habits, sports, arts, affairs of all kinds from which he draws images have greatly changed, so that we have to use more imagination in reading him.

52-4] Dante is puzzled at being mistaken for Pope Boniface VIII, the personage in the world of whom he most disapproves. 'The writing' is that of the book of Destiny, which is to some extent known to the damned, although they do not know the present as it passes in the upper world. Canto x. 94-108.

To grasp this grimly comic situation one has to be living in imagination in April of the Jubilee year of Grace, 1300, when Pope Boniface was full of vigour and ambitious expectancy. But as we have the advantage over him of being able to turn

'the accomplishment of many years
Into an hour-glass,'

we know that he has before him in this world but three years and six months—space too brief for his vast designs. Now Nicholas, son of the she-bear, being well-read in

'the Great Book where black on white
is set down ineffaceably' (*Par.* xv. 50),

knows that Boniface is to fall headlong into this hole; but, perceiving the figure waiting above him, he fancies he must have been deceived in the date. Insensitive must be the critic who deems Dante wanting in the sense of humour!

57] The references to the Church as the Lady, or the Bride of Christ, and by extension to the Pope as the Vicar of Christ, are so frequent that comment is, in most cases, superfluous.

67-72] The ex-Pope Nicholas III, who is speaking, was of the Orsini family, whose cognizance was the 'orsa' ('ursa', she-bear). He is not the first simoniacal pope, nor to be the last. Each on the arrival of his successor is jammed down flat into the fissure awaiting him—a narrow room contrasting with the great place he had occupied above.

82-7] Referring to Clement V, the Frenchman, tool of Philip the Fair. See 2 Maccabees iv and v.

Unless Dante himself was a prophet this must have been written after Clement's death in 1314.

90] Dante does not pay him the compliment of the *You*. Cf. Canto xv. 30, note.

95] Matthias was elected to the apostleship to take the place of Judas Iscariot (Acts i).

106-11] Revelation xvii.—The woman is the corrupt Church; the spouse, the Pope; the seven heads and ten horns the sacraments and the commandments.

115-17] This donation of Constantine was at a later time proved to be fictitious. Dante lived before historical sources were critically analysed. Milton's translation of this apostrophe will be remembered.

124-33] Virgil carries Dante from the bottom of the canyon up the bank and then up to the pinnacle of the arching bridge, from which he can look into the fourth bolgia.

CANTO XX

Soothsayers walking backward with heads wrenched around so that their copious tears fall upon their hinder parts.

4-5] Dante is looking down from the crown of the arching bridge to which Virgil had borne him up from the gulch of the Simoniacs.

9] Slowly as pace the chanting clergy or monastics. As in Catholic lands the penitential liturgical service is long heard before the slow procession is seen, it is natural to transfer the word 'litany' to the procession itself; the figure was either popular or instantly comprehensible.

28] Dante who had been commended by Virgil (human Reason) for his indignation against Filippo Argenti, is now rebuked for his sympathy with these distorted sufferers.

34] The soothsayer Amphiaräus, in the course of the expedition of the Seven against Thebes, was swallowed up by the earth. Dante gets the tale from the poet Statius, whom we shall meet in Purgatory.

40] This singular story of the metamorphosis of the Theban soothsayer is from Ovid, *Met.* III.

46] Aruns, Etruscan soothsayer who, according to Lucan (*Pharsalia*), prophesied the Civil Wars of Rome.

47] The Poet's visit to the beautiful Lunigiana (named from the ancient Etruscan and Roman Luni) at the foot of the marble snow of the Carrara Mountains, is commemorated in the lovely eighth Canto of *Purgatorio*.

55] Manto was daughter of Tiresias.

61] This long digression, geographically so vivid and accurate as to the origin and situation of Mantua, is one of the few passages not vitally—

at least not obviously—connected with the scheme of the whole. No other long poem has so few such excrescences, whose 'moral is in being fair'. A different account of the origin of Mantua is given in the *Aeneid*, Book X. Here, for some reason not now understood, our Poet makes Virgil correct himself.

67] The pastor (bishop) gives the benediction only within his diocese. The place where the three dioceses met was in or near the lake. For the other geographical references, see a detailed map of the region of Lake Garda.

70] Five centuries later Peschiera became one of the four fortresses of the famous (or rather infamous!) Quadrilateral, military centre of Austrian rule in northern Italy.

79-93] Browning, in the first Book of *Sordello*, faithfully pictures the region:

'In Mantua territory half is slough,
Half pine-tree forest; maples, scarlet oaks
Breed o'er the river-beds; even Mincio chokes
With sand the summer through: but 'tis morass
In winter up to Mantua walls.'

95] Referring to a bloody *coup d'état* in the course of which Pinamonte first duped and then expelled the lord of Mantua, Count Casalodi.

112] *Aeneid*, Book II, l. 114.

113] Dante refers to his Poem as Comedy (Canto xvi. 128). In his Letter to Can Grande, he distinguishes between Comedy and Tragedy, saying, in substance, that Comedy begins by treating of matters unpleasant and ends happily, while Tragedy does the reverse. There is also a vast difference of style and diction. Thus, ignorant of ancient classic drama, he adopts a new definition of the terms, applying them to narrative poems. As to diction, it is quite true that Dante studiously employs the simple speech of everyday life. But he is not bound by any theory of diction: in the later and nobler parts of the Poem he can rise to the height of his great argument in language as stately as the theme demands.

116-23] Michael Scot (or the Scot), a scholar greatly trusted by the Emperor Frederick II. Scholars, especially astronomical and medical students, were apt to be suspected of sorcery. Guido was an astrologer at the court of Frederick II. Asdente was a cobbler who dabbled in divination. As to the witches, the melting of the image of the person to be put to death is perhaps the commonest tale in folk-lore and no uncommon theme in literature, ancient and modern.

124-30] The Man in the Moon was popularly Cain carrying a bundle of thorns, the sorry 'fruit of the ground' that he harvested. The sky is of course invisible in Hell, but Dante will not forgo his astronomical allusion. The moon is one day past the full and sinks into the sea south of Seville (taking Jerusalem as the point of observation). That is, it is about 6 a.m. The final words of the speaker may mean this: Dante should remember that, while in distress of mind in the deep wood, the moon exempted him from her malign influence which might have made him insane. Cf. the origin of the word *lunacy*.

CANTO XXI

Venal politicians, and others who had secretly defiled their hands with funds entrusted, plunged neck and crop into boiling pitch. • Barrators are not essentially different from political bosses and other parasites of the public treasury such as to-day thrive at the expense of the helpless taxpayer who is no longer able to solace himself with vivid belief in the retribution here described. Dante evidently wrote these two Cantos (xxi-xxii) with great glee.

38-54] Dante here gives some pregnant hints about Lucca, as he elsewhere does of Siena and many other famous cities intimately known to him. Santa Zita is patroness of Lucca, a maidservant whom her master could not seduce—'the Pamela of legend'—whence the expression 'Elder of Saint Zita' suggests the tale of Susannah. The Holy Face is an ancient image of Christ still venerated in the cathedral there; the Serchio flows near the city wall. Bonturo is excepted as who should say—all grafters except Boss Tweed.

63] See Canto ix where Virgil tells of his previous descent to the lowest Hell.

91 ff.] It has been suggested that Dante here refers to the trumped-up charge of barratry which was one of the pretexts for his banishment from Florence in 1302. Cf. note below on the names of the fiends.

95] Caprona, a Pisan fortress on the Arno, was surrendered in 1289 to a force with which Dante served. This was shortly after the campaign so splendidly commemorated in *Purgatorio* v. The ruin of Caprona can still be seen from the train shortly before reaching Pisa from Florence.

112] The arch was shattered when Christ after the Crucifixion descended into Hell. It is now, therefore, mid-forenoon of the Saturday after Good Friday, 1300.

118] These are humorous travesties of names of Florentine families which Dante regarded as fair game. To this day Florence is noted for family names which seem humorous or ironical.

139] Devils were conceived to be not only malignant but foul and obscene. See the note to the introductory lines of the next Canto, and that on the place of the flatterers, Canto xviii.

CANTO XXII

Continuation of the preceding scene.

1-12] This mock-heroic treatment of an obscene theme was relished by robust medieval taste and is of a piece with the gargoyles and other grotesque plays of fancy which the cathedral builders delighted in. This and the preceding Canto afford example of spirited comic relief of rather high flavour.

19-21] References to the belief that the leaping of dolphins or porpoises is a sign of coming storm are common in literature. The superstition is said to persist among sailors and fisherfolk. Cf. the talk of the fishermen in the play of *Pericles*, II. i.

52] Thibaut II, King of Navarre in the time of the royal Saint Louis IX, of whom he was son-in-law and companion in arms. The contemporary poet, Rutebœuf, praises him. Of the Navarrese barrator we know no more than is told here. Old commentators say his name was Ciampolo (Jean Paul). With this satirical tale of an 'unjust steward' may be contrasted the touching account of the just Romeo (Romieu) in *Paradiso* vi, closing lines.

81] Gallura and Logodoro are two of the four provinces into which the Pisans divided Sardinia. Michael Zanchë was victim of an atrocious crime recorded at the close of Canto xxxiii. We meet a just and gentle magistrate of Gallura in *Purg.* viii. Now this 'noble judge Nino' had as trusty deputy-governor the crafty Friar Gomita; but convicting him of gross corruption in office the noble judge hanged him. Such was the short way with grafters in that simple age!

125] Alichino, whose incautious suggestion had enabled the Navarrese to escape.

141-51] Thus the prosecutors are themselves entangled: so difficult is it to convict those guilty of malversation in office. If for 'pitch' we read 'oil', the parable takes on for the American reader a singularly modern application.

CANTO XXIII

Just able to move beneath the gilded burden of deceit upon deceit—a lifelong accumulation.

3] Minor Friars, i.e. Franciscans, who were advised by the Saint to walk in this way, although they do not now always observe the rule. In this Canto ecclesiastical imagery is noticeable (Minor Friars, monks in Cologne, college of hypocrites), while Caiaphas and Annas are substituted for the usual examples from Greek or Roman antiquity.

4-9] A frog, while towing a rat across a stream, dives; but seeing the commotion a kite swoops upon both. The 'outset' is the attack upon Alichino by Calcabrina; the 'end' is that both alike suffer.

37-51] This is one of the instances in which our tersely graphic Poet chooses to describe an incident with much illustrative detail. Raphael took the rescue of the child by the mother as the subject for a painting. The reference to absence of the smock is explained by the fact, fully borne out by many allusions in our older literature, that the wearing of a shirt in bed was of old not customary.

57] That is for other regions of Hell. We have seen one of them engaged in passenger traffic with Lucca.

58] The Hypocrites.

63] There is here much to be said in favour of the reading 'Clugnì' (Clugny or Cluny) instead of 'Cologna' (Colonia, Cologne). In the Oxford text the line is metrically very irregular. Moreover the historical rôle of the celebrated Benedictine Abbey of Cluny in Burgundy furnishes a strong *a priori* argument for this reading, which seems to be that of the Trivulzian codex of 1336, and is adopted by the most eminent recent Italian editors (*Testo Critico*, and Professor Casella). Nothing seems to be known about the shape of the cowls at either place, the explanations of the early commentators looking as if they had been invented after the fact, as was too often the case.

66] Geoffrey, Archdeacon of Norwich, had a cope of lead put over his head and shoulders, in which he was starved to death for whispering the news of the excommunication of King John. Evidently that heavy penalty was not invented by Frederick II. The symbolism is a solemn one: the mask of hypocrisy gradually gathers weight until it becomes a clog upon every gesture that might betray the wearer.

Inasmuch as no record is found of the use of the punishment of the leaden cope by Frederick II, it is not improbable that this—as well as other cruelties practised by the severe Emperor Henry VI—has been ascribed to Henry's far humaner son by chroniclers with a case to prove.

70-8] Dante and Virgil were walking as usual, but their pace was swift to that of the hypocrites. That all speed is relative was understood before the day of the automobile, the airplane, and the Einstein theory.

103-8] During the year when these two were partners in the mayoralty of Florence the palaces of the great Ghibelline family of the Uberti were razed. The Gardingo was anciently a Longobard fortress, standing about where now is the Palazzo Vecchio and its Square. All this was done under the pretence of pacification in the critical period after the important battle of Bene-

vento (1266). These 'jolly friars' were really tools of Pope Clement IV. Cf. the story of Manfred, *Purg*. iii.

115-21] Caiaphas and Annas. Virgil, here representing Rome, would not understand. (Cf. lines 124-6.)

123] 'Daughters of Jerusalem, weep not for me, but weep for yourselves and for your children,' said Christ as he went to be crucified.

139-42] Malacoda had said there was a bridgeway across this gulch (xxi. 111).

142] Friar Catalano was born of Guelf family at Bologna and no doubt educated at the university there. He is making game of Virgil.

144] Directly quoted from the vulgate gospel of John, viii. 44: 'quia mendax est et pater ejus.'

146] The references to the perplexity and indignation of the high-souled pagan are telling.

CANTO XXIV

Thieves, who in life disguised themselves and crept covertly on their errands, are punished by an eternal series of transmutations from snake to man and man to snake.

1-15] In February, when the grass is already lush and when snow is a calamity to the shepherd. The Poet's magic gives us a moment's respite from horror, transporting us to a bright morning scene on an upland of southern Italy. The peasant's demonstrative behaviour is thoroughly Italian. In the half-light of early dawn the heavy hoar-frost is mistaken for snow, but with the rising sun the dainty artistry of the frost-work fades out. Frost (*la brina*) and snow (*la neve*) are feminine and therefore sisters. Jack Frost is altogether a different being, evolved by the imagination of a race too sorely familiar with winter to mistake frost for snow.

22-30] This is not the only passage where Dante shows himself familiar with mountain-climbing. He had clambered over the weary heights between Lerici and Turbia (*Purg*. iii), and perhaps over the Alps more than once.

A distinguished mountain-climber remarks in the *Alpine Journal* that this passage reads 'like a modern description of an Almer or a Devouassoud at work' (cited in the notes of H. F. Tozer). It is well to stress this, inasmuch as Ruskin, with a perversity not singular in his stimulating writings, asserts that Dante knew little of mountain-climbing. He did not indeed, like some modern scholars, climb for the sport of it; climbing was at certain periods of his wanderings just part of the day's work (Ruskin's numerous *obiter dicta* on Dante have been arranged and printed in a little volume by the late Charles Eliot Norton).

The allegory here is that of the difficulty of re-nouncing a course of dissimulation.

34-40] We are descending towards the centre of a vast funnel-like hollow, the sides of which are cut by the ten concentric *bolgie* (pockets, pouches, valleys, or gulches), so that the inner bank of every one of these channels is lower than the other. The valley of the hypocrites seems unusually deep.

45] It is noteworthy that here only, in the whole course of the journey through Hell, does Dante allow himself to sit down by reason of weariness. The noble rebuke he receives for this weakness may be accounted one of the many devices where-by the journey is marked as a continuous pil-grimage, the pauses in which are not for repose but for observation and instruction. Even during the long digression about Mantua Dante remains on his feet leaning against the hard parapet of the rocky viaduct (Canto xx. 25).

55-7] It is not enough to forsake error; one must practise active virtue, action typified by climbing the stair of the Penitential Mountain.

82-90] This Passage is based upon one in the ninth book of Lucan's *Pharsalia,* where all these snakes are fancifully described. There is a similar swarm in the tenth book of *Paradise Lost.*

93] Heliotrope, a mineral, possibly bloodstone, which was supposed to possess the virtue of so turning the sun's rays that the wearer became invisible.

100] *I* has no dot in medieval writing. These are the exceptional letters that require but a single stroke of the pen.

106-11] The passage is a freely rehandled and abbreviated rendering of Ovid's lines in *Met.* xv. 393-400.

114] It was then supposed that a stroke, as of epilepsy, was caused by stoppage (oppilation) of the passages through which the vital spirits went from heart to brain. Even as late as Shakespeare, literature is full of allusions to this physiology in which the vital spirits play a part similar to that now ascribed to the blood.

129] Dante, who had known this John (Gio-vanni) Fucci, is surprised that he is not among the violent (see Canto xii). Only a debased and desperate character would rob a church. Cf. the treatment of Bardolph for stealing the 'pax of little price' (*Henry V*, III. vi).

145] The thunderstorm of war from the valley of the Magra (Lunigiana) is Moroello Malaspina, whose family received and protected Dante in 1306. There is a noble tribute to this family at the end of *Purg.* viii. The physical theory underlying the imagery here is explained in the note to *Par.* xxiii. 40-2.

CANTO XXV

The story of Vanni Fucci continued. Cf. the similar connexion of Cantos in xxxii-xxxiii, Paradiso *v-vi, and* Paradiso *xxxii-xxxiii.*

2] An insulting gesture called by Ancient Pistol 'the fig of Spain'.

12] A reference to the desperadoes who followed Catiline—traditional founders of Pistoia.

15] Capaneus (Canto xiv).

19] The serpents in this and the preceding Canto are of course symbolic of the stealthy nature of the crime which they punish.

20] For the Maremma, see the first note to Can-to xiii.

25-33] Cacus, probably an ancient cowboy of the pre-Roman Campagna, appears in legend as the cattle-thief centaur, who made the mistake of driving off the herd of a stronger personage. The Aventine may have been a wild retreat before the foundation of Rome. For the full story in vivid detail cf. *Aeneid,* Book VIII, from l. 193.

35] These three who appear first are Agnello Brunelleschi, Buoso (of the Donati or Abati), Puccio the lame. The six-footed serpent turns out to be Cianfa Donati. Finally comes Guercio of the Cavalcanti in the form of a little fiery serpent, changing form with Buoso and taking flight in human shape. Puccio is the only one of the five who suffers no transformation. These, like the company of usurers (Canto xvi), all seem to be of distinguished families. A Brunellesco much later moulded the famous dome; Dante's wife was of the Donati, and his best friend a Caval-cante.

40-5] The manner in which Dante gradually gathers, by attentive listening to their talk, the names of four of the five Florentine thieves, is an example of his unobtrusive art. The gesture with the finger beside chin and nose is frequent in Italy.

69]
> 'Property was thus appalled
> That the self was not the same,
> Single nature's double name
> Neither two nor one was called.'

> (*The Phœnix and the Turtle.*)

If Shakespeare be the author of the poem, the lines form one of several passages in which he appears to owe an idea or a graphic phrase to Dante.

94-102] The Poet's exultant challenge to two whom he esteemed among the greatest of anti-quity, is fully borne out by the vividness of these scenes and the picturesque variety of the imagery. Cf. Canto iv. 90.

106-16] Milton surely had these lines in mind

INFERNO

when he described the transformation of Satan. *Paradise Lost, x. 511-14:*

'His visage drawn he felt to sharp and spare, His arms clung to his ribs, his legs entwining Each other,...'

But the Miltonic lines suffer by comparison with Dante's vivid rush of description cunningly merged with narrative.

144-5] The Poet seems to feel that the 'novelty' of these scenes has led him to dwell somewhat too complacently upon them; perhaps also he wishes to temper a little the bold self-confidence of his challenge to the elder poets.

151] The last line refers to the only one not named, possibly out of consideration for the Cavalcanti family, to which he belonged. The spirited peasantry of the little village of Gaville had killed the scoundrel, and now weep the vendetta wreaked upon them by the family.

CANTO XXVI

Souls wrapped in swirling flames like Elijah's 'chariot of fire', but numerous as fireflies.

7-9] Prato, although so near Florence, having distinct self-consciousness and local pride, is naturally impatient of subjection. The thought that dreams coming just before dawn are prophetic— a common belief in ancient times—is most beautifully developed at the beginning of *Purg.* ix.

25-32] When Dante, usually so terse, chooses to say a thing in a round-about way, he does so in a series of pictures. Here he places the reader in an Italian hillside vineyard at the close of a long summer day, when the fly gives place to the mosquito, to look down with the tired peasant at the fascinating splendour of the myriad fireflies.

54] The story is that when the bodies of Eteocles and Polynices were incinerated together the flame divided, showing that even in their ashes lived the wonted fires of fraternal hate.

61-2] Thetis, to save her son from a foretold fate, was so simple-minded as to place him, disguised as a girl, among the daughters of a king. The guile of Ulysses consisted in persuading the hero to break from this effeminate life, forsaking his sweetheart Deidamìa. But all these classical references are familiar.

72-5] It is hard not to find a symbol in the modest forbearing of Dante, despite his yearning, from direct speech with the Greeks. Likewise Petrarch, although a half-century nearer to the Renaissance, never mastered the language of Homer.

90 to end] The noble tale of Ulysses, as well as the preceding splendid series of images is in refreshing contrast to the horrible scenes we have witnessed. Dante owes nothing to Homer, whom he could not read. It is interesting to contrast Tennyson's ornate rehandling of this plain tale.

112-17] The Pillars of Hercules (on either side of the Strait of Gibraltar) marked for Dante, as for the ancients, the western limit of the habitable world. The southern hemisphere was supposed to be covered by the ocean. To embark upon this unknown deep was to encounter real dangers enhanced by imagined and unimaginable terrors.

133] The mountain is supposed to be that of Purgatory. The age of the great voyagers was yet distant, and anything could be imagined, for the other side of the world was as unknown as is the other side of the moon.

CANTO XXVII

The artistic parallel with the preceding Canto is notable. In the Paradiso *we shall find explicit illustration of the principle that the spiritual state of the Christian who stoops to guile is more deplorable than that of the pagan.*

7] The brazen bull in which were roasted alive the victims of the tyrant Phalaris, who first tested it upon its maker—very properly, subjoins Dante.

28] The Romagna is a rather indeterminate but persistent designation for that part of Italy between Apennine and Adriatic, south of the Po. The men of that region are exceptionally strong and independent in character, and often turbulent in action. Cf. *Purg.* xiv. 92 and following lines.

41] The Polenta family from which had sprung Francesca, and which was to be Dante's best shield.

43] Forlì, where a French army had suffered a bloody defeat by the person addressed.

46] The Malatesta of Rimini, the bloody, treacherous tyrants to whose fangs poor Francesca had been thrown.

49-54] Faenza and Imola, as well as Cesena, are named by their rivers. As in the case of Forlì the cognizance of the ruling family is mentioned. The renegade is Maghinardo of the Pagani, who is called the demon of the family in *Purgatorio* xiv. South of the Apennine, he is a Guelf; in his own country, a Ghibelline. Winter and summer, in Dantean metonymy, are north and south. The cognizance of the Pagani was 'a lion azure on a field argent' (*nido bianco,* l. 50). The 'green paws' of l. 45 designate the green lion on the shield of the Ordelaffi, then masters of Forlì.

56] *Another,* i.e. Dante himself.

61] Guido da Montefeltro, the astute Christian, is contrasted to his disadvantage with the noble pagan Ulysses. There is another contrast between Guido and his son Buonconte in Purgatory

Canto v). These are three of the longer tales in the Poem.

70] Pope Boniface VIII.

85 ff.] Palestrina (ancient Praeneste), stronghold of the powerful Colonna family, could be seen from the Lateran, then the seat of the popes. Boniface, at the instance of Guido, promised amnesty and then destroyed the place. The barbarous vengeance of the Colonna at Alagna shocked even Dante, hostile as he was to Boniface, and is sublimely commemorated in *Purg.* xx.

94-7] As Emperor Constantine sought out Pope Sylvester who had taken refuge in a cavern of Mount Soractë, so the Pope sought the speaker in his monastic retreat.

112 ff.] For the soul of Guido's son, Buonconte, there is a similar contention (*Purg.* v). Both were probably suggested by the old story of Michael and the Devil contending for the body of Moses (Jude, 9). In both cases the truth emphasized is that salvation depends upon the state of the soul at the end. In the case of Guido the absolution of a pope proves unavailing. Similarly, in the case of Manfred (*Purgatorio* iii), excommunication proves impotent.

118-19] So the King in *Hamlet* reasons: 'May one be pardoned and retain the offence?'

121-9] For the significance of the serpentine windings of the tail of Minos, see the beginning of Canto v. But his gesture in biting his tail! How all human values are reversed! Guido, after an eminently successful career at the close of which he had humbled himself to make his peace with God, finds after death the arms of the holy Francis open for him. Against him whom even Francis would pardon, the executor of Divine vengeance is singularly indignant. And it is all so sudden: 'Saint Francis came for me when I was dead!' But even Francis cannot prevail against the devil who plants himself upon the Categorical Imperative.

'The sin that practice burns into the blood,
And not the one dark hour which brings remorse,
Will brand us after, of whose fold we be.'
(Tennyson, *Merlin and Vivien*, ll. 760 ff.)

136] Who add by dividing—making up their load of sin by disuniting others.

CANTO XXVIII

'*That moat of Hell wherein is paid their due to those who, severing, make up their load.*'

10-18] Trojans for Romans; the rings picked up on the field of Cannae; Robert Guiscard, Norman conqueror of Apulia; Ceperano, an important strategical point on the river Liris. Its betrayal to the enemy is regarded as leading up to the defeat of Manfred at Benevento. Even so it is not clear why Dante should have written Ceperano for Benevento (*Purg.* iii). Tagliacozzo, where young Conradin, nephew of Manfred, was captured, was gained by the prudence of the Frenchman Erard de Valéry.

25-31] Mohammed was regarded as a Christian schismatic. According to Benvenuto these disgusting particulars symbolize the conversion of the good doctrine in the mind of Mohammed to pollution which infects the world.

32] The name of the famous son-in-law and successor of Mohammed is commonly printed 'Ali'. The form 'Alee' more closely represents the sound to the English ear.

In the original it will be noted that this and its accompanying rimed lines have the final ictus or stress on the ultimate syllable. Cases of this kind are extremely infrequent—seven only in the Inferno. Such verses in Italian are exceedingly abrupt, almost startling. This effect cannot, of course, be imitated in translation, because of the utterly different nature of our language, which is so prevalently monosyllabic that in a long poem the ictus necessarily falls, for the most part, on the final syllable of the line, so that what is a rare exception in Italian becomes the rule with us. Our poets vary the so-called heroic verse of five beats by more or less frequent use of the hendecasyllabic verse, i.e. verse in which the final stress falls on the penultimate syllable of the line.

In the present instance the three lines (32, 34, 36) seem to be cut off by a sharp sudden blow, like that of the scimitar which mutilated Alee.

55-60] Fra Dolcino wished to lead men back to apostolic simplicity and was cruelly punished after having made a brave fight. The Novarese are his pursuers, the men of Novara.

73-5] This Pietro (Peter) of the ruling family of the small town of Medicina in the Romagna is said to have been persuasive in setting greater lords by the ears. Hence the emblematic slitting of the windpipe. The lovely plain is of course the regions of Lombardy and Venetia sloping from Vercelli in eastern Piedmont to the fortress of Marcabò, commanding the mouths of the Po.

76-91] This tyrant who sees but with one eye is Malatestino, now tyrant of Rimini, where Curio had advised Caesar not to delay his advance on Rome. Focara is a squally headland on the Adriatic near La Cattolica, between Rimini and Fano. Of the two worthies of Fano made victims of the tyrant, little more is known. These warnings that Dante is asked to bear back to the world were perhaps suggested by Luke xvi. 27 ff., where Dives begs to have Lazarus go back to 'testify unto them, lest they also come into this place of torment'.

102] No explanation is made why Curio should be punished for promoting an enterprise which Brutus and Cassius are punished for opposing! Curio's advice seems to be cited with approval in Dante's seventh epistle.

106] Mosca of the Lamberti clan was he who advised the murder of young Buondelmonte, to which the origin of the great feud of the Guelfs and Ghibellines was attributed by tradition. See *Paradiso* xvi.

134] This Provençal poet was the friend of Henry, called the Young King, eldest surviving son of Henry II of England.

CANTO XXIX

Covered with itching scabs and scratching busily with their nails. ⁄ The falsifiers of four different kinds (alchemists, impostors, debasers of coin, malicious liars) are afflicted with disguising or deforming diseases. As everywhere, there is some congruity of punishment and sin. Here, as at the close of the next Canto, Virgil takes Dante to task for being too deeply absorbed. Dante's apparent adhesion to the un⁄Christian custom of the vendetta is one of the several inconsistencies between creed and sentiment, without which he would not be like all the rest of us.

27⁄9] Geri, a cousin of Dante's father, had been killed by one of the Sacchetti. The two families became formally reconciled about a score of years after the Poet's death. He 'who once held Haute⁄fort' is Bertran de Born.

46⁄51] Undrained malarial regions. The Tuscan Maremma, so often referred to, is the wild moor⁄land country near the seaboard south⁄west of Siena. The river Chiana stagnated in the level, marshy region between Tiber and Arno, where Lake Trasimene lies. The Arno, indeed, in pre⁄historic time, flowed into the Tiber. The region is now drained.

58⁄64] One of Ovid's tales. *Met.* vii.

103⁄8] The sympathy betrayed by these words and the whole bearing of the Poet is in strong contrast to his indignant contempt for the illus⁄trious Guido da Montefeltro (in Canto xxvii).

109⁄17] The story is that a bishop of Siena, who called Albert son, ordered the burning of Grif⁄folino, the Aretine, who was probably an ingen⁄ious precursor of those who have invented the aeroplane. Such were of old the rewards of the inventor and the student of nature! Griffolino is punished in both worlds.

125] Examples of fashionable, ostentatious spend⁄thrifts. Cloves imported from the far East at enormous expense. Siena, gay, elegant, rich, was

the garden in which such seed took root. The club was of young men of fashion, who tried to see which one could run through his fortune most swiftly and merrily. They were eminently successful in this enterprise, and their fame is still alive in their beautiful city.

139] Shakespeare calls Julio Romano the ape of nature, one of the instances in which he may be echoing our Poet.

CANTO XXX

Falsifiers: Personators, Counterfeiters, Malicious Ac⁄cusers.

1⁄12] Juno brought woe upon the royal house of Thebes on account of her jealousy of Semelë, daughter of Cadmus and mother of Bacchus by Jupiter. Ino, sister of Semelë, who had cared for Bacchus in his childhood, was punished as de⁄scribed here through the insanity of her husband, Athamas.

13⁄21] Dante knew nothing of 'Thebes or Pe⁄lops' line or the tale of Troy divine' except as told by the Latin poets. These terrible details of the legends of Ino and Hecuba are derived from Ovid. How much more would Hecuba have been to him had he been able to read *The Trojan Women* of Euripides, of which Gilbert Murray has made the glowing translation!

31] See preceding Canto, lines 109 ff. and note.

32] This gentleman of the house of Cavalcante was so famous an impersonator that his son ap⁄pears to have adopted the ape as a family emblem (cf. Toynbee's *Dante Dictionary*). His story or legend has recently been popularized by the co⁄mic opera, *Gianni Schicchi*.

37⁄41] The sensational tale of Myrrha is found in Ovid, *Metam.* x. Dante felt that she deserved worse punishment than that of Dido and Tris⁄tram. Since Dante is fond of coupling classical with Biblical examples, it is rather strange that the similar incest practised by the daughters of Lot is not mentioned (Genesis, xix). Cf. lines 97⁄8.

65] Casentino, upper valley of the Arno, above Arezzo, shut in by two chains of Apennine and closed at the north by Monte Falterona. See *Pur⁄gatorio* v and xiv. Alvernia, where St. Francis received the stigmata, overlooks the Casentino. Scene of the battle of Campaldino, in which Dante took part, and of the spiritual drama splen⁄didly recorded in *Purgatorio* v, this lovely valley was a region upon which he dwelt in memory most fondly.

70⁄90] The florin had on one side the image of John the Baptist and on the other the Florentine lily. This and the Venetian ducat were the stan⁄dard gold coins of those ages. As the credit of the

Republic depended upon the faith that all the world had in the florin, to tamper with the coin amounted to treason.

Counts of Romena who, being in debt, employed Master Adam, the famous Brescian expert, to debase the florin. The picturesque ruin of Romena, and the nearly dried-up Fontëbranda that supplied it with water, are still there. That region and others, which in Dante's time were well wooded and well watered, are now denuded of forest and relatively arid.

86] In the ninth pouch the circumference is twenty-two miles (Canto xxix. 9). The Pit is therefore a rapidly narrowing funnel, enormously wide at the top.

97-8] Potiphar's wife and Sinon the inventor of the famous 'wooden horse'. Such parallel instances from Scripture and classic Greek or Roman legend are a constant feature of the *Purgatorio*.

117] Every single counterfeited florin being reckoned as a separate sin.

128] In this smart retort Master Adam shows a familiarity with Greek mythology which comes well in play in such a contest of wits with the Homeric deceiver. There may be some moderns who will not resent being told that the mirror of Narcissus is a pool of clear water.

133 ff.] Dante's shame is, perhaps, not so much for his idle curiosity as at being for the first time treated with something like contempt by the dignified Virgil. It is incident to our Poet's very human nature that he should be for the moment diverted by this lively exchange of amenities between the Greek falsifier and the Italian forger. We should not forget that this Poem is a record of the author's spiritual life with all its lights and shadows. If it be, as he terms it, 'the sacred poem', it is one to which not only *Heaven* has set its hand, but also *Earth* (see beginning of *Par.* xxv). If men have called it Divine, he himself called it simply his Comedy, thus greatly enlarging the scope of the art of comedy.

CANTO XXXI

Emerging from the tenth and last of Malpouches, the Poets cross a plain in the midst of which is the Pit, surrounded and sentinelled by giants.

4-6] This magic spear, of power to kill and cure, fascinated the symbolizing mind of the Middle Ages.

18] According to the *Chanson de Roland*, after the defeat at Roncesvalles the horn of the dying Roland (Orlando) was heard by Charlemagne at a distance of thirty leagues.

41] Montereggionë still stands, as here described, a circular turreted wall surrounding a village, a

few miles north of Siena, of whose domains it was once a strategic point.

59] An enormous antique cone, some ten feet high, of gilded bronze, now in the garden of the Vatican. For interesting citations concerning the history of this *pina*, see Longfellow's notes.

64] Three men of tall stature placed end to end would not have equalled his height from the waist up.

67] This gibberish, like that at the beginning of Canto vii, is not meant to be understood.

115-21] The first battle here referred to is that of Zama where Hannibal met his Waterloo; the other that of Phlegra (cf. Canto xiv. 58). Antaeus is said by Lucan to have had his abode in a cavern near Zama.

136] Carisenda (or Garisenda) is one of a pair of leaning towers standing side by side at Bologna. This is 160 feet high; the other, which slants less, 320. Perhaps the Carisenda was once as high as its mate. Dante's choice of this, rather than of the more beautiful and famous tower at Pisa, is one of many reasons for thinking him to have been a student at Bologna. The writer has tested the vividness of the comparison under the slant both of this tower and that of Pisa. The impression is strong that the tower is falling.

142 ff.] Lines 143, 145 of the Italian text present another rare instance like that explained in the note to l. 32 of Canto xxviii.

The word 'lievemente' (lightly) certainly indicates nimble rather than gentle action. The temper of Antaeus is as far as possible from that of Virgil when he set Dante down on the top of the rough cliff (cf. close of Canto xix).

CANTO XXXII

In the First Ring, Caïna (Canto v, l. 107), are betrayers of kindred; in the Second, Antenora, traitors to country. — Unlike other sinners, who so often and so touchingly show desire to be remembered, the traitors feel that to be recognized by Dante is to have their obloquy commemorated on earth. This is the last thing they desire. But Camicion de' Pazzi basely betrays the names of his neighbours in the ice and finally, to anticipate reprisal, reveals his own, adding that he is looking forward to the advent of a still living relative so much worse than himself as to make his own crime appear only a peccadillo. The whole moral of the Inferno is here. The essence of the torture of Hell consists in the perpetual recurrence of evil passion, that chronic inward plague which has been the death of the soul. For those who do not succumb to this cancer of the soul, the perfect cure, as we shall see, is to be found in Purgatory.

9] Such description calls for other art than that of him who speaks and understands as a child.

26-30] Here in the original the cutting off of the final unaccented syllable of the lines (26, 28, 30) strikes the ear with a shock, as of collision. Lines 62, 64, 66, are another example. It is by no accident that two of the seven instances of this device found in the Inferno occur in a canto which begins as this one does with a wish for harsh, grating rimes. Cf. notes to xxviii. 32 and xxxi. 142. Tambernic and Pietrapana are tall rocky peaks.

31-33] In the Italian harvest season when the overworked peasant-girl goes over the tasks of the day as she dreams through the short sultry night. This sudden plunge into midsummer and back again makes the reader's teeth chatter too!

57] This Albert, Count of Mangona, ruled the valley of the Bisenzio, a little northward of Florence. These sons, who rejoiced in the names of Napoleon and Alexander, killed each other quarrelling over the inheritance.

61] According to the old French romance of Lancelot, when King Arthur's lance was pulled out of Mordred (or Mordrec), it left a hole through which passed a ray of sunlight, piercing the shadow of the traitor's body.

68-9] After mentioning five traitors against kin— three, at least, Tuscan—he names himself, intimating that his still-living kinsman, Carlino, will commit a crime so great as to excuse his own. Carlino's traitorous surrender of a castle held by his party (the Whites, Dante's party too) to the Blacks, in 1302, was to occasion the death of many fellow inmates. Of the other wretches referred to 'let us not speak of them, but look, and go'.

70] At this point we pass from Caïna into Antenora, so named from Antenor, who was supposed to have betrayed Troy, although of this neither Homer nor Virgil knows anything.

76-123] This is Bocca of the Abati, who, at the crucial moment of the battle of Montaperti, the most cruel defeat Florence suffered in the time of the Republic, cut off the hand of the Florentine standard-bearer. To this choice example of traitorhood Dante devotes more than forty dreadful lines.

115-116] Bribed by the French to betray Manfred. Cf. Canto xxviii. 16.

118-23] Ganelon is the notorious traitor of the Chanson de Roland. He of Beccherìa, abbot of Vallombrosa, a Ghibelline of Pavian origin. His execution for alleged correspondence and collusion with Ghibelline exiles in 1258 brought about the excommunication of Florence and troubles with Pavia. Gianni of the Soldanieri was an unsuccessful leader of a coup d'état against his own party (Ghibelline) in the tumultuous year of Benevento (1266).

124] Here begins the famous episode of Ugolino della Gherardesca and Archbishop Ruggieri. Ugolino was originally so great a Ghibelline that he could marry his eldest son to a granddaughter of the great Emperor Frederick II. Turning Guelf and becoming governor of Pisa, he was overthrown by a mob headed by Ruggieri. Ugolino seems to be condemned to Antenora for treason to the Imperial cause; Ruggieri for treachery to him.

130] The story of Tydeus and Menalippus, which doubtless suggested this gruesome situation to the Poet, is from the Thebaid of Statius, Bk. viii.

CANTO XXXIII

1-78] Francesco De Sanctis, in his Storia della Letteratura, makes a celebrated comment upon this episode. Ugolino is attached to Ruggieri by hate as Francesca by love to Paolo. In both cases the betrayed one is the only speaker. Nothing is said, except by implication, of the crime of Ugolino; the indignation that makes the verse is all against the archbishop. This is an ideal case of retribution (il contrapasso). The betrayed one, who was murdered by starvation, feeds his undying revenge by for ever gnawing the skull of the traitor, and so doing is executor of Divine Justice.

32-3] Three powerful families of Pisan nobility, friends and allies of the archbishop.

80] Italian was the 'lingua di sì' (language, originally, of 'sic' for 'yes') just as Provençal was the 'langue d'oc' ('hoc' for 'yes'), whence the name of the great region of Languedoc.

82] Caprara and Gorgona, islands off the mouth of Arno. Looking down the river from the Leaning Tower on a clear day, one seems to see them lying across the outlet.

91] Ptolomea, third Ring of Cocytus, named for the Ptolemaeus who slew Simon Maccabaeus and his sons at a banquet (1 Maccabees xvi). Here betrayers of guests shed icy tears.

118-151] This gentleman to whom Dante had, by an ambiguous oath, promised a courtesy, had murdered two of his kin at his dinner-table, the signal to the assassins being: 'Bring in the fruit!' Obviously Dante here acts in harmony with what he conceives to be Divine Justice. Let the betrayer feel in his own person what treachery is like! Matter-of-fact critics, forgetting the symbolism, gravely censure the Poet, as if this had been an action committed in our world by the man Dante!

137] Of the most distinguished family of Genoa. He had murdered his father-in-law, Michael Zanchë, whom we heard of among the barrators (Canto xxii. 88). Apparently the body of Ser

Branca continued to go through the motions of life on earth until Dante himself ceased to be met with down here. Our Poet seems to have felt that he bore the keys of Hell and Heaven!

CANTO XXXIV

Betrayers of lords and benefactors. ⁄ 'Vexilla Regis prodeunt infermi.'

1] Virgil parodies (in Latin of course) an ancient hymn: 'Vexilla Regis prodeunt Fulget crucis mysterium.' Since Dante rimes Latin with Italian, the translator must either sacrifice the rime or the Latin. It has seemed best, in general, to translate *everything* into English.

38] The three faces of the Author of evil are doubtless designed as an awful parody of the Divine Trinity, the vision of which Dante describes at the very close of the Poem.

61⁄7] 'Dante consistently regards Julius Caesar as the first of the Roman Emperors... and it is as traitorous to Caesar, representative of the highest civil authority, that he condemns Brutus and Cassius to the lowest pit of Hell, along with Judas, the betrayer of the representative of the highest spiritual authority.'—Toynbee's *Dante Dictionary*, s.v. Cesare.

92] Possibly some who are not dullards may be willing to be told that the Point in question was the Centre of the Earth, so that we are now under the southern hemisphere. Purgatory, toward which we are climbing, being opposite Jerusalem, we have gained twelve hours of time. It would now be Saturday morning again, so that twenty⁄four hours are allowed for the passage from the Centre to the foot of the mountain of Purgatory. If we can do it at all, we ought to be able to do it in that time, for we are not, as in descending, to make a thousand stops by the way.

112⁄17] Dante's feet are planted on a disk opposite that of the Judecca, so that he is now beneath the point in the southern hemisphere opposite the place of the Crucifixion.

121⁄26] The land of the southern hemisphere shrank away from Satan as he fell, and, after he was planted in the Centre, the ground forming the island and mountain of Purgatory fled up from him, leaving that passage open.

127⁄36] Beelzebub for Satan; his tomb is Hell; the upper part of his enormous bulk projects into Cocytus, the legs into this passage, which extends 'as far as his tomb', but in the opposite direction —that is, it leads, as described, to the surface of the Earth, to which the Poets now make the difficult but uneventful ascent.

139] Each Cantica closes with the word 'stelle', stars. This the stubborn English rime cannot always manage to the letter.

PURGATORIO

CANTO I

SCENE: *An island in the Southern Ocean, at foot of a loftier Teneriffe. ✦ TIME: The action begins before dawn on Easter Sunday, A D. 1300. ✦ CHARAC-TERS: All, save the pilgrim-poet, shades of the dead. ✦ Virgil and Dante appear on the plain slop-ing from seashore to mountain-cliff.*

7] Poesy is spoken of as dead hitherto because relating to the spiritually dead: so the words are generally understood. But does not poesy really die in the final Canto of the *Inferno*? It certainly seems benumbed with the chill of Cocytus, and the Satan of Dante is by no means a lofty or heroic figure like the Satan of *Paradise Lost* in the first two books. We must, however, beware of making our definition of poetry too narrow: it is enough to say that, while *Inferno* xxxiii and *Purgatorio* i are great and noble poetry, *Inferno* xxxiv is in places grotesque, in other places studiously plain.

11] The Magpies are the transformed princesses (the Pierides) who had presumed to vie with the Muses in song.

15] The first circle is that of the horizon.

19] The sun being in Aries (Ram) the morn-ing-star (Venus) is in the sign of Pisces. Medieval artists, picturing the Creation, showed Venus among the stars of that constellation. Since the English word 'comfort' has fallen from its high estate and its noun is making the tour of the world as 'le confort', it may be well to remind the reader of the original noble sense the word bore. Dante's line is: 'Lo bel pianeta che ad amar conforta': the fair planet whose influence makes strong to love.

23] As he is facing towards the dawn-star, the four symbolic stars are near the South Pole. These 'sacred stars', which appear again in Canto xxxi, probably symbolize the four pagan or cardinal virtues of Prudence, Justice, Fortitude, and Tem-perance. Dante had doubtless heard of the South-ern Cross, but, having no authentic information about the world south of the terrestrial equator, was happily free to give play to imagination.

31] The shade of Cato of Utica, warden of this region outside of Purgatory. Examples of other just pagans who appear among the redeemed are given in *Paradiso* xx. These examples are espe-cially interesting as showing how the tender Poet strove to soften the harshness of dogma.

58] Norton, whose renderings are almost always meticulously close to the literal meaning, here renders *non vide mai* by the words *has not yet seen*, evidently understanding the reference as to Dan-te's physical death. But the context surely shows that not the death of the body but that of the soul is meant. It was not physical death that his folly

put him in peril of, and it was to escape far other peril that the mystic journey was undertaken. This is not the only case in which the rime is faithful not only to the spirit but to the very letter of the significant word of the terse Poet.

89] The law is that in Heaven 'there is neither marriage nor giving in marriage'. Cato being one of the blest and Marcia on the wrong side of Acheron, she has become to him as a stranger. However one may judge this sentiment, Cato remains true to the type of the Roman of inflex-ible austerity. Dante puts into the mouth of Virgil such an allusion to Cato's suicide (71-5) as proves that the act is interpreted as a sublime sacrifice for freedom.

94-6] Symbolic cleansing and girding of Dante. The reed is symbol of humility: Dante's beset-ting sin, as we shall see, is pride.

115] The Oxford text reads *ôra*.

115-17] Impossible to render the enchanting ripple of the magical verse, 'Conobbi il tremolar della marina'. There is some dispute as to whether the Poet wrote *ora* (hour), or *aura* (ôra, breeze); but it is difficult to suppose that he conceived of the morning breeze, which blows off shore, as fleeing from, or in front of, the dawn. What is emphasized is the sudden imperceptible emer-gence of the light. The reading I follow is that of the Italian Dante Society in its critical text. of Torraca, of Passerini in his monumental edi-tion, and others, including that nice translator, C. E. Norton.

132] Cf. the fate of Ulysses, *Inferno* xxvi.

CANTO II

Contrast the opening of Inferno ii. ✦ The sun is rising here at Purgatory, night is falling at Jerusalem, it is midnight on the Ganges. For another great astro-nomical image to designate the time, cf. the beginning of Canto xxvii.

1-8] As the sun is with Aries, night, being opposite, is with Libra. Night is conceived as a female figure carrying the scales which fall from her hand when she exceeds: that is, at the au-tumnal equinox when the sun enters Libra and the night becomes longer than the day. Now, returning from this great flight of imagination to where we stand on the shore of this isle of the southern ocean, we see Aurora's cheeks changing from pearl to saffron as she swiftly ages. If this note seems insufficient, see Dr. E. Moore's essay on the *Astronomy of Dante*, or the note in Grand-gent's useful edition of the *Purgatorio*. This pas-sage it may be which fired Milton's imagination to one of its noblest flights:

'...from eastern point
Of Libra to the fleecy star that bears
Andromeda far off Atlantic seas
Beyond the horizon.'

46] *In exitu Israel de Aegypto.* Psalm 114. This passage refers, says Dante, by allegory to Redemption, morally to Conversion, anagogically to the departure from earthly slavery to eternal freedom. Cf. letter to Can Grande, Sec. 7.

55-7] The Ram being with the sun on the horizon, the Skygoat will be in the zenith. This is a good example of the native terseness of Dante in the idiom of the Greek myth.

70-5] 'Friends flocking round', as on the occasion of 'good news from Ghent to Aix'—a modern instance in Dante's day, when a galloping horse or a human runner relayed tidings good or bad from town to town.

91] Of his friend Casella, whom Dante 'met in the milder shades of Purgatory', little is known more than what the Poet here tells.

98] Three months since Christmas when the Jubilee Year of peace and pardon had begun.

101] The Isola Sacra at Tiber mouth seems to typify the Church, islanded amid the tumults and corruption of the human world. The happy souls are ferried by the angel from island to island!

112] The first line of that canzone which Dante analyses in his *Convivio*, Third Treatise. Beginning with the disappearance of Cato (i. 109), the close of the first Canto and the whole of the second constitute a complete symphonic composition in sweet and tender contrast with the crashing discords of the later Cantos of the *Inferno*. Here is set the key of the *Purgatorio*, the note of which is the serenity of blessed hope. The first chords of the allegro sweep over us with the quick coming of dawn, revealing the level expanse of water ruffled by the off-shore breeze. Then in soft and solemn chords the washing of the stains of Hell from the cheeks of the Pilgrim of Eternity and the girding with the reed of humility plucked from the lonely shore. At the beginning of Canto ii, in deep andante the majestic spectacle of the heavens, followed by the equally sublime emergence of the bright Bird of God, piloting the expectant souls from Tiber mouth. Now melting notes, conveying the helpless feeling of the stranger in a strange land, are interrupted by the intense surprise of the spirits on meeting a breathing man and the dramatic recognition of Dante by Casella. The pathetic tenor notes of his lovely aria are too soon interrupted by the harsh bass of stern Cato, when the whole is resolved in scurry and whir of swiftly fleeting wings, as of an affrighted flock of doves. What composer ever had a nobler theme?

CANTO III

Souls unjustly excommunicated wander round the island at foot of the first precipice for a period thirty-fold that of their exclusion from the communion of the Church.

14-15] *Che 'nverso il ciel più alto si dislaga.*

16-27] Dante for the first time sees his shadow, and missing that of Virgil beside it is startled. Virgil died at Brindisi (Brundusium) on the return from Athens in the suite of Augustus, who piously carried the body to Naples, where the supposed tomb is still shown.

39] Our Poet's references to the Virgin Mother are invariably tender and touching, bearing evidence that the devotion to her cult (unsympathetically termed by some mariolatry) had such a grip upon human nature as perhaps no other form of Christianity has ever fastened.

49] The Riviera from Turbìa (near Nice) to the Gulf of Spezia was traversed by a mountain-path.

55-72] This is a novel region for Virgil—a country where the mere inward light of reason is at fault. The observant Christian Poet is able to make a suggestion to his pagan Guide. The rule here is always to keep moving to the right, as the movement in Hell was always to the left. The rapid counter-movement of our two pilgrims towards the left evidently appeared to the shades alarming and possibly aggressive.

88-90] By the shadow knowing Dante to be in the body.

103-17] There is here an undercurrent of significance which it would be a pity to miss for want of familiarity with one or two historical facts. When the heroic young king Manfred lost life and kingdom at the battle of Benevento, 26 February 1266, Dante was but a babe of nine months, while Manfred's daughter Constance was old enough to have been married four years to Peter III of Aragon, and was probably already the mother of at least one son. Now when Manfred suddenly sees Dante in the flesh, apparently a man of about his own age, he makes nothing of the intervening years: 'Take thought if you ever saw me over there,' he exclaims. Although aware that his daughter is already mother of two kings, he can think of her only as young and fair as when he bade her farewell. Truly, 'Time takes no measure in Eternity'.

112 ff.] For Manfred's grandmother Constance, cf. *Paradiso* iii and final note there. His daughter Constance was mother of three kings, two of whom, James of Aragon and Frederick of Sicily, are referred to near the close of Canto vii and again near the close of *Paradiso* xix. Of the tragic historical significance of the defeat and death of

Manfred at the hands of the Frenchman, Charles of Anjou, who had been called in by Pope Clement IV, there is here no room to speak. We stand at one of the turning points of history.

130 ff.] Treating the body as that of an excommunicated ruler.

136 ff.] Manfred cannot enter Purgatory proper until thirty times the period of his excommunication shall have elapsed: that is the rule, but 'good prayers' may avail to shorten this period of hope deferred.

CANTO IV

This canto alone would suffice to confute the assertion sometimes made that geographical knowledge had died out in the Middle Ages. The placing of the Mount of Purgatory at the antipodes of Jerusalem— making these points the centres of two hemispheres of which the Equator is the common horizon—is enough to prove that Dante was keenly alive to the fact of the sphericity of our planet. And when, in carrying us southward on that last voyage of Ulysses, he makes us aware of the shifting of the horizon as the northern constellations gradually sink into the sea, while those of the south emerge, he is virtually re-stating one of Aristotle's major proofs that the earth is indeed a globe.

1-12] The *Timaeus* of Plato expounds the theory of a mortal and an immortal soul in man. If this were true we could attend to two things at the same time. But we have single-track minds. The soul indeed has three different faculties: vegetative, sensitive, intellective. Dante's intellective faculty had been bound and inoperative, while his sensitive faculty was listening. This psychological problem is dealt with in the *Convivio* and will come up in the Poem from time to time. Cf. Canto xxv.

16] So that it is now about nine o'clock.

19] So he does in Italy to-day.

25-6] Noli, then a port of some importance (36 miles west of Genoa), could be reached by the land-traveller only by a precipitous descent, cf. note to Canto iii. 49. San Leo, a lofty hill-town west of San Marino. Bismantova, a steep mountain some 25 miles southwest of Modena. Some fancy that the Poet fashioned after it his Mount of Purgatory.

26] Oxford text reads: *Su'n Bismantova e in Cacume;* a peak of the Monti Lepini, near Frosinone, in the Province of Rome, named Cacume, being perhaps referred to here.

42] Steeper than an angle of forty-five degrees.

55] Looking eastward in the southern hemisphere.

58-66] Dante is surprised to see the sun between himself and the north wind, as he looks eastward in the forenoon. Virgil explains that, if the sun were in the sign of Gemini (the Twins, Castor and Pollux), instead of in Aries (the Ram) as it is, he would see it blazing still further northward. The sun rides with the Twins from 21 May to 21 June, when it reaches its farthest north. To Dante's apprehension the changing positions of planets and constellations are not puzzling, for he seems to picture them to his mind as distinctly as he does the map of Italy, and to make them equally an element of poetry. It is worthy of note that the Eternal Twins are referred to here as being of singular significance to Dante. Cf. the splendid close of *Paradiso* xxii.

68-75] Jerusalem is conceived as at the antipodes of Purgatory. The course of the sun must therefore be north of Purgatory and south of Jerusalem. See the beginning of Canto ii.

79-84] That the celestial equator which is always between sun and winter is as far north of Purgatory as it is south of the Jewish capital. When the sun swings northward on the ecliptic it is winter south of the equator and *vice versa.*

123] The soul of Belacqua (Drinkwater), an old friend of Dante's who though indolent of temperament has the characteristic Florentine shrewdness of wit. He chaffs Dante for needing this elementary astronomical instruction.

137] It is noon in Purgatory; therefore the other hemisphere, from the Ganges to Morocco, is in darkness—the night just beginning in Morocco.

CANTO V

A lower slope of the Mountain. Early afternoon of the first day.

16-18] Implying, perhaps, that these souls had neglected action through 'some craven scruple of thinking too precisely on the event'.

37-9] The reference is to meteors and to lightning, which were both supposed to be due, according to the theory of Aristotle, to ignited vapours, i.e. what we term gas.

64 ff.] Jacopo del Cassero, a distinguished nobleman of Fano, waylaid near Padua by assassins in the pay of Marquis Azzo, lord of Ferrara. Charles's, i.e. kingdom of Naples, under Charles of Anjou. The land between the Romagna and that of Charles is the March of Ancona, southward from Rimini along the Adriatic.

75-80] The sons of Antenor were the Paduans. Antenor having been considered in the Middle Ages a typical traitor, it is probable that Dante means to hint at some collusion between the Paduans and the tyrant Azzo of Este. La Mira and Oriaco are places in the lowlands along the

Brenta between Padua and Venice. He thinks that, had he only fled in the other direction, he would still be in the land of the living, able to bear fruits meet for repentance!

88 ff.] Buonconte da Montefeltro, son of the renowned captain who speaks in *Inferno* xxvii. Dante himself fought in this battle of Campaldino (1289). The contrast between the story of the son and that of the father is marked with artistic intention. He begins by referring to the contrast between his greatness on earth and his present humble state; no one takes thought for him now, not even Joan (Giovanna) his wife. After that line of Dantean reserve, 'io fui di Montefeltro, io son Buonconte', the translator limps helpless as the wounded and dismounted knight.

112 ff.] Since the Devil, embodiment of Evil Will, finds himself foiled of the soul, he raises a great storm whereby to wreak spite upon the body of the unfortunate hero. An exceptionally interesting parallel to this is found in Calderon's *El Magico Prodigioso* (nobly translated by Fitz-Gerald under title of *The Mighty Magician*). In both the contrast is drawn between the power of the Fiend over the elements on the one hand, and on the other his impotence in conflict with Human Will.

116] The Pratomagno (great meadow) is the mountain chain between the Valdarno and the Casentino. The Great Yoke is the main range of the Apennine, cf. *Inferno* xxx. 64-6 (note).

127] He had crossed his arms over his breast in prayer.

130-6] Pia, of the great house of the Tolomei, flung by a faithless husband from his castle-crag in the wilds of the Tuscan Maremma. Pia thinks first of Dante and begs his prayers only after he shall have rested from the long pilgrimage. She names not her family nor her brutal husband; there is no word of blame; she mentions only her birthplace and place of death and the central event of a woman's life, her wedding. How she died *he* knows; *we* may infer, if we will, that she may have been a victim of the miasmatic Maremma. Perfect lines, such as these in the liquid Italian, are of course untranslatable.

CANTO VI

First day, mid-afternoon. Up the lower flank of the Mountain.

13-24] Those curious to see these old woes 'step on the stage again' are referred to Toynbee's *Dictionary*, Vernon's *Readings*, &c. Of that picturesque gentleman-bandit, Ghin di Tacco, Boccaccio tells a good story (*Decamerone*, x. 2). Pier de la Brosse was the favourite of the weak King

Philip III of France, son of Saint Louis. After the second marriage of Philip to Marie, beautiful daughter of the Duke of Brabant, the eldest son and heir to the throne was poisoned, apparently as the result of an obscure court intrigue. In satisfaction of justice Pier was hanged, but Dante finds him innocent and more than hints at the guilt of the young queen. Philip himself is mentioned in Canto vii. 103 (*Quel Nasetto*—He of the small nose).

28-46] *Aeneid* vi. 376: 'Cease to expect to bend the divine decree.' Virgil proceeds to point out the obvious distinction between the case of the pagan Palinurus and the cases before us, and then counsels Dante to look to Beatrice for more authoritative elucidation of 'doubt so deep'. Supreme reverence for Virgil is exhibited here; he is cited and questioned as if he were one of the sainted fathers of the Church. The expression Top of Judgement (Cima di Giudizio) is used by Shakespeare, *Measure for Measure*, II. ii. 75-7:

'How would you be
If He, which is the top of judgement, should
But judge you as you are?'

47] In the Earthly Paradise.

61-75] Sordello, a Lombard by birth, who, on account of an intrigue with the Cunizza whom we shall meet in Canto ix of *Paradiso*, was obliged to take refuge abroad. After residing at various courts of France and Spain he was some time in Provence, where he became celebrated as a troubadour in the time of Count Raymond Berenger, one of the great potentates of the western world (see close of *Paradiso* vi). Sordello returned to Italy in the train of Charles of Anjou, who rewarded him for great services. Browning, in his diffuse, elliptical, magnificent poem, gives a quite other impression of Sordello than that given here.

76 ff.] Political chaos of that age.

88-90] Of what avail the law without a power to enforce?

91 ff.] The claim of the clergy to temporal power.

97] Albert, son of the Emperor Rudolph, absentee King of the Romans.

106-8] Warring families in Guelf and Ghibelline feuds.

111] The counts of Santafiora of the great Aldobrandesco family, gradually suppressed by Siena (cf. Canto xi).

124-6] Every upstart demagogue thinks to play a part against the Empire like that of a Marcellus (there were three!) against Caesar, who was regarded as founder of the Empire.

The burst of eloquence that fills the second half of this Canto has been regarded by Italians as a chief justification for setting up the figure of the divine Poet as the venerated prophet of their national unity, finally consummated at such heroic cost, six centuries after the birth of Dante.

CANTO VII

Late afternoon of the first day. Same place on the mountainside.

15] Embracing either knees or feet: cf. Matthew xxviii. 9... 'took hold of his feet and adored him'.

16 ff.] Cf. the eulogy upon Virgil, *Inferno* i.

21] As in *Inferno* xxix. 40-2, the divisions of Hell are referred to as the cells of a monastery.

22-39] It is to be noted that Virgil does not, as heretofore, speak of himself as the guide of Dante, of whom Sordello takes no notice until, in the middle of Canto viii, he is startled to learn that this silent follower of Virgil is still in the first life.

31-3] Unbaptized infants. Cf. the explanation of the importance and efficacy of baptism in *Paradiso* xxxii.

43-60] Sordello, explaining that there is no possibility of ascent by night, proposes to lead them to a pleasant place where the First of the three nights upon the Mountain may be spent. One walks by sunlight; night is for profitable converse and study, and for sleep attended by symbolic visions. The allegorical significance of all this may be left to the reader's consideration.

73-9] The medieval taste for brilliant colouring, and for an abundance of particulars heaped up rather than grouped, appears in these lines. Nature seems to be painting

'Upon a background of pale gold
Such as the Tuscan's early art prefers'.

There is much question about line 74: Norton understands *indigo* to be meant, translating: 'Indian wood bright and clear blue'. So also Torraca, perhaps the best of modern editors. Grandgent, who commonly follows Torraca, here decides that the substance referred to is *amber!* But Dante would hardly have omitted a colour so common in nature as the blue of the sky or that of violets.

103-14] Philip III of France and Henry I of Navarre; the 'plague of France' is Philip the Fair; the stalwart King is Peter of Aragon husband of the Constance of Canto iii. He of the virile nose is Charles I of Anjou, who defeated Manfred at Benevento.

121-3] Chaucer (born a few years after Dante's death) translates these lines in the tale of the 'Wyf of Bathe':

'Ful selde up ryseth by his branches smale
Prowesse of man; for god, of his goodnesse,
Wol that of him we clayme our gentilesse.'

127-9] Dante here condenses into three lines more than even he could make clear to one not fully acquainted with all the facts involved. In *Paradiso* vi. 133, we read: 'Four daughters had Count Raymond Berenger and each of them a queen.' Of these Margaret was married to Louis IX (Saint Louis) and Beatrice to his brother, Charles of Anjou, the conqueror of Manfred. Constance, whom we already know as the fair daughter of Manfred (conclusion of Canto iii), was wife of Peter the Great of Aragon and mother of Frederick and James. All these personages were well known to Dante's contemporary readers. Now the Poet has one of those sudden visions that come to the great dramatic poets: the vision of a meeting between Constance and the two sisters who were the queens of the two royal brothers. Naturally they talk of husbands and children. 'Peter was kind and good, as well as great,' boasts Constance. 'So much,' confess the sisters, 'we cannot claim for our husbands; but if they were inferior to your lord, your own children, as well as ours, are equally inferior to them.' (Cf. *Paradiso* xix. 127-38). The only objection to this interpretation is that it places Louis IX much on a level with his brother 'of the virile nose'. Accordingly we may, if we like, consider the Margaret in question to be the second wife of the first Charles of Anjou—Margaret of Burgundy. But that would be relatively prosaic!

130 ff.] Harry of England is Henry III, father of Edward I. Marquis William is the good but unfortunate ruler of Montferrat (in Piedmont). The citizens of Alessandria and Asti are said to have taken him by treachery, thrusting him into a cage where he died. His son attempted to avenge him but was repulsed by help of the Visconti, whence his subjects lament in Montferrat and the *dolce terra* of the Canavese. In the *Convivio* (IV. 11) he is one of the examples of the virtue of liberality.

CANTO VIII

Nightfall in the beautiful mountain-nook where wait the princes.

13 ff.] *Te lucis ante terminum:* 'To Thee before the close of light'. The first words of the hymn of Saint Ambrose sung at the office of Compline after the Angelus. The following is the rendering used by the Anglican Church:

'Before the ending of the day,
Creator of the world, we pray
That Thou with wonted love wouldst keep
Thy watch around us while we sleep.'

These disembodied spirits of the negligent, who had postponed making their peace with God and are not yet admitted to happy purgatorial penance, are supposed by the Poet to be still subject to the terror of the Evil One, if not to assault by him, and are in need of reassurance by night from guardian angels. As to the further meaning of the allegory to which the Poet calls especial attention, terming it easy of discernment, I think it may safely be left to the meditative reader, but desire to add the following comment by Dante's own son, Pietro: 'The broken swords represent our defence against the temptations of the Devil. For we ought to flee, not to fear, these temptations... For we cannot kill the Devil, but only fly from him after the example of Christ, who said to the Devil wishing to tempt him, "Begone, Satan, thou shalt not tempt the Lord thy God".'

53] Judge Nino Visconti, Pisan governor of the Province of Gallura, Sardinia.

57] The reference to the 'far waters', and again in line 70 to the 'wide billows', is in exquisite dramatic keeping in the mouth of one who had spent his life as an island proconsul.

62] Sordello has been preoccupied with Virgil and, the sun being behind the Mountain, Dante's shadow was not visible.

70-84] He sends word, as Manfred had done, to his daughter, who was then only about nine years of age. She was married to the great lord whose assassination is predicted by Cunizza in *Paradiso* ix. 50-1. This was in 1312 when she was still little more than twenty. Afterwards pensioned for a time by Pisa, she finally found refuge in Florence where, notwithstanding an allowance from the Commune, she lived in poverty, dying at about the date of the appearance of the earliest *codex* of the *Divina Commedia* that has come down to us (1336). It is reasonable to believe that the reference to her in the Poem must have been a consolation. This can hardly be supposed of her mother, who at the date of the mystic pilgrimage was looking forward to marriage with Galeazzo Visconti, son of the tyrant of Milano, whose cognizance was the Viper.

89-93] Symbolizing the Christian virtues, as the four mentioned in Canto i symbolize the pagan virtues of everyday life.

97 ff.] This incursion of the Serpent into the abode of the dead is purely allegorical. See note to lines 13 ff.

112-14] If it be 'illuminative grace' that leads him up, it is evidently unavailing without being fed by the free will of the pilgrim. Upon reaching the 'sommo smalto' at the top of the Mountain, Dante will be given over to the guidance of Beatrice.

118-20] The elder Conrad was married to Constance, sister of King Manfred. The present spirit is his grandson and cousin of the lord who later entertained the Poet.

133 ff.] Dante was the honoured guest of the Malaspina in the Lunigiana in 1306.

CANTO IX

The sensitive reader will not fail to feel the singular loftiness of the allegory to which the Poet expressly calls attention. The scenery wherein the falling asleep and the awakening of the Poet are framed; the imagery of the lunar Aurora in the great constellation of the Scorpion; the dim imaginations of his dream and the contrast between its seeming violence and the placid action which it shadows; then the effect of Virgil's narrative upon Dante's mind and mood—all these circumstances form a symmetrical avenue of approach flanked by the converging lines of the dream and its answering reality. Hitherto we have been delayed outside the Christian Acropolis, first in the plain by the seaside, then upon the lower slopes of the Mountain; now we draw near to the mystic Propylaeum. Invited by the courteous Gatekeeper, we are drawn with our good will up the three symbolic steps. The first of these may be taken as an emblem of the white purity of Christ wherein we behold, as in an accusing mirror, the stains which we have come to purge away. The second step, dark and rough and scorched, of massive stone cracked lengthwise and across, brings the broken and contrite heart in contact with the Cross of Christ; while perhaps the third, which seemed porphyry flaming like blood from a master vein, denotes acceptance on the part of the pilgrim of the redeeming blood of Christ. The Bird of God who sits above the threshold of adamant typifies the priest receiving confession by authority of the Church. Here should be borne in mind the Poet's explanation in his letter to Can Grande of the various ways in which his poem may be read: it has meanings literal, moral, allegorical, anagogical—now this meaning and now that one shining out, and sometimes two or three different meanings dazzling the reader with their iridescence. Thus here the threshold of adamant is a member of an architectural structure, while allegorically it refers to the solid foundation upon which Christ built the Church, morally to the steadfastness appropriate to the confessor, and anagogically (as Torraca suggests) to the light of Grace. The purpose of the invocation to the reader (l. 70) is, in the light of these considerations, clear. The reader will not have failed to note how habitually Dante descends at the close of a Canto to some moral exhortation, some bitter invective, some piece of satire; and the loftier the theme of the Canto the more studiously homely is the phrasing of such descent to earth. There is such a descent to the language and needs of little people (mulierculae) at the close of the preceding and of the succeeding Canto. Such descents are more frequent as we go up and on. But in this Canto there is no descent, and the Poet challenges the reader not to wonder if he uses more art to support the exalted matter of his song.

1-6] The lunar Aurora appears around the constellation of the Scorpion.

10-18] The other four, having cast off the inheritance from Adam, apparently do not sleep. Dreams just before dawn are deemed prophetic or in some way true. The reference to the woes of the swallow recalls the tragic story of Procne (the nightingale) and Philomela (the swallow). Cf. Canto xvii. 19-21.

44] Awakening two hours after sunrise, Dante learns that his dream was indeed symbolically true.

55] It will be remembered that Dante is especially devoted to Saint Lucy, as we learned from the narrative of Virgil in *Inferno* ii. She was supposed to be an embodiment of 'illuminative grace', as well as the especial patroness of those who suffered from weakness of the eyes, to which Dante's severe studies are thought to have made him subject. Indeed he himself gives an interesting account of one occasion when he so suffered (*Convivio*, III. 9, near close).

112-14] P stands for Latin *peccatum;* the sins which are to be washed away are the deadly seven, from which all specific sins are supposed to spring. We are to see how, before quitting each terrace of the expiatory Mountain, one of these P's vanishes from the brow of the Pilgrim at the touch of an angel wing.

118-29] The silver symbolizes the knowledge of human nature which enables the priest to judge of the genuine nature of the penitence; the golden, the power of absolution.

133-8] According to the poet Lucan, the Tarpeian rock bellowed when Caesar put aside the Tribune and violated the treasury. The reason why the door of Purgatory creaks is mentioned at the beginning of the next Canto.

CANTO X

Second day: middle of the forenoon. On the first of the seven terraces, that where the Sin of Pride is expiated.

1-12] The hinges creak, therefore, because 'strait is the gate, and few there be that find it'; and the symbolism is sustained by the loneliness of the way upon which they enter. In the narrow pass where the walls undulate, the Poets are careful to go straight ahead. 'The evil love of souls which makes the crooked way seem straight' implies familiarity with the Poet's belief, to be fully developed later, that all actions, good or bad, are prompted by love of the good.

17-33] The mountain 'gathers back' leaving a terrace or 'cornice', as wide as three lengths of the human body, projecting from the upright cliff, whose marble surface is carven with wonderful figures speaking thrillingly of the vice or its antithetical virtue, so that the sensitive observer feels each picture to be either a *check* or a *goad*. In fact, on every one of the seven successive shelves of the purgatorial hill, this system of incitements to the virtue, or curbs to the vicious disposition, is in various ways enforced. It is to be noted that the first example of the virtue is invariably from some episode in the life of the Virgin Mary.

34 ff.] This first subject, as described in the first chapter of the gospel of Luke, has of course been since the time of Dante a favourite one with painters. Almost every one of the great masters has made a lovely picture of the Annunciation.

55-7] 2 Samuel vi. 3-7.

64-9] 2 Samuel vi. 12-16.

75] It was believed that Trajan was removed from Hell and redeemed in answer to the prayers of Gregory the Great. Cf. the great place given to the just Emperor in *Paradiso* xx.

94-105] Dante knows well that the plastic arts cannot tell a story, much less pronounce a dialogue, and therefore pauses to remind us that this 'visible speech', so novel and strange to us, is produced by Him to whom the strangest novelties 'are but dressings of a former sight'.

106-20] Dante attributes to the reader that Sin of Pride which he acknowledges to have been his own (as will appear later). The exhortation is doubtless addressed to himself as much as to the reader. The gradual way in which these obscure figures are perceived is very significant. These personages who in life were 'the observed of all observers' are now 'quite, quite down'. There is deep intention too in the carrying over of this episode from this Canto to the next. Another marked example of this exceptional handling is seen in the story of Ugolino, which is likewise introduced at the end of a Canto (*Inferno* xxxii).

130-9] Just as the caryatids of the Erechtheum (or the living caryatids whom one sees to-day in Italy) give pleasure by appealing to our sense of beauty, so these bended and contorted figures give pain. But if so, how much more the pain to see examples of the long expiation which we ourselves are doomed to suffer!

CANTO XI

The scene, as in the preceding Canto, is on the lowest shelf or cornice of the Mountain; time, before noon of the second day in Purgatory.

22 ff.] The prayer 'Deliver us from the Evil One'

is no longer needed, but is made for us who are still subject to fall. How then should we remember *them* when we pray!

46-8] The great personage who replies to Virgil's adjuration is so crushed down under the expiatory stone that he is hardly noticeable, even to Dante's quick eye.

59-66] Once one of those great counts of Santafiora mentioned in Canto vi. They boasted of having a castle for every day in the year. The Aldobrandeschi were known at least as widely throughout Europe, probably, as the Malaspina, whose fame is celebrated at the close of Canto viii. Therefore the humility expressed in l. 60 may seem somewhat exaggerated. It must be remembered that Humbert is only in process of purgation of the most insidious of all dispositions. Of all evil tendencies, that of Pride is the only one of which the victim is proud. The acquirement of the habit of humility will be gradual, and its expression is at first bound to be dogged by the shadow of affectation. How Pia died *he* knows— he only who espoused her. How I, Humbert, died, is known throughout the great state of Siena, and to every child in Campagnatico (where he was assassinated)! The pride is unconscious; the humility conscious, because conscientious.

82-7] Another example of the difficulty of acquiring the habit of humility. He professes to believe Franco his superior in his art, but immediately afterwards takes it back!

91-3] The famous man is like a tree withering at the top, and therefore soon cast into the shade by taller shafts of fresh growth, except in the event that seasons of decadence set in when the stunted tree still remains conspicuous.

94-9] Cimabuë, older than Dante by some twenty-five years, died in the year of the Poet's exile. Giotto, a year or two younger than Dante, outlived him by sixteen years. The examples of literary celebrity are Guido Guinizelli, whom we shall meet in Canto xxvi, and Guido Cavalcanti, whose father we met in *Inferno* x. The third poet is doubtless Dante himself. With delicate self-betrayal he thus illustrates that he was not exempt from 'that last infirmity of noble mind'.

108] The circle that turns in Heaven most slowly is that of the fixed stars, whose sphere was computed to revolve at the rate of one degree in a century.

109 ff.] The lord of the splendid city of Siena at the time of the signal defeat of the Florentine Guelfs at Montaperti (1260).

127-38] Dante desires to be informed why, in the case of Provenzano Salvani, an exception has been made to the rule under which we have seen

Buonconte and sad Pia wandering on the lower slopes, awaiting the hour for beginning penance. It was because of a dramatic display of humility which greatly struck the medieval imagination. One of his friends having assisted the last unhappy Hohenstaufen, Conradin, was flung into prison by the conquering Charles of Anjou and a huge ransom demanded. Unable to raise the sum in any other way, Provenzano posted himself as a mendicant upon the civic centre of Siena, the noble oval Campo or Piazza, which is still so unmodernized that little imagination is required to revive the scene.

139 ff.] Dante is also to know what it means to depend upon the charity of strangers.

CANTO XII

The time is near noon of the second day: the place further to the right around the Terrace of the Proud. The symmetrical rhetoric corresponds with the formal arrangement of the pictures. Carven tombs in the pavement of the church are common in Italy; but the most notable example of a pictured floor is in the Cathedral of Siena (the 'graffiti'). Any reader with a Bible and a dictionary can look up the examples. Series of stanzas beginning alike are frequent: e.g. the three beginning with the word 'Love' in Francesca's story (*Inferno* v), and the more elaborated series in *Paradiso* xix-xx. In the case before us, four stanzas begin 'I saw' (vedea), four 'O', four 'Showed' (mostrava), finally one sums them all up (*ll.* 61-3). In each group of four there are two examples from Scripture and two from classical mythology or history. As has already been observed, such parallel treatment of Scriptural and classical examples runs through the whole Poem.

49-51] Amphiaräus, whom we saw in the Pouch of the diviners (*Inferno* xx), foreseeing his death if he went with the Seven against Thebes, hid himself. His wife was bribed to betray his hiding-place by a tempting magic necklace from the forge of Vulcan. Her son Alcmaeon avenged his father upon her, so that she paid for the 'sventurato adornamento' with her life.

55-7] Herodotus tells the story in his first book; Dante found it in Orosius, the popular historian of the Middle Ages.

61-3] Toynbee suggested that, in the original text, the initial letters of the foregoing twelve terzine, viz. V, O, M (here repeated in a single terzina), may have a special significance, as representing the word UOM (i.e. UOMO), 'Man', whose root sin, the principal cause of his Fall, was pride (cf. *ll.* 70-1). By this device Dante may have intended to emphasize the lesson inculcated by the instances of pride given in *ll.* 25-60.

64-72] These floor-carvings are so masterly that, as Dante bends over them, his imagination is fired so that the figures leap to life and the scenes are re-enacted before his eyes. All these scenes are warnings againt vanity and presumption, but haughty sons of Eve will not so much cast down their looks as to consider them.

80] The sixth hour—so that noon is near.

100-5] Rubaconte is the ancient name of the upper bridge at Florence, in modern times called Ponte alle Grazie. After leaving the bridge, one first turns a little way to the left and then to the right, in order to reach the foot of the steep flight of steps leading to San Miniato—built before the public accounts and standards of measure were tampered with. If indeed the convenient steps by which people ascend there to-day be the same as those made in the good old time, all Dante's difficult mountain climbing is now over. As for the public scandals referred to:(1) A certain salt commissioner had enriched himself by taking a stave out of the measure with which he dealt out the commodity to the people. To the family of this gentleman any reference to the bushel was thereafter painful. See *Paradiso* xvi. 105. (2) As to the 'audit-book', a member of the great Acciaiuoli family had torn a leaf out of the municipal record in order to conceal a false entry.

118-36] The touch of the Angel's wing had erased one symbolic *P* from the Poet's brow.

CANTO XIII

Early afternoon of second day. Terrace of the Envious, who are sitting along the cliff with eyes sewed up as falconers used to 'seel' the eyes of wild hawks. Here the whips and checks are no longer appeals to the eye, but are voices recalling famous instances.

29] Mary at the marriage at Cana.

32] Pylades, wishing to die for his friend.

37-42] The Envious are scourged by voices of unselfish love. The bridle or curb to Envy is found voiced at the close of Canto xiv. The Pass of Pardon is the easier stairway to the next terrace above, where the first accents they hear are the gentle and forgiving ones of Mary and Pisistratus (Canto xv).

61-6] The services at the churches where indulgences could be obtained were, by a natural metonymy, called *perdoni* or *perdonanze*—pardons or indulgences. Thither flocked beggars—the poor and the maimed and the halt and the blind —to sit before the church-doors in disconsolate array craving charity of those whose hearts were melted by the warmth of Divine Grace.

94-6] No dividing lines of race or tongue or land or colour.

114] Life is here compared to an arch: at about the age of thirty-five one reaches the summit and then begins to descend. For the elaboration of this image, see the *Convivio* (Banquet), IV. 23. Cf. *Inferno* i. 1.

115-17] Here in 1269, nine years after their crushing defeat at Montaperti, the Florentine Guelfs had their revenge. This defeat of her own countryman, Provenzano, was what the envious woman prayed for. Cf. close of Canto xi.

123] The story goes that the merle comes out some fine midwinter day, singing: 'Lord I take no heed of thee, for winter is past.'

129] Peter the comb-maker, so unusually honest as to be still remembered in Siena.

133-8] Dante confesses that his besetting sin is pride.

151 ff.] Talamonë was a malarial seaport which the Sienese tried to develop; the Dian, an underground stream, they tried to tap. The Sienese 'admirals' are like those of Switzerland. For other references to this fascinating city, see Cantos v and xi, and *Inferno* xxix.

CANTO XIV

The Terrace of the Envious: mid-afternoon, second day. The spirits sitting along the cliff as in the preceding Canto. - SPEAKERS: Guido del Duca, Rinieri da Calboli.

16-54] Course of the Arno from its mountain source to the sea, Falterona being the mountain at the head of the poetic valley of Casentino. Indeed to Dante the map of Italy is everywhere material for poetry. Of his especial love for the rivers of Italy we have already had many examples. Here indeed there is indignation and scorn, as almost always when he refers to Florence, but we plainly perceive his wrath to be the grief of an injured lover. Some readers may be interested to compare Spenser's sweet and leisurely enumeration of the rivers of England and Ireland (*Faerie Queene*, IV. xi).

31-3] The Apennines, interrupted by the strait of Messina, may be considered to be continued in Sicily by the range now called the Pelorian (from Pelorus). The region of Falterona and Casentino, then well wooded and well watered, has become, owing to deforestation, rather dry. Heavy rains, like that described in Canto v, were then more common.

43] Porciano.

46] Arezzo.

50] Florence. The Florentines are again called wolves in *Paradiso* xxv. 6.

53] Pisa.

58-66] The ferocious Podestà (chief magistrate)

of Florence in the first year of Dante's exile. Here of course the language is wholly figurative. Since the Florentines are wolves, the city itself becomes a grim wood containing their dens.

86-7] These lines are text for a noble lesson in the next canto.

88-123] Dante considered all these names, like those in *Paradiso* xvi, 'on fame's eternal bede-roll worthy to be filed'. Doubtless they are as worthy of remembrance as the great, or the near-great, who bulk big in our biographical dictionaries, which are a recent invention. Unfortunately our knowledge as to *Who was Who* in those days is in many cases virtually limited to what the Poet himself chooses to set down. Those who desire to know more of the deeds and lives of these forgotten worthies are referred to Toynbee's entertaining *Dante Dictionary*.

91] The Romagna, bounded by Po, Reno, Apennine, Adriatic.

112-17] The counts who formerly ruled Bretti-noro (near Forlì) and Bagnacavallo (near Ravenna), have left no heirs, and it would be better if the same were true of those of Cunio (near Imola) and Castrocaro (near Forlì).

118] This human demon ought to be remembered for his sonorous name: Maghinardo Pagani da Susinana. He was lord of Faenza and Imola. Dante gives him three lines in *Inferno* xxvii (49-51).

133] Cain.

139] Apparently for coveting her sister's handsome lover.

143] The bridle-bit or check-rein of Canto xiii, line 40.

CANTO XV

Late afternoon of second day. Encounter of the Angel and profitable discourse on the ascent by the Pass of Pardon to the next Cornice.

1-6] The sphere is surely not the Ecliptic but the visible heavens, our sky, conceived as always in happy, innocent activity. Vespers is the time from 3 to 6 p.m. At 3 in Purgatory it would be midnight in Italy.

7-24] Although the light of the setting sun shines full in his eyes, an incomparably greater light strikes them at the same instant. In describing it he refers to the physical law, then less familiar than now, that the angle of reflection of a ray is equal to the angle of incidence, so that the departure of each from the perpendicular is the same. To this day one may see in Italy a stone used as a plummet.

37 ff.] Ascent to the Terrace of the Wrathful through the Pass of Pardon of xiii. 42.

44] Guido del Duca: lines 86-7 of Canto xiv.

46-75] This seems to me one of the most sweetly consoling passages in the Poem, foretelling a region where the earthly pilgrim may find wealth of a nature to be increased, rather than diminished by sharing. In Dante's time the chief end of man appeared to be to prepare to emigrate from this world where we are slaves of Avarice and where Envy works the bellows for our sighs. But as the Heavens, which then seemed so near, recede before our advance like the desert mirage, we begin to feel the need of realizing on this side of the dark waters values incommensurable, subject to no shrinkage like our *peau de chagrin,* and capable of being bequeathed to coming generations exempt from any devastating inheritance-tax.

83] The Cornice where the sins are purged that have their root in Wrath.

85-114] Three visions of Forbearance: lessons to the Wrathful.

88] The Virgin Mother.

101-5] Pisistratus, lord of Athens, whose daughter was publicly kissed by her lover to the great indignation of the mother. But Pisistratus gave a gentle answer and gained a son-in-law, presumably desirable, thus giving a lesson to over-anxious elders, prone to think ill of the rising generation.

106 ff.] The stoning of Saint Stephen.

117] *Non falsi errori*: false only as matters of fact; true as poetry and parable are true.

118-32] It is peculiarly appropriate that just here the Poet should be rapt and drunken with these noble visions in an ecstasy as intense as that whereby the soul is swept away in the storm of ignoble wrath. If himself somewhat quick to anger, he seems to hear his Master admonish:

> 'O gentle son,
> Upon the heat and flame of thy distemper
> Sprinkle cool patience.'

143] The symbolic smoke of wrath.

CANTO XVI

Terrace of the Wrathful: late afternoon of the second day.

19] The *Agnus Dei,* with its petition for compassion and peace, is of all offices perhaps best suited to allay the brief madness of anger.

27] 'In Dante's time the ancient usage still existed of terming the first day of the month calends' (Torraca). The speaker infers from Dante's inquiry that he has not yet passed over into eternal conditions, where time is no longer artificially divided as among the living on earth.

42] Modern, i.e., since the time of Saint Paul. Cf. beginning of *Inferno* ii.

46] Marco Lombardo: a great figure in his day, who left a reputation for sagacity, wit, brusque candour, liberality, honour. If he was prone to ire, he probably had good reason. Villani relates that Count Ugolino, having arranged a splendid festival, made a great display of his pomp and power to Marco, who held his tongue until Ugolino inquired: 'Marco, what say you to it?' Whereupon the sage quickly replied: 'You are in a fairer way to be subject to mischance than any baron of Italy.' 'Why?' faltered the Count. 'Because,' retorted Marco, 'because all you lack is the wrath of God!' And surely, subjoins Villani, the wrath of God soon enough came upon him!

65 ff.] Dante proceeds, in accordance with the psychology of the age as expounded by Saint Thomas Aquinas, as well as by earlier sages like Boethius and Saint Augustine, to point out that the influence of the stars upon human fate has certain limits, and that the Will can make head against that influence. The opening lines recall the words put by Homer into the mouth of Jove:

'O how falsely men
Accuse us Gods as authors of their ill!
When, by the bane their own bad lives instil,
They suffer all the miseries of their states,
Past our inflictions, and beyond their fates.'

(*Odyssey*, Book I, Chapman's translation.)

The best illustration of the main drift of the exposition is found in the words of Saint Augustine: 'The human mind that is not over-ruled by the Heavens is the soul in so far as it is free and rational, in which aspect it is superior to all material nature.' (*The City of God*, v. i.).

94-7] Where, if the pastor (or shepherd) lead the flock astray, is the mere layman, even if he be a magistrate, to look for the tower of the true City of God? Where but in that Rome of which Christ is a Roman (*Purgatorio* xxxii. 102)? On what map is shown that metropolis and see? Did He not say: 'The kingdom of God is within you'?

98 ff.] Chewing the cud (ruminating) is the business of the Pastor. The cleft hoof, which does not easily slip, symbolizes the practical wisdom of the magistrate. But the Pastor has usurped the functions of the Magistrate. Dante's political theory of the proper division of the functions of Church and State, of Pope and Emperor, is developed in his *De Monarchia*. To what he regarded as the usurpation on the part of the Ecclesiastic Power of the functions of the Secular Power Dante is everywhere consistently hostile, tracing to the temporal power of the Papacy most of the moral and political corruption of the age.

106-8] The clergy had long and strenuously taught that the spiritual rule was the Sun and the temporal rule only the Moon, shining by light reflected from the greater luminary. And so great was the force of such metaphors upon the mind of man at that time, that Dante in the *De Monarchia*, before proceeding to his constructive argument, was obliged to enter upon an elaborate discussion in order to dissipate the influence of the specious analogy.

115-26] Before the long struggle waged by Emperor Frederick II against a succession of popes, the people of Lombardy and Venice were noted for courtesy and valour. Now, on the other hand, one who for reasons of his own desires to avoid the searching glances of good men, may go his ways in security. The little that is known of the three good men so briefly mentioned is to be found in Toynbee's *Dante Dictionary*.

140] This somewhat indefinite allusion doubtless involves a compliment to a great lady who inherited and increased the honour of a stainless name. Any other interpretation is both baseless and graceless. It has been suggested that her name Gaia, as connotive of good breeding and courtesy, may be applied descriptively to her father, who would thus go by the double designation of the good and courteous Gerard (Gherardo).

142-4] The white radiance of the Angel who guards the foot of the next following 'Pass of Pardon', or ascent to the Terrace of *Acedia*.

CANTO XVII

Sunset of second day: Terrace of the Wrathful.

16-18] To this question the psychology of that time afforded the answer here succinctly given: the receptive fancy is stirred by immediate stellar influence, or by the direction of Divine Will. 'In the imagination of man by Divine inspiration are sometimes formed phantasms, which express divine things more perfectly than those impressions which we receive naturally from sensible objects, as appears in prophetic visions.' Saint Thomas Aquinas, *Summa Theologica*, from which many other passages are cited by commentators. Boccaccio gives a striking example of Dante's abstraction over a book at Siena. *Vita di Dante*, § 8.

20] Procne (or Progne), see Canto ix, 14. Dante follows Ovid. There is a more common version of the myth that makes Philomela the nightingale.

20-39] These three examples of the devastating effects of Wrath are parallel to the three contrasting examples of gentleness cited in Canto xv. It is significant that of the six examples four are of women. As this is unusual we must look for a reason, which is perhaps the following: Just as gentleness is more characteristic of woman, so wrath is in her uglier and more deforming.

25] Haman (Book of Esther). The *Vulgate* in one place terms the scaffold a 'cross'.

34] Lavinia, whose mother had killed herself at a false report of the death of Turnus, *Aeneid* xii.

52-7] These effects of light, from the appearance of Cato in Canto i, and the coming of the Angel Pilot in Canto ii, notable as they are, will be used with ever greater frequency, and with a variety that appears superhuman throughout the Poem, especially in the *Paradiso*. The passage before us probably stimulated Milton's sensitive (if imitative) imagination in such passages as that in *Paradise Lost,* iii. 375-82, and v. 598-9. Cf.

'Dark with excessive bright thy skirts appear;'

and,   '...whose top
Brightness had made invisible'.

70-2] Second nightfall.

85 to end] The discourses of Love and Free Will explain the radical difference between the classification of sins in Hell and that which is set forth here (cf. *Inferno* xi). In Hell specific sinful deeds are punished; here the Will is purified Thus the generic vice which Dante calls Avarice may be the occasion of a great variety of specific sins. To repent of a given sin is one thing; to have the crooked Will so straightened that Love is awakened for the corresponding virtue, is quite another. The Avaricious, for example, desires to continue his cleansing and straightening process until unselfish generosity becomes a passion in him.

85-7] Inactive or 'empty' (scemo) love of the good is purged on this shelf of the Mountain by severe athletic discipline. Here the exercise suggested is that of rowing; later, for obvious reasons running is preferred. Whatever it is let it be strenuous! Dante uses the theological term *Accidia* only once (Canto xviii. 132). That he calls those gurgling ones of *Inferno* vii. 118 ff. 'accidiose' is significant: a warning of the sunken state to which 'empty' virtue may fall. These terms are dropped in this translation.

94 ff.] Two kinds of love: innate and self-directed.

100 ff.] When love of worldly goods is not moderated, or when love of spiritual good is torpid.

103-11] Even if we harm ourselves, we do so actuated by mistaken desire for our own good. And since we are effects of the First Cause, 'in whom we live and move and have our being', and apart from whom we cannot be conceived as existing, to hate Him would be equivalent to hating ourselves. The pregnant comment upon

this passage is the following by George Santayana: 'The good—this was the fundamental thought of Aristotle and of all Greek ethics—the good is the end at which all nature aims. The demands of life cannot be radically perverse, since they are the judges of every excellence. No man, as Dante says, could hate his own soul; he could not at once be, and contradict, the voice of his instincts and emotions. Nor could a man hate God; for if that man knew himself, he would see that God was, by definition, his natural good, the ultimate goal of his actual aspirations.'

115 ff.] Pride.

118 ff.] Wrath.

124] These three affections purged in the lower terraces.

130 ff.] Sloth.

136 ff.] Perverted love takes three forms, as will be seen later.

CANTO XVIII

Second night: Terrace of the Slothful. Philosophical discourse continued.

13 ff.] Dante himself, in the *Convivio,* iii. 2 gives an interesting parallel treatment of this theory that all human actions are prompted by love well directed or misdirected. A sentence or two may be acceptable to the reader: 'Love, truly considered and subtly analysed, is nothing but spiritual union between the soul and the beloved object; into which union of its own nature the soul runs swiftly or slowly accordingly as it is free or hampered.' 'And since it is most natural to wish to be in God... and since its being depends on God and is conserved by Him, it naturally desires and wills to be united with God for its own strengthening. And since in the excellencies of Nature and Reason the Divine is manifested, it follows that the human soul unites naturally with those excellencies in a spiritual way, and that the sooner and more firmly the more perfectly they appear... This union is what we term Love, and its quality within the soul can be discerned by looking at those things outside that are beloved.'

29] 'Form' means essential nature: thus the form of fire is its entity by virtue of which it is fire and not something else. It is the form of fire to rise into the sphere of fire (cf. close of *Paradiso* i).

35] The Epicureans.

44] 'Foot,'—i.e., motive.

46] Virgil stands merely for human reason.

49] Scholastic phrasing: soul, although joined with matter, is yet distinct from it.

62] Reason watches at the threshold between this instinct and free desires.

67] Aristotle and Plato recognized free will as the corner-stone of Ethics.

76-81] Briefly, the moon, which was full at the beginning of the journey (*Inferno* xx. 127) is now gibbous in its third quarter, and has backed so far against the course of the heavens that it appears, on rising, in that constellation in which the sun appears when the Roman sees it setting a little south of west—over the strait between Sardinia and Corsica. For a full explanation of this complicated series of allusions I must refer the curious reader to Moore's *Studies in Dante*, iii. 71-3.

83] The modern name of Virgil's birthplace.

89 ff.] The purgation of the slothful in spirit.

93] Their patron god.

99 ff.] The voices in the air that 'scourge' the indifferent.

121 ff.] Albert, lord of Verona, had made the priorate a berth for his lame natural son. In Leviticus xxi are enumerated the blemishes excluding men from the priesthood. The rule of the Church there stated is flagrantly violated by this arrogant lord.

133-8] Those lukewarm Children of Israel who were left in the wilderness, and those followers of Aeneas who chose to stay in Sicily.

142 ff.] The medley of thoughts that lapse into dream.

CANTO XIX

Fourth Terrace for purgation of the slothful in spirit. Before dawn of the third day: Dante's Dream.

1-6] A combination of stars appearing in the eastern sky a little before sunrise at this season when the sun is in the Ram.

7 ff.] This woman, whatever her name, is the original of that monster who is 'of so frightful mien as to be hated needs but to be seen.'

22] Dante, who knew Homer only by tradition and comment, perhaps confuses the Siren with Calypso.

28 ff.] There is dramatic contrast between this dream of Virgil's negligence and his real watchfulness.

31-3] This description of the Siren and that of Satan at the close of the Inferno are the two cases where the supposed requirements of the hateful allegory deface the beauty of the Poem, like pustules upon a fair face. As we compare the *Divine Comedy* with other medieval poems the wonder grows that this Poet, alone among a host, was able with such methods and such materials to make Beauty triumph so signally. How soon, as at the beginning of this Cantica, does dead Poesy arise again! Spenser, imitating this passage

in the stripping of Duessa, gloats and stares where Dante bids us look and pass (*Faerie Queene*, I. 8, stanzas 46-9).

43] The voice of an Angel who stands at the entrance of the passage from the terrace of spiritual sloth (*acedia*) to that of avarice and prodigality.

61-6] A significant image from falconry. At call of the falconer announcing the appearance of the game, the famished hawk looks down at her feet fastened to the perch by jesses, and impatiently bates to be loosed for flight, which she performs in a series of circlings. Falconry was considered the pre-eminently *royal* sport. Here the Eternal King exhibits the lure of the great circles far above; man is no longer to look down at his feet but to use them for a start towards the lure to which he yearns to soar. Dante draws comparisons and metaphors from hawking scarcely less frequently than does Shakespeare, and quite as effectively.

69] That is he went up through the cleft in the rock until he came out upon the circle of the Fifth Cornice.

70] Fifth Terrace: Purgation of Avarice and Prodigality.

73] Needless to say, Dante uses the *Vulgate*. where this reading is found (Psalm cxviii. 25). In King James's version it is Psalm cxix, and the reading 'cleaveth unto the dust', less to the purpose. Those whose hearts are fixed upon earthly goods keep looking down until they are drawn down to the pavement, so that they are fain to use that as a bed which should be only a passageway. These penitents would fain be looking with the Poet up to the lure of the Eternal King, but are compelled to turn their backs to all the glory of the heavens and to water with their tears the unresponsive ground.

81] Turning to the right, their right hands would be on the outside, 'where borders the void' (*ove confina il vano*, Canto x. 22). In Purgatory they turn always to the right, just as in Hell their movement was, as a rule, to the left.

82-7] Virgil had asked the way to the next ascent—that to the Sixth Cornice. In the answer, 'If ye come free from lying prone,' Dante had detected something unspoken which he wished to probe. He had already heard them sighing, rather than saying, 'My soul hath to the pavement cleaved!' but was not yet aware that this lying with faces to the ground was symbol of their expiation. A wistful look is sufficient to communicate his desire to the Master who discerns his thoughts, as we have often seen. The common interpretation of line 84 is that the thing hidden is the front part of the spirits' bodies. The more significant interpretation I have adopted is that suggested by the subtle and scholarly Torraca.

97 ff.] Adrian V, who was pope for little more than a month in July and August of 1276, was of the great Fieschi family of Genoa, who were lords of the rich valley of the Entella and its affluents, chief among them the Lavagna. Near the little town of Lavagna are the church and palace built by Pope Innocent IV, uncle of Adrian. The mournful words are those of a man who has spent a lifetime in pursuit of a prize which turns to dust and ashes in his grasp.

133 ff.] The saying of Christ, 'They neither marry nor are given in marriage,' is supposed to symbolize the union of Christ and the Church. He is no longer the proxy of the Spouse of the Bride.

141] His tears ripen fruit meet for repentance: the allusion is to lines 91-2. There Dante had addressed him with the usual 'thou', 'thee'. In line 131 he changes to the 'your' used in addressing those of greatly superior station.

142] Wife of the Malaspina who befriended the Poet in 1306. The speaker leaves Dante to infer why the lady is mentioned. See close of Canto viii.

CANTO XX

Third day: morning hours. Fifth Terrace, where Avarice is purged. Hugh Capet surveys the history of his dynasty in France, predicts the betrayal of Dante's party in Florence by Charles of Valois (brother of Philip the Fair), as well as the outrage done to the Pope and the suppression of the Templars by Philip.

10-15] This terrible Wolf appeared to the Poet at the beginning. The Hound who shall expel the Wolf typifies some future way of salvation from the evils attending the pursuit of riches. Cf. *Inferno* i. 88-111.

19 ff.] Examples of the corresponding virtue.

25] Refused the bribes of Pyrrhus.

32] St. Nicholas threw dowries into their windows to save them from dishonour.

43-52] Hugh Capet: founder of the dynasty now the bane of France, Flanders, Italy. His father would be called to-day a great rancher or 'packer'. Dante was soon to see the vengeance here invoked upon Philip the Fair, who was compelled to concede the independence of the Flemings.

61] Provence came to the French crown by the marriage of Charles of Anjou, brother of St. Louis, to Beatrice, daughter of Count Raymond Berenger (1246). For Count Raymond and his daughters, cf. *Paradiso* vi. 133, and *Purgatorio* vii. 127-9.

65-9] Charles of Anjou did to death the last of the Hohenstaufen and (so Dante supposed) St. Thomas Aquinas. The repetition of the riming

phrase, 'for amends', puts poison on the arrows which he here proceeds to shoot. The emendation ('per vicenda' in line 67) by which a modern editor (Vandelli) blunts the point of this terrific irony, is deplorable. There is a similar repetition of a rime-word for especial emphasis in *Paradiso* xxx. 95-9.

70-8] Charles of Valois, whose nickname was Sansterre (Lackland). Brother of one of the most mischievous of kings, he left no very good reputation. Although never a king, the royal House of Valois proceeds from him. Old Villani records a popular saying: 'Messer Carlo came to Tuscany to make peace and left the land at war; he went to Sicily to make war and wrought a shameful peace.'

79] Charles, the second king in Naples of the house of Anjou (called 'the cripple of Jerusalem', *Paradiso* xix).

85-90] The outrage done to Pope Boniface by agents of Philip the Fair. Villani gives a full, vivid account of the proceedings of Sciarra Colonna and Guillaume de Nogaret upon seizing Boniface in his retreat at Alagna (Anagni), his native town, in September, 1303: 'And coming into his presence Sciarra and the other foes reviled him with villainous words, arresting him with such of his household as had stayed. Among those who reviled him was William of Nogaret who had managed the capture on behalf of the King of France, and who now threatened to take him in fetters to Lyons on the Rhone, and there to have him deposed and condemned in general council.' Finally, after the brutal soldiery had pillaged the palace for three days, the stout townsmen rallied and drove out the invaders, compelling Sciarra and Nogaret to fly for their lives. But the shock was too severe for the proud old man, who went mad and died at Rome a month later. Cf. especially *Paradiso* xxvii. 22, and the note there.

91-93] The destruction of the Order of the Temple by Philip. Dr. Döllinger considered the October day of 1307 when the great *coup* was carried out against the Order of Templars as in its consequences one of the most fatal in human annals. By all accounts, the proceeding was prompted by rapacity and carried out by help of the Inquisition with refinements of cruelty beyond the imagination of barbarians. Within the compass of a few tercets (ll. 67-93) the Poet here condenses the most illuminating and trenchant 'footnote to history' ever penned by a contemporary. Cf. Browning's *The Heretic's Tragedy*.

97] The only bride of the Holy Spirit is Mary, whom the shade was celebrating as Dante approached: ll. 19-24.

99-102] In the daytime they praise the virtue; at night they stigmatize the vice.

103] First told by Venus to Aeneas (*Aeneid*, Bk. I, from line 340).

109] For Achan's crime and punishment see the whole of the seventh chapter of Joshua.

113] 2 Maccabees iii. 25 (The other examples can readily be found).

117] The story was that the Parthians, having defeated and killed Crassus, poured molten gold into the mouth and sent the head to their king, so contriving, although unlettered, to compose allegorical poetry.

130] Delos had been, according to the poets, a floating island, but not more unstable than the Mountain now appears. As the birthplace of the Sun-god and the Moon-goddess it was peculiarly sacred; from it Diana takes the name Delia (as in Canto xxix. 78), and Dante elsewhere terms Apollo, Delius.

CANTO XXI

Terrace of the Avaricious: forenoon of the third day.

1-3] Dante begins his *Convivio* with 'that buoyant and immortal sentence' (Santayana) of the master of those who know: 'all men naturally desire to know'; and goes on to explain that this is because, as all things crave their perfection, the perfection of man consists in knowing. Here he suggests that such thirst is quenched only by draughts from the inward well-spring of everlasting life (Saint John iv. 5-15).

18] In this Canto, as in Canto vii and elsewhere, the contrast is startling between the theological disgrace of Virgil and the human honour which is pre-eminently his due. The antinomy is of course hopelessly insoluble; but those who press this point are too prone to forget that we are dealing, after all, with theology only as it appears in suspension in the poetry. The genuineness of the Poet's faith makes more poignant the dramatic conflict in which we participate on seeing these redeemed souls doing homage to one who was believed to be lost.

43-5] These lines form the theme which is developed in the lines that follow. That which comes from Heaven and is received back into it is the soul; not physical but spiritual causation is to be looked for here. Below the three symbolic steps at the entrance to Purgatory proper (described in Canto ix), the system of nature as set forth by philosophers holds good: there for example earthquakes are caused, as Aristotle explains, by wind somehow shut within the ground; there rain and fog are caused by humid vapour and winds by dry vapour. But here only deeper causes

obtain. In fact the Mountain quakes at the deliverance of each soul from penitential sufferings. Such deliverance, we are further instructed, takes place whenever will and desire are finally brought into harmony. There are two kinds of will, absolute and conditioned. Will absolute always seeks the Good; conditioned will, however, may be led astray, in the exercise of its freedom, to the choice of apparent good—that is to evil choices, leading to sin. Now this conditioned will causes the soul to desire to continue its painful process of purgation until, perhaps after hundreds of circlings of the sun, it is surprised by a sudden sense of purity caused by perfect harmony of will and desire.

50] Iris, the rainbow.

52-7] Aristotle's explanations of the causes of wind, earthquakes, lightning, and thunder were accepted not only by poets but by philosophers centuries after Dante's time. Francis Bacon, in the 'Inquisition Concerning the Winds', speaks of 'some that are subterraneal and underground... getting an issue by earthquakes'. Cf. Shakespeare's *Venus and Adonis*, 1046-7.

58] The soul desires its punishment until wholly purified of its sinful disposition. (See note to Canto xvii. 85.)

82-4] *Paradiso* vi. 91-3; vii. 19-51.

85] The name of Poet.

93] The Poem about Achilles is the 'second load'.

108] Norton translates literally, 'that in the most truthful they least follow the will'. The sincerest men are most apt to betray their feelings.

130-6] But in Canto vi we saw Sordello embrace Virgil! It is unsafe to assume that the Poet had forgotten this detail. Some purpose must be supposed. Possibly in the former case Virgil was taken by surprise, while here his sense of fitness declines the embrace of one who is on the threshold of a world where affection for the lost (such was the theory) is cancelled.

The thirty-four lines following Statius' declaration that, for the sake of acquaintance with the living Virgil, he would gladly have delayed for one circle of the sun (i.e., for a year) his release from the banishment of Purgatory, set dramatically before us an exceedingly sweet and tender scene. In subtle insight which it is now the fashion to term 'psychological', in humour and pathos, in swift seizure of the essential and corresponding suppression of unconcerning things, in mastery of dialogue, Dante here transcends all classic models known to him. This Canto is not as celebrated as some of the more powerful passages of the Inferno, but to those who have a quiet taste for delicate draughtsmanship its appeal is sure.

CANTO XXII

*Third day: late forenoon. Ascent to the Sixth Terrace:
Virgil and Statius with Dante.*

4-6] For the rest cf. close of Canto xxiv. The
word 'thirst' is supposed to be appropriate to the
souls who are repenting of Avarice, transferring
their thirst for gold to a worthy object. To 'hunger
after righteousness' is appropriate to the intemperate in food and drink, so that this part of the
beatitude is reserved for the Angel of the Sixth
Cornice.

31-45] The passage translated in lines 40-41 is
the well-known exclamation of Aeneas (*Aeneid*
III. 56):

> 'Quid non mortalia pectora cogis
> Auri sacra fames.'

Just how Dante interpreted the Virgilian adjec-
tive *sacra*, which he merely repeats, is a moot
point. The most scholarly of the early commentators, Benvenuto Rambaldi, who lectured on
Dante at Bologna a half century after the death
of the Poet, rightly paraphrases the words *auri
sacra fames* as meaning 'O execrabilis cupiditas
auri'—accursed craving for gold. But Francesco
d'Ovidio, discussing the passage at length, takes
refuge in the assumption that Dante misunderstood the words as meaning 'holy or just desire',
with reference to blameless acquisition and dis-
pensing; and Professor Grandgent, in his useful
edition, follows this interpretation. These are
doubtless good authorities, but Dante himself is
an even better, and to believe that he so misunderstood his favourite poet seems indeed an ex-
pedient to which one should resort with great
reluctance. How then could an invective against
greed for gold be supposed to have had so powerful an influence upon one addicted to the contrary vice of prodigality? Obviously one who
spends too much must sooner or later be driven
to seek, by hook or by crook, the means wherewith to spend. Thus prodigality meets and col-
lides with greed, as in the grim jousts described
in Canto vii of the *Inferno,* and referred to here
in line 42.
There is another consideration which seems to
have been overlooked. A man's prodigality may,
by pauperizing beneficiaries, converting servants
into parasites and dependents into sycophants,
prove the cause of greed in others. Considered
in this light, the unholy thirst for gold is bred in
the breasts of those who are weakened or corrupted by inconsiderate bounty. The suggestion
then is that Dante wishes to show how the eyes
of Statius could have been opened to the fact
that lavish spending and random gifts were mak-

ing him accessory to the vice which he most
detested. The magic of the Poet gave Statius a
sudden glimpse of himself as a very breeder of
avarice! It may well be that a man of genius,
who had begun to perceive how scanty a harvest
his liberal hand was reaping—weeds and thistles
for corn—might have been awakened to profitable
thought by Virgil's words, without wresting them
from their true meaning. Such is, I believe, the
true and deep interpretation of a passage which
has been considered one of the most difficult in
the whole *Divine Comedy.*

46-8] For the hairless or cropped crowns of the
prodigals see note to *Inferno* vii. 39.

63] Saint Peter, as at end of *Paradiso* xviii.

70-2] The Cumaean Sibyl, Eclogue iv. This
eclogue had from very early times been interpreted
as prophetic of Christ. Dante's use of the passage
is therefore sanctioned by venerable tradition.

91] In the early ages of Christianity many converts concealed their faith like Joseph of Ari-
mathaea.

98] Oxford text reads *Varro.*

99] The tone of this question strikes the modern
reader as rather cold-blooded. Here, as in the
case of Cato, our Poet fails to make his redeemed
soul quite *simpatico.* Considering his longing for
the companionship of Virgil, the latter's enumeration of the great and noble souls confined in
the 'Prison Blind' must surely awaken in Statius
regret at missing so much good company! But
upon this topic his lips are sealed, as ours must be.

106-8] As elsewhere mentioned, Dante knew
these (and other) Greek poets only through references to them in Latin writings.

112] Hypsipylë, for whose story see note to
Canto xxvi. 94 ff.

113] Here Dante seems for once wanting in
accuracy. Cf. *Inferno* xx. 40-60.

118-20] The fifth Hour is now driving the chariot of the Sun: it is about 11 o'clock.

130 ff.] The emblematic fruit-tree which the gluttons cannot climb.

142-4] Mary's words, 'They have no wine,' cited
in Canto xiii as an example of affectionate
thought for others, are here referred to as an example of temperance.

CANTO XXIII

*Terrace of the Intemperate in food and drink: about
noon of the third day.*

3] This comparison is strikingly Italian, too
many of Dante's countrymen still holding it good
sport to spend hours in order to snare or shoot a
lark, a robin, or a nightingale.

11] This phrase of the Miserere (Psalm li. 15)

is appropriate to those whose sin is here purged. The prayer is for the noble use of the lips exemplified by the Virgin Mother at the marriage at Cana. Cf. Canto xxii. 142-4.

26] Erysichthon was, according to Ovid, a Thessalian prince who, having presumed to fell a grove sacred to Ceres was punished by the goddess with such insatiable hunger that, after devouring everything else obtainable, he at last began to gnaw his own body. Would that the divinities of our sacred Sequoia groves were today powerful enough to protect their own!

30] The dreadful tale is told by Josephus.

31-3] The Latin word for man, *homo*, by the dropping of the aspirate, gives the Italian (u)omo. In a skull the eye-sockets, with the median line of the nose, compose quite accurately the capital M as then written. Thus it became a saying that the word for man in the universal language is printed on the face. In his *Urn Burial*, chapter iii, Sir Thomas Browne makes interesting comment on this passage. For another fanciful modification of the M see *Paradiso* xviii.

49-51] Cf. Virgil's reference to the shadowy bodies of the spirits, Canto iii. 31-3. Also the recognition of Ser Brunetto, *Inferno* xv.

58] The 'you' is plural, referring to the whole class of souls here undergoing purgation. In making this distinction, which is obvious in Italian, the translator but revives a forgotten usage of our tongue.

72-5] The souls rejoice in their pain as Christ rejoiced in the utter agony of the cross. Cf. Matthew xxvii. 46.

Lines 74, 76, 78 of the original text are examples of the infrequent *versi tronchi*—verses lacking the final unstressed syllable and therefore having masculine endings.

79] If you repented only when too weak to sin more. See Belacqua's explanation, Canto iv. 130-5.

94-6] The Barbagia was a wild region where the people were uncivilized. The word is a vestige of the remarkable race who gave the name 'Barbary' to a large part of North Africa where they are still called 'Berbers'.

94-111] The stormy voice of the poet-prophet speaks through Forese.

100-2] The contemporary *Ottimo Commento* confirms the facts here adverted to, although mentioning no specific instance of such ecclesiastical admonition. Villani in his history records laws regulating the dress and deportment of women, and references are found elsewhere to their breaches of decorum.

106-11] After the exile of Dante and the disastrous coming of Charles of Valois (1302), many calamities befell Florence. Before the boys who are now infants shall have reached adolescence, the mothers of Florence will be sorrowful.

115-17] Referring to a period of intimacy which Dante does not recall with pleasure. Of this the only record we have is the *tenzone* (series of six coarsely abusive sonnets) between Dante and Forese. Four of these are translated by Dante Rossetti in his *Early Italian Poets*. The originals are printed in the Oxford *Dante*, pp. 164-5. Cf. the reproaches of Beatrice and Dante's personal confession, Cantos xxx, xxxi.

132] Statius has explained the spiritual cause of the earthquake, Canto xxi. 40-72.

CANTO XXIV

Third day: early afternoon. Terrace of the Intemperate.

10] We shall meet her in the Heaven of the Moon (*Paradiso* iii). The reader is urged to read Longfellow's notes on the present Canto.

19] Benvenuto pronounces Bonagiunta a man of honour and an orator, a facile rimester but a more facile wine-bibber. This poet probably died but little before 1300.

21-4] Pope Martin IV, once treasurer of St. Martin's of Tours, is said to have been in the habit of stewing the eels in the famous sweet Vernaccia wine, and to have died of a surfeit. There is an ancient satirical epitaph averring that the eels rejoiced at his demise.

28-33] This Boniface was an archbishop of Ravenna—not, of course, to be confused with the pope so often mentioned. In fact he was, like Pope Adrian V (cf. Canto xix), a nephew of Pope Innocent IV, and of the great Genoese family, Fieschi, counts of Lavagna. Ubaldin de la Pila is said to have been a brother of the famous Ghibelline, Cardinal Ottaviano, mentioned among the heretics of *Inferno* x. Of Messer Marchese of Forlì there remains the anecdote of his thirsty habit which may have suggested the tercet.

38] i.e., in his throat.

43] Referring probably to a lady named Gentucca, who had shown some kindness to the Poet in his exile.

51] A canzone of Dante's *New Life*, well translated by Rossetti.

55 ff.] Because we did not, like you, pen the dictates of the heart. Cf. the conversation with Oderisi, Canto xi, and also that with Guido Guinizelli, Canto xxvi. These conversations have the interest that the comments of a master upon his art and its contemporary practitioners cannot fail to possess. For Guittone and the Notary (Jacopo da Lentino) see Gaspary's *Early Italian Literature*. This pregnant reference to the source

of our Poet's inspiration found an echo in the heart of Sidney:

'Fool, said my Muse to me, look in thy heart and write.'

82-7] Prophecy of the violent death of his bro-ther, the famous Corso Donati, turbulent chief of the party of the Neri (Blacks), whose career is too much bound up in the history of the time to be summarized in a note.

103 ff.] Cf. the symbolic tree described near the close of Canto xxii. The tree now encountered had been concealed by the curve of the terrace round the Mountain.

121] The Centaurs (Ovid, Met. xii).

124 ff.] Judges vii. 4-7.

138] The Angel standing at the entrance to the last 'Pass of Pardon' glows with the colour sym-bolic of Love.

151-4] Here appears the second half of the bea-titude which the Poet chooses to split, as we saw at the beginning of Canto xxii: 'Blessed are they which do hunger and thirst after righteousness.' The Latin of the Vulgate, esuriunt justitiam, is in-terpreted by the last line: 'esuriendo sempre quanto è giusto', 'hungering ever in accord with right', or as Norton renders it literally, 'so much as is right'. Inasmuch as the inordinate appetite purged on the Sixth Cornice comprises intemperance in drink as well as in food, this splitting of the bea-titude may appear fanciful. Perhaps Dante uses the word 'hunger' with reference to the dearth suf-fered by those who undergo the purgation of this cornice.

CANTO XXV

Third day: mid-afternoon. Ascent to the Seventh Ter-race, where the lust of the flesh is burnt away.

1-3] The sun, in Aries (the Ram), leaves the meridian to the next following constellation, while the night, circling opposite, would be in the Scorpion. Cf. the opening of Canto ii.

40] The heart is the 'perfect place' of line 48. As a man picks food from the table, so the heart takes the purest essence of the blood, infusing into it formative virtue, thus generating the seminal fluid.

47] The blood of the male is said to be active, that of the female, passive.

50] The word 'coagulating' is taken from the Latin of the Vulgate, Job x. 10, and Wisdom vii. 2, translated in the English versions by the words 'curdled', 'compacted'.

53] The vegetative soul is the goal of the plant, but only an incident in the progress of the human embryo.

63-6] Averroës, 'che 'l gran comento feo' (In-ferno iv. 144), following Aristotle, finding no special organ for the intellectual powers, fell back upon a doctrine something like that of Emer-son's 'Oversoul', thus abrogating mere individual immortality and with it the whole system of re-wards and punishments after death. Possibly Aquinas and Dante misunderstood Averroës, as they did his name (Ibn Roschd). See Renan's well-known essay, Averroès et l'Averroïsme.

68 ff.] The Prime Mover (God) breathes a soul into the embryo.

82] The faculties of sense mute.

86] The two shores are that of Tiber-mouth, leading to the isle of Purgatory, and that of the dark river of Inferno iii.

108] The ninety lines from 19 to 108 form per-haps the supreme example in literature of the succinct handling in verse of an abstruse philo-sophical theme. Dante's doubt as to how bodies that have no need of food can pine for want of it opens up the larger question of the relation of soul and body, upon which hangs in turn the whole system of theology. The question being too difficult for Virgil (human reason) is referred to Statius who, being a redeemed spirit, may be supposed to have received 'the new knowledge'. Here, concentrated in a very palatable bolus, the student of the workings of the human mind is offered a taste of that 'bread of angels' which Dante had more amply spread upon his board in the Convivio or Banquet. It has been said that in the Middle Ages men had no philosophy, but only logic and theology. However this may be, it would savour of intellectual arrogance to des-pise or overlook an era which could produce a Dante. As to the inter-relation of matter and spirit, the dependence of intellect upon physical function, the possible survival of intelligence, who shall say that, after all advances in science, we have yet reached a much better working hypo-thesis than the doubtless very crude one offered in this Canto? Rehandling the same theme six cen-turies later in the light of all our gathered know-ledge, Bridges reports little definite advance:

'This picklock Reason is still a-fumbling at
                                        the wards,
Bragging to unlock the door of stern Reality.'
                    Testament of Beauty, i. 463.

109 ff.] While Statius was discoursing they were moving on, and are now come to the Seventh Terrace to which Virgil had promised to lead Dante (Inferno i. 118-20).

122] First words of a hymn containing a prayer for purity.

127] Words of Mary to the Angel, Luke i. 34.

130-2] Ovid, Met. ii. Cf. Paradiso xxxi. 32-3.

PURGATORIO

CANTO XXVI

Terrace of the Sensual. Sinners according to Nature and Sinners against Nature. Third day: late afternoon.

7] The three poets are stepping along the ledge with the purging fires on the left and on the right the border from which a false step might precipitate Dante. As they are facing southward, the sloping sun projects over the white flame Dante's shadow, reddening the surface as he moves along.

12] Not the mere eidolon described in Canto xxv.

28 ff.] Dante, who exhibits his taste for symmetry in a thousand details, perhaps intends a parallel between the two troops of the lustful, who meet and pass like files of ants, and the two opposing files of the panders and the seducers in the first circle of *Malebolge. Inferno* xviii, from line 26.

41] The 'falsa vacca' of *Inferno* xii. 13.

43-5] Everything here is imaginary except the sandy plain. The Riphaean mountains were supposed to be far north; the sandy plain is the Libyan desert; the two flocks would hardly be flying in opposite directions at the same season.

69] The Italian is intranslatably felicitous: *quando rozzo e salvatico s'inurba. S'inurba*, 'comes to town for the first time' (inurbs him). In general the reflexives in the Latin tongues have a compactness defying English equivalents.

78] Taunted by his ribald soldiery.

82] i.e., immoderate but not unnatural self-indulgence. The nymph Salmacis prayed to be fused with the youth Hermaphroditus, and had her wish granted.

92] Cf. xi. 97-9.

94-6] In meeting Jason, *Inferno* xviii, we learned the first thrilling vicissitudes of Hypsipylë's romantic career. By Jason she had twins from whom, before they had grown up, she was carried off by pirates and sold as a slave to King Lycurgus. Entrusted with the care of his little boy, she was one day in the fields, when the 'Seven against Thebes' came marching by, very much athirst. Leaving the child on the grass, she led them at their urgent entreaty to the fountain Langeia (Canto xxii. 112), but returning found only the dead body of the child who had been stung by a serpent. Crazed by this bereavement, Lycurgus was about to put her to death, when her two heroic sons rushed in at the last moment and took her to their protecting embrace. Our Poet is like them in his delight to find his father in Apollo safe from perdition, but for fear of the fire does not quite rise to the heroism of the embrace. Dante owes the story of Hypsipylë to Statius who, it will be remembered, is a silent witness to all this.

112 ff.] Guido Guinizelli, in Italian, and Arnaut Daniel, in Provençal, seem to be considered by our poet as the recent predecessors to whom his indebtedness is deepest. The first awakening of poetry after the Dark Ages was in Provence in the twelfth century. The literary judgements and references in this Canto and in xxiv are of so great interest that they cannot be treated with satisfaction to any one in brief notes. Those who know nothing of the subject may begin by looking at the translations of Dante Gabriel Rossetti in his *Early Italian Poets.*

120] Giraut de Borneil.

131] Cf. Canto xi. 19-24. Spirits in Purgatory are not subject to temptation.

139 to end] The eight lines here attributed to Arnaut Daniel are in the Provençal tongue and are without doubt of Dante's composition.

CANTO XXVII

Third and last night on the Mountain, with the symbolic dream of Rachel and Leah. Virgil's last words.

1-5] All the heavens, whether visible or not, circle round in the vast spaces of the Poet's imagination. It is important, however, not to forget that true imagination, such as Dante's pre-eminently is, must be founded on knowledge. Now according to the knowledge accessible to the man of that time, Ganges and Ebro mark the eastern and western bounds of the hemisphere of land, Jerusalem being its centre and the Mountain of Purgatory at the antipodes; whence it follows that at sunset on the Mountain it will be sunrise at Jerusalem and noon over Ganges, while Ebro will reflect the midnight stars of Libra (the constellation opposite to Aries in which now rides the sun). The river Ebro stands for Spain, of which it is a principal stream; instead of it the Poet alternatively puts now Seville, now the Pillars of Hercules, now Ceuta near the Straits, now Morocco. For a similar astronomical determination of the hour, with like references to Jerusalem and Ganges, cf. beginning of Canto ii.

22-3] Cf. *Inferno* xvii. 79-99.

37-9] According to the pretty legend of the immortal lovers of Babylon, the mulberry is empurpled with the blood of Pyramus. Benvenuto da Imola finds in their love a parallel to that of Dante and Beatrice. Cf. Canto xxxiii. 69.

58-63] *Matthew* xxv. 34 The speaker is the seventh and last angelic sentinel who, presumably, erases the last *P* from Dante's brow.

64-9] They turned towards the right to pass through the flame, so that now they are going east and the setting sun is casting the long shadow of the living body upon the stairway before them.

76-87] The double comparison is developed

into a little poem in the manner familiar to readers of Milton and the classical epics. The Poet here 'sows with the whole hand' (Lowell's phrase). This is the artist's device for beautifully marking the crucial importance of this last night upon the mountainside, just prior to the final solemn pronouncement of Virgil at the entrance to the Earthly Paradise.

97 ff.] Dante's third dream of presage: Leah and Rachel—the Active Life and the Contemplative.

127-42] These are the last words spoken by Virgil in the Poem, although he remains with Statius for a while by the side of Dante, who records their smiling applause of Matilda's graceful 'corollary' at the close of the next Canto. During the mystic procession of the Church Triumphant, Dante notes Virgil's astonishment; apparently Statius has gone on. After this Virgil quietly vanishes unnoticed. See Canto xxx. 43-57. With these noble words of his Guide, type of Human Reason, our Poet is initiated into that Universal Communion of which participate the wise and good of every era and every tongue, whose simple creed is 'the religion of all sensible men'. This is that Round Table where knights in the eternal crusade for the liberation of humanity all gather round the same Holy Grail. Dante has not yet, indeed, satisfied all the requirements of his particular faith; Theology, in the person of Beatrice, is about to wound him with a sword whetted by his own sensitive conscience; he has, however, attained the lofty dignity of King and Priest over himself.

> 'There is no danger to a man that knows
> What life and death is; there's not any law
> Exceeds his knowledge; neither is it lawful
> That he should stoop to any other law.'

CANTO XXVIII

Soon after sunrise on the fourth day. Dante, no longer guided but followed by the two great Masters, is walking on the level upland.

19-21] The Roman name of the port of Ravenna was Classis, modified in Dante's age to Chiassi, now Classe. The ancient Pineta, although sadly depleted, still borders the sea between Ravenna and Cervia. And when Aeolus looses the rain-bringing south-east wind over the troubled Adriatic, every pine-tree of the wide forest becomes a chorded harp intoning the same solemn music that the lonely Poet heard.

28] 'Here', i.e., in this mortal world.

40 ff.] This is the Lady of whom Leah, in the dream of Canto xxvii, is the presage, just as Rachel is the presage of Beatrice. No name is given

to this Lady until the very end of the Cantica (xxxiii. 119) where she is called Matilda. The early commentators, including Dante's son Peter, assume that the great Countess of Tuscany is meant. Modern writers challenge for weighty reasons this traditional view. Readers should be content to accept the Lady purely and simply as the 'ever-womanly' figure limned by the artist's pencil.

80] Psalm xcii. 4 (Vulgate, xci. 5), 'Delectasti me, Domine in factura Tua' (Thou, Lord, hast made me glad through Thy work).

82] Every word in the Poem is significant—this especially so. Virgil no longer leads, but follows in silence.

85 to end] This is one of the many Cantos wherein Dante tries to rib his poetry with positive science—unscientific as much of it proves to be. In Canto xxi. 40-57, Statius had explained to Dante that above the Gateway of Purgatorio proper—the uppermost of the three mystic steps whereon the Vicar of Peter has his feet—there is no earthquake, nor rain nor hail nor mist, in short, no climatic alteration or meteorological change, such as the lower parts of the Mountain, being purely natural, are subject to. Here, however, Dante sees a running stream, feels a breeze upon his brow, hears a soughing in the forest whose leaves and sprays are all bent towards the west under the steady stress of the eastern trade-wind. All this appears to contradict what Statius had told him, so that he is full of doubt and wonder. Accordingly, when the beautiful Lady invites him to ask questions, he begs her to explain this contradiction. The substance of her explanation is as follows: 'My smiling is explained by the ninety-second Psalm, "For Thou, Lord, hast made me glad through Thy work".' As to the wind (ll. 97-9), 'this passage,' says Moore, 'describes the exemption of the Earthly Paradise from the storms generated on the lower earth by the exhalations which, proceeding from the water and the earth, rise as far as they can, following the heat by which such exhalations are drawn up.' Here, as everywhere, Dante follows the science of his time, which itself followed Aristotle's *Meteorologica*. But the wind here on the upper mountain is due to a very different cause: the revolution of the Primum Mobile, *la prima volta*, or first moving sphere. It is this that, carrying with it the upper air from east to west around the stationary earth, causes the steady current or trade-wind which bends the leaves all one way and makes the forest murmur like that on Classe's shore (la Pineta di Ravenna). As to the water: in many places Dante deals with the action of the moisture in the air, for ever replenishing the rivers at their sources in the mountains. But here the two streams, Lethë and Eunoë, issue at two sides from a fountain, steady and sure, that is constantly fed by direct interposition of the Will of God. Thus Dante's doubts are solved, but the Lady volunteers a 'corollary', connecting the Earthly Paradise with the Age of Gold of the Poets, two of whom are present and are pleased.

123] The Poet must some time have dwelt by a torrent near its source in the mountain snow, which, melting in the sun and freezing at night, keeps the breast of the stream summer-long swelling and subsiding.

CANTO XXIX

Mystic Pageant along the Bank of Lethë.

3] Vulgate Psalm xxxi. 1, 'quorum tecta sunt peccata.' In the version of 1611: 'whose sin is covered' (Psalm xxxii. 1).

7-12] Dante had been walking eastward till coming to the left bank of the brook. He now turns to the right, walking up-stream, in front of Virgil and Statius and keeping step with the Lady on the right bank, until the stream sweeps round a sharp curve and they all turn towards the east again. As usual in this Cantica, as well as in the *Inferno,* the movements are so definite that they could be (and have been) charted.

37-42] This noble invocation is amply justified and supported by the splendid if somewhat stiffly brocaded eloquence of the whole Canto. Emblematic pageantry was a cunning and, of course, wholly legitimate device of the Church to fasten its hold upon the illiterate multitude, while among the cultivated few who enjoyed both learning (such as it then was) and leisure, allegorical symbolism was more than a fashion—a veritable passion. Nowhere else in medieval literature (and I know not where in any literature) is descriptive allegory at once so compact and so vivid. Here for once allegory becomes a living thing, healthy, full-blooded, high-coloured, fascinating. The Canto may be enjoyed without analysis, as one enjoys a gorgeous frieze or panel painting. Those will be best able to analyse it who best know the Bible, especially the Apocalypse and the Book of Ezekiel. It is the purpose of the present editor to interrupt the reader rather infrequently; the student of details will find in Vandelli's third issue of his eighth edition of Scartazzini precisely one hundred references, scriptural, Dantean, and profane, to illustrate this Canto alone! It is easier to take the picture to pieces than to put it together again.

50] The seven golden candlesticks of the Judaic cult, exalted by Christian symbolism, and in the imagination of Dante a more glorious Septentrion (Canto xxx, first line). Each candle leaves a trail of one of the colours of the rainbow.

55-7] Giving the final touch to the principle that Human Reason is impotent in the presence of Revelation.

60] Referring to the stately wedding processions of old time, of which there are interesting early paintings, e.g., 'The Wedding of Baccio Adimari and Lina Ricasoli' (reproduced by the photographer, Alinari).

77] The lunar and solar spectrum.

83] Books of the Old Testament.

92] The Gospels.

108] The Gryphon who draws the Car of the Church typifies the union of the Divine and the human in the Saviour. The middle stripe of the seven colours is between his wings.

122] Love.

126] Faith.

130-2] The Cardinal Virtues, Temperance, Justice, Fortitude, led by Prudence, who sees past, present, future.

136-8] 'Luke, the beloved physician' is the follower of the father of medicine, Hippocrates, whom Nature created for her favourite animals (Mankind). Cf. *Paradiso* xi. 4-5.

139] St. Paul: cf. the imagery of Ephesians vi. 11-17.

142-4] Minor Epistles and Apocalypse (Revelation of St. John the Divine).

147-8] The white lily being emblem of Faith; the flowers of crimson and rose, of Love.

CANTO XXX

1-6] The symbolical Seven Candlesticks are called the Septentrion of the First Heaven (or Empyrean) because they image forth such guidance in the moral or spiritual world as men in this lower world seek by anxious observation of that group of stars variously called the Pointers, the Dipper, *Ursa Major,* Charles's Wain: Spenser's sevenfold team of the northern wagoner

'That was in ocean waves yet never wet,
But firm is fixt, and sendeth light from far
To all that in the wide deep wandering are.'

10] Canticle of Canticles iv. 8. For the threefold repetition cf. the Vulgate.

15] The voice is thought of as taking on the vesture of the body.

19] Matthew xxi. 9.

21] *Aeneid* VI. 883.

47-8] *Aeneid* IV. 23. Scripture has now been twice quoted and Virgil twice. On the part of the Christian poet of poets this is at once a gesture of supreme reverence and perhaps also an implicit protest. Why should he who has saved others be himself a castaway? Alas! the Poet cannot do for Virgil what the saint did for Trajan (cf. Canto x. 73-93 and *Paradiso* xx).

55] The Poet here carves, or rather stabs, his own name into the substance of his masterpiece — prompted not by pride but by deepest humility, for here begins his public act of repentance.

67 ff.] As the Lady here assumes the rôle of accuser, she veils the 'living flame' of love.

73-5] In the first of these lines Beatrice puts the barrier of the queenly 'we', 'us', between herself and her lover; in the second she withers his pride with scorn; in the third there is implicit but tender rebuke.

83] Psalm xxxi. 1-8 (Vulgate xxx).

85 ff.] As the trees on the mountains of Italy are sheathed with snow by the cold north, and melted by the breezes from the African desert where, towards the equator, the shadows shrink, so, &c. Considering that the man, Dante, stands in the Poem both for his own person and also in a representative capacity, the image is not too stately.

109-17] By influences rained down from the great wheeling spheres guided by angelic intelligences and directing all seeds to the soil where they may best thrive, as well as by largess of grace divine raining down from an infinitely loftier source, this man was in youth potentially such that the highest hope should have been made good in him. For the development of the doctrine that in God's Universe 'nothing walks with aimless feet', see the latter part of the first Canto of *Paradiso*.

124-6] In his *Convivio* (*Banquet*) Dante explains that adolescence continues until the twenty-fifth year, when youth begins. It was on this second threshold, that of youth, that Beatrice died. What the other yearning was that seduced the young Poet from his ideal is a disputed question which cannot be here discussed.

136-8] From the wilderness of sin and error described at the beginning of the *Inferno* there was no means of rescuing the Poet except to show him 'the ultimate consequences of sin' (Scartazzini).

CANTO XXXI

1-3] The cutting edge that made Dante quiver is the intolerably sweet and unsparing review of his life in the foregoing address of Beatrice to the angels (cf. preceding Canto, l. 57).

22] The phrase 'in thy desires of me' translates 'perentro i miei disiri'—within *my* desires. Dante

often uses in his pregnant way this *objective genitive*. See especially *Paradiso* v. 105 and note.

36] For the 'your' instead of 'thy' cf. xxx. 74; xxxiii. 29 and 92. Several like instances occur in the Poem, notably *Paradiso* xvi. 10.

59] Who or what was this 'dainty maid' (*pargoletta*)? A woman of flesh and blood or an abstraction like her he celebrates in the *Banquet*? We do not know.

62] 'In vain the net is spread in the sight of any bird', Proverbs i. 17. But Dante, following the Vulgate, has the word 'pennuti'—full-plumaged birds.

77] The angels.

92-102] Matilda draws Dante through Lethë, which takes away grievous remembrance of personal sin.

104] The Cardinal Virtues (cf. xxix. 130-2).

110] The Christian Graces (Canto xxix. 121-9).

115-26] Dante sees the mystery of the union of the human with the divine nature, not directly, but reflected in the emerald eyes of Beatrice. Looking directly at the form, it appears still the same, while in her eyes the image is transfigured. So Shelley saw the ideal Athens reflected:

'Within the surface of Time's fleeting river
Its wrinkled image lies, as then it lay
Immovably unquiet, and forever
It trembles, but it cannot pass away.'

139 to end] Here, as often elsewhere, the Poet's expression of his despair of picturing things beyond the reach of language becomes the most suggestive of appeals to the imagination.

CANTO XXXII

Vision seen in the Earthly Paradise on the morning of the fourth day.

5-9] Too intense personal vision reproved by the three Christian Virtues. There is here perhaps a reference to the traces of the early flame (xxx. 48). The four beautiful Pagan Graces had bidden Dante gaze his fill (xxxi. 115) into those emeralds whose colour was held salutary to the eyesight as well as to the soul (colour of Hope). Hereafter Beatrice will likewise check him: 'Not in mine eyes alone is Paradise' (*Paradiso* xviii. 21). Too intense contemplation, untempered by various observation and activity, makes the visionary and the mystic. On the other hand the power to throw a 'wall of indifference' (*parete di non caler*) around oneself, shutting out intrusive impressions, is the condition of all fruitful thought.

13-15] The transfiguration of the image in the eyes of Beatrice transcends in glory even the stately solemnity of the procession.

16-24] An accurate description of the wheeling right about face of a medieval column, the squadron with the standard turning under protection of overlapping shields (the *Testudo*).

30] Behind the right wheel of the Car.

38] Tree of Knowledge. The Cross, whereof the wain-pole is symbol, was fabled to be of the wood of this tree.

40-2] In the second Georgic Virgil had told of trees in India so lofty that no archer could send an arrow to the top.

48] Matthew iii. 15 (Vulgate).

52-60] This tree, grafted with the Cross, blossoms anew, as in spring, when the sun is in the Ram just behind the sign of the Fishes, our trees renew verdure and bloom. Here we have lovely poetry; but what, the reader asks, can it mean in modern application, and what is this colour *men che di rose e più che di viole?* According to a beautiful legend, Seth brought from the Garden of Eden three seeds of the apple eaten by his father, Adam; from one of these sprang the tree from whose wood was made the cross upon which the Redeemer expiated the human taint caused by the ungoverned appetite of our disobedient first parents. So it comes about that this tree represents Divine Justice, satisfied by the sacrifice of the Son of God. But Eternal Justice is the foundation of the Universal Empire, of which, then, the tree serves as symbol. To make fast to it the wain-pole of the Car of the Church and leave Beatrice sitting upon the root of the tree, thus gloriously renewed, is simply a poetic rendering of Dante's great leading idea, so often referred to, of the political subordination of Church to State. As to the colours in line 60, it is significant that violet hangings are used by the Church in Holy Week in sign of mourning. Rose, as we have often seen, is the emblem of Love, a virtue more intense than Justice. 'More than violet', on the other hand, may refer to the Imperial Purple.

64] The tale with which Hermes lulled Argus.

83] Matilda.

85-8] Theology left to guard the Church, surrounded by the Seven Virtues.

101] The selection of Rome here (instead perhaps of Jerusalem) as type of the *Civitas Dei*, is an indication of medieval veneration for the City called Eternal. Its empty name was a ruling power.

1-105] So far the Canto is one of the most beautiful. The following historical allegory, much less charming because of its subject than that of Canto xxix, may be read as an example of the sort of poetry (if we allow it that name) which made a strangely powerful appeal to medieval taste. This penultimate Canto of the Cantica is the longest in the whole Poem; the penultimate

Canto of the *Inferno* is shorter by only three lines.

109 to end] Allegorical view of the history of the Church.

113] The Roman Eagle.

118] Heresy.

124-9] Donation of Constantine, *Inferno* xix. 115-17.

130-5] The schism between Greek and Roman Church, or perhaps Islamism.

136 ff.] Corrupting gifts.

142 ff.] Corrupt relations of Papacy and French Monarchy. The scourging of the whore may refer to the outrage upon the person of Pope Boniface (Canto xx. 85-90). Dante perhaps here personifies in himself the enemies of Philip the Fair.

157 ff.] Removal of Papal See to Avignon. The strange animal must be the Car bestialized by the heads, representing the mortal sins.

CANTO XXXIII

1] Beginning of seventy-ninth Psalm (Vulgate, seventy-eighth).

10 ff.] Gospel of John xvi. 16. Allegorically, the restoration of the Church.

15] The Lady Matilda; the sage Statius.

29] Dante addresses her with the ceremonial 'You', as if she were a great personage. Cf. l. 92.

34 ff.] So the ardent prayer of Canto vi shall be answered; the Hound of *Inferno* i shall come. The DXV, whatever be the date foretold, may be an anagram for DUX, leader, or it may be the emblem of Christ.

36] This is a famous *crux*. The frank old commentator, Buti, remarks: 'I know not where Dante dug this up.' Others seemed to have devised the explanation commonly given, for which there is no known basis. Torraca finds that *suppe*, which he thinks Dante wrote in the form *iuppe*, meant cuirasses. This at least makes sense.

49] Dante read in his Ovid that the *Naiads* were the solvers of the riddle of the Sphynx. The correct reading is now known to be *Laiades*, i.e. Son of Laius, or Oedipus. The editors must conserve Dante's error; the translator is equally bound to remove it. Cf. Ovid, *Met.* vii. 759 ff.

52 ff.] Do not let the fear of the mighty hinder thee from telling men that the deed of Philip the Fair is such another crime as that of the disobedience of our first parents.

57] First by the Devil, now by Philip the Fair (the giant).

61] *Paradiso* xxvi. 115 ff.

67-9] Worldly joys stain, as did the blood of Pyramus the mulberry. Vain thoughts harden round the mind as Elsa water encrusts objects immersed in it. The Elsa is a small river of Tuscany which receives, at a point near Colle di Val d'Elsa, a spring strongly charged with subcarbonate of lime and carbonic acid. For the origin of the stain of the mulberry, see note to Canto xxvii. 37-9.

77] In remembrance of the pilgrimage.

90] The Primum Mobile, most distant and swiftest of the circling spheres, communicating motion to the successive spheres enclosed by it.

91 to end] The last six Cantos of the *Purgatorio* form a tragic Symphony the loftier strains of which die away in the tremulous words of the Poet to Beatrice at line 30. Then follows a passage of didactic and hortatory Recitative changing toward the close to pure and grave Allegro. Now, from about line 91, the strain alters again, and the theme is pursued in a subdued Scherzo, handled with utmost delicacy, exhibiting unmistakable gleams of tender mirth. The Poet, about to enter the Kingdom of Heaven, is become as a little child, and as such is indulgently humoured by the two noble woman spirits. His intellect seems for a moment staggered by the shock of new impressions and his otherwise retentive memory at fault. How like a child his assertion in lines 91-3! The formal logical tone of the answer of Beatrice to this is only a playful mask, which she deftly passes over to her charming companion, who keeps up the play: 'This and other things have been told to him by me; and I am sure that the water of Lethë has not hidden them from him' (Norton's version). Whereupon Beatrice archly excuses him. The tender purpose of both is, under cover of the comic mask, to give the mighty Poet a breathing-while to steady himself in the flood of rapture sweeping over him. So the composer, instead of finishing in an operatic flourish, feels for the common chord again and finds his resting-place in 'the C Major of this life'.

103] It is noon when the sun appears to come to a halt upon the meridian which (the astronomer in the Poet is careful to add!) shifts with the point of view. Therefore, if it be noon when the lovers begin their ascension, that is a fact relative only to their starting-point, and matters little in the absolute or eternal sense (cf. *Paradiso* xxiii. 12).

115-23] Canto xxviii. 121 and following lines.

119] The historical identity of this personage, as well as all the other moot points—riddles, prophecy, symbolism, dark allusions—of the last six Cantos (matters not to be settled, hardly to be summarized in succinct glosses) are discussed at length with scholarly fairness and competence by the late Dr. Edward Moore in his *Studies in Dante*, Third Series. See note, *Purgatorio* xxviii. 40.

127] The Pilgrim of Eternity, who has already drowned in Lethë all hauntings of sin committed or of evil suffered, is now, by baptism in Eunoë, to be sealed to remembrance of the Good.

136-41] Evidently the Poet meant the three parts of the Poem to be of equal length. He has now gone slightly beyond the limit set by the incomparably terse *Inferno*.

PARADISO

CANTO I

1-12] Subject of the Poem.

13-36] The Invocation. Beginning the other *cantiche* the Muses, daughters of Memory, were invoked; here he must look not only to these but to Divinity itself for inspiration.

31] Since Daphne (the laurel) is daughter of the river-god Peneus, the bay-leaf is called Peneian.

34-6] The Poet expresses the modest hope that better poets may some time be animated by his example to treat more worthily of his great theme. Cyrrha, ancient port of Delphi, here stands by metonymy for Apollo.

37 ff.] Here the action begins. The place of starting is the Earthly Paradise at the summit of the Mount of Purgatory. The time is Wednesday of Easter week, 1300, at noon. It is now some three weeks after the vernal equinox, when the circles of the celestial Equator, the Zodiac, and the Equinoctial colure cross the circle of the Horizon—a moment when the influence of the sun, merging with that of Aries (the best constellation), is most favourable. As the sun rises to mortals through a different gate every day, the conditions cannot be exactly those of the vernal equinox, but almost all the southern hemisphere is lighted and the northern correspondingly darkened. As the Mount of Purgatory is in the centre of the southern hemisphere, it follows that the hour is nearly that of noon 'yonder', while 'here', in Italy, it is evening. At Jerusalem, the centre of our hemisphere, opposite Purgatory, it is midnight.

55] As in line 44, 'yonder' refers to the garden at the top of the Mount of Purgatory; 'in this place', to the actual world in which the Poet was writing.

64 ff.] Near the close of *Purgatorio* xxxi, the mediatory power of the eyes of Beatrice is emphasized. Here they begin to raise Dante above the things of this world. The tale of Glaucus is found in Ovid, *Met.* XIII.

70] No words can set forth the loosing of the ties that hold the soul down to earth.

73-5] The soul, as is expounded in *Purgatorio* xxv. 67-75, is breathed into man after 'the organizing of the brain has been completed in the embryo'. The allusion is to the declaration of St. Paul, 2 Corinthians xii. 2-4.

76-84] The desire for union with God causes the eternal movement of the outmost swiftest of the spheres, which is the prime motor of all the others. The Poet is already so raised and 'transhumanized' that he can hear the music of the spheres.

121-6] In the tranquil empyrean, which is lighted with the presence of the Creator, whirls the Primum Mobile '(that which first moved). See note to ll. 76-84.

127-35] The Poet here suggests an analogy between the Creator and the earthly artist who often finds his material 'repugnant to command'. Moreover, the Eternal Foresight endowed man with free will whereby he may deviate from the course along which the whole creation moves. Human nature, like fire, is endowed by the Creator with an inherent tendency, or instinct, to rise heavenward; 'Descent and fall to us is adverse'. If we resist the 'prime thrust' (*l'impeto primo*) it is because our wills make choice of some false semblance of the good.

This Canto, together with the first eighteen lines of the following, may be considered as a kind of proem to the *Paradiso*. The only action is the ascent of Dante with Beatrice through the region of fire between earth and moon. Cf. ll. 79-81; also ll. 58-63. As a whole, the Canto consists of the statement of the subject; the invocation to the God of Poesy; the description of the astrological conditions prevailing at the season when the young sun is in the Ram, and finally the succinct exposition by Beatrice of the universal force by virtue of which all natures move to their different ports across the vast sea of being. It is this force which bears the transhumanized Poet ('whether in the body or out of the body') up through air and fire and the impalpable ether.

CANTO II

1-6] This warning doubtless implies that such sublime interpretations of Nature in its real underlying meanings, ethical and symbolic, as that with which the foregoing Canto closes, and such as the Poet intends to continue in this Canto, are likely to be rocks of offence to the superficial. He wishes to spare Beatrice the mortification of wasting her words upon listless ears. She is expected to deliver to him a moral philosophy loftier than that which he has heard even from Virgil, who, indeed, has more than once referred him to Beatrice for difficult solutions.

7-9] It is significant that the Poet exhibits no hesitancy or self-distrust, as at the outset (*Inferno* ii. 31-42). Upon beginning the *Purgatorio* he especially invokes Calliope (Muse of epic poetry); here, secure in the guidance of all the Muses and of Apollo himself, turning his prow to the high seas he shakes out his sails to the steady breeze breathed forth by the Goddess of Wisdom.

10-12] This metaphor is here a terse repetition of that in the very first section of the *Banquet* (*Convivio*). As to the thought, the suggestion is probably correct that comparatively few continue the voyage of discovery. But those few may enter the true El Dorado.

16-18] The Poet's hand is stronger than that of the hero who yoked the fire-breathing bulls and ploughed the field for the sowing of the dragon-teeth.

24] Order of verbs reversed to suggest instantaneous action.

31] Heaven of the Moon.

37 ff.] Mystery of the union of the human with the Divine.

49-51] Spots in the Moon. For the legend of Cain and the thorns, cf. *Inferno* xx. 126; also *Midsummer Night's Dream*, v. i:

'This man,with lanthorn, dog, and bush of Presenteth Moonshine.'   [thorn,

52] The smile of Beatrice, illumined more and more with the radiance of the Divine, is a *leitmotif* of the *Paradiso*.

59] Dante's former opinion.

63] The correct view (scholastic reasoning).

64 to end] The astrological theory of the time was that the starry heavens, although of one substance, vary in quantity and kind, and to these differences correspond the diverse influences they are supposed to exercise on the earth and on human affairs. The same principle, it is argued, must apply to the spots in the moon. These appearances proceed from causes much deeper than mere rarity and density. The spots, then, are no mere fortuitous or meaningless physical phenomena, but rather signet-marks of creative intellect, and therefore full of significance, could one decipher the hieroglyphics.

70-8] Albertus Magnus (Albert of Cologne), whom we shall meet later as master of the master, held this curious theory of rare and dense. But from the belief in starry influences (inflowings), which nobody thought of controverting, it seems to follow that we must look for fundamental forms (principles). The comparisons are intended to simplify the inference that, if the dark spots were not rare all the way through, then the rare and dense matter would be stratified, like fat and lean in a body, or lying one upon another like the leaves of a book.

94] The Experiment (the modern method).

112] Within the still Empyrean circles the swift Primum Mobile, communicating motion and Divine influences to the heaven of the fixed stars, and so down, through the successive interior and less swiftly whirling spheres, to earth at the centre.

115] Fixed stars.

124 ff.] The foregoing process of reasoning must appear to the modern mind quaint, and the experiment is certainly too crude to lead to any accurate result. It is, however, notable that there should be any experiment. It exhibits a properly directed curiosity and a method certainly unusual among the schoolmen. What then is the truth, if any, that is to enable the seeker 'to keep the ford alone' in the swirling stream of things? Evidently it is that one must look beneath and behind natural phenomena, for what was then called 'the form', which Plato had named 'the idea'. Beatrice is trying to encourage Dante not to be obstructed by 'unconcerning things, matters of fact', —of supposed fact.

'One Spirit's plastic stress
Sweeps through the dull dense world, compel-
ling there
All new successions to the forms they wear.'
(Shelley's *Adonais*, xliii.)

127] Celestial intelligences.

147] This metaphysical principle has baffled many readers, beginning with Dante's own son Pietro, who frankly records his want of comprehension. Its profound significance has been best set forth by George Santayana in his noteworthy essay on our Poet.

CANTO III

2] That the supreme intellect of the age should have accepted such reasoning as the foregoing, is interesting proof of the state of knowledge then, and of the danger of proceeding upon a false theory.

7-18] Marvellous vision: Dante mistakes spirits for reflected images. The lovely apparitions, glimmering like pearls on a white brow, are so dim as to seem but shadows, causing the Poet to fall into error contrary to that of Narcissus.

24] The smile of Beatrice, growing in radiance from sphere to sphere, a recurring theme treated with many beautiful variations.

41 and 58-65] 'Thy' is the singular; 'your', 'ye', the plural, referring to the whole company of spirits. This distinction, far more obvious in the Latin tongues than in ours, is observed throughout this translation; together with the use of the plural forms (you, your) to personages who should be addressed with especial formality.

49] Piccarda Donati (see *Purgatorio* xxiv, near the beginning; also the prediction of the fate of Corso Donati in same Canto).

57] Remiss in execution of vows.

65] Degrees of beatitude.

85] *E 'n la sua voluntate è nostra pace:* 'and in His Will is our peace'. The very nature of our tongue renders impossible anything like a literal translation of this noble line in verse, either as to meaning or as to music. To break the line, as does Longfellow, is to make this solemn truth appear a mere *obiter dictum*. The words 'will' and 'peace' are but two brief, terse syllables better suited to the word of command than to song; whereas the Italian equivalents, in filling out the measure, satisfy both ear and mind. Any reader willing to take the little pains required to know the sounds of the Italian vowels, may perceive the majestic swell of *voluntate* culminating like a great wave in the middle of the line, and having as neighbours mere ancillary vocables over which the voice glides without rest or stress; until at last this mighty force, without display of violence, gently rolls upon our human shore with the whisper *Pace*. As to meaning, one may ask wherein consists our beatitude if not in bringing desire into harmony with Will or Law that governs the world, with Nature, with the Will of God, however variously man may conceive Him?

97 ff.] Santa Clara of Assisi.

106 ff.] Violence done to Piccarda by Corso Donati. Piccarda's reference to her brother reminds one of that of Pia to her husband, although perhaps less tender (*Purgatorio*, close of Canto v).

119] The three blasts of Swabia are Frederick Barbarossa, Henry VI, and Frederick II. For the fate of her grandson, Manfred, see *Purgatorio* iii. She herself, being heiress to the crown of Sicily, became wife of Barbarossa's son Henry, and mother of the most illustrious monarch who ever bore the name of Frederick. During the latter's minority, Constance ruled firmly and prudently. That she had been at one time a nun was a popular tradition accepted by Dante but not by modern historical students.

CANTO IV

1-9] Sophism which passed into a proverb as that of Buridan's ass starving between two exactly equivalent 'bottles' of hay. It is in artistic keeping that a Canto dealing so largely with the dilemma of the broken vow should begin with this ancient paradox. Buridan himself is younger than Dante but the sophism is older than either.

10-24] Beatrice reads in Dante's face the two questions. The first arises from observing that Piccarda and Constance, who would have kept the vow but for violence, occupy a relatively low place among the blest. The second arises from seeing their souls apparently relegated to the sphere of the moon.

13] The dream of Nebuchadnezzar is told in the second chapter of the book of Daniel. For Dante's most elaborate use of it, cf. *Inferno* xiv. 103 ff.

27-36] The second question is the more poisonous in being contrary to the Christian doctrine that all the blest are citizens of that Rome where-of Christ is a Roman (*Purgatorio* xxxii. 102), 'fellow-citizens with the saints and of the household of God' (Ephesians ii. 19).

37 ff.] The appearances in the various spheres emblematic.

49 ff.] Beatrice goes on to show that Plato's error leads naturally to polytheism, but concedes that it deserves respectful consideration as shadowing forth the astrological doctrine (so often referred to by Dante as well as by our own classic poets) of the varying influences of the planetary spheres by whose virtue in our world 'nothing walks on aimless feet'.

64 ff.] The other doubt is the reverse of heretical, because an indication of faith. Cf. ll. 130-2.

73 ff.] Violence done to human will, due to laxity which abets. The question leads inevitably to a discussion of the freedom of the will. Cf. Milton: 'Thou canst not touch the freedom of my mind' (*Comus*, l. 663). Shakespeare touches the same note with his peculiar power:

> 'Though my gross blood be stained with this abuse,
> Immaculate and spotless is my mind;
> That was not forced; that never was inclined
> To accessary yieldings, but still pure
> Doth in her poisoned closet yet endure.'
>
> *Lucrece*, ll. 1655-9.

83 ff.] As so frequently a Christian and a pagan example: Mucius burned off his right hand for having failed in the crisis against the arch-enemy of Rome. St. Lawrence derisively begged his tormentors to turn him over and grill the other side.

97 ff.] Analysis of the assertion of Piccarda about Constance.

105] Cf. *Purgatorio* xii. 46-51. Out of piety to his father he became pitiless to his mother (Amphiaräus and Eriphylë). In connexion with the mention of Amphiaräus (*Inferno* xx. 28) there is similar word-play: 'Here piety lives on in pity dead.' In Italian, *pietà* means either piety or pity.

106 ff.] Aristotle had remarked that deeds performed through fear proceed from a mingling of the voluntary and the involuntary. There are two kinds of will, the absolute, which does not, and the conditioned which does consent to evil. St. Thomas Aquinas in the *Summa* defines the conditioned will as that which consents for the avoidance of greater evil.

115 ff.] Now the poet speaks.

122] Note the 'your'. But to a being really Divine 'thou (thy)'. Compare St. Bernard's prayer to the Virgin Mary (final Canto). So, after Beatrice has taken her place among the sainted, Dante in prayer to her reverts to the intimate form of speech appropriate to communings with the divine (*Par.* xxxi. 79-90).

130-2] 'With me, faith means perpetual unbelief
Kept quiet like the snake 'neath
Michael's foot,
Who stands calm just because he feels
it writhe.'
Browning's *Bishop Blougram*.
And from an older poet:
'You see, oft shaking of the cedar-tree
Fastens it more at root.'
Duchess of Malfi, 1. i. 270.
136] Can good deeds make amends for broken vows?

CANTO V

1-12] The light of Beatrice, an emanation of Divine Love increasingly bright as we rise toward God, beats down at first and blinds the weak eyes of flesh, to which it must in mercy be tempered; as the face of Moses, for its intolerable radiance, had to be veiled to his purblind people, when he came down the mountain after he had talked with the Most High.

13 ff.] All readers of history must have noticed how common in the Middle Ages and even later is that transaction between man and saint or divinity known as the Vow. The votary, in return for some immediate help or favour, solemnly promises some great future concession or sacrifice. Permanent foundations of churches, chapels, hospitals, convents, colleges, crosses, and other monuments were frequently the result of vows on the part of the rich and powerful. A vow of celibacy and its final nullification is the central feature of the plot of the most celebrated of Italian prose romances, Manzoni's *I Promessi Sposi* (the Betrothed). Dante's treatment of the subject is a good example of his ethical soundness.

28 ff.] The vow sacrifices the will, for which, as it is the most precious of possessions, nothing else can be substituted.

If, after the will has sacrificed itself by its own act, you revoke the gift, you by so doing become a thief who seeks to atone by making good use of ill-gotten treasure.

43] Two elements of the vow: first, the thing pledged (e. g., money, some treasured object, refraining from some indulgence); secondly, the pledge or covenant itself, involving the renouncement of self-will.

57] Cf. *Purgatorio* ix. 117.

67 ff.] Cases of Jephthah and Agamemnon. For the case of Jephthah, see Judges xi. 29 to end. The tale of the noble Iphigenia echoes through all our poetry from Euripides to Goethe and Tennyson; but Dante seems to have known it chiefly from Tully's *Offices* (Cicero, *De Off.*, III.

xxv). It is interesting to note the agreement of Dante and Cicero that such a vow would be 'more honoured in the breach than the observance'.

86-7] That happy age could still look beyond the remotest stars to a quickening fountain of life!

91 ff.] Slipping into the Heaven of Mercury. This image of the bowshot to indicate the rapid smooth flight to the prime star is here repeated with an unforgettable addition. Cf. Canto ii. 23-30.

97-9] The joy of Beatrice brightens the sphere on her arrival; if the star suffers a laughing change, how much more the mercurial nature of man and poet!

105] Torraca sees here an allusion to Dante's mission in writing his Divine Poem: to increase man's love for the Supreme Good, 'our love' being the love of others for us. As they are perfect beings, our love for them will be the measure of our love of perfection. Cf. *Purgatorio* xxxi. 22 (note on frequent use of this *objective genitive*).

110] The Reader thus addressed is one of those invited, at the beginning of Canto ii, to follow in the wake of the singing keel. Some there are who would have suffered a more painful dearth through the loss of the sequent Cantos (had the Poet really broken off here) than through the loss of all the ephemeral literature for the printing of which our forests are being converted into paper.

115] Dante is accosted by a spirit.

124] The Poet does speak.

139] This mode of introducing the next Canto is unique in the Poem, as the Canto thus introduced is itself unique in being from beginning to end the speech of one person.

CANTO VI

The soul of Justinian the lawgiver is made the mouthpiece of a philosophy of history. The Eagle, which had followed Aeneas from Troy to Italy, is made by Constantine to wheel eastward again to Byzantium not far from the mountains of the Troad (Ida), its original haunt.

10 ff.] Conversion and work of Justinian. With line 10, cf. *Purgatorio* v. 88: 'Io fui di Montefeltro; io son Buonconte', and the humility of the soul of him who had been Pope Adrian V (close of *Purgatorio* xix). The little brief authority, in which they here were dressed, counts for nothing over there.

12] Through the codification of the laws made under his direction, 'the public reason of the Romans' (as Gibbon says) has been transfused into the institutions of the modern world.

13-21] Theodora, wife of Justinian, over whom

her ascendency was all but complete, was an ardent adherent of the Monophysite wing of the Christian communion, while he (at least during her lifetime) appears to have been orthodox. She shared the throne with him and, although religion was then literally a *burning* question, their harmony was unbroken. Brunetto Latini makes the statement about Justinian's conversion to orthodoxy, and his *Trésor* is presumably Dante's authority here.

31 ff.] Victorious flight of the Roman Eagle from the time of Aeneas on. The story is recounted for the purpose of the practical application made toward the close of the Canto. The Ghibellines, who make the public ensign a party badge, the Guelfs who set against it the *fleur de lis* of France, are both condemned.

36] The heroic death of young Prince Pallas ('owing nothing now to any of the gods') is told in the *Aeneid* (see Bk. X. and beginning of Bk. XI). As to the following fifty lines, it would be pedantic and therefore impertinent to stuff these notes with a hundred glosses historic, biographic, geographic, mythologic.

73] Augustus.

81] With the shutting in of Janus, we may pause for breath; indeed this is the great pause of history:

'No war or battle's sound
Was heard the world around;…
And kings sate still with awful eye
As if they surely knew their sovran Lord was by.'

It is instructive to compare this poetical survey of Roman history with that made by Virgil in his description of the shield of Aeneas (*Aeneid*, VIII, last 106 lines). Virgil's survey is scenic, processional, stately like a triumph; selecting a small number of scenes, he dwells upon each in turn. Dante, on the other hand, darts across the landscape of history like a meteor; no sooner is the eye caught by a scene than another and another swim into ken. The adjectives are factual rather than ornamental: the Nile is 'torrid'; Cleopatra is taken by 'sudden and black death'; the Poet is well aware that the nouns and verbs are descriptive enough to those who know; others will not be helped to see by any number of adjectives and figures of speech.

86] Tiberius.

88-93] The Eagle executes Divine Justice for man's sin, and does vengeance on the Jews.

94-6] When and how, during the two centuries between the death of Justinian and the conquest of the Lombard kingdom by Charlemagne, the Empire was transferred to the west again is not explained. In fact there was no such west-ward course of empire; the successors of Justinian still ruled at Byzantium, and the Byzantine Empire was yet to continue for centuries. But the coronation of Charlemagne at the end of the ninth century by the Pope of Rome powerfully impressed all western Europeans, and that impression, deepened by the downfall of the exarchate, the abandonment of Italy by the eastern garrisons, and other circumstances, led willing minds to yield to the colossal delusion of the Holy Roman Empire.

97-111] Application of the lesson to Dante's time (cf. ll. 29-33). This condemnation of both parties is the more solemn as coming from the mouth of a blessed spirit who on earth had been (as was rightly or wrongly thought) the greatest lawgiver since Moses. In this survey, as in that more personal and impassioned one in *Purgatorio* vi, Dante appears, in his own dimensions like himself, a *national* poet.

106] Charles II of the Angevin dynasty in Naples and Apulia: 'young' (*novello*) to distinguish him from his father. He was much older than Dante, who frequently mentions him, never very favourably.

113] 'That last infirmity of noble mind'.

127 to end] The four daughters of this great Count of Provence are Margaret, married to Louis IX of France (St. Louis); Eleanor to Henry III of England; Sancha to Richard of Cornwall, 'King of the Romans'; Beatrice to Charles of Anjou, founder of the French Kingdom of Naples. Through this marriage of Beatrice, Provence came to be united to France (cf. *Purgatorio* xx. 61).

This pathetic legend of Romeo, minister of Count Berenger of Provence, affords the poetic relief that Dante is in the habit of giving after his intenser moods and loftier flights. In the tale there is admixture of truth and fiction; those who care most for historical accuracy may consult Toynbee; here we are concerned chiefly with poetic and human values. No sympathetic reader can help thinking of the exiled and wandering Poet under the figure or parable of the disgraced official. 'Through almost all regions where this language is spoken have I gone a pilgrim, almost a beggar, displaying against my will the injury of Fortune, for which the injured one is many times unjustly held to blame' (*Banquet* or *Convivio*, I. 3). The last three lines are on the part of the proudest of poets a touching appeal for sympathetic comprehension,—so much more desirable than fame, and alas! perhaps even rarer.

CANTO VII

The terse and noble treatment of the familiar theme calls for but brief annotation. It can hardly be said that Milton's more diffuse handling of the scholastic argument in Paradise Lost *is any improvement upon this 'reasoning august'.*

14] He reverences the very syllables of her name.

19 ff.] With a reassuring smile Beatrice states the tremendous dilemma which his tongue could not utter, and then proceeds to solve the apparent antinomy. Cf. Canto vi. 88/93.

25 ff.] It is all very well to find some of the theological implications of the doctrine of original sin repugnant to our sense of justice, and to cry with Omar:

'O Thou who man of baser earth didst make
And even with Paradise devise the snake;'

but the fact remains that we do find the earth whereof we are made growing baser because of hereditary taint resultant upon ancestral false choices. Modern science perceives human society to be an infected tissue: few individuals quite normal and sane; crime a pathological symptom; legal and moral remedies merely palliative. Is there any human cure in sight? Perhaps, after all, some wholesome truth may lurk in the legend of the forbidden tree and the free choice from which springs infinite woe calling for infinite redemption!

32] 'For God so loved the world.'

41] The just penalty.

55/7] Why did not God let man ransom himself?

67 ff.] That which distils from God is permanent, free and in the Divine likeness.

76/8] These coigns of vantage are freedom, life eternal, likeness to the Maker. By the fall man lost his freedom and Divine likeness, thus becoming subject to death.

97 ff.] Why human atonement might not suffice.

103 ff.] Necessity of the Incarnation. Line 105 simply anticipates, the two ways being justice and mercy.

121 ff.] The rest is a descent to reasoning more scholastic and somewhat less august. The elements, animals, plants, being indirectly created, are transitory and corruptible. Man, even as to his body, being a direct creation of the Divine hand, is immortal. Hence the resurrection of the 'spiritual body' which was given to our first parents (cf. St. Paul, 1 Cor. xv).

133 ff.] The elements not distilled directly from the Divine, but through the secondary influences of the stars.

143/6] 'Your', as always, is plural (referring here to mankind); while 'thou' is used in addressing the individual (here the man Dante).

CANTO VIII

3] The old astronomers, contriving 'to save appearances', were obliged to assume that the planets move in epicycles, which themselves are carried from east to west with the (supposed) general motion of the spheres around the earth. Milton, living in an age when the Copernican theory was about to be confirmed by Newton, suggests that God is moved to 'laughter at their quaint opinions wide' (*Paradise Lost,* viii. 75 ff.)

11/12] 'The planet fair that is love's comforter' (*Purgatorio* i. 19) is personified as coquetting with the sun, now in front as Phosphor or Lucifer (morning star), and now close behind as Hesperus (evening star).

15] Evidence of the ascent.

22/3] According to the meteorology of Aristotle, winds are caused by cold and, when ignited, become lightning or meteors. Cf. *Purg.* v. 37/9.

34/7] The celestial Princes are the angelic order usually called Principalities. The courteous spirit quotes the first line of a canzone of Dante apostrophizing the intelligences controlling the third sphere in which we are. The poem was presumably the great literary novelty (as Grandgent remarks) at the time when the young prince and the young Poet became friends.

44] The critical reader may note the polite *you* here, while *thou* and *thy* appear in ll. 85/91. The discrepancy is singular, I believe, both in the text and in my translation.

58 ff.] Charles Martel, heir presumptive to many kingdoms: Provence, east of the Rhone (*Purgatorio* xx. 61); Ausonia (Italy), south of the Tronto and the Verde (Garigliano), i.e., the kingdom of Naples (or Apulia), and Hungary; while, as he was son of Charles II of Anjou and son/in/law of Kaiser Rudolph, Trinacria (Sicily) would have been governed by his heirs but for the misrule of his grandfather culminating in the Sicilian Vespers.

67/70] Here we see the whole east coast of Sicily and the Gulf of Catania overhung by the fumes of the colossal volcano. The prevailing wind over that sea is the stormy rain/bringing *scirocco*. The fable of the giant writhing under the mountain must of course be condemned by a soul in Heaven. Seldom has so much geography, history, mythology been packed into a few lines as in this passage!

73 ff.] The Sicilian Vespers (A.D. 1282).

76/84] Robert, younger brother of Charles Martel, had been detained in Aragon for a number of years as a hostage. In 1295 (year of death of Charles Martel) Robert returned to Naples with a following of needy and greedy Catalonian fortune-hunters who, being installed in lucrative posts, proceeded to the same extortions as those which had provoked the revolt of 1282, known as the Sicilian Vespers. On the death of the father in 1309, this Robert was to usurp the throne despite the hereditary right of Charles Robert, son of the present speaker (see beginning of next Canto). In line 147 this brother, Robert, is again referred to: his hobby was preaching and 289 titles are extant of sermons by him. The father, Charles II of Naples (and titular king of Jerusalem), is referred to as generous: what Dante really thought of him is seen in Canto xix. 127-129, and in *Purgatorio* vii. 124-9, where, in a curiously cautious round-about fashion the first Charles of Anjou, grandfather of Charles Martel, is rated as at worst better than his son and heir. See especially *Purgatorio* xx. 79-84. It is true that in all these passages Dante is speaking through the mouth of his characters; but here, of course, Charles Martel is made to speak of his father as a son should speak.

93] How can a bad son descend from a good father?

94 ff.] Arguing in the manner of a professor at Paris or Bologna.

112-20] Uniformity of son with father would make social life impossible. The abstract argument is greatly lightened by this little dialogue, as between master and student.

124-6] One a lawgiver, one a king, one a priest, another an inventor (Daedalus).

131] Quirinus, the name of Romulus considered as a divinity.

138] The corollary: an application of the lesson.

147] Cf. the long note to lines 76-84. For Dante's preoccupation with the question of degeneracy in good families see especially *Purg.* xiv, and *Par.* xvi.

CANTO IX

1-6] Both the wife of Charles Martel and his daughter bore the name of Clemence. It is a matter of conjecture as to which is here apostrophized. The younger Clemence became queen of France in Dante's time; the mother seems to have died before 1300, or about that time. The form of expression surely points to the mother! The son, Charles Robert, was deprived of the throne of Naples by an usurping uncle Robert.

13] Cunizza da Romano.

25-8] The country between the mountains whence those rivers descend and the lagoons of Venice is for poetical purposes the March of Treviso. The hill of Romano is not far from Asolo, which readers of Browning will remember.

The Piava (Piavë) River is familiar as the line where the Italians in the Great War turned defeat to victory.

29] This firebrand is the notorious Ezzelino da Romano who enjoys the bad eminence of having been the worst of Italian tyrants—no small distinction! Dante's son Peter in his Latin commentary tells the story of the dream of the mother that she was about to bring forth a firebrand which should lay waste the March of Treviso. Frederick the Second, with politic cruelty, sacrificed a daughter to this Minotaur. Symonds devotes an edifying chapter to him in his *Age of the Despots*. In Browning's 'Sordello' he figures as Ecelin; his very name is torn to tatters—Azzolino, Eccelino, Icilinus, &c. He does appear to have been loyal to the great Hohenstaufen through thick and thin. Adopting the marking system applied by Dante to another, we may, to be just to him, rate his virtue at I and the *per contra* at M (cf. *Paradiso* xix. 127-9). His sister must have been a charming creature not without a certain engaging frailty.

32-6] Remorse for sin disappears in Lethë (*Purgatorio* xxi). Cunizza contemplates without regret the influence of the genial planet which had shaped her destiny.

37 ff.] Folco (or Folquet) of Marseilles, first troubadour then monk then bishop. It is difficult to share Dante's warm admiration for this personage. Certainly the prophecy of his fame was a rash one!

43-60] There is so much local geography and provincial chronicle here that the allusions become rather too complicated for clear summary elucidation. First it is prophesied that Paduan blood shall stain the pool formed by the Bacchiglionë near Vicenza (victory of Can Grande in 1314). Secondly that Richard of Camino, lord of Treviso (son of the good Gerard of *Purgatorio* xvi), shall be assassinated (1312). Thirdly that the treacherous bishop of Feltre shall give up to the governor of Ferrara some refugees to be decapitated—an act which renders this obliging priest the agent of their murder (1314). There was a papal prison called Malta in the Lake of Bolsena. Cunizza, herself a native of that land, adds that such gifts (surrender of political refugees) match the custom of the country. Finally she excuses her apparent bitterness by explaining that she beholds these judgements divine in angelic mirrors, called in human speech 'thrones'.

71] 'What is laughter if not a coruscation of the joy of the soul?'—*Convivio*, III. 8.

73 ff.] Dante prays the soul of Folco to reply to his unspoken question.

82-93] 'The greatest valley into which the water

flows from the ocean enwreathing earth runs from west to east the whole distance between meridian and horizon (i.e. an arc of ninety degrees of earth's surface). On the coast of that valley I dwelt between the Ebro and the Magra whose short course divides Genoa from Tuscany. Bougie sees the sun rise and set at the same time as my town whose blood once warmed its port.' The answer to this geographical historical astronomical puzzle is: Marseilles. Dante's notion of geography seems in many respects to be no great advance upon that of Strabo. The ocean surrounds the habitable part of the globe—which is all in the northern hemisphere. The valley forming the bed of the Great Middle Sea spreads west to east one fourth the distance round the globe (an enormous exaggeration!). Marseilles is only very slightly east of north from Bougie, which was then the most important seaport of northwest Africa. Reckoning upon the meridian, as apparently Dante here did, Marseilles is almost exactly half-way between the mouth of the Magra (ten degrees east of Greenwich) and that of Ebro. When Caesar 'struck at Marseilles' (*Purgatorio* xviii. 102) the blood, according to Lucan's *Pharsalia* iii. 572-7, reddened the sea-foam. The passage is a notable example of the poetry of the map. 97-102] The examples, being all of tragic love, suggest that Folco's passion may have had unhappy consequences. Dido and Phyllis of Rhodope took their own lives; the passion of Hercules for Iolë brought about his own death, that of Dejanira and that of Lichas. But when Folco's locks began to grey he became a monk and later an episcopal persecutor of the Waldenses.

103 ff.] He can speak truly and serenely of his time of sin (*Purgatorio* xxxi).

116 ff.] For Rahab the harlot see Joshua ii, vi. 17-25, also Hebrews xi. 30-1; James ii. 25. From Matthew i. 5, we learn that she was an ancestress of Jesus the Christ. Theological allegory found in her 'line of scarlet thread in the window' the prophetic symbol of His blood shed for the remission of sin. The word 'palm' (l. 122) means of course *token;* the reference in the next line is to the lifting of the hands in prayer of which the uplifted hands of Christ on the Cross are a symbol.

118] Here ends the shadow cast by earth, its length being estimated by Ptolemy as 871,000 miles. Allegorical significance was doubtless attached to this supposed fact. Souls in the spheres of the moon, Mercury and Venus are obviously persons whose behaviour here below was at times somewhat incorrect.

130] The golden florin with the stamp of the lily.

133 to end] The study of ecclesiastical law is more profitable for the ambitious and the avaricious than that of pure theology.

139-42] Another unfulfilled prophecy.

CANTO X

In the preceding cantos we have passed through the spheres of the Moon, of Mercury, and of Venus, all of which are more or less subject at times to the influence of the overshadowing cone of darkness projected from the Earth (Canto ix. 118-19). Here we emerge beyond the reach of such an occasional moral cloud into the splendour of the sphere of the Sun. In the first twenty-seven lines of this canto the Poet seems deliberately to mark the transition by a succinct consideration of the art of the Creator shown in the deviation of the Ecliptic from the Equator.

1-3] The three lines of this first tercet (terzina) refer to the three Persons of the Trinity. It is believed that Dante was moved to his choice of the *terza rima* for the *Poema Sacro* by the mystic connotations of the number three and its multiples.

8-21] The intersection of the Equator and the Ecliptic (cf. Canto i. 37-9) which occurs at the vernal equinox when the sun is in Aries. The 'oblique circle' whereby the road of the sun and planets deviates from the equator, thus producing alternation of seasons, appeared even more admirable in that age when the habitable part of earth was supposed to be only the north temperate zone. There are some similar observations, less directly and clearly expressed, in *Paradise Lost,* Book x, lines 668 ff.

28] The sun to which Dante had imperceptibly arisen.

31] Referring to ll. 8-9 where attention is called to the junction of the path of the sun and the plane of the Equator at the vernal Equinox. It is well to remember that our ideal pilgrimage takes place at the very season of the Canterbury pilgrimage, when

> 'the yonge sonne
> Hath in the Ram his halfe cours yronne.'

32-3] The apparent track of the sun at this season is a spiral one, the line coming a little farther northward every day, as any observer of the point of its emergence morning after morning can easily perceive.

37-40] Oxford text would read: 'O Beatrice, leading so suddenly from good to better that her act extends not in time, what must her own brightness have been.'

40-60] In these lines, what exhilaration, what rapture of spirit! One thinks, perhaps, of certain lines of Wordsworth, who never, however, achieves such release. Passing insensibly from the sphere of Venus, where the apex of earth's shadow still somehow clouds the moral sky, we enter a region of effulgent splendour wherein circle rainbow-like the souls of those great thinkers who have come nearest to true vision of things divine. First, at the suggestion of Beatrice, the poet soul springs aloft on wings of prayer to such altitude that even she is for a moment 'in eclipse forgot'. But such concentration comes and goes ere one can say, 'it lightens'; and the next moment attention is scattered among the new objects soliciting the eye.

67] The garland of the souls is like the halo around the moon, when the air, pregnant with moisture, retains the thread whereof is woven the rainbow tissue of her girdle.

79] Dancing the successive stanzas of the ballata.

83] Speaks the great Dominican theologian, Thomas Aquinas, Doctor Angelicus.

96] Note this line; cf. l. 114.

98] Albertus Magnus, Doctor Universalis.

104] Gratian, whose text-book of Canon Law helped both the ecclesiastical and the civil court.

106] Peter Lombard.

109] Solomon.

114] The reader will save time by taking mental note of this line and 96, for they will be discussed later.

115] Dionysius.

118] Orosius.

125] Boethius.

128] Church of the Golden Ceiling, at Pavia.

131] St. Isidore of Seville; the Venerable Bede; Richard of St. Victor, the Great Contemplator.

133-8] Dramatic interest is aroused and the harmony of Heaven illustrated when it is understood that St. Thomas Aquinas had publicly controverted opinions of Siger, who was one of the most daring of thinkers. He is said to have questioned the freedom of the will, the immortality of the soul, and even the existence of God. Cited before the Roman Curia for heresy, he was stabbed to death at Orvieto by a fanatical cleric. An alternative translation of *invidiosi veri* is 'truths which brought him envy' (Toynbee). But cf. *inveggiar*, Canto xii. 142.

136-8] Siger of Brabant, who lectured at Paris on theology. The mention of the *Vicus Straminis*, or *Rue du Fouarre* (Straw Street) in the Latin Quarter, tends to confirm the tradition that Dante studied at Paris.

140] The Bride is throughout the Poem, of course, the Church.

CANTO XI

1-12] The *Aphorisms of Hippocrates* was the great text-book for medical students; at Montpellier, in the full tide of the Renaissance more than two centuries after Dante, Rabelais still had to study it. It is noticeable that Dante mentions the professions of law, medicine, priesthood, diplomacy, politics, and theft all in the same context. In some old MSS. the reference to the priesthood is erased! In *Convivio* III. 11, he had said: 'He should not be called a true philosopher who is friend of wisdom merely for practical purposes (*per utilità*), as are lawyers, physicians, and almost all the professors of religion (*li religiosi*) who study not to know but to gain money or advancement.' *Acquistar moneta o dignità:* words that have the snap of a whip!

16] St. Thomas Aquinas, Doctor Angelicus.

25-6] Canto x. 96, 114.

26] Oxford text reads: *nacque:* has been born.

37-9] Francis is likened to 'the rapt seraph that adores and burns'; Dominic, preoccupied with doctrine, is 'a splendour of cherubic light'. St. Thomas Aquinas (who, it should be remembered, is the speaker) in his *Summa* defines *Seraphim* as by derivation signifying 'ardour of love' and *Cherubim* as so named for their knowledge.

43 ff.] Assisi lies out on the mountainside facing westward towards Perugia, whose old southeast Sungate (Porta Solë) lets in the reflected glare of summer heat and winter snow from Monte Subasio, a spur of Apennine rising behind Assisi to a height of more than four thousand feet. Between this mountain and the Roman Apennines to the east in the narrow valley lie shadowed Gualdo and Nocera washed by the Topino. This little river, whose course resembles that of upper Arno, flows southward until, escaping from the mountains and curving in a sharp elbow round Monte Subasio, it shapes its course northwestward to join the Tiber, but not until it has received the Chiascio flowing down from the hills about Gubbio, on one of which was the hermitage of St. Ubald. To those familiar with that district the Poet presents a picture. The map of Italy contains the materials of poetry in 'God's plenty'.

52-4] Assisi, supposed to be derived from 'Ascesi' (I rose); there is also allusion to Zacharias vi. 12 (*Vulgate*): 'Behold a man the Orient is his name' (Ecce vir Oriens nomen ejus).

58 ff.] He loved the Lady Poverty, but the father opposed the match.

64] The Lady's first husband was Christ.

68] Caesar, in a crisis of his struggle with Pompey, being in need of a boat, knocks at night at the wretched hut of the poor fisherman, Amyclas, who was not in the least startled. Dante found the anecdote in the *Pharsalia* of Lucan (v. 515/31), and dwells upon it in the *Convivio*, IV. 13: 'The empty/handed traveller would sing in the very presence of robbers'—as indeed Francis is reported to have done.

70/2] This parable of the marriage with Lady Poverty, the central idea of Francis as it is the culminating point of the Canto, has been handled by modern textual critics and commentators with defective sympathy. The Italian *Testo Critico* of 1921 reads 'pianse in su la croce' (wept upon the cross). It is true that some of the best and oldest manuscripts so read, but equally true that the best early commentators read *salse* (mounted). Passing over weighty considerations in favour of what Dr. Edward Moore terms the bolder, and therefore more probable, metaphor, 'mounted', I have to call attention to the very words of the saint himself—words strangely overlooked by commentators—upon which Dante obviously bases the noble line: 'During thy passion she alone did not forsake Thee. Mary thy mother stopped at the foot of the cross, but Poverty mounted it with Thee and clasped Thee...' The whole wonderful prayer is given in the fine article, 'Francis of Assisi', in the *Encyclopaedia Britannica* (Eleventh Edition; in the later edition the prayer is omitted). The reader of that article will, indeed, find these notes hardly necessary.

93] Sealed by the Church.

96] Not merely thus related, but sung by the Seraphic choirs.

98] Sealed by the Holy Spirit.

106/8] Sealed with the stigmata of the Crucified God. The seat of the order, founded by Francis on the rocky crest of La Verna, is a lovely place to which men of every faith can make devout pilgrimage.

118] Judge of the worth of my master Dominic, worthy colleague of such a saint.

124] Degenerate Dominican friars.

138/9] The qualifier is the subjoined clause, which has now been explained as promised. The line is repeated from x. 96.

CANTO XII

1/30] Rising from the mood of depression incident to the conclusion of the preceding Canto, our Poet here soars up into 'the high reason of his fancies with his garlands and singing/robes about him'.

15] When Love had sun/dried all the moisture of her body, Echo was mercifully transformed to a cliff about which her voice for ever wanders.

19] The great Doctors of the Divine forming a double halo of circling and singing flames.

29] The incidental reference to the magnetic needle gives proof that the mariner's compass was familiar to Italians of the thirteenth century.

31] Speaks the Franciscan Doctor Seraphicus, St. Bonaventura, in praise of Dominic.

35 ff.] The military imagery of these lines is certainly more in harmony with the character and methods of Dominic than with those of his far more Christ/like contemporary, Francis. But Dante deemed the deplorable corruption of the clergy to spring from laxity of doctrine; the Church required the support of the stern measures of Dominic. Although the latter seems a less poetic figure than Francis, it is significant that the Poet has lavished a greater wealth of fancy upon this Canto than upon its pendant. Here, as there, the reading of a brief sketch of the life of the hero may exempt the reader from being too frequently 'edified by the margent'.

53] Royal arms of Castile.

71/5] No other word is permitted to rime with the name of Christ. Cf. the identical rime in xiv. 104; xix. 104; xxxii. 83. The first counsel was, 'sell that thou hast and give to the poor'. Matthew xix. 21.

83] Authorities in medicine and canon law (the Decretals). Cf. opening passage of Canto xi.

90] Boniface the Eighth.

106 ff.] The two wheels of the Chariot of the Church (cf. *Purgatorio* xxix. 107). In the corresponding passage of the eulogy of Francis, St. Thomas uses the familiar symbol of Peter's bark.

114] A violent shift of metaphor! Dante, like Shakespeare, often defies the rules of the rhetoricians. From the rim of the wheel to the hoop of the cask, then from the container to the contents —the wine with its mould instead of the preservative beeswing.

115/27] Line 117 has been found 'very puzzling'. Yet the reader has only to imagine a man swinging his foot round to go back on his tracks. To one who follows the Poet's swiftly changing fancies the picture is vivid indeed. For the image of the tares and the good wheat in the following terzina, cf. Matthew xiii. 30.

124/6] Ubertino of Casale, leader of the 'spiritual' faction of the Franciscans, was so impracticably severe in interpreting the rule that he was finally driven from the order. Matthew of Acquasparta, cardinal bishop, general of the order, and confidential agent of Boniface VIII, went to the other extreme. He was papal legate at Florence at the very time when the office of prior was held by Dante, who had good reason to suspect the crafty churchman to be no very de/

voted lover of the Lady Poverty. The sting of the allusion lies in the implication that the cardinal evaded the rule for personal profit.

129] In his administration of the Franciscan Order and as bishop, he subordinated the temporal to the spiritual; with allusion to Proverbs iii. 16: 'in her left hand riches and honour'.

130 ff.] The other lights of the outer wreath of saints. For these names cf. Toynbee's *Concise Dictionary*.

CANTO XIII

1-24] There are some who can never read this vast period (perhaps the longest in the Poem) without an upleap of heart. The mighty sweep of the twelve opening lines is in harmony with that of the northern heaven as visible to us on a clear calm night; the relative diffuseness is true to the impression made by those unsounded interspaces between the solemn stars.

10] The Horn is the constellation of the Little Bear, the small end of the horn or trumpet being the pole-star. In Chapter XX of *Don Quixote*, Sancho refers to '*la boca de la Bocina*', 'the mouth of the buccina'; and Lope de Vega mentions '*el carro y la bocina*', 'the Wain and the Horn'.

13-18] The seven stars of the Dipper (Charles's Wain), the two at the mouth of that Horn which begins at the North Star, and fifteen stars of first magnitude are to be fancied as forming two concentric clusters, like the Crown of Ariadne, whirling together.

24] See note about the Chiana, *Inferno* xxix.

34 ff.] St. Thomas Aquinas now explains his attribution of highest wisdom to Solomon (x. 114).

37-48] Adam and Christ, both direct creations of the Divine, must have been superior in wisdom to Solomon. The words cited at end of l. 48 of the English version repeat the 'non surse il secondo' of Canto x. 114.

52 ff.] 'A religious hymn breathing the sense of mystery that surrounds the Divine' (Torraca).

67-72] Whatever is produced by the 'plastic stress' of the moving heavens is compared to wax, and the comparison, developed into a continued metaphor, does duty as an argument. Everyone who respected himself then had his signet; no document was valid without the seal; no amount of wit could rail the seal from off the bond. The peculiar relation of signet and wax lent the resultant metaphor such various significance that its frequent use in poetry became inevitable. In Shakespeare as in Dante it is common, though never commonplace.

73-8] As the creative idea, the seal, is handed down from sphere to sphere, it finds the wax less perfectly tempered to receive the impression, while the secondary creative powers (vaguely termed Nature) are like the skilful craftsman who cannot quite control the tremor of his hands. Natural products are all, it seems, subject to some flaw. Cf. the latter part of Canto viii.

91 ff.] St. Thomas now 'distinguishes'. Cf. the beautiful story of the dream of Solomon at Gibeon, 1 Kings iii.

97-102] The four highest branches of knowledge, as taught at the University, were theology, logic, metaphysic, geometry. As examples of what Solomon might have asked, one problem is cited from each one of these sciences. The second question involves the logical problem whether in the syllogism a necessary premiss coupled with a contingent one can ever result in a necessary conclusion. Any such syllogism conceals a quibble.

103 ff.] Solomon asked and got practical wisdom for his trade of king.

106] Cf. l. 48 and note.

116-17] Here, as in l. 109 and in Canto xi. 27, Dante uses the words *distinction, distinguish* as technical terms of logic. The premisses must be sharply scrutinized before proceeding to any inference.

121-3] Here St. Thomas, possibly feeling that he has already been somewhat discursive, does not succeed in saying quite all that he means. Obviously, an unskilful fisherman may return as he went—that is empty-handed. Does not Fitz-Gerald's Omar tell us that such was the case with his quest for the truth when he did eagerly frequent doctor and saint? But what our present saint has in mind is the converse danger of getting one's net encumbered with monsters of the speculative deep, such as the sharks of heresy.

124-31] Of the three Greek philosophers Aristotle had spoken with severity; the doctrines of the two Christian theologians had been condemned by councils of the Church: that seemed to Dante sufficient basis for using them as examples. It would be wrong in us, who live in an age enlightened by historical criticism, to treat the Poet as he treats these celebrated thinkers, else we might with some justice accuse him of the very fault he is condemning.

CANTO XIV

1-87] The voice of Thomas had come from the rim; that of Beatrice flows back from the centre.

18] Torraca insists that 'visible' is here used in the sense of 'capable of seeing', to which Grandgent adds the explanation 'with bodily eyes'. But does that interpretation harmonize with the context? These 'sightless substances' (as Shakespeare might have called them) are made manifest to the bodily eye of the Poet only by the brilliant light that flowers out of them. This and the voice are the 'accidents' of their 'substance'. The subconscious question that Beatrice perceives lurking in Dante's mind relates to the mystery of the assumption of the glorified body after the resurrection: how can bodily vision subsist unimpaired in the midst of such vivid splendour? It is a doubt attesting childlike faith. Whatever the reader's attitude towards such faith, it need not deprive him of the imaginative flexibility and reverence requisite to the enjoyment of the glorious burst of poetry to which the question leads. It may be well to note here that, with the exception of the shadowy faces in the Heaven of the Moon and perhaps of those in Mercury which come swimming like fish in pellucid water, Dante sees no bodily figures in Heaven until after his eyelids have drunk of the River of Light (Canto xxx. 88). Thereafter bodies are made visible to him such as all the blest are at last to receive. The glorified body may be conceived as the visible symbol of the eternalized human individual.

28-30] The chiastic structure, symbolic of the Cross, pregnantly expresses the great mysteries of the triune God and the double nature of Christ.

34 ff.] The light that speaks so modestly, in tones perhaps like those of the Seraph in making to Mary the tender annunciation, is that of the royal sage, Solomon. Cf. *Purgatorio* x. 34 ff. and *Paradiso* x. 109 ff.

61-6] In their supreme glory, so unimaginable that all this imagery of splendour is felt to come short, they still yearn for those features that stamp and identify the individual, linking him, amid the flux of things, to the humble and toilsome past, and this not so much for themselves as for those whom they loved:

> 'So mayst thou watch me where I weep,
> As, unto vaster motions bound,
> The circuits of thine orbit round
> A higher height, a deeper deep.'

67] Here begins the transition into the higher sphere of Mars: at first the vision appears uncertain as when the straining eye catches and loses and catches again the first faint glimmering stars in the fading daylight. Then comes the sudden unmistakable sparkling from which his dazzled eyes take refuge in the unspeakable love radiated from the smile of Beatrice.

79] The smile of Beatrice always marks the rise into a higher sphere.

86] The ruddy Heaven of Mars.

97 ff.] Imagine the 'Milky Way' in the form of a cross.

104] For the rime, cf. Canto xii. 71, 73, 75.

112-17] The image of the Galaxy forming a cross is of sublime still splendour; the image of the motes dancing in the isolated sunbeam shot through a darkened chamber simply adds the notion of movement, and prepares the mind for the return to the starry splendour after the music pauses at the beginning of the next Canto.

122 ff.] Hymn of the Warrior-Saints.

130] Because the eyes of Beatrice reflect the divine (cf. *Purgatorio* xxxi, the closing strain).

136-7] In plain prose, as translated by Norton: 'May excuse me for that whereof I accuse myself in order to excuse myself, and may see that I speak truth'. In ll. 79-81 is described the smile of Beatrice at the moment of leaving the sphere of the sun. But in this new world the vision of the starry cross and the rapture of the heavenly hymn transcend in charm any previous experience; and not yet since arriving here has he turned to look into her eyes. The two lines of verbal legerdemain are certainly in strong contrast with the noble simplicity which rules this great Canto—they even set it off! Many commentators will have it that 'the living seals of every beauty' are the spheres, apparently failing to perceive that what the Poet is celebrating is the supreme loveliness of Beatrice; and what gives the quickening seal to beauty, if not the eye?

CANTO XV

1-12] We learned in *Purgatorio* xviii, in the course of that philosophic conversation during the second night on the Mountain, that we are left perfectly free to direct our love either to the fashion of this world, which passeth away, or to the things that are abiding. It is the corner-stone of ethics. Those heavenly substances here give him example of benignant love by silencing the rapturous chords that had entranced him. Overwhelmed by the thought that this was done to facilitate his will to pray to them, the Poet exclaims that he well deserves his fate who, for love of perishable goods, robs himself of a love so considerate of our weakness:

> 'And is there care in Heaven? And is there love
> In heavenly spirits to these creatures base,
> That may compassion of their evils move?'

13 ff.] The light of Dante's greatest ancestor slips down the shaft of the mystic cross like a 'shooting star'.

28-30] Cacciaguida begins speaking in Latin,

then the universal tongue of Church, law, di‑plomacy, education. The greeting *sanguis meus* (kinsman mine) is taken from the *Aeneid,* vi. 835, where it is addressed to Julius Caesar by the ancestor of the Julian *gens.* Cf. also the meeting of Aeneas and Anchises, *Aeneid,* vi. 679 ff. Ob‑viously, the question implies no exclusion of the case of St. Paul. Cf. *Inferno* ii. 13‑33.

34] Here is the Poet's vindication from the in‑dictment brought against himself at the close of the last Canto.

50 ff.] The Great Book in which he reads, the Mirror in which they gaze, are images of the Divine Mind.

73‑82] The Divine Being is called the Prime Equality because having wisdom, power and love in equipoise. The blest are so imbued with His light (intelligence) and heat (love) that to do is as easy as to know what 'twere good to do; thought and action are convertible. Dante here humbly urges his moral inadequacy to the form of action called for—that is, discourse with a being in whom performance duly follows on desire. Shakespeare has often given classic expres‑sion to our human disparity of will and deed.

> 'The flighty purpose never is o'ertook
> Unless the deed go with it.'

91‑6] So Dante comes honestly by that beset‑ting sin of pride to which he confessed in the conversation with Sapía (*Purgatorio* xiii. 133‑8) He did not meet his great‑grandfather on that weary first cornice of the Mountain where pride is purged away. To have introduced his ancestor there would have rendered the present passage less artistically effective.

109‑10] Hills from which travellers from the north got the first view, respectively, of Rome and of Florence.

112‑17] Great citizens in their day (cf. *Inferno* xvi. 37, and next Canto).

120] Before Dante's time members of the great guilds were trafficking farther afield than France: in Bruges, London, Constantinople. The mer‑chant or traveller who ventured so far seldom returned in the same year, if ever.

127‑8] A woman of doubtful reputation, and a man whom Dante detested.

133 ff.] Tireless research has disclosed little more of Dante's ancestry than can be inferred from these lines. For the invocation of Mary in child‑birth, cf. *Purgatorio* xx. 19‑24.

142 ff.] Second Crusade, preached by St. Ber‑nard (1147); heroic death in such a cause was accounted martyrdom.

CANTO XVI

10 ff.] Dante addresses his ancestor as if he were royal ('you' instead of 'thou'). This use of the plural pronoun to a single person was then erro‑neously supposed to have been introduced in servile respect to Julius Caesar. But even at this day the people of Rome 'least persevere' in this usage. The smile of Beatrice at our Poet's beset‑ting sin of pride, reminds him of the warning cough of the lady‑in‑waiting when Guenevere first betrayed her passion for Lancelot. For the *you, your,* instead of *thou (thy),* cf. *Purgatorio* xxxi. 36; xxxiii. 92. Several other instances will be recalled by the reader of these notes.

25] Modern Florence is the city of the Baptist as the ancient was the city of Mars.

37] $580 \times 687 +$ (the number of our days re‑quired for the revolution of the planet Mars) gives about 1091 as the birth‑year of Cacciaguida.

46‑8] The city lay between the Church of St. John and the Ponte Vecchio with the mutilated statue of Mars. Populations were small in those days. Villani says that in 1300 Florence had 'more than 30,000 citizens capable of bearing arms'. London, in Shakespeare's time, three cen‑turies later, had perhaps as many. If, however, we counted only those 'on fame's eternal bead‑roll worthy to be filed', the census to‑day might seem less congested.

49 ff.] Dante was as far as possible from being a 'booster' of a 'greater Florence'. He was so medieval as not to confuse greatness with bigness; nor did the movement from the farm to the city seem to him a wholesome social symptom. The reader will not look to this place for a local gazetteer. Longfellow fills thirteen pages with interesting notes to this Canto; it would be easy to fill many more. Dante's contemporary, the historian Villani, confirms and illustrates many of the Poet's allusions.

58 ff.] That is to say, if the clergy had kept hands off. The Papal Curia had promoted the Guelf league against the Empire. Semifontë, a fief of the Empire, had been so effectually destroyed that its very name has perished from the coun‑tryside (a strange, unusual occurrence!). The destruction of the feudal strongholds, leaving the peasantry unprotected, caused a rush to the city.

88 ff.] For biographical information and anec‑dote Toynbee's *Dictionary* is the obvious reper‑tory. The reader will find profit in looking up Bellincion Berti and his daughter, the good Gual‑drada (*Inferno* xvi. 37). The historical student soon perceives that the viewpoint in these Cantos is very much that of an old Tory. The new fam‑

ilies, like the Cerchi, were often useful citizens. And the institution of the guilds is nowhere here referred to, although economically, politically, socially, even intellectually, of primary importance and immeasurable influence.

97-9] The Counts Guidi (cf. l. 64) descended through the good Gualdrada from Bellincionë (or Bellincion) Berti, of the ancient Ravignani family.

105] The great family who 'blush for the bushel' has been already alluded to but not named. *Purgatorio* xii. 105.

112-14] Two great families owed their wealth to the reversionary right to the episcopal revenues between the death of a bishop and the appointment of a successor.

115-17] The Adimari, one of whom had possession of Dante's property after his exile, here get a stab where they would feel it most.

124-126] The marvel is that even a minor gate to the old city should have been named for a family so obscure as the della Pera, from whom had arisen the opulent new house of the Peruzzi, hardly second to the Bardi among the bankers and merchants of that age. The veracious chronicler, Giovanni Villani, qualifies his statement with a 'some say', perhaps hesitating to remind these *nouveaux riches* of their humble origin. Dante certainly had no such hesitation. Had he lived a little longer he might have seen in the decline of the fortune of the Peruzzi a striking instance in harmony with the tenor of this canto. The repudiation by English Edward III, in 1339, of his enormous debt to the Bardi and the Peruzzi brought about the fall of their great houses, which had branches in all the financial centres of Europe and the Levant. This was, according to Davidsohn, the most serious financial crash of the Middle Ages.

127-32] Hugh of Brandenburg, Imperial Vicar about the year 1000, ennobled certain families, from one of which came Giano della Bella, the stalwart tribune of the people, whose scutcheon was that of the great baron with the addition of a border of gold.

136 ff.] The Amidei, whose murder of young Buondelmonte for slighting their alliance is the traditional origin of the factions of Guelf and Ghibelline.

152 ff.] The old banner showed a white lily in a red field; the Guelfs reversed the colours. This Canto may remind the reader of Homer's catalogue of ships. Probably nowhere in any literature has so much history and tradition and sentiment and satire been packed into so little room.

CANTO XVII

1-27] It is the unfortunate result of Apollo's indulgence of Phaëton that is supposed to make fathers chary to children. Phaëton, proud of divine origin, having heard that the god was not in fact his father, put the question to his mother, Clymenë. Similarly Dante, having heard heavy tidings about himself from Farinata (*Inferno* x), Ser Brunetto (*Inferno* xv), Vanni Fucci (*Inferno* xxiv), Conrad Malaspina (*Purgatorio* viii), Oderisi (*Purgatorio* xi), now questions his great forebear who can see in God things contingent: those that, while future to us, are all present in eternity. There the future is as certain as the plainest mathematical proposition.

37 ff.] A stock argument of the Christian schoolmen. While the events of Dante's life are foreseen, his will is left free.

'If I foreknew,
Foreknowledge had no influence on their fault,
Which had no less proved certain unforeknown.'
Paradise Lost, III. 117.

46-54] As the innocent Hippolytus was driven out of Athens by the false witness of a perfidious accuser, even so must Dante depart from Florence; indeed the plot is already schemed at Rome (apparently in April, 1300, before the priorate of Dante) and will soon be carried out by him who presides over the exchange where every day Christ is bought and sold (Boniface VIII, cf. the whole of *Inferno* xix). The vengeance may be indeterminate or it may refer to the outrage at Anagni (*Purgatorio* xx. 85 ff.).

61-9] We know only that Dante after his exile at the beginning of 1302 was a man of light and leading among the *fuorusciti* (outs), that their attempts to gain access to Florence by force were vain, and that he separated himself from the Whites. As to details reports are somewhat conflicting and conjectures more so.

70 ff.] The *gran Lombardo,* to whose courtesy the exiled Poet first turned for refuge, is an elder brother of the famous Can Grande della Scala, who is separately referred to and eulogized. The word Scala (ladder) made the ladder their obvious punning device, and as imperial vicars they placed the eagle above the ladder on their crest. Dante was received at Verona by the Scaligers (ladder-bearers) during the minority of Can Grande. who succeeded to the lordship in 1312, at the age of twenty-one. The deception by the Gascon Pope Clement V of Henry VII was at the time of that Emperor's coming to Italy in 1311. After the death of Henry in 1313, Dante hoped in Can Grande as a regenerator of Italy. He is probably the Hound of *Inferno* i. 101 ff. The best illustration of these lines is found in Rossetti's noble poem, 'Dante in Verona'.

101⁄2] Images from the textile industries, on which the prosperity of Florence was based, are not very common. Cf. Canto iii. 95⁄6; *Purga⁄torio* xxxi. 96; *Inferno* xvii. 16⁄18.

106 ff.] 'Whosoever in writing a modern history shall follow Truth too near the heels, it may haply strike out his teeth.' Dante understands this at least as well as Sir Walter Raleigh. But Dante feels still more the truth stated by Emerson with Dantean brevity: 'He who writes for him⁄self writes for an eternal audience.' His boldness in affixing the brand to the powerful of his time is hardly equalled in the history of poetry or prophecy. And though the instances he gives are far from being for us modern ones, yet the withers of men now living are not unwrung where he strikes the probe.

129] Dante's forebear, speaking with the forth⁄right plainness of a simpler age, seems to teach by example that in moral diagnosis all squea⁄mishness is out of place. To resent the occasional 'low' images of a lofty poet would be as foolish as to resent the studied harshness of phrasing that sometimes varies symphonic harmony. Cf. Canto xvi. 33.

136 to end] Our Poet's fine dramatic instinct leads him to bring in all his personages in an apparently casual manner; here, however, he declares a distinct purpose in their selection. Some commentators endeavour to draw a distinction between those who are shown to him by Virgil or Beatrice and those others who are merely re⁄cognized by himself; but most of both these classes exemplify the melancholy reflections on the vanity of fame set down in *Purgatorio* xi. 91⁄117. For example, how shadowy has grown the figure of that Folco (Folquet or Fulk) of Mar⁄seilles whose immortality is so confidently pre⁄dicted (*Paradiso* ix. 40)! If Sordello is somewhat better remembered it is not because he was on earth distinguished, 'col nome che più dura e più onora' (*Purgatorio* xxi. 85); Folco was a poet too. It was Dante who set Browning on the track of Sordello, and it is to Dante that all but a few of the historical personages of the Poem owe the rescue of their names from oblivion. The eulogy of Can Grande della Scala, to whom the *Paradiso* was dedicated, is embedded in the very middle of this central Canto. This is thought to be a de⁄liberate feature in the architecture of the Poem.

CANTO XVIII

1⁄18] The soul of Dante's ancestor is called a blest mirror as being a reflector of the Divine Wisdom, while the eyes of Beatrice are reflec⁄tors of the Divine Love. Here we should recall the sublime allegory set forth in *Purgatorio* xxxi. 121⁄6. Looking into her eyes his troubled thought is to give place to the peace which passeth all understanding.

28⁄30] The heavenly spheres are compared, col⁄lectively, to a tree in every way contrasting with trees on earth, in that it 'lives from the top', that it bears fruit always, and does not shed its leaves. Cf. Revelation xxii. 2.

43⁄8] These personages, known to our Poet through semi⁄legendary history, and as heroes of the romances of chivalry, were either defenders of the Christian world against the Saracen, or Crusaders. Robert Guiscard was more or less directly an ally of the greatest of the popes (Gre⁄gory VII) in his epochal conflict with the Empire.

55] The smile of Beatrice marking ascent to the Heaven of Jupiter.

64 ff.] The transition from the rubeate glory of Mars to the silvered tones of Jove is as soft and silent as the paling of the blush on a fair cheek.

82 ff.] 'Diva Pegaseä', nymph of the spring which burst from the mountain of Helicon at touch of the hoof of the flying horse: hence, 'di⁄vine (or heavenly) Muse'. The precise identity of the Muse is left to the reader's fancy. Urania, who represents the knowledge of the heavens, would perhaps be the most inspiring of the 'sacrosante vergini', whom the Poet invokes at his most need. Compare especially the noble invocation in *Purgatorio* xxix. 37⁄42.

91 ff.] 'Love Justice, you that are judges of the earth': first words of the book of Wisdom, for which see the Catholic Bible, or *Vulgate*.

97⁄129] One must picture to the mind the me⁄dieval capital M resembling the outline of the human face, as observed in *Purgatorio* xxiii. 33, where the M is also a rime⁄word. This with slight calligraphic variation becomes the *fleur de lis* of France (or the heraldic lily of Florence), from the medial summit of which buds forth the head of the Eagle. The M symbolizes the *Monar⁄chia* whereof Dante discoursed and dreamed; the union of this with the lily and the crowning of the whole with the emblem of Rome signifies the subordination of France to the Universal Em⁄pire—this not, of course, as an accomplished fact but as an ideal consummation. The Poet, with the freedom of prophecy, leaps forward from the period to which the vision is assigned, as indeed he is supposed to have done at the close of *Pur⁄gatorio* xxxii. The pope referred to here is probably not Boniface but John XXII, who from his seat at Avignon excommunicated Can Grande in 1317, withholding for political ends the sacra⁄

mental bread which 'the pitying Father grudges none'. The Florentine scholar, Parodi, points out that this interpretation explains the transition at the end to invective and irony. Here, and at the close of the next Canto, the Poet proceeds to vigorous practice of the precepts uttered by his great ancestor at the close of Canto xvii.

130 to end] The florin, with the lily on one side and the image of the Baptist on the other, prompts this avaricious pope to neglect Peter and Paul. The allusion here is the same as that in *Inferno* xix. 112 ff. The pope is so devoted to the Baptist as to worship him in hundreds of his images. It is curious to note that in Canto ix. 130 the florin is referred to with the same sad irony, there designated by the figure stamped on the reverse as here by that on the obverse.

CANTO XIX

The tremendous denunciation of several of the monarchs of the time is a signal instance of that buffeting of the summits for which the Poet is commended by his great ancestor in the concluding lines of Canto xvii. Only the supreme authority of the Empire can set right a world thus out of joint. This idea—a favourite one with Dante—is systematically developed in the De Monarchia. *In the Second Book of that work, chapters II and VIII, is a formal statement of the theological doctrine of this canto.*

1 ff.] Only a cold and superficial glance can fail to catch the majestic beauty of this symbol of living justice based on love, speaking with the voice of many souls at one together, and exhaling the blended fragrance that lingers in human remembrance of noble achievement.

22-4] 'Only the actions of the just
    Smell sweet and blossom in their dust.'

25-33] Dante prays that his great fast be broken, aware that the Eagle sees not as through a glass darkly, although the hierarchy called 'Thrones' are the special mirrors of Divine thought (cf. Canto ix. 61).

34] The image of the falcon, delighted at the removal of the hood, was most effective at a time when hawking was universally the fashionable sport.

40] The image of the compasses may be suggested by Proverbs viii. 27. Milton expands the image (*Paradise Lost,* vii. 224 ff.).

46-51] If the most perfect of created beings was unable to apprehend the Infinite Good, how scant a container of it is poor human nature! This, granting the premises, is most cogent.

52-7] The reading of these lines varies, as does the interpretation. The simplest and most natural rendering is that here followed. Passerini explains the word 'principio' in line 56 (meaning beginning, source, origin) as follows: 'The source of your sight (or vision)... is God, whose mind discerns far beyond that which is manifest to the perception of mortals.' Others make the word 'origin' the object of the verb. Thus Norton translates: 'Therefore our vision... cannot in its own nature be so potent as not to discern its origin far beyond that which is apparent to it.' That is, the divine source of our vision lies beyond the scope of our vision.

70-8] The problem: How can the virtuous heathen be condemned? In the following Canto Dante will open a very wide way for their salvation. The baptism here referred to is merely that of John, not that of the spirit.

90] The argument culminating here should be compared with that of St. Paul in Romans ix. It is perhaps introduced as a basis for what follows. Effective vindication of Divine Justice is found in the assurance that baptized potentates, whose deeds differ in no respect from those of pagan kings, are held to strict account.

101-2] The heraldic sign of the Eagle. Cf. the beginning of Canto vi.

103 ff.] The stormy voice again strikes the highest peaks (note the rime on the sacred name).

120] Philip the Fair, thrown from his horse, which had been crazed by the bristly wild boar darting between his legs.

127] Charles II of Naples, to whose crown is attached the title of Jerusalem. The moving pen of the Recorder will leave his account badly unbalanced.

130 ff.] Frederick, King of Sicily, whose misdeeds will crowd the page. His brother is James of Aragon. Cf. the story of Manfred, *Purgatorio* iii. Their uncle was James of Minorca. James and Frederick, sons of Manfred's Constance, are mentioned slightingly in *Purgatorio* vii. 119.

135] The translator here appropriates, with slight change, a magnificent line from Marlowe—such a line as Dante would have written had he written in English.

141] The Venetian ducat and the florin were the standard coins everywhere. Counterfeiting them was a form of repudiation which the integrity of needy rulers was often unable to resist. Cf. the story of Master Adam, *Inferno* xxx. 70-90.

144] The speaker foresees that the mountain-rampart is soon to prove of no avail, since the Queen of Navarre has become the consort of Philip the Fair of France.

145 ff.] Henry of Lusignan, a beastly little king, who keeps pace with the 'great powers' in evil-doing.

CANTO XX

This Canto seems intended to qualify and temper the harshness of the solution given to those 'obstinate questionings' of ll. 70-8 of the foregoing Canto. The lines celebrating the six just princes—David, Trajan, Hezekiah, Constantine, William the Good, Rhipeus—are ranged in symmetry as formal as that of the statues in the Sainte Chapelle.

10 ff.] If we could hear the emerging stars of evening sing vespers, as once those of morning sang matins, we might realize this sublime appeal to the Poet's eye and ear.

19 ff.] The voices of the Just, blending in the neck of the Eagle, issue like the sound of falling water, or of musical notes. Perhaps these lines suggested to Byron the noble comparison,

'the voices of the dead
Sound like a distant torrent's fall.'

37] David. Cf. 2 Samuel vi; *Purgatorio* x.

37-72] With these twelve tercets in elaborate parallel construction may be compared, for the form, the thirteen in *Purgatorio* xii (25-63).

43-45] Trajan. *Purgatorio* x. 73 ff.

49-54] The fullest account of the answer to the prayer of Hezekiah is that in Isaiah xxxviii, with which cf. 2 Kings xx. 1-7 and 2 Chronicles xxxii. 24-6.

55-60] Constantine. *Inferno* xix. 115; *Paradiso* vi. 1. The supposed Donation of Constantine, the consequences of which were thought by Dante to have been so disastrous, was long afterwards proved to be, as Bryce puts it, 'the most stupendous of medieval forgeries'.

61 ff.] William the Good of Sicily and Apulia (1154-1189), whose reign seems to have given Sicily the happiest and most peaceful score of years in the entire history of an island which has endured more (and far longer) misgovernment than even Ireland. Here was a king whom Dante could wholly praise, as he could not St. Louis.

68] Rhipeus the Trojan (*Aeneid*, II. 426).

104-5] One of the passages that defy literal translation: 'firm in faith, he (Rhipeus) in the feet that were to suffer and he (Trajan) in the feet that had suffered'.

106-17] St. Gregory made effectual fervent prayer for Trajan, who returned to this life long enough to repent and be redeemed. The legend was accepted by St. Thomas Aquinas and presumably by the Catholic world.

118-120] The image recalls that of *Purgatorio* viii. 68:

'Him... who doth so hide
His own first wherefore that it has no ford.'

The primal wave—first fountain-head whence issue the waters of grace—is at the bottom of a spring unfathomed by the most piercing eye.

128 ff.] Cf. *Purgatorio* xxix. 121-9. The orthodox Poet, who had appeared to close the door of grace to the unbaptized heathen, here by a large interpretation of the rite of baptism opens that door so wide that we wonder at the exclusion of such a soul as Virgil. Old Benvenuto da Imola aptly points out that this passage is a pendant to lines 106-14 in the preceding Canto. The obscurity of Rhipeus, whom we know only from two lines of Virgil, gave full scope to the Poet's imagination. The Eagle rewards him for the abnegation of his mere human sense of justice by revealing to him that two of the most glorious of all these souls had received baptism through faith and hope and love.

CANTO XXI

4 ff.] Ascending to the Heaven of Saturn, Beatrice withholds her smile. Bound by an oath, Jove reluctantly appeared in full glory to his beloved Semelë, who was consumed by the splendour. Cf. Exodus xxxiii. 18 ff., 'Man shall not see me and live.'

12] Aristotle, the scientific authority whose views were current for so many ages, held that thunder, rather than lightning, is the destructive agent. Hence the references all through modern poetry to the thunder-bolt, thunder-stone, and the blasting effect of thunder.

13-15] While Dante's eyes and mind have been intent upon the face of Beatrice in expectance of the wonted smile, he has been borne into the sphere of the contemplative planet, which seems really to have been then in the Sign of Leo. Thus the chilling influence, attributed by astrology to the rays of Saturn, is tempered.

28 ff.] Corresponding to the cross in Mars (symbol of crusading knighthood) and to the eagle in Jupiter (symbol of imperial justice), here in the contemplative planet is the golden ladder by using which man becomes taller than his reach. Bright spirits come flocking down like those Jacob saw in his dream in the desert of Luz. The comparison of these to such plain corvine birds as daws (or rooks) is an example of that plainness of speech, 'understanded of the people', referred to in the *Epistle to Can Grande* as suitable to comedy.

52] Dante humbly asks two questions of the spirit.

61] The eyes of Dante could not bear the smile; his muddy vesture of decay is impervious to the music.

67-78] The spirit has fully answered the second

of Dante's questions. To the other he only replies that he has come through love, not indeed greater love than that which informs the others, but because so allotted by the high love that makes all eager to serve Supreme Wisdom. But the Poet craves to know more than this—to know why among so many this particular spirit has been selected: a question that probes, and probes in vain, for the hidden roots of human experience. Infinite must be the wisdom of the historian who could lay bare the springs of those apparently casual contacts that, once made, appear inevitable, as they certainly are inalterable.

91 ff.] Cf. Canto xix. 52-7, and note.

106-26] He who makes the pleasant journey from Gubbio to Fano has before his eyes for a while a little to the right of his road the great arch or 'hump' of Monte Catria on which, in a lovely echo-haunted nook beneath the mountain brow, lies the venerable Benedictine monastery ('hermitage') of Santa Croce di Fonte Avellana. There in the eleventh century (1041) Peter Damian became abbot. He tells us that, in the house of Our Lady on the shore of the Adriatic, he had humbly gone by the name of Peter the Sinner. He was so useful and outstanding a supporter of Hildebrand (afterwards Gregory VII) that he was forced, against his will, to accept an appointment as cardinal-bishop ('the hat that shifts from bad to worse'). There is a persistent tradition that Dante tarried awhile during his exile in this lonely place of contemplation, where his spirit seems still more than elsewhere to hover.

127-35] In these lines, especially in the last one, is the most concentrated expression of the contrast between the primitive follower of Jesus and the modern false shepherd to be found anywhere even in the DIVINE COMEDY. For one of these whom Dante may have had in mind, though their name was legion, see the note to *Paradiso* xii. 124. The *Ottimo Commento,* by one who lays claim to personal acquaintance with the Poet, remarks: 'This lesson is clear; everybody has seen it. A beast is the rider because, issuing from the rule of his order, he is like the beast governed by appetite instead of reason; and a beast is the palfrey, and both are covered with a single cardinal cloak.' Cf. also the comments of Benvenuto da Imola (who lectured at Bologna on the comedy of Dante in the fourteenth century), cited by Longfellow and by Vernon.

CANTO XXII

7] Stricken with bewilderment, the Poet is reassured by Beatrice.

31] Speaks St. Benedict.

37 ff.] The Monastery of Monte Cassino, one of the most venerable monuments of Christendom.

49] There were two saints in Egypt named Macarius, both of whom were disciples of St. Anthony and both died near the end of the fourth century. St. Macarius of Alexandria stood in much the same relation to monasticism in the Orient as did St. Benedict in the West. St. Romuald reformed the Benedictine Order five centuries after its foundation, and in 1012 founded the monastery of Camaldoli in the mountains of the Casentino not far from La Verna (*Paradiso* xi. 106). For their beauty as well as for their sacred associations these spots, as well as Monte Cassino, are still visited.

52] Dante's prayer to Benedict.

68] The heavenly ladder, whereby contemplation may climb beyond eyeshot. Cf. Canto xxi. 29-30.

73 ff.] The 'dread voice' again.

78] The women of the people (*mulierculae*), in whose language the Poet says he composes his comedy, will not be slow to understand what he means by comparing the contents of the monks' cowls to maggoty flour. (Cf. *Epistle to Can Grande,* Sec. 10.)

88] Acts iii. 6; *Inferno* xix. 94-5.

100 ff.] Ascent to the Heaven of the Stars.

109] The translation misses here a vivid touch: 'Thou wouldst not have been so quick to draw out and put thy finger in the fire'; the thing happens so quickly that the touch and go appear simultaneous—in fact the finger is *out* before it is well *in*. A like effect is aimed at in the striking inversion in *Paradiso* ii. 24.

112 ff.] Dante invokes his natal constellation, the Eternal Twins, in which the sun was rising and setting when first he drew the breath of life. This passage fixes the season of his birth. We know that the year was 1265; in that year the sun was in Gemini from May 18 to June 17. So much can positive science derive from the lines. Interesting as is the fact, it has very little to do with the exhilaration communciated to the spirit by the noble invocation.

133 ff.] Survey of the solar system.

139 ff.] The Poet, assuming that the reader is by this time familiar with the deities identified with the planets, enumerates them by allusion to their parents—all save Jove, whose complexion was supposed to be tempered by the counter-influences of cold Saturn and hot Mars.

140] That other side of the moon 'Unseen of herdsman, huntsman, steersman, blank to Zoroaster on his terrace'—and without the spots discussed in Canto ii.

153] The whole spread of the land from the mountains to the mouths of the rivers. The foregoing passage perhaps suggested the description of Satan's view of the universe in *Paradise Lost*, III. 555-61. If so, Milton's lines afford an instructive example of the manner in which a poet's imagination may be kindled at another's fire.

CANTO XXIII

Now, far away from all the planetary circles, in the Eighth Heaven among the mysterious stars, we are granted a symbolic preliminary glimpse of Christ soaring swiftly to highest heaven with all the fruit harvested from the whirlings of all these spheres. No wonder the enlarged spirit of the Poet breaks loose from conscient self! His sweet guide, however, recalls him, bidding him look again upon her smile to which the forgotten vision has tempered his eyes. The splendid succession of images marks a division of the theme, an unbridged chasm which the Sacred Poem must leap. What can this be but the wide transition from the world of matter to the world of pure effluence? Here again, as at the outstart, the Poet warns back the unprepared voyager. The high song concludes with the lyric homage of the winged Sapphire to the divine Mother.

10] Beatrice expectant.

19 ff.] The pilgrim of eternity here receives a handsel of that fullness of spiritual vision which is to be. The passage may have been suggested by Luke xv. 7. The imagery of this Canto is peculiarly lovely nor are there any jarring chords of wrath or scorn such as blare out in almost all the preceding Cantos, especially towards the conclusion of each.

26] Trivia is one of the synonyms for Luna or Diana that Dante found in the *Aeneid*. Other synonyms are Delia, Phoebe, daughter of Latona, one of the twin eyes of Heaven.

40-2] According to medieval physics, following the teachings of Aristotle, lightning is ignited vapour generated in the upper region of the air. When surrounded by a heavy cloud of watery vapour this igneous vapour is so constricted that it seeks the easiest way of escape. If this path of least resistance chances to be the under side of the cloud, the lightning breaks through with the sound of thunder and, contrary to its aspiring fire-nature, darts to earth. Aristotle 'compares this to the way in which a nut, or the stone of a fruit, when squeezed between the fingers will, in spite of its weight, shoot upwards' (Moore, *Studies*, I. 130). For this violent image of the fiery vapour bursting the cloud, cf. close of *Inferno* xxiv. This theory seems to involve some notion of the expansive force of gases.

46 ff.] Dante's eyes given virtue to see the smile of Beatrice.

67] Cf. beginning of Canto ii.

73-5] The Rose is the Virgin Mary; the lilies are the white-robed host of the triumph of Christ, who make manifest the fragrance of his knowledge (2 Corinthians, ii. 14).

85] The Sun of Heaven shows just so much light as the mortal eye can bear.

94] The splendour and music of Gabriel.

99] See note to ll. 40-2.

112] Probably the ninth sphere, 'that first moved' (Primum Mobile). We are looking up from the sphere of the stars to the under side (*interna riva*) of that swiftest wheeling sphere whose function it is to convert Divine creative energy into the various motions of the universe, shedding down secondary influences upon the lives and fates of men.

121-6] They had received 'the kingdom of God as a little child'.

130-5] Those who have been faithful husbandmen in the Vineyard of the Lord during the life on earth, which is compared to the Babylonian exile, have now become coffers or chests of spiritual treasure. The image is perhaps suggested by the Scriptural *Vas electionis* (vessel of election or chosen recipient of grace) of Acts ix. 15. Cf. also *Inferno* ii. 28.

136 ff.] Here St. Peter is introduced at the very end of the Canto, linking it up with the next. Striking examples of this method of leading up to something of special importance are the conclusion of *Paradiso* v, of *Inferno* xxxii, and of *Paradiso* xxxii.

CANTO XXIV

1-9] Beatrice prays for Dante.

13] Cf. the comparison at end of Canto x.

22] The fairest carol sweeps around Beatrice.

25] Cf. xxiii. 62. It is as impossible to put this divine music into words as to depict Paradise in the face of Beatrice. Dante well knew that no art can be expressed in terms of another: a lesson which those who attempt to 'illustrate' the Poem with the pencil have not learned.

34] The light of St. Peter.

46 ff.] Picture of an examination such as the Poet had undergone at the university.

64] Definition of faith drawn from St. Paul (Heb. xi. 1).

69] The word substance appears to be used in its medieval philosophical sense of *substrate*: the being or essence that underlies the subordinate categories which schoolmen distinguished as quantity, quality, relation, action, passion, place where, time when, posture, habit. Milton, more than three centuries later, personifies all these in his college poem, 'At a Vacation Exercise', so proving that much the same scholastic philosophy still held sway in the schools, even after the time of Francis Bacon. Faith, like substance, while itself invisible, is the proof of things unseen.

74] Faith is the substance—that which stands under and supports hope.

91] Faith based on Scripture.

100] Divine because attested by miracle.

103/5] 'This is arguing in a circle', objects the examiner.

106 ff.] The conversion of the world through the agency of a few humble men would have been more wonderful than a miracle.

126] By faith did Peter first enter the sepulchre, although John had reached it first. John xx. 1/8.

127] Dante's own belief and its grounds.

141] That it is correct to make the name of the Holy Trinity the subject either of a singular or a plural verb.

152] The light of St. Peter now encircles Dante as it had first encircled Beatrice.

CANTO XXV

The Apostle James is less obviously identified with the virtue of Hope than are Peter with Faith and John with Love. But the repeated mention of Peter and James and John together in the Gospel narrative probably influenced Dante in the choice of James for the function he here performs. This apostle, who was put to the sword by Herod, does not appear to have been clearly distinguished in Dante's time from the other James sometimes styled 'the Less'. A widespread and romantic tradition had accrued about the name of this composite saint. He became (so ran the legend) an apostle to Spain, but returned to die in Jerusalem, whence his body was miraculously wafted to the coast of Galicia in the north/west corner of Spain. To his sacred burial place a bishop was long after/wards led by a star, and for this reason the spot came to be called 'Compostela', 'the Field of the Star'. This had early become one of the three chief goals of the Christian pilgrim who, confusing the words 'Galicia' and 'Galaxy', gave to the star/sown ne/bulae now sometimes called the 'Milky Way' the name of the 'Way of St. James'. A list of Dante's frequent references to these matters will be found in Toynbee's 'Dictionary'.

1/12] These lines have been cut into the stone just outside the door of the Baptistry by the exiled Poet's repentant fellow/citizens; but they are far more indelibly engraved upon the Italian heart. Even a poet of Dante's stature (there has been but one!) would fail to do justice to them in English except under stress of conditions hard as those which extorted this lyric cry. The appro/

priateness of prefixing them to the Canto of Hope hardly requires comment.

17] Froissart also terms St. James a 'baron'. He was believed to be buried at Santiago de Com/postela, 'The Jerusalem of the West'.

28] Beatrice, smiling, addresses the light of St. James.

34] Cheering words of the Apostle to the Poet.

52 ff.] Beatrice answers for Dante as to the sec/ond question, that he might not appear to boast.

67] Definition of hope.

70 ff.] Dante first drew it from the Psalms; next from the Epistle of James.

91/6] The passages in Isaiah referred to are lxi. 7 and 10: 'Therefore shall they receive double in their land', and 'he hath clothed me with the garments of salvation: and with the robe of righteousness he hath covered me, as a bride/groom decked with a crown, and as a bride adorned with her jewels.' Dante connects the two passages and doubtless regards the 'garment of salvation' as distinct from the 'robe of justice' (righteousness), the one being attributed to the bridegroom, the other to the bride. Of course Dante's only authority for the Scripture text is the *Vulgate,* from which the inference in question would be easier than from the version of the Westminster divines. The reference in line 94 is to perhaps the best/known passage in the Apo/calypse (vii. 9/17).

100] If the Sign of Cancer had a star as bright as the light of St. John, the winter night would be abolished.

113] The pelican, supposed to feed her brood with her own blood, is an emblem of Christ in medieval art.

114] For the 'great trust' cf. the Gospel of St. John xix. 26/7.

124] Compare Dante's desire to see the glorified body of St. Benedict, Canto xxii. There was a legend, based on John xxi. 22/3, that the beloved disciple was translated bodily into Heaven.

136/9] The Poet's momentary blindness is attri/buted in the devout commentary of Madame de Choiseul to his untimely curiosity about the body of St. John. 'It is this poor curiosity that blinds him, keeping him from seeing loftier things' — namely, the glorious depth of love personified by the Apostle. (*Dante: Le Paradis d'après les Com/mentateurs,* by the Comtesse Horace de Choiseul).

CANTO XXVI

8/12] St. John assures the Poet that Beatrice will do for him what Ananias did for Paul. Acts ix. 10/18. (Not to be confused with that other Ananias referred to in *Purgatorio* xx. 112.)

PARADISO

16-18] 'That Supreme Good wherein consists the blessedness of Heaven is the beginning and the end of the writing which Love reads in a voice more or less distinct from the book of my heart.' With this it is interesting to compare the canzone which Casella, 'met in the milder shades of Purgatory', begins to sing: 'Amor che nella mente mi ragiona'. *Purgatorio* ii. 112.

28] Aristotle taught that the world is moved by the desire of all things for God.

42] 'Omne bonum', 'all good', in the *Vulgate* (Exodus xxxiii. 19).

44] The Apocalypse, or 'Revelation of St. John the Divine'.

51] The Poet has been censured for the harsh metaphor, as being out of keeping with the 'sweetness of the subject'. But the Poet, with sure taste, attributes to the Apostle such homely imagery as is everywhere found in the Gospel narratives in dealing with the things of the 'kingdom of Heaven'. These plain images are the teeth with which Dante's lines bite into the memories of men.

64-6] The image is suggested by that of the vine and the branches in the Gospel of John xv. The sense is, briefly, that Dante loves his fellow-men in proportion to their participation in the Divine nature. As he is undergoing examination he is bound to follow very closely his theological authorities. The commentators support this by the appropriate citations from St. Thomas Aquinas and others.

70 ff.] The return of the Poet's eyesight scientifically described, as science was then understood.

82] The light of the first created human soul.

97 ff.] A similar screen of radiance, through which joy palpitates, surrounds the spirit of Charles Martel (Canto viii. 52-4).

106-8] Adam sees Dante's immost desire in the mirror of the Divine Essence, wherein are perfect images of things, although no created thing is capable of reflecting an image (pareglio) of the Deity. *Pareglio* or *parelio* may also mean 'parhelion', as Longfellow renders it. The reader will recall several instances in the Poem of such readings from the 'Divine Mirror': see especially Canto xv. 49-63; also ix. 61-2.

109 ff.] What questions would you ask if face to face with him who was supposed to be not only the progenitor but the most perfect of the race? Possibly the questions of an intelligent being at the present day would not be essentially different from these: What is the antiquity of the human race? How long did man remain in the state of innocence? What was the true reason for the wrath of God? What was the first language? The question considered most important is first briefly

answered: God's wrath was due to overstepping the mark, transgressing the bound. This fault, largely interpreted, consists in failure to bring one's will into harmony with the will of God. The stars in their courses fight against him who presumes to resist the stream of tendency in what we call Nature. As to the historical question, the earth has spoken and has extended our views of the history of the race almost as sublimely as astronomy has extended our conception of the immensity of the universe. As to the language spoken by man in the old stone age, we are as ignorant as was Dante of the dialect of Adam. Finally, as to the legend of the Garden, let me quote a few words from a distinguished scientist: 'In the Garden of Eden there is a tree... not guarded at all, perfectly open; guarded by a word of command...: You must not, but you can if you choose... It is a very beautiful parable, and it is true... In it is a great instinct for religious truth.' (Greatly condensed from an article by Sir Oliver Lodge.) Cf. notes to *Paradiso* iii. 85 and vii. 25.

139 ff.] Adam states that he remained in Paradise but seven hours! This was tradition.

CANTO XXVII

10] The lights or 'torches' are the three apostles and Adam.

11-15] The light of St. Peter grows ruddy with holy indignation.

22 ff.] St. Peter denounces Pope Boniface as a usurper. The contradiction between this passage and *Purgatorio* xx. 85-90 is apparent rather than real. St. Peter is here judging Boniface *sub specie eternitatis*: in the eyes of the Son of God, Boniface is a usurper and the See of Peter is vacant. The Office itself is sacred, however unworthy the incumbent, and before the world the only recognized incumbent is Boniface. That an earthly prince should presume to constitute himself the instrument of Divine vengeance is contrary to both reason and Scripture. It is noteworthy that the great denouncer of Boniface is at the same time the adequate expresser of the horror of the Christian world for the outrage done upon the Pope at Anagni by the agents of the rapacious Philip the Fourth of France.

37 ff.] The same 'dread voice' that speaks in Milton's 'Lycidas' (109-32).

58] Clement V was a Gascon; John XXII from Cahors, which was a financial centre noted for the extortionate practices of its usurers. It does not appear that the career of John XXII did much to redeem the reputation of his native town, although before the close of his long pontificate he founded a university there. Cf. *Inferno* xi. 50.

64-6] As Cacciaguida had done (Canto xvii, final lines), so Peter commands the Poet to speak.

70] An upward fall of snow.

79-87] Dante had revolved with the Twins through ninety degrees of the 'first climate', and could now see that portion of the earth from the Eastern Mediterranean to where Ulysses voyaged the Atlantic (*Inferno* xxvi). This superbly exhil-arating passage should be read in connexion with the conclusion of Canto xxii; the note on Canto ix. 82 ff. may also be consulted. At that time the habitable part of the globe of earth was sup-posed to be confined to the strip between about twelve degrees and about fifty north latitude, bounded east and west by the river Ganges and the river Ebro (principal Spanish tributary of the Mediterranean, and poetically synonymous with Cadiz, Pillars of Hercules, &c.). This por-tion of earth was divided longitudinally into seven zones or climes, in the middle of the first (southernmost) of which is the meridian of Jeru-salem. If the sun is on the meridian of Cadiz it is setting at Jerusalem—a circumstance which explains why Dante does not quite see the Phoe-nician shore where Europa became a sweet burden for the Bull (i.e. for the god so disguised). This geographical theory more than doubles the relative length of the Mediterranean. For full discussion cf. Moore's *Studies*, III.

98] The nest of Leda by metonymy for the con-stellated twins, Castor and Pollux.

106 ff.] The crystalline heaven, 'that first moved'.

118-19] Since this invisible sphere imparts mo-tion to the bodies whose apparent daily revolu-tion gives man his unit of time, to image it as containing the roots of time is both philosophic and sublime. This remark might have appeared superfluous had not an American editor stigma-tized the metaphor of the vase as 'grotesque'!

121] The transition may seem abrupt, but Dan-te's imagination never soars so high as to lead him to forget the moral needs of his audience. To his poem Earth has set its hand as well as Heaven.

136-8] The sun is called 'father of all mortal life' (Canto xxii. 116); his daughter is the human race. The metaphor appears to suggest that the moral experience of the individual, as described in the foregoing lines, has its parallel in the life of the race, the candid innocence of whose childhood becomes blackened with the soilure of guilt. The terzina falls short of our Poet's usual lucidity and has been made the subject of much learned and ingenious comment.

142] Roughly estimated, the error in the calendar amounted to a hundredth of a day every year (the difference between 365.25 days of the mean

calendar year and 365.24 days of the supposed tropical year), so that in some thousands of years January would have been wholly 'unwintered', i.e., become a spring month. The reverse of this had happened when Julius Caesar corrected the calendar. When a still more correct calendar was finally adopted in England in 1752, the error was eleven days, in Dante's time about nine. In 1582 Gregory XIII ordered October 5 to be called October 15, and introduced the 'leap-year', &c.

148] The Poet's wayward fancy leaps suddenly back to the metaphor of lines 124-6. This shift can only be justified by the principle that the king is above the law.

CANTO XXVIII

We have now reached the outermost and swiftest of the nine moving spheres which were supposed to circle daily round Earth as a centre. This so-called Crys-talline sphere had been invented to account for the apparent 'trepidation of the equinoxes'. Some theorists imagined a tenth sphere, called Primum Mobile:

'Then pass the planets seven, and pass the fixt,
And that crystalline sphere whose balance weighs
The trepidation talk'd, and that first mov'd'.
(Paradise Lost, Book III, ll. 481-3).

But Dante identifies the Crystalline sphere with 'that which first moved' and to which, as we have seen, most important virtues and influences were attributed. It is evident that he considered this heaven as neither spatial nor material:

'And in this heaven there is no other Where than in the Mind Divine.' (Canto xxvii. 109-10.)
Combining this with his further statement that this 'inverted bowl' contains the roots of time, we are confronted with something that might be considered an anticipation of Einstein's theory of time-space. Here, too, the observer gets a lesson in relativity, for here the swiftest movement is that of the inner ring nearest to the mystic central Point, while all the others move slower as they are more distant from the centre.

Beyond this Ninth sphere and enveloping the whole system of the universe there is the mysterious Em-pyrean, home of the Divinity, containing the 'many mansions' of the blessed.

1-18] It is in the eyes of Beatrice that the Poet first catches sight of the luminous spaceless Point —mystic symbol of the Deity—just as in her eyes he had found the revelation of the double na-ture of Christ. Cf. *Purgatorio* xxxi. 118-26. The image of the mirror in both cases seems to direct attention to the correspondence of the passages. Readers who find my notes to this Canto insuf-ficient are referred to the succinct 'argument' in

Professor Grandgent's admirable edition as well as to his 'Preliminary Note' to the *Paradiso*.

22] The first circle is about as far from the luminous Point as is the halo from the star which projects it upon dense mist. The very indeterminateness of the comparison gives it truth to our experience of such phenomena. Cf. Canto x. 67-9.

25 ff.] The nine orders of Angels.

32] Though the rainbow were a complete circle. Juno's herald is Iris, identified with the rainbow. Cf. xxxiii. 118.

46 ff.] The Poet's scientific notion of space (and therefore of time) seems here upset and reversed.

56] Apparently the sensible universe reverses the pattern.

64 ff.] The larger corporeal circles are more excellent; in the world now suddenly revealed the order is reversed, so that the sphere 'that first moved' corresponds to the inner circle of Intelligences.

81] Referring to pictures of the winds on old maps (cf. Shakespeare: 'Blow winds and crack your cheeks').

91-3] The squares of the board reduplicated by arithmetical progression. In line 93 the rime word is *s'immilla*, from *mille*, thousand. Dante creates several such words which can be reproduced in our less fluid idiom only by paraphrase. The ancient story is that the inventor of the game of chess, offered by the king his choice of a reward, claimed only a grain of wheat for the first square, two for the second, and so on, doubling to the sixty-fourth. The king thought it a small request, but not all the acreage of the kingdom could furnish so much grain.

100] The 'bonds' are those of love, attracting them to nearness to God. A sublime theory of gravitation in the spiritual world!

109-11] Love flows from knowledge.

117] The constellation Aries appears in our sky at the time of the falling leaf.

130 ff.] Dionysius learned the truth from St. Paul, so that he, rather than St. Gregory, is the trustworthy authority concerning the constitution of the kingdom of Heaven—the only world that is real and eternal and that deeply matters. Can it surprise any one that the Poet, believing thus, should devote two of his hundred Cantos to the celestial Intelligences?

These lines constitute a virtual disavowal of the statement in the *Convivio*, Book II, chapter 6. There the Thrones are the first of the final triad (or third from the bottom) where here the Principalities stand. In *Par.* ix. 61, Cunizza makes a somewhat obscure reference to the Thrones, a reference in which some find a trace of Dante's earlier opinion.

CANTO XXIX

1-6] The setting sun and the rising full moon at the equinox—the one under the Ram, the other under the Scales (Libra). The image is one which anyone may test by going to a clear lookout point at the right moment and using his eyes. How long do they balance there in the invisible scales hung from the zenith?

13] Why the angels were created.

16] Outside time and space.

22 ff.] Pure form or act is identified with intelligence (angels); matter is the pure potency, passive in character; the combination of form and matter is found in created things, especially in man.

31-6] These substances at the top of creation are the angels, which are pure act or form (i.e., intelligence). This interbraiding of spirit and matter cannot be severed by death.

37 ff.] The angels, movers of the spheres, could not be conceived as inactive—therefore could not have existed without their proper theatre of action.

49] The rebellious angels fell to earth before one could count twenty.

57] Cf. *Inferno* xxxii. 3.

71 ff.] Memory cannot be predicated of beings outside of time and space, who never forget.

79] They do not 'look before and after and sigh for what is not.'

85] The stormy voice again—unmistakably the voice of Dante rather than of gentle Beatrice.

97 ff.] Concerning the extent of the darkening from the sixth to the ninth hour (i.e., from noon until three) the *Vulgate* is more positive than the ordinary English versions: instead of 'over all the land' the words are 'super universam terram' (Matthew), 'per totam terram' (Mark), 'in universam terram' (Luke). 'Over the whole earth', reads Challoner's version of St. Matthew. Dante took these words to mean what they say. As a good astronomer, he knew that a mere natural eclipse caused by the interposition of the moon would not cause darkness over the whole earth. Reason therefore co-operated with faith to make him reject rationalizing explanations of an event that he regarded as supernatural of origin. Moreover he held that pseudo-scientific or philosophical speculations are out of place in the pulpit which, in an age when ability to read was confined to the few, was much more than at present a place of religious exposition.

100 ff.] The translation follows the reading of the third edition of the Oxford text, and differs sharply from that of the fourth edition, which is, usually, here followed. The latter represents the Poet as flatly giving the lie to those who assert

the retrocession of the moon, and asserting that the light withdrew of itself, because the light was eclipsed for the nations at the ends of the earth (Indians in the extreme east, Spaniards in the extreme west) as well as for the Jews in the middle. The later reading doubtless has the support of the majority of the codices, but it seems to some improbable that Dante would have used the ugly word 'lie' of such authorities as St. Jerome, Thomas Aquinas, and Dionysius.

103] Common nicknames in Florence: 'Lapo' corresponds to 'Jake' (Jacopo) (cf. xiii. 139).

118] A devil lurks in the tail of the monk's hood like a black bird close at the ear of the speaker and, doubtless, inspiring the sermon. One thinks of Milton's Satan

'...found
Squat like a toad close at the ear of Eve.'

Chaucer makes his shameless 'pardoner' give a frankly cynical description of his methods of hoodwinking the ignorant in the name of religion (Prologue to 'Pardoner's Tale').

124] St. Anthony put the hog under his feet as a symbol of his conquest of the sensual cravings of the body; but, as is almost universally the case, the symbol was regarded as itself sacred, until for long ages the 'tantony pigs', as they were called in England, roamed about medieval cities at will, fed by the pious, exactly as the sacred bulls roam the streets of Hindustan. In return for this free entertainment of their herds, as well as for the fat proceeds of their shameless begging, the monks of St. Anthony gave false indulgences. Dante more than intimates that the monks and their minions were more swinish than their pigs. The reader may be amused by consulting Boccaccio's *Decameron*, VI. 10.

130 ff.] Number of the angels countless. The numbers mentioned in Daniel vii. 10 are manifestly indefinite.

142 to end] The Eternal Worth (*Eterno Valore*) remains one in essence, although reflected with infinite diversity in those wonderfully individualized angelic creatures. Converse with them would afford as perpetual a variety of interest as is afforded here to the student of nature.

CANTO XXX

1-9] According to Dante's conception the globe of earth was considerably smaller than it really is, so that when the sun is in the zenith at a point about six thousand miles east of us it will not yet have risen where we are. As the brightest handmaid of the sun, Aurora, approaches our place of observation, the stars rapidly grow dimmer and dimmer until even the brilliant morning

star is shut from sight. Meanwhile the vast conical shadow of earth will be sinking as the sun rises until, at a given moment, sun and shadow will balance each other on the plane of the horizon, just as in the picture at the beginning of the preceding Canto the rising full moon is balanced against the setting sun. So, as Dante soars with Beatrice into the empyrean, the angelic circles are quenched in that excess of light. Such is the comparison, at once precise and sublime, which stands as a pylon or stately gateway before this noble concluding series of Cantos.

27] The memory suffers, as Torraca puts it, 'a solution of continuity'. Cf. xiv. 81; xxiii. 61-3. This may have suggested to Lowell his sad witticism, 'My memory has become a reminiscence of itself.' More and more frequently in these later Cantos the Poet confesses the despair of the artist who endeavours to render by means of conventional signs on paper not only the processes of thought but also all combinations of form and colour, harmonies of sound, and even signals from the great deep of the unconscious. But the marvel is that he contrives to convert the very confession of impotence into a vividly beautiful mode of description.

40 ff.] We enter here upon holy ground, where we must not only put the shoes from off our feet but school the voice to quiet utterance if not to reverent silence. All is beauty and significance; comment seems impertinence if not profanation; as well interrupt a symphony with explanation. In short, these final Cantos are not to be merely read, but to be brooded over, as a painter broods over a landscape in order to realize its appeal to the imagination.

43] The host of the Angels and that of the redeemed.

52-4] The blinding excess of light prepares the soul for the vision of the Divine radiance. The Poet may have had in mind the case of Saul of Tarsus blinded by revelatory light from Heaven (The Acts, chapter ix).

64-9] 'Some interchange of grace' between the living sparks of the river of light and the flowers blooming and exhaling fragrance upon the banks.

76 ff.] The stream of grace, the flowers, and the ruby-sparks are but symbols.

82] The tender and familiar image recalls Faust's cry:

'Wo fass ich dich, unendliche Natur?
Euch Brüste wo? Ihr Quellen alles Lebens...'
Cf. the image of the hungry child refusing the breast, l. 140; and that of the child grateful for being fed, Canto xxiii. 121-3.

88] Dante's sight exalted to see the reality behind these symbols.

95 ff.] The identical triple rime upon 'saw' has the same solemnity as that upon 'Christ'. Cf. Hugh Capet's discourse, *Purgatorio* xx. 65-9.

107] Striking upon the outermost surface of the universe it gives motion to all the spheres.

128 ff.] The last words of Beatrice.

132] Dante did not realize, as the thoughtful now do, that

> 'We are ancients of the earth
> And in the morning of the times.'

142 ff.] Clement V, who secretly opposed Henry VII while pretending to favour. He of Alagna is Boniface VIII. The best commentary is *Inferno* xix.

CANTO XXXI

7] The comparison with the bee was merely suggested in Canto xxx. 64-9.

16-18] The peace and love acquired by the angels *ventilando il fianco*—i.e., flying on their divine errands—they impart to the assembly of the blest.

32] Helicë was turned into the Great Bear (the Wain or Dipper), her son, Arcas, into the Lesser Bear, which is elsewhere called 'that Horn beginning at the point of the axle round which the first circle goeth', i.e. round the North Star (Canto xiii. 10-11).

36] The Lateran, first palace of the popes and still in Dante's time their seat, stands here for Rome itself, which, even after Constantine had transferred the seat of Empire to Byzantium, still remained the most stately city in the world.

39] The contrast memorably expressed in a dozen lines at the beginning of Canto xi is here concentrated into one lightning-flash. Excluded *there*, admitted *here!*

55-64] During Dante's absorption in this unexampled vision, Beatrice has imperceptibly returned to her place among the blessed. There is a studied likeness in contrast to the vanishing of Virgil (*Purgatorio* xxx. 40 ff.).

65] St. Bernard speaks.

79-90] Dante's prayer to the Heavenly Beatrice.

104] The touching legend is that a woman, Berenice (of which Veronica is an altered form) offered Jesus on the way to Calvary a kerchief to wipe his face; when the cloth was returned the features of the Lord were stamped upon it. This kerchief or veil, the *santo sudario*, was shown in Holy Week, and is now kept at St. Peter's. The word Veronica, used by Dante for the relic itself, may be derived from *verus* (true) and *icon* (image). Cf. Section 41 of the *Vita Nuova*.

115] Bernard directs the Poet to look up to the Queen of Heaven.

142] The quieter tone of this Canto, with its lovely, familiar images of the bees, the Northman in Rome, the pilgrim in the temple of his vow, the Croatian gazing upon the picture of his Saviour, the angels at their games—is in marked contrast with the splendours and intensity of the thirtieth.

CANTO XXXII

4] Mary. 5] Eve. 8] Rachel.

10] Sara, Rebecca, Judith, Ruth.

15] For the diagram see Gardner's *Dante*.

33] Between his own death and that of his Lord. Here he sits on the opposite side of the vast amphitheatre on the seat corresponding to that of the Mother of the Saviour.

37 ff.] In Dante's vast intellect, reasoning power balanced—perhaps sometimes overbalanced—imagination. Parts of this Canto, like *Inferno* xi and the second half of *Purgatorio* xvii, appeal rather to those studious of system than to lovers of poetry. They bear much the same relation to the Poem as a whole that an architect's draft bears to the finished miracle of stone. The books of reference contain diagrams of the 'Mystic Rose', but the diagram banishes the mystic. 'The parting genius is with sighing sent.' Those whose minds are overstrained by the poetry will do well to construct the diagram from the data so clearly furnished by the verses. After the passages of *récitatif* (which may no doubt be artfully introduced for relief) how gloriously the symphony is again intoned! Some of the positions assigned are significant of Dante's judgements of men. Eve, as directly created by God and as a type of eugenic perfection, is placed only below Mary: St. Francis *en face*. The contemplative, scholarly Benedict sits opposite the contemplative Rachel (cf. *Purgatorio* xxvii. 100-8), by whose side is Beatrice. Nothing is said of Dominic. By the fancy of the artist, the elect who have believed since the crucifixion have assigned to them exactly the same number of places as those assigned to believers of the old dispensation. Below the horizontal line of division, nearest the mystic sea of light, are the multitudes of innocent children saved by the faith and obedience of parents.

72] The different complexions of Jacob and Esau symbolize the variations in the gift of grace.

83-7] The rime again on the sacred name.

106] St. Bernard.

112] The Archangel Gabriel.

140] The Poet of the Divine does not need to take thought for the dignity of his allusions. Let us call him an architect, with an eye to symmetry. *Paradiso* exceeds *Purgatorio* by only three lines.

151] Compare the close of Canto v.

PARADISO

CANTO XXXIII

Profound intellect and simple taste, animated by some-thing deeper which some would term Genius and others would reverence as Grace, have shaped this final canto into one of the summits of all poetry. Here is no theatrical décor, no player king orientally enthroned. In the fluctuant auroral splendours of Cantos xxx and xxxi the Deity is present only as the invisible source of all light. In this 'safe and happy kingdom' the beings who partake most of the Divine Nature seem to be women—Mary, Rachel, Beatrice. Previously the Deity had been seen only as a Point of supreme brilliance. Now that the Poet is graced with a nearer view, the Point appears widened to a Circle containing the features of the human face. By this symbol the mind is baffled as the geometer is baffled by the problem of the qua-drature of the circle. How does the image fit the circle and how does it 'inwhere itself' there? To the brooding, eager mind the conclusion comes in a flash: the symbol denotes the final repose of the human will in the encirclement of the Divine Will. For this solution we have been prepared by the great words of Piccarda: 'in His will is our peace' (Canto iii. 85, and note).

1-21] Compare the invocation to Mary by Chaucer in the prologue to 'Second Nun's Tale'; also the prologue to 'Prioress's Tale'—both free imitations of this prayer of St. Bernard.

22] This nethermost pool may be the frozen pool of Cocytus at the bottom of Hell and centre of earth; although some think it to be Hell as a whole, wherein Dante made some notable ob-servations of perverted spirit-natures.

35-9] After the unexampled exaltation of the Beatific Vision Dante is to return to this world to be subject to all the insidious temptations to which flesh is heir, and well is he aware that he requires to be especially safeguarded. Nowhere does the proud, indignant poet give more signal proof of true Christian humility. Dante's beset-ting sin may be, as he himself admits, pride (see his conversation with Sapía, *Purgatorio* xiii. 133-8). But his pride never is spiritual pride—that odious malady of shallow self-complacence, a cancer fatal to the life of the soul. And he knows that the highest ecstasies of art, music, literature, even

spiritual vision, are in themselves no insurance against falling back when the rapture is past.

65] Cf. *Aeneid* III. 441-52.

76-99] Note the contrast between the '*credo*' (methinks), of ll. 77 and 91, and the triumphant 'I saw' thrice repeated instead of the rime in Canto xxx. 95, 97, 99. The Poet has caught a fleeting glimpse of That which infinite vision is required for really seeing; That wherein substance and accidents are interfused. His consciousness of having seen the Ineffable, Alpha and Omega of created things, is ratified by the ampler beati-tude with which the statement fills him. He recalls only enough to be aware that of the one Point he has forgotten more than in twenty-five cen-turies men have had time to forget of the memor-able emprise of those heroes who sailed in the Argo: that first ship whose shadow, clouding for a moment the light of Neptune's submarine palace, caused the god to look up with forebod-ing and to murmur:

> 'Can such things be
> And overcome us like a summer's cloud
> Without our special wonder?'

For 'substance and accidents' cf. xxiv. 69, note.

106-8] There is a reminiscence of this in the prologue to 'Prioress's Tale':

> 'But as a child of twelf month olde or less
> That can unnethës any word expresse.'

Cf. the same tender image in xxx. 82-4.

118-20] So the Son emanates from the Father and the Holy Ghost emanates equally from both, as one rainbow is reflected by another.

130 ff.] The circling which appeared effluence of divine reflected light seemed to contain our ef-figy: emblem of the god-man. The circle is the image of perfection and, as we have seen, the act of circling is the image of beatitude. While Dante is absorbed, like the geometer who would square the circle, in studying the conformity of the effigy and the circle, his desire is in a flash fulfilled. Then, as the wings of imaginative vision flag, he finds will and desire moved, like a wheel turn-ing evenly, by the Love that moves the sun and stars. In the original the word *stelle* (stars) is the last of each one of the three *cantiche*.

The Circle of the Lustful